The Complete Guide to Adventures in Odyssey®

The Complete Guide to Adventures in Odyssey

By Phil Lollar
and the Adventures in Odyssey Team

PUBLISHING
Colorado Springs, Colorado

THE COMPLETE GUIDE TO ADVENTURES IN ODYSSEY

Library of Congress Cataloging-in-Publication Data

Lollar, Phil
The complete guide to Adventures in Odyssey / Phil Lollar
p. cm.
Includes index.
ISBN 1-56179-466-X
1. Adventures in Odyssey (Radio program) I. Title.
PN1991.77.A38L66 1997
791.44'72—dc21 97-6691
CIP

Published by Focus on the Family Publishing,
Colorado Springs, Colorado 80995.

Focus on the Family books are available at special quantity discounts when purchased in bulk by corporations, organizations, churches, or groups. Special imprints, messages, and excerpts can be produced to meet your needs. For more information, write: Special Sales, Focus on the Family Publishing, 8605 Explorer Drive, Colorado Springs, CO 80920, or call (719) 531-3400 and ask for the Special Sales Department.

Editors: Betsy Holt and Keith Wall
Cover Design: Rick Mills
Cover Illustration: Len Smith, Ken Johnson, Rick Hemphill, Pamela Long, and Rick Mills

Printed in the United States of America

97 98 99 00/10 9 8 7 6 5 4 3 2 1

This book is dedicated to:

Paul M., Chuck B., Dave A., Bob L., and Steve H.
for your creativity.

John C., Charles H., Stephan S., Mike S., and Jeff P.
for the laughter.

Leslie and Ian
for your love.

Mom
for life.

and Owen Dale Lollar, my father,
whose life inspired so much of what finally became
John Avery Whittaker.

Contents

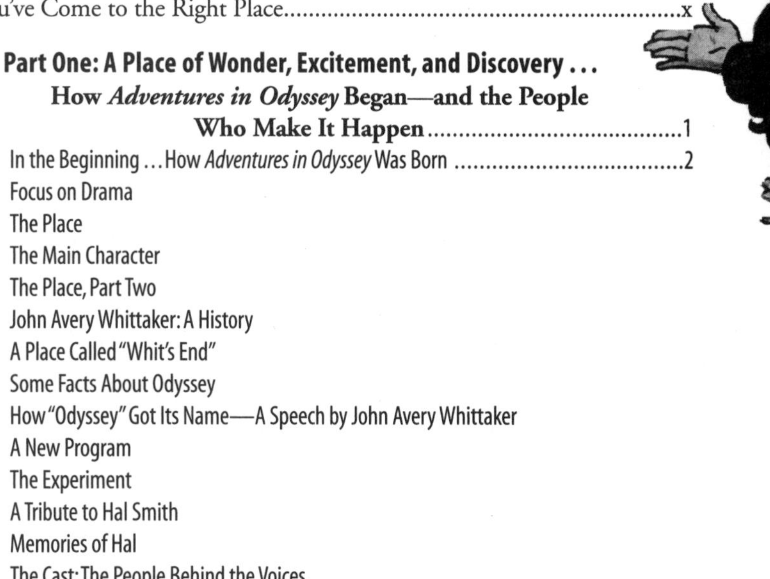

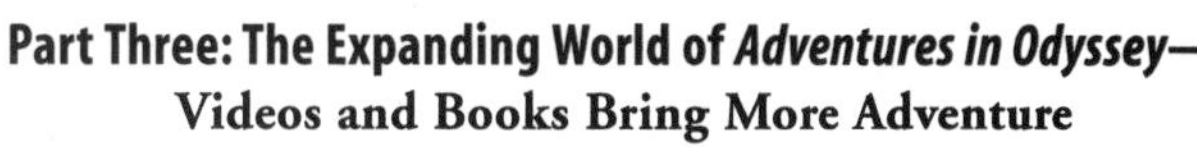

Acknowledgments

Though book writing is probably one of the loneliest professions, no one ever really writes a book alone—especially a book of this type. It takes many people many long, hard hours to pull together a project like this. My thanks go to all of them, especially:

Paul McCusker and Dave Arnold, for their thoughts, memories, and corrections; Bethany Stokka for her computer work and her kind voice; Al Janssen, Keith Wall, and Betsy Holt with Focus on the Family Book Publishing, and Clark Miller, for their patience, expertise, skill, and guidance; all of the writers, directors, producers, actors, musicians, and production engineers who bring *Adventures in Odyssey* to life; the radio stations that air *Adventures in Odyssey*; and you, the listener, for supporting the show and making it a part of your life.

Thanks also go to the many people in Focus's Correspondence Department who reviewed the episode summaries for accuracy. They include: Kari Andresen, Linda Beck, John Blackburn, Jamie Botdorf, Sally L. Brown, Mary Jo Campbell, Ed Cantu, Charles Carr, Donna Cliff, Paul Crotser, Barb Cruikshank, Cheryl Davis, Jill Farmer, Barb Faust, Karen Genandt, Jane Gillett, Kyle Hall, Sharon Hancock, Madeline Hoherd, Alice Jacob, Scott Johnson, Frank Keller, Kristy Kellner, Brad Mazzocco, Earle Morgan, Barney Royalty, Barb Siebert, Cari Stone, Carol Stuart, Barbara Verstag, John Vose, Amy Ward, Chrissie Williamson, and Steve Wilsey.

A very special thanks to my wife, Leslie, and my son, Ian, for their encouragement, confidence, and unconditional love . . . and to our Lord Jesus Christ for making it all happen.

Acknowledgments

Introduction

If You've Ever Had a Question About *Adventures in Odyssey*, You've Come to the Right Place

"It's a place of wonder, excitement, and discovery! Welcome to *Adventures in Odyssey!*"

When I first wrote those words 10 years ago, I had no idea the impact they would have on young—and not-so-young—minds and hearts across the country and around the world. And I certainly didn't think the fictional goings-on of a little town would become one of the most popular programs on radio.

But, by God's grace, that's exactly what happened.

As of this writing, more than 370 original *Adventures in Odyssey* radio programs have been produced. These shows air weekly on more than 1,400 radio facilities across the United States plus another 125 throughout the world, and then the shows are syndicated daily on over 800 radio facilities. Many of these episodes comprise the 29 six-cassette albums and 14 CD collections that have been continual best-sellers.

And that represents just the *audio* program! Eleven animated videos based on the series have each sold thousands of copies, and more are planned. A dozen novels based on the series have been published to great popularity, and more are in the works.

Each week, hundreds of thousands of people listen to *Adventures in Odyssey (AIO)* on the radio, watch it on video, and read about it in novels. Hundreds of fans write in to ask questions about the town, its characters, and the broadcast in general—also asking questions about the videos and novels—such as:

"Where is Odyssey?"

"Is it a real place?"

"Where did Whit come from?"

"How old is Connie?"

"How does the Imagination Station work?"

"How is a program put together?"

"Where do you get the ideas for your scripts and stories?"

"How come some of the characters on the radio program don't appear in the videos or the novels?"

People write in requesting information on a specific show we've aired, or conversely, asking if we've done a show that addresses a specific subject. Some want to track the general changes in the program (such as increases and decreases in Odyssey's population or modifications to the town), and some want to track the growth and development of an individual character (such as when Connie became a Christian). Most want pictures of Whit and the other characters or of the town itself. All want to know more about *Adventures in Odyssey.*

In contemplating all of this, I thought: Wouldn't it be nice to have a book that answered all of these questions? A book that tells *Adventures in Odyssey* fans what they want and need to know about every *AIO* broadcast, video, and novel—and more? A book that:

- Gives detailed story lines, themes, Scripture references, and study questions.
- Suggests ways parents can make the most of each program by using it to teach godly values to their children.
- Provides a detailed history of the town and its characters, complete with pictures and floor plans for Whit's End.
- Tells the story of how the program was created, who created it, and how it is still put together today.
- Provides interviews with and pictures of the creators, producers, and performers who make the program come to life each week.
- Shares trivia and "inside information" about the program that will enhance peoples' enjoyment level.

In short, wouldn't it be nice to have *The Complete Guide to Adventures in Odyssey*, written and compiled by someone who was there from the start?

After three years of many meetings and discussions, and countless hours of hard work later, that idea became the reality you're holding in your hands.

Over the years, many of you have told us that *Adventures in Odyssey* has been a great source of enjoyment, inspiration, and education for you and your families. It is my hope that *The Complete Guide to Adventures in Odyssey* will make the show more enjoyable—and meaningful—to everyone who listens, watches, and reads.

Getting the Most out of This Book

This guide can be enjoyed on many different levels. If you're already an *Adventures in Odyssey* fan, you can use it for more information about the characters and episodes. Plus, you'll find in these pages a gold mine of trivia, behind-the-scenes information, and the "inside scoop" on the world of *AIO.* If you're new to the series, you might want to look through it to become more familiar with *Adventures in Odyssey* characters and get caught up on stories you've missed.

We've included study questions and the theme of each program so Sunday school teachers, home-schoolers, and parents can use this book as a study guide in conjunction with the audio episodes or videos. Listen to the program or read the synopsis with your child or class, and use the study questions to reinforce the point of the episode. (Keep in mind that these questions are just to get the ball rolling. You can make your discussions more in-depth by adding your own questions.)

Many of our regular listeners write in to tell us they use *Adventures in Odyssey* as a sort of "bedtime story." (In fact, several radio stations air the daily and weekly broadcasts at night for that very reason.) Parents can use this guide to read the episode summaries ahead of time to determine if particular stories are appropriate for their children ("parental warnings" are also provided for those few episodes that are geared toward older listeners).

Above all, have fun! That's what this book—and *Adventures in Odyssey* in general—is all about: teaching timeless truths in the most fun way imaginable.

A Place of Wonder, Excitement, and Discovery . . .

How *Adventures in Odyssey* Began—and the People Who Make It Happen

In the Beginning . . .

How *Adventures in Odyssey* Was Born

As much as we'd like to tell you that the town of Odyssey and all of its inhabitants are real, we have to admit that Whit and the Odyssey gang are actually fictional characters living in a town you won't find on any map—at least on any map we have! (You'd be surprised at how many people have asked for directions to Odyssey.)

The truth is that *Adventures in Odyssey* is a production of Focus on the Family, a non-profit organization based in Colorado Springs. The behind-the-scenes personnel have changed a bit over the years, but the people primarily responsible for the program during its first 10 years have been: Phil Lollar (co-creator, writer, and director), Paul McCusker (producer, writer, and director), Dave Arnold (production manager/engineer), Bob Luttrell (production engineer), and Chuck Bolte (executive producer). Later additions to the team were Production Engineer Mark Drury and Writer/Director Marshal Younger. We also had three production assistants during our first 10 years: Joyce Blaine, Rodlyn Davis, and Paula Peterson. (You can hear from members of the *AIO* team on pages 23-26.)

But just how did *Adventures in Odyssey* get its start? To answer that question, we have to go back to the beginning.

Focus on Drama

Christmas 1983.

That was the birth of dramatic radio production at Focus on the Family. And it all started with a gentleman named Steve Harris, who was the Broadcasting Department's coordinator of promotion.

"I remember I was in a meeting with Broadcasting Director [now Vice President and co-host of the *Focus on the Family* radio program] Mike Trout and Broadcasting Manager [now Administrative Director] Bobbie Valentine," recalls Steve. "We were trying to decide what to air on the *Focus on the Family* (*FOF*) Christmas day broadcast. The traditional broadcast for that day was a program called 'Helen's Buggy,' a story Dr. Dobson would tell. However, after airing this same story for several years, we decided it was time to come up with something different."

That's when Steve had a great idea. Steve recalls, "I said, 'How about doing a drama? You know, a dramatic program?'"

"Great idea!" said Mike.

"Terrific!" said Bobbie.

"Yeah, let's go for it!" said Steve. "Uh, wait. . . . Who's going to pull it together?"

"*You are!*" said Mike and Bobbie.

Steve sought help from Dennis Shippey, a writer for the performing group Jeremiah People, and Dennis was commissioned to write a half hour Christmas program. The program became "Spare Tire," Focus on the Family's first dramatic production. It was produced on an ancient four-track recorder, which was pulled out of a crate in the back room for the occasion. Music for the

2 THE COMPLETE GUIDE TO ADVENTURES IN ODYSSEY

production was supplied by a young friend of Steve's named John Campbell—later *Adventures in Odyssey's* main composer—whose only credit to that point had been writing and performing songs for the teen night at First Baptist Church of Pomona, California. "Spare Tire" featured just two actors: D. J. Harner as the wife, Jennifer; and Chuck Bolte, director of The Jeremiah People, as the husband, Adam.

"Spare Tire" was a smashing success. Everyone loved it, not the least of whom was Focus on the Family President James Dobson. "He thought the drama went really well," Steve remembers, "so instead of every year at Christmas, he wanted to do one every three or four months."

Unfortunately, Steve's regular work schedule prevented him from producing another drama until the fall of 1984—and this one emerged from Steve's personal experience.

"My father had just undergone triple bypass heart surgery, and he stayed with me and my family during his recovery," Steve recalls.

It was a situation rich with dramatic possibilities. So Steve brought back Adam and Jennifer from "Spare Tire," added a father, and this time set the whole thing around Thanksgiving. The result was Focus's second drama, "House Guest." Joining D. J. and Chuck in the cast was a well-known actor and voiceover artist, best known for his role as Otis Campbell, the town drunk, on *The Andy Griffith Show.* His name was Hal Smith.

"I had worked with Hal on a Christmas album that he had narrated," remembers Chuck. "I admired him and wanted to work with him again. So when 'House Guest' came up, I called the number he had given me, expecting to reach his agent. But to my surprise, Hal himself answered! He had given me the number to his home!"

Hal was more than willing to work on the project, and it was another smashing success for Focus. But another year passed before Steve could produce the next drama, "Gone Fishin'," again featuring Chuck Bolte and Hal Smith. It was clear Steve could not keep up with the writing load by himself. So Steve sought help and, after the normal interviewing process, offered me a job.

I was an unemployed filmmaker at the time, looking for some place to vent my creativity, but I wasn't thrilled with the idea of writing for radio. On the other hand, film jobs were few and far between, and I had a pregnant wife to support. So writing for radio didn't sound so bad after all.

I started with Focus in January 1986 and in addition to dramatic programming, was hired to write scripts for *James Dobson Family Commentary,* a 90-second program featuring clips of wisdom from Dr. Dobson. The trouble was, "Gone Fishin'" had aired shortly after I came aboard, and there was no urgency to produce another drama.

The turning point came in the spring of 1986, when Dr. Dobson interviewed Bruce Wilkinson from the "Walk Through the Bible" organization for the *Focus* broadcast. The theme of the program was media influence in our society. After the interview, Mr. Wilkinson told Dr. Dobson that it isn't enough for Christians to simply decry the lousy programming on television and radio—they also need to produce high-quality alternative programming.

Soon thereafter, Dr. Dobson gave the marching orders: Launch into drama full force.

The Place

The Place

Steve and I got right to work. Or more accurately, we got right to *arguing.*

"What should the show's format be?"

"Who should be in it?"

"How should it be presented?"

"What are we going to do?"

No subject was left out of our "creative discussions." And our opinions couldn't have been more opposed.

I wanted to do a variety show, with music, fast-paced sketches, guest stars, and lots of wacky comedy. Steve wanted to do a 30-minute drama, much as we had been doing. We talked for hours, days, and weeks but were no closer to a decision than when we first started. Finally, Steve diplomatically explained that it didn't really matter what I wanted or even what *he* wanted. What mattered was what the leadership at Focus would *approve.*

Bing! The light suddenly went on in my musty, refrigerator-like brain. A 30-minute drama! What a wonderful idea!

More discussions, more debating, more brainstorming—but this time our sessions were productive. We agreed that the program needed to teach Scripture without seeming "educational" . . . that it needed to reflect the values of Focus on the Family . . . that it should hearken back to a simpler, kinder time in America. I took tons of notes and finally went back to my office and typed:

"A 30-minute weekly drama/comedy program set in a small town, centering on the problems, foibles, antics, relationships, and goings-on of the people within the town."

I wish I could say I loved it, but I can't.

In fact, I hated it.

I still wanted to do a variety show.

But I showed Steve what I had written, and he proclaimed it a good beginning. However, we needed more details, not the least of which was where the town was located and what it would be called.

The "where" part was simple for me. I was born in Klamath Falls, Oregon, a small town on the Oregon-California border. It is green and lovely, surrounded by farmland on one side and pine-covered mountains on the other. For me, the town was (and still *is*) Klamath Falls.

For Steve, however, the green part was all right, the lovely part was all right, the farmland and mountains part was all right—it was the Oregon part that he didn't like. He felt the town should be located in Ohio. (The fact that there are no mountains in Ohio didn't seem to bother him.) We finally decided not to place it in any *specific* state, just somewhere in the Midwest. That way it would be more universally appealing to everyone.

Next, we moved on to a much more difficult question: What would this town be called? Obviously, Klamath Falls was already taken, so we needed something else. We wracked our brains for the remainder of the day, but came up with a big, fat zero.

That night, I was lying on the floor of my office at home, trying in vain to think of something, *anything,* that would be an appropriate name for a small midwestern town. But nothing came. I rolled over on my side and stared at my bookshelf.

It jumped out at me. Sitting there on the second shelf was a book by William F. Buckley titled *United Nations Journal: A Delegate's Odyssey.*

Odyssey.

I looked it up in the dictionary. It said an odyssey is a long voyage, especially one filled with notable experiences.

Perfect.

The next day, I sat down at my computer and typed:

"The town is called 'Odyssey,' which, of course, is a long voyage. That's appropriate, because for some folks, the town is the start of this journey we call 'life.' For others, it's the finish. For still others, it's simply a resting place along the way. But whether they're starting, finishing, or just passing through, the town will affect each one of them profoundly and will become an unforgettable part of their voyage—an experience they'll always remember."

Suddenly, I started liking this program.

The Main Character

Okay, so the name of the town was Odyssey. But what about the people *in* the town? What would they be like? Would this be an ensemble cast, or would there be a central character?

More discussions, more talks, more debates. Finally, we decided there needed to be a central character. Steve wanted him to be a kindly, gentle, grandfatherly figure. I thought that was all right, but I also wanted him to be more eccentric, adventurous, and, for lack of a better term, *unpredictable.* I had just reread C. S. Lewis's *Chronicles of Narnia* series in which Aslan, the figure representing Jesus, is described as "good, but not tame." That's what I wanted most for this person.

So I went back to my computer and wrote: "The central character in Odyssey is an older man. As such, he is a grandfatherly figure, but also a Renaissance man: artist, builder, inventor, entertainer—and excellent at all of them. He has a mysterious dimension to his past. He's a widower but has living children and grandchildren. And, of course, he is a very strong Christian."

Things were taking shape. But our central character still didn't have a name. Try as we might, we just couldn't think of a moniker that suited our new hero. So, in desperation, we turned to the one reference source that contains practically nothing but names—the telephone book.

We started in the "A's" and worked our way down the list. Several hours and lots of discouragement later, we reached the "W's." By now, we were bleary-eyed and slumped in our chairs. Our conversation went something like this:

"Wade?"
"No."
"Wagner?"
"No."
"Walden?"
"Nah."
"Wallace?"
"Mmm—no."
"Wedgeworth?"
"You're kidding, right?"
"Wendel?"
"No."
"West?"
"Nah."
"Wheeler?"

The Main Character

"No."
"White?"
"That's my wife's maiden name."
"Oh. Whitehouse?"
"I don't think so."
"Whitehead?"
"No."
"Whittaker?"
Pause.
"Whittaker?"

It had definite possibilities, although we disagreed on whether it should be his first or last name. I voted for it being his first name. Steve thought it should be his last name. We finally compromised. Whittaker would be his last name, but most people would call him by a nickname: Whit.

He still needed a *first* name, though. By now, our brains were fried. We took a break. In the hall, I passed an open storage closet, and something inside caught my eye. It was a package of labels. Emblazoned across the front of the package was

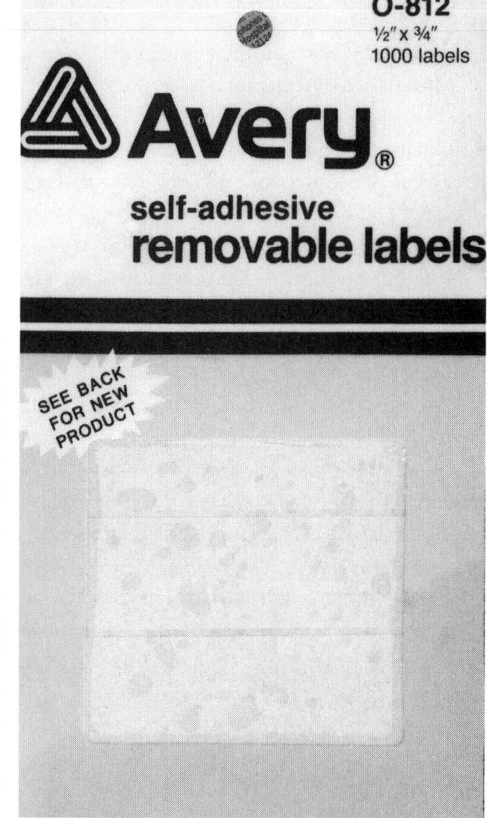

2645 Merger Cr. Univ
Electronic Resources Division
7641 Independence
Tasker Systems Division
110 E. Ramona Av 91
Water Management Products
6192 Pioneer Ln 9155
Whittaker Controls 226358 Sutherland Pl
Whittaker Jas E 221 Sturgis Rd . . . .
Whittaker Julie R . . . .
Whittaker Kellie 2263 Perry Park Dr . . . . .
Whittaker L . . . .
Whittaker L L . . . .
Whittaker M A . . . .
Whittaker Marjorie W . . . .
Whittaker Mary E . . . .
Whittaker Plastics Anjac Doron Division
24000 Cooper Dr Enc
Whittaker Plastics Anjac Doron Division
26266 Anchor Ln Enc
Whittaker Plastics Anjac Doron Division
26266 Anchor Ln Enc
Whittaker Richard & Janet
2949 Woodberry Park
Whittaker Robt J 10295 South Forty Rd . .
Whitted Clyde 1032 Jackhammer Rd . . . .
Whittem Jack 46223 Pioneer Ln South Be

the name of the company that produced them.

"Avery."®

It was perfect! Unusual, but still easy enough to remember and say. Not only that, but it was the last name of one of my favorite cartoon animators, Tex Avery! But I knew there wasn't a chance it would fly as a first name. The best I could hope for was to have it as a *middle* name.

The first name "John" followed automatically. I ran back to my computer and typed: "The central character of the town is named John Avery Whittaker. But you can call him Whit."

I was liking the program more and more.

The Place, Part Two

The Place, Part Two

Batman has the Batcave. Superman has the Fortress of Ice. The Shadow has the Inner Sanctum. I knew Whit also needed a place he could call his own.

I thought back to 1979, when my family and I attended my brother's wedding in San Rafael, California. While there, we visited my uncle, who lived in San Jose. He took us to a local mall for food and shopping. In that mall was something that is now commonplace, but at that time was rare—at least in *my* neck of the woods. It was a combination coffee shop and bookstore. You could go in, purchase or borrow a book, buy a cup of coffee or a soft drink, and read to your heart's content. Or play backgammon, checkers, or chess. Or join in one of several lively conversations taking place around the main room. It was absolutely wonderful! I felt right at home.

So when it came time to create Whit's haunt, I knew exactly what it should be. I told Steve all about it, and he caught the vision immediately. I sat down at the computer and wrote: "Whit spends most of his time in a combination coffee shop/ice cream parlor/discovery emporium he owns, which is filled with books, games, his inventions, and lively conversation. The place is called Whit's End."

Things were really coming together now!

But I knew that before Steve or I or anyone else could ever write any scripts, I had to get to know this character and this town we had created inside-out and upside-down. I had read somewhere that before screenwriter Paddy Chayefsky ever wrote one word of his scripts for *The Hospital* and *Network*, he first wrote a complete and thorough history of both the hospital and the network, including everyone who was ever involved with them. I knew I had to do the same.

What follows is Odyssey's history. It was originally designed to provide potential writers with a clear view of the backdrop against which *Adventures in Odyssey* should be portrayed. Many of the details wouldn't be revealed to the audience for years; in fact, some are revealed here for the first time.

John Avery Whittaker: A History

John Avery Whittaker is not the type of person who stands out in a crowd. As a matter of fact, unless you get to know him really well, it might be easy to lose him in a large group of people.

There are, however, a few things that distinguish him from other men his age. For instance, he walks with a slight limp. He also has a small, "L"-shaped scar above his right eyebrow, but it's noticeable only when his face is flushed. He has a full head of silver-colored hair, which is worn longish to cover the upper half of his ears. This might be considered unusual for a man of his age, but there is a reason for it: The top part of his right ear is missing. Because of his hair, even some long-time residents of Odyssey have yet to notice this war wound. He also sports a full mustache, which is, of course, the same color as his hair. Someone once said that he looks like a cross between Mark Twain and C. S. Lewis.

John Avery Whittaker was born on October 1 in Aberdeen, Scotland (though he *doesn't* have a Scottish accent). His father was an American history professor (making John a U.S. citizen) who was teaching in Scotland at the time of John's birth. John's mother died shortly after his fifth birthday, and his grief-stricken father later married a Scottish lass named Fiona Donneral. It was this great lady (tragically blinded in a horse-riding accident) who instilled in John a profound love for God, and he accepted Jesus Christ as his Savior shortly before his eleventh birthday.

John attended County McClaren Lower School in Aberdeen and received the equivalent of a first-grade education before his family moved back to the United States. He also received something else at that little Scottish school—the nickname "Whit."

Upon arriving in the U.S., his family settled in North Carolina (the Durham area), where he attended Robert E. Lee Elementary School. He graduated with honors from Durham High School and, on the strength of his grades, enrolled at Duke University on an academic scholarship, majoring in philosophy and literature.

Whit was only three units short of graduation when the United States entered World War II. He was drafted into the navy in January 1942. After boot camp, he was trained as a signalman.

Whit was assigned to the battleship U.S.S. *Nimitz* and saw three separate assignments in the Pacific. In April 1943, he received the Purple Heart for wounds sustained during the battle of Guadalcanal. (While helping to unload a transport ship, mortar fragments took off the upper part of his right ear and some lodged in his left leg.)

It was during his hospital stay that he became a published writer when his humorous piece "Making Waves in the Navy" appeared in *Stars and Stripes.* A field promotion brought him to the rank of ensign, and he transferred to the cargo ship U.S.S. *Horvath* as communications officer for the duration of the war. He was honorably discharged in September 1945.

Upon his discharge from the service, Whit apprenticed as a carpenter/furniture maker for Smith and Sons in Pasadena, California, for two years while he completed his college education. He received concurrent bachelor's degrees in philosophy and literature from the University of Southern California.

Because books were always a love of his, Whit also studied for and received a librarian certification later in the summer of that same year. He began working for the Pasadena Library that fall, a job he would hold for the next five years.

It was in post-war Pasadena that Whit met, courted, and married Guinevere (Jenny) Morrow. They were married in 1947 and stayed together for 37 years until her death in 1984. The marriage produced three children: Jeremiah ("Jerry," born in 1951), Jana (born in 1953), and Jason (born in 1959).

Whit also continued to write for both local and national magazines, and in 1950, his first book was published. Entitled *The Long and the Short of It,* the book is an anthology of allegorical stories on a variety of Christian themes. It was well received, and it was followed in the next two years by two more books with historical themes.

Then in 1953, Whit used funds from his books and outside backing to start the Universal Press Foundation, a publishing firm, in Chicago. (Although UPF publishes a variety of educational and school texts, the centerpiece of the organization is Whit's brainchild, *The Universal Encyclopedia.*) Apart from traveling and writing, he also tinkered with inventing during his Chicago days, receiving several patents for his efforts, including one for a successful, new type of bookbinding process. The Whittakers stayed in Chicago from 1953–1971, with Whit making several trips around the world, gathering research data for his encyclopedia.

But in 1970, tragedy struck when Jerry was reported missing in action in Vietnam. When his death was confirmed six months later, the Whittaker family nearly fell apart. Whit felt that the "big city" life was contributing to the breakup of his home. So, in desperation, he divested himself of active involvement in the extremely successful Universal Press Foundation and moved his family to the midwestern town of Odyssey.

The Whittaker family spent their first year in Odyssey in virtual seclusion. Whit felt that the only way to repair the broken relationships was by concentrating 100 percent on accomplishing that task. The strategy met with varying degrees of success, and the Whittakers soon turned their attention to their new surroundings. The kids got involved in school affairs. Jenny was active in civic, volunteer, and church work. And, ever one to expand his horizons, Whit earned an education certificate and began teaching English to seventh and eighth graders at McCallum Junior High School.

Because of his world experiences and his way with words, Whit soon became one of the most popular teachers at McCallum, garnering several awards for excellence in education during his 14-year stay there. He became well known throughout the city as an expert in the art of verbal communication, especially with kids. And he continued to write, publishing several books for youngsters, including a series of young-adult novels based on the works of William Shakespeare.

He might have remained on the McCallum faculty indefinitely, had it not been for the death of his wife. When Jenny died, teaching no longer interested Whit. Once again, he became a virtual recluse, only this time, he was really alone. His beloved wife was gone, and his children had long since grown up and moved away. Jenny's death nearly devastated him.

Then something happened that would change his life for good.

A Place Called "Whit's End"

Teaching junior high English was an eye-opening experience for Whit. Having just gotten his own family back into relatively good order, he was extra sensitive to what he perceived to be the decay of society and, more specifically, the effect it was having on children. Whit began to notice that many kids—even in Odyssey—were suffering from the "signs of the times": broken homes, single-parent households, relaxed standards on morals and ethics, pressure to grow up too fast. He wanted to do something about it, but he really didn't know what. The answer would come in an unexpected way.

In 1984, Jenny had become involved in a controversy that was raging around Odyssey, concerning the old Fillmore Recreation Center in McCalister Park. The shell of the old place was in fair shape, but the interior was almost rotted out from lack of upkeep. Many people saw the building as a hazard and wanted it torn down, while others felt that the center was a cultural landmark and should be saved and protected by the city. In the last cause in which she was ever to play a part, Jenny joined the preservationists.

The battle dragged on for months. At first Whit sided with those who wanted to tear down the place. Unfortunately, politics had seeped into the picture, and it looked as though the Fillmore Recreation Center was doomed.

But the final vote was postponed when Jenny collapsed at city hall and had to be rushed to the hospital. She was diagnosed as having a serious kidney disease, and she tragically died later that day. One of her last requests before she died was that Whit should purchase the old building and use his knowledge and experience to turn it into something good for kids.

So, partly out of a sense of civic duty and partly out of respect for his wife's last wishes, John Avery Whittaker opened up "Whit's End." Officially billed as "an ice cream and discovery emporium," it is really a conglomeration of things—part museum, part penny arcade, part bookstore, part activity center, and part soda fountain, with just a dash of carnival funhouse thrown in for good measure. Some of its attractions include the state's largest handmade electric train set (with the cars made by the patrons themselves), an "inventor's corner" (where kids are encouraged to make their ideas come to life), a small audio studio (from which "Kid's Radio" emanates), a little theater, a well-stocked library, and the Bible Room, where artifacts, museum pieces, displays, and an incredible invention called the "Imagination Station" help the Bible come alive in the imaginations of the kids.

As a world traveler, Whit knew that discovery is important to building character. He felt that keeping kids involved in the good things in life—classic books, hands-on crafts and activities, wholesome conversation, the search for knowledge and truth, taking the time to develop friendships—can serve two functions: (1) keep idle (and potentially destructive) minds occupied with positive activities, and (2) help kids build respect, both for other people and for themselves. Whit's End is a place of adventure and discovery, a place where people can experience the excitement of learning, a place filled with books and activities, fun and games, arts and crafts, uplifting conversation, and some of the best ice cream in the state.

But most of all, "Whit's End" is a place where kids—of *all* ages—can just be kids.

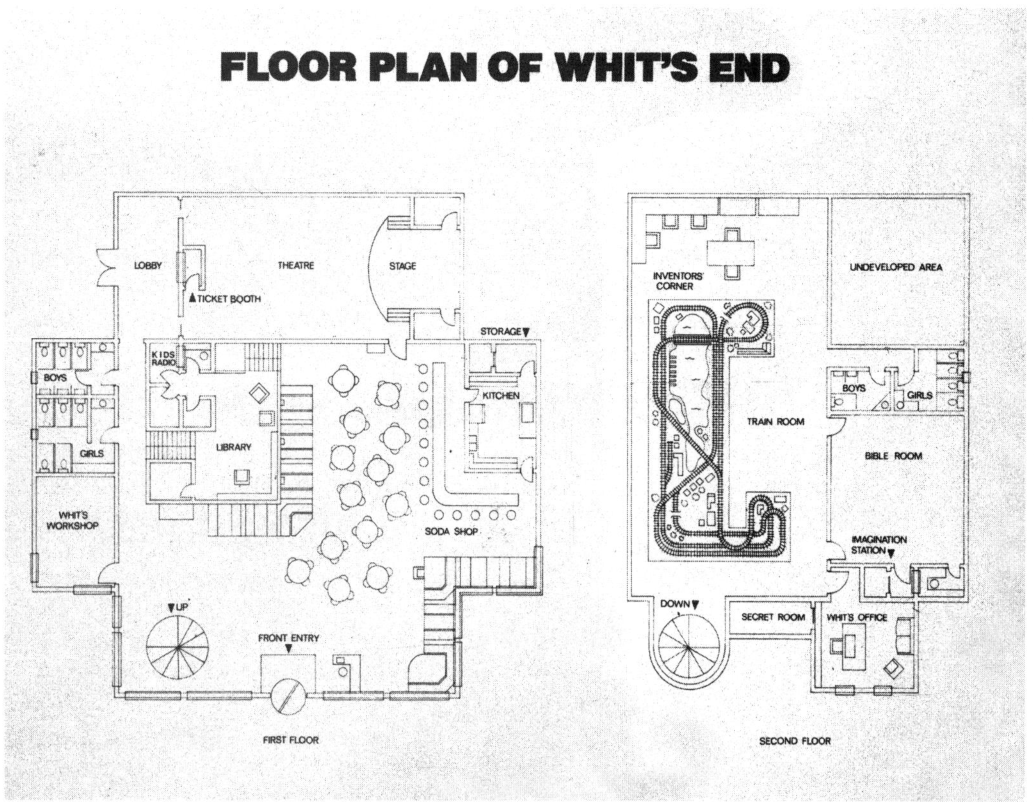

Some Facts About Odyssey

Some Facts About Odyssey

Whit chose to settle in Odyssey for several reasons. Its relatively small population (approximately 35,000 people) makes it ideal for civic involvement, which was therapeutic for Jenny. Because it is surrounded by farmland, Odyssey has a small-town feel about it, and most folks there still live by the traditional values that often characterize such places. The kids, of course, make every effort to appear as cool as can be, despite their basically rural roots. And, yet, it's close enough to a major metropolitan area (about 150 miles away) for a family to take advantage of the cultural opportunities offered by a large city, should they choose to do so.

Odyssey also has cultural advantages of its own. It has a fully-accredited four-year college, supplying degree programs in 30 different fields. There is also a well-supported civic center that boasts a 350-seat theater and a 1,500-seat music hall. An amateur theater troupe performs four or five full-scale productions per year, and a variety of traveling orchestras and musical groups make the town one of their stops when touring through the Midwest.

Odyssey is also no slouch when it comes to economy. While agriculture is a major industry in the area, there are also more than a few industrial and manufacturing plants in town. Some of these include Odyssey Automotive (the largest manufacturer of turn-signal flasher units in America), Commark Corporation (a marketing communications firm), and Valmar, Inc. (a company that makes both electronic and manually-operated occupational "games" that test an employee's mental and physical dexterity).

The town also has a fairly large shopping mall with all of the usual department stores and specialty shops. And there are a number of small but lucrative businesses scattered throughout the community, such as restaurants, assorted clothing and hardware stores, movie theaters and, of course, an unusual place called "Whit's End."

Once we had these background facts outlined, I could finally write something for Whit. What follows is the first speech he ever gave.

How "Odyssey" Got Its Name

How "Odyssey" Got Its Name

A Speech by John Avery Whittaker

Back in the early 1800s, this place had an Indian name, and that makes sense, seeing as how most of the denizens at that time were Indians. They called it "Wey-Aka-Tal-Ah-Nee-Tee," which, roughly translated, means "Land That Stinks Like Swamp." Funny thing is, there's not a real swamp within 200 or 300 miles of here.

But the Indians knew what they were talking about. You see, while we don't have a swamp, we do have a lake—Trickle Lake—about 2,000 feet up on this side of Forrest Mountain. And every year when the rains would come, Trickle would turn into a torrent and overflow and flood most of the flatlands surrounding the town. It'd stay that way for weeks at a time and after a while the place did smell somewhat . . . well, gamy.

Anyway, long after the Indians hightailed it toward sweeter-smelling pastures, the farmers finally put their heads together and came up with a bright idea. Instead of waiting for the rains to water their crops, they'd dig irrigation and drainage ditches and let the lake water do it. The less water there was in Trickle Lake, the less chance it had of becoming a gusher—which, in turn, meant that the ground had more time to dry out.

Well, that solved the odor problem. Unfortunately, it did nothing for the town's name problem. Very few of the pioneers who settled in this area fancied being known as citizens of "Stinking Swamp." So one night about 150 years ago, the folks gathered together to duly appoint this new little hamlet a proper and fitting title.

By the way, most people think this place ended up being named after the famous epic poem by the Greek writer Homer, but that's not really true. A man by the name of Horace McCalister, in a roundabout way, finally settled the matter. After the folks at that meeting exhausted all the variations on the Indian name, they started asking themselves what made this area such a nice one to settle in, now that the smell was gone. When it came around to Doc McCalister (who wasn't really a doctor—he owned the drug store in town and knew a few Latin words, so the name kinda stuck), he said it was because of where the settlement was situated. "It's in a beautiful valley," he said, "a place everyone oughta see."

Well, nobody at the meeting said a word after that. And aside from a little spelling change, that's how we've been known ever since.

And even though the real name of the town is "Ought to See," I think Homer would've been pleased to have this town named after his poem. After all, when you look it up in the dictionary, odyssey means "a long voyage, especially one filled with notable experiences."

I think that describes this place pretty well.

A New Program

It was a start. We were on our way. Steve presented all of this information—along with a request to hire another writer—to the Focus leadership. Both the concept and the new hire were approved. Steve and I screened several potential candidates and finally settled on a fine writer and poet named Susan McBride.

The three of us launched into brainstorming sessions, story conferences, and finally, scripts. Mike Trout retained Chuck Bolte's services to direct the programs. To produce them, Mike found Bob Luttrell, an experienced engineer who had single-handedly produced the Salvation Army's radio drama, *Heartbeat Theatre*, for several years.

There was only one thing we lacked—a title for the program! After more discussions and debates, Steve walked into my office and typed two words on my computer: "Family Portraits."

The Experiment

It was decided that the first 13 *Family Portraits* episodes would actually serve as a "test" to see if Focus's listeners—and Christian radio in general—would accept a weekly dramatic series. The shows would be aired every Monday within the *Focus on the Family* broadcast time slot.

As with every new series, there were painful moments during its creation. The original decision was to make the program for children, so we started brainstorming ideas for kids. But a few weeks later, word came down that we really needed to target the program more for adults, since they were the ones who would be most able to respond to it. We switched tracks and started brainstorming ideas for adults. Another week passed, and the target was again moved back to kids. We moved accordingly. Finally, word came down that the show would be for kids *and* adults—one week we'd do one, the next week we'd do the other. Since we had been working on both kinds of stories anyway, this ended up being the best decision of all—at least for the initial 13-week test.

Steve, Susan, and I wrote frantically. I finished my episode, "The New Kid in Town," first, but it really didn't strike everyone as the show we should use to launch the program. That distinction went to a script Steve and I wrote together, entitled "Whit's Visitor."

The first three programs were recorded in November of 1986. Bob Luttrell produced them during December, and on January 5, 1987, *Family Portraits* officially premiered.

FAMILY
PORTRAITS
Thirteen radio dramas on cassette
presented by
Focus on the Family
featuring comments by
Dr. James Dobson

A Tribute to Hal Smith

(John Avery Whittaker from 1988 to 1994)

Once we had the go-ahead to begin airing *Family Portraits* (the forerunner to *Adventures in Odyssey*), we turned our attention to finding an actor to play the critical role of Whit. Of course, it was really a no-brainer. There was only one possible choice. The best—and *only*—person for the role of Whit . . . was Hal Smith.

Harold John "Hal" Smith was born on August 24, 1916, in Pestoskey, Michigan, one of four children. Shortly after his birth, his family moved to Wilmington, North Carolina, then Suffolk, Virginia, finally settling in Messena, New York, when Hal was eight years old.

He was bitten by the "showbiz bug" at age 14 when he joined a local band as a vocalist—although he was fond of saying his "official" start in the entertainment business came when he was cast as an elf in a Wilmington production of "The Story of Pandora" at the ripe old age of six.

Hal's memories of his early days were right out of a Norman Rockwell painting. A favorite story was how his father bought him and his brother, Glen, a Shetland pony and a wagon. They would ride all over town in that wagon and give rides on the pony to the neighborhood kids in exchange for rides on their bicycles.

Young Hal and Glen also had a vaudeville act, the Smith Brothers (also known as "Cough & Drop" and "Trade & Mark"). It was a variety act—songs, impressions, and comedy—and the brothers performed in local amateur shows until they were told to stop coming because they were too good and monopolized the winnings.

Hal then went solo, joining a local band called Krazy Kats as a vocalist, filling in on guitar and piano when needed. For a while, he even had his own band, the Hal Smith Orchestra, which played all over the Massena region.

After high school, Hal started his professional career in radio. He was a vocalist/announcer at station WIBX in Utica, New York, and also had his own morning program, "The Yawn Patrol," where he sang, told jokes, played piano, and read the news.

Hal would have stayed in New York-area radio indefinitely had it not been for World War II. He signed up for the Army Air Forces in 1943, serving his country as—what else?—an entertainer in special services. Hal's war years were especially important to him, and he and several of our other cast members who served their country in WW II would spend literally hours during recording sessions rehashing old stories and memories for their own—and everyone's—immense pleasure.

After the war, Hal headed to Hollywood. His first job was in radio, at station KIEV in Glendale, and later at KFI, the largest station in Los Angeles. It was in L.A. that Hal met a lovely beautician named Louise Curtis. They fell in love, were married in 1947, and had their only child, Terry, in 1950.

During this time, Hal also became one of the pioneers of television broadcasting, appearing regularly on several of the first programs to air on Los Angeles's first television station, KTLA-TV. From there, his career soared.

That Hal was famous goes without saying. But it's not an overstatement to add that he was a bona fide show biz *legend*—especially in the voiceover industry. Hal's list of credits reads like a history of television, motion pictures, and radio.

His films include several of the "Ma and Pa Kettle" and "Francis the Talking Mule" series; *The Apartment* with Jack Lemmon and Shirley MacLaine; *The Three Stooges Meet Hercules*, *Son of Flubber* with Fred MacMurray; *The Great Race* with Tony Curtis and Jack Lemmon; *$1,000,000 Duck* with Dean Jones and Sandy Duncan; *Oklahoma Crude* with George C. Scott and Faye Dunaway; and *18 Again* with George Burns.

He appeared in dozens of television shows, including *The Adventures of Ozzie and Harriet, The Red Skelton Show, Bonanza, Gunsmoke, Lassie, Leave It to Beaver, Dennis the Menace, My Favorite Martian, Perry Mason, The Lucy Show, The Brady Bunch, The Odd Couple, Gomer Pyle, U.S.M.C.,* and *Little House on the Prairie.* He also starred in a children's show called *The Pancake Man* and, of course, as Otis Campbell on *The Andy Griffith Show.*

As for voiceover work, Hal was heard on everything from McDonald's commercials (as a soft drink cup and a McNugget) to Kellogg's cereal (as Tony the Tiger, Jr.). Among his best-known voice roles were the original voice of Goofy, the original Barney Rubble in *The Flintstones* (as well as the voice of Dino), Goliath in *Davy and Goliath,* J. P. Gotrockets in *The Jetsons,* Owl and Eeyore in the *Winnie the Pooh* series (he also took over the voice of Pooh when Sterling Holloway retired), Grape Ape on *Grape Ape,* Sludge on *The Smurfs,* Flintheart Glumgold, Gyro Gearloose, and Ludwig von Drake on *Duck Tales,* and Philippe the horse in *Beauty and the Beast.* To say we were thrilled to have him on *Adventures in Odyssey* would be a vast understatement!

But Hal was so much more than his credits. He was one of the kindest, gentlest, most generous, and genuinely *happy* men you would ever meet—and he was that way no matter how upsetting the circumstances of his personal life may have been. During his tenure on *Adventures in Odyssey,* Hal had both hips replaced, was placed on heart medication and a diuretic for glaucoma, got into a car accident on the way to the recording studio, had his house broken into, and most devastatingly, lost his wife to cancer (and these were just the things we *knew* about). Yet through it all, he still showed up at the studio with a smile and a joke, wearing his light-blue sweater, ready to work.

On January 27, 1994, Hal Smith died at his home in Santa Monica, California, listening to radio dramas on a local station, appropriately enough. All of us who worked with Hal were shocked and grief-stricken. We had lost not only a talented actor but a friend whom we all loved dearly.

Memories of Hal

He played our main character, he was the center of our cast, and he touched our lives in so many different ways. Hal Smith *was* Whit—his voice, his mannerisms, inflections, sense of humor, his very feel all came from Hal. When Hal Smith died, he left a huge void not just in the program, but in our lives. Here are some favorite personal memories of Hal, provided by those of us who worked most closely with him:

Paul McCusker (writer/director/producer):

"My favorite memory was when Hal recorded his personal 'thank you' to the staff at Focus on the Family for their prayers on behalf of his wife, Louise. He was deeply touched by our prayers, and I was moved by his expression of gratitude. I also remember his strength of character when we recorded 'The Mortal Coil' right after Louise passed away. We were worried that it might upset him because the program dealt with death, but he was determined to go on with it. His performance had us in tears—and yet he stayed resolved and professional. Those two memories don't do him justice, though. He was kind, generous, loving, gentle, and ego-less—a breed of 'gentleman-actor' that is hard to find these days (except, maybe, among the other radio actors we work with)."

Chuck Bolte (executive producer):

"In many ways, Hal's death affected me more deeply than the death of my own father. I honestly don't know why that is. I just know that when Paul McCusker called me at the National Religious Broadcasters conference to tell me Hal had died, I was calm and unshaken, perhaps because in some strange way we all expected it to happen within a few years. But when I hung up the phone, I lost it. It was as if someone had cut a chunk out of my heart, and I knew that even after the hurt had healed, there would always be a hole there.

"As far as memories go, how can you think of Hal and not think of his silly jokes? Or when he indulged us with his Otis character? (I still cherish the video I have of him ad-libbing a routine as Otis.) And how can you forget his touching 'thank you' to Dr. Dobson and the staff at Focus for their loving concern for Louise prior to and after her death, and how that was masterfully used in the 'Gone' episode? Acting-wise, I loved playing opposite Hal. One of the most fun and memorable times for me was when we did 'Gone Fishin'' because it was just Hal and me for most of the show."

Dave Arnold (production engineer/producer):

"I remember flying to California from Colorado for a recording session. We finally got to the studio and as usual, Hal was already there, sitting at the kitchen table, drinking a cup of McDonald's coffee, and sporting a big smile. After a warm greeting, Hal mentioned that he had something he wanted to give me. He opened up a sack and pulled out a beautiful sweatshirt, embroi-

In Loving Memory of

Hal Smith

Born
August 24, 1916
Gaylord, Michigan

Passed Away
January 28, 1994
Los Angeles, California

Service
Wednesday, Feb. 2, 1994, 1:00 p.m.
Pierce Brothers Moeller Murphy Chapel

Officiating
Rev. Inez Tarbell

Service concludes in the Chapel

Entombment
Woodlawn Mausoleum

Directors
Pierce Brothers Moeller Murphy Mortuary

From the funeral service for Hal Smith

dered with the logo of *The Andy Griffith Show.* He said they sent it to him as a gift, but it was an extra large. Hal had lost a lot of weight over the years and the shirt was far too big for him. He said he had thought of me, since I was a big guy, and handed it to me. I was so touched that I forgot to have him autograph it for me! But two months later, I brought the sweatshirt back with me to have him sign it. As always, he was more than gracious.

"But my most cherished memory of Hal happened in December of 1993. He asked Phil Lollar and me out to dinner at his favorite steak place. We met after the recording sessions and sat and talked for hours about Hal's life—his time in the service, how he got started in show business . . . everything. Phil and I plied him with questions, and he volleyed the answers right back. We were there for three hours, riveted by the conversation. Hal wanted us to have the king cut prime rib, but after seeing the price ($40 a pop), we decided on the regular cut. After the meal was over, Hal pulled out a $100 to pay for the meal and didn't ask for change. We left the restaurant and chatted for a few more minutes. I walked over to Hal's white Cadillac and looked inside to make sure everything was okay. He laughed at me for being so cautious. After a warm hug, we parted. That was the last time we ever saw each other. Hal passed away three weeks later.

"I still have dreams about him. He was a wonderful friend and a great loss."

Bob Luttrell (production engineer):

"I have so many favorite memories of Hal—every session was a memory! But if I had to pick one, I'd say it was just after his wife died. My mother died less than two weeks later. Hal and I would go outside the studio and cry together."

Phil Lollar (writer/director/producer):

"I have many fond memories of Hal: his willingness to do Otis, Winnie the Pooh, or any of his countless characters at the drop of a hat . . . his incredible lion roar into a trash can and horse-whinny into a cup (for added effect) . . . his endless supply of funny stories . . . his breaking into a song whenever there was even the slightest lull in the recording session . . . his ever-present pack of Raleigh cigarettes (a nasty habit we tried to get him to break) . . . his coughing into the microphone at the worst possible moment (thanks to the Raleighs!) . . . his throaty "Ooooooh!" . . . his impish grin and twinkling eyes.

Hal Smith and Chuck Bolte enjoy themselves while recording an early *Family Portraits* episode. Hal would later become John Avery Whittaker, and Chuck would take the reigns as executive producer of *Adventures In Odyssey* and play the voice of George Barclay.

"But my fondest and most cherished memory of Hal occurred in the summer of 1992. My birthday was approaching, and I knew my wife had a surprise party planned for me. When we returned to our house after dinner, I realized just how big the surprise was. My wife had invited not just our friends, but all of the people I worked with—including all of the *Odyssey* regulars. And sitting right in the middle of everyone was Hal Smith. He was holding court—telling jokes, singing songs, doing all of his characters for the kids, and laughing long and loud. Everyone had an absolutely wonderful time, and I was stunned, overjoyed, and completely honored that a man of Hal's stature would consider me a good enough friend to drive all the way across town just to attend my birthday party.

"So my most cherished memory is Hal's friendship, and I am honored that he counted me among *his* friends. I shall always miss him and never forget him for as long as I live."

18 THE COMPLETE GUIDE TO ADVENTURES IN ODYSSEY

THE CAST

The People Behind the Voices

Undoubtedly, Hal Smith as the original Whit was at the center of *Adventures in Odyssey* for many years. But there have been *hundreds* of talented actors and actresses who have helped make our program what it is. After all, *Adventures in Odyssey* would only be words on paper if it weren't for those who bring the characters to life. Here are quotes from *some* of the actors who have appeared in major roles on *AIO* during its first 10 years.

CHRIS LANSDOWNE *as CHRIS*

Other credits include: The voice of Barbie and many other toys.

"Bob Luttrell brought me on board with *Adventures in Odyssey*. He used to work at a studio in Hollywood where I did a lot of voiceover work, and he saw the fish symbol on my car's bumper and approached me. He explained about the program and said they were looking for a perky, bubbly voice for the show's announcer. I wasn't sure at first, but when he mentioned the name 'Dr. James Dobson,' I said, 'I'm in!'

"I count it a joy to be on this show. Because I do the voices of so many toys, I feel a real sense of responsibility because my voice is going into their homes. I want to be like a good friend—a comforting presence to them. And I think I do that on *Adventures in Odyssey*. It's also great to work with such wonderful people. It's like a second family, really."

WILL RYAN *as EUGENE MELTSNER and HARLOW DOYLE*

Other credits include: Rabbit and Tigger in Disney's Welcome to Pooh Corner*; the seahorse in Disney's* The Little Mermaid*; Petrie in the Don Bluth/Steven Spielberg/George Lucas production* The Land Before Time; *Elmo Aardvark; creative director of* Snappytoons.

"I came aboard at the suggestion of Bob Luttrell, who had duplicated my voice demo tape. I had also worked with Hal Smith on *Pooh Corner.* One day at the studio, Hal told me, 'I just met with this really smart guy named Jim Dobson. His company is putting together a dramatic radio show, and he said they want to do 2,000 episodes!' That sounded pretty good to me!

"I love radio. One reason working on this program is so great is because *radio* is so great! In a sense, the listeners are co-creators of the show because they supply the mental picture for what they're hearing. Also [*Adventures in Odyssey*] shows remind me of the old Jack Benny radio programs or *The Alan Young Radio Show,* because there is development of individual characters. At the same time it's an anthology-type program, so we get to play lots of different characters. My first two episodes were a good example. The first was dramatic ['Life of the Party'] while the second was wacky ['Gifts for Madge & Guy'].

"It's fun to work with pals like Katie Leigh Pavlakovich and Ed Walker [the voice of Tom Riley and Bart Rathbone]—and, of course, Hal—as well as with people I haven't worked with before. Plus, the scripts are intelligent—far superior to the television scripts that they're churning out at present."

KATIE LEIGH PAVLAKOVICH *as CONNIE KENDALL*

Other credits include: Baby Rowlf in Jim Henson's Muppet Babies*; Sunni Gummi in Disney's* Gummi Bears*; Honker in Disney's* Darkwing Duck*; Dumbo in Disney's* Dumbo Circus.

"I had the radio on while I was driving to an appointment in Arcadia, California, and I heard 'Gone Fishin'' [one of Focus's first dramatic programs]. I recognized Hal Smith's voice. I knew Hal from when we did *Dumbo Circus*, and I was familiar with Focus on the Family, but I had never heard the dramas before. I thought, *Wow! If they're going to do dramas now with actors like Hal, I want to be a part of it!* And since I just happened to be in Arcadia [where Focus was located at the time], I called them up and dropped off one of my demo tapes to Steve Harris, because I wanted to work with Christians.

"The character Connie is so much like me, especially before she got saved. I was just like that. And the really great thing is that the scripts always maintain the integrity of her character. It's not just about getting a message across. That's why I appreciate everyone who works on *Adventures in Odyssey*—they know that while our souls change immediately when we become Christians, it takes our personalities much longer to change. We may get better, but there are always going to be certain areas where we struggle. The *Adventures in Odyssey* characters and programs ring true in that respect. They do what real people would do in those situations. And I learn something from the character I play. When I started with the show, I hadn't been a Christian very long. All of the things I was struggling with in my life would show up in the scripts. I've been ministered to just by showing up for work."

DAVE MADDEN *as BERNARD WALTON*

Other credits include: Reuben Kincaid on The Partridge Family*; recurring roles on the TV classics* Laugh-In *and* Alice.

"I'd do the show every week if I could. Bernard is a lot of fun to play. And *Adventures in Odyssey* is a family show presented in a nonsectarian way, which is a pleasure. I've said many times before, if you couldn't pay us anymore, I'd still show up and do the program. It's not the kind of thing you do for money. It's the kind of thing you do for love."

TOWNSEND COLEMAN *as JASON WHITTAKER*

Other credits include: The Tick in the Fox animated series The Tick*; Michaelangelo in* Teenage Mutant Ninja Turtles*; Corporal Capeman in the animated series* Inspector Gadget*; the voice of NBC TV's "Must See TV" and "Tonite Show" promos.*

"I became involved in *Adventures in Odyssey* through Katie Leigh Pavlokovich. We had done a lot of voice work together in town, and she knew I was a Christian. So when the role of Jason came up, she encouraged me to read for it.

"Much of my day is spent doing commercial things for secular programs. My work life is largely about selling stuff that I really couldn't care less about. So when something like *Adventures in Odyssey* comes along—a program that has meaning—it is such a breath of fresh air.

"Every recording session, the thing I look forward to the most is reading the letters from listeners—both pro and con. I rarely hear from listeners or viewers about my other work, but *Adventures in Odyssey* listeners are really paying attention to the program and following what happens with the characters. The show *reaches* them. And that's why I like to do it."

ALAN YOUNG *as JACK ALLEN*

Other credits include: Scrooge McDuck in Disney's Duck Tales*; Wilbur on television's* Mr. Ed*; Filby in the classic movie* The Time Machine.

"Right away, I enjoyed working on the program. I was saddened by the stuff on television. *Adventures in Odyssey* reminds me of the old days of radio, where the whole family would gather around together and listen to a show. You know that working on *Adventures in Odyssey* is nothing you're going to be ashamed of."

PAUL HERLINGER *as JOHN AVERY WHITTAKER*

Other credits include: 25 years in TV production, specializing in writing and producing documentaries and public affairs programs; narrator of more than a dozen PBS documentaries, as well as hundreds of films, videos, slide shows, and commercials.

"Stepping into Hal Smith's place (no one can fill his shoes) has been challenging and very satisfying. Personally, working on *Adventures in Odyssey* has meant getting to know an incredibly talented and good-hearted group of professionals, knowing that the shows are reaching out to many people of all ages and backgrounds. Playing Whit and being accepted by my fellow actors, as well as the writers, producers, and engineers, has been fun and gratifying.

"I look back on the recording sessions I've done with a sense of warmth and camaraderie that made the sessions feel like we were a family and not just actors doing a job. My most touching experience so far occurred when I received a recent out-of-the-blue phone call one evening from a little girl in Amarillo, Texas. She is an *Adventures in Odyssey* fan who looked up my name on the Internet and just wanted to talk to the new Whit in person—sort of a telephone 'autograph.' "

STEVE BURNS *as RODNEY RATHBONE*

Other credits include: Co-starred in Centennial, *a Universal Pictures mini-series; co-starred in the movie* Casey's Shadow; West Wind, *a TV series; and* Blinded by the Light, *a made-for-TV movie; also has done numerous background voices.*

"My kids live and breathe *Adventures in Odyssey.* They love the fact that I'm Rodney—although I'm not sure how my being the bad guy will play out in the future.

"*Adventures in Odyssey* transcends age. It doesn't matter what age you are when you listen to it. It touches you. Plus you're getting a great spiritual message, which is so unlike what you get with TV. The only thing *Adventures in Odyssey* needs is more Rodney Rathbone shows!"

A 1989 photo of some of *Adventures in Odyssey's* core cast members: (back row, left to right) Kyle Fisk, Genny Mullen Long, David Griffin; (front row, left to right) Chad Reisser, Azure Janosky, Donald Long, Joseph Cammarato.

THE ADVENTURES IN ODYSSEY *TEAM*

The People Who Make It All Happen

Many talented and creative people have contributed to the success of *Adventures in Odyssey* over the years. Here are some thoughts from just a few of the people who have been integral parts of the *AIO* world.

DAVE ARNOLD
PRODUCTION ENGINEER; PRODUCER (1988– PRESENT)

"*Adventures in Odyssey* has been the most rewarding work I have ever done. Having the opportunity to do something fun, work with incredibly talented people, and fulfill a desire to impact our generation in a creative way is a tremendous blessing. When I read the letters from both children and adults who have been changed by the power of God through the show and even accepted Christ as Savior, I am brought to tears. It is a truly humbling experience.

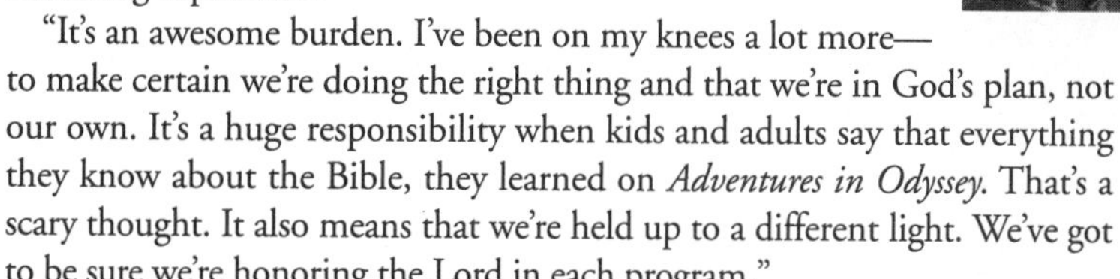

"It's an awesome burden. I've been on my knees a lot more—to make certain we're doing the right thing and that we're in God's plan, not our own. It's a huge responsibility when kids and adults say that everything they know about the Bible, they learned on *Adventures in Odyssey.* That's a scary thought. It also means that we're held up to a different light. We've got to be sure we're honoring the Lord in each program."

CHUCK BOLTE
EXECUTIVE PRODUCER (1988 –1996)

"Being on *Adventures in Odyssey* stretched me creatively, spiritually, and administratively. It is a great source of pride to know that we were able to be part of something that has had such a profound impact on so many families . . . more than any of us could have dreamed. It is also humbling to know that these programs may very well influence numerous future generations. I consider it a deep honor to have been part of the team."

The AIO Team

MARK DRURY
PRODUCTION ENGINEER (1993–PRESENT)

"*Adventures in Odyssey* has been a real revelation in my life. I can now look back on years of seemingly unrelated interests and experiences (music, photography, audio engineering, movies) and see how God used each one to prepare me for what I'm doing now. As a production engineer for *Adventues in Odyssey,* I have the three things I have always yearned (and begged God) for in a career: that it would make a difference in some kind of eternal way; that what I worked on would be of the highest quality; and that it would satisfy my need to be creative. Working on *Adventues in Odyssey* has been the perfect fulfillment of these three desires. Isn't God awesome?"

PHIL LOLLAR
CO-CREATOR; WRITER/DIRECTOR (1987–PRESENT)

"As for me, what more can I say about *Adventures in Odyssey* that hasn't already been said by these incredibly talented gentlemen? I would only add that I, too, praise God for allowing me to serve Him through this program, and for using *Adventues in Odyssey* to, in a small way, reflect the greater, grander Adventure that one day awaits us all."

BOB LUTTRELL
PRODUCTION ENGINEER (1987–1995)

"I've done many productions over the years, but *Adventures in Odyssey* gave me the opportunity to work on something I really believe in. It not only gave me the chance to expand my production skills, which I did in many ways, but it gave me a chance to do something unique. It's an entertaining show—as good as anything out there, and better than most—that touches and reaches kids."

PAUL McCUSKER
WRITER/DIRECTOR; PRODUCER (1988–PRESENT)

"It's difficult to say what *Adventures in Odyssey* has meant to me in a concise way since it now seems irreversibly integrated into my life and experiences. The creative dynamics of the team, the variety and scope of the episodes, the personal and professional relationships, the ministry opportunities . . . it's been a little bit of everything.

"I've learned a lot by working on *Adventures in Odyssey*—probably more than I could have learned elsewhere. More than anything, my experience with the program has given me an appreciation for the difference between my intentions as writer and how my writing is perceived by our audience. Focus's emphasis on listening to our audience has been formative in making me think and rethink what communication through drama is all about. The answers are still forthcoming, but it has taught me *a lot* along the way.

"The constant challenge and expectation of quality from Steve Harris and Phil Lollar, then later, Chuck Bolte, Bob Luttrell, Dave Arnold and the gang, and even our actors, stimulated me intellectually, emotionally, and spiritually. There is little tolerance for sloppy thinking or writing with our team. The variety of spiritual experiences within the team also forced a higher sensitivity to the spiritual realm of our work. In addition, we learned quickly that the program itself was often a reflection of where the team members were spiritually, for better or worse. What influenced us also influenced the direction of the show. That taught me an important lesson: I can't separate my spiritual condition from my writing."

STEVEN STILES
VIDEO EXECUTIVE PRODUCER/DIRECTOR/WRITER (1989–PRESENT)

"I was new to animation when we began producing the *Adventures in Odyssey* videos, and so the creative challenge has been a real 'E ticket' ride: moments of sheer panic followed by a series of blind switchbacks and disorienting loops after which I'd ask, 'Are we done?' But I've found great joy in trying to help craft stories which can offer hope and guidance to young viewers. Our prayer is always that, even though our efforts are flawed in various ways, the Lord can use these stories for redemptive purposes. I'm honored just to be involved—white knuckles and all."

ROBERT VERNON

VIDEO WRITER/PRODUCER/DIRECTOR (1990–PRESENT)

"Early in my professional career I had the opportunity of working for three years on a major network television series. That felt empty compared to the fulfillment I receive being involved with *Adventures in Odyssey.*"

"If you would have asked me in college what my dream was, I would have said, 'To be making quality films that entertain as well as teach solid Christian values.' *Adventures in Odyssey* has been the realization of that dream! And with new opportunities opening up for us in television—and a growing international market—that dream is being exceeded."

MARSHAL YOUNGER

WRITER/DIRECTOR (1993–PRESENT)

"When I was hired as a staff writer, it was a dream come true. To come right out of grad school and join a staff writing team—on *Adventures in Odyssey,* no less—was something I didn't think possible. But God worked things out in His own way. Since then, being around so many creative minds—all trying to do God's work—has been one of the greatest experiences of my life. I consider it an incredible privilege to be using my talents for something like this.

"At times, it is easy for me to write something simply for the benefit of trying to tell a good story, or be funny, or impress the rest of the team. But then, when I read the letters from listeners—especially the ones that say, 'My son accepted Christ because of this episode'—I have to step back and realize there is a higher purpose here. The number of children and adults I can influence through this show is staggering and humbling, and if [reaching those people] is not my main goal, my work here is meaningless. This attitude has carried over into all aspects of my life, and I have begun to realize that reaching others and influencing them [for Christ] should always be my main goal."

It's Not as Easy as It Sounds

How We Put Together an Episode

In our first 10 years, we produced more than 370 original programs. With that kind of output, it may seem like *Adventures in Odyssey* episodes just roll out of our studios easier than water off a duck's back.

But in reality, *hours* of work go into creating each episode. Every show is the result of a month-long process that culminates in the recording of the script, followed by a week or two of post-production (editing, adding sound effects, and so on). And though the process has changed somewhat from the early days of the program, we still produce each episode basically the same way.

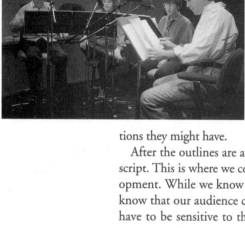

It all starts with the story concepts. The team will discuss ideas and decide which ones to pursue and which ones to toss. We then narrow down those ideas to the four we plan to use at the next recording session.

Once the story lines are hammered out, we then go about crafting the scripts. First, we fashion them into detailed outlines that break the story into scenes and acts. This gets passed around to the *AIO* team for any ideas, notes, and suggestions they might have.

After the outlines are approved, we move on to a first draft of the actual script. This is where we concentrate on dialogue, character, and story development. While we know our target audience is 8- to 12-year-olds, we also know that our audience contains both younger and older listeners, and we have to be sensitive to them as well. Another important consideration in scripting is trying to find the balance between making our characters behave like real kids—with all their foibles and failings—and making them behave like the role models listening parents want their kids to hear.

Once the first draft of the script is complete, it also makes the rounds among the *Adventures in Odyssey* team for more ideas, notes, and suggestions. Meanwhile, the casting of each individual program begins—often one of the most difficult parts of the process. Casting the regulars is easy enough, but finding just the right actor or actress to fill new roles is a chancy affair at best—not because the actors and actresses aren't talented, but because the writers and directors often have specific ideas in mind for a role, ideas that are sometimes difficult to get across.

It's Not as Easy as It Sounds

While the casting is being completed and recording studio dates are booked, we finalize changes to the scripts—anything from line and word changes to complete rewrites of scenes. Copies of the scripts are then made, and we're ready for the studio.

Finally, the big day arrives. Cast and crew meet in the morning at the southern California based studio where the recording is done (since most of the actors live in the Los Angeles-Hollywood area). The actors are shown to their proper places, and the director gives them a brief rundown of the story while they mark their scripts, often adding notes or highlighting their lines. After a few last-minute adjustments of the microphones and gulps of coffee, we're ready to record.

In this 1990 photo, Corey Burton is shown recording one of his numerous roles for *AIO*.

Ideally, all of the actors are assembled for the recording, but occasionally someone is missing, either because of a scheduling conflict or because we haven't found just the right person to voice a character. In that case, we're forced to "wild" record—that is, record those missing lines later and drop them in during the editing phase.

Each episode typically takes three or four hours to record, and we record two programs in a day. During the session, if an actor makes a mistake or the director wants a scene acted differently, everyone stops and re-records. Normally, complete scenes are recorded before moving on to the next one.

Once the scripts are recorded, our production engineers take the tapes—called *tracks*—back to their studios at Focus on the Family headquarters. There they edit the tracks to take out all the mistakes, get the show down to time, then add appropriate sound effects. Most of the sound effects are from sound effects libraries created over the years or compiled by other sound designers. Those sound effects not in our library are created by the engineers on our foley stage.

While sound effects are being added, a copy of the edited tracks are sent to our composers, who write custom music—underscores and bridges between scenes—for the show. Our production engineers then assemble the voice tracks, sound effects, and music, mix it all together on one master track, and play it for the *AIO* staff for still more ideas, notes, and suggestions. From start to finish, one *AIO* show can take four to six weeks to complete.

This is an early shot. Phil Lollar, Paul McCusker, and Chris Lansdowne work on "wrap-arounds"—the segments that open and close each episode.

After the program passes a final inspection, it goes to our Cassette Duplication Department, where copies are made and sent to radio stations all over the country—including the one where you live.

And once the tapes are shipped, we can sit back for a well-deserved rest . . . for about five minutes! Then we remember we have a show to do next week, and the whole process starts up again!

Old Tape and Kitty Litter

How We Make All Those Cool Sound Effects

An audio drama without sound effects is . . . well . . . just a lot of people talking. We may have great actors and exciting dialogue, but the scene still sounds very empty without *growls, gurgles,* and *gongs.* That's why sound effects are so important—they fill out a scene and make it seem real. But just how do our production engineers come up with all those neat sounds? *Adventures in Odyssey* Producer Dave Arnold tells all about it:

The easiest way to describe the sound design for *Adventures in Odyssey* is that we try to make a movie soundtrack for each program. The idea is to create an audio picture that listeners can "see" in their imaginations. To do that, we start by putting ourselves mentally in the location of each scene.

For instance, if the scene is in a home, we ask ourselves, What's happening there? Is the TV on? How about a dishwasher? Washer or dryer? Is someone taking a shower? What season is it? If it's summer, you might have an air conditioner or a fan on. If it's winter, a fireplace may be stoked up, or perhaps the furnace is running. What's the weather like outside? If it's sunny, then birds may be singing, or a dog might be barking, or perhaps someone is mowing or watering their lawn. If it's winter, perhaps someone is chopping wood or using a chain saw. Maybe it's raining or thundering outside. These are just a few of the questions we ask ourselves—and that's just for *one scene!*

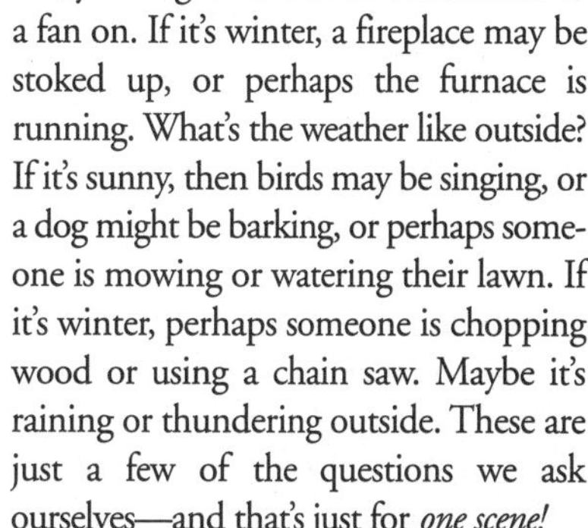

We also use sound to create emotion. If it's a somber scene, rain may be appropriate. If it's a scary scene, we use thunder and lightning. If it's a happy scene, birds chirp. Adding all these sounds is called *layering,* and we do as much of it as we can to create a world that sounds as real as possible.

But that's only *part* of the process. Next comes something called *foley,* which is simply adding live sound to an existing soundtrack. In the movies, foley artists watch the scene on the screen, then physically "act out" things like footsteps, punches, falling bodies, and other effects needed to make the scene come alive. We do the same thing for our programs. We listen to the recorded dialogue, then act out the physical movements of each character.

Perhaps Whit is cleaning up dishes, or Connie is wiping down the counter. Or Eugene may be tinkering with some invention.

But adding those sounds isn't always easy. For one thing, real sounds don't often work. An actual recording of an arrow flying through the air and hitting a target sounds nothing like what you *think* it should sound like. That's because movie sound artists have beefed up those kinds of sounds, and in doing so, have created an *expectation.* So now we have to use not the *real* sound, but rather what our ear *expects* to hear.

But just where do we get all those sound effects? A couple of different places. The first is our sound effects library. It's made up of lots of compact discs with hundreds of sounds on them—everything from a ticking clock to a door opening to a phone ringing to a baby crying to a *nursery* full of babies crying to a crowd of people to a cattle stampede to a whole army!

Still, even though we have all these effects right at our fingertips, almost every show has a scene that calls for a sound we just don't have on disc. And that's when we have to actually *use* our fingertips and create the sounds ourselves.

Say a scene calls for the characters to run on a dirt road, then run through bushes in the forest. Well, neither one of those effects is in our library, so we have to look for substitutes that *sound* like the real thing—and sometimes those substitutes can be pretty weird! For instance, the bushes are old, used recording tape . . . and the dirt road is kitty litter!

Old tape and kitty litter. It may sound strange—but that's the world of sound effects!

A Note About the Notes

The Music of *Adventures in Odyssey*

It is one of the most important aspects of every *Adventure in Odyssey.* It can make or break each program—and mean the difference between whether a production is a classic or a dud. And if it's done right, you hardly even notice it's there.

It's the music.

Adventures in Odyssey is blessed with some of the finest composers in the country. They include John Campbell, Martie Echito, Tim Hosman, James Gabriel, Pat Woodland, Jack Ballard, and Barry Young. Their melodies not only tie the shows together, but also lift the words, sound effects, and performances into the realm of art. And it all starts with that familiar seven note theme, written especially for *Adventures in Odyssey* by our main composer, John Campbell.

"When Steve Harris first asked me to write the theme for the show," John remembers, "I tried a couple of different passes, but they really didn't seem to be right. They didn't have that sense of whimsy that was needed to start off the show. So I shelved them. A few days later, I sat down at the piano and the theme just came to me. Within about 30 minutes, I had it all written out. Then I went to Martie Echito, who had a bigger studio than I did at the time, and we laid it down on tape using synthesizers. We were so excited about it that we called up everyone we knew and said, 'Listen to *this!*'"

Like some of the other *AIO* composers, John also works on TV and movie projects. "I've learned a lot writing music for Hanna-Barbera cartoons and Fox shows, and I bring those sensibilities to *Adventures in Odyssey*," he says. "Each show, I try to say, 'How can I make it better than the last one?' Of all the shows I work on, though, *Adventures in Odyssey* is by far the most challenging because each episode is a different style—comedy, drama, suspense, mystery, and so on.

"It's been a very rewarding experience. We've become such a close crew, I now consider the *AIO* guys to be some of my closest friends. Even though I do tons of TV stuff, I'll always make time for *Adventures in Odyssey*."

Part Two

Take a Ride into a Land of Excitement . . .

Explore the Radio Drama of *Adventures in Odyssey*

1987

The first 13 *Family Portraits* episodes were an experiment. We tinkered with who our target audience would be and wondered whether anyone would like the series. After a lot of hard work and discussion, on January 5, 1987, *Family Portraits* premiered.

After writing several episodes, the pressure was on—especially on the writing side. Steve Harris and I were the only writers, and we needed help. So Mike Trout and Steve found another writer. They gave him a completed but unscripted story to see how he could modify it for *Family Portraits*. That writer's name was Paul McCusker.

Family Portraits was a resounding success. We received over 4,000 responses from listeners—every one of them positive and enthusiastic. Christian audiences wanted good stories that reflected their worldview—which was just what *Family Portraits* was bringing to them.

We laid a solid foundation with those test episodes, but we still needed to make some changes. First, we narrowed our target audience to 8- to 12-year-olds. Then we fleshed out the characters and locations we had already created, adding new characters to the program as well. To do that, we met with Chuck Bolte and Joe Glauberg, who was a staff writer on *Happy Days* and *Mork and Mindy*. We booked a conference room at the Embassy Suites Hotel in Arcadia, California, and had an all-day brainstorming session.

One of the big things that came out of that meeting was "Connie." We needed another strong main character, and the upbeat, explosive Connie Kendall was brought into the picture. The character of Officer David Harley also popped up during this time. We wanted a purely comical character on the program and decided that this bumbling policeman would be the one. (Little did we know the trouble Harley's character would bring us.) Finally, we rounded out Tom Riley's character, giving him a history that coincided with Odyssey's.

During this time, we also came up with the opening musical theme for the program, composed by John Campbell. John wrote the distinctive, dramatic seven-note theme still heard on the program today.

The program was so well received that it got its own time slot. In the *FOF* time slot, the "wrap-arounds"—introductions and conclusions for each episode—had previously been handled by Mike Trout and Dr. Dobson. But we decided that in addition to its own time slot, the show also needed its own announcer. So after a round of auditions to find the right person, Chris Lansdowne joined the team. The "wrap-arounds" Chris did were also handled differently. They became skits to introduce the show, which then tied up any loose ends at the program's conclusion.

A big change was in progress at Focus as well. The ministry had outgrown its Arcadia facilities and had purchased two large buildings in Pomona, California. Remodeling plans in the new facility called for us to get a large, new 8-track recording studio.

Our biggest change, however, was in the title of the show. *Family Portraits* was fine for an all-encompassing family show, but since we were narrowing the audience's age range, we needed something new. We couldn't simply call the program "Odyssey"—it was too generic a term, and too many other programs and products already used the word as part of their titles. Finally, after a long day of brainstorming, Steve and I came up with the name—and on November 21, 1987, *Odyssey USA* premiered.

FAMILY PORTRAITS

FAMILY PORTRAITS

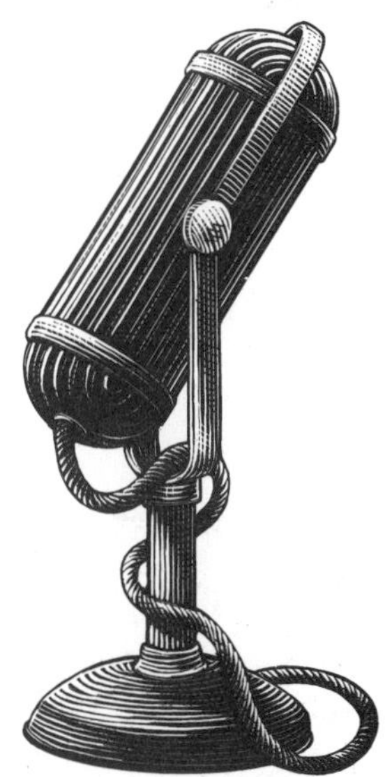

Episode #1 "Whit's Visitor"

Theme: The effects of divorce on children.
Scripture reference: Malachi 2:13-17
Written and directed by Steve Harris and Phil Lollar
Production engineers: Steve Harris and Bob Luttrell
(Original air date: 1-05-87)

Whit settles down for the evening with a cup of hot cocoa and a good book. Suddenly, he is startled by a noise in the basement. He investigates and discovers eight-year-old Davey Morrison, who lives across the street. At least, he did until tonight. Davey has set up housekeeping in Whit's basement. Whit finds that after months of chronic bickering, Davey's father has moved out of the house. Davey dreads choosing between his mom and dad and feels responsible for the conflict between them, which is why he decided to move into Whit's basement.

As the conversation continues, Davey touchingly describes his life in a disintegrating family. Whit encourages his young friend and tries to help him understand some of the tough realities of grown-up relationships. Finally, Davey realizes that he can't help his family unless he goes home. As he and Whit emerge from the basement, Davey sees his father's car parked in its usual spot on the driveway. Did his dad come home to stay? It's not clear. But either way, little Davey has done some serious growing up tonight.

the *Adventures in Odyssey* archives:

"Whit's Visitor" marked the first appearance of Whit, Tom, and Whit's End. Whit's opening monologue gives you a good idea of our intentions for the series, but it really belonged at the beginning of "The New Kid in Town" (*Family Portraits* #3), which was the first episode written.

STUDY QUESTIONS:

1. Why did Davey think he was responsible for his parents' argument?
2. Whit said, "Sometimes the only difference between an adult and a child is that the adult is taller." What did he mean?
3. Read Malachi 2:13-17. How does God feel about divorce?

Episode #2 "Dental Dilemma"

Theme: Teasing; dealing with fear.
Scripture reference: Psalm 27:1
Written by Susan McBride
Directed by Steve Harris and Chuck Bolte
Production engineers: Steve Harris and Bob Luttrell
(Original air date: 1-12-87)

Seven-year-old Emily Forbes is scheduled for her very first dental appointment. She can hardly wait to go—until her older brother, Mark, describes an imaginary visit to the dentist that would scare the Marquis de Sade. His horror story is so severe that when "D day" arrives, it's a wonder Emily can even be found. But Mark is also scheduled for an appointment. He promises Emily that she will survive the treatment if she imitates her courageous brother, who never flinches, no matter how much blood or pain.

Emily sees Dr. Graves first, and her anxious questions show her terror. Dr. Graves gently gets to the source of Emily's warped information. The good dentist promises not to hurt Emily, and together they devise a plan to turn the tables on Mark, giving him a taste of what it feels like to be afraid.

the *Adventures in Odyssey* archives:

Chad Reisser played Mark Forbes. Chad later played the recurring role of Monty, Whit's grandson. He was also Digger Digwillow, the young man who meets Jesus in the first Imagination Station episode. Emily Forbes was played by Sage Bolte—who was later cast as Robyn Jacobs. Sage's father is Chuck Bolte. He codirected this episode and later became executive producer of *Adventures in Odyssey.*

STUDY QUESTIONS:

1. Why was Mark wrong to tease Emily? Have you ever teased anyone that way?
2. Were Emily and Dr. Graves right to get back at Mark?
3. Do you think *all* teasing is bad? Why or why not? How do you think Jesus feels about it?

Episode #3 "The New Kid in Town"

Theme: Making new friends.
Scripture reference: Proverbs 18:24
Written by Phil Lollar
Directed by Steve Harris and Chuck Bolte
Production engineers: Steve Harris and Bob Luttrell
(Original air date: 1-19-87)

During his morning walk, Whit notices that a new family has moved into the neighborhood—Larry Walker; his wife, Colleen; and their 13-year-old daughter, Shawn. Lately, Shawn has been causing problems for her parents. The Walkers move frequently because of Larry's job, and all the moving has made Shawn insecure.

Whit believes that Shawn's insecurity is a problem and decides to help her. As Shawn leaves school later that afternoon, she meets a seemingly confused elderly gentleman who asks directions to an establishment called Whit's End. After some prodding from the gentleman, Shawn agrees to take the old man there. The two end up having a wonderful conversation.

When they finally arrive at Whit's End, the old man invites Shawn to come inside and meet some of the kids. Shawn hesitates, believing they won't talk to her because she's new. The older man reminds her that *they've* just finished having a great talk, and they were complete strangers when they started their conversation.

As Shawn thinks about this, a Whit's End employee pokes his head out the door and tells the old gent he has a phone call. Astonished, Shawn realizes the old man is Whit! Whit apologizes for the deception, explaining that sometimes the only way to help someone is to make them think *they're* helping *you*. Just then, a boy from school walks past Whit's End. Shawn screws up her courage and talks to him. Shawn is pleased to find that the boy talks back! They go inside, and Whit smiles—a new friendship has begun.

Dear Chris
I realy like
ODYSSEY
and I listen
to it whenever
I can. for a suggestion
I think there
should be a ODYSSEY
Where Whit, Connie and
Eugene go to Hawaii.

the *Adventures in* ODYSSEY archives:

Although it's third on the list, "The New Kid in Town" was actually the first *Family Portraits* episode written. Chuck Bolte played mailman George Poindexter—foreshadowing *another* George he would later play: George Barclay.

STUDY QUESTIONS:

1. Why did Shawn have trouble talking to people?
2. Have you ever come across anyone at school or church who acted like Shawn? How could you help them overcome their shyness?
3. Name three ways to make friends.

Episode #4 "No Stupid Questions"

Theme: Respect for the handicapped; the value of seeking knowledge.
Scripture reference: Proverbs 18:15
Written by Susan McBride
Directed by Steve Harris
Production engineer: Bob Luttrell
(Original air date: 1-26-87)

Meg Stevens and her mother, Carol, a new beautician in town, have a problem: Carol is divorced and there is no place for Meg to go after school except to the beauty shop. Meg is an inquisitive little girl, and unfortunately, she's beginning to get into the clienteles' hair!

Whit learns of Meg's situation and realizes who might be just the right mentor for her. Whit makes a call to the Odyssey Public Library and tells Chris Gottlieb to expect Meg Stevens—she has some questions no one but Chris can answer.

Chris is surprised when the inquisitive one turns out to be a 10-year-old girl. But a surprise also awaits Meg—Chris is in a wheelchair. There are a few moments of uncomfortable conversation. Soon, though, the two become fast friends and end up filling an important gap in each other's lives.

STUDY QUESTIONS:

1. Whit told Meg, "There are no stupid questions." What did he mean by that?
2. Why was Chris so angry about everything?
3. What's the best way to treat someone who has a handicap?

Episode #5 "You're Not Gonna Believe This . . ."

Theme: The importance of a good reputation.
Scripture references: Proverbs 18:7; 22:1
Written and directed by Phil Lollar
Production engineer: Bob Luttrell
(Original air date: 2-02-87)

Jonathan Charles Michael Stephen Wentworth III is on restriction . . . *again.* No one knows why he does so many nutty things. But his cousin, Jamie, thinks that carrying around four first names for 14 years has made him a bit strange. Of course, no one calls him by his full name; everyone who knows him calls him by his nickname, "Budgie."

Budgie isn't a bad kid—he just tends to exaggerate the truth. This time Budgie exaggerates about a small, black umbrella, which belongs to his mother. Or, rather, *belonged* to his mom. Budgie used her umbrella and ended up giving it away to an old west saloon girl, who, according to Budgie, drove up in a large, purple fire engine.

Cousin Jamie tells Whit about Budgie's little escapade and finds all this a little hard to swallow. Jamie wonders why he can't have a normal cousin like everybody else does. Whit tries to get Jamie to appreciate Budgie's unusual personality. Whit nearly succeeds when Budgie walks in a few moments later, apparently with proof about the outrageous umbrella affair.

Unfortunately, it turns out that Budgie exaggerated yet *again* to turn up that proof. Jamie gets so angry at his cousin, he storms out of the room. Budgie doesn't understand Jamie's behavior until Whit explains how Budgie has violated Jamie's trust. "When someone you trust lies to you," Whit says, "that's the worst hurt of all." Budgie finds Jamie and apologizes to him, promising to try to do better. Jamie says that he'll try to be more trusting of Budgie from now on, too.

TRIVIA QUIZ

The Town of Odyssey

1. What is the name of the man who first settled in Odyssey?
2. What was Whit's End before it was the Fillmore Recreation Center?
3. What is Wonderworld and who built it?
4. The Odyssey Coyotes play what sport?
5. How did Camp What-a-Nut get its name?
6. Which two rooms in Whit's End are painted green, and why?
7. What historic landmark sits on Tom Riley's farm?
8. What used to be located on the site where the Electric Palace now stands?
9. What do the Odyssey War Memorial and Whit's End have in common?
10. What are the names of the mountain and lake located just outside Odyssey?

1. Horace McCalister. 2. It was the mayor's house. Before that, it was a church. 3. It's a tree house, built by Digger Digwillow. 4. They actually play three: Baseball, basketball, and softball. 5. From an Indian phrase "Wey-Aka-Tal-Ah-Nee-Tee," which means "land that stinks like swamp"—same as the area surrounding Odyssey. 6. The hidden attic room from "The Treasure of Le Monde!" and the basement secret room from "The Case of the Secret Room" are painted green to remind everyone of the greed at the center of both stories. 7. Timmy's cabin, once used by Johnny Appleseed. 8. Blackgaard's Castle, which burned down at the hands of Dr. Blackgaard and Richard Maxwell. 9. They are both located in McCalister Park. 10. Forrest Mountain and Trickle Lake.

the *Adventures in* ODYSSEY archives:

"You're Not Gonna Believe This..." was rewritten and remade as *Adventures in Odyssey* episode #44, "It Sure Seemed Like It to Me." See that episode for study questions.

Episode #6 "My Brother's Keeper"

Theme: Sibling conflict.
Scripture reference: Proverbs 12:18
Written by Paul McCusker, from a story by Phil Lollar
Directed by Steve Harris and Phil Lollar
Production engineer: Bob Luttrell
(Original air date: 2-16-87)

Twelve-year-old Phillip Callas has a problem—namely, his six-year-old brother, Dean. Dean is constantly getting himself and Phillip into trouble. Once, Dean nearly destroyed a special school project Phillip had recorded on his tape player. Then, later at baseball practice, Dean embarrassed Phillip by making a pre-supper snack out of a large bug. Phillip blows up at Dean, then sends him home, alone. Phillip half-jokingly wishes that something would happen to his little brother—until the phone rings, and his mother informs him that Dean never made it home. He's missing.

With Whit's help, Phillip searches for Dean. They find him in the bottom of a large hole at a construction site. Dean has taken a nasty fall and is unconscious. They rush him to the hospital. Phillip is upset, believing the whole thing is his fault. He hadn't *really* wanted anything to happen to Dean. Whit comforts Phillip and prays with him. As Phillip talks to God, Phillip realizes that Dean isn't such a bad kid after all.

Fortunately, aside from having a small concussion and some bruises and scratches, Dean is all right. Phillip goes into Dean's hospital room. There, Phillip apologizes for treating Dean so badly and says that Dean can play with anything he wants when he gets home. And of course, the one thing Dean wants to play with is Phillip's tape player.

the *Adventures in* ODYSSEY archives:

This was Paul McCusker's first script contribution to the world of *Adventures in Odyssey.*

STUDY QUESTIONS:

1. How should Phillip have handled the situation with Dean?
2. Have you ever treated your younger brother or sister, or even a friend at school or at church, the way Phillip treated Dean?
3. What does it mean to love your brothers and sisters?

Episode #7 "While Dad's Away"

Theme: Absentee fathers.
Scripture reference: Malachi 4:6
Written by Phil Lollar
Directed by Phil Lollar and Steve Harris
Production engineer: Bob Luttrell
(Original air date: 3-02-87)

As a favor to a friend, Whit shows Peter and Sarah, a young married couple, a house that's up for sale. Sarah loves the place, but Peter is wary, especially when Whit mentions that the previous owners, Michael and Janice Brettman, were forced to sell quickly. Peter thinks the Brettmans moved because the house is built over a graveyard or something, but the reason is far more serious than that.

Whit explains that Mike Brettman is vice president of sales for Odyssey Automotive. His job requires him to spend a lot of time away from home. Fortunately, Janice and the kids, DeWayne and Laura, are very supportive and understanding. While they're not pleased with their dad's frequent absences, they're determined to make any necessary adjustments.

Those adjustments slowly become more clear to Mike when he calls home during each trip. Janice recounts the day's activities, and Mike realizes that his family is getting too good at functioning without him. But Mike's not yet willing to change anything.

After one particularly depressing call, Mike decides to get a bite to eat at a local fast-food restaurant. A boy approaches him and asks if Mike will sit next to the door. The boy points to a sign that reads, "All children must be accompanied by parent or guardian." He explains that his mom is at work, and his dad is gone. He wants to play in the playground, and he can only if Mike pretends to be the boy's father. Mike agrees to help and suddenly realizes that lately he's had a lot of practice being a pretend father.

When Mike returns home, he tells Janice he misses being part of his own family. He asks her if she would like to move closer to his work so he can spend more time at home. Janice agrees wholeheartedly, and the Brettmans become a *real* family again.

STUDY QUESTIONS:

1. Was Mike wrong for wanting to be vice president? Explain.
2. Did Janice handle the news of Mike's promotion the best way? How could she have handled it better?
3. Janice and the kids learned to function without Mike. Are fathers and husbands *really* necessary in a family? Why?

Episode #8 "The Letter"

Theme: Communication with teens.
Scripture reference: Ephesians 6:1-4
Written and directed by Steve Harris
Production engineer: Bob Luttrell
(Original air date: 3-09-87)

Whit tells the story of Stan and his daughter, Stacy. Lately, things have been a little tense between the two of them—the usual friction that occurs between teenagers and their parents. One day, Stan gets home from work and finds Stacy on the phone. He interrupts Stacy's conversation and hangs up on her friend. Stacy declares that she hates her father. Each feels insulted and goes to an opposite corner of the house.

At this point, Stacy's mom intervenes. She finds a letter Stan had written for Stacy on her first birthday. It is filled with memories and hopes for the future, intended to be read at Stacy's high school graduation. Reading her father's words causes Stacy to rethink her attitude.

Meanwhile, Stan is busying himself in the garage with a woodworking project. Suddenly, he notices a note from Stacy on the floor near the door. Copying her father's style, Stacy recounts her own memories of early childhood and the special relationship she enjoyed with her father. She apologizes in the letter for their earlier confrontation. Stan opens the door to the workshop and finds Stacy standing there. Stan apologizes for their fight and suggests they go eat someplace where Stacy won't be embarrassed to be seen with her father. But Stacy has a better idea: dinner with her dad—at the hottest teen hangout in town.

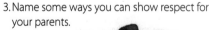

the *Adventures in* ODYSSEY archives:

Stacy, the daughter, was played by Katie Leigh Pavlakovich. Katie reappeared in *Adventures in Odyssey* as Connie Kendall. The father, Stan, was played by Alan Bergman—who plays Connie's father, Bill Kendall.

STUDY QUESTIONS:

1. Do you think Stacy was acting disrespectfully toward her father? Why or why not?
2. How well do you think Stan handled things with Stacy? Could he have acted any differently? Explain.
3. Name some ways you can show respect for your parents.

38 THE COMPLETE GUIDE TO ADVENTURES IN ODYSSEY

Episode #9 "A Different Kind of Peer Pressure"

Theme: Peer pressure.
Scripture reference: Romans 12:2
Written and directed by Steve Harris
Production engineer: Bob Luttrell
(Original air date: 3-16-87)

The Hudson Family—Richard, Ruth, and 14-year-old Blair—are shopping at Odyssey Mall. The tension is thick between Blair and Richard. It escalates into a full-blown argument when they run into Mickey, a childhood friend of Blair's. Blair treats Mickey like he has some sort of disease, and he leaves quickly. Blair excuses her rudeness by telling her parents that the gang at school has decided that Mickey is "out." Richard finds Blair's behavior inexcusable, and he grounds her for three weeks.

But Richard learns that peer pressure isn't just for the young. The next day at work, he puts down Jerry, a friend and co-worker, just because Jerry doesn't fit the corporate image. Jerry finds out about Richard's betrayal and blasts him for it, then quits.

Richard feels guilty and goes to Whit for advice. Whit tells him some prayer is in order, then strongly suggests that both Richard and Blair patch things up with Jerry and Mickey. Richard agrees, thanks Whit, and goes home. He asks Ruth if they have plans after church that Sunday.

Ruth says, "No, why?"

"Well," says Richard, "there are a couple of people I'd like to invite over for dinner. . . ."

STUDY QUESTIONS:

1. How could both Blair and Richard have better handled their situations?
2. Have you ever treated anyone the way Blair and Richard treated Mickey and Jerry? Has anyone ever treated you that way?
3. Is it *always* wrong to go along with the crowd? List some ways peer pressure can be good.

Episode #10 "In Memory of Herman"

Theme: Life after death; salvation.
Scripture reference: 1 Peter 3:1-2
Written and directed by Phil Lollar
Production engineer: Bob Luttrell
(Original air date: 3-23-87)

The Hardwick household is feeling gloomy: Seven-year-old Randy's turtle has died. On this particularly cold morning, the family is out in the backyard preparing a final resting place for poor "Herman." The Hardwicks have mixed feelings about this solemn occasion. Randy is in mourning. His mother, Amanda, sees this as an opportunity to teach Randy more about eternal life in Jesus Christ. But Vic, Randy's father, thinks the whole situation is silly. He is not a Christian, and the main thing that concerns him right now is getting out of the cold.

When the service is finally over and Randy goes off to school, Vic confronts Amanda. He claims she unfairly used the situation to influence their son toward Christianity. Amanda successfully turns the conversation around to talk to her husband about his own salvation. He gives his usual flippant and evasive retorts, and their discussion quickly turns into a philosophical debate. Then Vic stomps off to work.

After he is gone, Amanda turns to her only solace: prayer. She asks God to communicate to Vic the importance of following Jesus.

At a Bible study that afternoon, Amanda tells Whit about what happened, asking him how she can make Vic understand her faith. But before Whit can respond, the phone rings. Amanda answers, and a friend tells her that a terrible accident has occurred downtown at the Harrigan building where Vic works. Vic could be hurt—or even dead. Amanda starts off for the hospital when the phone rings again. It's Vic. He's all right, but his partner, Hank, is in critical condition. When Vic hangs up, Amanda nearly collapses. If Vic had died, she would have lost him for eternity! Whit comforts her, then gently suggests that maybe she is pushing Vic too hard. *She* can't save Vic, only *God* can.

Later, Vic comes home, upset about the accident. He walks outside to see his son, who is in the backyard. Randy is tearfully standing at Herman's grave. Randy is angry at God because He took Herman away, forever. Vic takes a deep breath and says that he's been wrong to tell Randy that life ends at death. Vic relates that today he discovered life is fragile—now, he believes there must be more to the world.

Then he approaches Amanda, and they both apologize for their earlier behavior. Vic asks if Amanda can share more about her faith. Amanda says, "Of course," and they walk back to the house—Amanda filled with hope, and Vic taking his first step toward eternal life.

STUDY QUESTIONS:

1. Was Amanda wrong to confront Vic like she did? Why or why not?
2. How should we share the Gospel with unsaved relatives?
3. Give a few reasons why it is so important for husbands and wives to share the same faith.

Episodes #11 & 12

"A Member of the Family," Parts One & Two

Theme: Discipline; family conflict.
Scripture references: Proverbs 3:11-12; Exodus 20:12; Ephesians 6:4
Part One: Written by Susan McBride and directed by Steve Harris
Part Two: Written and directed by Steve Harris
Production engineer: Bob Luttrell
(Original air dates: 3-30-87 & 4-06-87)

Whit and Tom are at the airport, waiting excitedly for Whit's grandson, Monty, to arrive. Monty is going to spend the summer in Odyssey to take a break from a difficult home situation. Whit's daughter, Jana, and her husband have split up, and the divorce has been difficult for Monty and his sister, Jenny.

Unfortunately, Monty is a first-class spoiled brat. Whit deals with Monty as best he can, trying to be patient. Finally, Whit lays down some ground rules: No more sassiness, no more rudeness.

The next day, at Whit's End, Whit shows Monty a few chores he can do to earn some spending money. But when Whit's gone, Monty calls his mother long distance, lies about how mean Whit is to him, and begs her to come take him home. Jana says she can't come until the end of the week. So, to make matters worse, Monty steals money from the cash register and goes to the movies.

When Whit finds out, he does *not* spare the rod on his grandson. Afterward, Whit explains to Monty why he had to be spanked. Monty responds positively. Over the next week, he and Whit start having fun, and Monty even helps the Odyssey Coyotes win the Little League championship. Everything is going well—until Jana shows up at Whit's door, very upset.

Whit tries to explain what happened, but Jana is too stubborn to listen, and their discussion becomes an argument. When Jana stomps upstairs to take her son away, Monty isn't there. He has run away. Whit and Jana go to the sheriff's office to report Monty missing, but surprisingly, Monty is already there. He was picked up for breaking a window at Whit's End.

The three return to Whit's house and finally talk things out. When Whit and Jana are alone, Whit explains some Whittaker family history to Jana. Whit tells her that when her brother, Jerry, died in the Vietnam War, they all handled their grief differently. Whit spent more time with Jana's younger brother, Jason, partly because he missed Jerry so much, and partly because soon Jason would be draft age himself. Unfortunately, Jana got lost in the whole ordeal, and before Whit knew what had happened, there was a huge gap between them.

Whit tells Jana he'd like to try and close that gap. Jana agrees, and for the first time in years, both father and daughter are happy.

the *Adventures in* ODYSSEY archives:

"A Member of the Family" marked the first appearance of Whit's family members and revealed important facts about them. These episodes explained why the Whittakers moved to Odyssey. They also revealed that Whit's older son, Jerry, died in Vietnam, and that Whit has a younger son, Jason. "A Member of the Family" also showed that Whit isn't perfect—like many godly men in the Old Testament, Whit has made some mistakes in dealing with his family.

STUDY QUESTIONS:

1. Do you think Whit had a good reason to spank Monty? What does the Bible say about spanking? Could Whit have handled the situation in any other way? Explain your answers.
2. Why was Jana so angry with Whit? Why was Monty so rude to Whit and Tom?
3. What mistakes did Whit make in raising Jana? How could he have avoided those mistakes? Corrected them?

Episode #13 "A Simple Addition"

Theme: Sibling rivalry.
Scripture reference: Romans 12:10
Written by Susan McBride
Directed by Steve Harris and Phil Lollar
Production engineer: Bob Luttrell
(Original air date: 4-13-87)

The Rogers household is about to add a new member, and Joe and Shelly are happy about the prospect of having a baby. But four-year-old Nicky is only excited about the prospect of getting some new boots. Joe promises Nicky they will go shopping, but before they can, Shelly goes into labor. They all rush to the hospital, and Shannon Rogers comes into the world. Everyone is excited, except Nicky. He'd rather have his boots. Nicky feels even worse when Joe and Shelly bring little Shannon home. Shannon gets Nicky's old baby bed and pacifier (thoroughly sanitized, of course), not to mention most of Joe and Shelly's attention. Nick feels rejected and seeks comfort from the only family member who will still listen to him: Jingle Bells, the dog.

A few hours later, Joe finds Nicky and talks with him about his responsibilities as a new big brother. Joe reassures Nicky that his parents still love him more than ever. Nicky feels better and even gets a little excited about being a big brother. But he still wants his boots.

Just then, a package arrives for Nicky from his grandparents, who are missionaries in Brazil. Inside the package is a pair of boots. God knew all along.

STUDY QUESTIONS:

1. Why was Nicky upset when he saw Shannon in his old baby bed?
2. Have you ever felt like Nicky? If so, explain how.
3. Joe told Nicky, "Not even Mommy and I can love you more than God does." Do you think that's true? Name some ways God shows that He loves you.

ODYSSEY USA

ODYSSEY USA

Episode #1 "Whit's Flop"

Theme: The importance of failure.
Scripture reference: Romans 8:28
Written by Phil Lollar
Directed by Phil Lollar and Steve Harris
Production engineer: Bob Luttrell
(Original air date: 11-21-87)

Davey Holcomb is a walking disaster. It seems everything he touches or attempts ends up in failure. At a Little League baseball game, Davey strikes out three times, knocks over the portable backstop, runs into his own second baseman, and causes the entire team to trip over him when he bends down to tie his shoe.

After the game, the team goes to Whit's End to commiserate about their loss. There, Davey meets Whit, who shows him around. As they talk, Whit learns that Davey is interested in inventing things. Whit suggests Davey try out the Inventor's Corner, but Davey is afraid he'll fail again. So Whit asks Davey to help him bring out a new display called "Whit's Flop." It's an invention Whit couldn't get to work. Davey tries to fix it and nearly succeeds, but then he accidentally breaks off a lever on the machine.

Davey runs out, dejected. Whit follows to lure him back inside, telling Davey that he must fix what he has broken. So Davey returns, and he and Whit work on the flop together, creating a new invention. They unveil it later that afternoon. But when Davey proudly turns it on, it shorts out and nearly blows up. He leaves again, feeling sorry for himself.

A short time later, Whit finds Davey and offers him a piece of freshly-made pizza. They talk, and Davey learns that the machine fizzled out because of a short in the wiring at Whit's End, not because of anything Davey did. The machine, a convection oven, works wonderfully and is a big hit with the kids. Davey has succeeded—without even knowing it! Whit explains that this is an example of how "God works all things together for good."

Adventures in ODYSSEY the archives:

"Whit's Flop" was full of firsts. It was the first *Odyssey USA* episode we aired. We got our first good look around Whit's End, the Train Station, the Inventor's Corner, Whit's workshop, and the displays. It was the first time Whit identified himself as an inventor, and the first time we introduced a food besides ice cream at Whit's End—mini pizzas. Whit also admitted, for the first time, that he had failed at something.

Many people thought it was strange that we started out a new series with a show about failure. But I actually loved the irony—it took off some of the pressure. After all, if Thomas Edison failed hundreds of times before he got the electric lightbulb right, then maybe we could have a few chances to get *Odyssey USA* right.

STUDY QUESTIONS:

1. Why did Whit say failing is important?
2. How long should you keep trying to do something at which you've failed?
3. List some ways God has worked things out for good in your life.

Episode #2 "The Life of the Party"

Theme: Friendship.
Scripture reference: 1 Samuel 20
Written by Paul McCusker
Directed by Phil Lollar and Steve Harris
Production engineer: Bob Luttrell
(Original air date: 11-28-87)

Craig Moorhead is a funny guy. No matter what anyone says to him, he always responds with a joke. In the three weeks he and his family have been in town, Craig has made a lot of friends by keeping them in stitches. Unfortunately, Craig takes his humor too far when he razzes Freddy, whose parents are getting a divorce. Freddy storms off, and Craig goes home, where he faces his own family problems.

Craig's dad moved the family to Odyssey to start a handyman business. But business isn't going so well, and Craig's mom wants to go back to Columbus, where they previously lived. This conflict erupts into a full-blown argument. Craig, who likes living in Odyssey, is distraught by his parents' conflict. He tears out of the house and races away on his skateboard, which he ends up crashing. Craig's friends see him crash and rush over to check if he's all right. But instead of offering sympathy, his friends ask him to tell more jokes. Craig angrily refuses. His friends leave him feeling bruised, hurt, and alone.

Craig wanders into Whit's End and tells Whit the whole story. Attempting to explain things to Craig, Whit uses some melting orange sherbet and raspberry ice cream to illustrate the biblical principle of sowing and reaping. Craig has sown nothing but jokes with his friends, so how can he expect to reap their sympathy? Craig understands and promises to put what he has learned into practice—a promise he gets to keep immediately when the door opens, and in walks Freddy.

the Adventures in ODYSSEY archives:

One of the most interesting things about "The Life of the Party" was that we had to "make a fix" on one of Whit's lines. The line should have read, "What you sow you shall also reap." But for some reason, it was written in the script and recorded as, "What you reap you shall also sow." It took some doing, but Bob Luttrell and Steve Harris were able to fix the line without re-recording it. Listen carefully—can you tell?

behind the scenes:

"I showed up at the Focus on the Family address. It was an abandoned, three-story building in Arcadia, California. I walked around yelling, 'Hello!' like a baffled parrot. No one was there. No one had told me that Focus was in the process of moving to Pomona, California. I finally found everyone in a sound-proof studio behind several closed doors on the third floor. Turned out, the part was refreshing for me because it was a straight acting role instead of the animals and wacky characters I usually did."

—Will Ryan, "Craig's father," on his first recording experience for *Adventures in Odyssey.*

STUDY QUESTIONS:

1. Why did Freddy get so angry at Craig?
2. Is it wrong to tell jokes? Why or why not?
3. List some qualities of a true friend.

Episode #3 "Lights Out at Whit's End"

Theme: Communication; fellowship.
Scripture reference: 1 John 1:7
Written and directed by Steve Harris and Phil Lollar
Production engineer: Bob Luttrell
(Original air date: 12-05-87)

The kids at Whit's End are scurrying around getting ready to shoot their first video production on the subject of communication. But just as they're ready to roll, the lights flicker, and the power goes out—all over town. The kids think their afternoon is ruined, but Whit, Tom, and Officer David Harley help the kids put on an impromptu stage show, lit by makeshift footlights made from candles and aluminum pie tins.

The skits include a humorous visit with the 3,000-year-old man (son of the 4,000-year-old man), Gutenberg's printing of the first Bible, and a talk *with* a telephone. This all leads to the grand finale, a rap song. The success of the show proves to the gang that they don't need electrical power and high-tech equipment to communicate and have fun.

the Adventures in ODYSSEY archives:

Officer David Harley made his first appearance here. "Light's Out at Whit's End" also contained our first—and, thankfully, our last—attempt at rap music.

STUDY QUESTIONS:

1. Why is communication important?
2. The Bible is one of the ways God communicates with us. What is the best way we can communicate with God?
3. How well do you communicate with your friends? Your family?

Episode #4 "Connie Comes to Town"

Theme: Being content.
Scripture reference: Philippians 4:11-12
Written and directed by Phil Lollar and Steve Harris
Production engineer: Bob Luttrell
(Original air date: 12-12-87)

It's a busy day at Whit's End. The phone is ringing, kids are demanding sundaes, Tom Riley is making deliveries—everything is in an uproar. Yet, despite all this, Bobby is bored silly. He wants excitement and new activities, not the same old Bible Bowl every few months. Whit tells him to stay alert—excitement could be waiting right at the other side of the door. And right on cue, the door opens, and in walks a teenager named Connie Kendall.

Connie is looking for a job to earn money to get back to Los Angeles. After hearing a bit about her, Whit hires Connie on the spot. Connie proves to be popular with the kids—especially with Bobby, who develops a big crush on her. Bobby is so smitten, in fact, that he plans on sitting next to Connie when she flies back to L.A.

Connie won't take any responsibility for the situation, but Whit tells her she can't simply drift through life thinking she won't influence anyone—God made us dependent on each other. Connie claims she's not into God, but Whit says that her attitude won't solve the problem. But Whit does know how Connie can help.

Later that day, Tom coaxes Bobby to come to the Bible Bowl—with surprise guest emcee, Connie Kendall. Connie gets Bobby to participate in the bowl, and they both have a lot of fun. Afterward, Connie convinces Bobby—and herself—that instead of looking for happiness in California, maybe they should try to find it right here in Odyssey.

behind the scenes:

"After my first appearance in *Family Portraits* ('The Letter' #8), Steve Harris told me about Focus's future plans for *Adventures in Odyssey*. I was really excited about it, and I told Steve to call me. Nine months went by before Focus actually did. By that time, I'd just had a baby—so I had to turn them down! But they waited to record this episode, 'Connie Comes to Town,' and the next one, 'Promises, Promises,' and I recorded with them a few weeks later."

—Katie Leigh Pavlakovich, "Connie Kendall"

STUDY QUESTIONS:

1. What does it mean to be content?
2. Bobby was bored with his life in Odyssey. Have you ever been bored? How did you escape your boredom?
3. Whit told Connie that God made us dependent on each other. In what ways do you depend on others? How do they depend on you?

Episode #5 "Gifts for Madge & Guy"

Theme: Giving.
Scripture references: Matthew 1:18-25; Luke 2:1-20
Written and directed by Phil Lollar and Steve Harris
Production engineer: Bob Luttrell
(Original air date: 12-19-87)

It's Christmastime at Whit's End. Whit, Tom, and Officer Harley are setting up the tree, and Connie is doling out hot chocolate. Two of the kids are arguing about the meaning of giving gifts. Whit tries to convince them that "it's not the gift but the thought that counts," and "it's more blessed to give than to receive."

When the kids scoff at this, Whit comically presents for them the O. Henry story, *The Gift of the Magi,* told in the style of a "Fractured Fairy Tale." In it, Madge cuts off her lovely hair to buy "her guy, Guy," a new chain for his watch. But Madge doesn't realize that Guy has sold his watch to buy Madge some beautiful combs for her hair. Each of them sell their most prized possession to give the other a gift—much like God did for us when He sent His only begotten Son to die so that we may have eternal life.

the *Adventures in* ODYSSEY archives:

"Gifts for Madge and Guy" was the first time Whit told a story to the kids. It was also one of only three episodes where our announcer, Chris Lansdowne, appeared as a character. The other two are *AIO* #92, "The Ill-Gotten Deed," and *AIO* #107, "Bad Luck."

"Gifts for Madge and Guy" was also the first episode that stretched *AIO's* creative bounds. We used wacky, off-beat humor in a classic story to teach a lesson about giving. It was our homage to the radio comedian Stan Freberg and the cartoon *Rocky and Bullwinkle.*

STUDY QUESTIONS:

1. Madge and Guy sacrificed their greatest possession for one another. Have you ever sacrificed to give someone a gift? Why is sacrifice important?
2. What is the greatest gift you've ever received? The greatest gift you've ever given?
3. Have you accepted God's gift of eternal life?

Episode #6 "The Day After Christmas"

Theme: Caring for the poor.
Scripture reference: Matthew 25:31-46
Written by Paul McCusker
Directed by Steve Harris and Phil Lollar
Production engineer: Bob Luttrell
(Original air date: 12-26-87)

It's the day after Christmas, and Annie McNeal is bored, despite the fact that she got everything she wanted—and more—for the holiday. She wanders into Whit's End looking for something to do. Annie finds Whit hard at work preparing boxes of food for the poor people at Foster Creek ghetto. Whit asks if Annie would like to help, and she agrees.

At Foster Creek, Annie meets a young boy named Tommy who lures her out on the dangerous streets—against Whit's orders. When the two kids are spotted by a gang, Tommy runs off, and Annie is pulled into a house by old Mrs. Rossini, the local crazy lady. Only, Annie soon learns that Mrs. Rossini isn't crazy. She's a lonely widow who is pleased to have company for the first time in years. She and Annie have a delightful afternoon tea, and Mrs. Rossini tells Annie about her life, describing how the Lord has brought her through some very difficult times.

Suddenly, the gang shows up again. They smash Mrs. Rossini's windows and threaten to break into the house. But they disappear as quickly as they came—thanks to some quick thinking by Whit, who shows up with several deputies from the sheriff's department. They all head back to Reverend Pike's church for a delicious day-after-Christmas lunch, where Whit informs Tommy and Annie that since their disobedience led to the broken windows, they'll have to work to replace them.

Tommy is disappointed, but Annie doesn't mind. She's glad to have something worthwhile to do with her time. Her afternoon with Mrs. Rossini has taught her a valuable lesson: The fun of getting Christmas presents can quickly disappear, but the excitement of giving lasts all year long.

STUDY QUESTIONS:

1. Why do you think Annie got bored so quickly with her Christmas presents?
2. Why didn't Whit want Tommy and Annie to leave the church?
3. Mrs. Rossini said her faith in God got her through some very difficult times. Can you think of times when your faith helped you? Explain.

ODYSSEY MATCH-UP

Match these characters to the items or actions they are best known for (answers below).

1. Jack Allen	A. The Electric Palace
2. Donna Barclay	B. Zappazoids
3. Eugene Meltsner	C. The *Odyssey Times*
4. Connie Kendall	D. National Security Agency
5. Jason Whittaker	E. Fergeson and Normal
6. Lucy Schultz	F. The Imagination Station
7. Rodney Rathbone	G. A wheelchair
8. Jimmy Barclay	H. Dreams
9. Zachary Sellers	I. Being late
10. Dale Jacobs	J. The Bones of Rath
11. Bart Rathbone	K. Computers
12. John Whittaker	L. The *Odyssey Owl*

Answers:

1.H; 2.E; 3.K; 4.I; 5.D; 6.L; 7.J; 8.B; 9.G; 10.C; 11.A; 12.F

1988

It was a hectic year. Focus on the Family had just moved to Pomona, California, and because of other problems, we quickly found ourselves behind schedule again. We needed help—especially with the writing. So Paul McCusker came to work with *Odyssey USA (OUSA)* in January. Having him come on staff as a full-time writer relieved much of our load.

At the same time, Chuck Bolte also joined the team as executive producer. One of the first administrative moves Chuck made was to have Steve Harris and me write our scripts separately, which freed each of us up, allowing us to do twice the work. Chuck also decided to re-air some of the *Family Portraits* episodes to buy us more time and get the team back on schedule.

In the beginning of 1988, Dave Arnold came on board to co-produce the show with Bob Luttrell. Dave had already been working at Focus in the Creative Services Department. But soon it became obvious that Bob couldn't keep up with the weekly broadcast alone—so Dave began helping Bob by editing the voice tracks for him. When an extra production engineer position was approved, Dave immediately joined the team. Dave remembers, "Steve Harris offered me the job, and after 10 seconds of deep contemplation, I accepted."

Finally, the core team was in place. We buckled down and got to work.

But a couple of months later in April 1988, *OUSA* experienced another significant change. Debate had raged for months about the show's title. Broadcasting Vice President Mike Trout rightly believed that the name *Odyssey USA* would alienate our Canadian listeners, as well as potential audiences overseas. So finally, after much brainstorming, arguing, and prayer, we decided on a new title. And although it didn't make everyone happy, at least we all agreed we could live with it. We decided to call the program . . . *Adventures in Odyssey.*

Episode #7 "Promises, Promises"

Theme: The folly of making promises you can't keep.
Scripture reference: Romans 3:23
Written by Phil Lollar
Directed by Phil Lollar and Steve Harris
Production engineer: Bob Luttrell
(Original air date: 1-02-88)

Odyssey's most recent resident, Connie Kendall, writes about her new home in a letter to her friend Marcy back in California. Connie describes various places and people in Odyssey: Whit's End, an ice cream parlor and discovery emporium; Tom Riley, a retired farmer and city council member; Officer David Harley, "whose brain takes an occasional vacation"; and most of all, an amazing fellow named John Avery Whittaker.

Connie describes Whit: businessman, writer, and all-around storehouse of information. Connie also tells Marcy about Whit's devotion to God. His devotion guides everything he does, even how he looks at world events—which, Connie explains, is what got her into a bit of trouble.

In a flashback, Connie and Whit listen to a news report on the radio about wars. Connie laments the world's violence. She remarks that if people would just get to know each other, they'd see how much they have in common, and all wars would end. Whit feels this is a noble idea, but not very realistic. Connie believes Whit is wrong. She says that peace would be possible if everyone simply promised to treat one another with kindness, gentleness, and patience.

To prove her idea is realistic, Connie makes that promise herself, on paper. She will try to be patient for four weeks. Everything goes well—for the first few days. Connie puts up with impatient customers and other irritations with grace and ease. But later, when the kids fail to figure out a simple riddle Whit tells them, Connie becomes so impatient she explodes. She belittles the kids and completely embarrasses herself. Whit explains to her that no matter how much we may *want* to conquer our sinful nature, we can't. It's too strong. That's why we need Jesus. Only He can transform us—and only He can change the world.

the *Adventures in* ODYSSEY archives:

"Promises, Promises" was the first episode that spelled out the key characters of *Adventures in Odyssey* at the time. They were: Whit, Tom Riley, Connie, and Officer David Harley. Officer Harley was a comical police officer who appeared in several of our early episodes—including this one. But we received some criticism for portraying a police officer as a buffoon. So Harley had to "go the way of all good things" and leave *Adventures in Odyssey.* Some of the episodes he appeared in were redone completely. In others, like "Promises, Promises," we simply replaced him.

This episode reflected Connie's early days. One of the great things about Connie's character back then was that she *wasn't* a Christian. It gave us, the writers and producers, an opportunity to try and figure out how we would bring her to Jesus. What kinds of experiences would she need to have? What kinds of lessons would she have to learn? In this program, Connie needed to learn that deep down inside, we humans aren't basically good, but basically sinful.

STUDY QUESTIONS:

1. Why did Connie fail to keep her promise?
2. Connie said that "people are basically good." Why was she wrong?
3. Read Matthew 5:33-37. What does Jesus say about making promises?

Episode #8 "Dental Dilemma"

Theme: Teasing; dealing with fear.
Scripture reference: Psalm 27:1
Written by Susan McBride
Directed by Steve Harris and Chuck Bolte
Production engineers: Steve Harris and Bob Luttrell
(Original air date: 1-09-88)

This episode was re-aired from the original, *Family Portraits* #2. See that episode for study questions and story.

Episode #9 "Doing Unto Others"

Theme: The Golden Rule.
Scripture references: Matthew 7:12; Luke 6:31
Written by Phil Lollar
Directed by Phil Lollar and Steve Harris
Production engineer: Bob Luttrell
(Original air date: 1-16-88)

Johnny Bickle knows the Bible. When Whit asks his sixth-grade Bible study group their memory verse, Johnny's hand always shoots up first. On this particular day, the verse happens to be Matthew 7:12, the Golden Rule. But Johnny is confused. He knows the verse says, "Do unto others as you would have others do unto you." But he doesn't know what kinds of things he should do or how he should do them. Class ends before Whit can explain this, and unfortunately, Johnny takes advice from the next adult he runs across—Officer Harley. After a confusing conversation, the two of them conclude that "doing unto others" means that whatever Johnny likes is what other people will like, too. He tries putting this into practice and has disastrous results.

Later at Whit's End, he explains his problem to Connie. She says the true meaning of "doing unto others" is helping people without expecting anything in return. Connie suggests that Whit is the perfect candidate on whom Johnny can practice the Golden Rule. Connie reveals that Whit doesn't have a television. Johnny can't believe it. So with Connie's help, Johnny immediately rushes out to buy one for Whit.

When they deliver the gift to Whit, though, Johnny and Connie learn that Whit doesn't have a television because he doesn't *want* one, not because he can't afford one. When Whit watches the tube, he turns into a TV junkie. Johnny is upset and begins to doubt whether "doing unto others" is even possible! But Whit quickly shows Johnny that following the Golden Rule is not only possible, it's the best way to live.

the Adventures in ODYSSEY archives:

This episode was remade to take Officer Harley out of the script. The new version is "Isaac the Benevolent," *AIO* #116. See that episode for study questions.

Episode #10 "Nothing to Fear"

Theme: Dealing with fear.
Scripture reference: 1 John 4:18
Recommended maturity level: 9 and up
Written by Paul McCusker
Directed by Phil Lollar and Steve Harris
Production engineer: Bob Luttrell
(Original air date: 1-23-88)

PARENTAL WARNING: The nightmare scene and the scene in the basement at Whit's End may be too intense for younger listeners.

Shirley is afraid of *everything*. When we first meet her, she is screaming at the top of her lungs at the sight of Jake's pet mouse, Luther. Whit notes Shirley's problem and tells her that Jesus' perfect love can cast out her fear. Whit suggests that most fears are really inside our heads. He coaxes Shirley into holding Luther just so she'll know that there is no reason to be afraid. All is well for a few seconds—then Luther moves. Shirley screams again and drops him, sending Luther scurrying off into the cracks and crevices of Whit's End.

This doesn't sit well with Jake, and he concocts a plan to teach Shirley a lesson about fear. With the help of his friend Danny, Jake sets the plan: He'll lure Shirley down to the basement of Whit's End, where he's rigged up some boxes to fall on her. Danny's job is to turn out the lights once they're down there and then distract Connie, who is working upstairs. Whit is at a meeting.

Shirley comes in, and Jake puts his plan into action. Down in the basement, Shirley is frightened. Jake laughs, especially when the lights go out. But when he tries to take Shirley back upstairs, he trips over his own booby trap and ends up spraining his ankle. They yell for help, but Danny is doing his job so well that no one hears them. Jake can't walk, so it's up to Shirley to face her fears and go for help. She remembers Whit's words about fear and turns to God for strength. Shirley sets her mind on Jesus, and her fear disappears. Jake is rescued, and all learn a valuable lesson about the power of Jesus' perfect love.

the Adventures in ODYSSEY archives:

Shirley's mother was played by Janna Arnold, wife of Production Engineer Dave Arnold.

This was the first episode that garnered any noticeable negative reaction, due to the nightmare scene with Luther the Mouse. The episode was supposed to help children better deal with their fears by teaching them to call upon Christ. But ironically, parents wrote in saying their children had never been afraid—until they heard this episode.

STUDY QUESTIONS:

1. Why do you think Shirley was so afraid of everything?
2. Why was Jake wrong for wanting to teach Shirley a lesson?
3. What makes you scared? How do you deal with your fears?

Episode #11 "Addictions Can Be Habit Forming"

Theme: Addictions.
Scripture reference: 1 Corinthians 6:12
Written by Steve Harris and Jim Adams
Directed by Steve Harris
Production engineer: Bob Luttrell
(Original air date: 1-30-88)

Stefanie has a problem—she's never met a meal she didn't like. She wants to lose weight, but it seems she just can't. So her friend Joey decides to help her. Joey goes to the library at Whit's End to get a dieting book for Stefanie and runs into Officer Harley. After a typically confusing conversation with Harley, Joey believes that the best way she (yes, Joey is a girl) can help Stefanie lose weight is to follow her and literally take food out of her mouth.

A desperate Stefanie agrees to this. But Joey ends up being too good at her job, making Stefanie even more desperate for food. Frantically, she dashes into Whit's End and pleads with Connie to make her a small pizza. Connie makes one for Stefanie. Just as she's about to scarf it down, Joey races in, yelling for Officer Harley—who is passing by—to stop Stefanie. Officer Harley assumes a crime is being committed and holds up Stef with a cucumber.

Whit hears the commotion and demands to know what is happening. Joey tells Whit the whole story, saying she only wanted to get Stefanie to "just say no" to food. Whit says that may be a good strategy for drugs, but not for dieting. Besides, Stefanie's food problem probably goes much deeper than simply eating too much. Whit says the best things Joey can do for her friend are talk with her about her problem, be willing to listen, and most of all, pray for her. This advice really *does* work, and Stefanie is soon on the road to healing.

the *Adventures in* ODYSSEY archives:

Stefanie and Joey were played by Rebekah (Leck) and Amy (Slivka) Trout, respectively—real-life sisters and the daughters of Mike Trout, vice president of broadcasting for Focus on the Family and cohost of the *Focus* broadcast. "Addictions Can Be Habit Forming" was another episode that was pulled from distribution because of Officer Harley.

STUDY QUESTIONS:

1. Read 1 Corinthians 6:12. Why is it wrong to always overeat?
2. What was wrong with Joey's solution to Stefanie's problem?
3. Stefanie had an addiction to food. Name some other things to which people become addicted.

Episode #12 "The Tangled Web"

Theme: Lying.
Scripture reference: Proverbs 12:22
Written and directed by Phil Lollar
Production engineer: Bob Luttrell
(Original air date: 2-06-88)

Connie's friend Debbie has gotten tickets to the hottest concert of the year—a concert Connie is sure her mother wouldn't want her to attend. In order to go, Connie deceives her mother into thinking she is just spending the night at Debbie's. Next, Connie works at trying to persuade Whit to let her take the afternoon off.

Whit appears, carrying a box of manuscripts—old stories he's written that he thinks the kids might enjoy reading. Connie makes her request. Whit says "yes"—if they finish cataloguing the manuscripts. They dig into the box, and Connie comes across a story called "The Tangled Web." Whit asks her to read it aloud.

It's a tale about a youngster named Jeremy, whose mother asks him to go to the store for her after school. Jeremy doesn't want to go to the store—he'd rather go to Whit's End to get free ice cream and see a display on how movie cameras work. Rather than miss out on fun at Whit's End, Jeremy decides to do both. But somewhere along the way, he loses the money his mother gave him. When she questions him about it, Jeremy panics and says someone took the money.

Mom interprets this to mean that someone stole it, and Jeremy picks up on this theme. He concocts a wild tale about a teenaged thug who pushed him into an alley and threatened to hurt Jeremy unless he handed over the cash. Mom is horrified and takes action. Soon the police force is out looking for the thug, and the school board, town council, and mayor are singing Jeremy's praises. The mayor even decides to honor the youngster for bravery! Jeremy realizes that his lie has gotten way out of hand. When it's time to receive his award, though, he steps nervously to the podium . . . and graciously accepts it!

Connie is dumbstruck—the kid got away with it! But Whit points out that he really *didn't*. Jeremy's lie would haunt him for the rest of his life—just like *Connie's* lie will haunt *her* if she goes through with it. Whit leaves Connie to think about this. She sighs . . . then reluctantly calls her mom.

the *Adventures in* ODYSSEY archives:

"The Tangled Web" also had to be redone to take out Officer Harley. Fortunately, Harley was only in one scene, so we replaced his character with another bumbling—but less comical—police officer, played by Bob Luttrell.

The story within "The Tangled Web" almost had a different ending. The original ending had Jeremy walking up to the platform to receive his reward—only to break down and confess that the whole thing was a hoax. But instead, we had him accept the award, shake hands with the mayor, and sit down. It was a totally unexpected twist, and it gave added emphasis to the message of "The Tangled Web."

STUDY QUESTIONS:

1. Connie believed that half-truths aren't really lies. Why was Connie wrong?
2. Have you ever lied like Jeremy did? Like Connie did? If so, how did it affect you?
3. Why does God hate lying so much?

the Adventures in ODYSSEY archives:

The title of this episode was named after the producer of the *Focus on the Family* broadcast, Bobbie Valentine. This episode was another Officer Harley redo, remade as "The Trouble with Girls," *AIO* #117. See that episode for study questions.

Episode #13 "Bobby's Valentine"

Theme: Crushes; puppy love.
Scripture reference: 1 Corinthians 13
Written by Paul McCusker
Directed by Phil Lollar and Steve Harris
Production engineer: Bob Luttrell
(Original air date: 2-13-88)

It's Valentine's Day in Odyssey, and Bobby is flustered. There is a note in the mailbox addressed to him. The note is from Amy, who thinks Bobby is the cutest boy in school. She wants to go steady with him. Bobby, however, wants to stay as far from Amy as possible.

Later, in the cafeteria, Bobby tells his friend Jeff about the problem. Jeff thinks Bobby should tell Amy to get lost, then throw mud on her. Fortunately, Bobby knows there are better ways to handle this. He resolves to talk to Amy, but the bell rings before he can do it.

After school, Amy sits at the counter in Whit's End, waiting for her true love. Connie walks over, and the two talk about Bobby. Amy says she's written Bobby several notes and poems, but he hasn't responded to her. Connie suggests a trick that once worked for her: ignoring him.

Meanwhile, Bobby and Jeff run into Officer Harley, who is on a stakeout in the middle of the sidewalk. Bobby explains his problem to the well-meaning officer, who suggests that Bobby should tell Amy he's madly in love with her. Harley says that if Amy thinks she can have Bobby's affection, she won't want him.

Both youngsters put their plans into action. Unfortunately, once Bobby professes his "like" for Amy, she vows to be his forever and to never leave him—then rushes off to record her feelings in her diary. The following week, Amy dotes on Bobby, writing him more notes and poems. She even gives him flowers while he's playing softball.

Finally, Bobby seeks out Whit. Whit suggests that Bobby just wait until the crush passes, but Bobby doesn't want to wait. So Whit says the best thing to do is be direct and honest with Amy. Tell her the truth. Bobby screws up his courage and starts to confront Amy—but before he can say anything, she breaks up with him. Much to Bobby's relief, Amy has a new crush: Officer Harley! Bobby is amused by Amy's crush on Officer Harley but is generally bewildered by the whole experience. Isn't love grand?

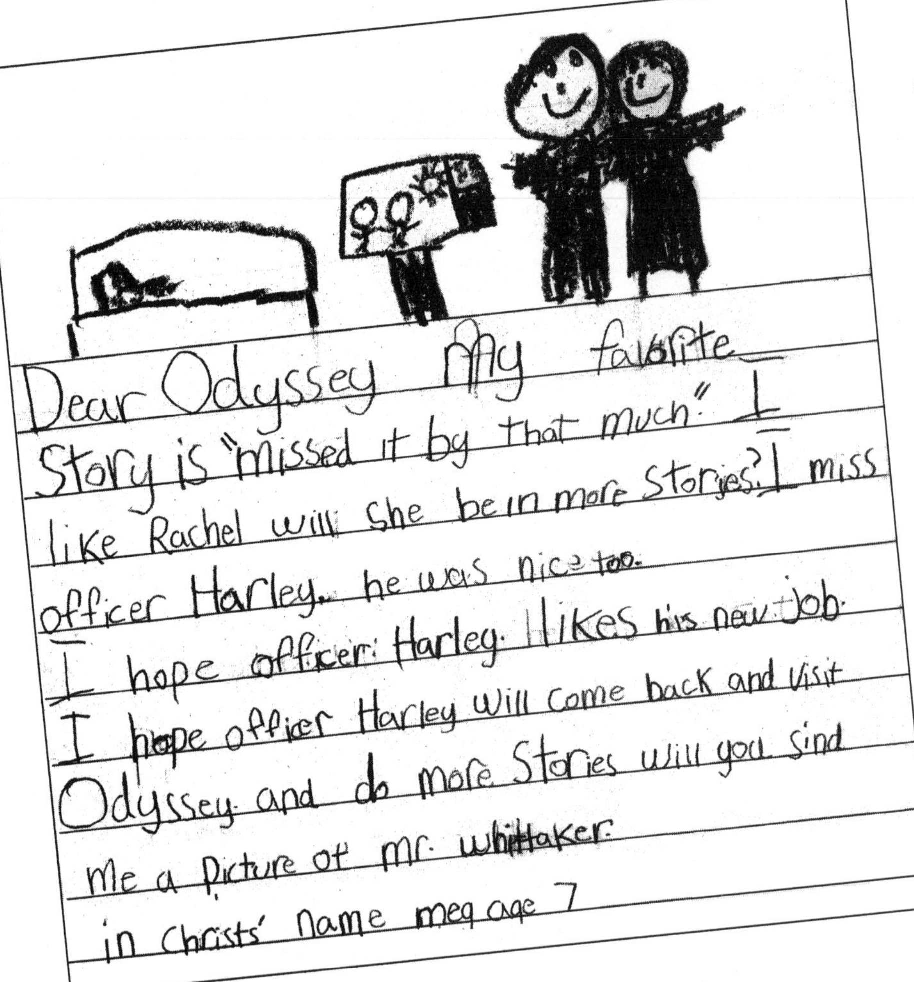
Dear Odyssey My favorite
Story is "missed it by that much." I
like Rachel will she be in more Stories? I miss
officer Harley. he was nice too.
I hope officer: Harley. likes his new Job.
I hope offier Harley will come back and visit
Odyssey and do more Stories will you sind
me a picture of mr. whittaker
in Christs' name meg age 7

Episode #14 "Missed It by That Much"

Theme: Tardiness.
Scripture reference: Matthew 25:1-13
Written by Paul McCusker
Directed by Phil Lollar and Steve Harris
Production engineer: Bob Luttrell
(Original air date: 2-20-88)

Rachel Weaver is always late. Everyone knows it, especially the kids at Whit's End. They're gathered there, waiting for Rachel to show up so they can leave for a roller-skating trip that Connie is going to chaperone. Finally, Connie decides to leave. She yells for the kids to hop in the bus outside. Then she tells Whit to inform Rachel that they got tired of waiting. Connie adds that if Rachel isn't on time for the volleyball tournament the next day, she's off the team.

They leave, Rachel shows up, and Whit delivers Connie's message. Rachel makes all sorts of empty excuses for her tardiness, but finally realizes that it really *is* her fault. At home, her father agrees and says that habitual lateness is downright rude. Later, a depressed Rachel falls asleep in front of the television and has a terrible nightmare. She meets Rod Serly and takes a trip into the Twilife Zone! There, she is late for every important event in her life—even her funeral! She wakes up from the nightmare in a cold sweat, determined not to be late for anything again. Especially for the next day's volleyball tournament.

But getting there the next morning proves to be its own real-life Twilife Zone. First, her parents oversleep. Then, her dad's car won't start. Rachel takes off on her bicycle and gets a flat tire. She cuts across a neighbor's backyard and is chased by a ferocious dog into the woods, where she falls in a creek. Just then, Whit drives past. Rachel hops into Whit's car, but when he steps on the gas, it, too, dies!

At the school, Connie is just about to boot Rachel from the game when Rachel walks in—wrinkled, disheveled, and soaked, but ready to play volleyball! The kids cheer. Later at Whit's End, the team has a grand celebration. Rachel's team lost, but more importantly, she showed up on time.

the Adventures in ODYSSEY archives:

The name "The Twilife Zone" reappeared much later as the title of an entire episode. This show was remade as "Better Late than Never," *AIO* #119. See that episode for study questions.

behind the scenes:

"The name 'The Twilife Zone' originally appeared in a sketch I wrote a few years before, in a collection called 'Souvenirs.' Also, the header on this original script calls the program *Focus on the Family Clubhouse/Odyssey, USA.* This name came from an old memo I recently found from Focus management, asking us to introduce the show as, '*Focus on the Family Clubhouse* presents *Odyssey USA.*'"

—Paul McCusker

Episode #15 "My Brother's Keeper"

Theme: Sibling conflict.
Scripture reference: Proverbs 12:18
Written by Paul McCusker, from a story by Phil Lollar
Directed by Steve Harris and Phil Lollar
Production engineer: Bob Luttrell
(Original air date: 2-27-88)

This episode was re-aired from *Family Portraits* #6. See that episode for study questions and story.

Episode #16 "No Stupid Questions"

Theme: Respect for the handicapped; the value of seeking knowledge.
Scripture reference: Proverbs 18:15
Written by Susan McBride
Directed by Steve Harris
Production engineer: Bob Luttrell
(Original air date: 3-05-88)

This episode was re-aired from *Family Portraits* #4. See that episode for study questions and story.

Episodes #17 & 18 "A Member of the Family," Parts One & Two

Theme: Discipline; family conflict.
Scripture references: Exodus 20:12; Proverbs 3:11-12; Ephesians 6:4
Part One: Written by Susan McBride and directed by Steve Harris
Part Two: Written and directed by Steve Harris
Production engineer: Bob Luttrell
(Original air dates: 3-12-88 & 3-19-88)

These episodes were re-aired from *Family Portraits* #11 & 12. See those episodes for study questions and story.

the *Adventures in* ODYSSEY archives:

We re-recorded a couple of scenes for the re-airing of "A Member of the Family" on *Odyssey USA*. The original episode had a young man helping out at Whit's End. But in order to make it current with the show, we replaced the young man with Connie.

Episode #19 "Recollections"

Theme: Fighting for your convictions; making good out of bad circumstances.
Scripture reference: Galatians 6:9
Written by Phil Lollar
Directed by Steve Harris
Production engineer: Bob Luttrell
(Original air date: 3-26-88)

Connie rushes in late, making excuses to Whit, who is kneeling behind the counter. Only, it isn't Whit, it's Tom. Whit has gone to his wife's grave to pay his respects, something he's done annually for the past four years since she died. Tom tells Connie the story of Jenny Whittaker and how she was responsible for saving Whit's End.

In a flashback, Jenny delivers a fiery speech before Tom and the other members of the city council. She pleads with them to save the Fillmore Recreation Center—what is now Whit's End—from destruction. Jenny's main opponent on the council is Philip Glossman, who wants to destroy the building and sell the property to a firm that will turn it into a mini-mall. Jenny argues so passionately that she collapses and is rushed to the hospital. There, Whit learns that Jenny has been suffering from a chronic ailment that has caused her kidneys to deteriorate. There is so much damage, the doctors can do nothing.

Out of respect for Jenny, the city council puts off voting on the Fillmore for a month. Tom and Officer Harley visit Whit, hoping that he'll carry on the fight. But Whit refuses. He is bitter and believes that fighting to save the old building is what killed his wife.

Later, he visits the old place. He sees children playing happily on the grounds. There, a young girl says sadly that after the Fillmore is destroyed, the kids won't have a fun place to play anymore. Whit listens and is touched. Then the girl is called by her mother. The girl's name is Jenny.

Whit takes that to be a sign from God to keep fighting. Right after the city council votes to sell the building, Whit bursts in the room with an offer to buy it for more than the mini-mall firm is offering. The buyer Whit represents is the Universal Press Foundation, publishers of the *Universal Encyclopedia*. UPF proposes to turn the building into "a place of adventure and discovery, filled with books and activities, fun and games, arts and crafts, and uplifting conversation." The city council votes hands down to sell the building to UPF.

Coming out of the flashback, Connie learns that the Universal Press Foundation is owned by John Avery Whittaker! A remarkable man indeed.

the *Adventures in* ODYSSEY archives:

"Recollections" was our first show about the history of Whit's End. Here we met Jenny Whittaker and Philip Glossman, who both play important roles in future episodes. We also learned that there is much more to Whit than meets the ear: He was a schoolteacher and is very wealthy, which ended up being a convenient story device in later shows.

STUDY QUESTIONS:

1. Why did Jenny Whittaker want to preserve the Fillmore Recreation Center?
2. Is it important to preserve buildings, items, and memories? Why?
3. What's the most significant memory you have?

Episode #20 "Mike Makes Right"

Theme: Pride; handling power; dealing with bullies.
Scripture references: Proverbs 16:18; Matthew 20:25-28
Written by Paul McCusker
Directed by Phil Lollar and Steve Harris
Production engineer: Bob Luttrell
(Original air date: 4-02-88)

Fight! Fight! All the kids at Odyssey Elementary are gathered around to watch Billy Barton, the biggest bully in school, beat up poor Donny. As the fight progresses, Mike Caldwell walks over. Mike tells a kid named Freddy that Billy should cut it out, then Mike yells for Billy to pick on someone his own size. Billy hears this and is insulted. He finishes up with Donny, then turns his anger on Mike. Fortunately, Mike is literally saved by the school bell signaling the end of lunch. But Billy tells Mike to meet him the next day for the thrashing of his life. Mike is naturally petrified.

At the fight the next day, Mike gets predictably whipped—until Billy grabs Mike's shirt and tears it. Mike is enraged! He attacks Billy, punching him wildly. Billy backs away from the onslaught as best he can, but a sidelong punch connects solidly with Billy's nose. The blood flows, and so do Billy's tears. Beaten, Billy runs away.

Mike's an instant hero! Everyone is proud, heaping praises upon him. But soon, Mike gets arrogant about the fight and begins taking over Billy Barton's place as the school bully! "Magnificent Mike" generally abuses and pushes around the other kids. Then he runs into Sam, a new kid who's never heard of Billy Barton. Mike tries his conceited routine on Sam, who responds with a swift punch to the Magnificent One's stomach. Suddenly, the kids have a new hero! Lying on the floor, gasping for breath, Mike realizes that his pride has gone before his enormous fall—a lesson he won't soon forget.

Adventures in the ODYSSEY archives:

"Mike Makes Right" was the first show where John Campbell didn't do the music. Martie Echito—John's friend and a music mixer—created the score. Martie did a great job of rendering the fight scene. His music added just the right amount of tension, comedy, and triumph to make the scene soar. Along with the score, Martie also wrote an *Adventures in Odyssey* song. Bob Luttrell added the lyrics later. Unfortunately, the song never made it on the air or in a cassette package, and it has not been heard by anyone other than the *AIO* staff.

Paul McCusker came up with a clever way of handling the fight scene. For radio, the scene wouldn't have sounded exciting at all—mainly a lot of scuffling and grunting from the participants, with screaming and yelling from the onlookers. So Paul added the character of Freddy and made him a miniature sportscaster in order to have someone provide a funny, blow-by-blow description of the fight. That way, the listeners would know everything that was happening—*without realizing* they were hearing all about it.

STUDY QUESTIONS:

1. Should Mike have stood up to Billy Barton? Why or why not? When is it more appropriate to "turn the other cheek"?
2. How could Mike have kept himself from becoming a bully?
3. Read Matthew 20:25–28. What does Jesus say about being the greatest?

Episode #21 "The Case of the Missing Train Car"

Theme: Forgiveness; unconditional love.
Scripture references: Matthew 18:21-35; 1 Corinthians 13:7
Written and directed by Phil Lollar
Production engineer: Bob Luttrell
(Original air date: 4-09-88)

Michelle Terry has a bad reputation. Fortunately, that reputation doesn't matter to people like Tom Riley and Whit. Tom and his wife, Agnes, are sponsoring Michelle on a "parole" from reform school. Whit has given Michelle free run of Whit's End, treating her the same as the other kids. Their good intentions are working—Michelle seems to be responding. She's built a fine miniature—blue-colored—caboose. Warren, however, informs Michelle that to be *truly* authentic, the caboose should be red. Saying that, he proudly holds up his perfect replica of a Silver Streak engine.

Both Michelle and Warren are pleased with and protective of their work, which is why Warren panics the next day when he goes to Whit's End and discovers his Silver Streak is missing! Officer Harley is there and takes over the investigation. Unfortunately, all fingers seem to point at Michelle Terry. Officer Harley takes them all for a ride out to the Riley farm to question Michelle and finds that she had both the motive and opportunity to steal the caboose. Whit and Tom refuse to believe it, though.

Officer Harley takes Michelle down to the station for further questioning. Tom follows, dropping off Whit and Warren back at Whit's End along the way. Whit questions Connie about the Silver Streak and learns that she cleaned up around the Train Station after the kids left the previous day, throwing away several items. It's possible that Connie accidentally threw away the Silver Streak! They race down to the trash bin outside to see if it's there. Unfortunately, the garbage men have already emptied the dumpster, but they still find the evidence: a set of wheels from the Silver Streak.

Warren ends up apologizing to Michelle for accusing her of stealing. Michelle accepts the apology, but during the conversation that follows, she lets information slip that proves she really *did* steal the Silver Streak! What's more, she doesn't care! She's tired of all these "do-gooders" and tells Officer Harley to take her away from them, back to reform school.

Later, Connie looks in on a distraught Whit. He can't believe that Michelle behaved the way she did, despite all the kindness they showed her. Connie shrugs off the whole incident. She says Michelle was just a bad apple, and if she doesn't want to be helped, there's nothing more Whit can do. But there *is* one last thing Whit can do. As Connie leaves, Whit sinks to his knees in prayer.

the *Adventures in* ODYSSEY archives:

"The Case of the Missing Train Car" was our first mystery. In this episode, we found out that Tom has a wife, Agnes—although we didn't actually hear her. This episode was remade as "Whatever Happened to the Silver Streak?" *AIO* #118. See that episode for study questions.

Episode #22 "A Simple Addition"

Theme: Sibling rivalry.
Scripture reference: Romans 12:10
Written by Susan McBride
Directed by Steve Harris and Phil Lollar
Production engineer: Bob Luttrell
(Original air date: 4-16-88)

This episode was re-aired from *Family Portraits* #13. See that episode for study questions and story.

ADVENTURES IN ODYSSEY

ADVENTURES IN ODYSSEY

Episode #23 "The Quality of Mercy"

Theme: Mercy.
Scripture reference: Matthew 18:21-35
Written by Paul McCusker
Directed by Phil Lollar and Steve Harris
Production engineer: Bob Luttrell
(Original air date: 4-23-88)

Duuuum-de-*dum*-dum! The city is Odyssey. Young Scott Williams is nabbed by Officer David Harley for trying to steal apples from Tom Riley's farm. Scott breaks a fence in the process, and Tom figures the damage comes to about $30. Scott professes poverty and begs Tom to forgive the debt, which Tom does. But instead of passing the favor along, Scott immediately hunts down Robb Holt and demands repayment of a $2 loan. Robb only has $1, so Scott throttles him and pushes him into a stack of garbage cans.

Tom Riley hears of this and has Officer Harley find Scott and bring him back to the farm. Once there, Tom tells Scott to fix the fence and pick up all the apples around the area to pay back the debt he owes Tom. Scott protests that Tom said the debt was clear! It isn't fair! But Tom says he's being as fair with Scott as Scott was with Robb Holt. When Tom adds that Scott's father agrees, Scott realizes that he's run out of appeals. He groans loudly, then picks up the hammer and nails and begins making restitution.

the *Adventures in* ODYSSEY archives:

This was our first *AIO* episode —a "parallel parable," which retold the parable of the unmerciful servant. The title comes from a line in Shakespeare's play *The Merchant of Venice*. "The Quality of Mercy" was also the first show where Tom did the teaching instead of Whit. We were slowly changing him from a "country bumpkin" to a "wise mentor." This episode was remade—to write Officer Harley out of the script—as "An Act of Mercy," *AIO* #115. See that episode for study questions.

Episode #24 "Gotcha!"

Theme: The occult.
Scripture reference: 1 John 4:1-6
Written and directed by Phil Lollar
Production engineer: Bob Luttrell
(Original air date: 4-30-88)

There's been a rash of practical jokes around Whit's End, and Philo Sanderson is the culprit. After he pulls three successive jokes on Whit, Tom, and Officer Harley, Tom warns Philo that the problem with pulling practical jokes is that someone will usually retaliate. Philo says he doesn't have to worry about that because he has a lucky rabbit's foot. Whit immediately dismisses this notion, but Philo says Connie told him he needed the rabbit's foot after she read him his horoscope that morning.

Concerned, Whit borrows the foot and marches off to find Connie. Whit asks for an explanation and finds that Connie didn't know there was anything wrong with horoscopes and good-luck charms. When Whit tells her that they're all a part of the occult, Connie is horrified. She apologizes and reminds Whit that horoscopes are cheap and are everywhere—after all, they're in the paper every day.

This starts Whit thinking, and he expresses his concern to Tom the next day. Tom suggests that they simply need to make the message of the Bible more exciting to kids than the occult or horoscopes. Whit agrees, then excuses himself and gets to work.

Later that week, he unveils Whit's End's newest and grandest attraction: the Bible Room, designed to bring the Scriptures literally to life. In it are displays such as the full armor of God and the city of Jericho—complete with collapsible walls and a talking mirror that speaks Bible verses. Other displays are in the works. The room has also been inspired by Connie, Tom, and especially Philo, whose practical jokes helped Whit see that horoscopes and the occult are Satan's practical jokes on us.

Speaking of practical jokes, Philo enters the Bible Room, covered with blue paint. He was setting up another practical joke that backfired on him. Everyone has a good laugh—and silently wonders what kinds of adventures this new room will bring.

the *Adventures in* ODYSSEY archives:

"Gotcha!" introduced the Bible Room, which soon became one of the most popular attractions in Whit's End. Thanks to Officer Harley, portions of "Gotcha!" were redone in "Pranks for the Memories," *AIO* #120, and were excerpted as flashbacks in "It Began with a Rabbit's Foot," *AIO* #266. See *AIO* #120 for study questions.

Episodes #25 & 26 "Harley Takes the Case," Parts One & Two

Theme: You can't run away from your problems.
Scripture reference: Luke 15:11-32
Written by Paul McCusker
Directed by Phil Lollar and Steve Harris
Production engineer: Bob Luttrell
(Original air dates: 5-07-88 & 5-14-88)

It's carnival time in Odyssey, and young Steve Larson is missing. Officer Harley gets the call from the chief, and immediately, the good officer goes to Steve's house and interviews his father, Al. Al is impatient and thinks that Harley isn't doing enough to find Steve. When Harley suggests that Steve might have run away, Al gets angry and walks off to the woods, where Steve was last seen going to softball practice that morning.

Harley then makes his way over to Jay Brandt's house. Jay, Steve's best friend, mentions that Steve skipped out on softball practice because he hates the game, so there's no use looking for Steve around there. After that, Harley talks to Old Mr. Webster, who saw Steve heading for the woods carrying a bat, a glove, and a knapsack. Harley goes to search the woods and runs into Al again. Harley updates Al and again says that Steve might have run away. Al refuses to listen. Then, a neighbor runs up, saying he's searched the woods all the way out to Gower's field, and there's nothing there but a rusted-out tractor and an old barn.

Just then, Harley gets a static-filled call from the chief on his walkie-talkie. Someone thinks she saw Steve at the carnival. The chief tells Harley to finish what he's doing and join the rest of the searchers there. Al overhears this and tells everyone to head over to the carnival.

Everyone leaves—except Harley. He continues to search the woods, trying to imagine he's a young boy running away. His method works: Near Gower's Field, Harley finds Steve's abandoned bat and glove. Harley suspects that Steve is in the old barn. Inside the barn, Harley finds a raccoon eating a cupcake. Harley, confident that Steve is there, calls out to him. Steve finally answers from the loft, saying he wants to be left alone. Harley pleads with Steve to come out of the barn. It's a dangerous place—so old, a sneeze could blow it over. Steve refuses, so Harley starts to climb to the loft. Suddenly, the barn creaks, shudders, then collapses on both of them.

At the carnival, a lady tells the chief and Al Larson that she saw Steve talking with a man who is standing by the merry-go-round. The chief tries to handle it, but before he can, Al Larson yells at the man, who starts running. The chase is on. When they finally corner the guy, Al wants to kill him. Fortunately, before he can, the man's son runs up—and he looks almost exactly like Steve. Al apologizes, and the chief tells a trooper to take Al home. Once at home, Al and his wife pray.

Meanwhile, back at the barn, Steve and Harley are trapped under a bunch of rubble. When they realize they're all right, Steve finally explains why he ran away. He feels his dad doesn't care about him. Harley tries to tell Steve otherwise, but Steve thinks Al will only love him if he plays softball. Harley disputes this and tells Steve that it's foolish to run away. Harley knows because *he* did it once, and it broke his father's heart.

Suddenly, they hear noises. They think it might be a rescue team—until they hear growling. It's a pack of wild dogs. Harley tells Steve to cover himself up as best he can. Steve does, and the dogs break in and start to attack. The dogs kick the walkie-talkie over where Harley can reach it. He calls in, telling the chief he has a present for him, and it's trapped under some rubble in the old Gower barn.

Later, after the rescue team arrives on the scene, Steve and Al agree to talk about the softball issue. Al reaffirms his love for his son, then apologizes to Harley. The chief congratulates Harley and offers to buy him a cup of coffee. Harley says "fine"—but first, he's going to call his dad.

Adventures in Odyssey — the ODYSSEY archives:

"Harley Takes the Case" was *AIO*'s first two-parter. It was designed to show everyone that Officer Harley wasn't a complete buffoon. These two episodes were remade as a single, non-Harley episode, "Missing Person," *AIO* #121. See that episode for study questions.

Episode #27 "A Change of Hart"

Theme: Salvation; living a changed life.
Scripture references: 2 Corinthians 3:18; 5:16-17
Written by Paul McCusker
Directed by Phil Lollar and Steve Harris
Production engineer: Bob Luttrell
(Original air date: 5-21-88)

Freddie Hart would love to be someone else—*anybody* except himself. He's so unpopular, he's the poster child for Geek World. All the kids love to make fun of him and pick on him. Freddie is so miserable, he asks his dad if the family could move to a new city. Dad doesn't think that's practical, so Freddie suggests that he move instead to a different school—Odyssey Academy. No one knows him there, so he could be a different person. Dad doesn't think running away from problems is a good answer for Freddie, though, so Dad tells Freddie to stick it out.

But the next day, Freddie gets beat up. Mr. Hart tries talking to the school principal, but he's not at all helpful. So Freddie gets his wish—a transfer to Odyssey Academy. He's elated. At last, it's a chance to start fresh! Only, almost immediately, the familiar pattern starts: the teasing, the cruel jokes, the snickering. Freddie thinks he's found a friend in Gordie, but after Gordie offers some blunt advice to Freddie about changing his clothes, his hair, and his hobbies, Gordie avoids him like the plague. Soon Freddie is right back where he started.

That night, Freddie tearfully (again) asks his dad if he wouldn't mind moving the family to another city. Dad comforts him, and Freddie says he's tried everything he knows to make friends. He's changed his appearance, his manners, and even his school just to be liked, but nothing works. Dad says that the only way Freddie can really change is on the inside, in his heart. Everyone wants to be loved and accepted, but the important question is, To whom do we want to be acceptable? The answer, of course, is God. Dad tells Freddy that, fortunately, we don't have to change for God—we just have to let God work His changes in and through us. The way we do that is by asking Jesus Christ to come into our hearts. Dad asks if Freddie wants to do that. Freddie says he does. The two of them kneel, and Freddie finally gets his wish—he becomes a new creation.

Adventures in Odyssey — the ODYSSEY archives:

"A Change of Hart" was the first *AIO* episode that didn't have any of our "regulars" in it.

STUDY QUESTIONS:

1. Why did Freddie try to change himself?
2. Have you ever changed something about yourself just to please someone else? What was it?
3. When is it good to change something about yourself?

Episode #28 "The Price of Freedom"

Theme: God's control; patriotism; the price of freedom.
Scripture reference: Ecclesiastes 3:1,8
Written and directed by Phil Lollar
Production engineer: Bob Luttrell
(Original air date: 5-28-88)

Kirk McGinty idolizes his war-hero father, who died in Vietnam. But when his teacher, Mr. Altman, tells him that the soldiers who fought in southeast Asia were killers, it shakes Kirk's faith to the core. Altman tells Kirk that the men who lost their lives in Vietnam died for nothing. Then Altman gives him a book, which details some of the atrocities that happened at the hands of U.S. soldiers. After reading the book, Kirk isn't sure he wants to participate in the unveiling of the Veterans' Monument at Odyssey's annual Memorial Day picnic, even though he and his mother, Joyce, worked very hard to make the monument a reality.

Joyce tries to comfort Kirk, but when he sleeps that night, Altman's words and the book's images invade his dreams. Kirk wakes up convinced that his father did, indeed, die for nothing.

Meanwhile, Whit visits Altman and questions the wisdom of his actions. Whit informs Altman of the fate of Kirk's father. Altman, in turn, bitterly reveals that he lost a brother in Vietnam.

Later, at the unveiling of the memorial, Kirk is subdued until his mother reads a portion of the last letter Kirk's father ever wrote to her. The letter reveals his sense of duty and the gratitude of the Vietnamese people, and how those things make paying the price of freedom worthwhile. Kirk is touched by his father's words and proudly cuts the ribbon, unveiling the memorial.

Then Altman shows up and apologizes to Kirk for damaging his image of his father. Kirk and Joyce take a closer look at the monument. Altman says he noticed his brother's name carved on the memorial and passes on veiled thanks to Whit, who is the only other person in town who knew about Altman's brother. Altman also says he noticed another name on the monument—Jerry Whittaker. Whit tells Altman that Jerry was his son. The two share a moment of silent pain, mourning their losses, and Altman better understands Memorial Day.

Adventures in the ODYSSEY archives:

"The Price of Freedom" was the first episode that had an "adult" theme. The War Memorial also appeared in several subsequent episodes. "The Price of Freedom" received a lot of positive response. Many veterans wrote in to tell us how the episode affected them and to thank us for remembering their sacrifice.

On a lighter note, Bob Luttrell and Paul McCusker played the soldiers at the beginning of this episode. We all like to tease Bob for the trouble he has saying, "He's motion-n-n-ning us forward!"

STUDY QUESTIONS:

1. Why is it important to remember those who have fought and died in wars?
2. Should Christians fight in wars? Why or why not?
3. What kind of freedom do you have as a citizen? What kind of freedom do you have in Jesus Christ?

Episode #29 "Rumor Has It"

Theme: The dangers of gossip.
Scripture reference: James 3:5-12
Written by Paul McCusker
Directed by Phil Lollar and Steve Harris
Production engineer: Bob Luttrell
(Original air date: 6-04-88)

There is a new family in town, and they are giving all the kids at Odyssey Elementary the creeps—especially Jack and Lucy. They have to walk by the family's house every day, and Lucy is spooked by the young boy she sees staring at them through the window. At school, they hear further rumors about the family from Alice Pringle. Alice's brother saw the strange family's father leaving the house early in the morning, carrying what looked like a big sack with a body in it. Jack deduces that the father is a Mafia scientist.

Later at Whit's End, Whit tells Jack and Lucy the name of the family: Kirban. Whit says they are very private people, which just makes Jack even more curious to find out about them. Lucy, on the other hand, wants nothing to do with the family. She even refuses to walk by the house with Jack the next morning. At school, Jack informs Lucy that the boy wasn't in the window that morning. Just as Lucy wonders where the boy went, the teacher introduces a new student . . . John Kirban! No one even gets close to John all day, which makes Lucy feel guilty.

After school at Whit's End, Jack reveals plans to spy on the Kirbans and wants Lucy to help him. She refuses. Jack storms off angrily, bumping into Connie on the way. Connie talks to Whit and tells him that she saw John Kirban sitting on the curb by himself, crying. Whit goes to Lucy and asks her to do him a favor: Walk to school the next morning with John Kirban! Lucy tries, but when she reaches the Kirban's house, John's father nearly slams the door in her face, telling her that John isn't going back to school that day or any other.

Lucy runs from the house, terrified, and runs into Jack. He tells her not to worry—he's going to spy on the Kirbans that night and expose the whole Mafia/mad-scientist family! But thanks to a stray cat and several trash cans, it is *Jack* who winds up exposed, caught by Mr. Kirban! Officer Harley is summoned and gets to the bottom of things. The bag the father carries out to his van contains . . . a carpet. Mr. Kirban is a carpet maker. The family seemed unfriendly and mysterious because they are from a different country. Jack is released back to his parents' custody, Whit decides to buy a new carpet, Lucy has a new friend in John Kirban, and everyone learns that you can't always believe what you hear.

the *Adventures in* ODYSSEY archives:

"Rumor Has It" was the first time Jack and Lucy appeared on *AIO*. Jack and Lucy were played by Donald Long and Genesis Mullen. Donald and Genny knew each other outside of *Adventures in Odyssey*. In fact, they grew up and went to school together. They also fell in love, and in 1993, began a new and different kind of adventure—marriage.

"Rumor Has It" was another show that originally had Officer Harley in it. He was the policeman who collared Jack for trespassing on the Kirbans' property. We replaced Harley with a normal police officer—played by Executive Producer Chuck Bolte.

STUDY QUESTIONS:

1. What was Jack and Lucy's first mistake when it came to the Kirban family?
2. Why is it wrong to listen to rumors about people? What does the Bible say about gossip?
3. When someone starts to tell you a rumor, what should you do?

Episode #30 "Honor Thy Parents"

Theme: Respecting parents.
Scripture reference: Exodus 20:12
Written and directed by Phil Lollar
Production engineer: Bob Luttrell
(Original air date: 6-11-88)

School's out, and Laura Fremont is ecstatic. Sixth grade is over, and she is planning a party at Whit's End to celebrate. As she and her friend Kelly walk to the popular emporium, Kelly says that she's looking forward to meeting Laura's parents at the party. Laura quickly replies that her folks are out of town. The girls turn a corner just in time to witness an employer chewing out one of his employees. Kelly feels sorry for the employee, but Laura callously remarks that the man probably deserved it. When Laura and Kelly get to Whit's End, Laura's mom, Eula, is already there, talking with Whit. Laura is embarrassed that her mother is there (especially since her parents are supposedly out of town). When Laura's father, Homer, shows up a few moments later, Laura is mortified. Homer is the man they saw getting yelled at in the alley. Homer and Eula are friendly to Kelly, but Laura quickly shuttles Kelly away, then turns on her parents. She tells them they embarrass her and yells that she wishes she'd never been born into the Fremont family!

The next day, Whit talks with Laura about why she treats her lovely parents like dirt. "Because they're *hicks*!" Laura blurts out. Whit can't believe Laura feels that way and decides to show Laura why her folks are honorable. First, he has Laura meet Homer's boss, who tells Laura that Homer is his best employee. Then Whit takes Laura to the mission where Homer and Eula volunteer their services. Laura sees the wonderful work the mission is doing and discovers that her parents helped start it. Laura meets people who literally owe their lives to her parents.

Whit informs Laura that the things her parents have done are worthy of her respect. But the most important reason Laura should honor her parents is because the Bible says children must do it. The lesson sinks in, and at her party that night, Laura introduces all of her friends to her special guests of honor: her folks, Homer and Eula Fremont.

the *Adventures in* ODYSSEY archives:

"Honor Thy Parents" featured the debut of Dave Madden to the show. Dave later became Odyssey's favorite window washer, Bernard Walton.

STUDY QUESTIONS:

1. Why is it important to honor and respect your mom and dad?
2. How can you show respect for your parents?
3. What is God's promise to those who honor their father and mother?

Episodes #31 & 32

"Family Vacation," Parts One & Two

Theme: Family togetherness.
Scripture references: 2 Corinthians 13:14; Hebrews 10:25
Written and directed by Paul McCusker
Production engineer: Bob Luttrell
(Original air dates: 6-18-88 & 6-25-88)

It's vacation time, and the Barclay family is off like a herd of turtles. Well, almost—they haven't even left yet. Young Jimmy is going to journal about the trip. One of the first things he records is that his older sister, Donna, doesn't want to go. She prefers to remain in Odyssey, but her parents have overruled that notion, so Donna is not a happy camper. Jimmy also documents a brief, pretrip visit with Whit, who has given him a new invention, "Whit's Boredom Buster"—to be used only when Jimmy is "absolutely, without question, no doubt about it, as bored as you've ever been in your life."

At last, the Barclays are on the road . . . and aren't 20 minutes into their trip when trouble starts. Donna and Jimmy argue about backseat space; George runs over something that everyone thinks is a small animal but turns out to be a piece of tire rubber; they have a chewy lunch in an old diner; they sing every praise chorus they know; and the batteries go dead in Donna's tape player, further souring her mood.

To top it all off, the car suddenly dies. When George gets out to investigate, Jimmy sees a man they passed on the road rapidly approaching them. Donna speculates that he's an ax murderer. She screams for her father to get back in the car. Just as the man walks up, George pops the cap off the hot radiator, sending up an explosion of water and steam.

George falls back before the hot water and steam can scald him. The strange man runs up and turns out to be anything but an ax murderer. He and George walk back to the station and tow in the Barclay car, which will take at least a weekend to be repaired. Chester, the strange man, invites the Barclays to come home with him. The Barclays are wary at first, but it turns out that Chester and his family are Christians, so they accept.

Chester lives in a big house with his wife, Grace, and their youngest boy, Ted, who is Jimmy's age. Ted and Jimmy hit it off immediately and, after doing a few chores, run off into the forest to play. Mary and Grace enjoy each other's company, as do George and Chester.

The next day is Sunday, and the Barclays attend a church picnic with great food, a three-legged race, horseshoes, softball, egg-tosses, and other games. Donna is the only one not having a good time. She sits and sulks under a tree, and no one can move her. Jimmy says that if all Donna is going to do is think about Odyssey, she might as well hold a piece of it. So he gives her Whit's Boredom Buster puzzle.

Donna slowly starts working on it and soon is completely engaged. After a few hours she finally figures it out, and the puzzle comes to life in a beautiful array of swirling colors, lively music, and a nice message from Whit saying that boredom is under your control. Donna finally gets the message, just in time to participate in the last event of the day—the tug-of-war. After a few good pulls, Donna ends up in the mud, followed by everyone else in her family, much to their great amusement. The next morning, Chester finishes fixing the car, and the Barclays continue on their way, knowing that their vacation has gotten off to a great start thanks to a little Christian fellowship.

the *Adventures in* ODYSSEY archives:

"Family Vacation" marked the first appearance of the Barclay family on *AIO*. Although Jimmy and Donna were played by the same actors throughout the series, George and Mary were played by several *different* people over the years.

The Barclays' first names came from the Frank Capra movie classic *It's a Wonderful Life*. The character of George Bailey was played by Jimmy Stewart, and Mary Bailey was played by Donna Reed—thus, George, Jimmy, Mary, and Donna.

STUDY QUESTIONS:

1. What was the meaning of Whit's message, "Boredom is under your control"?
2. Why is it important for families to have fun together?
3. Describe some fun times you have had with your family.

Episode #33

"The Day Independence Came"

Theme: American history; freedom; our Christian heritage.
Scripture references: Proverbs 28:16; Acts 5:29; 2 Corinthians 3:17
Written and directed by Phil Lollar
Production engineer: Bob Luttrell
(Original air date: 7-02-88)

Irwin Springer loves history—especially about the American Revolution. So he is excited when Whit leaves a book about Ben Franklin for Irwin in the library. Unfortunately, Irwin's enthusiasm causes him to temporarily lose good sense. Irwin climbs on a rolling chair to reach the book, which is on top of a tall bookcase. The chair slips, Irwin falls, and he's knocked unconscious.

When he awakens, he's in a forest, where a man is telling him to run. Suddenly, a bullet whizzes by Irwin's head and splats into a tree. Irwin runs, and he and the man hide in some bushes. The men chasing them run up, and to Irwin's amazement, they're Redcoats from the

British Colonial Army! Irwin has been transported back in time. He and the man narrowly escape the Redcoats by pulling down a wasps' nest onto the men, but then Irwin and his companion are attacked by the wasps. They jump into a nearby pond and swim to the opposite shore. There, the man introduces himself—as Nathan Hale!

Hale takes Irwin back to the Continental Army camp, where he meets George Washington. Irwin can't believe any of this is happening. He's especially awed when General Washington asks him to take a message to the Continental Congress in Philadelphia. Irwin doesn't know how to ride a horse, but he certainly can't refuse a request from George Washington. So Irwin runs off to Philadelphia.

In Philadelphia, he meets the patriots, who are debating over whether to sign a document called the Declaration of Independence. Irwin delivers his message, the debate rages on, and finally the Declaration is signed. Ben Franklin tells Irwin to spread the news to every village and town—the United States are free! Irwin does, but his horse stumbles and falls, knocking him unconscious again. When he awakens this time, he's back in the library at Whit's End. It was all just a dream . . . or was it?

the Adventures in ODYSSEY archives:

"The Day Independence Came" was our first historical adventure and first time-travel adventure. We originally wanted to do a wacky, comical look at our nation's founding, but Chuck Bolte, our executive producer, suggested a more serious episode.

Irwin traveled back in time by getting conked on the head—a story device borrowed from Mark Twain's *A Connecticut Yankee in King Arthur's Court* (at least, the movie version with Bing Crosby). We enjoyed doing this time-travel adventure, but we couldn't keep knocking out our characters to do it. So we started thinking about alternatives—which we played out in other episodes.

The cast performances and Bob Luttrell's production really shine here. When Irwin and Nathan Hale came out of the water after escaping the wasps, the effects blended so well with the actors' performances that they sounded like they were actually wet. The splat of the bullet that hit right above Irwin's head also sounded remarkably real. Our standard of production went up a notch with this one.

The episode generated negative mail. Some people wrote in objecting to the scene in which Washington prays in Jesus' name. But the prayer came from Washington's own daily prayer journal. The words are *his*, and he prayed them almost every day, morning and night.

STUDY QUESTIONS:

1. Why is it important to know the history of your country?
2. How did the signing of the Declaration of Independence change America?
3. Read Proverbs 28:16. How does God feel about unjust rulers?

Episode #34 "Stormy Weather"

Theme: Courage; faith; friendship.
Scripture references: Psalm 103; Ecclesiastes 4:9-12
Written by Paul McCusker
Directed by Paul McCusker and Phil Lollar
Production engineer: Bob Luttrell
(Original air date: 7-09-88)

Rain, rain, rain—it's been storming in Odyssey for days, and Connie is sick of it. Sick of that and the way Whit, Tom, and everyone else in town seem to be "preaching" at her. It all escalates when Whit assumes Connie will emcee the upcoming Bible Drill. Connie blows up, then takes a walk in the rain. She goes to a friend's house, but finds no comfort there. Finally, she ends up at home, where she begs her mom to let her go back to California—permanently. Mrs. Kendall says she'll have to think about it. To Connie, that means it's a done deal. Suddenly, Mrs. Kendall remembers that she called Whit because she was worried about Connie, and Whit went looking for her out in the storm.

Connie dons a slicker and rubber boots and takes off in search of Whit. They meet up in a neighbor's shed, and Connie informs Whit of her decision to go back to California. Whit is bothered but suggests that they go back to Whit's End to talk about it. The storm gets much worse. Whit and Connie barely get inside the door when the front window explodes! Glass flies everywhere, and a large chunk embeds itself in Whit's leg. Connie panics, but Whit steadily issues instructions to her while quietly quoting a psalm to calm himself.

Just when things seem their darkest, Mrs. Kendall arrives. She and Connie take Whit to the hospital where he gets stitches. Connie tells Whit that she didn't realize how much Whit meant to her until the accident. Whit tells Connie virtually the same thing, then asks if she's still going to California. Connie says maybe around Christmas. Then she adds that she'd be happy to judge the Bible Drill. Whit and Connie hug, and Connie realizes that Whit is much more to her than just a nice employer. He's her friend.

the Adventures in ODYSSEY archives:

The original title of this episode was "A Stormy Afternoon." Connie's mother, played by Maggie Malloy, made her debut here.

One of the key story lines we wanted to develop during our early days was moving Connie toward accepting Jesus. "Stormy Weather" was another stepping-stone in the right direction for her as she witnessed firsthand how Whit relied on his faith in God to see him through a major crisis.

STUDY QUESTIONS:

1. Why was Connie so anxious to get back to California?
2. Why did Whit want Connie to stay in Odyssey?
3. Why did Whit start reciting the psalm?

Episode #35 "V.B.S. Blues"

Theme: Sharing your faith; God's provision in tough situations.
Scripture references: Daniel 3; Hebrews 4:12
Written and directed by Phil Lollar
Production engineer: Bob Luttrell
(Original air date: 7-16-88)

Ned Lewis is a nervous wreck. His sixth-grade class at Vacation Bible School is set to perform a sketch Ned wrote and directed about Shadrach, Meshach, Abednego, and the fiery furnace. The problem is, the class isn't ready, not by a long shot. And, as he explains to Whit, the kids playing the lead characters—Mugsy Mumford, Hank Shorter, and Junior Bascomb—are the closest thing in Odyssey to gang members. Whit says things can't possibly be that bad, so Ned explains in a flashback just how disastrous the V.B.S. week has been.

Mugsy, Hank, and Junior continually disrupted the class, took over the main parts of the sketch, and generally made nuisances of themselves. To make the disaster complete, the pastor told Ned how much he's looking forward to the sketch. The pastor said if it goes well, he may approve the drama program Ned's been wanting to start at the church.

Talking to Whit, Ned reveals that he's mostly disappointed because his reason for doing the sketch was so the kids would learn something. Now it doesn't seem that they're gaining anything from it. Whit disputes this and tells Ned that God works in ways we can't possibly understand. Whit encourages Ned and tells him to trust in God.

That night, Ned and his class perform their sketch, leaving the audience in stitches. Ned believes the whole thing flopped. To his surprise, Whit, the audience, and Pastor Williams compliment Ned on a job well done. The pastor even wants to talk more about the drama program. Best of all, Mugsy, Hank, and Junior thank Ned for letting them be in the show. They also apologize for disrupting the class during the week and ask if they can come to Ned's weekly Sunday school class. Ned says "absolutely," and he and Whit marvel at the faithfulness of the Lord.

STUDY QUESTIONS:

1. Why did Ned feel that the kids weren't getting anything out of his class?
2. Ned told Whit that everything that had happened was his "fiery furnace." Can you think of a time when it seemed like you were in a "fiery furnace"? How did God help you through it?
3. What is your favorite Old Testament story? How has it helped you?

Episode #36 "Kid's Radio"

Theme: Perseverance; commitment.
Scripture reference: Hebrews 10:36
Written by Paul McCusker
Directed by Paul McCusker and Phil Lollar
Production engineer: Bob Luttrell
(Original air date: 7-23-88)

Brad Dillard loves radio. He tells Whit that he wishes a radio station existed just for kids. Whit is intrigued by the idea and shows Brad all sorts of old broadcasting equipment that came with the building when he bought Whit's End. Whit says he'll provide the equipment if Brad will run the station. Brad agrees and calls all the kids together. Everyone is enthusiastic, especially a nerdy little kid named Sherman who is a whiz at electronics. The gang all agrees to help Brad get "Kid's Radio" off the ground.

But soon Brad and Sherman learn that what kids promise and what they deliver are two different things. The only ones who put any real work into the station are Brad and Sherman! They work hard to get it on the air, and once they do, they work to *keep* it on the air.

After a while the work starts to take its toll, making both Brad and Sherman frazzled. Brad's father tells Whit that Brad is endangering his health by working so hard. Brad cannot continue. Whit agrees. He goes on the air to praise Brad and Sherman for their commitment and mildly scolds the kids listening for not following through on their promise to help. Whit also announces that everyone interested in keeping Kid's Radio on the air should meet at Whit's End at 3 P.M. the next day. Unfortunately, no one shows. Brad, Sherman, and Whit are disappointed—until the manager of a local station walks in the door. The manager says he loves the show and wants it for his Saturday morning lineup. Brad and Sherman happily agree, having learned firsthand the value of perseverance.

This episode was the first time Kid's Radio appeared—one of *AIO's* best storytelling devices.

STUDY QUESTIONS:

1. Why didn't anyone help Brad and Sherman get Kid's Radio on the air?
2. Why did Brad apologize to Sherman?
3. How can you become a good promise keeper?

Episodes #37 & 38

"Camp What-a-Nut," Parts One & Two

Theme: Having fun at camp; building character.
Scripture reference: 1 Samuel 16:1-13
Written and directed by Phil Lollar
Production engineer: Bob Luttrell
(Original air dates: 7-30-88 & 8-06-88)

Summertime means going to camp, and in Odyssey, the camp everyone goes to is Camp What-a-Nut. It's Donny McCoy's first year as a camper, and he records every minute of his experience in his journal. He starts with Camp Director Whit's explanation of how the place came to be called "What-a-Nut." It's an acronym for the camp's *real* name, "Wey-Aka-Tal-Ah-Nee-Tee"—an Indian phrase meaning "land that stinks like swamp."

Donny's week takes off from there. It's filled with both exciting and ridiculous incidents. First, his sister, Gloria, seems to fall in love with Donny's counselor, Ned Lewis. Gloria appears so smitten, she crafts a heart-shaped necklace. Then, to make matters worse, Donny learns that one of his cabinmates is Chas Wentworth, a notorious bully. Chas has a run-in with the camp's Italian cook, Marco Dibiasi. Chas vows revenge. Unfortunately, Chas also zeroes in on Donny, teasing him about being short.

Donny tries every activity available and fails at each one because of his small stature. Whit notices this and takes Donny on a walk in the forest. Suddenly an enormous bear lumbers right toward them! The bear is protecting her cubs. She charges Donny and Whit, who run! Whit trips and falls. The bear rushes closer and closer.

Donny helps Whit to his feet, and they both climb a nearby tree. The bear starts up after them, but she's too heavy to get far, so she tries shaking them down from the tree. Donny and Whit hang on tight, feverishly praying to God for safety.

Meanwhile, back at camp, Chas has discovered a way to get even with Marco—by luring a skunk into his cabin with a trail of popcorn. But the skunk escapes and follows Chas to the mess hall, causing a panic. Everyone clears the room but Chas, whom the frightened skunk blesses with a special present—his spray.

Later, Ned, who has received Gloria's necklace via Chas, meets up with Gloria and discovers that she made the necklace for a *different* fellow, not him.

Ned's worries are over, but Whit and Donny's are just starting. The bear finally leaves, but when Whit and Donny try to return to the camp, they get lost. Nighttime is coming fast, and they have to do something. Suddenly, Donny gets an idea: He'll climb a tree all the way to the top to see if he can spot the camp. His smallness works in his favor, and once at the top, he quickly sees both the camp and the route back. The two of them make their way back, and Donny has quite a tale to tell his journal—and everyone else—about how the thing he always disliked about himself ended up saving his and Whit's lives.

the Adventures in ODYSSEY archives:

"Camp What-a-Nut" was originally written with Jimmy Barclay in the lead role, to continue his summer journal. But David Griffin, who plays Jimmy, was on a real-life vacation with his real-life family at recording time. So the lead was changed to Donny McCoy. The origins of the "What-a-Nut" title provided a little background into the history of Odyssey—which we explain further in later episodes.

STUDY QUESTIONS:

1. Why did Chas treat Marco—and everyone else—so badly?
2. Read 1 Samuel 16:1-13. Why does God think what's on the inside is more important than what's on the outside?
3. How can you become better at seeing people's hearts rather than their appearances?

Episodes #39 & 40

"The Case of the Secret Room," Parts One & Two

Theme: Greed; justice.
Scripture references: Matthew 6:24; 1 Timothy 6:10
Recommended maturity level: 10 and up
Written and directed by Paul McCusker
Production engineer: Bob Luttrell
(Original air dates: 8-13-88 & 8-20-88)

PARENTAL WARNING: This is a mystery about a 40-year-old murder. It contains subject matter that may be too intense for younger children.

Whit is in his basement working on an "automatic freezing machine" when Tom and his great-niece, Jami, come to visit. Whit shows the invention to Tom and Jami and accidentally drops an important part. It rolls under a large cabinet. Tom and Whit move the cabinet to recover the part and discover an ancient, hidden door. When they wrench open the door, they find a small room. Sitting in the middle of the room is a fully-clothed skeleton with a bullet hole in its shirt. They immediately call the police, and an inspector named Ralph Howards answers a few questions for them.

The skeleton is Spencer Barfield, a man who came to Odyssey in 1946. He worked as a maintenance man at Whit's End when it was known as the Fillmore Recreation Center. He disappeared the day after Odyssey Bank was robbed of $25,000. The police assumed Barfield was in on the robbery and searched all over the country but never found him—until now. Howards says that Barfield had a partner who double-crossed him, shot him, then ran off with the money.

Whit wants the police to look for Barfield's killer, but Inspector Howards says they wouldn't even know where to start looking. As far as he's concerned, the case will just have to remain a mystery.

But that's not good enough for Whit, so he and Jami head to the library to dig up some clues. They read the microfilm of newspaper articles dating from the approximate time of the robbery. From those, Whit and Jami learn that the bank was managed by Percival Fenwick. Percival now lives as a semi-recluse in his family's mansion on Chatwick Hill.

Whit and Jami also discover another interesting bit of news from the microfilm: A rookie policeman was making his rounds at the bank when the robbery occurred. The man was knocked unconscious by the robbers. His name? Ralph Howards.

Whit and Jami go talk to Percival Fenwick. He's a strange old man with an extensive collection of African weaponry (spears, shields, blow darts, etc.). Fenwick says the robbers cut the alarm and slipped in through a back window. Only he, the bank president, and the police knew where the alarm box was located. Fenwick thinks somebody on the police force tipped the robbers off in exchange for a share of the money.

Whit and Jami leave, more puzzled than ever. They go talk to Inspector Howards again. They reveal what they learned about him in the newspapers and tell Howards what Mr. Fenwick said. Howards says he wasn't knocked out, he *blacked* out. He adds that the police commission cleared him of any wrongdoing in the matter. The whole incident has been an embarrassment—he just wants to put it all behind him. Howards tells Whit to stop pursuing the case.

That night, Whit goes back to Whit's End, where Connie tells him a strange woman came by that afternoon asking all sorts of questions about the basement room and the skeleton. She left Whit an envelope. Inside is a headline dated June 7, 1946: "Police in Car Chase." More mystery!

Suddenly, they hear a crash in the basement. Whit goes down to investigate, and the lights go out. A harsh voice whispers for Whit to stay out of things. Then Whit is pushed into a stack of boxes and is knocked unconscious!

Whit ends up all right but is still at odds with Inspector Howards about investigating the case. Howards insists that Whit drop it. Whit suspects that Howards might be hiding something—and continues his quest to solve the mystery. The plot is further complicated when Whit learns that Howards was involved in a car chase that led to the death of a man named Alfred Myers. In the man's car, the police found a .38 caliber pistol (the same caliber as the bullet found in the skeleton).

Just then, the mysterious lady arrives and introduces herself as Spencer Barfield's sister. She's determined to clear her brother's name and help Whit in any way she can. She claims that Alfred Myers was in cahoots with Percival Fenwick, the bank manager! Fenwick later denies the claim. He says he had hired Myers as a private investigator to keep an eye on Howards, who Fenwick thinks was in on the bank robbery, too. Whit, Connie, and Jami can't figure out who to believe. Then Tom Riley comes up with an idea of his own: What if the money is buried in the basement of Whit's End?

That night, Whit goes down to dig for the buried box and is surprised to find that it's there! That's only the first surprise, as he is suddenly interrupted by someone. Who? It would be unfair to solve the mystery for you. But you can be sure that justice is served—and everyone involved learns an important lesson about greed and how it can lead even the best people into trouble.

Adventures in the ODYSSEY archives:

The blow dart at the end of "The Case of the Secret Room" was originally a gun. We changed it to dispel potential audience fears about violence. These episodes also show how Whit's End can become as big or small as we need it to be. We needed a secret room with a secret door, and —poof!— one magically appeared.

STUDY QUESTIONS:

1. Why was Whit so intent on following the case?
2. Whit said that he was exercising his rights as a citizen by pursuing the case. What did he mean?
3. Whit lamented that this whole incident was caused by greed. When have you felt greedy? What's the best way to keep your greed under control?

Episode #41 "Return to the Bible Room"

Theme: Obedience; biblical history: Jonah.
Scripture references: the book of Jonah; Ephesians 6:1-3
Written by Paul McCusker
Directed by Phil Lollar
Production engineer: Bob Luttrell
(Original air date: 8-27-88)

Jack is upstairs in the Bible Room when Lucy approaches him. She's upset with Jack. He isn't following through on a promise they made to their parents. Jack and Lucy have committed to help with the church cleanup day, but Jack would rather stay at Whit's End and look at all the Bible displays.

Whit walks up and demonstrates the attractions in the room: the Talking Mirror, the "Full Armor of God," the Walls of Jericho, and so on. Finally, they come to a big fish, which represents the story of Jonah. Lucy says they should leave, but Jack asks Whit to tell them the story. Whit does, and he insists that Jack and Lucy help by using their imaginations. They do—and end up inside the action!

They're sailing on a stormy sea. Jonah is trying to run away from God. When the sailors learn this, Jonah tells them the only way to save themselves is to throw him overboard. The crew tosses Jonah over, and a wave sweeps Jack and Lucy overboard as well! All three are swallowed by a whale. Later, in the belly of the whale, Jonah does some serious soul searching—and in the process he manages to convict Jack of not obeying his parents.

Finally, having escaped from the whale's belly, they all arrive in Nineveh, where Jonah delivers a message from God. He says that the Lord will destroy the city's inhabitants. But the city repents, and God spares it—much to Jonah's displeasure. God reproves Jonah, and his tale ends.

At the story's conclusion, Jack asks Whit if Jonah learned a lesson. Whit asks the same thing of Jack. Jack realizes he's disobeyed his parents, but now that the church cleanup day is over, it's too late to make things right. Fortunately, Whit says the cleanup day was postponed until the following Saturday, so Jack and Lucy can keep their promise after all. In the meantime, Whit has a suggestion: Anyone for a little fishing?

Adventures in the ODYSSEY archives:

The crowd of sailors heard in the background throughout the storm scenes was performed by only three guys: Hal Smith, Ed Walker, and Will Ryan. Talk about talent! "Return to the Bible Room" also created a little controversy among some listeners over whether Jonah was swallowed by a whale or a big fish.

STUDY QUESTIONS:

1. What does it mean to "cast lots" for something? What other story in the Bible uses this phrase?
2. Jonah asked Jack if he always listened to his parents. Do you always listen to your parents? To God? Why or why not?
3. Why is it foolish to try to run from God?

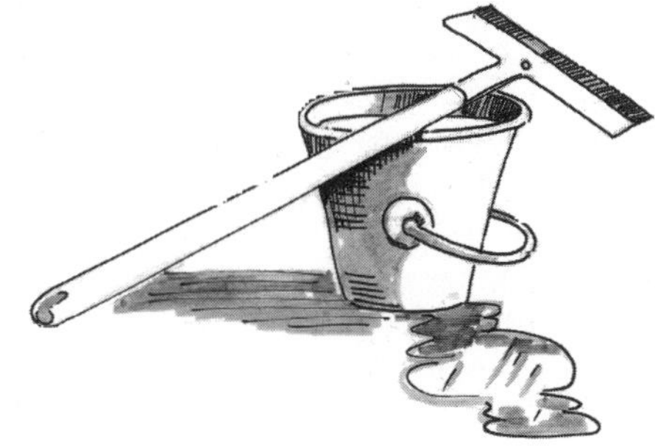

Episode #42

"The Last Great Adventure of the Summer"

Theme: God's protection; Dad as a hero.
Scripture reference: Proverbs 23:24
Recommended maturity level: 10 and up
Written and directed by Phil Lollar
Production engineers: Steve Harris and Dave Arnold
(Original air date: 9-03-88)

PARENTAL WARNING: This adventure about spies and international intrigue may be too intense for younger children.

Terry Johnston is having the worst summer of his life. He tells Whit that all he and his overprotective dad have done is go to church, the library, and Whit's End. Whit sympathizes with Terry, then Dad picks him up to go see an educational film. Whit asks if they would drop some garbage bags in the dumpster on the way outside. But as they approach the dumpster behind Whit's End, a strange man suddenly steps out of the shadows. He greets Dad as "Catspaw" and demands that he hand over "the formula."

Dad looks frightened until the stranger takes a step toward Terry. Suddenly, Dad springs into action, dropping the stranger to the pavement with some karate chops. Then Dad tells Terry to run. They hop in Dad's car and race away. Terry can't believe any of this is happening. He is even more stunned when his dad reveals that he's with the CIA. Unfortunately, the stranger after Terry's dad is hot on their heels. He ends up chasing them into an open boxcar at the train depot. There, Terry and Dad are knocked unconscious with sleeping gas. They wind up in London, trapped in the penthouse apartment of an evil man named Maxim. Maxim is their strange pursuer's boss. The room is filled with aquariums. Maxim enters and demands the formula. When Dad refuses, Maxim threatens him with a tank full of piranhas.

This time Terry takes action, stomping on the stranger's foot, then smashing the piranha tank. Dad grabs Terry, and they escape to the roof. Maxim and his henchmen clamber up after them. Dad and Terry are trapped! . . . Or are they?

Just in the nick of time, Scotland Yard and the CIA appear to capture Maxim and his cronies. But Maxim won't be robbed of his revenge. He suddenly pushes Terry's dad off the roof. The agents drag Maxim away as he laughs at his "victory." Once Maxim is gone, a horrified Terry discovers that his father is safe—on a window washer's scaffolding just below the roof.

The window washers were also agents. Terry finds that everything that has happened was planned from the start. Now that Maxim thinks Catspaw is dead, Terry's father can retire from the agency and spend more time with his son! But the irony is, because everything is top secret for security reasons, Terry can't tell *anyone* about his adventure.

"The Last Great Adventure of the Summer" was a complete departure from our normal adventures. This time, we didn't portray the adventure as a fantasy or a dream. Yes, international intrigue reaches even into Odyssey!

STUDY QUESTIONS:

1. Should Terry's dad have kept his profession a secret from Terry? Why or why not?
2. How would you feel if *your* mom or dad were a secret agent?
3. Can you think of something heroic that your mother or father has done? How about caring for you, providing for you, and loving you? Are those things heroic? Explain.

Episode #43 "Back to School"

Theme: Making new friends.
Scripture references: Ecclesiastes 3; Hebrews 13:8
Written by Paul McCusker
Directed by Phil Lollar
Production engineer: Bob Luttrell
(Original air date: 9-10-88)

Leslie has a reputation around Whit's End for telling stories—exaggerated ones. Most of the time, they're pretty funny. But today they're covering up something more serious. First, she describes the Turners' dog as being bigger than a horse. Then Leslie tells Whit a wild tale about her first day at school: Her mother made her wear a torn dress and a hot sweater. The bus was driven by "Crazy Eddie," who only drives slower than 65 mph when he has to slow down for turns. All her friends deserted her at school. The principal put her in Mr. Gutwrench's class, who immediately made fun of her torn dress, gave her a 10,000 word essay to write, and yelled at her for hanging out with her friends during the summer.

Whit, of course, questions the truthfulness of these statements. After a bit of probing, he discovers that Leslie is actually upset because her best friend, Cindy, isn't hanging around with her anymore. Cindy is good friends with Krista now, even though Cindy and Leslie promised to be best friends forever. Whit suggests the promise was one neither of them could keep. But Leslie ignores him and confronts Cindy at her house. Leslie tells Cindy that if they can't be *best* friends, then they won't be friends at all! Cindy shrugs this off as a sign of Leslie's immaturity.

Leslie runs home, feeling sorry for herself. She ends up treating another friend, Anne, the same way Cindy treated her. When Anne leaves in tears, Leslie's mother gets to the bottom of the situation and explains to Leslie that people change as they get older. Sometimes friends grow apart, and Leslie and Cindy are starting to do that. But there is a friend who will never change: Jesus.

Leslie feels terrible about her actions. She calls Anne to apologize. Anne forgives her, and Leslie learns a valuable lesson about friendship and life.

STUDY QUESTIONS:

1. Why was Leslie upset with Cindy? Did Leslie have a right to be upset with her? Why or why not?
2. Have you ever grown apart from your best friend? How did you feel? What did you do about it?
3. Leslie had trouble when her friendships changed. What kinds of changes are hardest for you?

Episode #44

"It Sure Seems Like It to Me"

Theme: Exaggerating.
Scripture references: Psalm 19:14; Ephesians 4:29
Written and directed by Phil Lollar
Production engineer: Bob Luttrell
(Original air date: 9-17-88)

In this remake of *Family Portraits* #5, "You're Not Gonna Believe This!" Leslie is back. This time she gets into trouble because of her exaggerated stories—especially with a tale of how she gave her mother's new umbrella to a cowboy riding a purple fire engine. The catch? The cowboy story turns out to be true!

STUDY QUESTIONS:

1. What's the difference between exaggerating and lying? Is there a difference?
2. Why didn't anyone believe Leslie's story about the cowboy and the purple fire engine?
3. How can you learn to trust someone who has lied to you? How can you build back trust with someone you have lied to?

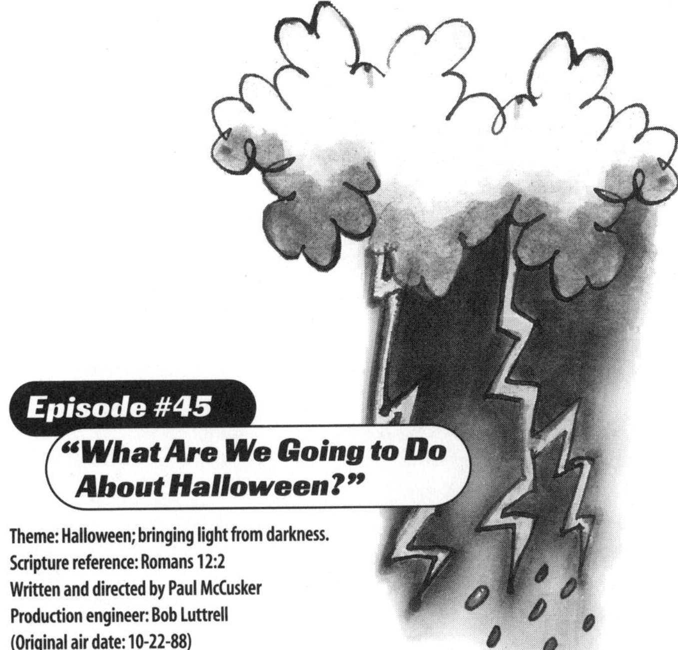

Episode #45

"What Are We Going to Do About Halloween?"

Theme: Halloween; bringing light from darkness.
Scripture reference: Romans 12:2
Written and directed by Paul McCusker
Production engineer: Bob Luttrell
(Original air date: 10-22-88)

Halloween—a time for witches, ghouls, goblins . . . and controversy. There is dissension in the air, especially at Odyssey Community Church. There, Tom moderates an elder's meeting at which Mr. Renfield expresses his disapproval of Halloween. Renfield believes that Halloween is not only harmful, it's a slap in the face to Christians everywhere. He wants the pastor and the elder board to recommend that parents not celebrate Halloween in any way. The following Sunday, the pastor preaches against the observance, which leads the parents of the congregation to ignore Halloween.

This makes the kids at Whit's End extremely unhappy. They elect Brad and Leonard to talk to Whit about it. Whit says he won't go against their parents' wishes, but he will let them learn all about Halloween by reading library books. Brad and Leonard start researching and learn the history of "All Hallow's Eve"—a night where it was traditionally thought that demons would run wild, pulling pranks and tricks on people. The boys sadly decide that Halloween really *isn't* a good thing to celebrate. Brad suggests that maybe instead they should celebrate All Saints' Day and have a Biblical Character Costume Party. Whit agrees and offers Whit's End as the celebration site.

This seems to be an acceptable solution for everyone—except Mr. Renfield. He visits Whit and asks him to cancel the party. Mr. Renfield says it's causing a ton of trouble in his household because his children aren't allowed to participate. Whit suggests that Mr. Renfield reconsider—after all, the party is a celebration of the saints, not demons. Renfield disagrees.

The party goes on as scheduled and is a great success. Everyone has a good time. At the end of the evening, families gather together as Whit helps to focus everyone's attention on God—a perfect example of letting light shine through the darkness.

STUDY QUESTIONS:

1. Why was Mr. Renfield so opposed to Halloween?
2. Is Halloween really bad? Why or why not?
3. Does your church have a biblical character costume party on Halloween?

Episode #46
"The Shepherd and the Giant"

Theme: Biblical history: David and Goliath.
Scripture references: 1 Samuel 16; 17
Written and directed by Phil Lollar
Production engineer: Dave Arnold
(Original air date: 10-29-88)

Whit is in the Bible Room working on another invention designed to make the Scriptures come to life. Connie enters, and Whit shows her "The Environment Enhancer." It's a set of headphones hooked up to a machine that, through the imagination, places you inside a biblical adventure. Connie is disappointed that the adventures are from the Bible, but Whit tells her not to knock it until she's tried it.

Connie puts on the headphones and is almost immediately transported to a pastoral setting where a young man is watching over a flock of sheep and playing a harp. The young man's name is David. He reads Connie one of his "poems." She watches as he fights a lion with nothing but his staff. Later, Connie witnesses this young shepherd being anointed king of Israel by an old prophet named Samuel.

Connie then accompanies David as he visits his brothers on the battlefield in their war against the Philistines. A giant bully named Goliath taunts the Israelites. Connie is stunned when David volunteers to go one-on-one against Goliath in battle, armed with only a sling and five smooth stones. Goliath ridicules David, but David calls upon the Lord. Connie watches as the giant falls to the ground, then David cuts off Goliath's head with his own sword. Spurred on by David's heroism, the Israelites surge forward and attack the Philistines, defeating them soundly.

Connie discovers that the Bible is anything but boring, moving her another step closer to a relationship with God.

the *Adventures in* ODYSSEY archives:

"The Shepherd and the Giant" was the first and last time we ever used the Environment Enhancer, a forerunner of the Imagination Station.

behind the scenes:

"'The Shepherd and the Giant' was a challenge to produce. One of the effects I had to create was the sound of Goliath's head being chopped off. So I brought a cantalope into the studio and chopped it in half with a machete. It worked great—but was kind of messy."

—Dave Arnold, on his first solo production

STUDY QUESTIONS:

1. Connie thought there were much better stories to tell than those in the Bible. Why do you think she believed that?
2. Why did God reject all of David's brothers?
3. Why did David pick up *five* stones to fight Goliath?

Episode #47
"A Single Vote"

Theme: Voting; civic duty; participating in democracy.
Scripture reference: Matthew 22:21
Written and directed by Phil Lollar
Production engineer: Bob Luttrell
(Original air date: 11-05-88)

Horace Higgenbotham is running for president of the student body at Odyssey Elementary. Whit has let the candidates hold a rally at Whit's End. Thanks to some free ice cream, the kids are all there and are excited. But Connie is sick of the whole thing. She feels that one vote can't possibly make a difference. So Whit proceeds to prove her wrong.

He tells her and everyone listening about a man named Jamison Shoemaker, whose story *ends* in the territory of Texas during 1845. Territorial President Sam Houston waits anxiously for word on the vote for Texas statehood. Texas needs 36 congressional votes, and Houston is not certain they have them. Suddenly, a messenger bursts in to deliver the news: Texas has become the 28th state—by a margin of one vote, cast by Harrigan, a senator from Indiana.

This leads to the next phase of the story, which happened six years earlier in Indiana. The legislators had gathered in Indianapolis for an important vote to elect a senator. One of those legislators was a man named Madison Marsh. Marsh elicited advice from his advisors, then decided to cast his vote for Harrigan, who was confirmed as a senator—by Marsh's one vote!

All of this finally leads to Jamison Shoemaker. It's Election Day, 1837. Shoemaker is out plowing his field and nearly misses his chance to vote, rushing to town and casting his ballot just before the polls close. The ballots are counted, and the new representative to the Indiana state legislator is Madison Marsh. Shoemaker realizes that's the fellow *he* voted for—*and Marsh won by that one vote!*

One ordinary man with one ordinary vote was directly responsible for Texas becoming a state. As Whit tells us, it's all a part of our Maker's plan.

the *Adventures in* ODYSSEY archives:

"A Single Vote" generates a lot of mail every time it is aired. The main question people ask is, "Where did you get this story?" We got it from a *Focus on the Family* broadcast. In an effort to encourage listeners to vote, Dr. Dobson relayed the basic facts I used in the story about each election being decided by just one vote. I filled in the details, fictionalizing some—but not all—of the characters in the episode. The basic facts have since been confirmed by other sources such as Ann Landers's newspaper column.

Jimmy attends Lightning's basketball workshop. His devotion to the man grows, despite Lightning's attempts to quell it. Later, at Whit's End, Howard slams Lightning, accusing him of using drugs. Jimmy flies into a rage and yells at Howard, who tells Jimmy to go ask Lightning about it himself.

Jimmy rushes to Lightning's sports shop and confronts Lightning about his rumored drug problem. Jimmy can't believe it, but Lightning admits that it's true. Jimmy runs off, upset.

The next day, Lightning makes a statement from the steps of city hall, admitting his problem and crediting Jesus with changing his life. Unfortunately, Jimmy misses the press conference because he's apologizing to everyone he yelled at the previous day.

When Jimmy gets home, Lightning is there waiting for Jimmy. Lightning confesses he made a terrible mistake using drugs, but Christ turned his life around. He asks Jimmy for forgiveness. Jimmy does, having learned a valuable lesson—that the only hero any of us will *ever* need is Jesus.

STUDY QUESTIONS:

1. Why is it important to vote?
2. Read Matthew 22:21. In our country, who is the ruling authority?
3. Name some other instances where one person made a big difference.

Episode #48 "Heroes"

Theme: Hero worship.
Scripture reference: Hebrews 7:26
Written and directed by Paul McCusker
Production engineer: Dave Arnold
(Original air date: 11-12-88)

Extra! Extra! Read all about it! Former basketball star Lightning Livingston has moved to Odyssey after retiring from the game. Frank Malone, a reporter from the *Odyssey Times,* interviews Lightning at the site of his new sports store. Frank tries to find out why the star retired from the game so young. Lightning refuses to answer questions about his retirement. He says he'd like to conduct some basketball workshops with the youth of Odyssey—much to the great satisfaction of Jimmy Barclay, Lightning's greatest fan.

Malone isn't satisfied with that, however. He digs further, talking to Livingston's only friend in town, John Avery Whittaker. But Whit has no comment for Malone about Lightning's retirement, either—even when Malone suggests that the star quit the game because of a drug problem. Unfortunately, Jimmy is also present and is upset to hear this. Jimmy says the assertion is a lie, but Malone vows to reveal the truth.

behind the scenes:

"At the time of recording, no one had been cast for the lead role of Lightning. But we went ahead and recorded all the other parts—while we continued our search. Finally, we found the perfect Lightning right under our noses. Focus on the Family staff member Bill D'Anjou was cast, and all of his lines were recorded separately. I had to edit the tracks together to make it sound like the characters were all in the studio at the same time. Can you tell the difference?"

—Dave Arnold

STUDY QUESTIONS:

1. Frank Malone said "the people have a right to know." Why did he say this? Was he correct?
2. Why did Whit believe that the stories about Lightning's former drug abuse shouldn't have been printed in the paper?
3. Was it wrong for Jimmy to make Lightning his hero? Why or why not? Do you have a hero?

Episode #49 "Thank You, God"

Theme: Thanksgiving; salvation; making the best of a bad situation.
Scripture references: Romans 8:28; Ephesians 5:20
Written and directed by Phil Lollar
Production engineer: Bob Luttrell
(Original air date: 11-19-88)

It's Thanksgiving, and Whit has invited Connie and her mom, June, along with Tom Riley and his wife, Agnes, to Whit's End for dinner. With the Rileys is a boy named Rodney. He's without family today because his father is traveling, and his mother abandoned him when he was a small child. Before everyone sits down to eat, Whit asks them to participate in a tradition his wife started years earlier.

On each plate is a kernel of corn. Whit passes around a basket, and each person is to place their kernel in the basket and tell one thing for which they're thankful. Many of the answers are predictable—Connie and June are thankful for each other, as are Agnes and Tom, and Tom is also thankful for the time of year. But Rodney says his lack of family leaves him without anything to be thankful for. Whit disagrees. He says that as a Christian, Rodney can give thanks in all situations—even difficult ones.

To illustrate, Whit recounts, via flashback, the story of his stepmother, Fiona Donneral. She was a devout Christian woman who did her best to raise Whit after his real mother died. They lived in rural North Carolina where Whit's father was a professor at Duke University. Whit and Fiona did many things together, including ride horses.

As they rode one afternoon, Fiona's horse galloped under a tree, and she was knocked out by a low-hanging branch. When she awoke later, she had lost her sight. Young Whit was devastated. First, he'd had to deal with his natural mother's death, and now, his stepmother's blindness. But Fiona's Christian faith gave her courage and the ability to cope. She pulled both of them through the difficult times. Her faith was so great that it helped lead young Whit to Jesus—which is what his kernel represents.

Fiona's story inspires even Rodney, who decides he really does have much to be thankful for after all.

the *Adventures in* ODYSSEY archives:

"Thank You, God" was one of the first times we delved into Whit's past. This show also marked our first anniversary. We couldn't believe it—one year and still on the air! In addition, this is the first time we hear Connie's mom's name, June. And for some reason, Chuck Bolte as Professor Harold Whittaker actually says, "There are no need for lights." It's not in the script, Chuck just said it.

STUDY QUESTIONS:

1. What Thanksgiving traditions does your family practice?
2. How can Christians be thankful in all situations?
3. What does Romans 8:28 mean when it says that God works all things out for the good of those who love Him?

Episode #50 "Karen"

Theme: Dealing with death.
Scripture reference: Psalm 23
Recommended maturity level: 10 and up
Written and directed by Paul McCusker
Production engineer: Dave Arnold
(Original air date: 11-26-88)

PARENTAL WARNING: This story is about the sickness and death of a young girl. While told sensitively, it contains subject matter that may be too intense for younger children.

A group of kids at Whit's End disclose the topic of the hour: Young, vivacious, outgoing Karen Crosby has cancer. It's in her leg bone, and it's spreading. Whit and Donna Barclay, Karen's best friend, are on their way to see her in the hospital. Donna is nervous before entering, but a quick prayer and encouragement from Whit see her through the visit.

Karen is surprisingly chipper. She's cheered when Donna tells her that everyone misses her, especially Fergeson, her cat, which Donna is watching. After a brief visit, a nurse enters and announces that visiting hours have ended. Whit and Donna start to go, but Karen calls Donna back. Karen tells Donna to make sure the school saves her a place in the Fall Festival program. Donna agrees. At school three days later, she persuades the organizers of the program to keep Karen's spot open.

That afternoon Donna goes to the hospital to deliver the news. She is met by Karen's mom, Mary. Mary sits Donna down and tells Donna that Karen had an operation earlier that morning. The cancer was worse than anyone thought, and the doctors had to amputate Karen's leg to stop the cancer from spreading.

A few days later, Donna visits Karen, who seems to be in better spirits than ever. Karen tells Donna about an incredible dream she had during the operation: She saw Jesus, and He was healing people. There were several people whom He didn't heal, and when they asked Him to heal them, Jesus said, "I have something better for you." Then He turned to Karen and said, "I have something better for *you*, too." Karen says there's a good chance she'll be released soon, to appear in the Fall Festival. She has something special planned.

The following week at the Festival, Karen doesn't disappoint. She hobbles on stage on crutches and recites the words of a special hymn.

A few days later, Donna bursts into Whit's End in a panic—Fergeson the cat has run away! Fortunately, Karen, very weakened, takes it all in stride. She's sure Fergeson will return—just as Karen's sure she will die soon. Donna can't bear to hear that, but Karen comforts her that one day, they'll both be together again in heaven.

A week later, Donna sits by herself in the Bible Room, thinking about Karen, who has just passed away. Whit enters, and they discuss Karen's funeral. Whit offers comfort from Scripture. This helps lift Donna's spirits, but she's still afraid she'll eventually forget her friend. Just then, Connie enters, bearing a special package: Fergeson the cat has returned. Cheered by the presence of the cat and the hope of Jesus, Donna now knows she will never forget Karen.

the *Adventures in* ODYSSEY archives:

"Karen" was based on a true incident that happened to a friend of Sage Bolte's, who plays Karen. This episode was also yet another stepping-stone to bring Connie to Jesus.

STUDY QUESTIONS:

1. How could Karen be so peaceful about her illness?
2. In Karen's dream, what did Jesus mean when He said He had something better for her?
3. Why *shouldn't* Christians fear death and the grave?

YOU KNOW YOU'RE ADDICTED TO ADVENTURES IN ODYSSEY WHEN . . .

- You measure time and miles by *Adventures in Odyssey* episodes
- You name your dog "Normal"
- You're late for church because you just have to know what happens to Digger Digwillow
- You know the difference between Greenblatt's Department Store and Greenway's Department Store
- You go to your local soda fountain and order a "wod-fam-choc-sod"
- You know why the dog walked on water
- Your conscience talks to you in the voice of Whit
- You're intellectually stimulated by Harlow Doyle
- You plan a vacation in Pokenberry Falls
- You know who the Goat-Man is
- You know why Whit doesn't own a television
- You read the Bible and hear Bernard's voice telling the story
- You know the words to "Seasonal Felicitations"
- You name your first child Bruno Chainbreaker
- You know the color of Eugene's eyes
- You wonder why every kid in Odyssey has grown up, but Connie has been 16 forever
- You know the postal code for Vancouver, B.C., Canada
- You send valentines to Rodney Rathbone

Episodes #51 & 52

"Connie," Parts One & Two

Theme: Salvation.
Scripture references: John 3:16; Romans 5:8
Written and directed by Paul McCusker
Production engineers: Bob Luttrell and Dave Arnold
(Original air dates: 12-03-88 & 12-10-88)

Wintertime has come again to Odyssey—and so has Connie's trip to California. Everything is settled. All that's left now is getting time off from work. Whit grudgingly gives it, adding that he'll have to look for part-time help while Connie is away.

Enter Eugene Meltsner, student and recognized genius at Campbell County Community College. Whit hires him on the spot, and Eugene immediately goes about trying to change everything in sight.

Soon it's the day of Connie's big departure. Whit and June Kendall see Connie off on her trip. Whit gives her an early Christmas present to open on the bus. He and June hug Connie good-bye, and she leaves on her two-day bus ride to California.

The next morning, just outside Los Angeles, Connie awakens to find an elderly woman, Mrs. Nelson, sitting next to her. They talk, and Connie discovers Mrs. Nelson is a Christian. Connie muses that Whit probably arranged this, but Mrs. Nelson says it wasn't Whit—it was God. She tells Connie that God loves her, and He has put people in her life who have shown her that love. It's up to *her* to believe. Connie ponders this.

Finally, Connie is in sunny California, lying on the beach with her friend Marcie. Connie asks Marcie about one of their old friends, Pamela. Marcie says the old crowd hardly sees Pamela now because she's become a Christian. Connie is surprised—Pamela was the wildest one of them all. But Marcie says that's all in the past. Then Marcie tells Connie about a great party that night at a house in Beverly Hills. Connie isn't sure she wants to go, and Marcie thinks she's off her rocker.

Meanwhile, back at Whit's End, Eugene has changed everything from how the electric trains run to the way ice cream sundaes are made. Tom comes in and tells Whit that some of the kids are complaining about all the changes. Whit promises to have a talk with Eugene to get the place back to normal—right after Whit and Tom pray for Connie.

Back in California, Connie is having trouble spending time with her father. Bill Kendall is too busy to even have dinner with his only child. But Connie isn't totally alone. The doorbell rings, and in walks Pamela. She and Connie talk briefly about Pam's new life. Connie states emphatically that she's *not* a Christian. Pamela tells Connie about God's love for her, then invites her to a beach bonfire that night with some Christian friends. Connie says she'll think about it.

Later, Connie sits by herself, trying to watch television. She is agitated and frustrated. Finally, as a last resort, she attends Pamela's beach bonfire. Pamela is happy to see Connie and introduces her to their group's sponsor—Mrs. Nelson, the woman Connie met on the bus! Connie doesn't know how to handle all this, but Mrs. Nelson repeats that God is working on Connie. With that, Connie makes a decision to go back to Odyssey.

Once there, she immediately visits Whit. She tells him about her trip and why she returned so early. Then Connie says the words Whit has prayed for over a year to hear: "I want to ask Jesus Christ to come live in my heart." Whit cries tears of joy, praising God as they kneel to pray. In the center of the Bible Room, Connie Kendall becomes a new creation . . . and her *real* adventure finally begins.

the Adventures in ODYSSEY archives:

"Connie" marked the first time we used flashbacks to previous episodes—a dramatic device that allowed us to quickly recap her journey to Christianity. "Connie" also led to quite a few other stories which chronicle how Connie and the kids at Whit's End learn about the basics of our faith.

Also at this point, we knew we needed to expand our cast. After our comical character, Officer Harley, was transferred out of town, we needed a new comic foil. So we brought in Eugene Meltsner. Eugene was inspired in part by a listener who wrote in suggesting that we create a character like her dad—brilliant, but always losing his keys.

Thanks to Paul McCusker's writing and Will Ryan's performance, Eugene seemed to be fully developed right from the beginning. A hilarious intellectual, Eugene provided—and continues to provide—some of our funniest and most poignant moments. By the way, Paul got Eugene's name from two editors—a Eugene and a Meltsner—who were listed on the masthead of a magazine he was reading.

"Connie" was arguably the sweetest of our "conversion" episodes. Actually, the last scene of the program was so emotional that it brought everyone in the studio—including the actors, writers, and directors—to tears.

STUDY QUESTIONS:

1. Why did Connie want to get back to California so badly?
2. Tom told Whit that what happened to Connie in California was God's business. What did he mean by that?
3. Both Mrs. Nelson and Pamela told Connie that God was putting people in her path to influence her. Can you think of people who have influenced *you* for God? How?

Episode #53 "The Sacred Trust"

Theme: The folly of making promises you can't keep.
Scripture references: Matthew 5:33-37; 1 John 2:29
Written and directed by Phil Lollar
Production engineer: Bob Luttrell
(Original air date: 12-17-88)

Connie rushes into work, late as usual, and finds Lucy sitting at the counter. Lucy tells her that Whit is working with Eugene in the Bible Room. Whit and Eugene walk up, and Whit tells Connie that he wasn't expecting her back at work until after the holiday. Connie immediately tries to jump back into work, though only to learn that Eugene's inventions have virtually eliminated her jobs. Whit suggests that she vacuum the floor. Connie happily rushes to the task.

Whit notices Lucy, and they talk about her plans for the weekend. She's invited her friend Heather to sleep over. They're going to make a "sacred trust" with each other—a promise to always be faithful friends and never reveal any secret they tell each other. Whit thinks it's nice that the two of them want to deepen their relationship, but he is concerned about the idea of a sacred trust.

Before he can explain his concerns, though, the vacuum cleaner goes wild. Eugene increased the suction power of the machine, and now it's nearly wrecking the place! By the time Whit gets things under control again, Lucy has already left.

That night, Lucy and Heather go ahead with their sacred trust. To seal their pact, they exchange valuables—Lucy gives Heather an angora sweater, and Heather gives Lucy a necklace and locket. Lucy then tells Heather a special secret: Bobby Reynolds kissed her! But Heather has an even bigger secret: A couple of weekends ago, she skipped out of Sunday evening church service and went to a teen dance club!

Lucy is stunned and nearly falls over when Heather reveals that she's going again this coming Sunday night. Lucy tells her she can't—Heather's underage, and it's wrong! Heather says she just wants to have fun and suggests that Lucy come along. Lucy says absolutely not and begs Heather not to go, either. Heather tells her not to worry about it, then reminds her of the sacred trust they just made—no revealed secrets.

Lucy wrestles with her conscience—should she tell? The next morning, Lucy talks with her mother and decides that she should tell about Heather's secret. Lucy loses Heather's friendship as a result, but Lucy realizes that she's done the right thing.

STUDY QUESTIONS:

1. Did Lucy make the right decision? What would you have done? Why?
2. Why were Heather's actions wrong?
3. Do you agree or disagree with what Whit told Lucy about revealing secrets? Why? Have you ever kept a secret that you shouldn't have kept?

Episode #54 "Peace on Earth"

Theme: The peace of God; the reason for the season.
Scripture references: Luke 2:1-21; John 14:27; Philippians 4:7
Written and directed by Paul McCusker
Production engineer: Dave Arnold
(Original air date: 12-24-88)

It's the afternoon of Christmas Eve, and Whit's End is bustling with customers. Connie, Eugene, and especially Whit are rushing around frantically. He has packages left to wrap, phone calls to family members to make, church programs to participate in, and the Barclay family to visit. Tom comes in and literally makes Whit slow down. The customers slowly dissipate, and Whit and Tom enjoy the splendor and quiet of freshly fallen snow on Odyssey.

After the church services that evening, Whit and Eugene visit with the Barclay family. George boasts of the wonderful Christmas they've prepared for the kids that year, while Jimmy obsesses over his presents. Whit tries to remind them of the reason for the season, just as he was reminded earlier by Tom. George assures Whit that they always take a few moments during the day to read the Christmas story. Then Mary brings in hot chocolate, mugs are lifted, and good wishes are shared by all.

The next morning, George and Mary are awakened by Jimmy and Donna, who want to get downstairs and open some presents. The family rises and goes downstairs—only to find an empty living room! They've been robbed—cleaned out completely! The thieves even took their Christmas dinner.

The family is filled with gloom and doom until George reminds them that God kept them safe through the ordeal. They still have each other. The family decides to make the best of this bad situation, and George pulls out his Bible. He starts to read the Christmas story.

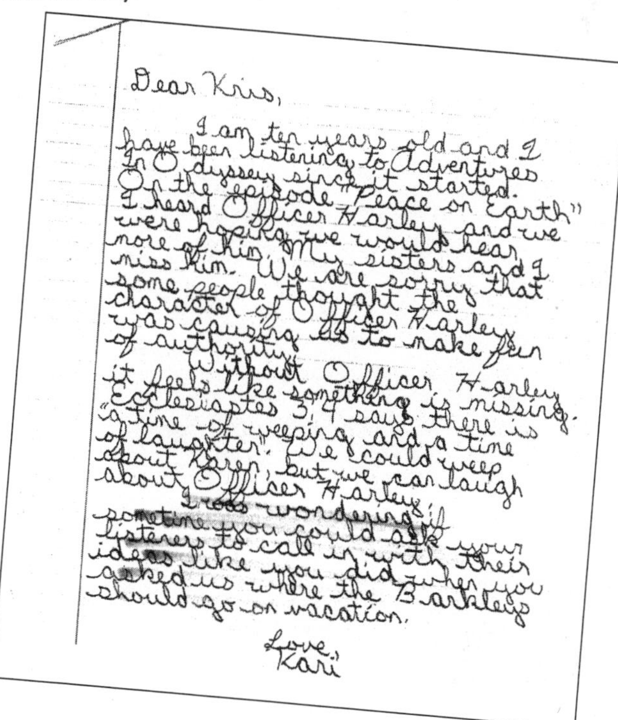
Dear Kris,
I am ten years old and I
have been listening to Adventures
In Odyssey since it started.
On the episode "Peace on Earth"
I heard Officer Harley and we
were hoping we would hear
more of him. My sisters and I
miss him. We are sorry that
some people thought the
character of Officer Harley
was causing us to make fun
of authority.
Without Officer Harley
it feels like something is missing.
Ecclesiastes 3:4 says there is
"a time of weeping and a time
of laughter". We could weep
about Karen, but we can laugh
about Officer Harley.
I was wondering if
sometime you could ask your
listeners to call in with their
ideas like you did when you
asked us where the Barkleys
should go on vacation.
Love,
Kari

Audio Dramas 71

Just then, the doorbell rings. George answers it, and there stand Whit and Eugene along with just about everyone else in town! They all heard how the Barclays had been robbed during the night and have come to share Christmas with them. George quietly thanks Jesus and welcomes them all inside. This holiday season, the Barclays have discovered the true spirit of Christmas.

the Adventures in Odyssey archives:

The original concept for this episode dealt solely with Whit being too busy to enjoy Christmas. Chuck Bolte came up with the idea of the Barclays getting robbed, and Paul McCusker blended the two stories.

STUDY QUESTIONS:

1. Why did Tom want Whit to slow down?
2. Why was Connie so eager to celebrate Christmas?
3. How does your family celebrate Christmas?

Episode #55 "Auld Lang Syne"

Theme: The importance of memories; reflecting on your life.
Scripture reference: Revelation 22:13
Written and directed by Phil Lollar
Production engineers: Bob Luttrell and Dave Arnold
(Original air date: 12-31-88)

Should old acquaintance be forgot . . .

It's New Year's Eve, and there's a party going on at Whit's End. Only, the party's host, Whit, is sitting by himself in a back room. Tom finds him. The two of them look back over the past year, taking us along for the ride with clips from "Gotcha!" "The Tangled Web," "Kid's Radio," "The Day Independence Came," "Return to the Bible Room," and "Connie." Whit and Tom conclude that they've been extremely blessed during the past year—and they're looking forward to what God has in store for the future.

. . . we'll drink a cup of kindness yet, for Auld Lang Syne.

STUDY QUESTIONS:

1. Why are memories important?
2. Is there anything that you would like to change about the past year? If so, what? What would you like to have continue?
3. Think about some special things that have happened to you during the past year. How has God worked in your life?

Draw Your Own Whit

Here's how to draw Mr. Whittaker.

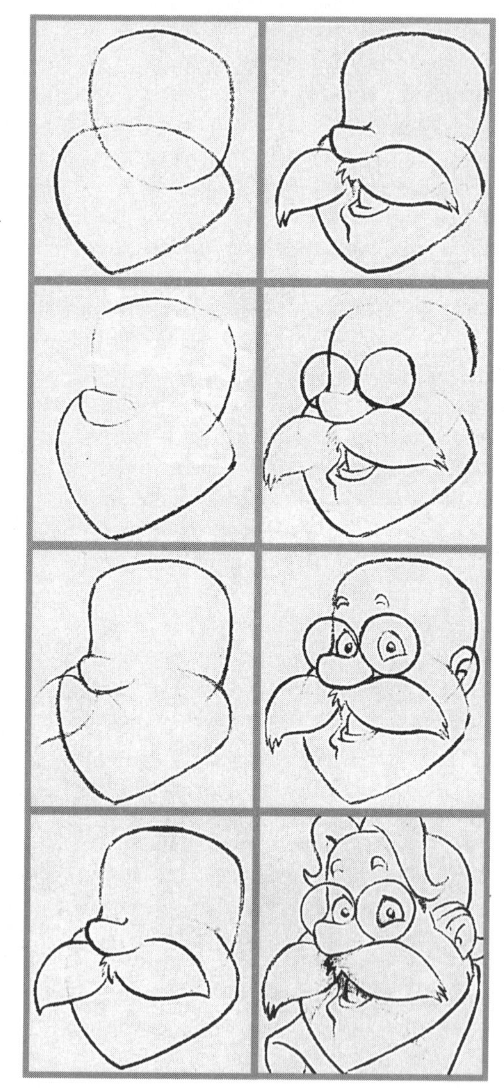

1989

The main story line of 1988 was Connie's salvation. But once Connie became a Christian, we knew we needed to provide episodes that would allow her to mature spiritually. So the team came up with a series of programs designed to teach Connie—and indirectly, the audience—all about the basics of the faith.

We began with a show about faith in 1989—and throughout the year, we included programs with themes on repentance, obedience, Bible study, prayer, church attendance, being Christlike, stewardship, loving one another, choosing friends wisely, dealing with authority, and finally, evangelism. We also introduced the Imagination Station and Dr. Regis Blackgaard during this year.

One other important—but difficult—event occurred in 1989. Steve Harris, one of our core team people, decided to leave *Adventures in Odyssey* to pursue other avenues. Steve's creativity and leadership were vital to the creation of *Adventures in Odyssey*, and we were sad to see him go.

Episode #56 "By Faith, Noah"

Theme: Faith; biblical history: Noah.
Scripture references: Genesis 6-9; Hebrews 11:7; 1 Peter 1:8-9
Written and directed by Paul McCusker
Production engineer: Bob Luttrell
(Original air date: 1-07-89)

In an effort to illustrate the meaning of faith, Whit tells Jack and Lucy a comical version of Noah's Ark.

Noah reveals to his wife that God is going to destroy the earth by flood. According to Noah, the Lord also told him to build a gigantic boat called an "ark." In the ark, he, his family, and two of every kind of animal on earth will be saved. Noah works on the ark for the next 120 years, proceeding by faith. He puts up with obstacles such as jeering neighbors, city health inspectors, the president of the Arkbuilders Union, an attorney representing the Pre-Antediluvian Civil Liberties Association, and a member of the Society for the Protection of Cruel Animals, among others.

Finally the ark is built, and the flood comes. Noah, his family, and the animals are safe, but Noah still must trust that the Lord will take care of them and eventually return them to dry land. He sends out the raven and the doves, and eventually his faith is rewarded. God commissions Noah and his family to go out of the ark and be fruitful and multiply, then sets a rainbow in the sky as a sign that He will never again destroy the earth by flood.

Whit's point about faith is made.

STUDY QUESTIONS:

1. Why is Noah such a good example of someone who had great faith?
2. In 2 Peter 2:5, the Bible says that Noah preached to others while he was building the ark, even though the others made fun of him. Would you share your faith with friends who made fun of you? If so, how would you do that?
3. Rainbows are signs of a promise from God. What are some other promises that God has made to us?

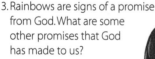

Episode #57 "The Prodigal, Jimmy"

Theme: Repentance; forgiveness; the parable of the prodigal son.
Scripture references: Luke 15:11-32; 1 John 1:9
Written and directed by Phil Lollar
Production engineer: Dave Arnold
(Original air date: 1-14-89)

Jimmy Barclay is rolling in dough—almost $50 worth, to be exact. He decides to spend the money and his entire Saturday playing video games at the arcade. But his father, George, nixes that idea, thanks to the C-minus Jimmy got on his spelling test. George rightly surmises that the poor grade is due to Jimmy's lack of study and his tendency to goof off lately. George orders Jimmy to stay home, finish his chores, and study.

But Jimmy's money is burning a hole in his pocket and his piggy bank. He decides that he's old enough to come and go as he pleases. So when George goes to work, Jimmy sneaks out and heads off to Pizza City. His plan is to have some fun in the morning, then return home before his dad does that afternoon at 3:30.

At Pizza City, Jimmy meets up with two unsavory men named Mook and Howie, who con Jimmy into spending all his money on them. They teach him how to play video games and tell him jokes, living it up at Jimmy's expense. But when his funds run out, Mook and Howie quickly leave. Jimmy is embarrassed and hurt at being taken for a sucker—until he remembers to ask about the time. It's 3:30.

Jimmy is so scared, he doesn't go home. He goes to Whit's End and plays with the trains. Whit, who has already talked with George, wheedles the story out of Jimmy, who doesn't know what to do.

For guidance, Whit tells him the story of another fellow who disobeyed his father, spent all his money on no-good friends, and ended up feeding pigs for a living. Jimmy recognizes the story as the parable of the prodigal son. With Whit's help, Jimmy realizes that just like the son in the story, he, too, must repent and return home.

Whit takes Jimmy home, and he immediately confesses his sins to George. Jimmy waits for his punishment. But before George punishes his son, he welcomes Jimmy with a hug, showing him the real meaning of the prodigal story: forgiveness.

the *Adventures in* ODYSSEY archives:

The last scene, between George and Jimmy, was performed "free-form." Chuck Bolte and David Griffin merely glanced at the script to get an idea of where things needed to land emotionally, then ad-libbed the scene. It worked nicely—they both sounded more natural, which gave the episode a warm, touching ending.

STUDY QUESTIONS:

1. Jimmy said he was old enough to make his own decisions. Was he? When *is* someone old enough to make his or her own decisions? Explain.
2. Why was Jimmy so afraid to go home? Was his fear justified?
3. What does it mean to repent?

Episode #58 "A Matter of Obedience"

Theme: Obedience.
Scripture references: John 14:15; 1 John 5:3
Written and directed by Paul McCusker
Production engineer: Dave Arnold
(Original air date: 1-21-89)

Tom Riley is filling in for a sick Sunday school teacher. He's trying to teach on obedience, but the class can only tell him the original Greek meanings of the word. So Tom decides to illustrate the principle through storytelling.

Tom begins by describing his boyhood. He grew up during the Great Depression, and his father, Tom Sr., was a country doctor. In Tom's story, his father is just about to deliver some much-needed medicine to Mrs. Sawyer when he gets a phone call from Frank Roth. Frank's wife has just gone into labor. Tom Sr. needs to deliver the child, so he sends Tom Jr. and his sister, Becky, to deliver the medicine.

Mrs. Sawyer lives on the other side of Gloomy Woods, and Tom Sr. gives his children several strict instructions to follow: Pack a knapsack of food to take along with you. Take Single Path all the way through the forest, even though there are other paths that might seem shorter. If you meet a stranger, be polite but keep moving. No playing around or having imaginary adventures. Finally, when you get to the end of the woods, stay on Single Path until you come to a house with a blue door. That's your destination.

Tom Sr. makes the kids repeat the instructions, then leaves. Tom Jr. and Becky begin their journey. Almost immediately, they forget their father's instructions. Young Tom pretends he's an acrobat and loses the knapsack of food in a stream. Tom and Becky meet a man who wants them to join him. Tom almost goes, but Becky stops him. On the other side of the woods, they knock on a red door instead of a blue one and end up trapped in the house's basement by its elderly occupant. Thanks to quick thinking and skillful maneuvering, Tom and Becky finally free themselves and are able to carry out their father's instructions.

Tom concludes by saying he learned a valuable lesson about obedience that day . . . and he hopes the Sunday school class has, too.

the *Adventures in* ODYSSEY archives:

"A Matter of Obedience" was unique in several ways. First, the young actors who played brother and sister Tom and Becky Riley are also brother and sister in real life. This was also one of the few early programs without Whit in it. And we got a glimpse of Tom's early years, along with what Odyssey was like during the Great Depression of the 1930s.

STUDY QUESTIONS:

1. Why do you think Tom and Becky so quickly disregarded their father's instructions?
2. Why does God ask us to be obedient?
3. Can you explain and define "obedience"? What does it mean to you?

TRIVIA QUIZ

The People of Odyssey

1. Why doesn't Whit watch television?
2. Why is Whit's granddaughter, Jenny, so special?
3. What musical instrument does Jenny play? How about Eugene?
4. What did Tom Riley's father do for a living?
5. What is Coach Fred Zachary's catch phrase?
6. What was Eugene's father's name?
7. How many episodes has Robert Skeed appeared in?
8. What is Bernard's wife's name?
9. Why did Connie's mom choose to move to Odyssey?
10. Name Connie's only other relative in Odyssey.

Answers:

1. He became "addicted" to it after his wife, Jenny, died. He saw that it was taking over his life, so he got rid of his televisions and hasn't watched TV since. 2. She's a gifted student, with a genius-level IQ. 3. Jenny plays the violin. Eugene plays the ukulele. 4. He was a town doctor and, like Tom, an apple farmer. 5. "Whatchacall." 6. Leonard. 7. None. However, he is referred to in five episodes. 8. Maude. 9. She grew up there. 10. Her great uncle Joe Finneman, owner and operator of Finneman's Market.

Episode #59 "A Worker Approved"

Theme: The importance of Bible study.
Scripture reference: 2 Timothy 2:15
Written and directed by Phil Lollar
Production engineer: Bob Luttrell
(Original air date: 1-28-89)

For a school report, Robyn Jacobs shares the testimony of how and why she became a Christian. When she's finished, her teacher, Mr. Southworth, asks if there are any questions. Oscar raises his hand. He asks several probing questions, but because he's usually one of the more slow students, everyone thinks he's joking.

After class, Oscar corners Robyn and asks her: Why did Jesus have to die? Robyn scolds Oscar for making fun of her, but Oscar is earnest—he really wants to know. The only problem is, Robyn doesn't have an answer. She hems and haws and finally says that some things must simply be taken on faith.

This doesn't satisfy Oscar. He goes to Whit's End to ask Whit, who has been coaching Connie in Bible verse memorization. Whit tells Connie to put her newfound knowledge to use, and Connie recites Scripture to answer Oscar's question. Oscar and Connie continue to talk in the library, and Robyn is impressed. She wants to know how Connie can quote Scripture so well. Whit says Connie has been studying every day since she became a Christian. Then Whit asks Robyn how much she studies. Robyn sheepishly admits she doesn't study at all. Whit mildly reproves her—Connie spends a half hour every morning searching the Bible, and she studies a chapter from both the Old and New Testaments every night.

Robyn resolves to follow suit and embarks on a regimen of study. First, she gets up early like Connie, but Robyn falls asleep at her desk and is almost late for school. Then she tries reading in bed, but again Robyn nods off before she gets through one page. After several more tries, she reports back to Whit that she isn't cut out to study the Bible. Whit tells Robyn that Bible reading is important. He gives her several suggestions on how to commit Scripture to memory. Whit is especially emphatic that Robyn join a Bible study group. Robyn agrees to follow his suggestions, then Whit tells her of a study group she could join. He leads Robyn back to the library, where Connie and Oscar are intensely studying the Word. Robyn joins them, taking another step toward enriching her faith.

Adventures in the ODYSSEY archives:

"A Worker Approved" marked the first appearance of two of our best kid characters: Robyn Jacobs and Oscar—whom we never got around to giving a last name.

STUDY QUESTIONS:

1. Why did Robyn think she didn't have to study the Bible?
2. Why is Bible study important?
3. Do you know all the scriptures Connie quoted? If someone asked you the question Oscar asked Robyn, would you be able to answer it? What would you say?

Episode #60 "And When You Pray..."

Theme: Prayer.
Scripture reference: Mark 11:24
Written by Paul McCusker
Directed by Phil Lollar
Production engineer: Bob Luttrell
(Original air date: 2-04-89)

It's Saturday morning at the Barclay household. Jimmy is sitting by himself in the garage. Donna enters and tells Jimmy to shovel the snow off the sidewalk to prepare for their grandfather's visit that evening. Donna wants to know why Jimmy's out there. Jimmy says he's waiting for a bicycle. He prayed hard for one the previous evening. His friend Brad prayed for a bike and *got* one, so Jimmy believes it'll happen to him, too.

Donna is skeptical. She tells Jimmy prayer doesn't work that way. But Jimmy sticks to his guns. And that night, Grandfather Barclay informs Jimmy that while cleaning out the basement, he found George's old bicycle and thought Jimmy would like to have it.

Donna is stunned—Jimmy's prayer really worked! So, in bed that night, she decides to give it a try herself. As a test, she prays that God will make it rain on Monday so she won't have to go out for gym class, which she hates. To prove she really believes in the power of prayer, she dresses for school on Monday in a raincoat and galoshes. Everyone thinks Donna's crazy, including her mother and especially her gym teacher, Mrs. Butchfield. Mrs. Butchfield orders Donna out of the rain gear and into her gym outfit. Donna is bitterly disappointed and believes that God doesn't really answer prayer.

Later that day, she and Jimmy go to Whit's End. Whit has heard about Donna's prayer fiasco and is working on an invention to better explain the nature of prayer. It's a vending machine for prayers. You decide on a prayer, push a button, and out comes the answer. Jimmy thinks it's great, but Donna is understandably skeptical.

Then Whit tells them it's a joke but says many people do think that God will give us what we want if we just push the right prayer buttons. Whit sets Jimmy and Donna straight about the *real* meaning of prayer. Donna says she understands—right as a peal of thunder sounds and a rainstorm begins. Doesn't God have a wonderful sense of humor?

Adventures in the ODYSSEY archives:

The original wrap-arounds for "And When You Pray . . ." featured a skit between Chris Lansdowne, our announcer, and an Odyssey mailman named Roger. Roger delivered several letters from listeners to Chris, which the two of them read on the air.

STUDY QUESTIONS:

1. Did God really answer Jimmy's prayer, or was it a coincidence that he received a bike? Explain.
2. What was wrong with the way Donna prayed? What about Connie? What do your motives have to do with prayer?
3. Read Mark 11:24. What do you think Jesus meant?

Episode #61

"The Boy Who Didn't Go to Church"

Theme: The importance of regular church attendance.
Scripture reference: 1 Corinthians 12:12-31
Written and directed by Phil Lollar
Production engineer: Dave Arnold
(Original air date: 2-11-89)

In the Little Theatre at Whit's End, Whit, Connie, and the kids are about to run through a dress rehearsal of a play Whit has written. Jack, one of the kids, has stopped by to watch the rehearsal and is talking to Whit. Whit tells Jack that the play will be performed at church the following evening. Jack is puzzled. He wonders when the church started doing plays on Sunday nights. When Whit says the pastor announced it quite a while ago, Jack sheepishly admits that it's been a few weeks since he's attended church.

Just then, Connie walks up and says they can't run the rehearsal because their main character is too nervous. Everyone is disappointed until Whit volunteers Jack to fill in the role. Jack enthusiastically agrees. Whit hands him a script, and the play begins.

It's a tale about a group called the Brotherhood of Dutiful Youth, or the BODY. The cast includes Mr. Headly, Miss Lippman, R. U. Listnin, Hans Armstrong, and John LaFete, which is Jack's part. The BODY is dedicated to helping people, and each member has a specific job. But John LaFete isn't happy with his task. He wants to do something else. When the others refuse to give him another job, he leaves the BODY to form his own group, the LaFetes.

The LaFetes go searching for people to help, but because all of their experience, talent, and ability is only in one area, they fail miserably. Finally John learns his lesson, breaks up the LaFetes, and rushes back to the BODY—only to discover that it has disbanded! When John left, no one was there to do his job. Without all of its members, the BODY couldn't function effectively, so it died.

The play ends on this down note, but the lesson isn't lost on Jack. He realizes that the church is a body, too. If its members fail to attend church, it can't function effectively—it might even die. Jack assures Whit that from now on, he (Jack) will be a vital part of the church body.

STUDY QUESTIONS:

1. Were John LaFete's feelings about doing the same old thing valid? Explain.
2. Why is it important for *every* church member to be active in church ministries?
3. Do you attend church regularly? Are you involved in any activities? What are some of your gifts of service?

Episode #62

"Let This Mind Be in You"

Theme: Being Christlike.
Scripture references: 1 Corinthians 11:1; Philippians 2:5
Written by Paul McCusker
Directed by Phil Lollar
Production engineer: Dave Arnold
(Original air date: 2-18-89)

Whit is going out of town for a couple of days. He puts Connie and Eugene in charge of Whit's End. Connie is nervous about it—she doesn't want to do anything wrong. But Whit tells both her and Eugene that he's left a note that explains everything they need to know. Whit has even included the phone number where he can be reached if they have any questions. Connie still isn't sure about the arrangement, but Whit says all they have to do is run the place the way *he* would run it. Eugene tells Whit not to worry because everything will be under control. With that assurance, Whit leaves.

The next day, Connie shows up for work dressed like Whit. She figures that if she's supposed to *be* like Whit, she might as well *look* like him. Meanwhile, Eugene tries to decide what to do with a delivery of paint. He wonders where Whit is planning to use it. Eugene recalls Whit saying something about repainting the Bible Room and decides to complete the task himself to surprise Whit.

Dear Chris,

My name is Jeremy. I am 9 years old and I really enjoy listening to Odyssey. I have listened to your program for about two years now and I even have some of the Adventures in Odyssey tapes. Odyssey is my favorite radio program. I listen almost every night on 96.3 FM. My favorite program is the one where Mr. Whittaker goes on a business trip and leaves Connie and Eugene to look after Whitts End.

Audio Dramas 77

Downstairs, Connie takes on Whit's role with a vengeance. First, she interprets for Jack and Lucy the biblical story of Jacob wrestling with the angel. Then Connie attempts to fix the malfunctioning Bible Room mirror. Finally, she helps Jimmy solve an ethical dilemma, advising him not to tell his father about being sent to the principal over a shoving match. Connie's attempts to be like Whit fail dismally: Her biblical explanation confuses Jack and Lucy; she breaks the Bible Room mirror; and Jimmy's father, George, mildly reproves Connie for her poor advice to Jimmy.

Connie is upset. She removes her "Whit sweater" and tells Eugene about her failures. Eugene tells her that being *like* Whit doesn't mean Connie has to *be* Whit. Connie can't be anyone else. She has to be herself.

Unfortunately, Eugene hasn't handled things perfectly, either. When Whit returns and sees the Bible Room, he informs Eugene that the paint was for a storage shed outside. Whit asks Eugene if he and Connie read the note. Whit's instructions about the paint and the Bible Room mirror were clearly spelled out there. If they had questions, all they had to do was call!

Connie and Eugene sheepishly admit their mistakes, having learned about both imitation and obedience.

STUDY QUESTIONS:

1. In this episode, who did Whit represent? What did his letter signify? If Connie and Eugene had called Whit, what would their call have represented?
2. Why did Connie try to be Whit? Why didn't she succeed?
3. What does it mean to be an "imitator of Christ"? How can you best do that?

Episode #63 "A Good and Faithful Servant"

Theme: Stewardship.
Scripture reference: Psalm 24:1
Written and directed by Phil Lollar
Production engineer: Bob Luttrell
(Original air date: 2-25-89)

Budget. The word conjures up feelings of grief and doom to teenagers and families everywhere. And when Jimmy, Donna, and Mary Barclay keep cornering George for money, he decides a budget is just the ticket. Donna is especially unhappy about having a budget. She believes that it will spell the end of her fun. She tells Whit this before she heads home to learn about her father's plan. Whit tells Donna to keep an open mind—it might not be as bad as she thinks.

That night, George and Mary present the budget to the kids. Though it is strict, the plan allows Donna the flexibility to spend and save. It teaches her and Jimmy responsibility in the process. Despite that, Donna still isn't very thrilled about the idea.

After three weeks of being on the plan, George and Mary decide to test the budget and let Jimmy and Donna shop by themselves at the mall. After shopping, the family will meet up at Whit's End.

Later, while waiting for the kids, George and Mary tell Whit about the situation and wonder how their daughter and son—as well as their financial experiment—fared. They don't have long to wait. Jimmy enters and says that he only purchased a small tank for his soldier collection. But the big test is Donna. A few moments later, she enters. To the Barclays' surprise, Donna has purchased nothing!

Donna explains that while shopping, she was reminded of something Whit said: Christians are God's stewards—all things are God's gifts to us, and they should be used wisely. So instead of spending money on herself, Donna went to church and put part of her money into the missionary fund. Her parents and Whit are pleased, Jimmy is impressed, and Donna has learned an important lesson about stewardship.

the *Adventures in* ODYSSEY archives:

The financial plan George and Mary implemented for their kids was based on a plan devised by Ron Blue in his book *Money Matters for Parents and Their Kids*.

STUDY QUESTIONS:

1. Both George and Whit said, "Money is a great motivator." What did they mean by this?
2. Are you and your family on a budget? What are its advantages? Disadvantages?
3. How can you be a faithful steward of God's gifts?

Episode #64 "The Greatest of These"

Theme: Unconditional love.
Scripture references: John 15:12; 1 Corinthians 13
Written and directed by Phil Lollar
Production engineer: Dave Arnold
(Original air date: 3-04-89)

Robyn Jacobs is madder than a wet hen. The focus of her anger? Oscar. She tells Whit that not only did Oscar lose a spelling bee for her team at school (thus creating extra homework for them that night), but Robyn has also been paired with Oscar for the upcoming science fair! Robyn believes that their project will be an absolute disaster.

Whit tells Robyn to calm down. When Oscar joins them a few moments later, Robyn is surprised to learn that Oscar has a good idea for the fair. He wants to build a working model volcano. They decide to begin gathering research, but Whit tells Robyn to go ahead without Oscar—Whit first wants Oscar to help with something.

Robyn leaves, and Whit asks Oscar to read the big menu board above the counter. Oscar tries his best, but he can't even get past the second word. This confirms Whit's suspicion that Oscar is dyslexic. Unfortunately, Whit doesn't get a chance to tell Robyn, and she and Oscar proceed with their science project together.

At the end of the week, they're ready to test their model volcano for Whit and Connie. It works nicely—the lava is pushed through the volcano orifices via a pump controlled by a dimmer switch, which Oscar operates. But when Robyn tells Oscar to turn the dimmer off, everything turns chaotic. The pump goes crazy, and the volcano erupts, slathering everyone in glop! Oscar turned the switch all the way *on* rather than off. Before Whit can stop Robyn, she chews Oscar out, almost completely sinking his fragile self-esteem.

Later, when Robyn is cleaning up the room, Whit talks to her about her outburst and reveals Oscar's dyslexia problem. Robyn says she feels terrible for Oscar. But Whit tells Robyn that her words aren't good enough. The Bible teaches us to *practice* agape love—unconditional love—even if people don't deserve it. Whit explains that's the kind of love Jesus had for us. Robyn sees her mistake. When Oscar pops in to help with the cleanup, Robyn apologizes and suggests that they build a newer, better volcano. Oscar agrees . . . and Whit smiles at agape in action.

behind the scenes:

"One of the challenges in producing a show like 'The Greatest of These' is finding just the right sound effects. I had to improvise with the model volcano. The pump motor sound was from a generator, which I speeded up when Oscar turned up the pump speed. As for the glops of lava, they were hair gel! I brought a bottle in from home and blew into the container with a straw to get the blurping sounds. The faster the generator went, the harder I puffed. Then I made a bunch of mud in a wastepaper basket. When the volcano blew, I slopped the mud against the floor in big splats."

—Dave Arnold

STUDY QUESTIONS:

1. Did Robyn have a right to be angry with Oscar? Explain.
2. Do you know anyone with dyslexia? If so, how would you handle working with him or her on a project?
3. How can you practice agape love today?

Episode #65 "Bad Company"

Theme: Choosing friends wisely.
Scripture references: Psalm 1:1-4; 2 Corinthians 6:14
Written and directed by Paul McCusker
Production engineer: Bob Luttrell
(Original air date: 3-11-89)

Donna Barclay is on her way out the door to meet her friend Rachael at the mall when Donna is stopped by her mother. Mary isn't sure Donna should hang around Rachael, whose reputation is less than sterling. Donna defends her friend, and Mary finally relents and lets Donna go. Mary expresses her reservations to George, but he says they have to trust that they've raised their daughter to choose her friends wisely.

Meanwhile, Connie stops by to visit Whit at home. He's sick with a cold. Connie needs to borrow a Bible from Whit because she's on her way to a Bible study with friends from school. Whit warns Connie about attending just *any* study taught by just *anybody*. Connie promises to be careful.

At the mall, Donna and Rachael talk about various things, including Donna's beliefs. Rachael cuts the conversation short when she sees some earrings. Donna goes to look at blouses. Later, the mall security guard confronts the girls and demands to see the contents of their purses. Donna immediately hands hers over, but Rachael spitefully turns her purse upside down and spills the earrings. Rachael runs, but Donna is too shocked to move and gets caught.

Connie fares no better at the Bible study. There, a Mr. Grayson clouds her mind with a lot of nonbiblical baloney, saying that Jesus never claimed to be the Son of God. Connie leaves the study feeling confused and goes back to Whit. He sets her straight and offers to teach a Bible study for Connie and her friends that focuses on the truth. Whit tells her to be more careful about whom she associates with.

Donna heeds this advice as well. She catches up with Rachael and scolds her for stealing the earrings and running away. Rachael brushes off the lecture. When Donna tells her to take back the earrings, Rachael brushes *Donna* off as well. Donna returns home and, along with Connie, learns an important lesson about the hazards of associating with bad company.

the Adventures in ODYSSEY archives:

The scenes between Connie and Whit were adjusted in the studio to accommodate Hal Smith's cold. Hal's voice was so affected, there was no way to hide or disguise his flu bug. So we included it in the program.

behind the scenes:

"'Bad Company' was the first episode where Bob Luttrell and I worked together on the foley (live sound effects). We used lots of different and weird things to make noise—like coconuts cut in half for horse hooves, cornflakes under a sheet for ice, corn starch boxes for walking in snow, and bubble-packing wrap for fireplace sounds (the crackles and pops).

"We also have a different pair of shoes for each character—Whit has his own pair, Connie has hers, and so on."

—Dave Arnold

STUDY QUESTIONS:

1. How do your friends affect your faith? If you're a Christian, do you think it's appropriate to have non-Christian friends? Explain.
2. Read Psalm 1:1-4 and 2 Corinthians 6:14. What kinds of friends do you hang around with?
3. How can you be sure that you and your friends believe the same things about God?

Episodes #66 & 67

"The Imagination Station," Parts One & Two

Theme: The crucifixion and resurrection of Jesus Christ.
Scripture references: Mark 11:1-10; 14:12-16:13
Written and directed by Phil Lollar and Paul McCusker
Production engineers: Bob Luttrell and Dave Arnold
(Original air dates: 3-18-89 & 3-25-89)

Tom visits Whit to talk to him about a student in Tom's Sunday school class—Digger Digwillow. Digger doesn't show any interest in learning about Scripture and thinks the Bible is boring. So Whit decides to work on an invention that may raise Digger's interest. When Digger visits, Whit introduces him to the Imagination Station. Whit explains that it's an invention which, through the imagination, helps people to experience the Bible and history.

Digger doesn't think it will work on him, but he climbs in, pushes the red button, and soars back to first-century Jerusalem. There, Digger lives through the last week of Jesus' earthly life—from the Triumphal Entry to the Last Supper; to the trial, the crucifixion, and the resurrection. Digger also personally encounters the Savior. In the process, Digger gets nearly trampled by a crowd, arrested by Roman soldiers, thrown into prison, and learns to believe.

the Adventures in Odyssey archives:

"The Imagination Station" marked the premiere of Whit's greatest invention. From the first airings, it quickly became one of our most popular episodes. But we almost didn't cast the central character in the program. It was easy to find a Digger, John Mark, Mary, and even a Peter. We couldn't agree on who should play Jesus, though. How do you cast the Creator of the universe? Recording time drew closer and closer, and we had to make a decision. So we read everyone on the *AIO* staff, and we all agreed that the best person for the job was Dave Arnold.

STUDY QUESTIONS:

1. If Digger's adventure were real, could he have stopped Jesus from being crucified? Could *anyone* have stopped Jesus from being crucified? Why or why not?
2. What would you learn if you could be taken back in time to Jesus' death and resurrection?
3. Why is Jesus' death and resurrection so important?

STATION INFORMATION

To this day, none of us can agree on what the Imagination Station actually looks like. Early descriptions made it out to be an old-time phone booth, the cockpit of a helicopter, and the holodeck on *Star Trek: The Next Generation*'s U.S.S. *Enterprise-D*. We even get another different description of the Imagination Station in "A Prisoner for Christ," *AIO* #80. Nicholas says it looks like "a big hot-water tank lying on its side." And that's part of the Station's beauty—it can be whatever you imagine.

We had several lengthy discussions to carefully define what the Imagination Station is. It is not a time machine. It is a vehicle that helps us visualize history and the Bible through our imaginations.

In addition, we had to decide how we were going to tell the Imagination Station stories. So we settled on what we call "The Ben Hur Approach." That is, we'd focus on an extra-biblical character (in this case, Digger) whose adventure parallels an event in the Bible or world history.

"The Imagination Station" generated a great deal of positive response. One 16-year-old young man wrote to tell us that "The Imagination Station" made Jesus' death and resurrection real to him and clarified things. "Your show," he wrote, "really made it come alive."

Episode #68 "Choices"

Theme: Dealing with authority; standing up for your faith.
Scripture references: Romans 14:23; 2 Timothy 1:7
Written and directed by Phil Lollar
Production engineer: Dave Arnold
(Original air date: 4-01-89)

Lucy receives the best and worst news of her academic career on the same afternoon. First, her teacher, Mr. Winthrop, informs her that she's been chosen to write a report that will be published in the *Educator*, a newspaper that goes to all of the teachers in the district. Lucy is excited—until she learns that the subject of her report is evolution.

Lucy's Christian beliefs are at odds with this prevailing scientific theory. She asks if she can write about something else, but the report is also part of a class assignment, and thus a part of her grade. If she doesn't do the report, she fails the assignment. Lucy is cornered.

That night at home, she relates the dilemma to her father, who leaves the decision up to Lucy. Dad says she's responsible enough to figure this one out for herself. He and her mother will support Lucy, whatever she decides to do. Lucy mulls the situation over and over in her mind. She even has a nightmare about it. Finally, on Sunday, she receives some spiritual guidance from Whit. He says the Bible teaches that if you believe in your heart that something is wrong, you shouldn't do it, because "everything that does not come from faith is sin" (Romans 14:23).

Lucy makes up her mind. Monday at school, she gives Mr. Winthrop her decision: She's not writing the report. Mr. Winthrop is naturally disappointed and asks why. Lucy explains that her Christian beliefs conflict with the theory of evolution. She can't in good conscience write the report, even if that means she'll get a failing grade. Mr. Winthrop is impressed with her convictions and the courage she shows in living by them, so much so that he comes up with a solution: Write about evolution from a Christian perspective. Lucy agrees, and life returns to normal.

behind the scenes:

"The SFX—sound effects—of the film reel in 'Choices' were fun to create. I wanted the reel to have that old projector sound, where the hub rubs when it rotates, making the audio sound warbled. I layered the sound tracks for the film onto a reel-to-reel deck, and I thumbed the reel so it would drag, making everything sound warbled. It took a lot of 'takes' to get it right, but it was fun!"

—Dave Arnold

STUDY QUESTIONS:

1. Why was Lucy so opposed to writing the report?
2. Did Lucy's dad do the right thing in letting Lucy make the decision about writing the report?
3. Has anybody ever asked you to do something you didn't believe was right? How did you handle the situation? Did you pray about it?

Episode #69 "Go Ye Therefore"

Theme: Witnessing; evangelism.
Scripture references: Matthew 28:18-20; Mark 16:15; Luke 24:46-48
Written and directed by Paul McCusker
Production engineer: Dave Arnold
(Original air date: 4-08-89)

Connie arrives at Whit's End, frustrated. She has been attempting to carry out the Great Commission to evangelize—with disastrous results. She says that she got her ideas about witnessing from a book. Then, in a flashback, Connie tells Whit how poorly the ideas worked.

First, she and a friend, Robert, try handing out pamphlets in the park to strangers. Connie gets snubbed so often that when someone actually wants a tract, she ends up snubbing *him*. Next, she and Robert try putting the pamphlets into books at a local bookstore and end up getting booted from the establishment. Then Connie plasters her mother's car with Christian bumper stickers—and Mom reacts by nearly plastering Connie to the wall!

Finally, Connie follows the book's advice about being bold at school. During a study hall, several friends begin talking about a drunken party they had attended the previous Friday. When one of them thinks she saw Connie at the party, another denies it before Connie can say anything. The girl uses the opportunity to criticize Connie for her new beliefs. Connie attempts to turn the conversation into a discussion about the condition of her friends' souls, but the harder she tries to convince them of their lost state, the more they make fun of her. Another disaster.

Connie tells Whit that she simply isn't cut out to spread the Gospel. She doesn't even care to try anymore. Just then, the door opens and Cheryl, another friend of Connie's, enters. Whit excuses himself, and Cheryl and Connie talk. Cheryl says she's noticed a change in Connie over the past few months—especially in Connie's happiness. Cheryl wants that kind of joy. At first, Connie is a bit taken aback, but then she shares the source of her happiness with Cheryl. Cheryl becomes a new creation, and Connie discovers that the best way to spread the word of God is one person at a time.

STUDY QUESTIONS:

1. What is "the Great Commission"?
2. Should Connie and Robert have handed out tracts in the park? Placed them into books at the bookstore? Why or why not?
3. What is the best way to share your faith with others?

Episodes #70 & 71

"The Return of Harley," Parts One & Two

Theme: Controlling your imagination.
Scripture reference: Proverbs 14:7,25
Written and directed by Phil Lollar
Production engineers: Bob Luttrell and Dave Arnold
(Original air dates: 4-29-89 & 5-06-89)

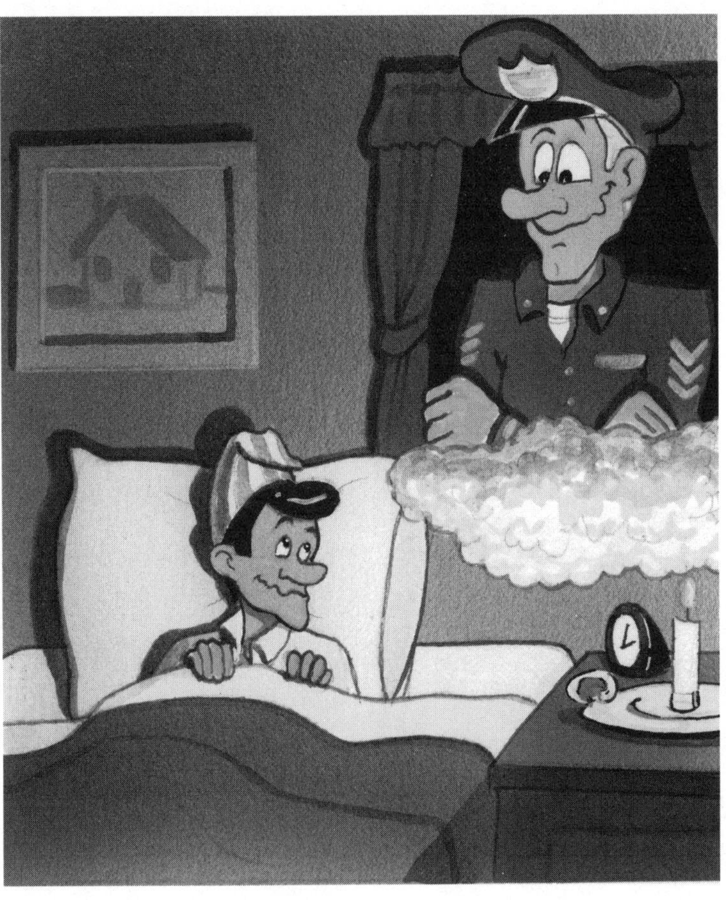

Officer David Harley is back! He comes into town to take Steve Larson on a promised motorcycle ride. But Steve is no longer in town, so David takes Jack Davis for a spin instead. They're on their way up to Trickle Lake when Jack spots a deserted road. Officer Harley and Jack investigate and discover a van on the road, parked in front of a hidden cave. Two guys are loading boxes into the van from the cave. David tells Jack to hop off and stay put. Then Officer Harley races up the road toward the cave and van to investigate.

On his way up the hill, his motorcycle hits a booby trap. Harley's motorcycle careens out of control and crashes down a steep embankment. Jack runs back to town and is followed by one of the men from the van. Jack gets Whit, Connie, and his parents to return with him to the cave. But once they get there, everything is gone—the van, boxes, motorcycle, and even Officer Harley! And since Jack tends to have an overactive imagination, no one believes him.

Later that night, the man who followed Jack into town suddenly appears in Jack's backyard. The man tells Jack that if he ever wants to see David again, Jack had better make sure no one believes his story.

Meanwhile, David regains consciousness and finds himself in the home and care of a kind farmer named McKinney, who found him the night before. David thanks him for his hospitality and races off.

Jack's parents don't believe his story, but they allow Jack to go back to the mysterious cave—where they are startled to see Whit. Whit has thought it over and has decided that Jack's story is worth investigating. Just as Whit deduces that Jack's story is true and that they are, in fact, dealing with bootleggers, they're captured and taken to the bootleggers' hideout. It's now left to David Harley to rescue Whit and Jack. And rescue them Harley does, as only our intrepid Officer Harley can! There's one other twist to the story—how David, Whit, and Jack are going to escape. You'll enjoy finding out for yourself *and* discovering that appearances can be deceiving.

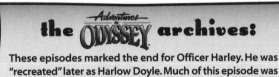

These episodes marked the end for Officer Harley. He was "recreated" later as Harlow Doyle. Much of this episode was remade, with different characters, as *AIO* #255, "The Boy Who Cried 'Destructo!'" See *AIO* #255 for study questions.

Episode #72

"An Encounter with Mrs. Hooper"

Theme: Compassion for the elderly.
Scripture reference: Colossians 3:12
Written and directed by Paul McCusker
Production engineer: Bob Luttrell
(Original air date: 5-13-89)

Whit takes his Sunday school class to visit the elderly at the Odyssey Retirement Home. Once there, Donna Barclay ends up assigned to the meanest, cruelest senior in the facility, Mrs. Mary Hooper. The only thing Mrs. Hooper cares about are her plants. When she first meets Donna, Mrs. Hooper treats her so badly that Donna runs from the room, vowing to never return.

The next day, Whit convinces Donna to visit again and take Mrs. Hooper a mixture Whit has concocted for the woman's flowers. Donna reluctantly goes back, and this time she manages to break down a little bit of Mary's wall, thanks to Donna's knowledge of flowers.

During the next week, Donna visits Mary frequently, and the two become good friends. Donna even helps Mary with her physical therapy. Mary reveals that she was so devastated when her husband died, she withdrew from life. But she wants no pity, and she refuses to cry over her loss.

Donna decides to try and tear down the wall completely. She enlists Whit's aid to find Mary's daughter. However, on Donna's next visit, she finds Mary back to her former hardness, yelling, and ranting. After a great deal of prodding, Mary finally admits that today is her birthday. For the first time since her husband died, she wants to have someone say "Happy Birthday" to her. So Donna opens the door and delivers the best present Mary could ask for: her daughter. Finally, the tears come. The wall completely dissolves. Mary Hooper has a happy birthday, and Donna learns that just because people act a certain way on the outside doesn't mean they're always that way on the inside.

the *Adventures in* ODYSSEY archives:

This show marked the debut of the character Richard Maxwell, who would figure into future shows in far more prominent ways.

STUDY QUESTIONS:

1. How did Donna finally become friends with Mrs. Hooper?
2. Have you ever talked with a senior citizen who isn't related to you? Why is it important to befriend elderly people?
3. How can you learn to get beyond people's outsides? Why should Christians look first at peoples' hearts?

Episode #73 "A Bite of Applesauce"

Theme: Disobedience.
Scripture reference: Genesis 3
Written and directed by Paul McCusker
Production engineer: Dave Arnold
(Original air date: 5-20-89)

Whit has been busy working on a new project at Whit's End, and his secretive attitude is nearly driving Connie crazy—especially when Whit lets Eugene in on the secret. Whit shows Eugene a special computer room behind the bookshelf in his office. The room contains a huge computer named Mabel and an unusual program called "Applesauce." Whit shows Eugene how to use Mabel but gives him strict instructions: (1) to keep the room a secret and (2) absolutely, positively, under no conditions is he or anyone else allowed to even *look* at "Applesauce." Eugene promises.

Later that week, Whit is at a city council meeting when the electric train set starts acting funny. Eugene goes to take care of the problem. He starts off toward the office, telling Connie to wait where she is. But her curiosity and frustration at being left out get the best of her. She follows Eugene into the office . . . and the computer room. Eugene immediately orders her out, but Connie stubbornly refuses to go until Eugene shows her how Mabel works. So Eugene shows her, swearing Connie to secrecy. Unfortunately, she sees the "Applesauce" program on the main menu and wonders what it does. Eugene adamantly refuses to look at "Applesauce" and insists that they both leave. Connie agrees, and finally they go.

But the next morning when Connie is running the shop all alone, the train set acts funny again. Connie tries to get Mabel to fix it, but she accidentally loads "Applesauce." The program causes Whit's End to go crazy! Eugene arrives and tries to stop the computer, with limited success. Finally, Mabel uses "Applesauce" to shut down the shop *completely*, causing the place to become as quiet as a tomb. Connie and Eugene are mortified.

When they finally face Whit, he is anguished that his two most trusted employees—and his friends—would disregard his wishes and instructions. Eugene and Connie apologize profusely, and Whit forgives them, but the damage is done. They must face the consequences. Effective immediately, Connie and Eugene can no longer work at Whit's End. They're fired.

the *Adventures in* ODYSSEY archives:

"A Bite of Applesauce" was the first time we ventured into Whit's association with intelligence agencies and ultra-secret computer programs—revealing yet another side of his character.

STUDY QUESTIONS:

1. When Connie first entered the computer room, what should Eugene have done?
2. Describe a time when you realized the benefits of having rules. What would have happened if (or when) you broke those rules?
3. Why has God set rules for us? Why does He command obedience to them?

Episodes #74 & 75

"Connie Goes to Camp," Parts One & Two

Theme: Disobedience; setting our minds on Jesus.
Scripture references: Proverbs 6:16,18b; Philippians 4:8
Written and directed by Paul McCusker
Production engineers: Dave Arnold and Bob Luttrell
(Original air dates: 6-10-89 & 6-17-89)

After getting fired from her job at Whit's End, Connie decides to be a counselor at Camp What-a-Nut. She writes to her mother about the camp and the unusual activities that have occurred there during the past week. First, in her cabin are Lucy, Donna, Robyn, and Allison. Each has her own little quirk—Donna and Robyn love clothes and makeup, Allison is addicted to TV, and Lucy makes friends with a rebellious girl named Jill. Meanwhile, the boys—Jimmy, Jack, and Oscar—give athletics a bad name by severely botching both archery and canoeing, much to the dismay of their counselor, Fred Zachary.

Later, when the girls go on a nature walk/camp out, Jill persuades Lucy to sneak away—something that is strictly against the rules—to see a beautiful waterfall and a herd of wild horses. That night, the girls bed down in their tents. Donna and Robyn complain about the dirt, bugs, and rain, while Allison continues to bemoan her lack of TV. Suddenly, they hear strange noises outside. The girls are instantly terrified. Allison makes things worse by telling stories of "the Goat-Man," a supposed monster that roams the territory. The noise moves closer until it's right outside their tent. Something lifts their tent flap. The girls scream in terror.

Fortunately, "the Goat-Man" ends up being Lucy and Jill, who are just returning from their outing. Unfortunately, Connie and several other counselors have been out looking for the two girls. The next morning, Connie reprimands Lucy and sends Jill back to her group. Then Connie informs the girls that they'll be competing head-to-head against the boys in Mr. Zachary's cabin. There will be three contests: archery, canoeing, and a relay race.

Connie plays sports announcer and describes the tournament. As the games progress, Jill once again approaches Lucy about sneaking away. Lucy says no at first, but Jill shames her into agreeing. They meet that night outside Jill's cabin. But Lucy refuses to accompany Jill. Lucy says it's wrong of them to disobey, especially after they've already gotten into trouble for it once. Jill accuses her of wimping out, but Lucy is adamant. Before Lucy can make it back to her cabin, though, the two girls are caught by a counselor.

The next morning, Connie punishes them: She expels Lucy and Jill from Camp What-a-Nut. Connie writes to her mom that it was the toughest thing she's ever had to do. Now she understands how much it must have hurt Whit to fire her—and how hurt God must feel when He has to discipline His people. Connie wraps up her letter, signs off, then adds: "P.S. Tell Whit I said hello."

the Adventures in ODYSSEY archives:

Although a fun episode, "Connie Goes to Camp" was not without its controversy. The "Goat-Man" was meant to be a typical, scary, camp-type story, but it proved to be a little too scary for some listeners. Fortunately, the ghost story is only a small portion of the episode and provides parents a chance to teach discernment skills to their children.

"Connie Goes to Camp" is also interesting because the character of Mrs. Neidlebark is played by . . . a man! John Eldridge is a fine actor who does a great impersonation of Julia Child/Queen Victoria.

behind the scenes:

"'Connie Goes to Camp' presented some interesting production problems. One was the arrow—I couldn't find a good, comical arrow sound anywhere. The whooshing of the arrow ended up being the sound of air blowing through a straw. The arrow's impact was the sound of a pocketknife being thrust into wood, and the 'doiiing!' of the impact was a coil door stopper being slapped back and forth."

—Dave Arnold

STUDY QUESTIONS:

1. Connie gave Lucy and Jill a warning the first time they disobeyed. How many "second chances" would you give someone who disobeyed? Are there times when it's appropriate to punish without first giving a warning?
2. Lucy said she was sorry for hurting Connie. What did Lucy mean by that?
3. Donna and Robyn were obsessed with makeup and clothes, while Allison was addicted to TV. Do you have any obsessions that you need to let go of? If so, what are they?

Episode #76 "Eugene's Dilemma"

Theme: Doing what's right; responsibility; standing up for your friends.
Scripture reference: John 15:13,17
Written and directed by Paul McCusker
Production engineer: Bob Luttrell
(Original air date: 6-24-89)

After being fired from Whit's End, Eugene has wasted no time in getting a new job at Campbell County Community College. He's working in the school's computer center, in charge of the high security programming. It guards financial reports, students' grades, and other personal information. His boss, Mr. Burglemeister, introduces Eugene to his only other employee, a child genius named Nicholas Adamsworth. Nicholas's parents died when he was little, and he is being tested in a new program the college has started with the state orphanage to see if kids with his intelligence can adjust to higher learning. If Nicholas fails to adjust, the program will be canceled. He'll end up back at the orphanage, "trying to keep from being picked on."

The work runs smoothly for a while, but trouble starts when Mr. Burglemeister asks Eugene to run a random check on the students' grades. Nicholas acts very nervous, and his attitude worsens when they're suddenly visited by Nicholas's counselor—Richard Maxwell. Richard was up for Eugene's job, though he's not cut out for any responsible position.

After Richard leaves, Eugene runs the random check and discovers a discrepancy—a grade has been changed. Nicholas tries to downplay it. Eugene investigates the matter and discovers that not one, but *two* grades have been changed. Nicholas confesses. He says he had to change them or else Richard Maxwell would have given the college a bad report about Nicholas. Just then, Richard shows up and confirms what Nicholas has said. Richard informs Eugene that if he doesn't keep quiet about all this, Richard will make Nicholas's life even more miserable.

Later, Eugene comes up with a scheme to correct things—he and Nicholas will simply change the grades *back.* Unfortunately, Eugene is caught doing this by Mr. Burglemeister, who brings him before the college's board of trustees—one of whom is Whit.

Eugene takes full responsibility for the incident, but Whit's investigation reveals that Eugene is actually innocent. Whit tries to get the truth out of Eugene, but he refuses to implicate anyone but himself. Things look bleak for Eugene, but at the last minute Nicholas bursts into the room and tells all. The trustees fire Richard Maxwell, place Nicholas on indefinite probation at the college, and transfer Eugene . . . back to Whit's End! Whit feels Eugene has learned his lesson and has discovered the importance of sacrifice.

But all is not *completely* well: Richard Maxwell vows to return. . . .

Young Nicholas Adamsworth was played by a man well into his 60s!

STUDY QUESTIONS:

1. What should Nicholas have done when he was first threatened by Richard Maxwell?
2. Was it right for Eugene to take all of the blame the way he did? Why or why not?
3. Was Eugene dishonest to change the grades back? Should he have handled the situation differently? Explain your answers.

Episodes #77 & 78

"The Nemesis," Parts One & Two

Theme: Trusting God in times of trouble.
Scripture reference: Psalm 46:1
Written and directed by Phil Lollar
Production engineers: Bob Luttrell and Dave Arnold
(Original air dates: 7-08-89 & 7-15-89)

Odyssey City Council is in full session, and the item of the moment is whether or not the town should grant a business license to Dr. Regis Blackgaard. Blackgaard's biggest advocate is Philip Glossman—the man who opposed selling Whit's End to Whit—and the main holdout is Tom Riley. Tom's concern is that no one, including Dr. Blackgaard, really knows what kind of business "Blackgaard's Castle" will be. All that's certain is that it'll be a place for kids.

A heated discussion ensues between Tom and Glossman. Whit finally intervenes, suggesting that they wait a week to vote on whether they should grant Blackgaard a business license. Everyone agrees. The meeting breaks up, and Blackgaard tells Glossman that they'll have to make sure Whit and Tom are out of the way when the vote is finally cast.

Meanwhile, back at Whit's End, Eugene is concerned to see Lucy there with Richard Maxwell. Then Connie wanders in and is shocked to find that Eugene is working at Whit's End again. Connie and Lucy talk. Connie learns that Lucy is still resentful that Connie sent her home from Camp What-a-Nut. Lucy leaves. Connie feels disappointed by her visit and decides to leave—with Richard. On the way out, she runs into Whit and Tom. Connie has another brief, strained, and quiet conversation, and then she excuses herself.

Tom asks Whit why he didn't rehire Connie like he did Eugene. Whit sadly replies that Connie has to ask for her job back. Whit says he could rehire Eugene because he knew first-hand that Eugene has learned his lesson. But Whit can't say that about Connie. He doesn't know if she understands yet why he fired her. When she's ready, he'll be there for her. Until then, he'll pray.

Outside, Richard Maxwell tells a confused Connie that there are other places in town to work. Richard invites her to come and meet his boss. Connie agrees, and Richard takes her across town, where she makes the acquaintance of Dr. Regis Blackgaard.

Blackgaard interviews Connie, smoothly suggesting that her firing was all Whit's fault. Regis cleverly maneuvers the conversation around to the "Applesauce" computer program. Connie barely keeps from telling the men what the program did. Then Blackgaard offers her a job, and she says she needs to think about it.

After Connie leaves, Blackgaard asks Richard how "the plans" are proceeding. Richard says getting Whit out of the way for the vote is no problem, but he's nervous about the plan for Tom Riley. Blackgaard unleashes his wrath on Maxwell, who crumbles under the pressure and promises not to let down Blackgaard.

Meanwhile, at the Riley farm, Tom and Whit discuss the upcoming vote and the situation with Connie, agreeing that much prayer is in order. Back at Whit's End, Richard Maxwell is spinning Blackgaard's web of deceit—and his vehicle is Lucy. First, Richard charms Lucy into calling Connie's house to tell her that Whit wants to meet with her. Then Maxwell persuades Lucy to deliver a note to Whit saying that Connie wants to meet with him. This meeting is planned for the same time as the city council vote. Finally, as for Tom Riley, Richard takes care of him in a much more direct fashion—by setting his barn on fire. The ploys work—Whit and Tom miss the vote. Dr. Regis Blackgaard gets his license . . . and is here to stay.

the *Adventures in* ODYSSEY archives:

"The Nemesis" introduced Dr. Regis Blackgaard, our series's villian. We had discussed creating a "nemesis" for Whit—someone who believed in all the things Whit was against. The character took on a life of its own and wound up far more sinister than we had planned.

behind the scenes:

"My notes from the story meeting for these episodes show that 'The Nemesis' was originally called 'The Arcade,' and Dr. Blackgaard was named Jonathan Dark. Later, in one of Phil Lollar's outlines, Dr. Regis Blackgaard was named Dr. Janus Blackgaard. 'Janus' was the name of a two-faced Roman god."

—Paul McCusker

STUDY QUESTIONS:

1. Why were Whit and Tom opposed to "Blackgaard's Castle"?
2. Why was Lucy so easily influenced by Richard Maxwell?
3. Connie got her job back because Lucy lied. Is it okay to lie if something good can result from it? Why or why not?

Episode #79 "Our Best Vacation Ever"

Theme: Family togetherness.
Scripture reference: Ephesians 6:1-4
Written and directed by Phil Lollar
Production engineer: Dave Arnold
(Original air date: 7-22-89)

Summer is vacation time—for everyone except the Barclays. Mary has reviewed the family budget, and there isn't enough money to go anywhere. The family isn't too happy about the prospect of not having a vacation.

The next day, George stops in at Whit's End. He relays the depressing news to Whit, who suggests that the Barclays don't have to go anywhere to have a good time. They can have fun right there in Odyssey. George likes the idea and rushes home to tell the family. At first, they aren't sure about Whit's suggestion, but then they decide that it's better than sitting around feeling sorry for themselves. They decide to look for opportunities to have fun.

Those opportunities start the next morning when Jimmy accidentally squirts his dad with a sprinkler, which leads to a massive water fight. The rest of the week is spent in low-cost, but fun, activities. The Barclays visit the zoo, take a trip to Trickle Lake, go camping (in the Barclay living room, no less), and attend an old-fashioned barn raising at the Riley farm.

The Barclays have a wonderful time. They learn that a little creativity—and a lot of family togetherness—has given them their best vacation ever!

Adventures in the ODYSSEY archives:

The water fight was originally a food fight (and still appears that way in the recording script). But we changed it at the last minute because we felt that wasting food—even in pursuit of family togetherness—wasn't a great idea.

STUDY QUESTIONS:

1. George said that what makes vacations fun is not what you do, but who you're with. Do you agree or disagree? Why?
2. What are some of the most creative activities you've done, without having a lot of money?
3. Have you had any memorable family vacations? Why were they memorable?

Episode #80 "A Prisoner for Christ"

Theme: Biblical history: Philemon; forgiveness.
Scripture reference: The book of Philemon.
Written and directed by Phil Lollar
Production engineer: Bob Luttrell
(Original air date: 7-29-89)

Nicholas Adamsworth is back—and he's more afraid than ever. But it's not Richard Maxwell he's scared of, it's Eugene! Nicholas tells Whit that he and Eugene had to create computer programs for a class at the college. Eugene created a great one that Nicholas has managed to ruin! He's afraid that Eugene will kill him, so he's hiding out at Whit's End.

Whit says that since Nicholas is there, he can help test a new Imagination Station adventure. Nicholas agrees, climbs in, and is propelled back to first-century Rome, where he finds himself in the middle of an exciting chase. A slave named Onesimus is being pursued by Flavius, a centurion who's driving a chariot. With Onesimus, Nicholas manages to escape from Flavius, but Onesimus sprains his ankle in the process. Fortunately, they are helped by Epaphras, a countryman of Onesimus's, who witnessed the end of the chase. Onesimus pleads to Epaphras for sanctuary, so he takes them through the sewers to the only man he knows who has a house in Rome—the apostle Paul!

But after they arrive at Paul's house, Flavius shows up, claiming Onesimus. Paul grants Onesimus sanctuary, but the centurion still demands payment for the damages caused by the chase. Paul agrees to pay Onesimus's bill himself! This satisfies Flavius, and he leaves. Everyone is stunned by Paul's generosity, especially Onesimus. He wants to know why Paul would do such a thing. Paul says that someone special once paid a great debt for him—could he do anything less for others?

Onesimus wants to know more about this man who repays impossible debts, so Paul tells him about Jesus. Eventually, Onesimus becomes a Christian. He realizes that now he must return to his master, Philemon. Nicholas tries to talk Onesimus out of it, but Onesimus says that not going back would be like living a lie. He only wants to do the right thing. Nicholas realizes that he needs to do the right thing as well. He exits the Imagination Station and tells Whit that he's returning to the college to face Eugene.

Adventures in the ODYSSEY archives:

The baptism scene generates a bit of controversy every time "A Prisoner for Christ" is aired. Some listeners object to the apostle Paul baptizing Onesimus "in the name of the Father, the Son, and the Holy Spirit." We were just using the words of Jesus in Matthew 28:19.

STUDY QUESTIONS:

1. Why was Nicholas so afraid of Eugene?
2. Have you ever repayed someone's debt? If so, when?
3. Is it important to be baptized? Why or why not? What does your church believe about baptism?

Episode #81 "Good Business"

Theme: Honesty; a worker is worth his or her wages.
Scripture reference: 2 Thessalonians 3:6-12
Written by Paul McCusker
Directed by Phil Lollar
Production engineer: Dave Arnold
(Original air date: 8-05-89)

Robyn wants money—lots of it. The trouble is, she doesn't want to work for it. Her dad proposes that she get a paper route, which she tries. Unfortunately, she can't seem to handle getting up early enough to deliver the papers on time. One of her customers, Mrs. Maddux, suggests Robyn move into a different line of work and offers her $10 to mow the lawn. Robyn jumps at the opportunity, and when she's finished, Mrs. Maddux's next-door neighbor also hires Robyn to clip his yard. Robyn knows a good thing when she sees it. She decides to start Robyn's Rotor Company, a gardening service.

Business is good—too good, as it turns out. Robyn is so booked up with lawns to mow, she doesn't have time to spend or enjoy any of the money she is making. She relates this to Jack and Oscar on one of her rare afternoons off, and they say they *wish* they had her problem—they can't seem to find work anywhere. Another light-bulb goes off in Robyn's head, and she immediately hires the two boys for $5 per lawn.

The business works like a charm—Jack and Oscar do all the work, while Robyn takes phone calls and rakes in the money. But after a few days of this, Jack and Oscar wise up. They demand more pay and threaten to go on strike if they don't get a raise. When nothing happens, Jack and Oscar hit the picket line. Robyn is back where she started. She wants to fold the business completely, but her father won't allow it. They discuss what went wrong, and Robyn learns that she shouldn't try to get something for nothing. An honest day's work must merit an honest day's pay. Robyn meets again with Jack and Oscar and tells them they can have the whole $10 for their work. After all, "a worker must be worthy of [his] wages."

STUDY QUESTIONS:

1. Robyn wanted to make money without working for it. Is that wrong? Why or why not?
2. Do you think Robyn paid Jack and Oscar fairly at first? Explain.
3. What does Jesus say about the love of money?

Episode #82 "Heatwave"

Theme: Using your imagination properly.
Scripture reference: Romans 12:2
Written by Paul McCusker
Directed by Phil Lollar
Production engineer: Bob Luttrell
(Original air date: 8-12-89)

The town is Odyssey. It's summer. The weather is hot. Very hot. The kids on the street have a name for this kind of weather. They call it a heat wave. Or so Jack explains in his best detective monologue. He and Oscar sit on Jack's front porch, bored out of their wits—until they see a mysterious kid walk by with a knapsack and an armload of lumber. Jack and Oscar decide to investigate.

First, they check out the local hardware store and discover that the kid got the lumber there. The owner tells them that the kid, a loner, is building something called "Wonderworld." Next, Jack and Oscar go to Whit's End and learn from Robyn that the kid comes in frequently to check out books from the library. They look at the check-out sheet for his name, but the only thing written down is "D. D."

The next day, Jack and Oscar follow the kid into the forest where they discover the truth! "D. D." is Digger Digwillow, and "Wonderworld" is the tree house he is building. Digger tells them that Whit is helping him develop his imagination properly so that he won't use it to get into trouble.

the Adventures in ODYSSEY archives:
"Heatwave" marked the introduction of the Wonderworld tree house, another teaching device.

STUDY QUESTIONS:

1. Digger said that Whit had been teaching him how to use his imagination properly. What did he mean by that?
2. Do you have a place like Wonderworld where you live?
3. What's the most creative summer project you've done? List some other fun projects to do during the summer.

Episodes #83 & 84

"The Battle," Parts One & Two

Theme: God's protection in times of trouble.
Scripture references: Romans 8:18,28,31
Written and directed by Phil Lollar
Production engineers: Bob Luttrell and Dave Arnold
(Original air dates: 8-18-89 & 8-26-89)

Dr. Regis Blackgaard has finally opened Blackgaard's Castle. Whit and Eugene stop by for a visit and discover the place is the antithesis of Whit's End: noisy, rowdy, and full of unwholesome games. Blackgaard tries to dismiss all this with a "kids-will-be-kids" nonchalance. Soon Whit and Eugene have had enough, and they leave.

What they don't know is that the place is just a cover for Blackgaard and Richard Maxwell, who are trying to steal Whit's "Applesauce" computer program. They have a computer and modem of their own and log into Whit's computer, Mabel, causing "Applesauce" to wreak havoc on Whit's End. But they soon run into the password problem. Blackgaard tells Richard he must use Lucy to get more information about "Applesauce" from Whit. But Lucy overhears them and rushes off to tell Whit.

Meanwhile, Blackgaard has Richard use "Applesauce" to produce a power surge in the Imagination Station. Richard causes it to blow up right as Lucy rushes into the Station! Lucy is taken to the hospital. Because of her injuries, Whit must conduct an investigation. To do that, he decides to close down Whit's End.

Richard Maxwell is furious with Blackgaard that Lucy was the one who got hurt. But Regis has too much incriminating information about Richard. Blackgaard persuades Richard to calm down and get back to work on finding out the password to "Applesauce."

Meanwhile, Whit—who is discouraged by Lucy's injuries—and Eugene try to discover why the Imagination Station blew up. Whit informs Eugene that "Applesauce" isn't only a program for Whit's End. It is also a highly classified government program that contains a lot of top secret government information. Thanks to a "log" in Mabel's program, Eugene learns that it had been broken into—which caused the Imagination Station to malfunction. Whit and Eugene also discover that the culprit was Richard Maxwell or, more likely, Dr. Blackgaard.

Richard Maxwell goes to the hospital to apologize to Lucy and learns that she knows about Blackgaard's scheme to get "Applesauce." Lucy challenges Richard to do the right thing and go to the authorities. He feels terrible, but he says he can't. He leaves just as Whit arrives. Lucy tells Whit everything she knows.

Richard returns to Blackgaard's Castle and informs the doctor that he has gotten the password. Blackgaard is thrilled and rushes to go input it. But Richard is not the man we think he is: The password he tells Regis to type in isn't the password for Whit's computer. It's the password to destroy *Blackgaard's* computer. Everything at the Castle suddenly goes haywire. A fire breaks out. Blackgaard is insanely angry at Richard and pushes an arcade game on top of him, leaving him to die in the fire.

Whit arrives just in time to save Richard. The police arrest Richard but have little luck in finding Dr. Blackgaard. Whit destroys the "Applesauce" program, hoping that will put an end to the sad events that have plagued Odyssey since Dr. Blackgaard's arrival. Will things return to normal? Only time will tell.

the *Adventures in* ODYSSEY archives:

In these "Blackgaard" episodes, the actor who played Richard Maxwell, Lucy's "love interest," also played Lucy's *father* in *AIO* #68, "Choices."

STUDY QUESTIONS:

1. Dr. Blackgaard said that children already have too much structure in their lives and should be given more freedom. Was he right? Why or why not?
2. Was Richard Maxwell right to have wrecked Blackgaard's Castle? If you were in Richard's position, would you have done what he did?
3. Whit thanked God for protecting them throughout the summer. Can you think of a time when you felt God's protection around you? If so, explain.

Episode #85
"You Go to School Where?"

Theme: Home schooling.
Scripture reference: Proverbs 22:6
Written and directed by Phil Lollar
Production engineer: Dave Arnold
(Original air date: 9-16-89)

School has begun again. Robyn and Dale Jacobs visit Whit's End for their just-established, "time-honored" tradition—the annual back-to-school chocolate soda. While there, they run into Esther Langford and her mother, Helen. Esther has never been to Whit's End before, so while Robyn shows her around, Whit and Dale talk with Helen and learn that she home schools Esther.

Dale is intrigued—he needs material for a newspaper story and thinks home schooling might be a good subject. But Whit comes up with an even better twist for Dale's article: Since neither Robyn nor Esther is looking forward to the prospect of going back to school, why not have the girls switch places for a day, then report on their experiences?

Everyone is game, and Robyn and Esther step into each other's shoes—getting a good lesson about how the other half learns.

STUDY QUESTIONS:

1. What does "the grass is always greener on the other side" mean?
2. Why is it important to learn from others?
3. What are some of the advantages and disadvantages of home schooling? Of public schools?

Episode #86 "Isaac the Insecure"

Theme: Overcoming insecurity.
Scripture references: Psalm 139:14; Luke 16:15
Written and directed by Paul McCusker
Production engineer: Bob Luttrell
(Original air date: 9-23-89)

Isaac is no soccer player. After Isaac botches several plays, Coach Fred Zachary politely boots him from the team. But Isaac is definitely the "Péle" of the academic world, which he proves later in math class. He'd give up all his intelligence, though, if he could just be like Jack Davis, captain of the soccer team and the most popular guy in school.

In English class, Isaac and Jack are paired to do a report. Isaac thinks this could be his big chance to "catch" some of Jack's popularity, so he does everything he can to avoid making Jack upset. When it becomes obvious that Jack is uncomfortable having Isaac as a partner, Isaac resolves to work harder on the report so Jack will like him.

But their teacher corners Isaac and forces him to reveal how much work he's doing and how little work Jack seems to be doing. The teacher scolds Jack, who, in turn, rakes Isaac over the coals. Isaac determines to make it up to Jack by doing the *entire* report himself. But when Isaac gets to the library, the librarian tells him that someone else is already there, doing a report on Isaac's subject.

Isaac hunts down the copycat and discovers that it's Jack! It turns out that Jack didn't want to be Isaac's partner because *he* felt inferior around *Isaac*. Much to their surprise, they both have the same insecurities. They get down to work, and Isaac discovers he's made a new friend—one who has turned out to be a lot like him.

> **the *Adventures in* ODYSSEY archives:**
>
> **"Isaac the Insecure" introduced Isaac Morton, one of our long-term characters. This episode also started a mini-series of programs that bear Isaac's name.**

STUDY QUESTIONS:

1. Have you ever felt like Isaac and Jack? What did you do to regain confidence?
2. What are some of your special gifts?
3. How can you boost someone's self-esteem?

Episodes #87 & 88
"Elijah," Parts One & Two

Theme: God's sovereignty; biblical history: Elijah.
Scripture reference: 1 Kings 17:1-19:2
Written by Paul McCusker
Directed by Phil Lollar
Production engineers: Bob Luttrell and Dave Arnold
(Original air dates: 9-30-89 & 10-07-89)

Whit and Tom are repairing the damage that Dr. Blackgaard and Richard Maxwell have done to the Imagination Station. In addition to making repairs, Whit is also adding a few modifications to the machine. The most interesting of these changes is that the cockpit has been divided in half so that *two* kids can now have an adventure at the same time.

Once the repairs are complete, Whit and Tom move to the control room to do a little programming. Tom puts up a "Keep Off" sign on the machine, but it isn't enough to stop Robyn and Jack. First, Robyn climbs in the Station. Then Jack follows to "rescue" her, and together they are whisked out of Odyssey. The two find themselves in the middle of ancient Israel during the reign of evil King Ahab and his even more evil queen, Jezebel. The king and queen hold Robyn captive, while Jack joins one of the greatest prophets in the Old Testament: Elijah. Jack's and Robyn's lives are threatened several times as they witness the prophet's bravery, his confrontation with the king and queen, his challenge to the prophets of Baal, and God's magnificent victory and total sovereignty.

When Jack and Robyn get back, they've both learned three things: 1) The Imagination Station is working again; 2) God's power is greater than anything; 3) When a sign says "Keep Off," it means *"Keep Off!"*

the ODYSSEY archives:

"Elijah" revealed even more about the ever-changing Imagination Station. In this episode, not only was the cockpit divided in half, but the red button became a flashing white one—a slip of the writer's pen.

STUDY QUESTIONS:

1. Why was Elijah considered such a great prophet?
2. What are the biblical criteria for being a prophet?
3. Read 1 Kings 17:1–19:2. What eventually happened to King Ahab? Queen Jezebel?

Episode #89 "That's Not Fair!"

Theme: Fairness; God's grace.
Scripture reference: Romans 6:23
Written and directed by Phil Lollar
Production engineer: Bob Luttrell
(Original air date: 10-14-89)

Connie, Donna, and Oscar are sitting around Whit's End, looking glum. When Whit inquires about their sour moods, they all relay grossly unfair incidents that recently happened to them: Connie says her mother has given her too many chores. Oscar says he never gets to do the things his older brother, Tony, gets to do. Donna says Mr. Zachary gave her a homework assignment as a punishment when she didn't feel she did anything wrong.

Whit patiently hears them out, then says he thinks they're overreacting. All three explode and take him to task. They say they only want to be treated fairly—no more, no less. Whit thinks about this for a few moments, then tells them he'll see what he can do about getting them *absolutely fair* treatment for the next few days. They are delighted at the prospect, but Whit feels that they don't know what they're getting themselves into with this deal.

Sure enough, perfectly fair treatment isn't as wonderful as they thought. Connie's mom takes away her extra chores but refuses to awaken Connie in the morning, fix her breakfast, or pay Connie's part of the rent! Oscar's dad agrees that Oscar should be able to go everywhere Tony goes—and that Oscar's little brother, Henry, should be able to go everywhere *Oscar* goes. As for Donna, Fred Zachary apologizes for not hearing her out, but he refuses to take back the homework project because Donna has been late with *every* assignment the entire semester. The threesome learns an important lesson about the foolishness of demanding absolute fairness—and the wisdom of relying on God's grace instead.

STUDY QUESTIONS:

1. Did Connie, Oscar, and Donna have good reasons to be upset?
2. Are there people in your life who treat you unfairly? Who are they? How are their actions unfair? Who have you treated unfairly?
3. If we were all treated *absolutely* fairly, what do you think would happen to us?

Episode #90 "But, You Promised"

Theme: The consequences of lying.
Scripture reference: Colossians 3:9
Written by Diane Dalbey and Phil Lollar
Directed by Phil Lollar
Production engineer: Dave Arnold
(Original air date: 10-21-89)

Robyn has had a problem with responsibility lately. First, she hasn't been locking her bike up like she should. She's also putting off schoolwork and stretching the truth to her friends. Her parents debate over whether to step in and correct her or let Robyn suffer the consequences of her actions.

Robyn's parents decide on the latter and, soon enough, Robyn deals with her lack of responsibility. She fails to lock up her bike at the mall, and it gets stolen. To avoid the inevitable lectures from her parents, Robyn says that her bike was taken by two guys in a van who talk funny. Soon Robyn's world begins to crumble when Donna and Lucy confront her about the fibs she's been telling.

Things get really bad, though, when Officer Sedgwick from the Odyssey Sheriff's Department informs her that they've found two men who fit her description of the bicycle thieves—Italian immigrants named Angelo and Mario. Robyn doesn't want to implicate the men, but she doesn't do much to acquit them, either. When the two men come up with an airtight alibi, Robyn's story-telling is finally over for good. She is forced to admit the whole story, having learned that the trouble caused by telling lies is far worse than any trouble brought by telling the truth.

the ODYSSEY archives:

The first draft of this story was about Robyn making promises she couldn't keep—which is why we titled it "But, You Promised." Later, we changed the focus of the episode to lying. Unfortunately, the title remained, and now it has nothing to do with the episode.

STUDY QUESTIONS:

1. Robyn said she fibbed to Lucy because she didn't want to hurt Lucy's feelings. Is that a good reason to lie? Explain.
2. Have you ever told a lie that got someone else in trouble? If so, how did you remedy the situation?
3. Besides getting in trouble, what are some other consequences of lying?

Episode #91 "A Mission for Jimmy"

Theme: Supporting missionaries.
Scripture reference: Romans 10:14-15
Written and directed by Paul McCusker
Production engineer: Bob Luttrell
(Original air date: 10-28-89)

Jimmy Barclay is in a bad mood. His dad asks why, and Jimmy responds that he was put in charge of the missionary fund-raiser for his Sunday school class. Dad says that since Jimmy has to do it, he might as well do his best. But Jimmy's first effort produces a poster, which shows a missionary being boiled in a pot by cannibals. So, George gives him some books on the subject—including one by Dan Isidro, missionary to the Miskito Indians in Nicaragua. Jimmy starts to read and soon falls asleep—only to wake up in with Dan in Nicaragua!

Jimmy and Dan are on their way to pick up a sick boy named Pablo and take him to the doctor. But they are met with setback after setback along the way. The battery in their jeep goes dead, they run out of gas, and soldiers threaten their lives. Even though they manage to get through all the problems, the situation is still hopeless for little Pablo. Jimmy is distraught. They have to do something to save him!

He awakens from his dream with those words on his lips and realizes that missionaries do much more than stand on corners and hand out tracts. Jimmy decides to do something to help them. He puts his creativity to work and comes up with the best fund-raiser the church has ever had: a Christmas party for missions. Everyone gives money, the party is a success, and Jimmy is stunned when a special guest arrives—the missionary Dan Isidro!

the *Adventures in* ODYSSEY archives:

After Paul McCusker completed his script, he gave it to the International Ministries department at Focus on the Family. They translated the appropriate lines into Spanish and also helped with the casting. This gave the episode authenticity.

behind the scenes:

"For this show, we couldn't find the sound effects of a jeep on a bumpy road. None of us knew anyone who had a jeep, and there were no bumpy dirt roads in the concrete jungle of Los Angeles. So we went to an unpaved field in the back of the Focus parking lot, disconnected two of the spark plugs from my four-cylinder car, and raced the car over ruts and through weeds. Dave hung out of the passenger side window and held the microphone down by the wheels. That old car was never the same after that day, but hey!—we got the right sound effects!"

—Bob Luttrell

STUDY QUESTIONS:

1. Why didn't Jimmy want to be in charge of the fund-raiser?
2. Why was Jimmy so mistaken about what missionaries do?
3. Does your church support any missionaries? Have you ever met them? Written to them? Prayed for them?

Episode #92 "The Ill-Gotten Deed"

Theme: The folly of revenge; Odyssey's history.
Scripture reference: Romans 12:19-21
Written and directed by Phil Lollar
Production engineer: Dave Arnold
(Original air date: 11-04-89)

Calvin is mad at his brother, Ronny. So mad, in fact, he is searching the library at Whit's End for a book of mean tricks to play on his sibling. Calvin tells Whit that Ronny is always double-crossing him. Whit hears Calvin out, then Whit says he does have a book for Calvin after all.

The book is called *The Ill-Gotten Deed,* by John Avery Whittaker. It's all about two identical twin brothers named Horace and Grover who live in Virginia with their wives. Their father dies, leaving behind his land out west. But instead of dividing it up, the father's will states that the first of the brothers to reach the land gets it all! It's supposed to be a fair contest, but unfortunately Grover ends up double-crossing his brother. Grover wins the contest and cheats Horace out of the land.

Grover and his wife, Rachael, arrive first and the deed is signed over to them. But as soon as the deed is signed, they learn that the land is actually a swamp for most of the year. It's overrun by range cattle and, worst of all, surrounded by hostile Indians—who decide at that very moment to go on the warpath! Grover and Rachael fight the Indians off as best they can, but it looks hopeless. Suddenly, the Indians ride off, chased away by a huge herd of range cattle. And behind the cattle is Horace! He's saved Grover and Rachael, despite what Grover did to him.

Grover still has one more swindle up his sleeve, though. He insists that Horace take their father's land! Horace, not knowing all the land's drawbacks, agrees. He turns over his small farm in Virginia to Grover.

Calvin can't believe it until Whit reads the rest of the story to him: The swamp land turned out to be fine when a few strategic drainage ditches were dug. Horace built himself a lovely little town on the property, a town he ended up calling "Odyssey." Everything turned out all right for Horace in the end—and Calvin discovers why it's best not to overcome evil by evil, but to overcome evil with good.

STUDY QUESTIONS:

1. Calvin said his brother was always playing tricks on him. What's the difference between a practical joke and a dirty trick? How do you know when a joke has gone too far?
2. Why is it best to let God handle revenge?
3. What does it mean to "overcome evil with good" (Romans 12:21)? Can you think of any examples of this?

Episode #93

"Rescue from Manatugo Point"

Theme: God holds the future.
Scripture references: Psalm 90:12; Psalm 39:4; 2 Peter 3:8
Written by Paul McCusker
Directed by Phil Lollar
Production engineer: Dave Arnold
(Original air date: 11-11-89)

Whit is writing a magazine article for Sunday school teachers when Connie brings him the mail. In it is an airmail letter containing two words: "Manatugo Point." Reading the letter and later perusing old journals brings back a flood of memories for Whit.

Flashback to World War II: Young John Avery Whittaker is a signalman just assigned to the U.S.S. *Irongate,* headed for Guadalcanal. Once there, he is immediately assigned to a patrol boat that's on a mission to rescue a "coast watcher"—a member of the British navy who is hidden on the island. Coast watchers keep tabs day and night on the Japanese and relay their movements to the Allied forces. It's dangerous work, and this particular coast watcher—Leftenant Reginald Duffield—hasn't been heard from for days.

Young Whit and his commander, Lt. Evans, lead a team onto the island at Manatugo Point. There, they meet up with an island boy named Malanga, Lt. Duffield's co-worker. Malanga leads them on a tense journey to the injured Leftenant, who then guides them all back. Once there, Duffield realizes that Malanga would be safer back in his village and reluctantly decides to send him away. At last, the rescuers get back to the PT211, which scurries off just before a Japanese patrol floats ashore.

Back to the present. Whit closes his journal. He basks in the glow of fond memories, wondering if the mysterious letter means an old friend is coming back into his life.

Adventures in Odyssey the ODYSSEY archives:

"Rescue from Manatugo Point" contained a remarkable performance. The young boy, Malanga, was portrayed by Katie Leigh Pavlakovich, a.k.a. Connie!

STUDY QUESTIONS:

1. Read 2 Peter 3:8. What does this verse mean?
2. When did the Battle of Guadalcanal take place? Where is Guadalcanal?
3. Do you have any relatives who are war veterans? Have you heard their stories?

Episode #94 "Operation DigOut"

Theme: Spreading the Gospel; doing good.
Scripture references: Isaiah 40:28-31; Galatians 6:7-10
Written by Paul McCusker
Directed by Phil Lollar
Production engineer: Bob Luttrell
(Original air date: 11-18-89)

Connie is behind the counter at Whit's End when an elderly stranger walks inside. He asks to see Whit, who is absent at the moment. Connie offers to take a message, and the old gent gives her one: "Operation DigOut." Connie, of course, can barely contain her excitement. Finally, Whit returns, and once Connie has delivered the message, he tells her the story behind it, which once again involves Leftenant Reginald Duffield.

In a flashback, Reggie and young Whit are assigned to help land several transports of soldiers on the strategic island of Rubaku in Guadalcanal—an island held by the Japanese. The night before the invasion, Whit and Reggie discuss spiritual issues. Reggie is a nonbeliever but is intrigued by Whit's faith. The two make a date to discuss the matter over tea when the war has ended.

During the battle, Whit and Reggie both exhibit immense bravery, risking their lives to make sure the transport they're on arrives intact. Once the soldiers are on the beach, Whit takes his bravery a step further. He shields Reggie from an incoming shell and gets severely wounded. He wakes up in the hospital with a large gash in his leg and the upper part of his right ear missing, thanks to the shrapnel from the shell. His commander tells him that Reggie stopped by to see him while he was still unconscious and left Whit a message about a date for tea. Whit smiles, and we return to the present.

Whit takes a drive up to Trickle Lake, where he meets up with the former Leftenant Duffield. They have tea, and Reggie tells Whit that the seeds of Christianity he planted so long ago took root. For the last 25 years, Reggie has pastored a church in a little English village. The two old friends relive old times and catch up on each other's lives, marveling at how God works in the lives of His people.

the *Adventures in* ODYSSEY archives:

More about Whit's past was revealed in "Operation DigOut." This episode gave information about the wound in Whit's leg and the missing upper part of his ear—items that were included in the first description ever written about him. Also, Paul McCusker's wife, Elizabeth—a native of Great Britain—helped us Yanks to keep our accents authentic.

STUDY QUESTIONS:

1. Lt. Duffield asked young Whit if he was a "war-time convert." What does that mean? Do you know anyone who was a "war-time convert"?
2. Duffield marveled that Whit had been a Christian since he was a youngster. When do you think a person is old enough to become a Christian?
3. Reggie said that the seeds of faith Whit planted when they were young led Reggie to the Lord. Who could you share your faith with today?

Episode #95 "The Very Best of Friends"

Theme: Anger; dealing with death.
Scripture reference: 1 Corinthians 15:51-57
Written and directed by Phil Lollar
Production engineer: Dave Arnold
(Original air date: 12-02-89)

Jessie and the other kids at Odyssey Elementary have come up with a special surprise for Donna Barclay: They've chosen her to be the host of the annual Fall Festival. Everyone is excited about the choice . . . except Donna. She thanks her friends but says she doesn't ever want to have anything to do with the Festival again.

Jessie is confused and takes the dilemma to Whit. Donna is so talented and outgoing, Jessie wonders why Donna doesn't jump at this honor. But Whit believes he knows why Donna is acting so strangely. He takes Jessie over to the Barclay house to talk with Donna about it. Unfortunately, Donna refuses to admit anything is wrong and demands to be left alone.

Jessie thinks it's all her fault, but Whit tells her that Donna is feeling bad about a different friend—someone who was around before Jessie came on the scene—Karen. It's been a year since Karen died, and one of the last things she did was the Fall Festival. Whit knows Donna has to release her anger—anger toward Karen for dying, toward God for letting Karen die, and toward herself for having those feelings in the first place.

Whit arranges to take Donna to the one place where she can let go of her bitterness—Karen's grave. At the cemetery, Whit makes Donna confront her anger by turning it over to God. The healing begins, and Donna is finally able to tell Karen "good-bye."

the *Adventures in* ODYSSEY archives:

"The Very Best of Friends" was a sequel to "Karen," *AIO* #50. It was also the last we saw of Reginald Duffield.

STUDY QUESTIONS:

1. Have you ever lost a friend or loved one? How did you cope with it?
2. How can you cherish the memory of a loved one but also be able to tell them good-bye?
3. How could you encourage a friend who is grieving?

Episode #96 "The Reluctant Rival"

Theme: Treating others better than yourself.
Scripture references: Matthew 5:43-48; Philippians 2:3-4
Written and directed by Paul McCusker
Production engineer: Bob Luttrell
(Original air date: 12-09-89)

Whit's daughter, Jana, and her kids, Monty and Jenny, have come to town for the holidays. There is always some tension when Jana is around, and this visit is no exception. But this time, the tension centers on Jenny, and for an unusual reason: She is a gifted child. When it comes to brains, Jenny Whittaker-Dowd could give Eugene Meltsner a run for his money.

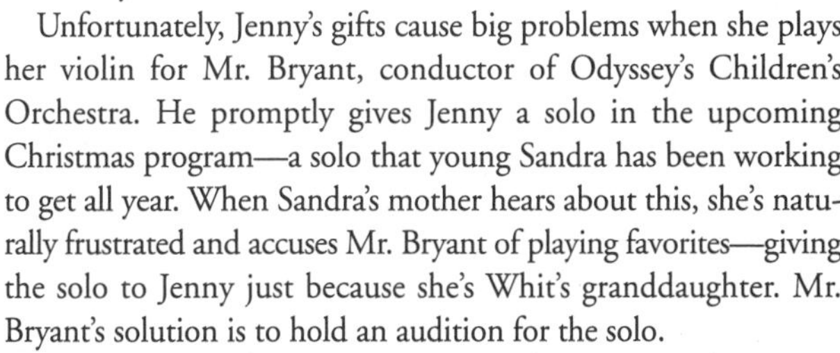

Unfortunately, Jenny's gifts cause big problems when she plays her violin for Mr. Bryant, conductor of Odyssey's Children's Orchestra. He promptly gives Jenny a solo in the upcoming Christmas program—a solo that young Sandra has been working to get all year. When Sandra's mother hears about this, she's naturally frustrated and accuses Mr. Bryant of playing favorites—giving the solo to Jenny just because she's Whit's granddaughter. Mr. Bryant's solution is to hold an audition for the solo.

Sandra and her friend run into Jenny downtown and are mean to her. Jenny tries to hide her hurt, but the tears finally come. She can't understand why people dislike her just because she's smart and talented.

The day of the audition arrives. Sandra does well. Then Jenny plays . . . and royally botches up the piece. Mr. Bryant has no choice but to give the solo to Sandra.

Later, at Whit's End, Jana asks Jenny why she performed so badly. Jenny says that getting to perform the solo is not worth hurting Sandra's and her mother's happiness. Whit and Jana couldn't be more proud. Somewhere beneath Jenny's brilliant I.Q. is an equally brilliant heart.

Adventures in the ODYSSEY archives:

"The Reluctant Rival" was the first episode to feature Whit's daughter and grandchildren since 1987's "A Member of the Family," *Family Portraits* #11 & 12. We also saw Whit uncharacteristically on the defense in this episode and the next—Whit was dealing with not only Jana's bitter feelings about him as a father, but also the pain of her divorce.

STUDY QUESTIONS:

1. Why did Sandra assume that she already had the violin solo? Should she have made that assumption? Explain.
2. What do you think is worth more: hard work or natural talent? Is one better than the other? Explain.
3. Did Jenny do the right thing by purposefully playing badly so Sandra could win? Would you consider that a deception or a gracious act? Explain your answer.

Episode #97 "Monty's Christmas"

Theme: The effects of divorce on kids; the importance of strong families.
Scripture reference: Malachi 2:16
Written and directed by Paul McCusker
Production engineer: Dave Arnold
(Original air date: 12-16-89)

The Whittakers are getting ready to celebrate Christmas. Everyone seems to be having a good time—except Monty. Something is bothering him, but no one knows what it is. The tension mounts when Jana jumps all over Monty after he accidentally drops and breaks an angel from the nativity scene. Then, when Monty decides to go to his room, he and Jana fight again. Monty leaves, and Jana remarks that Monty is just like his dad, Phil. Whit decides to try and reach Monty to see what's wrong, but even Whit can't break down the wall.

The situation worsens when Jana calls her ex-husband to inquire about the kids' Christmas presents. Jana and Phil exchange harsh words, and Jana hangs up before Monty can talk with Phil. This causes even more strain. Monty runs out, and Jana attributes Monty's behavior to him inheriting his father's disposition. But Whit thinks it's more simple than that: Monty probably just *misses* his dad.

Monty goes to the mall, where he runs into Connie, who is Christmas shopping. They talk, and through their conversation, Connie helps Monty understand that he's not the only one who is hurting—his mom is, too. Connie knows from her own situation that even moms are human and need love, sympathy, and compassion, just like everyone else.

They finish shopping and return to Whit's house, where they build a snowman and start a snowball fight on the front lawn. They are soon joined by the rest of the Whittaker family. Monty and Jana exchange apologies. Monty gives his mom a pre-Christmas gift: a small glass angel. It looks like they'll have a happy holiday after all.

STUDY QUESTIONS:

1. Why was Monty so upset?
2. Do you know anyone who is hiding their sadness? How can you help them?
3. Why was it so hard for Monty to understand that his mom was also hurting? How can you show a family member some love and understanding?

Episode #98 "The Visitors"

Theme: Charity; sacrifice.
Scripture references: Matthew 25:31-46; Luke 2:1-7; Ephesians 2:10
Written and directed by Phil Lollar
Production engineer: Bob Luttrell
(Original air date: 12-23-89)

The Barclay family is having a wonderful Christmas Day, filled with presents, laughter, and love. Jimmy and George go outside to play with Jimmy's favorite present, a remote-control dune buggy. Things go well—until George gets the control and ends up crashing the buggy against the side of an old tool shed.

While retrieving the car, George and Jimmy hear a strange noise coming from inside the shed. It sounds like the neighbor's cat, but when they open the shed to let him out, they are stunned to discover that the cat is actually a baby! It's lying in Jimmy's old cradle—and its parents are hidden farther back in the shed.

Inside the Barclay kitchen, we learn that the folks—Chris, Elizabeth, and baby Zack—were on their way home but got stranded in the snowstorm. Jimmy and Donna immediately make friends with the couple, but George and Mary privately express their reservations. They know nothing about these people, and Mary is uncomfortable with them staying the night. George agrees, but doesn't know who to call. He decides the best thing to do is contact Whit, who agrees to take in the strangers.

Later, just before the Barclays sit down to a scrumptious dinner, they discuss their previous Christmas—how they were robbed, and the incredible kindness that was shown to them. George reads the Christmas story. Or, he tries to read it. Midway through, the family feels convicted by their actions that morning—shuffling the young couple and their baby off to Whit. They decide to remedy the situation, and George calls Whit to bring the folks back. But Whit says they're gone!

The Barclays jump in their car and search for the strangers, but the people are nowhere to be found. The Barclays pray for help. Suddenly, they see the family rounding a corner into an alley. The Barclays quickly follow, but the alley is a dead-end—and the strangers aren't there! Then Jimmy sees a stairwell. They investigate and, sure enough, a family *is* hiding down there—only it's a different family! They are just as needy. The Barclays are confused, then begin to think that maybe these are the folks they were meant to find all along. They return home with the family, and the Barclays better realize the true meaning of charity.

the *Adventures in* ODYSSEY archives:

"The Visitors" was translated into Spanish and aired on *En Foque a la Familia,* Focus on the Family's Spanish language program. It was also adapted into story form and published in the December 1995 edition of *Focus on the Family* magazine.

STUDY QUESTIONS:

1. Mary said that they had "shuffled Jesus off onto Whit." What did she mean?
2. The Barclays couldn't find the strangers until they prayed. How did that prayer make a difference?
3. Who do you think Chris, Elizabeth, and little Zack represented?

Episode #99 "The Barclay Ski Vacation"

Theme: Family relations and togetherness.
Scripture reference: Luke 1:17b
Written by Jeff Parker
Directed by Phil Lollar
Production engineer: Dave Arnold
(Original air date: 12-30-89)

It's finally time for the Barclays to take their long-anticipated ski trip! Everyone is excited about it—except, oddly enough, Donna, who desperately wanted to go somewhere, *anywhere*, last summer. But despite her complaints, the Barclays head for the mountains and the slopes. Once there, George immediately signs the kids up for ski school. The next day, the family has a wonderful time shushing, snow-plowing, paralleling, and traversing. Even Donna. In fact, *especially* Donna. She seems unusually happy, and George and Mary soon discover why: a good-looking, young ski instructor named Robb. Donna has a crush on him, and George is beside himself about it.

That night, he tells Mary that he's concerned about their daughter. Mary tries to downplay the whole situation, but George goes off the deep end and tries to come up with ways to prevent Donna from seeing Robb again. Finally, George settles on a brilliant and cunning plan: Tomorrow, he'll take Donna out for a little "father/daughter" day. She'll be so wrapped up in having fun with her old man, she'll forget all about Robb. But Donna refuses to go with her dad. She wants to go to her ski class. George decides against making her go on their date and returns to bed, disappointed.

George isn't the only disappointed one, though. The next day, Donna discovers that Robb has a girlfriend! Donna skis back to the Barclay cabin, where she finds her dad brooding. They brood together, and after George comforts Donna, he realizes that his little girl is finally growing up.

STUDY QUESTIONS:

1. Why do you think it's so hard for parents to see their kids get older?
2. Do you think Donna was foolish to have such a big crush on Robb? Why or why not?
3. How else do parent-child relationships change when the child becomes a teenager?

1990

Adventures in Odyssey grew by leaps and bounds during 1990. In the summer, we had our first serious discussion about *AIO* spin-off programs and products. To start, Chick-Fil-A restaurants put *AIO* cassette tapes in their kids' meals. We also came up with a plan to have the program air daily on a rerun basis—though it wasn't implemented for another 16 months.

In 1990, Focus decided to launch a series of *AIO* novels for young readers—and asked Paul McCusker to write them.

At the same time, Focus on the Family was participating in the release of the popular *McGee and Me* video series. It was remarkably successful—so Focus decided to start production on a completely animated *AIO* video series and commissioned me to write the initial video scripts.

Since Paul and I were now writing for *Adventures in Odyssey* spin-off products, we needed to lighten our normal workload. One way to do that was to take the stories that contained the now-banned Officer David Harley and de-Harleyize them. The results made up the bulk of our 1990 summer schedule.

Around the fall of 1990, the flavor of our programs changed. The Focus leadership became concerned about the influence of daytime television on kids, especially latchkey children—kids who come home from school to an empty house because of their parents' work situation. This was a concern because these youngsters can turn on the tube and, unsupervised, see immorality at its worst.

To address this problem, Dr. Dobson requested that all the communications divisions at Focus on the Family—including *Adventures in Odyssey*—hit the issues of the day and present the godly response to them. So *AIO* ran programs that first dealt with issues of general morality, then proceeded with environmentalism, bigotry, illiteracy, and abortion. These shows comprised most of our fall schedule.

But the close of 1990 brought two of the biggest changes *AIO* had yet experienced. First, the Focus on the Family leadership decided to move the ministry out of southern California. The ministry had several offers pending, among them from Seattle, Washington; Raleigh, North Carolina; and Colorado Springs, Colorado. The leadership diligently sought God's help in making the right choice—and several factors had to fall into place before the move could be made, so it was at least a good year or more away.

Still, it meant a momentous decision hung over all our heads: Go with Focus, or stay in California? The first of us to make his decision was Paul. He decided to go instead to England, where he had always wanted to live. He and his wife, Elizabeth, packed up and moved—lock, stock, and barrel. With the advent of computer and modem technology, Paul would continue to write for *AIO* long distance, while pursuing other interests as well.

While the rest of us were excited for Paul, we were also concerned at the potential breakup of the core team. Dave kept repeating over and over, "It'll never be the same . . . it'll never be the same"—and he was right. But despite the stress and distance, we ended up producing some of our best episodes in the next year.

Episode #100 "Ice Fishing"

Theme: Self-esteem; you are unique in God's eyes.
Scripture reference: Psalm 139:13-14
Written by Campbell Freed
Directed by Phil Lollar
Production engineer: Bob Luttrell
(Original air date: 1-20-90)

A famous frog once sang, "It's not easy bein' green." Nor is it easy living with a super-intelligent sister, as Monty Whittaker-Dowd knows. Jenny has done *everything* during her visit to Odyssey. She has played the violin in the Children's Orchestra, been in a church play, and built a model of a Southern Pacific Railroad passenger car—and she's done it all with excellence. Monty, on the other hand, can barely manage to keep himself out of trouble. Whit notices this, and when Tom Riley decides to take Eugene on an ice-fishing expedition to broaden his horizons, Whit decides to join them and take Monty, figuring the trip might do Monty some good as well.

The foursome heads off for the wilderness, though Eugene, much to Tom's frustration, manages to bring along many of the comforts of civilization. Meanwhile, Whit has a wonderful bonding time with Monty, convincing him that just because Jenny is special doesn't mean that Monty isn't special, too. In fact, Whit says, even though there are billions of people in the world, no two are exactly alike. God loves each one of us. All we have to be is who He's made us to be.

The trip is a success. Everyone ends up having a good time, and Monty and Tom learn that if there is anything about us that needs changing, we should let God do it.

STUDY QUESTIONS:

1. Monty said he was tired of being "Jenny's brother" and "Whit's grandson." Do you know how he feels? If so, how do you deal with those feelings?
2. Why did Tom want to change Eugene? Should Tom have tried?
3. Name five things you're good at.

Episode #101 "Scattered Seeds"

Theme: The parable of the sower.
Scripture reference: Matthew 13
Written by Campbell Freed
Directed by Phil Lollar
Production engineer: Dave Arnold
(Original air date: 1-27-90)

Connie is reading through some of Whit's short stories and wishes aloud that she could write like Whit. She feels that something interesting is always happening to Whit, while she is as boring as a glass of water. But Whit disagrees and reminds Connie of an incident that recently happened to her, which would make a great story.

Connie directed one of Whit's plays, "The Sower and the Seeds," based on the parable of the sower. Everyone around Whit's End had roles. At first, they each were excited about their parts, but soon the actors began to behave just like the "scattered seeds" in the parable.

Eugene was snatched from the play by his college computer club, just like the seed in the parable was snatched up by the birds. Monty was like the seeds sown among the rocks—enthusiastic in the beginning about his part, but when things got tough, he left. Jenny was worried about what other people would think of her if she didn't do a perfect job. She was so worried, in fact, that she choked—just like the seeds sown among the thorns. And Tom and Lucy were similar to the good seeds who stuck with it, worked hard, and produced a good crop—the play.

Connie realizes she has lived out a modern version of one of Jesus' parables, and she thanks Whit for pointing that out. Whit smiles and tells her that we're surrounded by parables in our daily lives—we just have to learn to look for them.

the *Adventures in* ODYSSEY archives:

"Ice Fishing" (the previous episode) and "Scattered Seeds" were scripts that Paul McCusker and I started and then swapped—each finishing the other's. Instead of using both our names for the credits, Paul and I used the pseudonym "Campbell Freed." The name came from our mothers—Agnes Campbell Lollar (my mother) and Nancy Freed (Paul's mother).

STUDY QUESTIONS:

1. Monty was excited about his part at first, but then his enthusiasm petered out. Has that ever happened to you? How so?
2. Jenny choked and couldn't do her part at all. Have you ever "choked" on something you were involved in? What did you do?
3. Eugene became so busy with other things, he couldn't do his part. Is there something important you're neglecting because you are too busy?

Episode #102
"The Treasure of Le Monde!"

Theme: Greed.
Scripture reference: Proverbs 28:25
Written and directed by Phil Lollar
Production engineer: Bob Luttrell
(Original air date: 2-03-90)

Exciting things are happening at Whit's End. Connie has discovered a new room, which is boarded up in the turret attic! She, Whit, and Robyn tear down the boards and explore the forgotten room. Amid all the dust and cobwebs, tarps are covering an old pipe organ. Whit guesses the organ is there because Whit's End was once a church. The main sanctuary burned down, but the tower stayed up, and the rest of the building was built around it.

Robyn decides to play the organ, but the middle "C" key isn't working. Whit examines the pipe and discovers something stuffed inside it—an old, gray rag with writing on it. Actually, it's a poem. It says, "I, Rufus Cowley, do hereby attest / The words you now read are the truest and best: / Your course is now set, the path you're now on, / To the greatest of riches—the Treasure Le Monde! / This prize you may find by heeding said adage: / Start in the middle and play 'a deaf cabbage.'"

Apparently, Whit, Robyn, and Connie have stumbled across a clue to a hidden treasure! But Whit believes the only way to be certain is to talk to one of Whit's friends, history professor Alduous Webster. Webster confirms that there really *is* a Le Monde treasure, named after a French nobleman, Henri Le Monde. He became a missionary to the region just before the French Revolution, taking his family fortune with him. Henri hid his treasure so fortune seekers would have to wade through a series of clues to find it.

Rufus Cowley, writer of the poem, was a fortune hunter who moved to Odyssey in the late 1850s. He learned about the treasure and, through a series of circumstances, ran afoul of the law and ended up in the steeple of the old church, where he planted the piece of cloth in the organ!

Robyn becomes consumed with the idea of finding the treasure and figures out the meaning of "a deaf cabbage." Our heroes then quickly put together the remaining pieces to the puzzle of the treasure of Le Monde and find themselves in a secret bat-filled cave.

But they are not alone—Professor Webster has greedily followed them to claim the treasure for himself. Surprisingly, though, the treasure is not what the world considers a treasure—money or riches—but is the greatest treasure of all: the Bible! Le Monde certainly had his priorities right.

STUDY QUESTIONS:

1. What does "Le Monde" mean?
2. Did Rufus Cowley get what he deserved? What about Professor Webster?
3. Why is greed so bad?

Episode #103
"Front Page News"

Theme: Escaping responsibility.
Scripture references: The book of Jonah; Acts 5:1-11
Written and directed by Paul McCusker
Production engineer: Dave Arnold
(Original air date: 2-10-90)

Curt and Oscar are running laps in gym class, and Curt is sick of it. So much so, he'll do anything to get out of it. When he and Oscar find out that Lucy is working on the *Odyssey Owl* school newspaper, which meets during gym class, Curt decides that he and Oscar will become ace reporters—despite the fact that neither one of them has any experience or writing talent.

Mrs. Medloff, publisher and editor of the *Owl*, is skeptical of the boys' sincerity but agrees to give them a chance. Their first assignment? To interview their former P. E. teacher, Coach Stubbs. Stubbs just won an award for catching kids who try to get out of gym class. Curt and Oscar do the interview. But after they talk to the coach, they discover that their tape recorder wasn't working—it didn't tape anything Mr. Stubbs said. So they make up the interview.

Unfortunately, Mrs. Medloff doesn't share their enthusiasm for fictional news stories. The boys quickly find themselves back out on the track running laps, having learned a valuable lesson about why it's wrong to lie to get out of work. Or at least, *Oscar* has learned a lesson. . . .

Adventures in the ODYSSEY archives:

"Front Page News" introduced the character of Curt, played by Fabio Stephens. Curt is a boy who will do almost anything to get out of work. But his schemes always get him into more trouble than if he had simply done what he was supposed to do.

STUDY QUESTIONS:

1. Oscar went along with Curt's idea even though it was wrong. Have you ever done that? What happened?
2. What is the best way to stand up for the right thing?
3. Have you ever experienced peer pressure? Have you ever been the one to pressure someone else?

Episodes #104 & 105
"Lincoln," Parts One & Two

Theme: History: Civil War; Abraham Lincoln
Scripture reference: Romans 13:1-5
Written and directed by Phil Lollar
Production engineers: Bob Luttrell and Dave Arnold
(Original air dates: 2-17-90 & 2-24-90)

Jimmy Barclay thinks history is one long snooze and that the Imagination Station isn't nearly as exciting as the Zappazoids video game. But when Whit programs the Station to take Jimmy back to 1865, he soon discovers how wrong he is.

There, he meets a tall, elderly gent who teaches him how to hunt squirrels with a sling. The gent, it turns out, is the 16th president of the United States, Abraham Lincoln. Jimmy experiences firsthand the last days of the Civil War, including the Battle of Richmond, General Lee's surrender to Grant at Appomattox, and the assassination of Honest Abe. Zappazoids better than the Imagination Station? History boring? Not anymore, according to Jimmy Barclay!

Yet another element of the Imagination Station was introduced in "Lincoln"—a remote control that allows you to "fast forward" through the adventure. It didn't appear again, though, until almost four years later in "A Time for Christmas." Lincoln was played by Ed Walker, the voice of Tom Riley and Bart Rathbone.

STUDY QUESTIONS:

1. Why did Jimmy think history is boring?
2. When did the Civil War end? Why was it fought?
3. Why did Whit think Lincoln was the greatest president the U.S. has ever had?

Episode #106 "By Any Other Name"

Theme: Calling things what they are.
Scripture reference: Proverbs 11:3
Written by Paul McCusker
Directed by Phil Lollar
Production engineer: Bob Luttrell
(Original air date: 3-03-90)

Bernard Walton has changed the name of his company. Instead of "Walton's Janitorial Service," he tells Whit to make out his weekly check for Bernard's services to "Walton's Hygienic Maintenance and Engineering Company." The company's new title has come courtesy of a fast-talking, big shot, Chicago marketing consultant named Phil Phillips. Phil is advising the town's businesses to change their names to something more fast-paced and upbeat, even though those names may have nothing to do with the business.

Meanwhile, Curt is up to a scheme of his own, trying to run for Odyssey Middle School's student council because—why else?—he thinks it's an easy grade. He enlists Lucy's aid as his campaign manager. Curt makes impossible promises to the students if they'll vote for him. Lucy tells Curt he can't lie like that, but Curt says no one expects him to really follow through on those promises.

Lucy resigns her post, much to Curt's dismay. He complains to Whit about it, and Whit tries to explain that Lucy is right. Words are meaningful, and giving something a flashy name doesn't change what it really is. As a real life example, Whit, in front of Curt, exposes Phil Phillips as a con man wanted by the Chicago police. Phil tries to skip out of town, but is caught by the local authorities, and Curt learns a valuable lesson—at least until the election. . . .

Adventures in the ODYSSEY archives:

"By Any Other Name" marked the debut of Bernard Walton. During our frequent brainstorming sessions, we would come up with ideas for potential new characters. One of those ideas was about an Eeyore type person who, deep down, has a good heart but continually mumbles about how disgusted he is with everything. Paul McCusker wrote Bernard into the story, and Dave Madden played the character perfectly.

STUDY QUESTIONS:

1. Is exaggerating the same as lying? Why or why not?
2. Why is it so important to follow through on your promises? What promises has Jesus given us?
3. Describe something that sounds fancy but is actually ordinary.

Episode #107 "Bad Luck"

Theme: Superstitions.
Scripture reference: Exodus 20:3
Written and directed by Paul McCusker
Production engineer: Dave Arnold
(Original air date: 3-10-90)

Robyn Jacobs is worried. She's received a chain letter telling her that if she breaks the chain, she'll have all sorts of bad luck. Her friend Jessie strongly advises Robyn to do what the letter says, but Robyn isn't convinced it has any magical power. She tears up the letter. Jessie is horrified, completely convinced that Robyn will be plagued with bad luck. Robyn scoffs—until she starts experiencing several small disasters.

First, she walks under Bernard Walton's ladder, and his bucket falls on her, soaking her to the skin. Then, while searching the medicine cabinet for an aspirin, Robyn slams the cabinet door, breaking the mirror. At lunch the next day, she knocks over a salt shaker, spilling its contents. Quadruple bad luck! Jessie is so concerned for her friend, she gives her own good luck charm to Robyn—a rabbit's foot. But it doesn't work, because Robyn ends up being late for an important meeting at the library. On the way, she tries rubbing the rabbit's foot, and she nearly hits a car with her bike and plows into a tree.

Jessie tells Robyn she has to get that letter back. Robyn is finally convinced. She races back to Whit's End, where she threw away the letter, and searches through the trash dump for it. Bernard Walton finds her there, and he and Officer Winger take her home. When Robyn's feeling better, her dad has a serious talk with her about the folly of believing in silly superstitions. In the end, Robyn learns why it's always better to trust in the Lord.

the *Adventures in* ODYSSEY archives:

This was the first—and only—time (thus far) Bernard's wife, Maude, appeared on *AIO*. Maude was played by our announcer, Chris Lansdowne.

STUDY QUESTIONS:

1. Did Robyn do the right thing when she tore up the letter? Why do you think she had such a bad day after she got rid of the chain letter?
2. Is it wrong to believe in luck? Explain your answer.
3. What does the Bible say about luck?

Episode #108 "Isaac the Courageous"

Theme: Courage.
Scripture references: Joshua 1:6-7,9; John 15:13
Written and directed by Phil Lollar
Production engineer: Bob Luttrell
(Original air date: 3-17-90)

Isaac Morton wants to prove that he's not a coward—so badly, in fact, that he's agreed to go through the terrible, painful initiation to get into Rodney Rathbone's gang, the Bones of Rath. The initiation includes things like climbing a rope to the top of the gym and being flicked on the arm with a large rubber band. Among the worst of these initiations is running through the Line of Bravery. In this test, two rows of guys with paddles line up facing each other. Isaac and the other candidates run between the lines, while everyone with a paddle takes a swipe at them.

Lucy convinces Isaac not to go through with such nonsense. As Isaac walks away, Rodney and the Bones brand Isaac to be a chicken. Isaac is distraught and goes to Whit's End for some encouragement. Whit tells him the story of Joshua and how God had to *continually* remind the hero of Jericho to be brave as he led the children of Israel into the Promised Land. Isaac is encouraged.

Walking home, he sees the Bones engaged in yet another part of their initiation: When Rodney throws a pinecone out on the frozen river, the candidates must go retrieve it. Rodney again razzes Isaac about being a chicken. But when little Peter takes his turn, the ice breaks, and he falls into the water. This time, it's Rodney who turns yellow, and Isaac who springs into action. He forms the kids into a human chain. With God's help, they edge out onto the river and rescue Peter. Isaac learns the meaning of *true* courage, the kids learn not to run out on the ice, and we learn that Rodney Rathbone is 16 and still in middle school.

the *Adventures in* ODYSSEY archives:

"Isaac the Courageous" introduced Rodney Rathbone and the Bones of Rath to *AIO*—the closest thing to a gang in Odyssey.

STUDY QUESTIONS:

1. If you saw someone fall through cracked ice like Peter did, what would you do? How could you best help him or her?
2. Who is the most courageous person you know? Why?
3. Why is courage important? Why should Christians have courage?

Episode #109
"Two Sides to Every Story"

Theme: Considering another person's point of view.
Scripture reference: Proverbs 20:23
Written and directed by Paul McCusker
Production engineer: Dave Arnold
(Original air date: 3-24-90)

George and Mary Barclay are on their way home from a well-deserved night on the town, thankful that the kids are finally old enough to stay home by themselves. But as they turn up their street, they see a fire truck parked in front of their house! George and Mary race home, where the fire captain calms them. He says the kids just experienced a small electrical fire when they dumped water on their malfunctioning television set.

After the firemen leave, George and Mary attempt to find out from Jimmy and Donna *exactly* what happened. But both kids keep talking at the same time, so George and Mary decide to split up the kids and get their individual stories. George takes Jimmy, and Mary takes Donna. Each couple retreats to separate rooms to get the scoop.

When Donna tells her side, she blames Jimmy for the whole thing, while painting herself as a long-suffering saint. Jimmy does the same—Donna acted like a mean old witch to Jimmy, the handsome, young (and innocent) prince.

George and Mary find it hard to believe either one of them. They piece together what *really* happened and, not surprisingly, both kids were at fault. George and Mary decide on appropriate punishments for Jimmy and Donna, and the Barclay family illustrates that there are always two sides to every story.

the *Adventures in* ODYSSEY archives:

The inspiration for "Two Sides to Every Story" came from the movie *Rashomon,* a classic by Japanese director Akira Kurosawa. In that movie, four people involved in a crime tell varying accounts of what happened.

This episode also generated mail from firefighters who said we must inform our listeners to *never* put out an electrical fire with water, like Jimmy and Donna did. So we re-recorded Chris Lansdowne saying this in her wrap-up.

STUDY QUESTIONS:

1. Who lied in this story? Explain your answer.
2. Do you think that Jimmy and Donna meant to lie? Why or why not?
3. Why is it important to try and see both sides to every story? Do you think that's how God looks at things? Give a biblical example.

Episode #110 "A...Is for Attitude"

Theme: Positive thinking; trusting in God.
Scripture reference: Proverbs 3:5
Written and directed by Phil Lollar
Production engineer: Bob Luttrell
(Original air date: 4-14-90)

Connie has had it with studying. She turns on the television for background noise and hears positive-thinking expert Dr. Vincent Van Schpeele on the Opera Geraldohue show. Dr. Van Schpeele is promoting his new book, *Happiness Is a State, but You Can't Get There from Here.* In his book, he theorizes that performance is directly tied to attitude—good attitude results in good performance, and bad attitude results in bad performance.

Connie falls for this philosophy hook, line, and sinker. She immediately applies it to her life—starting with her geography test. She also begins spreading the gospel of positive thinking, convincing her friend Cheryl that she should try out for the school glee club—even though she's never sung before. Connie also tells Jimmy and Ben to let attitude win their next basketball game and encourages Peter to conquer his fear of heights by crossing the train trestle at Miller's Ravine.

Needless to say, none of this works: Cheryl makes a fool of herself, Jimmy and Ben get creamed, and Peter ends up frozen with fear at the top of the trestle. Whit and Connie race off to rescue Peter, which Whit does just before a train runs them down! And Connie winds up with a "D" on her geography test. She has learned that it's foolish to rely on positive thinking rather than on the Lord.

the *Adventures in* ODYSSEY archives:

"A . . . Is for Attitude" was another episode partly inspired by a movie. The train trestle climax was a tribute to Rob Reiner's movie *Stand by Me.*

STUDY QUESTIONS:

1. Why did Connie think Dr. Van Schpeele's book would help her?
2. Is there anything wrong with positive thinking? When does positive thinking present problems?
3. Why should you never, *ever* walk across a train trestle—or even on train tracks, for that matter?

Episode #111 "First Love"

Theme: Being unequally yoked.
Scripture reference: 2 Corinthians 6:14
Recommended maturity level: 10 and up
Written and directed by Paul McCusker
Production engineer: Dave Arnold
(Original air date: 4-21-90)

PARENTAL WARNING: This story is about whether it's right or wrong to date a non-Christian. Although handled delicately, the subject matter may be too mature for younger listeners.

Connie goes to a baseball game with her friend Cheryl. Afterward, Connie meets one of the team's star players, Jeff Lewis. The two of them hit it off famously and begin seeing more and more of each other. Soon, Connie has fallen in love.

Jeff is not a Christian, though. At first, Connie falls into the trap of believing that she's doing Jeff a favor by staying with him so she can win him to the Lord. Before long, she begins skipping Bible studies, then church services, just so she can be with Jeff. And he is no closer to Jesus than when they first met.

At last, Cheryl, and then Whit, confronts Connie with the danger of her actions. Connie realizes she must break off her relationship with Jeff. She goes through with the painful task and matures even more in her walk with Jesus.

behind the scenes:

"Though this episode deals with a 'teen' issue, it wasn't really written for them. I remember thinking—and still believe—that we should give our audience 'prescriptive' ideas before those issues become problems. The idea that kids shouldn't date non-believers had been instilled in me long before I thought much about dating, which made a big difference in my dating practices. In the few episodes we've done 'for teens,' we actually just wanted to plant the seed of the idea before the kids get to the age where it might be too late to influence them."

—Paul McCusker

STUDY QUESTIONS:

1. Why is it wrong for Christians to date non-Christians?
2. What excuses did Connie give for dating Jeff? What would you say to a friend who was acting like Connie?
3. Whit told Connie she was in the middle of a "tug-of-war" between Jeff and God. What did Whit mean by that?

Episode #112 "Curious, Isn't It?"

Theme: Minding our own business.
Scripture reference: 1 Thessalonians 4:11
Written and directed by Phil Lollar
Production engineer: Bob Luttrell
(Original air date: 4-28-90)

Ben is showing Esther a "shortcut" to Whit's End, which passes by a cemetery. As they pass it, they look over the rows of tombstones and see a familiar face: Whit's. He's talking to a lady that neither Ben nor Esther recognize. Esther is curious and moves closer to hear what they're saying. Whit is asking the lady, Emma, for an answer. She says, "Yes." Then Whit takes out a ring and gives it to Emma! They both walk off happily.

Esther is stunned. She quickly assumes Whit is getting married. But Ben warns her not to jump to conclusions. To get more proof, they follow Whit. They discover that he's bought a huge amount of flowers for Emma, and that he's ordered alterations on his tuxedo. That's enough to convince Ben. But when he later tells Connie, Eugene, and Bernard about it, they say they need more proof.

Later, Whit walks downstairs, dressed to the hilt. Whit says he'll be gone a couple of hours and that he's bringing back someone special for them to meet. After that, there's no doubt left in anyone's mind. Whit leaves, and everyone instantly springs into action. In a whirlwind of activity, they plan and pull together a party for the newlyweds. The whole town turns out for it—and Dale Jacobs even writes a front-page story about it for the *Odyssey Times.*

When Whit and Emma walk in, everyone yells "Surprise!" George Barclay presents them with their wedding present: a trip to the Bahamas. Whit and Emma are flattered and flabbergasted . . . but not married. Esther put together a series of circumstances and arrived at the wrong conclusion. The town is humiliated, but Whit graciously allows the party to continue. Esther learns not to let her curiosity take over her common sense—until she spies Eugene talking to a girl. . . .

STUDY QUESTIONS:

1. Esther drew the wrong conclusion about Whit. But even if she had been correct, why was it wrong for her to spread the news?
2. What should Connie, Eugene, and Bernard have done when they saw Whit in his tuxedo?
3. How do you decide if something is gossip? How can you avoid making assumptions about other people's business?

Episode #113 "Suspicious Minds"

Theme: Trusting each other; not jumping to conclusions.
Scripture reference: Isaiah 30:15
Written by Paul McCusker
Directed by Phil Lollar
Production engineer: Dave Arnold
(Original air date: 5-05-90)

It's closing time at Whit's End, and Whit is totaling the receipts for the day. Eugene and Connie make small talk. Connie mentions she needs $100 to buy a used car, while Eugene needs the same amount to purchase a new personal computer. But when $60 winds up missing from the register that day and another $40 disappears the next, Connie and Eugene end up suspecting one another. Eugene sets out to catch and "reform" Connie, while Connie decides to replace the money from her own bank account to keep Eugene from getting into trouble.

The whole thing comes to a head when Eugene actually booby-traps the cash register (a ploy which backfires on him), and Whit solves the mystery of the missing money. It was stuck in the back of the register drawer the whole time. Whit scolds his employees for their lack of trust in each other. Connie and Eugene promise to try to do better—a promise they keep for about 30 seconds.

the *Adventures in* ODYSSEY archives:

"Suspicious Minds" showed a quirky side of Bernard—he got a real kick out of Eugene and Connie's silliness. Dave Madden, who played Bernard, ad-libbed the continual chuckle through the last scene.

STUDY QUESTIONS:

1. Did Connie and Eugene have good reason to suspect one another of taking the money? Explain your answer.
2. Is it wrong to be suspicious of people? Why or why not?
3. What's the best way to keep your suspicions in check?

Episode #114 "The Big Broadcast"

Theme: The parable of the good Samaritan; creativity.
Scripture reference: Luke 10:25-37
Written and directed by Paul McCusker
Production engineer: Bob Luttrell
(Original air date: 6-09-90)

Tom and Whit move an old desk into one of the rooms at Whit's End. In that room, covered with tarps, sits Kid's Radio, gathering dust. No one has used it since Brad and Sherman launched the station. Tom says it's a waste to let the equipment sit unused. He suggests that he and Whit put on their own radio show, airing the classics of radio's golden age. Whit agrees, and the result is "Odyssey's Big Broadcast"!

First, they run the ever-popular game show "Fact or Fiction," in which Lucy and Jimmy compete head-to-head to answer the brain-teasing question: "Is it *fact,* or is it *fiction*?" Then, Eugene brings us the "Odyssey Sports Round-Up," in which he interviews Coach Fred Zachary.

After a few more twists and curves, we arrive at the centerpiece of the production, "Odyssey Theatre of the Air's" presentation of "Sam Maritan, Private Eye." Sam comes across "The Mystery on the Road to Jericho," in which he finds a man beaten and left for dead. Sam questions a Jewish priest and a Levite who saw the man but passed him on the road. After talking with them, Sam solves the attack, concluding that it was done by robbers.The Big Broadcast is fun, humorous, and a smashing success. It looks like Kid's Radio is back in business.

the *Adventures in* ODYSSEY archives:

Here's where we heard Lucy's *other* last name, Schultz, for the first time. "The Big Broadcast" was also the debut of composer James Gabriel to the show. James is well known for his compositions and arrangements—they appear on many of the "Praise" albums under the name James Stipeck.

STUDY QUESTIONS:

1. Why is creativity important?
2. What is the point of the parable of the good Samaritan?
3. Would you help someone you disliked? Why or why not? How can you learn to love your enemy?

Episode #115 "An Act of Mercy"

Theme: The parable of the unmerciful servant.
Scripture reference: Matthew 18:21-35
Written and directed by Paul McCusker
Production engineer: Dave Arnold
(Original air date: 6-16-90)

This episode is a remake of "The Quality of Mercy," *AIO* episode #23, which retells the parable of the unmerciful servant.

the Adventures in Odyssey archives:

Although he didn't yet have a name, we were briefly introduced to Rodney's father, Bart, in "An Act of Mercy."

STUDY QUESTIONS:

1. What does it mean to forgive someone?
2. How many times does Jesus say to forgive your neighbor?
3. Describe a time you have shown, or failed to show, someone mercy.

Episode #116 "Isaac the Benevolent"

Theme: The Golden Rule.
Scripture references: Matthew 7:12; Luke 6:31
Written and directed by Phil Lollar
Production engineer: Dave Arnold
(Original air date: 6-23-90)

"Isaac the Benevolent" was a remake of "Doing Unto Others," *OUSA* episode #9. Isaac Morton replaces Johnny Bickle (who was played by David Griffin, who later became Jimmy Barclay), Lucy Cunningham-Schultz replaces Linda (who was played by Sage Bolte, who later became Robyn Jacobs), and Eugene replaces Officer David Harley (who was played by Will Ryan, who later became Eugene). Whit is still Whit, and Connie is still Connie.

STUDY QUESTIONS:

1. What was wrong with the way Isaac thought we should "do unto others"?
2. Why is the Golden Rule important?
3. How can you apply the Golden Rule to your life?

Episode #117 "The Trouble with Girls"

Theme: Crushes; puppy love.
Scripture reference: 1 Corinthians 13
Written and directed by Paul McCusker
Production engineer: Bob Luttrell
(Original air date: 6-30-90)

"The Trouble with Girls" was a remake of "Bobby's Valentine," *OUSA* episode #13. Jimmy Barclay replaces Bobby (both played by David Griffin), Jessie replaces Amy, and Eugene again replaces Officer Harley.

STUDY QUESTIONS:

1. Why is it a bad idea to "play games" with someone's emotions?
2. What's the difference between acting friendly and being a pest?
3. List some ways that you can best deal with people who make you uncomfortable.

Episode #118 "What Happened to the Silver Streak?"

Theme: Forgiveness; unconditional love.
Scripture references: Matthew 18:21-35; 1 Corinthians 13:7
Written and directed by Phil Lollar
Production engineer: Bob Luttrell
(Original air date: 7-07-90)

"What Happened to the Silver Streak" was a remake of "The Case of the Missing Train Car," *OUSA* episode #21. Traci Needlemeyer replaces Warren, and (in a twist) Curt replaces Officer Harley.

the Adventures in Odyssey archives:

One of the most striking changes between versions one and two came near the end of the program. In the original version, just before Michelle leaves, Whit said, "I forgive you," and Michelle scoffed. In the second version, Whit asked Michelle, "Hasn't your time [at Whit's End] meant anything to you?" Michelle answered, "It's been one big bore"—a much stronger ending.

STUDY QUESTIONS:

1. Should Traci have accused Michelle? Should Whit and Tom have defended her? Why or why not?
2. Connie said Michelle was "just no good." Do you believe that? Does God believe someone is no good? Explain your answers.
3. Read Matthew 18:21-35. Why do you think Jesus wants us to forgive each other so often?

Episode #119 "Better Late than Never"

Theme: Lateness.
Scripture reference: Matthew 25:1-13
Written and directed by Paul McCusker
Production engineer: Bob Luttrell
(Original air date: 7-14-90)

"Better Late than Never" was a remake of "Missed It by That Much," *OUSA* episode #14. The cast is a virtual repeat of the original, except Robyn Jacobs replaces Rachel Weaver, and Officer Harley has been eliminated.

STUDY QUESTIONS:

1. Why is it so rude to be late?
2. What could Robyn have done to break her bad habit of always being tardy?
3. Read Matthew 25:1-13. How does Jesus feel about tardiness?

Episode #120

"Pranks for the Memories"

Theme: Pranks.
Scripture reference: Philippians 2:3-4
Written and directed by Phil Lollar
Production engineer: Dave Arnold
(Original air date: 7-21-90)

Only part of this episode is a remake of "Gotcha!" *AIO* episode #24. This time, Curt is pulling the pranks. Whit warns him about the problem with prank-pulling: You always have to be on the lookout for someone pulling a prank on you. Curt leaves, paranoid. But the situation worsens when Lucy decides to throw a surprise birthday party for Curt out at Tom Riley's farm.

The combination of Curt's paranoia and Lucy's trying to get him to the farm without revealing the surprise leads to all sorts of merriment—especially when Curt rushes out to the Riley barn and sets a trap for Lucy. Unfortunately, the trap he's set requires physical endurance on his part. Before long, his strength gives out. Curt's trap backfires on him, and he is humiliated. Whit, as usual, was right about pulling pranks—the only person Curt should have been on the lookout for . . . was himself.

STUDY QUESTIONS:

1. Is it wrong to pull practical jokes? Why or why not?
2. Did Curt take his joking too far with Lucy? Did he learn a lesson? Explain.
3. What are some "practical jokes" Satan likes to pull on us? How can we avoid them?

Episode #121 "Missing Person"

Theme: You can't run away from your problems.
Scripture reference: Luke 15:11-32
Written and directed by Paul McCusker
Production engineer: Dave Arnold
(Original air date: 7-28-90)

"Missing Person" was a remake of "Harley Takes the Case," Parts One and Two, *AIO* episodes #25 and #26. Now, it's one episode, Rodney Rathbone is the runaway, Isaac and Lucy find him, and no one is threatened by wild dogs.

STUDY QUESTIONS:

1. Why did Rodney run away?
2. The Bible tells us to honor our parents. Why was it dishonoring to Rodney's parents when he ran away?
3. How could you help a friend who is determined to run away?

Episodes #122 & 123

"Castles & Cauldrons," Parts One & Two

Theme: The dangers of fantasy role-playing games; Satan worship; the occult.
Scripture reference: Deuteronomy 18:10b-12a
Recommended maturity level: 10 and up
Written and directed by Paul McCusker
Production engineers: Bob Luttrell and Dave Arnold
(Original air dates: 8-04-90 & 8-11-90)

PARENTAL WARNING: This is a story about fantasy role-playing games and how they can lure their participants into satanic activity. It is very intense in spots and not meant for listeners under 10 years of age. Parents should listen along with their older children.

The Barclays have a visitor for the summer: Len, George's nephew. Jimmy is excited to have his cousin stay with them, especially when Len shows Jimmy a new game called Castles & Cauldrons—it's even better than Zappazoids.

Castles & Cauldrons (C & C) is a fantasy role-playing game. The players become medieval characters who use battle skills and other means to conquer their enemies. Len is "Luthor the Magician," and he names Jimmy "Jondel the Apprentice." Jimmy thinks the game is harmless—until Len takes it a step further, and imagination starts becoming reality.

Plastic swords ring with the sound of steel; epic battles are fought against the forces of darkness and won. Jimmy is amazed by these things, but Len wants him to go further still, into incantations, spells, and conjuring—which sounds suspiciously like black magic. What's worse, Len swears Jimmy to silence. He's not to tell anybody about the game, especially his parents or Whit, because "they won't understand."

But Whit already suspects something is wrong. One night, Donna's doll is mysteriously ripped apart, and she blames Jimmy and Len. Whit questions her about the boys' activities. Then George tells Jimmy that Len didn't come to Odyssey just to visit them. His parents thought it would be healthy for Len to get away from a "questionable group of friends."

That night, Jimmy and Len go camping out in the forest. Len decides to include Jimmy in the ultimate C & C initiation: a ritual to summon Shalman, the most powerful magician of all. Len starts the ritual. Jimmy resists, but Len gets so caught up in it, he begins forcing Jimmy to participate. Just before things get ugly, Whit and George show up to put a stop to the ritual—and to Castles & Cauldrons. Whit destroys the game. Len gets some professional help. The Barclay family retuns back to normal, and everyone realizes that even Odyssey isn't immune from Satan's wiles.

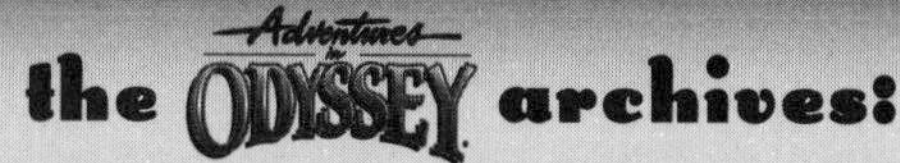

the Odyssey archives:

"Castles & Cauldrons" was the first episode in which Dr. Dobson came on the air with a personal warning.

STUDY QUESTIONS:

1. Are all role-playing games bad? Why is it a bad idea to play games like Castles & Cauldrons?
2. What should Jimmy have done when Len stopped Jimmy from telling his dad and Whit about the game?
3. Why do you think Whit "felt" something was wrong in Odyssey?

Episode #124 "The Winning Edge"

Theme: Competitiveness.
Scripture reference: Romans 15:2
Written and directed by Phil Lollar
Production engineer: Dave Arnold
(Original air date: 8-18-90)

Summertime in Odyssey means softball, and this summer is no exception. Robyn Jacobs is on the Coyotes, coached by Tom Riley. Traci Needlemeyer, however, is on the Stingrays, the biggest losers in their division. She isn't happy about it at all, until she meets their new coach, Bart Rathbone. He immediately gives Traci a pep talk and bolsters her self-confidence, doing the same for the rest of the team. Bart whips them into shape and makes them better players. But he also tells the team that winning is everything—and should be attained at any cost.

Traci isn't sure about this philosophy. But when the Stingrays begin rising in the ranks, Traci starts believing that winning is all that matters. And when the team clinches the Western Division title, Traci is a full-fledged convert. The Stingrays will meet the Eastern Division champions, the Coyotes, in the playoffs.

Bart sends Traci to the Coyotes' victory celebration at Whit's End to rattle Robyn. Traci does this by dumping a malt all over her.

Whit recognizes the symptoms of a deeper problem and talks to Bart about easing up on his win-at-all-costs message. But Whit's plea falls on deaf ears. The Stingrays find themselves in trouble in the championship game because of Robyn's powerhouse hitting. Over Traci's objections, Bart orders one of his players to "take [Robyn] out of the game." Zelda, one of the Stingrays, slides into Robyn, injuring her.

The Stingrays end up winning, but Traci is horrified and cannot enjoy the victory. She visits Robyn at the doctor's office and is relieved to learn that Robyn has suffered no permanent damage. Traci begs for her forgiveness, which Robyn grants. Everyone learns a valuable lesson about not letting their competitive spirit get out of hand.

STUDY QUESTIONS:

1. Is it wrong to be competitive? Why or why not?
2. Why was it so easy for Traci to give in to Bart's win-at-all-costs philosophy?
3. Is winning at all costs *always* wrong? Can you think of some instances where it might be okay? If so, explain.

ULTIMATE ADVENTURES IN ODYSSEY *TRIVIA*

Obscure Facts for Only the Most Devoted Fans

THE TOWN OF ODYSSEY

A Nativity scene has been set up on City Hall property in the middle of Odyssey since 1948.

In the state where Odyssey is located, it is against the law to ride a bicycle without a helmet.

If traveling by train, it is a day's journey from Chicago to Odyssey.

President Eisenhower once came through the town, as did President Teddy Roosevelt on a "Whistle Stop" train tour.

Before it was owned by Edwin Blackgaard, the Harlequin Theatre was owned by a Mr. Flynn, who moved to Florida.

Number of computer stores in Odyssey: 10 (according to Eugene Meltsner, who should definitely know).

Trickle Lake is the only place in Odyssey for boating. The town of Odyssey is only a few miles from the state line.

Episode #125
"All's Well with Boswell"

Theme: Responsibility.
Scripture reference: Luke 16:10-12
Written and directed by Phil Lollar
Production engineer: Bob Luttrell
(Original air date: 8-25-90)

Robyn Jacobs has gotten her first baby-sitting job—only, instead of a baby, she's sitting with Mrs. Fishbine's *cat*. Boswell is a huge feline, and Mrs. Fishbine thinks the world of him. However, she is a stern parent: Robyn must make certain that Boswell eats three solid meals during the day. Boswell also can't go outside (because he's recovering from a cold), and he must stay off the furniture. Robyn agrees to make Boswell behave, and Mrs. Fishbine leaves.

Almost immediately, the trouble starts. As Robyn prepares Boswell's breakfast in the kitchen, Boswell knocks over and breaks a small glass ballerina in the living room. Robyn realizes that she can replace the figurine with a duplicate from Greenblatt's department store. She phones Jessie and tells her to pick up the figurine and bring it to Mrs. Fishbine's house.

Jessie does, and that's when the trouble really begins. Thanks to a series of circumstances, Boswell ends up outside, Robyn and Jessie chase after him, and they all end up in a locked furniture van on its way to Connellsville!

Eventually, Robyn and Jessie get out of the van in Connellsville and see Tom Riley, who is delivering a load of apples. They sneak into the back of his truck and make it back to Odyssey and Mrs. Fishbine's house just in the nick of time. But Boswell gets in the last word as he knocks the *new* glass ballerina from the mantle. Mrs. Fishbine reprimands her cat for breaking it *again*. We can guess that Robyn will never cat-sit again.

behind the scenes:

"I actually dumped a complete bag of cat food all over my kitchen floor just to get the right sound effect. I also stayed locked up in my home studio for hours with a neighborhood cat, trying to get just the right 'meows' for Boswell. By the way, I don't recommend this to *anyone*."

—Bob Luttrell

STUDY QUESTIONS:

1. Do you think Robyn's problems with Boswell were due to lack of responsibility or to bad circumstances? Explain.
2. How could Robyn have better handled the catastrophes of her day?
3. Should Robyn have told Mrs. Fishbine everything that happened? Would you? Why or why not?

Episode #126 "Wishful Thinking"

Theme: Dealing with a pesky sibling.
Scripture references: Genesis 4; 27; 37:18-35; 1 John 2:10-11
Written and directed by Paul McCusker
Production engineer: Dave Arnold
(Original air date: 9-01-90)

Donna Barclay has had it with her little brother. Jimmy is becoming more annoying with each passing day. Every morning, he wakes her up by bouncing on her bed and telling her a corny riddle. He's always either telling dumb jokes, teasing Donna, getting her into trouble, or taking all her stuff. According to Donna, Jimmy's nothing but a big pain. Donna confesses to both her mother and Lucy that she wishes Jimmy had never been born. Mom then reminds Donna of what her great-grandmother always said: "Never make wishes—they might come true." But that would be okay with Donna. She goes to bed that night feeling her life would be better if she were an only child.

When she awakens the next morning, Donna realizes her wish has come true. Not only is Jimmy gone, but no one has ever even *heard* of him. At first, Donna thinks it's great. Then the reality of the situation hits her. She has to do extra chores, and her folks take great pains not to spoil her like she thought they would. But worst of all, she finds she truly misses Jimmy. Donna misses Jimmy's loudness and the way he tells dumb jokes. She even misses Jimmy's annoying habits and the way he chases her around in the rain. She's lonely, and she wishes that Jimmy would come back.

Then Donna awakens, realizing it was all a dream. Jimmy is standing right in front of her! Donna is ecstatic and immediately apologizes to Jimmy for being so mean to him. A bewildered Jimmy accepts her apology, and they both get back to the business of being brother and sister again.

the Adventures in ODYSSEY archives:

In keeping with the Barclay's history, "Wishful Thinking" is a twist on the plot of "It's a Wonderful Life." The episode plays off the movie's theme that we all touch each other in unimaginable ways, so we should treasure our lives as God has made them. He knows best.

STUDY QUESTIONS:

1. How could Donna have best handled her frustrations with Jimmy?
2. If you have a brother or sister, what do you think life would be like without them? If you are an only child, do you ever wish for a sibling? Why or why not?
3. Name five ways you can show your brother or sister that you love them.

Episode #127 "Have You No Selpurcs?"

Theme: Scruples.
Scripture references: Proverbs 14:8-9,15-16
Written and directed by Phil Lollar
Production engineer: Bob Luttrell
(Original air date: 9-08-90)

Lucy and Curt are waiting for Lucy's mom to pick them up from Whit's End. While they wait, Connie gives them a test she's come across in a magazine that measures your "HQ"—Honesty Quotient. Whit walks up just as they finish. To no one's surprise, Curt fails miserably. Lucy, on the other hand, scores a perfect 100 percent. She rubs Curt's nose in it a little bit, then the two of them leave as Lucy's mom pulls up.

Whit is intrigued by the test. He's not only dismayed that Curt scored so poorly, Whit's also upset that Lucy enjoyed pointing it out to everyone. So John Avery decides to come up with a game for Lucy and Curt based on the test. The game is called "Selpurcs." All Curt and Lucy have to do is follow the instructions contained inside a series of envelopes scattered around Odyssey. If they adhere to the directions, and if they figure out what "selpurcs" means, they are promised a fabulous surprise at the end of the game.

Curt and Lucy agree. Instantly, they are faced with a series of moral dilemmas involving Connie and a mail-order scarf, a quart of orange juice, Lucy's neighbor's newspaper, and a movie called *My Little Unicorn.* At each turn—and in typical fashion—Curt makes the wrong choice or helps others to make the wrong choice. By the end of the game, things are a mess. But the two have learned some things. Curt realizes that the disastrous results are due to the lousy choices he's made. Lucy is reprimanded for her prideful attitude—and both of them have figured out what "selpurcs" means. Have you?

STUDY QUESTIONS:

1. What should Lucy have done when Curt made the wrong decisions?
2. Why did Lucy need to learn a lesson?
3. Have you ever faced any dilemmas like the ones Curt and Lucy faced? If so, what did you do?

Episode #128 "One Bad Apple"

Theme: Taking care of the environment.
Scripture references: Genesis 1; 2:15
Written and directed by Paul McCusker
Production engineer: Bob Luttrell
(Original air date: 9-15-90)

Something unthinkable is happening at Whit's End. Kids are getting sick from food served there. Whit can't imagine what the cause might be, until he and Connie figure out it was a batch of apples Whit bought from Tom Riley.

Tom is having illness problems of his own, though. He thought one of his horses was down with colic, but instead it turns out to be a mild form of insecticide poisoning. When Curt informs Tom that his creek is filled with dead fish, Tom decides to launch a full-scale investigation.

He and Curt do some exploring upstream. They come across an empty barrel from Edgebiter Chemical Company lying in the middle of the creek. Further up, they discover the industrial complex that houses the Edgebiter offices. They try to get some information but end up getting the runaround. So Whit joins the investigation.

That night, the three of them examine the industrial complex more closely and discover a warehouse with an illegal drainage system that dumps into the creek. But their discovery does them little good—right then, an Edgebiter security guard catches them and takes them inside the offices. There, they confront Mr. Edgebiter himself.

Mr. Edgebiter admits that the warehouse has been illegally draining an accidental chemical spill into the creek. But he also points out that Whit, Tom, Curt, and the rest of America are quick to accuse big businesses of polluting the environment, but they hardly live up to their own responsibilities to keep the world clean. None of them recycles or conserves. They simply use things and throw them away. It is a point well taken. Both sides agree to try in the future to take better care of this planet God has loaned to us.

the *Adventures in* ODYSSEY archives:

Curt's part was originally written for Bernard Walton, but Dave Madden wasn't available, so the part was rewritten for Curt. That's why many of the lines still sounded like they should be coming from Bernard's mouth. We did learn something about Curt's family here, though: His dad's name is Frank, and he works in a factory.

STUDY QUESTIONS:

1. Were Whit, Tom, and Curt wrong to walk around Edgebiter after hours? Explain your answer.
2. Do you and your family recycle? Why or why not?
3. Why is it important to take care of our environment? Besides recycling, what else can you do to help?

Episode #129 "Not One of Us"

Theme: Bigotry.
Scripture references: Acts 17:26; Romans 3:29; 1 Corinthians 12:13;
Written and directed by Paul McCusker
Production engineer: Dave Arnold
(Original air date: 9-22-90)

Extra! Extra! Councilman Philip Glossman resigns in disgrace! He makes a racial slur against the Japanese!

Due to the excitement, Mrs. Medloff, editor of the *Odyssey Owl*, thinks bigotry is an excellent article for Lucy to tackle. She wants young Miss Cunningham-Schultz to explore the other ways prejudice shows up in Odyssey. Lucy reluctantly complies and interviews everyone she knows to find out if they've ever experienced discrimination. She writes a model article, which briefly and clearly presents a wide variety of opinions. But it also completely lacks heart.

Mrs. Medloff asks Lucy to try again—and this time to come at it from a more personal angle. So, at Bart Rathbone's suggestion, Lucy and Connie visit a small town called Sloughburgh, where the people supposedly know a lot about prejudice. But when they get there, they discover that the folks of Sloughburgh haven't been the objects of discrimination. These folks are the discriminators. They are prejudiced against people they call "sitters"—city folks.

Connie and Lucy are treated badly. The girls actually end up in jail, just because the Sloughburghians don't like them. They finally get bailed out by Bart Rathbone (whom the Sloughburghians like, for some mysterious reason). Now Lucy has more than enough information—and firsthand experience—for her article. Even Odyssey is not immune to the evils of bigotry.

behind the scenes:

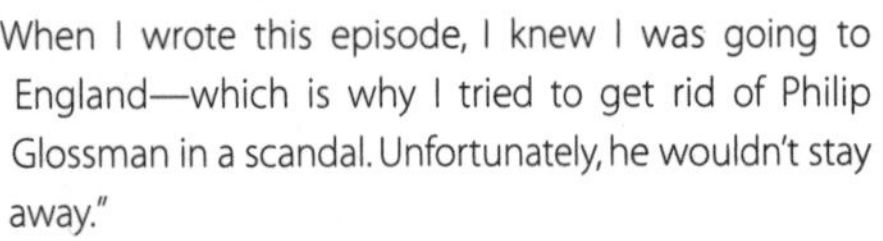

"When I wrote this episode, I knew I was going to England—which is why I tried to get rid of Philip Glossman in a scandal. Unfortunately, he wouldn't stay away."

—Paul McCusker (the voice of Glossman)

STUDY QUESTIONS:

1. What is prejudice?
2. Have you ever been discriminated against? Have you ever discriminated against anyone? What were the reasons?
3. How do you think God feels about discrimination? How did Jesus treat people who were different?

Episodes #130 & 131 "Bernard and Joseph," Parts One & Two

Theme: Biblical history: Joseph; God's sovereignty.
Scripture references: Genesis 37; 39-46:7
Written and directed by Phil Lollar
Production engineers: Dave Arnold and Bob Luttrell
(Original air dates: 10-27-90 & 10-30-90)

Artie Powell is not happy about coming from a large family. Having six kids around, he always feels he's merely one of the bunch. Artie loves his siblings, but sometimes they can be a real pain!

Then Bernard tells Artie a story about Joseph, a young man who had *11* brothers. Hearing about Joseph makes Artie realize that the trouble that he has with his brothers is nothing compared with the way Joseph's brothers treated him. Artie rethinks his ill feelings about his family, and Whit's End finds a new premier storyteller: Bernard Walton.

the Adventures in ODYSSEY archives:

"Bernard and Joseph" was the first of several stories narrated by Bernard. Also, the popular Christian comedy team Custer & Hoose provided several of the vocal characterizations in these two programs.

STUDY QUESTIONS:

1. Why did God bless Joseph so abundantly?
2. Name some ways Joseph pleased God.
3. How would you have treated your siblings if you had been in Joseph's position? Why was Joseph able to be so kind to them?

Episode #132 "Thanksgiving at Home"

Theme: Thanksgiving; being thankful.
Scripture reference: 1 Chronicles 16:8
Written and directed by Paul McCusker
Production engineer: Bob Luttrell
(Original air date: 11-17-90)

Another Thanksgiving Day has rolled around. Jimmy Barclay is looking forward to the smell of roasting turkey, a crackling fire in the fireplace, and that warm, cozy feeling of watching bowl games on TV. The only problem is, none of that is happening. George and Mary were visited by an unwelcome guest during the night—the flu bug. They are both so sick that if Jimmy and Donna want Thanksgiving this year, they'll have to provide it for themselves.

So Jimmy and Donna attempt to cook, with disastrous results. Donna tries to bake a frozen turkey. Jimmy struggles to whip whole, unpeeled potatoes. Donna makes stuffing out of torn-up pieces of white bread. Jimmy tries to light a fire in the fireplace without opening the flue. Once they've made a mess out of the dinner and the house, Jimmy and Donna decide to put on a play for their ailing parents—the story of the first Thanksgiving.

Finally, the Barclays all end up on George and Mary's bed, eating pizza and chicken soup. Jimmy reveals that he's learned the true meaning of the holiday—it's not *how* you celebrate it, it's *why* you celebrate it. And Donna has discovered she is most thankful for her mom and dad.

STUDY QUESTIONS:

1. Why was it dangerous for Jimmy to try lighting a fire?
2. When was the first Thanksgiving celebrated? When did Thanksgiving become an official holiday?
3. Describe a special Thanksgiving memory.

Episode #133 "Cousin Albert"

Theme: Illiteracy.
Scripture reference: Proverbs 23:12
Written and directed by Phil Lollar
Production engineer: Bob Luttrell
(Original air date: 11-24-90)

Lucy's latest interview for the *Odyssey Owl* is her own cousin—Albert Schultz, Odyssey High's star basketball player. The only problem is, he doesn't give a good interview. All he tells her is that he loves basketball, and he works as a stocker at Jenkin's Market. So, to get more information, Lucy decides to do a little investigating on her cousin.

Lucy shows up unexpectedly at Albert's job and witnesses him in the middle of what looks like a drug transaction. Albert promises her that the package he's just purchased is not drugs. It's a school report. Lucy is confused—why would Albert spend money on a school report? She presses Albert for an answer, and finally he admits a deep, dark secret: He can't read. He's completely illiterate.

Stunned, Lucy asks how this is possible. Albert explains that school has never been easy for him. What has made it tougher is that his family moves around a lot. He has never been with one teacher long enough to learn reading skills. But Albert doesn't mind. All he's ever wanted to do is play basketball, anyway. His plan is to graduate, then try out for the NBA.

Lucy tells Whit about Albert's illiteracy. She and Whit set up a plan to help teach Albert that reading skills are vital. The plan works, and Albert takes his first step into the world of the literate.

STUDY QUESTIONS:

1. Why did Albert stop trying to learn how to read?
2. Why is reading so important?
3. How could you help someone who doesn't know how to read?

Episode #134 "Pamela Has a Problem"

Theme: Abortion; the sanctity of life.
Scripture reference: Psalm 82:1-4
Recommended maturity level: 10 and up
Written and directed by Paul McCusker
Production engineer: Dave Arnold
(Original air date: 12-01-90)

PARENTAL WARNING: This story deals with abortion and the sanctity of life in an open and frank way. While the issue is handled sensitively, the subject matter may be too mature for younger listeners.

Connie is surprised when her friend Pam comes to Odyssey for a surprise visit. The real surprise, though, is Pam's news: She's pregnant. Connie is torn up over the situation. After all, Pam helped lead Connie to Jesus. Pam's a good Christian girl, too—things like this aren't supposed to happen to people like her. What's worse, she hasn't told her parents yet. Pam feels it would destroy them if they knew their little girl wasn't the princess they thought. In fact, she's actually considering terminating the pregnancy at a clinic in Connellsville.

Connie tries to talk her out of having an abortion, as does Whit. They both urge her to call her parents. Pamela finally does, but before she can tell them, Pam learns that her 16-year-old cousin is also pregnant. The family is devastated. This convinces Pam, more than ever, that she must get an abortion.

Pam goes to the clinic and meets Lynn, another girl who is also scheduled for the procedure. They talk, and Lynn's callous and flippant attitude toward her pregnancy hits Pamela like a bucket of cold water. Pam realizes that inside her womb is a *baby*—a human life. Snuffing out that life would be murder. She simply can't go through with the abortion.

Pam heads back to Connie's house, where Pam finds her parents waiting for her. They came to Odyssey because Pam's phone call disturbed them. They could tell something was wrong. Pam can't keep her secret from her parents any longer, and she tells them the truth. Pam's parents don't condone her mistake, but they're still ready to give their daughter the love and support she needs. It sounds like Pamela and her baby will have a happy ending after all.

STUDY QUESTIONS:

1. Why couldn't Pam go through with the abortion?
2. How could you best help a friend who is pregnant?
3. Why do you think human life is so important to God?

Episodes #135 – 137

"Back to Bethlehem," Parts One, Two, & Three

Theme: The birth of Jesus Christ.
Scripture references: Matthew 1:18-2:1; Luke 2:1-20
Written by Paul McCusker
Directed by Phil Lollar
Production engineers: Dave Arnold and Bob Luttrell
(Original air dates: 12-08-90, 12-15-90, 12-22-90)

Whit sends Connie and Eugene on a trip in the Imagination Station to witness the birth of Jesus Christ. Along the way, they encounter a cranky innkeeper, several smelly shepherds, a crazy but sincere Jewish teacher, a hot-headed but romantic young zealot, a callous but romantic Roman general, and a carpenter and his maiden bride. While the zealot and the general vie for Connie's affections, the teacher explains the strange star up in the sky to Eugene—and they both bear witness to the glory of the newborn King.

the *Adventures in* ODYSSEY archives:

"Back to Bethlehem," our first three-parter, was based on Paul McCusker's stage production, "Step into Bethlehem."

STUDY QUESTIONS:

1. Why was Eugene crying at the end?
2. Why was Jesus' birth so important?
3. How do you celebrate Christmas at your house? What does Christmas mean to you?

Episode #138

"The Adventure of the Adventure"

Theme: The story of *AIO*.
Written by Paul McCusker
Directed by Paul McCusker
Production engineers: Bob Luttrell
(Original air date: 12-29-90)

This episode features a behind-the-scenes look at the creation, history, and ongoing production of *Adventures in Odyssey.* It features clips from: "Whit's Visitor," "Whit's Flop," "Thank You, God!" "Operation DigOut," "A Member of the Family," "Recollections," "Kid's Radio," "Scattered Seeds," "Gotcha!" "The Case of the Secret Room," "The Treasure of Le Monde!" "The Shepherd and the Giant," "The Imagination Station," "Let This Mind Be in You," "Connie," "Two Sides to Every Story," "Our Best Vacation Ever," "The Greatest of These," "Choices," "Isaac the Courageous," "The Sacred Trust," "Castles & Cauldrons," "Ice Fishing," and "The Prodigal, Jimmy."

STUDY QUESTIONS:

1. What's your favorite adventure in Odyssey? Why?
2. How is Odyssey different from your hometown? How is it similar?
3. Which *Adventures in Odyssey* character do you think would make the best friend? Why?

1991

In 1991, we introduced a major change in the format of *Adventures in Odyssey.* Up to this point, we had done skits in the opening (and sometimes the closing) wrap-arounds—the introductions and conclusions to each program, done by our announcer, Chris Lansdowne. The skits were designed to introduce the subject of each particular episode.

They were fun to do but eventually became more elaborate. Sometimes the skits ended up so long that we were forced to cut time from the main story! They also became too complicated to produce—almost as difficult to do as the episodes themselves. So we cut the skits out of the program, and Chris simply gave a brief introduction to the episode.

At the close of 1991, the team also had to make a big decision—would we move to Colorado Springs or stay in California? For Dave Arnold, the choice was easy—move to the Springs. Being from Montana, the Rocky Mountains of Colorado seemed much more like home to Dave than southern California did. And as for Chuck Bolte, Colorado Springs was his hometown, so he also decided to move with Focus.

But two of us stayed behind. Bob Luttrell grew up in California—his whole family is there. So he decided to stay. My wife and I decided to remain in California as well, and I started freelancing for *AIO.*

We all worried about the impact the distance would have on the team. Chuck Bolte's responsibilities at Focus on the Family increased in many ways, and it was clear that a point person—or producer—was needed for the show. We played "eeny–meany–miny–moe," and the job fell to Paul McCusker, who volunteered to return from England. After a game of "musical chairs" with our job descriptions, the show rolled onward.

Episode #139 "Melanie's Diary"

Theme: Empathy; the folly of revenge.
Scripture reference: Deuteronomy 32:35
Written by Paul McCusker
Directed by Phil Lollar
Production engineer: Bob Luttrell
(Original air date: 1-05-91)

Robyn is having trouble hanging on to her school work. First, she loses the text of a speech about highway safety. Then, she misplaces a report she and Jessie wrote about Huck Finn. Her father gives her a few pointers about organization and suggests that Robyn put each of her projects in different colored folders. But Mr. Jacobs has given the last several folders to Robyn's sister, Melanie. Robyn goes to Melanie's room to retrieve them. Once there, Robyn demands Melanie's last two folders and reads her private diary.

Matters worsen when Robyn divulges the contents of what she read to Jessie and Eugene the next day at Whit's End. Melanie leaves, anguished and angry, vowing revenge against her big sister. And revenge is what Melanie pursues.

First, Robyn and Jessie's report mysteriously disappears. Then, Eugene gets a love note written in Robyn's handwriting. Finally, Robyn rushes in to deliver her award-winning speech, only to discover that it has been replaced by her report on Huck Finn. She is utterly humiliated.

This embarrassment causes her to think seriously about how she treated Melanie. Robyn feels so bad, she actually buys Melanie a *real* diary—which makes Mel feel about two feet tall for playing all those pranks on Robyn. Both the Jacobs girls learn an important lesson about revenge, empathy—and love.

STUDY QUESTIONS:

1. How else could Robyn have been better organized?
2. Is revenge really "sweet" in the long run? Explain.
3. What's the best way to handle someone who has hurt you?

Episode #140 "The Vow"

Theme: The sanctity of marriage.
Scripture reference: Matthew 19:5-6
Written and directed by Phil Lollar
Production engineer: Dave Arnold
(Original air date: 1-12-91)

Jessie and Donna are walking home one day when they see a friend of theirs riding in a car with her mother. Jessie informs Donna that the friend's parents are getting a divorce, then describes all of the symptoms that led up to their split. Donna is sympathetic—until Jessie implies that maybe *Donna's* parents are suffering from the same symptoms.

Donna denies it, but when she gets home, George and Mary seem to live out the symptoms right before Donna's eyes. Concerned, she talks to Jimmy about it. The two of them come up with a scheme to get their parents to sign a contract promising they will stay together.

After a series of comical circumstances, George and Mary finally learn of Donna and Jimmy's fears. George and Mary convince their kids that just because they argue once in a while doesn't mean they're getting a divorce. To prove their love and commitment for one another, George and Mary renew their marriage vows in front of their kids and before God—which is better than a contract any day.

STUDY QUESTIONS:

1. What should Donna and Jimmy have done when they suspected their parents were having problems?
2. Is arguing always unhealthy? Why or why not?
3. Why is marriage so important to God?

Episode #141 "Over the Airwaves"

Theme: Parables about the kingdom of heaven.
Scripture reference: Matthew 21:28-46
Written by Paul McCusker
Directed by Phil Lollar
Production engineer: Dave Arnold
(Original air date: 1-19-91)

Kid's Radio produces two of Jesus' parables about the kingdom of heaven, both with a twist. The first is the parable of the two sons. It is about a father and his two children, in this case played by George, Jimmy, and Donna Barclay. George tells Donna to mow the lawn. She refuses but later does as her father asked. Then George tells Jimmy to mow the lawn. Jimmy agrees, but he doesn't follow through. Although Donna didn't comply at first, she, unlike Jimmy, did what her father asked. This illustrates the point that even the worst sinners who truly repent will enter into heaven before those who were simply "good" or "religious."

Following this is the parable of the tenants. In this parable, a vineyard owner sends his servants, then his son, to collect rent from the farmers working the vineyard. But in the Kid's Radio version, the setting changes to the old West, the vineyard becomes Southspoon Ranch, and the owner is now Matt Cartwood. Although told humorously, the point is serious: The kingdom of heaven will be taken away from the chief priests and the Pharisees and given to people who follow God's will for His kingdom.

The Kid's Radio production of the two parables is a smashing success.

STUDY QUESTIONS:

1. When your parents ask you to do something, do you respond like Jimmy or Donna did? How *should* you respond?
2. Who did Mr. Cartwood represent? Jeremy? The Southspoon Ranch?
3. How do the lessons from these two parables apply to us today?

Episode #142 "Train Ride"

Theme: Pranks; breaking up the daily routine.
Scripture reference: Matthew 5:44
Recommended maturity level: 10 and up
Written and directed by Phil Lollar
Production engineer: Bob Luttrell
(Original air date: 1-26-91)

PARENTAL WARNING: This is a mystery in which Whit solves a murder on a train. Although told tongue-in-cheek, it may be too intense for younger listeners.

While Eugene and Whit are taking a train ride back to Odyssey from Chicago, Eugene meets an old enemy named Lawrence Chalmers. For several years, Lawrence has been Eugene's nightmare. Lawrence stole a term paper from Eugene at their previous college. This caused Eugene to get a lower grade and kept him from attending the university of his choice. Not only that, but Lawrence also stole Eugene's girlfriend, Margaret Hoffmeyer, and ended up marrying her! Seeing Lawrence again makes Eugene so upset, he can't eat that night and retires to his room to sleep.

Meanwhile, as the train rounds a corner, Whit looks at the rear baggage cars and witnesses a struggle between two figures, one of whom falls off the train! Whit rushes back to the baggage car and finds Margaret unconscious. She awakens in near hysteria, crying that her husband, Lawrence, was *pushed* out of the train. And she claims that Eugene did it! Did Eugene actually murder Lawrence? If he didn't, who did? Is Lawrence Chalmers really dead? For the answer to these questions, tune into "Train Ride"!

STUDY QUESTIONS:

1. How did Whit figure out what really happened on the train?
2. Do you think God likes jokes? Why or why not?
3. What kinds of things do you do to break up your daily routine?

Episode #143 "Muckraker"

Theme: Handling power responsibly.
Scripture reference: Proverbs 6:16,19
Written by Paul McCusker
Directed by Phil Lollar
Production engineer: Bob Luttrell
(Original air date: 2-02-91)

Lucy is hot on the trail of a great story for the *Odyssey Owl.* Apparently, the Calvin Bloom Company, a maker of fine skin and hair products, has been putting a harmful green dye in their Accu-Gel shampoo—despite the Food and Drug Administration's ban on it. Lucy talks with Calvin Bloom's public relations director, Mr. Norton. Norton tells her that the company has fully complied with government regulations.

But Lucy has already come across a former Calvin Bloom employee who disagrees. This informant has told Lucy that Calvin Bloom continues to use the green dye. The person also informs Lucy about "a lot of other things going on out there that people need to be warned about."

Lucy is excited about her scoop. She writes a defaming article about Calvin Bloom's alleged cover-up. She is proud of her work—until Mr. Norton informs Lucy that her informant was fired for cheating on her time cards. The woman used Lucy to get back at the company. Lucy is stunned and upset. She writes a retraction, which the *Owl* prints, and learns a difficult lesson about the power of the printed word and the importance of wielding that power responsibly.

STUDY QUESTIONS:

1. Why was Lucy so eager to uncover a story about the Calvin Bloom company?
2. How should Lucy have handled what Miss Sadler told her?
3. Why is the written word such a powerful thing?

Episode #144

"Someone to Watch over Me"

Theme: God's protection; guardian angels.
Scripture references: Psalm 91:11-12; Matthew 18:10
Written and directed by Phil Lollar
Production engineer: Dave Arnold
(Original air date: 2-09-91)

Jimmy Barclay is on the strangest Imagination Station adventure of his life! It starts out in the cockpit of a World War II bomber plane. Jimmy is on a mission over Germany with his copilot, Nagle. Jimmy is about to be shot out of the sky by the evil General Grimmstaad. The general seems to have a personal vendetta against Jimmy. In order to save his plane and crew, Jimmy parachutes out of the plane. He lands in a haystack—where he is again met by Nagle!

Now, however, they are secret agents in Cold War Europe. Jimmy and Nagle must smuggle secret papers out of the communist bloc, past the evil General Grimmkov. But they end up trapped on a cliff. The only escape is to high dive into the ocean below. Jimmy takes the plunge, grabbing on to a piece of floating driftwood. Soon, a three-masted schooner passes by and fishes him out of the water. Again waiting for him on board is Mr. Nagle, who is now a yeoman to Jimmy's admiral!

This time, they're being chased by the dreadful pirate Grimmbeard. An epic sea battle takes place. Jimmy's ship fights furiously, but it's no use. Grimmbeard boards the ship and nearly captures Jimmy. He escapes by going down into the hold. There, a door slides open. He then finds himself in a spaceship, copiloted by his old friend Nagle!

Now they're being chased by the vile Grimm, who is trying to vaporize them. But suddenly, Jimmy doesn't want to play anymore. The whole thing has become tiresome—the strangest Imagination Station adventure he's ever been on—and he wants Whit to let him out! But Nagle tells Jimmy that Whit *can't* let him out . . . because this *isn't* an Imagination Station adventure.

In a touching—and surprising—conclusion, Jimmy learns that there is a spiritual realm at work beyond his imagination—and that his life is, and always has been, in the hands of God.

the *Adventures in* ODYSSEY archives:

This story was based on a teleplay I wrote for the new (but short-lived) *Twilight Zone* TV series. The script revolved around the idea that, for a completely paralyzed man, dreaming would be a welcome escape from reality. It would allow him to move, jump, run, and have all sorts of adventures. *Twilight Zone* didn't want it, so I played with the idea a little bit and came up with what turned out to be one of our most popular episodes ever—thanks in large part to Dave Arnold's production.

behind the scenes:

"'Someone to Watch over Me' increased the dynamic range of the show on the production end. For the computer voice in the space adventure, I recorded myself and my wife, Janna, doing the lines together and ran them through a processor to get the digitalized sound."

—Dave Arnold

STUDY QUESTIONS:

1. Why didn't Jimmy have anything to fear from Grimmstaad, Grimmkov, Grimmbeard, and Grimm?
2. Read Matthew 18:10. Can you think of a time when one of God's angels protected you? If so, when?
3. Do you think what happened to Jimmy is really possible?

Adventures in ODYSSEY

SCRAPBOOK

The Odyssey Times

ALWAYS Free

THE ONLY ONE WE'VE GOT

"Odyssey" Takes

Whittaker Unveils New Invention

The Imagination Station 'brings the Bible to life.'

By Dale Jacobs

lending library, a theat
ve performances, craft
the Bible Room, a ne

Focus on the Fam
Children's Radio Dra

ODYSSEY USA
A RADIO JOURNEY

PURPOSE:

To effectively communicate scriptural principles with a special emphasis on traditional family values to youngsters primarily in the 8-12 age group using the entertainment-based medium of weekly radio drama.

PROPOSAL:

Develop a 30-minute weekly radio series called "Odyssey," based largely on "Family Portraits," aimed specifically at the 8-12 age group.

PROPOSED SCHEDULE:

We recommend commencing
would require appro
personnel. The prop
September 5, 1987.

Adventures in ODYSSEY
THE EARLY CLASSICS

BLUE PRINT: WHIT'S END

The Odyssey Times
Odyssey Takes to the Airwaves

Helps kids relate to police

BROADCAST news

Focus on the Family's

July 1988

ODYSSEY: WHERE ADVENTURES BEGIN!

"odyssey" (n.) 1. an intellectual or spiritual quest. 2. a small town in the middle of your radio, as in *Adventures in Odyssey*."

Move over *He-Man* and *Care Bears*! Watch out Batman and Road Runner! The airwaves have a new hero *and* a new power to deal with. The hero? Hmm. Must be a new costume-clad superbeing from another planet. And the

("Whit" for short). And the power? An old contraption

525 outlets in cities around the country are presenting a serious challenge to the commercial-induced antics of Saturday morning children's television characters. Their weapon in this "challenge"? A program entitled *Adventures in Odyssey*.

With more than a "nod" to the radio dramas of yesteryear, *Adventures in Odyssey* was created to blow the dust off of a little used national

Our Hometown

A colorful "icon" of Whit's End back when the show was called Odyssey USA

Whit's End

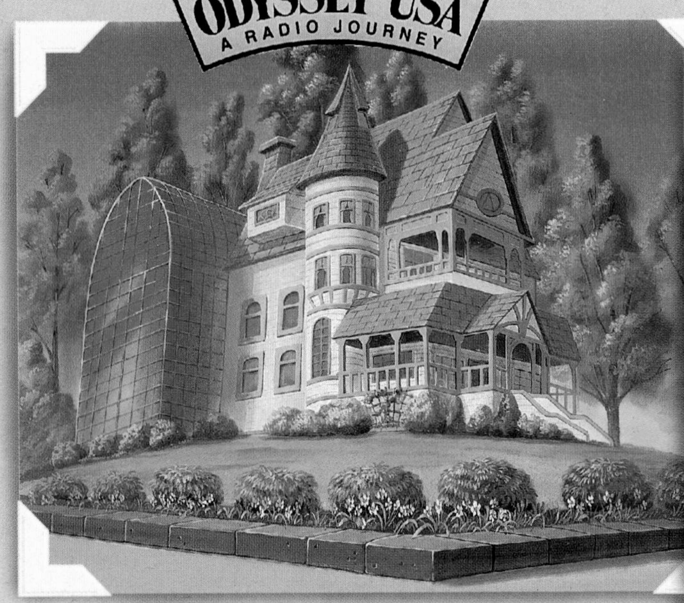

Outside Whit's End in the animated video world

Here is Whit's End by artist Bruce Day (for Clubhouse magazine and Chick-Fil-A meal bag). See how many items you can find beginning with the letter 'S'.

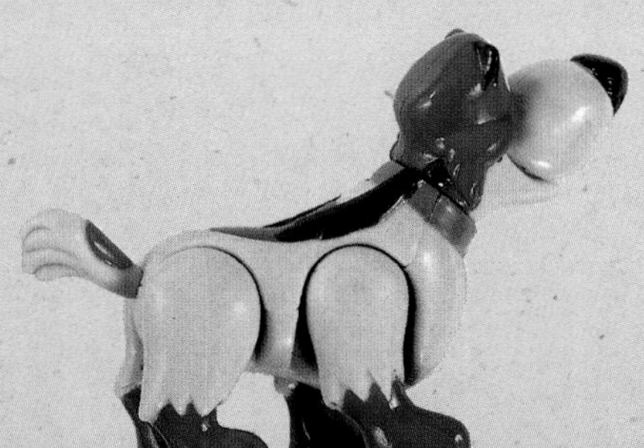

# of Odyssey

Through the Years

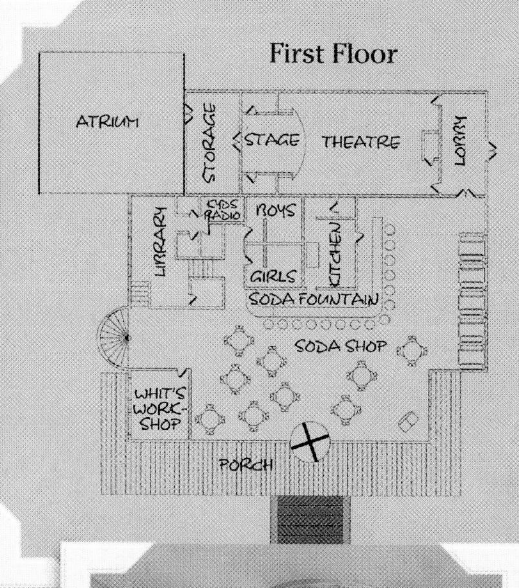

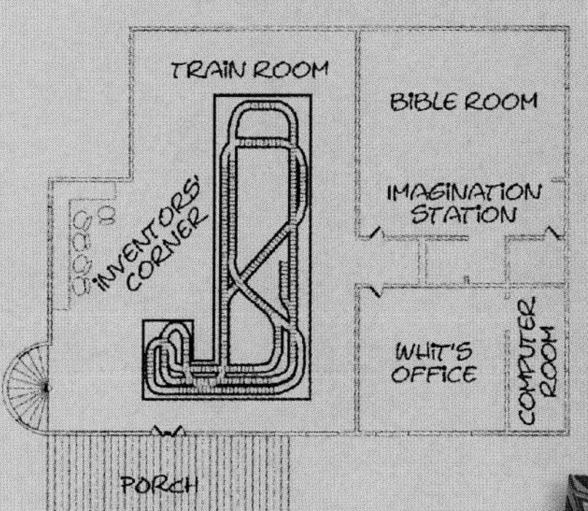

Here is a "blueprint" of Whit's End, as rendered for Clubhouse magazine. One fan pointed out that this "blueprint" wasn't accurate because the girls' bathroom doesn't have windows (which was Connie's means of escape in "This is Chad Pearson?").

Inside Whit's End in the animated video world

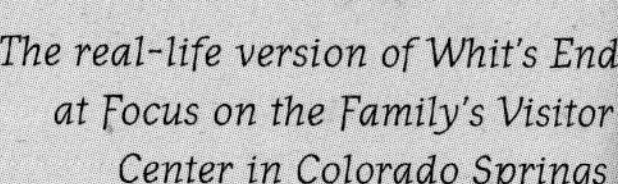

The real-life version of Whit's End at Focus on the Family's Visitor Center in Colorado Springs

John Avery Whittaker

a.k.a. Whit

Here are the different faces of Whit over the years

A T-shirt, circa 1987

Album cover, circa 1988

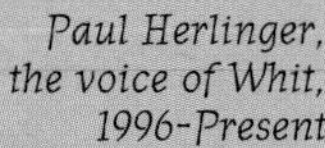

Paul Herlinger, the voice of Whit, 1996-Present

As drawn by Bruce Day for the cassette albums, circa 1989-1991

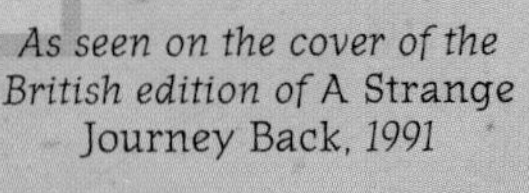

As seen on the cover of the British edition of A Strange Journey Back, 1991

The animated videos' version, 1991-Present

Whit, circa 1992

A "promotional" version, 1995

Hal Smith, the voice of Whit, 1987-1994

Whit of the future? (As rendered for A Twist in Time), 1997

From the book cover The Stranger's Message, 1997

What is your impression of Whit? Why don't you draw him and send him in to us?

Description:

Wild white hair and moustache (similar to Mark Twain). Round, friendly face. Blue, compassionate eyes (sometimes wears spectacles). Missing top part of his right ear and walks with very slight limp from war injury. Stocky build (sometimes overweight when animated). Considered wise, inventive, generous, creative, and deeply Christian.

ART GALLERY

A sampling of some of the cover art created for* Adventures in Odyssey *over the years

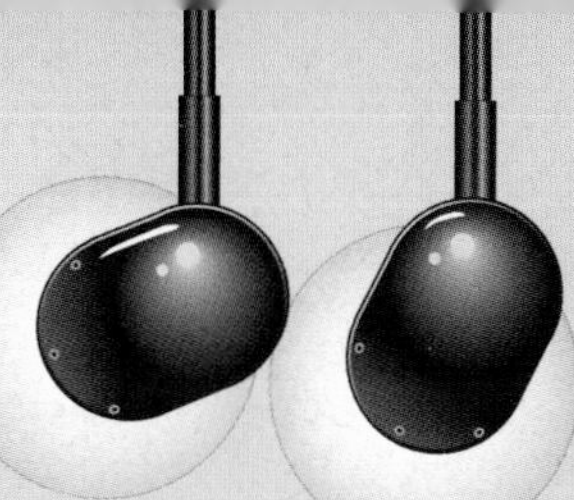

In Harm's Way, *the tenth animated video cover*

The art for the Darkness Before Dawn *compilation album*

Here is the cover art for Once Upon an Avalanche, *the sixth animated video. It won first place for best video jacket at the 1994 Christian Booksellers Association convention.*

The art from The Search for Whit, *our 27th compilation album*

Cover art for the fourth novel, Behind the Locked Door

Wish You Were Here *postcard motif for the 21st compilation album*

PHOTO

Co-creator and producer Steve Harris (foreground) with production engineer Bob Luttrell, recording an early episode of *Adventures in Odyssey* in our Pomona, California, studios

Will Ryan, Katie Leigh Pavlakovich, and Hal Smith crowd in for a "take."

(from left to right) Alan Young, Ed Walker, Will Ryan, Katie Leigh Pavlakovich, Dave Madden, Dave Arnold, and Paul McCusker. The ukelele in Katie's lap actually belongs to Will, who not only plays well but also composes songs for us.

Will Ryan (Eugene) in an earnest moment

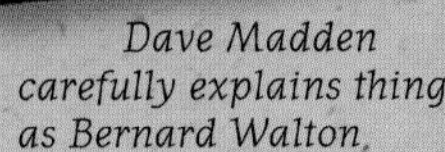

Dave Madden carefully explains things as Bernard Walton.

Alan Young puts on the face of Scrooge McDuck

Hal Smith laughing—as usual!

Parley Baer, who has played Connie's Uncle Joe, Reginald Duffield, and a first-century zealot, to name only a few

ALBUM

Maggie Malloy as June Kendall

Young Genny Mullen (Lucy) in 1988

Will Ryan and Katie Leigh Pavlakovich entertain guests at the Whit's End soda shop at Focus on the Family's Visitor Center. Will has put on the face he uses for Harlow Doyle.

Paul Herlinger, the "new" voice of Whit, stands next to his animated counterpart.

Young David Griffin as Jimmy Barclay in 1988

Paul McCusker, Dave Arnold, Marshal Younger, and Phil Lollar look like fairly normal guys.

The same crew after a not-so-normal Adventures in Odyssey *recording session*

Pictured in this early photo are Erin and Sage Bolte, who played Melanie and Robyn Jacobs.

Joe Cammarato as Oscar in 1988

CARE FOR THE FAMILY PRESENTS . . . Adventures in

ISSUE No.5 ALWAYS FREE

THE ODYSSEY™ TIMES

Guide to Odyssey

Some People Who Live There

Jimmy Barclay
Typical 10-year-old who gets into all sorts of trouble that isn't his fault (at least according to him). Often has a hard time of it!

Robyn Jacobs
11 years old. She's an expert at getting herself into situations too big to handle. But she's also an expert at learning lessons.

Donna Barclay
…mmy's older sister. …e complains some…nes, but loves her …mily and friends and …uld do anything for …m—even her brother.

Lucy Schultz
Bright 12-year-old. Lucy writes for her school newspaper, the *Odyssey Owl*—which sometimes gets her into unexpected trouble.

…nard Walton
…sey's expert …ow-washer.

Curt Stephens
Mischievous young man who's always attempting

ADVENTURES IN ODYSSEY™ 1
Family Vacation I
A production of Focus on the Family
Focus on the Family is a non-profit organization dedicated to the preservation of the home. James C. Dobson, Ph.D., President.

ADVENTURES IN ODYSSEY™ 1
The Day Independence Came
A production of Focus on the Family

…ES IN ODYSSEY™ 1
…S Radio
A production of Focus on the Family

JUNE 1991

Focus on the Family

…oadcast News™

"Adventures in Odyssey" to Go Da…

Focus Responds to Stations' Requests for Daily "Odyssey"

The "Adventures in Odyssey" radio drama series will soon be available for daily airing. According to Mike Trout, senior vice president of broadcasting at …

FOCUS ON THE FAMILY PRESENTS

Adventures in ODYSSEY

Where's Whit?!

Mr. Whittaker is needed at Whit's End. Can you find him somewhere in Odyssey? Also, what time is it? What's happening at Whit's End? (Hint: Find Connie.) How are the Odyssey *Coyotes* doing this season? What kind of trouble is Jimmy in now? What story is Lucy working on for the next issue of the *Odyssey Owl*? (Hint: Look for Eugene.)

…from … be 6 to 14 … local radio … the *daily* … Odyssey … entry blank … station … listen to Od… between M… (except Memorial Day weekend) to discover seven secret words. With them, you'll qualify to enter two separate drawings.

First, each station will pick two winners of an "Adventures in Odyssey" tape library. Second, Focus on the Family will draw the name of one grand-prize winner to be flown with his or her parents to beautiful Colorado Springs on Labor Day weekend. The winner will get to play a part in an Odyssey episode, take a ride in a hot air balloon, and do other fun stuff around town. So get your entry blank now!

9

MAY 1992

ADVENTUR…
Return to …

INSIDE Whit's End

by Paul McCusker

Imagine walking throu… American town on a … day. People smile and … day" as they pass, even … stranger to them.

Eventually you reach … Victorian house with a … door that says "Whit's E… find it's an old-fashioned … lor, but as you wander a… discover that it's much m…

Wait a minute, here's … called "The Bible Room," … working next to a machin… between a telephone booth … cockpit, is a tall, sparkly-e… with unruly white hair and … mustache. He wipes his ha… and steps forward to shake …

"Hi, I'm John Whittaker … But you can call me Whit."

Whit explains that the … called "The Imagination St… he invented to help kids us… nations to bring the Bible t… essence, it's a machine that … kids back to the moment w… defeated Goliath or Elijah b… down from heaven or, yes, e… fixion and resurrection of Je…

You stand back to take it … seems too good to be true. B… because you *believe* you're … It's the start of your own adv… in a town named Odyssey.

How Did It All Start?

The program began as an … In 1987, Focus on the Family … a limited-run family drama f… son's broadcast. Called "Fami… the series introduced the strug… conflicts of Odyssey's resident… wise and amiable John Avery …

Audience response was so … that Dr. Dobson asked Focus b… producers Phil Lollar and Steve… to develop a weekly series for c… Listeners to those early episod… remember that the program wa… nally called "Odyssey USA." It … changed to "Adventures in Ody… to give it more international ap…

Within a few months of its f… "Odyssey" executive producer … Bolte hired me to be writer and … Along with production enginee… Arnold and Bob Luttrell, we are … a team that brings scriptural prin… life through memorable characters… dramas, heartfelt comedy and eve… of fantasy using the "theater of th… Since 1987, we have written and … more than 200 half-hour episode…

The "Adventures in Odyssey" radio drama series has been a …away success since Focus on the Family introduced it six …s ago. Here, "Odyssey" producer Paul McCusker (left) …terviews main character John Avery Whittaker.

Episode #145 "The Second Coming"

Theme: The return of Jesus.
Scripture reference: Matthew 24:36-42
Written by Paul McCusker
Directed by Phil Lollar and Chuck Bolte
Production engineer: Dave Arnold
(Original air date: 3-02-91)

Melanie is excited. She's been reading a book by televangelist Henry Fernbank about the second coming of Jesus. Henry has used mathematics and symbols from Revelation to come up with a formula to predict when Christ will return. According to Henry, it's this Saturday!

Melanie is so convinced Fernbank is right, she makes a bunch of posters about the second coming and hangs them up around town. Her parents run after her, frantically taking down the posters. Finally, they talk with her and try to explain that the Bible says no one knows the exact day of Jesus' return.

That doesn't stop Melanie from believing that it will be Saturday, though. When the big day arrives, she sets up a tent in the backyard. Melanie takes her Bible, a Sunday school certificate, and a sleeping bag to await the Lord's return.

Although He doesn't return, the whole experience deepens Melanie's faith in Jesus and her excitement at His promised return. It also deepens her skepticism of television preachers. Melanie learns that you can't always believe what you hear.

STUDY QUESTIONS:

1. Why was it so easy for Melanie to believe Henry Fernbank?
2. Should Melanie have hung posters about Jesus' second coming all around town? Why or why not?
3. What's the best way to tell others about Jesus' return?

Episode #146 "Emotional Baggage"

Theme: Holding grudges.
Scripture reference: 1 Corinthians 13:5,7
Written and directed by Phil Lollar
Production engineer: Bob Luttrell
(Original air date: 3-09-91)

Connie is in a major snit. She has just learned that her Aunt Helen (who is only eight years older than Connie) is coming for a visit. But Connie's mother, June, can't figure out why Connie is so upset. Helen is June's ex-husband's sister. That should be a problem for *June*, not for Connie. Connie tells her mom that Helen has never liked her and is always mean to her. Refusing to take the grief this time, Connie decides to stay at Whit's End until Helen leaves.

Whit talks with Connie about it and discovers that her real problem with her aunt is that Helen introduced Connie's dad to the woman he left Connie's mom for. Whit acknowledges Connie's pain but says that she must release her bitterness. Connie refuses, so Whit comes up with a game involving bricks and feathers to tangibly illustrate the emotional baggage that Connie is carrying around. Whit tells her that the solution is to give it all over to God. Let Him take control, and He'll help Connie let go of her anger. Connie finally realizes that Whit is right. At long last, Connie sends her grudge packing.

Adventures in ODYSSEY the archives:

We learned a lot about Connie's family history in "Emotional Baggage." The name of her father's new wife and Connie's aunt were revealed—along with the fact that Helen is only eight years older than Connie. Some of this information set the stage for future episodes.

STUDY QUESTIONS:

1. What could Connie have done to avoid becoming bitter?
2. Why is it bad to hold a grudge?
3. Are you holding a grudge against anybody? How can you let go of it?

ULTIMATE ADVENTURES IN ODYSSEY TRIVIA

Whit's End and the Imagination Station

Whit's End has two secret tunnels underneath it, a secret staircase, a secret room in the basement, a secret room in the attic, and a secret computer room in Whit's office.

The Imagination Station has an emergency reset button.

Whit's End has a pizza oven, but no grill.

Whit's End will not take sides in an election.

At Whit's End, employees are never allowed to contradict parents in front of their children.

Whit's End is closed on Sundays.

Episode #147
"Where There's a Will…"

Theme: Knowing God's will.
Scripture reference: Ephesians 5:17
Written by Paul McCusker
Directed by Phil Lollar
Production engineer: Dave Arnold
(Original air date: 3-30-91)

George Barclay returns from a business trip to Washington, D.C., with some big news: His company's head office wants to give him a promotion and move him and the family to the nation's capital! Jimmy and Donna throw fits when they hear the news, but George and Mary tell them that they haven't decided anything yet. They're waiting until they know exactly what God wants them to do. George and Mary advise Jimmy and Donna to also seek God's will in the matter.

Jimmy and Donna aren't quite sure of how to do that. Donna enlists Jessie's assistance, while Jimmy goes to Whit. Whit tells Jimmy the biblical story of Gideon, who tried to discern God's will by praying for dew to appear on a fleece—which Jimmy attempts to duplicate that night with his wool sweater. Donna and Jessie pray over random Bible verses.

Unfortunately, both Barclay kids arrive at opposite conclusions. Donna's scripture search says they should stay, and Jimmy's sweater experiment says they should go.

Meanwhile, George's boss, Mr. Cole, comes for a visit. When George shows Mr. Cole around Odyssey, he realizes how much both the town and especially George's family mean to him. Mr. Cole tells George that he must decide if the job really is right for him—it will require not only a move to a new city, but also much more of George's time and energy. After thinking more about it, George decides it's not the right thing for him or the family. Odyssey will have the Barclays around for a while longer. It's God's will.

STUDY QUESTIONS:

1. Do you think God shows us His will today the same way He showed Gideon His will? Explain your answer.
2. What was wrong with the way Donna and Jessie searched for God's will?
3. Have you discovered God's will for your life? How? In what way?

Episode #148
"Isaac the Procrastinator"

Theme: Procrastination; laziness.
Scripture reference: Proverbs 10:4
Written and directed by Phil Lollar
Production engineer: Bob Luttrell
(Original air date: 4-06-91)

Isaac is doing a lot of heavy-duty praying. He has a report due today. It's not ready, so Isaac is praying that God will let the bell ring before his teacher calls on him to deliver it. Amazingly, that's exactly what happens—now, Isaac has the weekend to finish the report.

But Lucy finds Isaac in the mall on Saturday morning, looking at books on space travel. She confronts him about it. Then Lucy asks if Isaac has done any work on their joint geometry project, which is due in a week. He hasn't, but he promises to get to it immediately. Isaac leaves to go directly to the library. But before he can get there, he is distracted by a hot Zappazoids tournament.

Meanwhile, Lucy goes to Whit's End, where she learns that Isaac owes yet *another* project to Dale Jacobs! Lucy and Dale are ready to dump Isaac, but Whit asks them to be patient. He has a plan to cure Isaac of his procrastination.

The next day, Isaac comes into Whit's End. Whit convinces Isaac that he is suffering from a disease—chronic procrastinitus. Whit says he has the only known treatment for it, so Isaac begs for a dose of the medicine. Whit hands him the treatment. Isaac drinks it down and almost immediately feels it working! He instantly starts a flurry of work, completing Dale Jacobs's project in just a few hours.

Isaac is amazed at the effectiveness of Whit's treatment—until Whit tells Isaac that it was only lemonade. "Chronic procrastinitus" is just a fancy term for laziness. The reason Isaac was able to complete the work so quickly was because he finally decided to just *do it.* Isaac has learned his lesson and promises to—in the future—perform his tasks right away.

the *Adventures in* ODYSSEY archives:

Hal Smith was out of town when "Isaac the Procrastinator" was recorded, so all of his lines had to be recorded "wild" (separately) and added in later. Can you tell?

STUDY QUESTIONS:

1. Why did Isaac keep putting off his work?
2. How does God feel about laziness?
3. What's the best way to combat procrastination?

Episode #149 "By Dawn's Early Light"

Theme: American history: the War of 1812; sacrifice for one's country; respect for the flag; patriotism; God's place in U.S. history.
Scripture reference: Psalm 33:12-22
Written and directed by Phil Lollar
Production engineer: Dave Arnold
(Original air date: 4-13-91)

Curt and Lucy take an amazing trip in the Imagination Station back to the year 1812. They witness the British General Ross's tragic capture and torching of Washington, D.C., the British Admiral Cockburn's epic bombardment of Fort McHenry, and the composition of our national anthem by a young lawyer named Francis Scott Key.

the *Adventures in* ODYSSEY archives:

"By Dawn's Early Light" was written in response to all the flag burning that took place around the U.S. during this period.

Although it was one of our most popular episodes, "By Dawn's Early Light" contained an egregious error. Being Americans, we naturally pronounced the name "*Cockburn*" the way it's written—with a hard "ck" sound in the middle of the word. Little did we know that the British pronounce the name "*Coburn*"—with no hard "ck" sound.

STUDY QUESTIONS:

1. Lucy said she doesn't understand all the fuss over flag burning. Do you? Explain your answer.
2. Why did we fight the War of 1812?
3. Name some other examples of how God "preserv'd us a nation."

Episode #150 "Home Is Where the Hurt Is"

Theme: Dealing with an alcoholic parent.
Scripture references: Proverbs 20:1; Ephesians 5:18
Written by Paul McCusker
Directed by Phil Lollar
Production engineer: Bob Luttrell
(Original air date: 4-20-91)

Curt is scheming. He has called up the publisher of his math book to have the company send him a teacher's copy—which contains all the answers. It's a devious plan, and it almost works. Except the company that prints his math book is a subsidiary of Universal Press, the company Whit owns.

Lucy informs Whit of Curt's scheme. Whit tells her that a salesman will deliver the book *in person* to Curt's house! Lucy relays this to Curt, and he races home in a panic to meet the salesman before his father does. Lucy hasn't been to Curt's house before. Out of curiosity, she follows him home.

Once there, Lucy learns why Curt has never invited her over: His father is an alcoholic. Until now, Curt has successfully hidden it from everybody. He is so embarrassed that Lucy discovered his secret, he disappears for several days.

Finally, Whit and Lucy find Curt fishing at Trickle Lake. They offer their support, but Curt doesn't want any. He just wants to pretend that things are the same as before they knew about his father. Curt assures them that it's no big deal and asks to be left alone. Lucy and Whit honor his request. They go, leaving Curt alone with his thoughts, his fishing line, and his tears.

STUDY QUESTIONS:

1. Why didn't Curt want to talk about his dad's alcoholism?
2. Was it wrong for Lucy to follow Curt home, then tell Whit what she saw? Why or why not?
3. Do you know of someone in Curt's situation? If so, what's the best way to help them?

Episode #151 "...The Last Shall Be First"

Theme: The parable of the workers; salvation.
Scripture references: Matthew 18:12-13; 20:1-16
Written and directed by Phil Lollar
Production engineer: Dave Arnold
(Original air date: 4-27-91)

The Little Theatre at Whit's End is a mess. The kids have just finished re-enacting Jesus' parable of the workers. To clean things up, Whit enlists the aid of Jimmy and Artie, agreeing to pay them $15 for a job well done. Around noon, Donna drops by. Whit also hires her to help clean the theatre. Then, later that afternoon, Lucy and Curt wander in, and Whit engages their cleaning services for the going rate of $15.

Meanwhile, Connie is trying to get her great-uncle Joe Finneman to go back to church. He stopped going years ago, and Connie has made him her personal project. But no matter what Connie says, Uncle Joe stubbornly refuses to go. He feels church is for the young, like Connie—not for old folks, like himself.

Connie tells Whit about this, and he gets an idea. Whit has Connie bring Uncle Joe down to the Little Theatre to witness Whit paying the kids for a job well done. Just as in the scriptural model, those who were hired first complained that they were paid the same as the workers hired later in the day. But Whit sets them straight. Connie uses the illustration to point out to Uncle Joe that God's salvation is available to *all* people, no matter what "time of day" they come to Him. The following Sunday, Uncle Joe accepts Connie's invitation to come to church.

STUDY QUESTIONS:

1. Was Whit was unfair to pay everyone the same wage? Why or why not?
2. Uncle Joe thought he was too old to go to church. Why do you think he believed that?
3. How would you get an unsaved friend or relative to go to church with you?

Episode #152
"The Meaning of Sacrifice"

Theme: Sacrifice.
Scripture reference: 1 Samuel 15:19,22
Written by Paul McCusker
Directed by Phil Lollar
Production engineer: Bob Luttrell
(Original air date: 5-04-91)

Inspired by the pastor's sermon one Sunday morning, George suggests that each of the Barclays sacrifice something important to them: television. That means no soap operas for Donna and no Zappazoids for Jimmy, since the game is played on a TV. The kids don't really like the idea, but they finally agree: No TV for a month.

Jessie thinks Donna is crazy for giving up their favorite soap opera right when things in the story line are getting critical. So Jessie comes up with a way to keep Donna up to date without breaking her promise: Jessie will watch the show and then tell Donna what happened. Donna isn't sure about it, but she agrees.

At the same time, Jimmy discovers that Finneman's Market has a new Zappazoids game. Jimmy reasons that technically he won't be watching TV by playing the game at the store.

Jimmy's and Donna's schemes work—until they run into each other at Finneman's. Donna is buying a soap opera magazine, while Jimmy is in the middle of a hot Zappazoids game. They both blame each other. Whit, who also happens to be in the store, overhears the conversation. He explains that they have been following the letter, but not the *spirit* of the law. Jimmy and Donna both used a technicality to give into their temptation to watch television. The kids realize their error. They now understand the meaning of the verse, "To obey is better than sacrifice." This time, they'll give up TV—not for their parents or even for themselves—for God.

STUDY QUESTIONS:

1. What were Jimmy's and Donna's first mistakes?
2. Read 1 Samuel 15:22. What does "To obey is better than sacrifice" mean?
3. Have you ever sacrificed something for God? If so, what was it?

Episode #153
"Mayor for a Day"

Theme: Responsibility; leadership.
Scripture reference: Romans 13:1-7
Written by Paul McCusker
Directed by Phil Lollar
Production engineer: Dave Arnold
(Original air date: 5-11-91)

Cunning, conniving, irresponsible Curt Stevens wins a contest and becomes mayor of Odyssey for a day. His administration starts off with a bang. First, he orders his new secretary to have a Batphone installed in his office. He then unleashes a horde of crazy animals on the city and nearly causes the town to go bankrupt. Finally, he signs an order instructing Whit's End to be torn down! His administration is a nightmare—but no one would expect anything less from Curt.

STUDY QUESTIONS:

1. Why did Curt make such a terrible mayor?
2. What are the characteristics of a good leader?
3. Read Romans 13:1-7. Why do you think God wants us to obey our leaders?

Episode #154
"Coming of Age"

Theme: Adolescence; growing up.
Scripture references: Deuteronomy 31:6; Matthew 10:30; 1 Timothy 4:12
Recommended maturity level: 8 and up
Written and directed by Phil Lollar
Production engineer: Bob Luttrell
(Original air date: 5-18-91)

PARENTAL WARNING: This episode deals with Jimmy Barclay's entry into adolescence and all the embarrassment, anguish, and awkwardness that go along with it. Although tastefully handled, it may be too mature for younger listeners. It also may raise questions in older listeners' minds about the process of growing up.

After a three-year absence, Jimmy Barclay has returned to his journal to pen his thoughts and feelings about life. Lately, several "strange" things have been happening to him. Donna has been teasing Jimmy because he's started shaving. He's not getting along with his mom and dad. His body seems to be falling apart. His chest hurts, his bones ache, and his voice sounds like a cross between a frog with laryngitis and a country-western singer.

To top it all off, Jimmy's been thinking a lot about Connie lately. He gets a funny feeling in his stomach when she's around. Jimmy discovers what the strange feeling is while rehearsing *Romeo and Juliet* at the Little Theatre in Whit's End. Connie is playing Juliet to Jimmy's Romeo, and during the balcony scene, Jimmy realizes he's in love with Connie! But while he's trying to figure out how to tell her, he learns that Whit has cast Artie Powell in a role that Jimmy wanted to play. Jimmy confronts Whit about it, demanding to play the role. Whit refuses, so Jimmy quits the play and angrily storms out of the theatre. Unfortunately, he leaves his journal—which reveals his feelings about Connie—behind.

Jimmy rushes back to Whit's End and learns that Connie has seen his journal. Jimmy apologizes to her, feeling terrible that Connie discovered his feelings for her that way. But Connie tells him that she only *saw* the journal—she hasn't *read* it. Completely embarrassed, Jimmy retreats to the Wonderworld tree house. Whit joins him and talks to Jimmy about what's been happening to him. Jimmy thinks he's going crazy, but Whit says he's actually on the verge of adolescence. Whit explains that growing up is inevitable, so Jimmy should try to enjoy it. And it will be much easier by if he remembers that Jesus is always with him.

the *Adventures in* ODYSSEY archives:

David Griffin's voice was changing during this period, so we decided to handle it within the context of a show. "Coming of Age" was meant to take Jimmy out of *AIO*, but the Barclays were too popular as characters for us to abandon them completely.

STUDY QUESTIONS:

1. Why did Jimmy feel he couldn't talk to his father? What should he have done to overcome those feelings?
2. What do you think is the best part of growing up? The hardest part?
3. What did Whit mean when he said Jimmy was not alone?

ULTIMATE ADVENTURES IN ODYSSEY *TRIVIA*

The People and Pets of Odyssey

Richard Maxwell has a little sister, Rachael, who appeared in "Bad Company."

In the Barclay household, when family decisions are made, Mary and George get two votes each, and Jimmy and Donna each get one vote.

Jimmy and Lawrence are members of the Rick Rancid Fan Club—which has only two members.

Mary Barclay's maiden name was Benson.

Donna Barclay's middle name is Renee.

Normal, the Barclay's dog, was originally named "Harry."

Two of Lucy Cunningham-Schultz's cousins have appeared in *AIO* episodes: Albert, in "Cousin Albert," and Leslie, in "It Sure Seemed Like It to Me!"

Harlow Doyle is president of the local chapter of the Daniel Boone Fan Club.

Connie Kendall owns a golden Labrador retriever that has never appeared on the program.

Eugene Meltsner's eyes are periwinkle blue. Katrina Shanks's are gray.

Eugene Meltsner started college at age 13. Nicky Adamsworth started when he was 11.

Eugene Meltsner's mother's father's last name was Kronholm—no relation to the Kronholm who teaches geography at Odyssey High School.

In 1934, Tom Riley's father helped build the Fillmore Recreation Center—which eventually became Whit's End.

Jenny Whittaker, Whit's late wife, introduced Tom Riley to his current wife, Agnes.

Continued on page 123.

Episodes #155 & 156

"Waylaid in the Windy City," Parts One & Two

Theme: God is in control; the folly of revenge.
Scripture reference: Proverbs 29:25
Recommended maturity level: 8 and up
Written by Paul McCusker and Phil Lollar
Directed by Phil Lollar
Production engineers: Dave Arnold and Bob Luttrell
(Original air dates: 6-22-91 & 6-29-91)

PARENTAL WARNING: This two-parter deals with mystery and subterfuge. Although mild by today's television standards, some scenes may be too intense for younger listeners.

Whit takes Connie on a trip to Chicago. She's excited to visit the city. But when they get off the plane, a security guard demands to examine Whit's laptop computer. Apparently, a computer that looks just like Whit's was recently stolen. Whit proves the laptop is his, and he and Connie make their way out to the hotel van.

Inside the van, a strange young man is acting secretive. He demands to be let out on the way to the hotel. The driver stops, opening the back of the van to retrieve the young man's luggage. The young man grabs his bags and leaves.

Later, at the hotel, Whit and Connie turn on the TV and are stunned to see that the same young man is wanted for the disappearance of the stolen computer! The computer belonged to a member of the Department of Defense, and it contained top secret files. Whit and Connie head straight to the police.

Meanwhile, the young man is being interrogated by Dr. Regis Blackgaard. The young man was stealing electronic equipment out of cars for Blackgaard when he picked up the laptop as well. But, to further complicate things, the laptop the young man gave to Blackgaard doesn't have any Defense Department secrets on it. The young man grabbed the wrong computer—Whit's—when he got out of the van. Blackgaard leaves to find Whit.

But Whit is being questioned by Agent Phillips from the Defense Department. Phillips suspects Whit of stealing the computer. There is no proof, however, so Phillips lets Whit and Connie go.

When they return to their hotel, they find that someone tried to break into Whit's room! All of Whit's possessions are now in the hotel's safe. Connie is escorted upstairs by a bellhop, while Whit checks things out and examines the computer. Sure enough, it belongs to the Department of Defense!

Whit immediately calls Agent Phillips, who warns Whit that he could be in great danger. Whit suddenly remembers Connie. But it's too late. The bellhop was really one of Blackgaard's men. The evil doctor kidnapped her. Blackgaard arranges a meeting place with Whit—under a clock tower—to swap Connie for the computer.

Whit coordinates with Agent Phillips, who insists that his squad be there to capture the doctor. So, under the clock tower, Whit waits. The agents watch him closely through their surveillance equipment. Suddenly, Whit disappears! Whit has been grabbed by Richard Maxwell, Blackgaard's former assistant. Maxwell insists that he's out to get revenge against Blackgaard. Maxwell claims he's there to help Whit, but Whit is unsure of what to believe. Since Maxwell also claims to know where Blackgaard is holding Connie, Whit decides to trust him and go along.

Our story comes to a climax in a warehouse owned by Blackgaard. But there are a few more twists left in the story. Richard Maxwell forces Blackgaard to his knees, Whit intercedes, and there's at least one character who isn't who he pretends to be. Along the way, we learn important lessons about the folly of revenge, deception, and greed. And Blackgaard, who never seems to learn anything from his experiences, vows that he will have his own revenge against John Avery Whittaker.

behind the scenes:

"I had originally intended for these episodes to take place in London, not Chicago—but that wasn't practical because of the accents.

"The inspiration for 'Waylaid in the Windy City' came from a news item in England. Apparently, someone in the British military had been driving across London and stopped to use the bathroom. A laptop computer was sitting on the front seat of the car. The computer contained all kinds of military secrets. In the short time the man was away from his car, someone broke in and stole the laptop. The police and military were convinced that whoever took the laptop had no idea it was so important. I shifted the idea onto Whit getting involved in a luggage mix-up, and the show took off from there."

—Paul McCusker

STUDY QUESTIONS:

1. Was it inappropriate for Connie to get angry with airport security? Why or why not?
2. If you were Whit, would you have trusted Richard Maxwell? Do you think Richard had changed for better or for worse? Explain.
3. Read Proverbs 29:25. How has the Lord kept you safe lately?

Episode #157 "Last in a Long Line"

Theme: The importance of family heritage.
Scripture reference: Proverbs 17:6
Written and directed by Phil Lollar
Production engineer: Dave Arnold
(Original air date: 7-06-91)

Eugene and Bernard are both doing freelance work for the local Presbyterian church—Bernard on their windows and Eugene on their computer. They walk home together. Much against Bernard's wishes, they take a shortcut through the cemetery next to the church. Eugene chides Bernard for feeling spooked—until he sees a tombstone with "Meltsner" carved on it! When Eugene investigates further, he discovers that the full name on the stone reads "Leonard Meltsner"—Eugene's father!

Eugene is stunned. He has always believed that his father and mother died on an anthropological expedition in the rain forests of Zaire. Eugene tells Whit about the grave, and they decide to find out the truth. The city records reveal nothing, so they go back to the cemetery to see if the church has any records. That's when Eugene notices that the grave has been manicured! Its grass has been trimmed, and fresh flowers have been planted.

Just then, the church secretary walks up to them. She reports that the church's records don't reveal much information. But files do show that its upkeep is paid for each month by "The GHM Fund, Connellsville Bank." Eugene surmises that "GHM" stands for "Garvey Hiram Meltsner," his grandfather. Eugene is ecstatic at the thought that his grandfather may still be alive! Eugene had always assumed that he was the last living Meltsner.

Whit reminds Eugene that the check came from a trust fund—his grandfather might *not* be alive. Whit pulls a few strings and learns where G. Hiram lives. But when Whit and Eugene go there, they learn that Eugene's grandfather passed away just a few days earlier. Eugene is heartbroken.

G. Hiram did leave his grandson a piggy bank filled with silver dollars, though. Hiram originally gave it to Eugene for Christmas when he was two years old. Because Eugene liked it so much, Hiram promised to put a silver dollar in it every year for Eugene. But Eugene's father and grandfather had a fight, and Eugene never saw Hiram again. Hiram still put coins in the piggy bank every year, hoping that Eugene would visit. Eugene is touched. For the first time in his life, he understands the true meaning of family.

STUDY QUESTIONS:

1. Why was it so important for Eugene to know if his father was buried in Odyssey? Why was finding his grandfather so important to Eugene?
2. What would you do if you saw your family name carved on a tombstone in a cemetery?
3. What do you know about your heritage? Is your family history important to you? Why or why not?

ULTIMATE ADVENTURES IN ODYSSEY TRIVIA

The People and Pets of Odyssey

All of Bernard Walton's siblings are janitors, and all have names that begin with the letter "B": Bettina, Beulah, Benjamin, Boris, and Bosco.

Jack Allen taught Whit how to make ice cream curly cues.

George and Mary Barclay were high school and college sweethearts.

Mary Barclay dreams of going to Tahiti on vacation.

Jimmy Barclay's first trip in the Imagination Station was in "Lincoln."

Some of the professions Jimmy Barclay wants to have when he grows up: radio DJ, actor, paramedic, rugby player, preacher.

Edwin Blackgaard's first name is Ronald.

Erica and Hayley Clark had 27 stuffed animals—all with names—that they donated to the Whit's End "Share-A-Thon."

Cryin' Bryan Dern has worked at both Odyssey 106 FM and Odyssey 105 FM.

Harlow Doyle's office is a block south of Whit's End—which, of course, is in the middle of a park.

Jason Whittaker's NSA number is 1131. Tasha Forbes's number is 2632.

Philip Glossman resigned from the Odyssey City Council because he made racist comments about the Japanese.

Before coming to Whit's End, Connie Kendall was not terribly fond of kids.

Eugene Meltsner has seven years of college under his belt.

Eugene Meltsner wears Dumbo pajamas.

Continued on page 125.

Episode #158 "A Day in the Life"

Theme: Distinguishing truth from falsehood.
Scripture reference: John 8:32
Written by Paul McCusker
Directed by Phil Lollar
Production engineer: Bob Luttrell
(Original air date: 7-13-91)

Whit writes a story about the people of Odyssey called "A Day in the Life." He sends it to his agent, and the agent gives it to a publisher. The publisher brings it to the attention of a movie producer—who wants to make it into a motion picture. And so Hollywood descends on Odyssey.

Director Marty Scoresberg and his crew arrive and turn the place upside-down. They change not only Whit's story, but rewrite some of the characters, eliminate others, fabricate scenes, and add nonexistent structures and even a *beach front* to the midwestern town! Whit and the others complain loudly, but there is nothing they can do. Whit's agent sold all the story rights to the producer.

Finally, the movie is finished, and the premiere is held at the Bijou Theatre in Odyssey. Ironically, everyone *likes* it. The movie isn't Odyssey, but the townspeople hope everyone will know the difference. They all go back to Whit's End and, as Whit puts it, are "glad to be living and breathing in the *real* Odyssey, where the lights . . . burn late into the night, and we slip quietly to the end of yet another day in our lives. No movie could capture the wonder of that. Then again, who said it has to?"

STUDY QUESTIONS:

1. Why was it so hard for the people of Odyssey to see the movie script change so radically?
2. Whit said, "Maybe the people will know the difference" between the movie Odyssey and the real Odyssey. Do you think he was right? Explain.
3. How else does the media distort reality?

Episode #159 "The Homecoming"

Theme: Forgiveness.
Scripture reference: Matthew 6:12
Written by Paul McCusker
Directed by Phil Lollar
Production engineer: Dave Arnold
(Original air date: 7-20-91)

Richard Maxwell is back in town, and immediately everyone is on guard—especially Tom and Lucy. Tom is instantly suspicious of Maxwell, while Lucy just wants to steer clear of him. Richard asks to talk with Whit. In their conversation, Richard reveals the *real* reason he's back in town: He wants to apologize to the people he hurt. Whit is happy to hear it—but he clarifies the difference between merely apologizing and asking for forgiveness. The latter means that Richard needs their pardon for what he's done.

Richard says he wants to ask forgiveness. He starts with Whit, who immediately grants Richard's request. Richard moves on, asking Connie, Eugene, Lucy, and Tom for forgiveness. Connie forgives Richard almost instantly. Eugene grants him conditional forgiveness. That is, he will accept Richard's apology with the understanding that they won't become anything more than acquaintances.

When it comes to Lucy and Tom, however, Richard runs into large and painful brick walls. Lucy is still hurting from the way Richard used her during the Blackgaard/Applesauce fiasco. Tom refuses to trust Richard any further than Tom can throw him.

Richard decides to leave town. But just before he boards the bus, Lucy rushes up and tells Richard that she's done a lot of soul searching and realizes that she, too, must forgive him. Richard thanks her and leaves. Only Tom is left holding his grudge . . . which he and Whit later bring humbly and earnestly before the Lord.

STUDY QUESTIONS:

1. What is the difference between apologizing to someone and asking for their forgiveness? Which do you think is harder to do?
2. What does the Bible say about forgiveness?
3. Do you need forgiveness for something you've done? Do you need to forgive someone else?

Episode #160 "A Rathbone of Contention"

Theme: The folly of taking shortcuts.
Scripture references: Proverbs 21:5; 26:27
Written and directed by Phil Lollar
Production engineer: Bob Luttrell
(Original air date: 7-27-91)

A new business is going up on the old site of Blackgaard's Castle. It's called "the Electric Palace," and its proprietor is Bart Rathbone! Bart is on such an aggressive schedule to get the place up and running that he's cutting major corners. First, he hires Rodney to take care of the promotion. Rodney hires Lucy to write fliers, but he never bothers to pay her. Then, Bart "borrows" Eugene to set up the computer. And when Bart's certified electrician can't make it in time for the building inspector, he pulls Eugene off the computer installation to do the wiring for the building. Eugene protests—he doesn't know enough about electricity to wire a whole building! But Bart insists, so Eugene ends up giving it a try.

When Whit finds out about Bart and Rodney's shoddy business practices, he tries to stop them. But before he can, the building inspector comes. He okays everything in the structure but notices that the place is still operating off a generator. Bart says they were just about to switch over to city power. He orders Eugene to throw the switch. Everything seems fine for a moment. Then the place goes haywire, nearly blowing up! The Electric Palace doesn't get passed by the inspector—and Bart has plenty of time to dwell on the folly of taking shortcuts.

STUDY QUESTIONS:

1. Why is it usually best not to take shortcuts?
2. What are the benefits of taking your time?
3. Have you ever taken a shortcut on a project when you knew you shouldn't? When? Did you learn from your mistake?

Episode #161 "Isaac the True Friend"

Theme: Biblical history: David and Jonathan; friendship.
Scripture references: 1 Samuel 20; Proverbs 18:24
Written and directed by Phil Lollar
Production engineer: Dave Arnold
(Original air date: 8-03-91)

Isaac is looking for a friend. He tells Whit he has only acquaintances. So Whit sends Isaac on a trip in the Imagination Station to witness the friendship between Jonathan the prince and David the shepherd—one of the greatest friendships of all time. While there, Isaac meets a boy his age named Samuel. The two of them help Jonathan and David avoid King Saul's wicked plots to have David killed. Samuel and Isaac become steadfast companions, and by the end of the adventure, Isaac has learned what it means to have—and *be*—a true friend.

the Adventures in ODYSSEY archives:

"Isaac the True Friend" introduced the character of Sam Johnson, one of *AIO's* central kids.

STUDY QUESTIONS:

1. Whit told Isaac that to make a friend, you have to *be* a friend. What did he mean?
2. What made the friendship between Jonathan and David so strong?
3. Do you have friends like Jonathan and David? How do you show your love for them?

ULTIMATE ADVENTURES IN ODYSSEY *TRIVIA*

The People and Pets of Odyssey (Continued from page 123.)

Eugene Meltsner has great knowledge in the areas of computers, cars, law, electronics, circuitry, history, science, chemistry, radios, word origins, inventing, French, Greek, mythology, physics, math, astronomy, and literature ... but limited knowledge of the creative arts.

Bart Rathbone had a bad church experience as a child and has been working to undermine Sunday school ever since.

Lucy Cunningham-Schultz and Isaac Morton once saved Rodney Rathbone's life.

The known members of the Bones of Rath are: Rodney Rathbone, Rusty Gordon (or Malone), Butch Evans, Denver Thorpe, and Jay Brandt.

Tom Riley's apple orchard was originally planted by Johnny Appleseed.

Tom Riley is a member of the board of directors at the unnamed Bible college where George Barclay earned his degree.

Katrina Shanks is allergic to carnations.

Bernard Walton won the Golden Squeegee Award for Custodian of the Year.

Bernard Walton's favorite childhood singer was cowboy star Hip Hobson.

Jason Whittaker didn't laugh until he was two years old.

Whit wrote stories to help him deal with his wife's death.

Twelve animals have been featured in *Adventures in Odyssey* episodes: 4 cats: Boswell, Fergeson, Sasha (Dr. Blackgaard's cat), Jasper (videos); 2 dogs: Normal, Sherman (videos); 2 birds: Napoleon & Josephine (videos); 3 horses: Leah, Rachel, Little Joe; 1 mouse: Luther.

Other animals that have appeared in the series include: a pack of wild dogs, a bear, various farm animals, a skunk, a whale—or "big fish"—a tank of piranhas, a lion, a flock of sheep, all of the animals on the ark, a Goat-Man, a catfish, a wild bull, and Cryin' Bryan Dern.

Episode #162 "Peacemaker"

Theme: Being a peacemaker.
Scripture reference: Matthew 5:9
Written by Paul McCusker
Directed by Phil Lollar
Production engineer: Bob Luttrell
(Original air date: 8-10-91)

Whit gathers Connie, Jessie, and Donna together for a meeting. The church's elders have decided to make next week Compassion Week—seven days of programs designed to help those in need. Because of their particular talents, Whit wants the three young ladies to come up with an idea to help raise food, clothing, or money for the homeless. The three agree and immediately decide to discuss ideas.

Things get off to a slow start, though. After more than an hour of sitting and staring, Jessie decides to go home. Connie says the least they can do before they break up is decide who will lead their group. Donna volunteers, but Jessie thinks Donna always wants to be the leader. Donna hotly remarks that Jessie is too unreliable and disorganized to lead the group. This causes a huge rift between them, with Connie stuck in the middle.

Connie reports what has happened to Whit. He says Connie needs to play peacemaker in order to get the two girls speaking to each other and working together again. Connie tries, and at first she makes things worse. But finally, she gets Donna and Jessie to start working on their idea for helping the homeless, and it ends up being a smashing success. Blessed are the peacemakers, indeed.

behind the scenes:

"The Third World Banquet in this script was based on a real-life banquet of the same name held at my church. The young people of a church would eat the kind of meager food a good portion of the world eats every day. The experience was designed to teach them how blessed we are and move teens to want to help the poor."

—Phil Lollar

STUDY QUESTIONS:

1. Where did Connie go wrong when she first tried to get Donna and Jessie together?
2. What does it mean to be a peacemaker?
3. Does your church or community have a program to help the poor and homeless? Are you a part of it? Why or why not?

Episode #163 "A Model Child"

Theme: Vanity; the source of real beauty.
Scripture reference: 1 Samuel 16:7
Written by Paul McCusker
Directed by Phil Lollar
Production engineer: Dave Arnold
(Original air date: 8-17-91)

Bart Rathbone and the Electric Palace are sponsoring Odyssey's first beauty contest, junior division. Melanie and Traci are a bit disappointed because they know their parents won't let them enter such a silly contest. But one of their friends, Monica, has entered the contest, and she's taking it very seriously. Or rather, her *mother* is. Monica's mom insists that Monica act much older than her 11 years. She won't let Monica play or swim with the other girls. She buys Monica makeup and the latest teenage fashions. She places her daughter on diets—all to try and mold her into a model child.

Monica doesn't like all these restrictions, but she has too much respect for (and fear of) her mother to rebel. But when Monica can't fit into the dress her mother has bought her for the beauty contest, she runs away to the forest where Melanie and Ann find her. Monica is devastated—she knows her mother will be angry that she couldn't lose enough weight to wear the dress.

Ann and Melanie start to take her back to town when Monica collapses. They rush her to the hospital. Later, Monica and her mother both get counseling help. Monica won't be winning any beauty contests, but she *will* get back to being a normal little girl.

STUDY QUESTIONS:

1. Why did Whit and the Jacobs think beauty contests are silly? Do you agree? Why or why not?
2. Have you ever judged someone by the way they look? How can you start looking at people's hearts instead?
3. Read 1 Samuel 16:7. How does God define beauty?

Episode #164 "Sixties-Something"

Theme: God's unchanging nature; the consequences of drug use; the true source of peace, freedom, and love.
Scripture references: Hebrews 13:8; Revelation 22:13
Written by Paul McCusker
Directed by Phil Lollar
Production engineer: Bob Luttrell
(Original air date: 8-24-91)

Bart Rathbone is at it again. He has the whole town whipped up in a frenzy over a "Remember the Sixties" movement. Everyone is walking down the street in sandals, bell-bottomed jeans, paisley shirts, Nehru jackets, turtlenecks, and psychedelic headbands. Connie thinks it's interesting. Whit thinks it looks as silly now as it did in the '60s.

Bart tries to get Whit to join in the fun, but Whit flatly refuses. Connie, however, wants to know more. She goes to the library and checks out a volume of poetry and essays about the '60s written by a man named Josh Guthrie. Connie is very taken with Guthrie's musings about peace, love, and freedom. She searches him out.

Connie finds him directing a rehabilitation clinic under an assumed name. Asking Guthrie about his beautiful writing, Connie finds out that he has completely disassociated himself from the '60s. That turbulent decade left him and thousands like him as strung-out "junkies." They wanted freedom without responsibility. Guthrie tells Connie that they ended up with a drug epidemic, AIDS, and self-absorbed people. While everyone else is grooving to the tunes, he wants Connie to remember *both* sides of the story. Connie promises that she will. She tells Whit that she wants to introduce Josh to the true source of peace, freedom, and love: Jesus Christ.

STUDY QUESTIONS:

1. Why didn't Josh Guthrie want Connie to know who he was?
2. Why do some people take drugs? What would you do if a friend was trying drugs?
3. Is it wrong to chase after peace, freedom, and love? Why or why not? What does Jesus say about doing that?

Episodes #165 & 166 "Bernard & Esther," Parts One & Two

Theme: Biblical history: Esther; courage; God's protection and providence.
Scripture reference: The book of Esther.
Written and directed by Phil Lollar
Production engineers: Bob Luttrell and Dave Arnold
(Original air dates: 8-31-91 & 9-07-91)

Robyn wants to take Melanie on an Imagination Station adventure, but Whit has closed it down to work on it. The girls are disappointed—until Bernard tells them a wonderful, true story about a great king named Xerxes, a wicked knight named Haman, and a beautiful and brave maiden named Esther who saved her people from annihilation.

STUDY QUESTIONS:

1. Why were the Jews in captivity?
2. Where did Esther get her courage? Would you have done what Esther did? Why or why not?
3. What holiday do the Jewish people celebrate as a result of Esther's actions?

Episode #167 "Dobson Comes to Town"

Theme: Video/daily *AIO* promotion.
Written and directed by Phil Lollar
Production engineer: Dave Arnold
(Original air date: 9-14-91)

Through a series of rather remarkable circumstances, a special visitor comes to Odyssey: Dr. James Dobson! He isn't quite sure how he got into Odyssey or why he's there—and he's a bit disappointed when Connie and Eugene say they've never heard of him. But Whit has, of course. So Whit and Dr. Dobson take the opportunity to talk about some of the changes going on around town. They discuss the new animated video series and the daily release of *AIO*. While in Odyssey, Dr. Dobson also manages to help Melanie Jacobs. Then, he heads back to the Focus on the Family studios via—how else?—the Imagination Station!

Adventures in the ODYSSEY archives:

"Dr. Dobson Comes to Town" was an episode full of "onlys": the only time Dr. Dobson ever visited Odyssey, the only time anyone famous ever visited Odyssey as himself, and the only time anyone *real* ever visited Odyssey as himself.

STUDY QUESTIONS:

1. If you hosted a daily broadcast, what subjects would you cover? Why?
2. Dr. Dobson helped out Melanie Jacobs. Is there someone you know who needs help? How could you help them?
3. What famous person would you like to meet? Why?

Episode #168 "The Curse"

Theme: The folly of believing in curses.
Scripture references: Ephesians 6:12; 1 John 4:4
Written and directed by Phil Lollar
Production engineer: Bob Luttrell
(Original air date: 9-21-91)

Whit and Eugene have been hard at work preparing for a new addition to Whit's End—a microwave satellite dish that will beam Kid's Radio programs to Connellsville. They both have errands to run, leaving Connie and Lucy to manage Whit's End. Lucy is looking for an interesting news article to write. She doesn't have long to wait, for as soon as Whit and Eugene leave, in walks one of the most unusual characters ever to come into Whit's End. He's an Indian chief, complete with war paint, a blanket, leather clothing, and moccasins. He asks who the owner of the building is. When Connie tells him, he puts an ancient curse on Whit for defiling the lands of his ancestors!

Connie and Lucy don't believe any of this will happen. But the Indian tells them that when the signs start coming true, they *will* believe. The girls want to know what signs the chief is talking about, so he tells them: "Flying horses made of rock. Water that is not traveling up. Forest comes to building." They think the whole thing is bizarre and are about to dismiss it—until the signs start happening! Connie, Lucy, and even Eugene start believing in the Indian's nonsense. They are especially afraid since the culmination of the curse is Whit's death!

When Whit returns, he calms their fears, though. He reveals that the medicine man is really a con man. The "Indian" works at a radio station in Connelsville—he's merely trying to scare Whit out of putting up the microwave satellite dish.

STUDY QUESTIONS:

1. Why didn't Whit believe in the curse?
2. What does the Bible about say about curses?
3. How can you avoid being taken in by scams like curses?

Episode #169 "Hold Up!"

Theme: Mankind's basic nature; God's protection.
Scripture references: Ecclesiastes 7:20; Jeremiah 17:9; Romans 3:23
Recommended maturity level: 9 and up
Written by Paul McCusker
Directed by Phil Lollar
Production engineer: Bob Luttrell
(Original air date: 10-26-91)

PARENTAL WARNING: This episode is about a holdup at Whit's End. Though it is comical and no one gets hurt, several gunshots are fired during the end of the program, which may be too intense for younger listeners.

Connie and Eugene are closing up the shop one evening when they begin talking about the nature of man. Connie takes the Christian perspective that man is basically evil. Eugene takes the New Age theory that man is basically good.

A stranger sitting in the corner booth overhears their conversation and agrees with Eugene—that mankind is basically good, it's simply man's circumstances that cause him to do evil. The stranger, Hank Murray, uses himself as an example. He has no money and no job. He is basically a good person, but the only way he can pay for his banana split and make a little cash on the side is by holding up Whit's End! He does this, pulling out a gun to make his point!

Connie manages to set off the silent alarm, dispatching the police. The police don't want to have any unnecessary shooting, though, so they wait for Whit to arrive to see if he can show them a different way into the building. Whit, who has been delivering a lecture at Campbell County Community College, knows of a tunnel leading into Whit's End from the forest. Not only that, but he has a plan that will use the displays and attractions inside Whit's End to scare Hank Murray into surrendering. Through this, Whit proves that the emporium is really what you make of it. If you make it something good, it will be good. But if you make it something scary . . .

the Adventures in ODYSSEY archives:

Charles Knox Robinson, who played Hank Murray, is a versatile actor. He's played a thief, an Indian medicine man, Nathan Hale, and an angel for us!

STUDY QUESTIONS:

1. Why did Whit and Connie think that humans are basically evil? Why did Eugene and Professor Ronan believe that people are basically good? What do you think?
2. Why was Hank Murray so frightened by the displays in the Bible Room?
3. Did Connie and Eugene do the right thing when Hank Murray held them up? What would *you* have done?

Episode #170 "A Test for Robyn"

Theme: Procrastination; cheating.
Scripture reference: Psalm 51:17
Written by Paul McCusker
Directed by Phil Lollar
Production engineer: Bob Luttrell
(Original air date: 11-02-91)

Robyn Jacobs is bored with studying and wants to play a game of checkers with Melanie. But Melanie refuses because she's studying for an English test she has at the end of the week. Mel reminds her sister that Robyn *also* has a test, in history, at the end of the week. Robyn says that she'll cram for it on Thursday night.

The next day, however, Robyn discovers that there is much more to the test than she thought. She asks Whit and Eugene for help on how to study. They offer several theories and tips, which Robyn unsuccessfully tries. Finally, the night before the test, she turns to her parents in desperation. After admonishing Robyn for procrastinating, they help her cram for the test.

The next morning, Melanie tests Robyn all the way to school. Robyn discovers, to her delight, that she actually *does* know the material. But that afternoon when Melanie asks Robyn how she did, Robyn says she went blank. After dinner that night, Robyn is distraught. When her mother tries to comfort her, Robyn reveals the real reason for her distress—she cheated. Her mother comforts her, and the next day they figure out a solution to her dilemma. Robyn vows from now on to study for tests in advance.

STUDY QUESTIONS:

1. Why is it a bad idea to put off studying until the last minute?
2. Why didn't Whit's study methods work for Robyn?
3. Have you ever gone blank on a test? How did you handle it?

Episodes #171 & 172

"The Cross of Cortes," Parts One & Two

Theme: Greed; God's sovereignty.
Scripture references: Deuteronomy 6:13-15; Luke 4:8
Written and directed by Phil Lollar
Production engineers: Bob Luttrell and Dave Arnold
(Original air dates: 11-09-91 & 11-16-91)

Whit receives a mysterious package from Mexico. He opens it and discovers it's from Dan Isidro, his missionary friend from Nicaragua. Eugene wonders why Dan is in Mexico. The accompanying letter reveals that he is on furlough there. Since Whit and Eugene have planned a trip to the region, Dan has invited them to spend some time with him and requests that they bring along the enclosed parcel.

Whit and Eugene examine the parcel more closely and discover that it's an ancient map. Dan's letter cautions them to not let it out of their possession or sight. Whit and Eugene study the map and recognize certain landmarks and symbols. Among them are the ancient city of Tenochtitlán, which is modern-day Mexico City, and two volcanoes called Corozon del Diablo— "Heart of the Devil"—which has under them the symbol of a cross!

Whit and Eugene head off to Mexico to find Dan. When they arrive there, almost immediately they are met by a policeman named Cordova. He claims Isidro stole the map! Once Cordova leaves, Dan sneaks in through Whit and Eugene's hotel window. Dan tells Whit that Cordova is not a member of the Mexico City police, but of the Nicaraguan police. He has no authority in Mexico and, like Dan, is after the map.

The ancient map leads to an important find: the Cross of Cortes! It was worn by Hernan Cortes when he defeated the Aztec nation and conquered Mexico. Legend has it that the cross contains supernatural powers. It makes the wearer invincible.

Unfortunately, Dan can't read the map any better than Whit or Eugene can. So he's contacted an interpreter named Mendoza, who meets them at a bullfight the next day. Mendoza is a woman, and she is taken with Eugene, much to his discomfort.

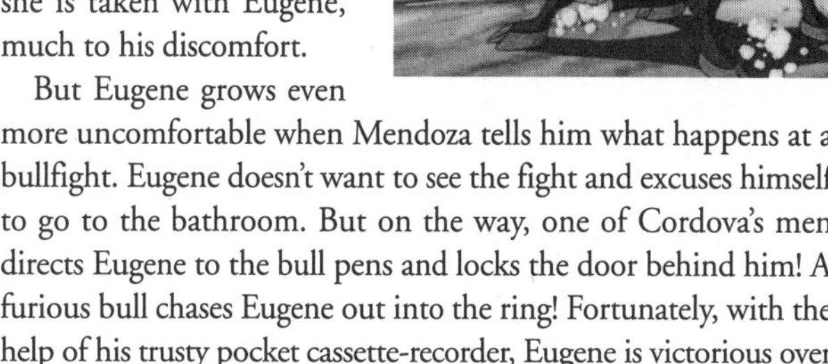

But Eugene grows even more uncomfortable when Mendoza tells him what happens at a bullfight. Eugene doesn't want to see the fight and excuses himself to go to the bathroom. But on the way, one of Cordova's men directs Eugene to the bull pens and locks the door behind him! A furious bull chases Eugene out into the ring! Fortunately, with the help of his trusty pocket cassette-recorder, Eugene is victorious over the bull.

When Whit and Eugene return to decipher the mysterious map, they learn that a key symbol on the map is missing. They decide they may be able to figure out what it was. They go to an old temple and, with the help of a sundial and a flashlight, they figure it out. But they're just about to go to the Cross of Cortes when friends suddenly turn into enemies and take the map! Whit, Eugene, and Dan Isidro are undaunted (since they cleverly had their own copy of the map). The chase is on to see who'll get to the Cross of Cortes first.

Our story is resolved in a dark cave where our characters meet. In the cave, we discover their true reasons for wanting the Cross of Cortes. We won't give away all the surprises, but you can be sure that an important lesson about the dangerous allure of power (even when people have the best of intentions) is clearly learned.

the *Adventures in* ODYSSEY archives:

We wanted to do several shows where Whit and the gang visit foreign lands. "The Cross of Cortes" was our first attempt. It highlighted several problems with these kinds of stories—not the least of which is finding actors with authentic accents.

behind the scenes:

"Bob Luttrell and I couldn't find any decent sound effects of bull vocalizations, so we both got in front of a microphone and took turns doing the roars and grunts. Then we pitched the tape down to create the bull sounds."

—Dave Arnold

STUDY QUESTIONS:

1. Why did everyone want the Cross of Cortes?
2. Do things like crosses *really* have supernatural power? Explain.
3. Why is the cross so important to Christians?

Episode #173
"A Thanksgiving Carol"

Theme: Thanksgiving; being thankful.
Scripture reference: 1 Thessalonians 5:18
Written and directed by Phil Lollar
Production engineer: Dave Arnold
(Original air date: 11-23-91)

Eugene and Connie are in the midst of yet another disagreement—this time about Thanksgiving. Eugene believes that, in this modern age, God isn't at all part of the holiday. Connie feels just the opposite. They both go to Whit to settle the matter. He does resolve things—by agreeing with Eugene! Whit explains that many people don't associate Thanksgiving with God. To most people, the holiday is just a lot of good food, a day off from work, football games, and a parade on TV.

But Whit has a plan to change all that, via a Kid's Radio production of "The Thanksgiving Carol"—an adaptation of Charles Dickens's "A Christmas Carol." The characters are all similar: the miserly money-lender Ebenezer Stooge, who has a stony heart and a mind dulled from greed; his overworked clerk Bob Wretched, who makes barely enough to feed his wife and 10 children; Teeny Tom, Wretched's crippled youngest son; the haunting Jacob Arley, Ebenezer's late partner who bears the chains he forged in life (and sounds suspiciously like a long-lost *AIO* character); and Terence Clodbody, the ghost of Thanksgiving past, present, and future.

Through their actions, Stooge learns the true meaning of Thanksgiving—including to whom we're all giving thanks. God bless us, every one!

the ADVENTURES IN ODYSSEY archives:

This was the last program recorded in our Pomona, California, studios. Focus on the Family had finally moved to Colorado Springs, Colorado. For *Adventures in Odyssey*, our new recording home would be a rented studio in Burbank, California, since most of our actors live in southern California.

STUDY QUESTIONS:

1. Why did Eugene think God has nothing to do with Thanksgiving? Was he right? Why or why not?
2. Why do you think some people would like to permanently take God out of Thanksgiving?
3. What are some other holidays in which God is no longer an important part? How can you focus on Him during those special days?

Episode #174
"Where's Your Daddy?"

Theme: Having a parent in prison.
Scripture reference: Matthew 25:31-46
Written by Paul McCusker
Directed by Phil Lollar
Production engineer: Dave Arnold
(Original air date: 11-30-91)

Whit and Connie are preparing a space for the Christmas tree inside Whit's End. They look out the window and notice a woman sitting on a park bench under a tree. She's been sitting there for some time, and now she's crying. Whit investigates and discovers that the woman's name is Julie Myers. She and her children—Eric and Brooke—moved to Odyssey a few weeks ago, and Julie hasn't been able to find a job. So Whit promptly offers her one.

Later, Tom brings a fresh tree in from his farm, which they all set up and decorate with envelopes from the Angel Tree Project. In the envelopes are the names of families who have a parent in prison. People from churches around Odyssey will come in, pick up an envelope, and help that family by giving clothing and toys.

Later, Whit and Tom discover that the Myers family is a candidate for such help: Julie's husband, Ernie, is in prison. Whit, Connie, and especially Tom resolve to help the Myers. Tom visits Ernie in prison and studies the Bible with him—unbeknownst to the rest of the family. Meanwhile, Eric is bitter about his dad and thinks that no one will be willing to help them. But Christmas morning proves Eric wrong. Brooke gets a new doll, Eric gets a bicycle, and Julie gets from Ernie the best present of all: A letter saying Ernie has become a Christian. After hearing this news, Julie decides to offer the kids a present of her own: a visit to their dad. And while they have nothing to give him, Tom believes that somehow their joy will be enough.

the ADVENTURES IN ODYSSEY archives:

Eric Myers was played by Joe Dammann, who also played Nicholas in the *McGee & Me* videos. Brooke Myers was played by Amber Arnold, daughter of Dave Arnold

STUDY QUESTIONS:

1. Why didn't anybody except Whit want to hire Julie Myers? Why didn't Whit have a problem with it?
2. Why was Eric so skeptical of Whit, Tom, and Connie?
3. Does your church have a prison visitation program or an Angel Tree project? If so, how can you participate?

Episode #175 "East Winds, Raining"

Theme: Don't judge others; trust in God.
Scripture references: Psalm 33:11-13, 16; Galatians 3:26-28
Written by Paul McCusker
Directed by Phil Lollar
Production engineer: Bob Luttrell
(Original air date: 12-07-91)

Bart Rathbone is ordering products from one of his distributor reps, David Saburo. Bart thinks David must be embarrassed by his Japanese ancestry, considering that it's Pearl Harbor Day. David tries to tell him that December 7 is an important day for him, too, because his father was at Pearl Harbor. Bart suggests that David not tell that to anybody around Odyssey—several families lost relatives when the Japanese bombed Pearl. David humbly accepts Bart's suggestion.

Meanwhile, Connie finds her great-uncle Joe sitting next to the war memorial in McCalister Park, remembering where he was on that fateful day in 1941. Connie says she would love to hear about his experience. Uncle Joe tells Connie he was actually in Hawaii, working as a courier for the U.S. Department of State and the Naval Base at Pearl. His close friend, Sam, worked as a decoder for the U.S. Naval Intelligence.

In a flashback, Sam says he's convinced that the Japanese Imperial Fleet is up to no good. He asks Joe to help him check it out. Reluctantly, Joe agrees and slowly becomes convinced that Sam is right. They set out to warn the American fleet at Pearl that the Imperial bomber planes are coming. But despite Joe's warning, no one listens. Sam insists they keep trying, but it is too late. Pearl Harbor is destroyed. Sam is killed in the process.

Uncle Joe is sad at the memory and at losing his best friend. Then David Saburo speaks. He stopped by to see the memorial and heard Joe's story. David mentions again that his father was at Pearl. He worked as a decoder for the U.S. Naval Intelligence. His name was Sam Saburo. David is Sam's son.

the Adventures in Odyssey archives:

Parley Baer, who played Uncle Joe Finneman, was a colonel in America's armed forces during World War II. It was one of the first times we featured an actor who had lived through the historical event. It was an honor to work with Parley. Parley was also a good friend of Hal Smith's. They both played characters in the *Andy Griffith* show—Hal was Otis, and Parley was the town mayor.

behind the scenes:

"I especially remember this episode because I had such a difficult time finding detailed information about the bombing of Pearl Harbor. I was living in England at the time, and it wasn't the sort of event the English would have much information about.

"One day, in a local bookstore, I finally found a helpful reference book. It was a big coffee-table edition about World War II, and I didn't want to spend the money on it—so I huddled in a corner with a piece of scrap paper, writing down all the information I could. I was nervous and kept waiting for a sales clerk to insist that I buy the book or leave. Fortunately, that didn't happen."

—Paul McCusker

STUDY QUESTIONS:

1. Why did Bart Rathbone warn David Saburo not to tell anyone in Odyssey that his father was at Pearl Harbor? Was Bart wrong for doing so? Why or why not?
2. Read 1 Samuel 16:1-13 and Matthew 7:1-5. How does God look at each of us? What did Jesus say about judging people?
3. Do you have a grandparent or other relative who lived through World War II? What is their story?

Episodes #176 & 177 "The Star," Parts One & Two

Theme: The Christmas story—the visit from the Magi.
Scripture reference: Matthew 2:1-15
Written and directed by Phil Lollar
Production engineers: Bob Luttrell and Dave Arnold
(Original air dates: 12-14-91 & 12-21-91)

Connie and Eugene take a voyage in the Imagination Station to ancient Judea to see the baby Jesus. But once there, they get separated. Eugene finds himself in the desert with three strange travelers who are known as the Magi, and Connie ends up with a kind man named Proclus, who takes her to Jerusalem.

There, she meets Mary, Joseph, and the Holy Child. What Connie doesn't know is that Proclus is a Roman soldier who works for wicked King Herod! Proclus tells Herod that the Messiah may be a child. Just as Mary and Joseph are about to leave the temple, Herod calls Mary over to him and takes Jesus from her! Fortunately, Herod returns Jesus to His parents, proclaiming there is no Messiah.

Connie and the holy family return to Bethlehem just as Eugene and the Magi arrive in town! The Magi tell Herod about their search and convince him that the Messiah really is a child—from Bethlehem. Herod sends the Magi off to find the new king, but he keeps Eugene behind—trapped in a dungeon—in order to get information from him.

Fortunately, Proclus is there. After questioning Eugene, Proclus discovers Eugene's connection to Connie. Proclus releases Eugene. The two take off after Connie and the holy family, finding them and the Magi in the small town of Bethlehem. The wise men bring the child some gifts, Connie holds the baby Jesus, and Proclus learns that a small infant can, indeed, be the light of the world.

STUDY QUESTIONS:

1. Why did Herod want to kill Jesus?
2. Why did the wise men travel to see Him? What significance did the gifts have?
3. What gift could *you* give to the King?

Episode #178 "Room Mates"

Theme: Family relationships; getting along with others.
Scripture references: Leviticus 19:18; Mark 12:28-31
Written by Paul McCusker
Directed by Phil Lollar
Production engineer: Bob Luttrell
(Original air date: 12-28-91)

The Campbell County Community College dormitories are getting their once-every-10-years fumigation, and Eugene finds himself homeless. Bernard runs into Eugene and opens up his home to him—after all, they are distantly related. Eugene accepts Bernard's offer, and the new odd couple is born.

The two of them unintentionally drive each other crazy. Despite this, Eugene feels obligated to not only stay with Bernard, but also to pay him back for his kindness. So Eugene tries to help Bernard with his work.

This leads to one disaster after another, culminating when Bernard's scaffolding collapses—while he's standing at the top of it! Bernard gets a severely sprained ankle and several bad bruises. Eugene feels terrible. He visits Bernard and apologizes for being so stubborn. Bernard, after a bit of prodding from Whit, also apologizes. They both understand a little bit better what it means to "love your neighbor as yourself."

STUDY QUESTIONS:

1. Why were Bernard and Eugene always so much at odds?
2. Why did Bernard find it so hard to apologize to Eugene?
3. What does it mean to "love your neighbor as yourself"?

1992

In 1992, we kicked off the year with a series of 12 episodes that dealt with various virtues. Among those virtues were wisdom, purity, integrity, justice, and moderation. Each episode began with the phrase, "It all started when . . ." The series was intended to teach lessons about attributes we felt had been neglected.

The year also brought some changes behind the scenes. Marshal Younger began working for *AIO* as a freelance writer. We also secured other writers who helped us to establish new characters we grew to love. Characters that were developed during this time included "Jenny," a blind girl who was the pen pal of Melanie Jacobs, and "Chunky," an affable young man who reminded us of the earlier character "Oscar." Another character arrived in 1992 as well—Harlow Doyle, our successor to Officer David Harley.

Our constant tinkering with the Imagination Station created some interesting and diverse plot turns. In one episode, it brought a medieval knight into present-day Odyssey. In another, it allowed George and Jimmy Barclay to experience some father-son bonding. And, finally, it gave us insight into the lives of Whit and Eugene as they both experienced a strange "life-after-death" program that Whit had developed for the machine.

We also looked further into some of our characters' lives and pasts. From Bernard's experiences as a young crossing guard, to Connie's efforts to reconcile her divorced parents, to the story behind the death of Tom Riley's son—each story helped make the world and people of Odyssey all the more real.

Episode #179 "You Gotta Be Wise"

Theme: Wisdom; discernment.
Scripture reference: Proverbs 22:6
Written by Paul McCusker
Directed by Chuck Bolte
Production engineer: Dave Arnold
(Original air date: 1-04-92)

It all started one evening at the Jacobs' household. Dale Jacobs tries to get Robyn to come downstairs for dinner. Dale is shocked to learn that Robyn and several other kids around Odyssey have become big fans of a new rock-and-roll band—led by Rodney and the Bones of Rath! As Robyn's father *and* the editor of the *Odyssey Times*, Dale investigates. He discovers that the band is yet another scheme by Bart Rathbone, this time designed to swindle money from Odyssey's young.

Aside from the ear-piercing noise, Dale is alarmed by Rodney's lyrics. Many of the songs have titles like, "I Wish You Would Hurry Up and Die," "Beasts of Hades," "Razor Blade Rag," and "Who Needs Parents?" Dale confronts Bart, but Bart shrugs things off. He says that Dale just doesn't understand modern teenagers. But other parents are angry as well. Several of them become so irate and concerned, they decide to use Rodney's tapes to fuel a gigantic bonfire. Suddenly, Dale finds himself torn in the middle of an argument about parental rights, censorship, and free speech—an argument that plays out between himself and his own daughter.

Things come to a head when the parents organize a march on the Electric Palace that nearly turns into a riot. Dale arrives in time to calm everyone. He suggests that an alternate course is to teach kids *why* the lyrics are offensive. In other words: Learn to discern.

STUDY QUESTIONS:

1. Why were Dale and the other parents so concerned about Rodney's lyrics?
2. Is it wrong to listen to rock-and-roll music? Why or why not?
3. What does it mean to be discerning?

Episode #180 "Isaac the Pure"

Theme: Purity.
Scripture reference: Matthew 5:8
Written by Paul McCusker
Directed by Chuck Bolte
Production engineer: Bob Luttrell
(Original air date: 1-11-92)

It all started one afternoon on the way to Whit's End. Sam notices that his good friend Isaac is unusually quiet. After a lot of coaxing from Sam, Isaac finally reveals that he feels bad about laughing when the gang starts telling dirty jokes after school. Isaac says the jokes make him feel dirty, and he wants to be pure.

Isaac first starts his purity campaign by ridding his house of all the things that make him feel impure—including his father's *Reader's Digest* and *National Geographic* magazines. Mr. Morton isn't pleased by this, though he does admire Isaac's desire to be pure. Then, Isaac gathers all of his possessions and takes them to Hamstrung's Junk Shop. He trades them for an old, useless clock. Isaac's plan is to keep himself so busy cleaning and repairing the clock, he'll have no time to think impure thoughts.

Unfortunately, later that week, Isaac runs across Sam. Sam tells him some of the gang's new jokes, the last of which turns out to be a little crude. Isaac laughs in spite of himself—then suddenly realizes that he's acted impurely again! As a result, Isaac concludes that he must seclude himself so he can remain untouched by the impurities of the world. Everyone thinks he's gone a little crazy, until Whit comes over and sets Isaac straight. Isaac learns from Whit the true meaning of purity. And, thanks to Isaac's efforts, he also winds up with a beautifully restored antique clock!

STUDY QUESTIONS:

1. What does it mean to be pure? Why is purity important?
2. Why did Isaac think that secluding himself from everyone would keep him pure?
3. What's the best way to stay pure?

Episode #181 "It Takes Integrity"

Theme: Integrity.
Scripture reference: Proverbs 10:29
Written and directed by Phil Lollar
Production engineer: Bob Luttrell
(Original air date: 1-18-92)

It all started when the Odyssey Middle School student council elections began. Lucy is upset that Curt Stevens is running for office again. This time he has his sights set on being student body president! He's asked Lucy to interview him for the *Odyssey Owl*, which Lucy refuses to do—she knows that all Curt wants is a fluffy story about himself.

What really gets Lucy, though, is that Curt is running *unopposed*! Lucy's incensed that the only kid at Odyssey Middle School who cares enough to get involved in their school elections is Curt. She tells Whit that the students need someone who stands for integrity!

Whit thinks Lucy is absolutely right. He says that the person the students need is Lucy! He convinces her to run for office against Curt, and the race begins. Both Curt and Lucy work hard to get votes. Curt says anything to get elected, while Lucy conducts an upright campaign that focuses on the issues.

Curt begins to get creamed in the polls. He is desperate to save his sinking campaign. So at Bart Rathbone's suggestion, Curt digs up some dirt on Lucy. He parades Lucy's past misreporting of the facts in "Muckraker," using it in a debate to make her look like a first-class hypocrite. Lucy is devastated and decides the only honorable thing she can do is withdraw from the race.

But Whit takes matters into his own hands and confronts Curt with his dirty politicking. Curt says all is fair in love and war—until Whit makes Curt believe that Whit is going to reveal the truth about Curt's alcoholic father to the *Odyssey Owl.* Curt panics, begging Whit not to do it. Whit says he'd never do anything so cruel—unlike Curt. For once, Curt gets the message and ends up beating Lucy to the punch: He withdraws from the race, leaving the office wide open for Lucy.

STUDY QUESTIONS:

1. Why was Lucy so upset that Curt was running for office?
2. Whit told Lucy, "If you're not willing to participate in democracy, then you can't complain when it goes sour." What did he mean?
3. Do you agree with Curt's statement that "all is fair in love and war"? Why or why not?

Episode #182 "The Scales of Justice"

Theme: Justice.
Scripture reference: Psalm 89:14
Written and directed by Phil Lollar
Production engineer: Bob Luttrell
(Original air date: 2-15-92)

It all started one afternoon. While walking through the woods near Gower's Field, Isaac literally stumbles across a plastic bag filled with $2,000! He takes it back to Whit's End. Whit advises him to take it to the police, and Isaac does. He files a "found property report" and waits for 90 days to see if someone claims the property. But on the *89th* day, Rodney Rathbone appears! He claims the money is his and says that Isaac tried to steal it!

The police know that Rodney is obviously lying. So, because of the special circumstances surrounding the case, and in the interest of giving the kids at Whit's End a civics lesson, Captain O'Ryan of the Odyssey Police Department agrees to let the matter be settled in a mock trial—held at Whit's End. Whit serves as Isaac's lawyer, and Bart serves as Rodney's. Connie is the bailiff, and Eugene presides over the court as judge.

Rodney and Isaac state their sides in the matter. In the end, Eugene decides that the money is Rodney's. Rodney and Bart are thrilled, while Isaac wonders if justice really does exist. It does—but not always in the ways we expect. In a news report, we learn that the money was, in fact, counterfeit—and Bart and Rodney have been taken to the police station for questioning.

STUDY QUESTIONS:

1. Do you think Eugene made the right decision?
2. Was justice ultimately served in this case?
3. What does God say about justice?

Episode #183 "Tales of Moderation"

Theme: Moderation.
Scripture references: Matthew 6:19-21; Luke 18:18-25
Written and directed by Phil Lollar
Production engineer: Bob Luttrell
(Original air date: 2-22-92)

It all started at Whit's house. Connie is there, helping him clean out his garage. There, she notices something: Although Whit is wealthy and owns lots of property, he chooses to live in a modest home. Connie asks Whit about it. She wonders why he doesn't live in a way that better suits his financial status. Whit tells Connie that wisdom and experience have taught him that it's much better to exercise moderation and live more simply.

Connie isn't convinced, so Whit gives her a book of three tales, which explains his reasons for living like he does. The first tale is about two farmers. The first farmer lives frugally through good times and doesn't suffer through bad times. The second farmer lives it up during the good times and has nothing when famine strikes. Whit's second tale is about a man who surrounds himself with every expensive and modern appliance available in order to become truly independent. Unfortunately, the man finds that his appliances soon start controlling his life—*literally.* Finally, Connie reads the story of a rich, young prince who asks a great teacher what he must do to gain eternal life. The teacher tells him to sell all his possessions and give them to the poor. The young prince leaves sadly—he loves his wealth more than he loves anything else.

The point is made—Connie understands the importance of moderation. In her prayers that evening, she thanks God for giving her a wise friend like John Avery Whittaker.

Adventures in the ODYSSEY archives:

As unbelievable as it seems, "Tales of Moderation" was the only *AIO* episode where a talking toaster appears.

STUDY QUESTIONS:

1. Connie felt that since Whit was wealthy, he should live like it. Do you agree? Why or why not?
2. What were Whit's reasons for living simply?
3. Why is it important to practice moderation? How can you practice moderation in your life?

Episode #184 "Isaac the Chivalrous"

Theme: Chivalry.
Scripture reference: Job 13:15
Written and directed by Phil Lollar
Production engineer: Dave Arnold
(Original air date: 2-29-92)

It all started at Whit's End. Isaac Morton wants to know about the meaning of chivalry. So Whit sends Isaac back in the Imagination Station to the time of knights and maidens. Isaac becomes the squire to Sir William of Marshall and helps him defeat the Black Knight. But when the adventure ends, Isaac exits the Imagination Station and informs Whit that he's rather disappointed. He didn't learn much about chivalry. Whit asks Isaac to write down how the program could be improved, and the first thing Isaac writes is "spend more time with Sir William of Marshall."

Suddenly, the door to the Imagination Station opens—*and out steps Sir William!* Being a typical thirteenth-century knight, Sir William instantly believes that witchcraft has brought him to the twentieth century. Isaac explains that it isn't witchcraft, but *Whit*-craft that's responsible. He takes the knight to Whit and Eugene. The only explanation they can come up with is that some sort of quirk must have occurred in the Station's programming.

Sir William has some difficulty understanding modern-day Odyssey. When he has an unfortunate run-in with Connie's portable radio, Whit suggests that Isaac take the knight around town to get him used to things in our time. Meanwhile, Whit and Eugene will figure out a way to get the knight back to *his* time. Sir William and Isaac have many comical misunderstandings on the streets of Odyssey. After visiting a local church and running into Rodney Rathbone, Isaac learns the real meaning of chivalry: "Though He slay me, yet I will hope in Him" (Job 13:15).

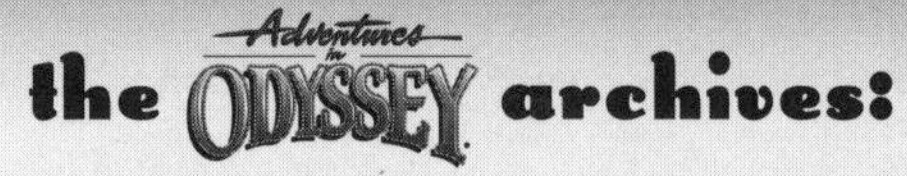

"Isaac the Chivalrous" was the first time we ever had a character come *out* of the Imagination Station and step into Odyssey.

STUDY QUESTIONS:

1. What is chivalry? Why is it important?
2. Sir William didn't know what a radio, a car, or ice cream was. Name some other items that weren't available in the thirteenth century.
3. What do you think Job 13:15 means? How can you apply it to your life?

Episode #185 "A Question of Loyalty"

Theme: Loyalty.
Scripture reference: Micah 7:5
Written and directed by Paul McCusker
Production engineer: Dave Arnold
(Original air date: 3-07-92)

It all started at Odyssey Middle School. The *Odyssey Owl* is having an important meeting. Mr. Burton, the school's sponsor and editor, makes an announcement about a county-wide newspaper contest—a competition to determine the best middle-school newspaper in the county. The contest is open to all middle-school newspapers—including the *Odyssey Voice.* The *Voice* is a fluffy, low-budget paper, put together by kids who don't know good writing from a hole in the ground.

The *Owl* staff is excited about the contest and thinks they have a good chance of winning. Lucy is especially involved in the contest. She even goes out of her way to encourage and coach a talented, shy, new girl named Emily Fowler. Lucy teaches her the basics of newspaper writing and helps draw Emily out of her shell. A friendship is born. Unfortunately, Emily and Lucy's friendship quickly withers when Emily begins to receive praise for her articles. Soon, Emily finds she simply doesn't have time for Lucy anymore. Things worsen when Emily goes to Mr. Burton and demands that her articles get front-page status. Mr. Burton asks Lucy to talk some sense into Emily, but it's no use. Either Emily gets the front page, or she defects to the *Odyssey Voice.*

The *Owl* refuses, Emily leaves, and the contest becomes heated. It is a hard-fought, close competition, but in the end the *Owl* wins! Only, Lucy doesn't feel like rejoicing. She's lost a friend. She has also learned a hard lesson about loyalty—that its betrayal can have long-lasting and heartbreaking consequences.

STUDY QUESTIONS:

1. Why did Emily suddenly decide she didn't have time for Lucy anymore?
2. Since their friendship turned out so sour, would Lucy have been better off not helping Emily in the first place? Explain your answer.
3. What was the worst act of betrayal in history? Why?

Episode #186

"The Conscientious Cross-Guard"

Theme: Conscientiousness; perseverance.
Scripture reference: Proverbs 20:6
Written and directed by Phil Lollar
Production engineer: Bob Luttrell
(Original air date: 3-14-92)

It all started when Bernard won the Campbell County Custodial Commission's highest honor, the Golden Squeegee Award. Bernard addresses the guests in attendance at the gala affair, telling them of a particular incident in his life that taught him the importance of perseverance.

The incident happened when he was in middle school. . . . Young Bernard and his best friend, Nick, are crossing guards—a position and responsibility they hold proudly. Of course, no job is completely without risk or an element of danger. In this case, the danger comes from a thug named Tanyer Hyde and his gang.

Tanyer likes nothing better than to break the rules and pick on young Bernard—and on this particular morning, Tanyer gets the chance to do both. Unfortunately for Hyde and his gang, they don't see the school principal drive up to them as they torment Bernard. The principal reprimands Hyde and his gang, giving them all detention that afternoon—subsequently forcing them to miss their big baseball game.

This makes them furious at Bernard, and they vow to get him back that afternoon after school. Bernard tries everything he can think of to get help facing the bullies, but circumstances and the cowardice of his friends leave him to fight all alone. Even his best friend, Nick, refuses to help. Nick tells Bernard: Just leave. No one will care. It's certainly not worth getting practically killed. But Bernard remembers some advice the old school janitor, Mr. Umphrees, once gave him: Turn to a higher power for strength.

Bernard does just that, and he stays to face Tanyer. Bernard is by himself—but not alone. Tanyer and his gang pick on Bernard, shoving him out into the street and into the path of an oncoming car! Mr. Umphrees saves Bernard by pushing him out of the way. In the process, the old janitor gets hit.

Later, at the hospital, Mr. Umphrees says that when he was young, he faced a similar situation. But Umphrees ran away. Helping Bernard was the old janitor's chance to redeem himself.

Back at the banquet, Bernard thanks Mr. Umphrees for teaching him the importance of sticking to his guns, doing his duty—and remembering that with God, you're never alone.

the Adventures in ODYSSEY archives:

"The Conscientious Cross-Guard" was yet another movie tribute—to the Gary Cooper classic *High Noon*. This episode was also nostalgic for us—young Bernard was played by David Griffin (who also played Jimmy Barclay), and Tanyer Hyde was played by Donald Long (who also played Jack Davis).

behind the scenes:

"An embarrassing thing from this episode occurred on the morning of the recording in Los Angeles. We were at breakfast, talking over the cast, when we realized we hadn't cast the part of Nick. In a panic, Paul McCusker ran to the phone and called Chad Reisser. Chad's mom got him to the studio just in time to do the part."

—Dave Arnold

STUDY QUESTIONS:

1. Why did Mr. Umphrees think it was so important for young Bernard to stay at his position? Was he right?
2. Why did everyone abandon Bernard?
3. Would you have stayed if you were Bernard? If you were his friend, would you have helped him? Why or why not?

Episode #187 "An Act of Nobility"

Theme: Nobility.
Scripture reference: Luke 22:24-26
Written and directed by Phil Lollar
Production engineer: Dave Arnold
(Original air date: 3-21-92)

It all started in Isaac Morton's history class. Isaac's teacher asks the class the meaning of nobility. Isaac pipes up and says that it's about kings and queens, dukes and earls. His teacher responds, however, that there's a whole lot more to nobility than that. He assigns Isaac a report about what nobility is and why it's important. Isaac relays all this information to Whit, who proceeds to tell Isaac a wonderful story about nobility—under the condition that Isaac doesn't use it in his report. Isaac reluctantly agrees, and Whit tells his story. . . .

In a small country called Muldavia, a young American named James Armor notices that the locals give him odd looks when he walks past. He doesn't know why until he's out in the forest and sees a small plane go down nearby. James rushes to the plane and helps rescue the pilot.

Two other men who have been following the plane help as well: General Farnham and Doctor Munroe. They also react strangely to James—for James and the pilot look *exactly* alike! What's even more amazing is that the pilot is actually the Crown Prince.

But the pilot is not a very responsible or good prince, according to the general and the doctor. This has made the pilot a target for a political coup, spearheaded by his illegitimate cousin, Baron Von Warberg.

Just before the prince flew off, Von Warberg drugged the prince's wine, hoping that he would crash his plane and die. Von Warberg could then step in and take over the country. The general and pilot are worried. The prince survived the crash, but he is in no condition to go through with the coronation. When he fails to show up, the general and doctor fear Von Warberg will certainly exploit the situation for his own political purposes. At the very least, Muldavia will be plunged into civil war.

So, James comes up with a plan: *He* will pose as the prince for the coronation. The general and the doctor agree with the plan and set it into motion. The plan works, but when the real prince finds out, he accuses James, the doctor, and the general of trying to steal his crown. The prince (who is now the king) orders James to be arrested. But before James can be taken away, Von Warberg shows up—he has also discovered the secret.

Von Warberg uses the mix-up to his advantage by making it look as if James, Roderick, the doctor, and the general all killed each other. Suddenly, James disarms Von Warberg and his sidekick, again saving the king. King Roderick finally realizes he's been a fool. He thanks James for teaching him the true meaning of nobility.

STUDY QUESTIONS:

1. What is the meaning of nobility?
2. Why did James show himself to be more noble than the prince?
3. James helped the prince even though he really didn't deserve help. Would *you* have? Was it right for James to deceive the people into thinking he was the prince? Why or why not?

Episode #188 "The Courage to Stand"

Theme: Courage.
Scripture reference: 2 Chronicles 32:7-8
Written by Paul McCusker
Directed by Phil Lollar and Paul McCusker
Production engineer: Bob Luttrell
(Original air date: 3-28-92)

It all started when Robyn tried out to be a cheerleader. Shannon, the head cheerleader, and Michelle, a member of the squad, are impressed with Robyn—they tell her she's definitely in the running. But, they inform her, there's more to being a cheerleader than simply knowing all the routines and showing up for the games and pep rallies. Robyn also has to "fit in." Her chance to do that is at a party Shannon is throwing Friday night at her house.

Robyn is excited about going—until her mom tells her that the party has to be chaperoned, or Robyn can't go. Robyn asks Shannon about it. Shannon makes light of the question at first, then tells Robyn that the party will have adults there. Only, Shannon isn't telling the truth: Robyn discovers that Shannon's parents aren't even in town and won't get back until the following Sunday. Robyn balks, and Shannon confronts her—if Robyn wants to be a cheerleader, then she needs to go to the party. Robyn screws up her courage and says she can't. It wouldn't be right. Shannon instantly snubs her.

Robyn is upset. She goes to Whit's End, where Connie comforts her. Connie tells of a similar situation she once faced. She relays that standing up for what's right is far more rewarding than compromising your beliefs.

Back at school the following week, one of Shannon's friends, Michelle, tells Robyn that the party got way out of hand. Everyone who attended got into trouble. Michelle says that because Robyn had the courage to stand up to Shannon, Michelle also refused to go to the party. Hearing that, Robyn understands Connie's words—it's best to have the courage to stand up for what you believe.

STUDY QUESTIONS:

1. Did Robyn have good reasons for wanting to be a cheerleader? Explain.
2. What did Shannon mean when she told Robyn that she'd have to "fit in" to be a cheerleader?
3. Have you ever been pressured to "fit in" with a certain group? How did you handle it? Is trying to fit in always wrong? Explain.

Episode #189 "No, Honestly!"

Theme: Honesty.
Scripture reference: Proverbs 12:22
Written and directed by Phil Lollar
Production engineer: Bob Luttrell
(Original air date: 4-04-92)

It all started outside of Whit's End. Rodney Rathbone is trying to sell Sam an "original, *signed* photograph of General Lee." But just as Sam is about to buy it, a stranger named Mark Reed walks up, mistaking the tower of Whit's End for a local church. He overhears Rodney's claim about the photograph and exposes the signature for the forgery it is. Rodney is upset that his scam was foiled. He investigates this stranger, believing there's more to him than meets the eye.

Apparently, Reed is a representative for a photography company that specializes in church membership directories. He talks to Whit, who promises to introduce Reed to the pastors in the area. Reed thanks Whit and leaves. Rodney again denounces Reed as a fake and a scam artist. Everyone, including Whit, tells Rodney to back down. But Rodney refuses. He sets out to prove his allegations, using an illegal device from his father's shop: a radio scanner that picks up on car phones. Rodney listens in on Reed's calls—and overhears him talking with a partner about how to break into people's homes! Rodney rushes around town to tell everyone what he's learned, but no one believes him! Rodney's past has caught up with him. He's pulled too many pranks to be taken seriously. In desperation, he turns to the only person in all of Odyssey who he thinks will give him a chance: John Avery Whittaker.

Whit takes the chance that Rodney is telling the truth. Whit, along with the police, sets a trap for the gang of thieves. For once in his life, Rodney does the right thing and helps save the day—but has he learned to be honest? What do you think?

the *Adventures in* ODYSSEY archives:

"No, Honestly!" was the only episode that Rodney Rathbone ever narrated. We had to walk a fine line with Rodney here. We didn't want to make him look too good, since he is our resident bully. So, even though Rodney is right in this episode, he still doesn't learn a lesson.

STUDY QUESTIONS:

1. Why was Rodney suspicious of Mark Reed?
2. Why was Whit angry with Rodney even after Rodney proved that Mark was out to rob houses?
3. Why is honesty so important?

LISTENERS' TOP NINE FAVORITES

Here's what listeners have told us are their top all-time favorite episodes. Are any of *your* favorites on this list?

- "The Underground Railroad," 1, 2 & 3
- "The Perfect Witness," 1, 2 & 3
- "A Name, Not a Number," 1 & 2
- "Aloha, Oy!," 1, 2 & 3
- "The Time Has Come"
- "A License to Drive"
- (tie) "Someone to Watch Over Me"; "The Imagination Station," 1 & 2
- (tie) "The Cross of Cortes," 1 & 2; "Waylaid in the Windy City," 1 & 2
- (tie) "The Case of the Secret Room," 1 & 2; "Pen Pal"; "Terror from the Skies"

Episodes #190 & 191

"Moses: The Passover," Parts One & Two

Theme: Biblical history: Moses; the Exodus.
Scripture reference: The book of Exodus
Written by Phil Lollar and Paul McCusker
Directed by Phil Lollar
Production engineers: Bob Luttrell and Dave Arnold
(Original air dates: 4-11-92 & 4-18-92)

This episode tells the story of Moses and the exodus of the Hebrews from Egypt—complete with the plagues, the angel of death, the pillar of fire, and the parting of the Red Sea—as experienced by Jimmy and George Barclay in the Imagination Station.

behind the scenes:

"The crowd that crossed the Red Sea was actually only made up of 15 people. Using the marvels of technology, I processed their voices to make them sound like millions."

—Bob Luttrell

STUDY QUESTIONS:

1. Why did it take so long for Pharaoh to release the Hebrews?
2. George said Passover was a "terrible night," but Moses disagreed. Why?
3. Why should we remember and observe Passover today?

Episode #192

"Modesty Is the Best Policy"

Theme: Modesty.
Scripture reference: 1 Timothy 2:9
Written and directed by Paul McCusker
Production engineer: Dave Arnold
(Original air date: 4-25-92)

George is trying to talk to Donna as she is getting ready for a party. As usual, George walks into Donna's room without knocking and is met with shrieks and howls of protest—Donna isn't dressed yet. George is confused by this turn of events and asks Mary about it. Mary tells him that Donna is getting older. From now on, George will have to expect this sort of behavior. George reluctantly agrees.

Just then, Donna comes downstairs wearing a new, revealing dress. George absolutely forbids Donna to go out like that, but Donna says all the girls are wearing dresses like this. Finally, Mary strikes a compromise: Donna can wear the dress as long as she also keeps on the coat that came with it. Donna reluctantly agrees and heads off to the party.

Once there, she grumbles and complains to Jack Davis that her parents aren't fair. Donna is standing there sweating in a coat, while everyone else is wearing what they want. She finally gets so upset, she removes her coat. Immediately, she gets reactions from the guys at the party.

Donna likes those reactions—until she learns throughout the next week at school that her reputation as a nice girl is suffering. Suddenly, rumors are spreading that Donna is not as pure as she lets people think. Shannon even nearly challenges her to a fight—she thinks Donna is using her slinky little dresses to steal Shannon's boyfriend. Finally, Donna realizes that things may have gone too far—and that modesty is the best policy after all.

STUDY QUESTIONS:

1. Why didn't George want Donna to go out the way she was dressed?
2. How much do you think your modesty (or lack of it) determines your reputation?
3. Why is it so important to be modest? How does God feel about it?

Episode #193

"A Tongue of Fire"

Theme: Watching your words.
Scripture reference: James 3:1-12
Written and directed by Phil Lollar
Production engineer: Bob Luttrell
(Original air date: 5-02-92)

Jimmy Barclay is on the air at Kid's Radio! He talks, he tells jokes, he trades barbs with his audience, and he is pretty entertaining for a kid in middle school. But he wants to be *very* entertaining. So, with Eugene's help, Jimmy's made a demo tape to take to the most popular disc jockey in town—Cryin' Bryan Dern.

Whit thinks the tape is amusing but warns Jimmy that he needs to be careful about what he says—some of his quips border on being insults. Jimmy sloughs off the advice and goes to Dern. Dern tells Jimmy to do exactly the *opposite*. In fact, one of Dern's secrets is to tape people covertly, make clips of their choicest comments, and put together well-chosen questions to make the speaker look ridiculous.

Jimmy quickly puts this device to use. He tapes Eugene as he reveals to Whit a surprising and private admission—he has failed his driver's test. Eugene is mortified that Jimmy would reveal this information on Kid's Radio. Whit is so angry about it, he pulls Jimmy's show off the air.

Jimmy doesn't understand what all the fuss is about—until he hears himself being made a fool of on Bryan Dern's program. It seems Dern did to Jimmy what Jimmy did to Eugene. Jimmy doesn't like it one bit. He apologizes to Eugene, and the two of them set out to make a new demo tape of the Jimmy Barclay Show—a kinder, gentler demo tape. And Jimmy learns an important lesson about the damage that the tongue can do.

STUDY QUESTIONS:

1. Why did Jimmy think it was okay to secretly record Eugene? Why was Whit so angry with Jimmy for what he did?
2. How can you learn to be more careful about what you say? Is that a struggle for you? Why or why not?
3. Read James 3:1-12. What did the apostle James mean when he said that "the tongue is a fire"?

Episode #194 "A License to Drive"

Theme: Diligence.
Scripture reference: Proverbs 10:4
Written and directed by Phil Lollar
Production engineer: Bob Luttrell
(Original air date: 5-09-92)

Whit is enjoying a calm afternoon at Whit's End when the quiet is suddenly shattered by an argument between Connie and Eugene. Whit wants to know what the fuss is. Connie tells him that she was just trying to share one of her goals with Eugene—her dream of being a teacher—and Eugene burst out laughing!

Whit reproves Eugene, but Eugene insists that he couldn't help himself. He says his reaction was involuntary. His brain finds the concept of Connie becoming a teacher to be absurd. Connie responds with a low blow, making fun of Eugene's lack of a driver's license. Another argument ensues. Whit again breaks up the fight. He asks them why they can't help each other instead of tearing the other person down all the time. Connie guesses that it's because they just don't see eye-to-eye. Eugene speculates that they rarely have opportunities to assist one another.

Whit doesn't buy their excuses. He immediately comes up with an idea to bring them together. Connie wants to be a teacher, and Eugene needs help to pass his driver's test—so Whit orders Connie to teach Eugene how to drive!

At first, the experiment is a disaster. Connie is an overbearing instructor, and Eugene believes the best way to learn how to drive is to memorize the Odyssey traffic manual and study the workings of the internal combustion engine. Despite their best efforts, Eugene again fails the test.

They are both ready to give up when Whit makes them try again. They take a practice drive around McCalister Park and come across a car with a pregnant lady inside who is about to give birth. Eugene is forced to face his greatest fear. He must drive them all to the hospital while Connie stays with the mother in the backseat.

Everything works out fine. Later, when Eugene, Connie, and Whit visit little Connie Eugenia in the maternity ward, Eugene proudly shows off his new driver's license—and thanks Connie for being such a good teacher.

the *Adventures in* ODYSSEY archives:

The title of "A License to Drive" was a play on the James Bond film *A License to Kill*, which was released around the same time as this episode.

STUDY QUESTIONS:

1. What are the qualities of a good teacher? Was Connie a good one? Why or why not?
2. After Eugene failed his driver's test, why didn't Whit let both he and Connie quit?
3. Have you ever wanted to quit a difficult task? What or who prevented you from doing so?

Episode #195 "Father's Day"

Theme: Dealing with parents' divorce.
Scripture reference: Malachi 2:14-16
Written and directed by Phil Lollar
Production engineer: Bob Luttrell
(Original air date: 6-20-92)

It's Father's Day, and Connie's dad, Bill, has come to town—and specifically to Whit's End—for a surprise visit. He's actually just passing through on his way to see his ailing mother in New York. He wants to take Connie with him. Connie is all for it but says she has to get permission from her mom first. She doesn't have long to wait. A few moments later, June Kendall walks through the door.

Things are a bit tense at first, but soon June gives her consent for Connie to go to New York. Bill and June even have a pleasant conversation about the old days and the happy times they had together. Bill insists on taking June and Connie out to dinner that night. He even walks June out to her car. Connie is so happy to see her folks "back together" again, she gets the wild idea that maybe she can do something to make the arrangement permanent.

Later, Bill and June come back to Whit's End to pick Connie up for dinner. They are stunned to find the place redecorated to resemble one of their favorite restaurants they used to go to when Connie was little. Connie tries her best to recreate the atmosphere of happier times—but both Bill and June gently tell Connie that it is impossible for them to get back together again. June explains that they are different people now, but Bill has a more fundamental reason: He's already remarried!

When Connie hears this, she gets upset. Things get even worse when she discovers that Bill married someone named April, a woman whom Connie doesn't even know. Connie storms out, telling her dad to forget about the trip to New York.

Later, June talks with Connie about her father's irresponsible ways, and Connie makes yet another discovery—her mother still has feelings for her father. June has simply learned to deal with the hurt and move on with life. Connie takes her mother's example to heart. The next morning, she informs Bill that she'll go with him to New York after all. She also determines that, even though she still loves her father, she won't look at him through rose-colored glasses anymore. From now on, she'll see him as he really is.

STUDY QUESTIONS:

1. Why did Connie think she could get her folks back together again?
2. Why was Connie so angry with her dad when she learned he was remarried?
3. Why do you think the Bible is so against divorce?

Episode #196 "Harlow Doyle, Private Eye"

Theme: Faith.
Scripture references: Luke 17:5-6; 2 Timothy 2:15; Hebrews 10:25
Written and directed by Paul McCusker
Production engineer: Dave Arnold
(Original air date: 6-27-92)

There is a new private detective in town. His name is Harlow Doyle, and his motto is, "No case too big, too small, or too unusual." And it's a good thing. Soon after visiting Whit's End and meeting Whit, Harlow gets hired by Jessie to find something she's lost—her faith!

Whit isn't sure about this, but before he can say anything, Harlow takes off to examine every aspect of Jessie's life. What he finds is revealing: First of all, Jessie has been spending Sunday afternoons at the local bookstore, browsing through teen magazines—hardly uplifting reading material. Second, the local soccer league has started playing their games on Sunday mornings, causing Jessie to miss church. Third, Jessie's Bible school teacher, Dale Jacobs, has been giving boring lessons. Finally, Jessie's parents haven't been as diligent as they should in making sure she attends church and her Sunday night evangelism class.

Harlow puts all the facts together and deduces that the culprit responsible for taking Jessie's faith is . . . Maybe it's better not to say. But the lesson that Jessie learns about faith as being a matter of obedience and discipline is one that applies to all of us.

the Adventures in ODYSSEY archives:

We wanted to bring back the wackiness of Officer David Harley. Harlow Doyle, PI, was the answer, thanks to the vocal characterization and performance of Will Ryan—who played both Doyle and Harley. We got Harlow Doyle's name from two places: "Doyle" was a twist on Hoyle playing cards and "Harlow" was the reworked version of Officer Harley's name.

STUDY QUESTIONS:

1. What were some of reasons Jessie stopped attending church and her Bible school class?
2. Why did Jessie think she had lost her faith? Did Jessie *really* lose her faith? Explain your answer.
3. Have you ever felt like Jessie? If so, how can you begin to feel closer to God again?

Episode #197 "The Midnight Ride"

Theme: American history: the Revolution; Paul Revere; duty; patriotism.
Scripture reference: Psalm 33:12
Written and directed by Phil Lollar
Production engineer: Bob Luttrell
(Original air date: 7-04-92)

It's American history time at Whit's End. When Marsha reads Longfellow's famous poem about Paul Revere's midnight ride, Whit tells her the *whole* story of Revere's ride, the Boston Tea Party, America's quest for independence . . . and "the shot heard 'round the world."

the Adventures in ODYSSEY archives:

Doing a historical story like "The Midnight Ride" is fun partly because of the research. You learn all sorts of fun facts. For example, did you know that after dumping the tea into Boston Harbor, the "Indians" swept up the boat? Or that Revere and company tried to row more quietly by wrapping petticoats around the oars? Or that Paul Revere was actually there for "the shot heard 'round the world"?

STUDY QUESTIONS:

1. Why did the American colonists throw tea into Boston Harbor?
2. Why was it important for America to gain its independence from England?
3. What made Paul Revere's ride so important?

Episode #198 "Treasure Hunt"

Theme: God's protection.
Scripture reference: Proverbs 10:29
Written and directed by Paul McCusker
Production engineer: Dave Arnold
(Original air date: 7-11-92)

The crowds are gathering at McCalister Park for the big Treasure Hunt and War Games Contest sponsored by Bart Rathbone's Electric Palace and Odyssey 105 FM. Bryan Dern is excitedly reporting on the competition as teams of two players race all over town to find the secret treasure. It seems as if everyone in town is participating—except for Whit and Tom. They want nothing to do with one of Bart Rathbone's schemes. At Tom's barn, while listening to Cryin' Bryan on the radio, they also hear that the infamous Hank Murray—who tried to rob Connie and Eugene at Whit's End—has escaped from Campbell County Jail. Whit wonders if Murray would be so bold as to come back to Odyssey. Sure enough, he does return. Murray shows up at the barn and takes Tom and Whit hostage!

Meanwhile, the unlikely team of Isaac Morton and Eugene Meltsner is doing well in the contest. But things get complicated when Isaac and Eugene disagree over a set of clues. Isaac ends up at Tom's barn, where he is also promptly taken hostage by Hank Murray. This leaves Eugene as their only hope for rescue!

Things look dim—until Eugene bursts into the barn just as Hank Murray is about to escape on one of Tom's horses. Eugene stops Hank by blowing a special whistle—which sends the horse into a fit! Murray is thrown from the horse, and Eugene disarms him. Eugene has saved the day, and everyone learns a lesson about God's protection.

STUDY QUESTIONS:

1. Why didn't Whit want to take part in the contest even though it was for a good cause?
2. Did Whit and Tom handle the situation with Hank Murray correctly? What about Isaac and Eugene?
3. Why did Eugene get so carried away with his squirt gun?

Episode #199 "The 'No' Factor"

Theme: Being wise with your time; the danger of overcommitment.
Scripture reference: Ecclesiastes 3:2-8; 11
Written and directed by Phil Lollar
Production engineer: Bob Luttrell
(Original air date: 7-18-92)

Connie is busy, busy, busy! First, her pastor has asked her to be part of an important ministry—visiting the sick and shut-ins, taking them medicine, and running errands for them. Then, Connie volunteers her time to work in the library at Campbell County Community College. Next, she agrees to be in a play Jack Davis is directing for the Odyssey Parks and Recreation Department. Later, Dale Jacobs convinces her to write an article for the *Odyssey Times* about her experiences at Whit's End. Finally, Marsha pleads with her to sponsor their Sunday school class picnic. All this is in addition to her school studies and extracurricular activities, church attendance, membership in the youth group, and her job at a certain ice cream shop and discovery emporium.

To say Connie's schedule is stretched thin would be an extreme understatement! She attacks each task with gusto and fervor—at *first.* But as time goes on, more and more details of each task begin slipping through the cracks. Soon, Connie is messing up on a regular basis—which culminates when she forgets all about her commitment to the pastor.

Fortunately, the pastor is forgiving. He even offers Connie a remedy for her situation, something he calls "The 'No' Factor"—in other words, learning how to say "no." It's a lesson Connie has learned the hard way—and hopefully, she's learned it well.

STUDY QUESTIONS:

1. Why did Connie take on so many tasks?
2. How could she have avoided becoming overcommitted?
3. Is it wrong to say "no" when people want you to help them? Why or why not?

Episode #200 "Feud for Thought"

Theme: Forgiveness.
Scripture reference: Ephesians 4:31-32
Written and directed by Phil Lollar
Production engineer: Bob Luttrell
(Original air date: 7-25-92)

Eugene and Bernard are taking a trip together to an annual family reunion. Bernard goes every year, so he couldn't be more bored by the prospect. But this is Eugene's first time since he discovered he and Bernard are related, so naturally he is nearly jumping out of his skin with excitement.

Eugene has a wonderful time meeting all of his newfound kin—until he meets Bernard's grandfather, Borealis P. Walton. When Borealis learns that Eugene is a Meltsner, he explodes with rage and demands that Eugene leave immediately! Borealis contends that the Meltsners are nothing but a pack of thieves and liars—and Eugene's grandfather, Hiram, was the biggest liar and thief of all!

Bernard finally calms Borealis enough to find out what's happening. Borealis tells Bernard that years ago, Hiram cheated him in a livestock deal, which involved pigs. Hiram's crookedness set the pattern for the Waltons' future. The Waltons could have been prosperous like the Rockerfellers, but instead they all went into the sanitation business.

Eugene begs Bernard to help him right this terrible wrong. Bernard reluctantly agrees. After digging for more information, they find that Hiram did, indeed, cheat Borealis out of his porcine property. Eugene says the only way to remedy the situation is for Eugene to pay Borealis back—even though the sum is astronomical!

But then, an acquaintance of both Hiram and Borealis, Mr. Harry Reems, enters and sets the record straight. He proves that Hiram Meltsner was innocent! Unfortunately, Borealis sees this as just another Meltsner trick and refuses to forgive Eugene. Eugene is crushed. But Bernard says that next year, they'll work together to change Borealis's mind. After all, Bernard chokes out, Eugene *is* family.

STUDY QUESTIONS:

1. Was Borealis justified in holding his grudge against Hiram for so long? Why or why not?
2. Did Eugene do the right thing when he found out why Borealis was so angry? Could he have remedied the situation in any other way?
3. Have you ever held a grudge against anyone? What does Paul say in Ephesians 4:31-32 about forgiveness?

Episode #201 "Fair-Weather Fans"

Theme: Friendship; discernment.
Scripture reference: Proverbs 18:24
Written by Charlie Richards
Directed by Paul McCusker
Production engineer: Bob Luttrell
(Original air date: 8-15-92)

Isaac meets a new kid in town named Derek, who is going door-to-door, selling electric fans. When Derek asks Isaac to join him as a partner, Isaac believes he's found a great friend. Isaac takes Derek around town and introduces him to everyone he knows—including Whit. Then, the two of them proceed to talk all those folks into buying fans. Derek even goes so far as to guarantee that the fans will last as long as the lifetime of the owner's house.

Isaac and Derek make money hand over fist. Things are going well—until Derek learns that Isaac has already introduced him to everyone he knows. Then, Derek disappears. Unfortunately, the fans begin to break. The customers start calling Isaac, demanding to know what the problem is.

Isaac and his dad go searching for Derek. When Isaac finds him, he discovers that their friendship and business partnership was a scam. Derek simply used Isaac to sell useless fans. Derek skips town, leaving Isaac to rectify the situation. With Whit's help, Isaac does. Together they fix the fans, and Isaac learns a painful lesson about choosing his friends wisely.

STUDY QUESTIONS:

1. Why were Isaac and the townspeople so easily taken in by Derek?
2. How would you have handled Derek?
3. What is the best way to choose your friends?

Episode #202 "Timmy's Cabin"

Theme: The importance of family memories; God's protection.
Scripture reference: Psalm 33:18
Written and directed by Phil Lollar
Production engineer: Dave Arnold
(Original air date: 8-22-92)

Philip Glossman is back—and this time he's after Tom Riley's farm! Or at least *part* of it. He wants the land to build a new state highway. Since he works for the state Secretary of Transportation, he has the governmental authority to back up his decision. But the piece of land Glossman wants happens to be the place where Tom's deceased son, Timmy, discovered and rebuilt an old cabin. Tom has decided to clean up the cabin and let the kids of Odyssey use it for a clubhouse.

When he, Whit, and Marsha check out the place, they discover someone is already living there! His name is Chapman, and he is a vagabond—a wandering "explorer of history." He agrees to help Tom around the farm in exchange for his temporary lodgings. But those plans are put in jeopardy when Glossman swoops down on the farm and informs Tom of his intentions.

Tom and Whit try to fight for the land, but it's no use. Glossman holds all the cards. He brings in his bulldozers. He's just about to knock down the one memory Tom has left of his son when Mr. Chapman notices an unusual marking on the door frame. Chapman recognizes the mark as being carved by Johnny Appleseed! In fact, Tom Riley's orchard may have been originally planted by Appleseed! This makes the cabin a historic landmark, which means that Glossman will have to build his highway elsewhere. Justice triumphs after all in Odyssey!

STUDY QUESTIONS:

1. Why did Tom tell Mr. Chapman not to cause any trouble about tearing down the cabin?
2. What was Johnny Appleseed's real name? Why did he plant so many orchards?
3. Have you been to any other historical landmarks? Which ones? Why are they important?

Episode #203 "Double Trouble"

Theme: Judging a book by its cover.
Scripture reference: 1 Samuel 16:7
Written and directed by Paul McCusker
Production engineer: Dave Arnold
(Original air date: 8-29-92)

Lucy goes to the local dinner theatre to interview its new owner for the *Odyssey Times*. There, she gets one of the biggest shocks of her young life. The new owner is Blackgaard—R. Edwin Blackgaard. He is the identical twin of the infamous Dr. Regis Blackgaard, although no one really believes this at first. Everyone is suspicious of poor Edwin, thanks to his notorious brother.

Edwin goes out of his way to prove himself. He puts up posters, does a newspaper interview, attempts conversation, and finally puts on a free performance at the gazebo in McCalister Park. But it's no good—no one shows up for the performance except Whit.

Later that night, Edwin comes to the back door of Whit's End to thank Whit for his support. Whit says that he believes Edwin is really Edwin—not Regis trying to pull a fast one. Edwin thanks Whit and asks for advice on how to win over the people of Odyssey. Whit doesn't have an answer for him. He can only say that it will take time for people to get over their bad feelings for his brother. Whit promises to help Edwin in any way he can and proves it by breaking one of the cardinal rules of Whit's End: He hangs up one of Edwin's posters in the window. Perhaps Edwin will make it in Odyssey after all.

the Adventures in ODYSSEY archives:

For those who are familiar with British television, Edwin Blackgaard and his faithful aide, Shakespeare, were loosely modeled after Edwin Blackadder and his faithful aide, Baldrick.

STUDY QUESTIONS:

1. Why did everyone believe that Edwin Blackgaard was really *Regis* Blackgaard? Were they justified in expecting the worst? Why or why not?
2. What's the best way to be discerning with people?
3. Have you ever felt like you had to prove yourself to someone? If so, explain.

Episode #204 "Wonderworld"

Theme: The proper use of imagination; creativity.
Scripture reference: Psalm 104
Written and directed by Phil Lollar
Production engineer: Bob Luttrell
(Original air date: 9-05-92)

Christopher Robin is leaving Pooh Corner. At least, that's what it feels like to Whit when Jimmy Barclay announces that he is getting too old to come to Whit's End and play in the Imagination Station. In fact, Jimmy is beginning to think that the whole imagination scene is just a bit too immature for him. He even takes on a heavy responsibility—baby-sitting for Donna. He watches a young, energetic bundle of pure imagination named Lawrence Hodges.

While Jimmy is baby-sitting, he and Lawrence go to Wonderworld, where Lawrence takes Jimmy on a roller coaster ride of fantasy fun. They stop at a prisoner of war camp, Nottingham Forest, the African veldt, and the headquarters of the evil agency Destructo. Jimmy tries his best to maintain his newfound "adult" composure. But little by little, Lawrence wears Jimmy down until the two of them jump headlong into the imagination river. They have a great time, and Jimmy realizes that you're never too old to be a kid again.

the Adventures in ODYSSEY archives:

"Wonderworld" marked the introduction of one of our most popular characters—Lawrence Hodges, played by Gabriel Encarnacion. Lawrence's mom is played by actress Janet Waldo, who also provides the voice of "daughter Judy" on the television cartoon *The Jetsons*.

STUDY QUESTIONS:

1. Why didn't Jimmy want to try out Whit's new program for the Imagination Station? Have you ever felt like Jimmy did? When?
2. Are you ever too old to use your imagination? Explain your answer.
3. Read Psalm 104. How does God feel about creativity?

Episode #205 "Flash Flood"

Theme: Friendship.
Scripture reference: Proverbs 17:17
Written by Rich Peterson and Paul McCusker
Directed by Paul McCusker
Production engineer: Dave Arnold
(Original air date: 9-26-92)

It's male bonding time. Whit, Tom, Bernard, and Eugene are going on a camping trip together. Tom and Bernard aren't thrilled about Eugene coming along, though. They believe he will ruin the trip. Indeed, Eugene *does* manage to smash their emergency radio and lead a bear to their camp. But on the whole, Tom and Bernard's barely disguised displeasure is barely noticed by Eugene. He is gratified at having the opportunity to commune with nature—and with "the guys."

Unfortunately, the foursome has picked one of the worst times of the year to go camping—flood season. The flood flashes up right on schedule, stranding the intrepid campers behind a 10-foot wall of water, nearly sweeping Tom away! Tom grabs on to a tree branch, which stretches over the rushing water.

Things look bad until Eugene comes up with a plan to save Tom. The plan means Eugene will have to risk his own safety. Eugene climbs out onto the branch with a long rope and helps Tom to loop it around himself. Whit, Bernard, and Eugene manage to pull Tom to the riverbank. Tom apologizes to Eugene for making fun of him, and everyone learns why it's important to be prepared.

STUDY QUESTIONS:

1. Why didn't Tom and Bernard want Eugene to go along with them on the camping trip?
2. Why is it a bad idea to throw food around in the forest?
3. Have you ever been treated like Tom and Bernard treated Eugene? Is there someone in your life with whom you are being less than patient?

Episode #206 "Pen Pal"

Theme: Friendship; compassion for the handicapped.
Scripture reference: Psalm 146
Written by Vann Trapp and Paul McCusker
Directed by Phil Lollar
Production engineer: Bob Luttrell
(Original air date: 10-03-92)

Melanie is ecstatic. Her pen pal, Jenny Roberts—a girl Mel has never met—is coming for dinner. But when Melanie meets Jenny, she is taken aback. Jenny is blind. Jenny lost her sight to a disease when she was seven years old. Melanie tries to be friendly, but she is unable to get past the fact that Jenny can't see.

What makes Melanie *really* upset, however, is that Robyn seems to be getting along better with Jenny than Melanie is. The two Jacobs girls take Jenny all over town and to all sorts of events, including a soccer match and a carnival. At the carnival, Jenny plays a trick on Melanie in the Maze of Mirrors. This sends Mel over the edge. She lashes out at Jenny and Robyn.

Later, at home, Jenny apologizes to Melanie and reads her a letter she was going to send before her visit—a letter revealing that she is blind. Jenny says Melanie has to realize that she's the same person who wrote all those letters—she loves to laugh and play and have fun, and they can do all those things together. Jenny adds that she knows Mel is scared of Jenny's disability and offers to help her get over her fear. Melanie agrees, and the two of them stop being pen pals . . . and start becoming good friends.

the Adventures in ODYSSEY archives:

"Pen Pal" introduced us to Jenny Roberts, who was the first handicapped character to regularly appear on the program.

STUDY QUESTIONS:

1. Why did Melanie react the way she did when she learned Jenny was blind?
2. Why was Melanie angry that Robyn and Jenny got along so well?
3. Do you know any special people like Jenny? How do you treat them?

Episode #207

"The Case of the Candid Camera"

Theme: Honesty; the consequences of sin.
Scripture reference: Numbers 32:23
Written and directed by Phil Lollar
Production engineer: Bob Luttrell
(Original air date: 10-10-92)

Harlow Doyle is on the case! Rodney Rathbone has had a camera stolen, and he thinks someone from Whit's End took it. It all started when he took his friend Denver to Whit's End to enter him in the Bible Bowl. Rodney set his camera down for a couple of minutes to go sign Denver up, and when Rodney came back, it was gone.

Harlow examines the facts and turns up nothing. Just as he's about to give up, Denver bursts in, conscience-stricken. He confesses that the whole thing is a setup: Rodney needs the camera back because he took pictures of the answers to give Denver so he could win the Bible Bowl! But Denver says he has been studying. He thinks he has a good chance without the pictures! Lucy, who is organizing the contest, decides to give Denver a shot, and he actually wins without cheating!

Or does he? While giving Denver his award, Whit mentions a well-known Bible verse, which Denver doesn't seem to know. Whit is also concerned that the camera hasn't turned up—which means there is still a thief on the loose. Denver is happy, though. He gets his picture in the paper for winning the contest, and he and Rodney plan to use the prize to enjoy themselves at Water World.

Later, during a visit to a nearby shop, Harlow Doyle learns that a roll of film has been dropped off there by Rodney Rathbone to be developed. Harlow puts two and two together and realizes that Rodney dropped off the film *after* the camera had been stolen! How was that possible?

Whit and Harlow get to the bottom of it. They discover that . . . well, we won't give away the ending, but you can be sure that the thief is caught, punishment is meted out—and Odyssey returns back to normal.

STUDY QUESTIONS:

1. Why did Rodney and Denver think they could pull a fast one on Lucy and Harlow?
2. Why didn't Lucy believe Rodney and Denver?
3. Read Numbers 32:23. Have you ever tried to hide your sin? Did it "find you out"?

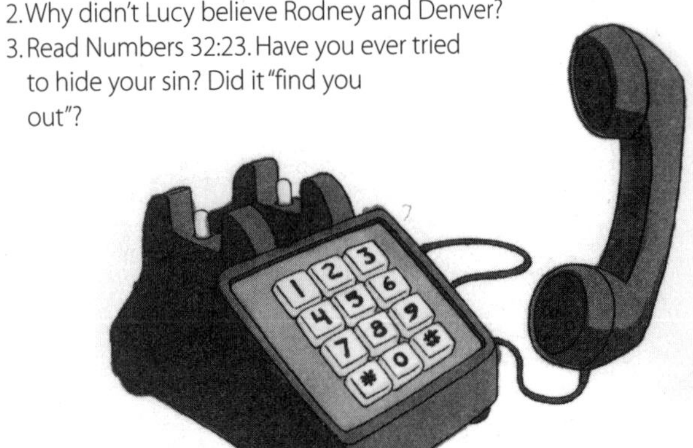

Episode #208

"Pipe Dreams"

Theme: Making the most of a bad situation.
Scripture reference: Luke 19:11-26
Written by Chris Fabry
Directed by Paul McCusker
Production engineer: Dave Arnold
(Original air date: 10-17-92)

It's Campbell County Government Day. The student chosen to represent Odyssey Middle School is Charles Edward Thompson, also known as "Chunky." Chunky is hoping to be assigned to the sheriff's department, but he winds up in "The Division of Fluid Management"—or in actual terms, the Department of Water and Sewage. It's run by a cranky, old woman named Mrs. Bavaqua who doesn't care for kids or Campbell County Government Day.

To make matters worse, a storm has blown in, and it's raining all over town. Chunky does learn a lot about water and sewers, but all in all, it's a dull experience. Things get more interesting when Mrs. Bavaqua gets called away on an emergency, leaving Chunky to answer the phones! The emergency nearly turns into a disaster when the rain causes the system to back up at the treatment plant. Odyssey's water supply is in danger of becoming contaminated. The only one who can stop it is Chunky!

Mrs. Bavaqua walks Chunky through the steps on the telephone, and Chunky saves the day! As a reward, he receives a citation from the city, a real sheriff's badge—and the knowledge that, no matter how big or small, every job is important in its own way.

STUDY QUESTIONS:

1. Why did Chunky think bad things always happen to him?
2. What would you have done if you were in Chunky's place during the emergency?
3. What have you learned about water and sewers?

Episode #209

"Columbus: The Grand Voyage"

Theme: History: Columbus; courage.
Scripture reference: Psalm 22:27–28
Written and directed by Phil Lollar
Production engineer: Bob Luttrell
(Original air date: 10-24-92)

Lawrence takes a trip back in the Imagination Station to the late 1400s, a time of great exploration and discovery. There, he runs into Queen Isabella of Spain. Lawrence tells her that he's looking for Christopher Columbus. Isabella is amused by the boy. She sends him to fetch Columbus. But when Lawrence finds Columbus, the explorer says he doesn't want to meet with the queen. He wants to sail to France.

Lawrence convinces Columbus to meet Isabella. After a series of setbacks, he and Columbus finally set sail. The voyage is rough, and the crew almost revolts. At last, just as their food is about to run out, they spot land—the New World! Columbus claims it for Spain and praises God for His goodness.

Just then, the Imagination Station winds down. Lawrence learns that Columbus was not only a great explorer, but a man of God as well. This makes such a strong impression on Lawrence that he decides to go on the adventure all over again!

STUDY QUESTIONS:

1. Why did Columbus want to sail west? What did he hope to find?
2. Why was he met with so much resistance?
3. Do you think God had anything to do with Columbus's discovery of America? Explain your answer.

Episode #210 "On Solid Ground"

Theme: Bible history: Abraham and Lot.
Scripture references: Genesis 13-14; 18-19:29
Written and directed by Phil Lollar
Production engineer: Dave Arnold
(Original air date: 10-31-92)

This episode gives the story of Abraham, Sarah, Lot, three angels, Sodom and Gomorah, and the Lord God—as reported by Kid's Radio's *O. T. Action News* team, which includes Lucy Schultz, Charles Edward Thompson, Eugene Meltsner, Connie Kendall, and Edwin Blackgaard.

behind the scenes:

"To get the sound effect of Lot's wife turning into a pillar of salt, I used an old Easter basket, twisting it and then speeding up the sound. I also adjusted the voice tracks to get them to break up and get that crystallizing sound."

—Dave Arnold

STUDY QUESTIONS:

1. Why did God love Abraham so much?
2. If you were faced with the same problem Abraham and Lot faced, which land would you have chosen? Why?
3. What does it mean to have a good, solid foundation under you? Why is it important?

WHAT'S IN A NAME?

William Shakespeare may have thought that "a rose by any other name would smell as sweet," but that certainly isn't true of character names. In fact, giving a character just the right moniker can be one of the most difficult parts of scriptwriting. The perfect name not only instantly communicates the personality and behavior of the character, but it can be a whole lot of fun as well. Below are some of the names we've used on *AIO*, the episodes in which they first appeared and, if applicable, where the names came from. Some characters are walk-ons, most are featured roles, a few are main characters—and all are fun.

Character Names Borrowed from Historical Figures

Bedford Forrest—"The Curse" *(Civil War general)*

S. L. Clemmens—"The Case of the Candid Camera" *(Mark Twain's real name)*

Fenimore Cooper—"A Victim of Circumstance" *(Famous American writer)*

Mr. Chapman—"Timmy's Cabin" *(Johnny Appleseed)*

Character Names That Are Parodies of Other Character Names

Rosecrantz Guildenstern—"My Fair Bernard" *(Two characters from Shakespeare's* Hamlet*)*

William Shattered and Mr. Schlock—"Hidden in My Heart" *(Famous actor and well-known Vulcan)*

Character Names That Are Parodies of Real Names

Rod Serley—First appeared in "Missed It by That Much" (Twilife Zone *storyteller)*

Mac Thuselah—"By Faith, Noah" *(Oldest man ever)*

Opera Geraldohue and Dr. Vincent Van Schpeele—First heard in "A . . . Is for Attitude" *(Three daytime talk show hosts and well-known author/positive thinker)*

Marty Scoresberg—"A Day in the Life" *(Two Hollywood directors)*

Cryin' Bryan Dern—First appeared in "A Tongue of Fire" *(Shock jock)*

Brink Chetley—First heard in "On Solid Ground" *(Newscasters)*

Van Scuddy and Port Rosser—First heard in "Our Father" *(Sportscasters)*

Continued on page 151.

NOV 21, 1992

Dear Mr. Bolte

Thank you for the Odyssey Tape If you make Whit die then Odyssey is gone. Dont ever make Whit die. I can't wait to hear the rest of Whits Adventure next week. but he better not die.

Your Friend
Travis

Episodes #211 & 212
"The Mortal Coil," Parts One & Two

Theme: Death; heaven.
Scripture references: 1 Corinthians 2:9; 1 Thessalonians 4:13-15; 2 Corinthians 4:18-5:2; Revelation 7:17; 21:4
Written and directed by Paul McCusker
Production engineer: Dave Arnold
(Original air date: 11-21-92 & 11-28-92)

Whit has been working long hours on a new program for the Imagination Station, and Connie is curious about what the program is. This time, Whit tells her it is an adventure that explores life after death.

Connie is taken aback by this—but is also eager to try it. She does, and the program seems to fizzle out on her. Then Whit gets in the Station to experience the program. While it's running, Eugene enters the Bible Room—just in time to hear Whit cry out! Eugene shuts down the Station. Whit steps out, very shaken.

Later, Tom visits Whit at home and speaks with Whit about the death program. For Christians, Tom says, death is a door to eternal life with God—but it's supposed to be a *locked* door until God opens it. Whit knows Tom is right, but the explorer in him outweighs Tom's good sense. Whit goes back into the Station. Only this time, something goes terribly wrong, and Whit winds up in a coma!

After putting Whit in the hospital, Tom and Eugene go back to Whit's End. There, Tom tries out the program for a fraction of a second. It's also too much for him, and he orders Eugene to destroy it immediately! But after Tom goes back to Whit in the hospital, Eugene hops into the Station—with disastrous results.

Meanwhile, on the doctor's advice, Tom talks to Whit, hoping that the stimulation might "bring him back." Tom tells Whit that he had no business messing around with life after death—only God should be the one to say when and how people are to die. But even as Tom speaks, Whit's heartbeat slows down and stops completely.

Whit is not oblivious to what's happening. He's aware of the doctors' attempts to save him. But suddenly, he seems to be transported a quiet and pleasant place, where he is surprised to meet his wife, Jenny. Meanwhile, the doctors stabilize Whit's condition. Whit's two children—Jana and Jason—arrive. Everyone prays for the best but prepares for the worst.

Back at Whit's End, Tom shows Jason the Imagination Station and realizes that Eugene hasn't destroyed the program. He must have tried it out for himself. No one knows where he is.

We rejoin Whit in his imagination as he basks in his wife's love and is eventually reunited with his dead son, Jerry. As far as Whit is concerned, he is in heaven. But Jenny assures him that he is not. He is, in fact, in a coma—merely playing out what he always imagined heaven to be. Jenny tells Whit that it is time for him to go back to living life. The real heaven will be much better than anything he could ever imagine. He agrees to "return."

In the hospital, Whit's family and friends are overjoyed when Whit wakes up. Whit concedes that toying with a life-after-death program was foolish.

Meanwhile, Connie tracks down Eugene at his dorm room. He is distraught. Yes, he had tried out the life-after-death program and experienced what Connie concludes was something like hell. Eugene is horrified. Connie talks to him about Christ, describing how we can escape hell because of His death on the cross. She then asks Eugene if it's something he can believe. Eugene isn't sure—but we know that this experience will stay with him for a long, long time.

the Adventures in ODYSSEY archives:

"The Mortal Coil" was one of our most popular episodes. The first part was written to be put aside in case Hal Smith (Whit) died. But we liked the story so much, we decided to finish it.

We recorded these episodes right after Hal Smith's wife died and were worried about how Hal might react to the content. But being the man he was, he insisted the show must continue.

Also, we got a lot of negative mail because Part One originally aired the weekend before Thanksgiving, which meant that a lot of people missed Part Two because of the holiday. Other listeners were upset that we put their kids through the torture of going a whole week, wondering whether or not Whit was still alive.

STUDY QUESTIONS:

1. Why was Whit so adamant about retrying the death program?
2. Why was Tom so insistent that Eugene destroy it? Why was the program so frightening to Eugene?
3. What do you think heaven will be like?

Episode #213 "Best Intentions"

Theme: Compassion.
Scripture reference: Matthew 25:36
Written by Paul McCusker
Directed by Phil Lollar
Production engineer: Dave Arnold
(Original air date: 12-05-92)

Whit is home from the hospital, recuperating from his ordeal with the death program in the Imagination Station. Or, *trying* to recuperate. Everyone in Odyssey has Whit's best interests at heart, and they keep coming over to his house to make sure he is resting. First, Connie and Eugene try to help, and they pamper him—too much. Then, Eugene refuses to let anyone—even Tom—visit Whit. This forces Tom to climb a tree and go in through Whit's bedroom window. Whit is happy to see Tom—until Tom insists on reading to Whit.

Meanwhile, Sam discovers that Whit's End is closed. Dissatisfied with the explanation, he wants to find out why the emporium is *really* shut down. So Sam allows Harlow Doyle to impose his aid and help find the answer.

Eventually, everyone but Sam ends up in Whit's room, causing all sorts of commotion. Dr. Morton enters and tries to get everyone to leave, causing even more uproar. But, in the ruckus, Whit slips out unnoticed. He finds Sam (who is sitting out in front of the house), and the two of them go where John Avery can get some rest—to Whit's End.

STUDY QUESTIONS:

1. Why was everyone so intent on helping Whit?
2. Why is it important to visit the sick and bedridden?
3. What's the best way to help someone who's sick? Explain.

Episode #214 "The Living Nativity"

Theme: Freedom of religion.
Scripture reference: Romans 13:1-7
Written by Marshal Younger
Directed by Phil Lollar
Production engineer: Bob Luttrell
(Original air date: 12-12-92)

When the nativity display on city hall grounds is vandalized and destroyed, Whit and the gang come up with a wonderful solution. They decide to do a "living nativity." It will be complete with narration, costumes, Connie as the virgin Mary, and Eugene as a donkey. Everyone in town thinks it is a smashing success—everyone, that is, except Bart and Rodney Rathbone.

The display is near Barney's Appliance Cave and is taking customers away from the Electric Palace. Bart decides the living nativity must go! He calls the mayor and files a formal protest, upon which the mayor has no choice but to act. The police shut down the display.

Whit comes up with a solution, though: Instead of celebrating *just* Christmas, use the city hall lawn to celebrate *all* of the cultural events that take place in December as well, such as Hanukkah. It isn't the perfect solution, but it is one that's legal and one that satisfies almost everybody.

the Adventures in ODYSSEY archives:

"The Living Nativity" was the first show written for us by Marshal Younger, who later joined the *AIO* staff. The controversial nature of this story launched an hour-long debate among our actors in the studio about the First Amendment and the true meaning of "separation of church and state." While the discussion was healthy, it sure ate up a lot of studio time.

STUDY QUESTIONS:

1. Why did Bart and Rodney want the living nativity stopped?
2. Is it illegal to have a nativity display on city hall property? Why or why not?
3. Do you think Whit's solution was a good one? Explain.

WHAT'S IN A NAME?

Original Character Names
(Continued from page 149.)

Philo Sanderson—"Gotcha!"

Mugsy Mumford and Junior Bascomb—"VBS Blues"

Marco Dibiasi—"Camp What-A-Nut" *(Dibiasi is my uncle's last name)*

Percival Fenwick—"The Case of the Secret Room"

Fiona Donneral—"Thank You, God"

Mook—"The Prodigal, Jimmy"

Digger Digwillow—First appeared in "The Imagination Station"

Thelma Thud and Mrs. Neidlebark—"Connie Goes to Camp"

Mr. Burglemeister—"Eugene's Dilemma"

Dr. Regis Blackgaard—First appeared in "The Nemesis"

Ambrose P. Schnook and Silas Van Kreeft—"The Ill-Gotten Deed"

Reginald Duffield—First appeared in "Rescue from Manatugo Point" *(Duffield is Paul McCusker's wife's maiden name)*

Traci Needlemeyer—First appeared in "The Barclay Ski Vacation"

Tanyer Hyde— "The Conscientious Cross-Guard"

Harlow Doyle—First appeared in "Harlow Doyle, Private Eye"

Borealis P. Walton—"Feud for Thought" (*Northern Lights*)

Don Iowa—"Aloha, Oy!" *(Pronounced "Ee-OH-way")*

Terence Bougainville—"The War Hero" *(Flower)*

Agent Burt Furter—"Tom for Mayor"

Hassn Ben-Sober —"Siege at Jericho"

Ewell Mosby —"Blackbeard's Treasure" *(Two Civil War generals)*

Howard J. Weizel and Trent Mackey—"A Victim of Circumstance"

Gabby Libbens—"Rewards in Full"

Armitage Shanks—First appears in "The Turning Point" *(British commode)*

Jellyfish—First appears in "Gathering Thunder"

Professor Bovril—First appears in "Moving Targets" *(British chocolate drink mix)*

Morton Dunkey—"Welcome Home, Mr. Blackgaard"

Episode #215 "Caroling, Caroling"

Theme: Celebrating Christmas; the birth of Jesus.
Scripture reference: Luke 2:1-20
Written by Paul McCusker
Directed by Chuck Bolte
Production engineers: Dave Arnold and Tim Jaquette
Music by John Campbell
(Original air date: 12-19-92)

As a special Christmas treat, Whit and Connie take several kids from Whit's End on a wonderful sleigh ride through Odyssey and out to Tom Riley's farm. Along the way, they meet up with Bernard, Eugene, and Dale Jacobs. They all learn several new holiday songs (including one by Eugene called "Seasonal Felicitations") and rediscover the "reason for the season": Jesus.

STUDY QUESTIONS:

1. Why is it important for us to remember and celebrate Christmas?
2. What does "Seasonal Felicitations" mean?
3. What does Christmas mean to you?

Episode #216 "Like Father, Like Son"

Theme: Judging others.
Scripture reference: Matthew 7:1-2
Written by April Dammann and Paul McCusker
Directed by Paul McCusker
Production engineer: Bob Luttrell
(Original air date: 12-26-92)

Eric Myers has been working hard, shoveling snow off people's driveways. He's doing his part to help his soccer team take a trip to France to see the World Cup. The team has earned almost all of the money they need—despite having some unwanted competition from Rodney Rathbone and his snow blower.

Rodney is earning the money for himself. He razzes Eric about everything from his lack of equipment, to the way the team is suspicious of him.

Rodney really arouses everyone's distrust of Eric later at Whit's End. The cash box containing the money for the team's trip turns up missing—and the last one seen near it was Eric. Rodney repeatedly points out that Eric's father, Ernie, is in prison. He reminds everyone of the old saying: Like father, like son. These comments earn Rodney a sharp reprimand from Whit and a punch in the nose from Eric.

But the fact remains that someone took the money, and the prime suspect is Eric. Even his mother suspects him when she unexpectedly walks in on him and sees him counting a large wad of cash! Eric actually got the money by shoveling snow from people's porches. He was going to use it to replace the team's missing money.

At Whit's End, Whit tries to convince Eric to wait before he replenishes the cash. The truth will come out. Eric says it doesn't matter, though. Everyone thinks he took the money because his dad's in jail. Nothing he does will change people's beliefs.

The truth *does* come out when Eric and Coach Bryan deduce that Rodney's younger cousin, Scrub, took the cash box. Scrub collects junk, and he thought the box was something no one else wanted. Everything is resolved, and the kids learn not to jump to conclusions.

the Adventures in ODYSSEY archives:

Due to scheduling problems, Steve Burns, the actor who does the voice of Rodney Rathbone, couldn't make the session. After a bit of scrambling, Matt Hurwitz stepped in and did an admirable job of covering for Steve. Also, Landon Arnold, son of Dave Arnold, played the part of Scrub.

STUDY QUESTIONS:

1. Did Rodney deserve to be punched? Why or why not?
2. If you were on the soccer team, would *you* have thought Eric took the money? How would you have reacted?
3. Have you ever been accused of something you didn't do? Have you ever accused someone without first knowing all the facts?

1993

In 1993, we introduced several new developments to *Adventures in Odyssey.* First, a couple of new inventions appeared at Whit's End. One was "BEAVRS," the Bible Education Audio/Video Research System. "BEAVRS" was designed to help the kids in Odyssey with Bible questions. We also brought the Room of Consequence into *AIO.* Similar to the Imagination Station, the Room of Consequence allowed kids to play out dilemmas so that they could see the consequences of their actions.

The Barclay family underwent many changes as well. Lawrence became more involved with the Barclays, and George lost his job. We had decided that things were running too smoothly for the Barclays. Listeners needed to be able to relate to them, so we implemented some shake-ups in the Barclays' lives.

All of these things happened in episodes which had titles that were taken from a verse of the Lord's Prayer. Some of the shows dealt directly with the Lord's Prayer—such as "Hallowed Be Thy Name" and "Thy Kingdom Come"—but most of the titles were just launching points for the show.

Finally, in November 1993, Marshal Younger came on staff as a writer. Around the same time, Mark Drury joined the *AIO* team full-time as a production engineer. Our crew had expanded.

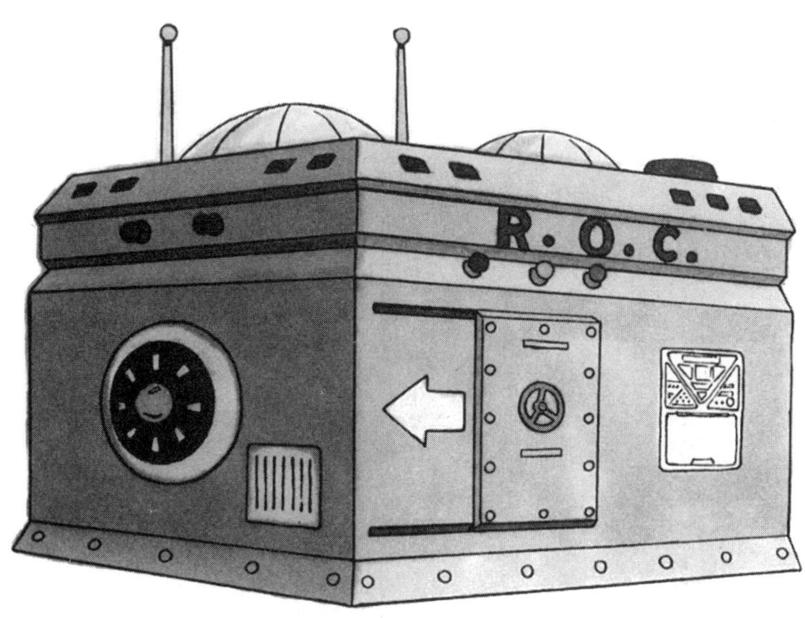

Episode #217 "Rights, Wrongs & Reasons"

Theme: Doing the right thing for the right reason.
Scripture reference: Romans 6:1
Written and directed by Phil Lollar
Production engineer: Bob Luttrell
(Original air date: 1-02-93)

Whit and Connie are playing a game called "Rights, Wrongs & Reasons" when Jenny walks up and asks what they're doing. Connie explains that it's a guessing game Whit created. It deals with actions and motivations. "Rights and wrongs" are the things we do in a given situation. "Reasons" are the motivations for those actions.

One person sets up a scenario. The other person has to guess which of four categories the scenario falls into: doing the right thing for the right reason, the right thing for the wrong reason, the wrong thing for the right reason, or the wrong thing for the wrong reason. For instance, Connie tells Jenny, giving a part of your allowance to the church because God wants you to is doing the right thing for the right reason.

Once Jenny understands, Whit and Connie present her with several scenarios involving two girls named Heather and Sherry. When Jenny guesses correctly every time, Whit and Connie move on to a tougher, Old Testament scenario: the death of Uzzah in 2 Samuel 6 and 1 Chronicles 13. Everyone enjoys the afternoon, and both Jenny and Connie know more about motives.

STUDY QUESTIONS:

1. Do you think all scenarios can fall into the categories Whit devised? Why or why not?
2. Why did Uzzah die? Was it possible for God to spare him? Explain.
3. Describe some right/right, right/wrong, wrong/right, or wrong/wrong scenarios from your life.

Episode #218 "A Class Act"

Theme: Honesty; relying on God; favoritism.
Scripture reference: James 2:1-4
Written and directed by Paul McCusker
Production engineer: Bob Luttrell
(Original air date: 1-09-93)

Edwin Blackgaard's Harlequin Theatre is in trouble. He can't ever seem to get a big enough audience. He is almost ready to throw in the towel when he receives an anonymous letter—it offers him a large sum of money to teach an acting class. There's only one catch: He cannot exclude anyone who wants to attend. Blackgaard is hesitant at first but soon decides to give it a try. He tells his loyal and trusty minion, Shakespeare, to inform everyone in Odyssey that his class is in session.

But, oh! what a class! It consists of Connie, a budding and terrible playwright; Eugene and his ukulele; Charles Edward "Chunky" Thompson; Jack Davis, now a pizza delivery boy; and Shannon Everett, whose father adores her. Edwin is forced to be nice to all of them because he doesn't know who his benefactor is. He lets them rehearse an awful play Connie has written. It is certain to damage Blackgaard's reputation as a teacher—and perhaps even the reputation of the Harlequin Theatre itself.

Instead of using his best judgment and confronting the situation directly, Edwin deduces that the benefactor could only be Shannon's father. After all, he is the only one with money. So Edwin replaces Connie's play with one of his own and treats everyone like dirt—except Shannon. Edwin makes Shannon the star and caters to her every whim. Unfortunately, this also means he doesn't give her any direction. As a result, her performance is terrible.

Edwin thinks that Shannon's father won't care as long as Shannon has the lead role. But Mr. Everett is outraged that Edwin would allow Shannon to make a fool out of herself. Shannon's father refuses to give the Harlequin any money and storms out of the theatre in disgust. He leaves Edwin right back where he started. And Edwin learns a hard lesson about not sacrificing his integrity for money.

> **the *Adventures in* ODYSSEY archives:**
>
> **We always try to write our episodes as closely as possible to the maximum time alloted for the broadcast—24 minutes, 55 seconds. When we're short, we make up the time with a longer wrap-around. When we're long, we have to cut material out of the show. In recording "A Class Act," we ended up going way too long—and unfortunately, we had to cut some hilarious scenes of Blackgaard butchering *Hamlet* and his students butchering acting in general.**

STUDY QUESTIONS:

1. Why didn't Edwin think he could be completely honest with everyone in the class?
2. What would *you* have done in Edwin's place? Why?
3. What does integrity mean? Why is it important?

Episode #219 "Treasures of the Heart"

Theme: Setting proper priorities.
Scripture reference: Matthew 6:19
Written by Paul McCusker and Geoff Kohler
Directed by Paul McCusker
Production engineer: Dave Arnold
(Original air date: 1-16-93)

The Barclay family is sitting around the dinner table when George asks everybody how their respective days went. Mary says she attended a meeting of the Odyssey Women's Committee, which wants to raise money for a new orphanage. Jimmy went shoe shopping—or browsing. He's thinking of buying a pair of $125 Jordo tennis shoes, to the dismay of his mom and dad. Donna tells the family about the interesting discussion she had in civics class. The

topic was priorities, and the question posed was, Imagine your house was on fire, but you knew the family was safe. If you could rescue only one thing before the house burned down, what would you rescue?

The Barclays dialogue about each family member's experience of the day. Over the next several days, these three stories teach the whole family not to place too much importance on things that don't last.

STUDY QUESTIONS:

1. Should Jimmy have been allowed to buy the shoes with his own money? Why or why not?
2. Why did Donna think George would be mad about what happened to his books?
3. How would *you* answer the question Donna's civics teacher asked?

Episode #220 "This Is Chad Pearson?"

Theme: The folly of hero worship.
Scripture reference: Philippians 2:3-11
Written by Marshal Younger
Directed by Paul McCusker
Production engineer: Bob Luttrell
(Original air date: 2-20-93)

At the Electric Palace one afternoon, Bart Rathbone notices Kim and Erica glued to the row of televisions. They are watching a show starring the character Chad Pearson. Bart notices how devoted the girls are to this TV personality—and he recognizes a potential money-making opportunity. He sponsors a contest. The winner gets to spend a day with the actor Nick Grant, who plays Chad Pearson!

The young girls of the town are ecstatic at the prospect—especially Erica. But she is terribly disappointed when the winner of the contest turns out to be . . . Connie Kendall! As it turns out, Connie couldn't be less interested in the whole situation. Nick ends up to be a nice guy who isn't at all like his television character—but who is lonely. And Connie ends up making a new friend.

STUDY QUESTIONS:

1. Was it wrong for Kim and Erica to be so devoted to a TV star? Why or why not?
2. Why was Connie so disinterested in Nick (Chad) at first? What made her change her mind?
3. Who are your heroes? Who should your main hero be ?

Episode #221 "It Is Well"

Theme: Trusting God through all life's circumstances; the power of faith.
Scripture reference: Philippians 4:12-13
Recommended maturity level: 10 and up
Written and directed by Phil Lollar
Production engineer: Dave Arnold
(Original air date: 2-27-93)

PARENTAL WARNING: Though this is an inspirational and moving story, it does contain a realistic shipwreck as well as several deaths. While handled tastefully, these scenes may frighten younger listeners.

Whit is in his office, listening to a tape of his church choir singing "It Is Well with My Soul." Lucy enters and comments on how pretty the song is. Whit agrees that it's a wonderful piece. He adds that the church has a rich tradition of hymns that are now almost forgotten. Whit and Lucy listen to part of a verse for a moment, then Lucy comments on how inspirational and poetic the words are. Whit says the story behind those words is extraordinary. He describes the life of the hymn's writer, Horatio G. Spafford.

Spafford suffered incredible tragedy in his life. He lost his business to the great Chicago fire and his son to disease. Then, if that weren't enough, he sent his wife and four daughters to England on an evangelistic tour and, on the way over, the boat sank in a storm. All four of his daughters drowned. Only his wife survived. Spafford left for England immediately. As his ship passed over the spot where his daughters were lost, Spafford wrote his most famous and inspirational verse: "When peace like a river, attendeth my way / When sorrow like sea billows roll / Whatever my lot, Thou hast taught me to say / It is well, it is well, with my soul."

Adventures in the ODYSSEY archives:

The story of Horatio G. Spafford is a true one, and we told it as faithfully to the real thing as our research allowed.

STUDY QUESTIONS:

1. Why did Whit say it is important to sing old hymns as well as more modern praise songs?
2. How could Horatio Spafford write "it is well with my soul" even though he lost all of his children and his business?
3. Could you say the same thing if something terrible happened to you? Why or why not?

Episode #222 "The Jesus Cloth"

Theme: The object of our faith.
Scripture reference: 2 Timothy 1:12
Written and directed by Phil Lollar
Production engineer: Bob Luttrell
(Original air date: 3-06-93)

Connie brings Whit a package that arrived in the mail from Alfred Brownlee, who used to send Whit unusual archaeological artifacts. The package contains an ancient, smelly leather pouch. Inside is a piece of very old cloth. A letter from Brownlee explains that he found the pouch and cloth at a dig site in the Holy Land. The cloth is dated from the time of Christ—and is possibly a piece of Jesus' robe!

Connie is excited about this and urges Whit to see if it is authentic. Whit says he will check it out. He tells Connie to keep quiet about it until they know something for sure. But Connie lets the news slip out, and soon Whit's End is besieged with people wanting to see the "Jesus Cloth." Whit tries to convince them that there is no conclusive proof that the cloth is from Christ's robe. But when he mentions that the only way to know if it's even from the right time period is by radiocarbon dating—which involves burning the cloth—the crowd nearly riots, and the police are called to Whit's End.

Whit sends the cloth to a museum in Jerusalem and sadly ponders whether we Christians are putting our faith in relics or in the risen Christ.

the *Adventures in* ODYSSEY archives:

"The Jesus Cloth" was written around the time the Dead Sea Scrolls were released to the public. Many people were conjecturing that the scrolls would contain material that was contradictory to Scripture. This led us to ask, "Upon what are we basing our faith?"

STUDY QUESTIONS:

1. Can you think of a real-life example of "The Jesus Cloth"? How do people act around it? What do you think should be the real purpose of relics?
2. Is it bad to believe in relics? Should we expect them to perform miracles? Explain your answers.
3. Upon what do you base your faith?

Episode #223 "Real Time"

Theme: God's protection; making the most of each moment.
Scripture reference: Luke 12:16-21
Written and directed by Phil Lollar
Production engineer: Dave Arnold
(Original air date: 3-13-93)

Connie pulls up in front of the Scheimholtz building in downtown Odyssey. She is dropping off Whit, who is scheduled to debate Cryin' Bryan Dern on the topic of Christianity vs. atheism on Dern's show. Connie doesn't want Whit to do it—she feels that Dern is just sponsoring the debate as a publicity stunt. But Whit says Dern has made some unqualified statements about the church and God that cannot go unchallenged. So Whit has decided to appear on the program.

Unfortunately, Whit doesn't know that Dern has rigged himself with a wireless microphone, hoping to catch Whit making an embarrassing statement. But what nobody knows is that two thugs named Benny and Lou have planted a bomb in the basement elevator shaft!

Later, when the elevator gets stuck between floors, it's Dern who ends up making a statement—revealing that he actually *does* believe in God. Dern begs God to help them. The timer ticks away, and the police evacuate the building. But there's no way to get Whit and Dern out in time. The countdown reaches its end, and the elevator shaft is shaken with an explosion. Whit and Dern are unharmed—except for being dizzy from a terrible smell that fills the building. The bomb was a *stink* bomb! Benny and Lou are caught by the police, and Cryin' Bryan Dern has to deal with the fool he's made out of himself on the radio.

behind the scenes:

"As you might guess from the title, we wanted to do an episode that took place in 'real time.' The minutes that were called off throughout the course of the show were the closest we could get them to the actual running time of the episode. The idea was inspired by a M*A*S*H episode that did the same thing. To accomplish this, we had to read through the script beforehand and get rough times—we wouldn't know the actual minutes until the editing was complete and the sound effects and music were added. So, first, we recorded four or five different phrases for each mention of the minutes. Then we cut in [added] the appropriate phrase when we knew what it would be."

—Phil Lollar

STUDY QUESTIONS:

1. Why did Whit want to debate Bryan Dern? Why didn't Connie want Whit to go on the show?
2. Were Lou and Benny justified in doing what they did? Why or why not?
3. Do you think Bryan Dern really believed what he said about God before he and Whit got stuck in the elevator? What about afterward, when Bryan thought he was going to die? Explain.

Episode #224 "Greater Love"

Theme: Jesus' love for us.
Scripture reference: John 15:12–13
Written and directed by Phil Lollar
Production engineer: Bob Luttrell
(Original air date: 3-20-93)

Tom and Whit are visiting the grave of Tom's son, Timmy, who died tragically 20 years ago. But when they arrive, they are surprised to see someone already there—a young man named P. D. Barnes. He was a friend of Timmy's who has also come to pay his respects. Tom visibly stiffens at the sight of P. D., makes a hasty excuse, and leaves. Whit apologizes for Tom's behavior, but P. D. says he understands Tom's reaction.

"It's the reason I'm here," he says. "You see . . . I killed Timmy."

Whit is stunned, and in a flashback, P. D. tells the story of his relationship with Timmy and with the Rileys. P. D. explains that he was a rotten little kid. Timmy befriended him and showed him love and trust. But P. D. feels he betrayed Timmy's trust—P. D. was responsible for Timmy's drowning accident. The boys were out on the lake when P. D. started fooling around in the boat. He fell in the water. P. D. couldn't swim, so Timmy dove in after his friend—and got entangled in some vines.

After all these years, P. D. wanted to tell Tom how sorry he is. Whit takes P. D. to Tom's farm, and P. D. gets his wish. Tom extends true forgiveness.

the Adventures in ODYSSEY archives:

In "Greater Love," we learned more about Tom's family and his early days. This story and the next, "Count It All Joy," began a series of programs on the fruit of the spirit. Unfortunately, we only got as far as "love" and "joy" before we were diverted to other topics.

Also, the splashing in the drowning scene was done in a small tub of water in one of the studio rooms.

STUDY QUESTIONS:

1. Why did P. D. think he killed Timmy?
2. Why did young P. D. steal from the Rileys? Did Timmy handle the situation in the right way? How would you have handled it?
3. Why did Tom blame himself for Timmy's death? Was he right to do so?

Episode #225 "Count It All Joy"

Theme: Joy.
Scripture references: Nehemiah 8:10; James 1:2-4
Written and directed by Phil Lollar
Production engineer: Dave Arnold
(Original air date: 3-27-93)

As Erica and Kim walk home from school together, Erica talks a mile a minute about how her life is so terrible and depressing. Kim listens patiently and tries to be sympathetic. But soon, she gets fed up and tells Erica that her life isn't that bad. She should try being happy once in a while.

Later, at Whit's End, Erica runs into Jenny Roberts. Erica asks Jenny why she always seems to be happy despite her blindness. Jenny quotes James 1:2-3: "Consider it pure joy, my brothers, whenever you face trials of many kinds, because you know that the testing of your faith develops perseverance." Jenny says she can be joyful about her blindness, because she knows that it brings her closer to Jesus. Whenever things get rough, she just says to herself, "Count it all joy, count it all joy." That usually does the trick.

Erica thinks that's a great idea and tries it. But what works so well for Jenny seems to completely backfire for Erica. Instead of relieving Erica's frustrations, "counting it all joy" actually *increases* them—leading Erica to blow her top at Kim.

Back at Whit's End, Erica relates her problem to Whit. Whit explains that Erica has confused joy with happiness. He says that everyone feels bad occasionally, but true joy has nothing to do with feelings. Joy is being rooted in Christ and what He did for us on the cross. Erica returns to Kim and apologizes. She understands now that she can't always be happy and shouldn't always be sad. Instead, she now wants to live on a higher ground—a foundation called joy.

STUDY QUESTIONS:

1. Why did Erica think her life was so depressing?
2. Did Jenny give Erica good or bad advice when she said to just repeat "Count it all joy, count it all joy"? Should Jenny have said something else instead?
3. Have you found the difference between joy and happiness? Explain your answer.

Episodes #226 & 227
"An Adventure in Bethany," Parts One & Two

Theme: Biblical history: Lazarus; the power of Jesus; sacrifice.
Scripture reference: John 11:1-12:11
Written and directed by Paul McCusker
Production engineers: Dave Arnold and Bob Luttrell
(Original air dates: 4-03-93 & 4-10-93)

The Sunday school committee has asked Lucy to write a series of articles about towns and cities of the Bible. So Whit sends Lucy back to first century Bethany, a suburb of Jerusalem. Later, he joins her there, and the two of them experience an adventure full of intrigue. They see an attempted murder, the anointing of a king, the raising of a man from the dead—and, best of all, the sacrifice, forgiveness, and love of Christ.

the *Adventures in* ODYSSEY archives:

"An Adventure in Bethany" was the first time Whit went into the Imagination Station to experience history.

STUDY QUESTIONS:

1. Lucy thought it was okay to miss a few church services in order to write the Bible articles. Why was that wrong to do?
2. Why were the rabbis and religious leaders of Lazarus's time so afraid of Jesus?
3. How would you have reacted if you were there when Jesus raised Lazarus from the dead?

Episode #228
"A Game of Compassion"

Theme: Helping others; sacrifice.
Scripture reference: James 2:14-26
Written by Jeff White
Directed by Paul McCusker
Production engineer: Dave Arnold
(Original air date: 4-17-93)

Eric Myers is one of the star players on Odyssey's soccer team. Thanks to his skills, the team has a chance to win the championship for the first time in 17 years. The big game is on Friday, and Eric is pumped for it.

After practice, he meets the locker-room cleaning lady, Mrs. Phillips. She seems distressed. Mrs. Phillips reluctantly tells Eric she is widowed and nearly destitute. She needs to move from her current place to a new apartment—but she doesn't have anyone to help her. Eric volunteers. He tells her that he'll be there first thing Saturday morning.

But the next day, the soccer coach announces that due to a problem with the field, the big championship game has been moved to Saturday. Eric panics! He knows the team needs him, but he's made a promise to Mrs. Phillips. Eric decides to keep his promise. He tells the team he can't be there. But Eric doesn't tell the team why, so they think Eric is a traitor.

Later, at Whit's End, Eric's little sister, Brooke, tells Whit about Eric's dilemma. Whit tells Eric that he's doing the right thing. Eric knows this, but he says it still won't help him win the game.

Saturday arrives, and Eric goes to help Mrs. Phillips. She has also heard about Eric's dilemma, though. Mrs. Phillips tells Eric to go to the game. But Eric says he made a promise, and he intends to keep it. Just then, there's a knock at the door. It's Whit—along with the entire soccer team. They all pitch in and help, and Mrs. Phillips is moved before the game.

behind the scenes:

"Mid-production on this show, I had a sports accident that took me away from work for a week. Since we were so close to the broadcast date, Mark Drury stepped in to finish the show and get it out on time."

—Dave Arnold

STUDY QUESTIONS:

1. Should Eric have kept his promise to Mrs. Phillips? Why or why not?
2. Why didn't Eric simply tell his coach or his mom or even Whit about his dilemma? Would you have kept quiet?
3. Have you ever faced a problem like Eric's? How did you handle it?

Episode #229
"The Marriage Feast"

Theme: The parable of the marriage feast.
Scripture references: Matthew 22:1-14; Romans 6:23
Written and directed by Phil Lollar
Production engineer: Bob Luttrell
(Original air date: 4-24-93)

It's another episode of "Adventures in the Bible!" This time, Whit begins by reading a letter from Brooke. It states: "Dear Mr. Whittaker—I have a friend who says that everybody is going to go to heaven no matter how good or bad they are, because God is love, and so He can't send us to hell. I say my friend's crazy. Who's right?"

Whit answers the question by narrating his own version of Jesus' parable of the marriage feast. The point is well made: God gives us many chances to come to Him. If we refuse Him and reject His Son, God can—and *will*—punish us. But there is hope. "The wages of sin is death, but the [free] gift of God is eternal life in Jesus Christ our Lord" (Romans 6:23).

STUDY QUESTIONS:

1. Why wouldn't the duke, earl, or countess accept the king's invitation?
2. Why did the vulgar man refuse to wear the king's wedding clothes?
3. Do you know anyone who believes what Brooke's friend believes—that because God is love, He won't send us to hell? What would you say to that person? How do you feel about God sending those who reject Jesus to hell?

Episode #230 "Our Father"

Theme: The importance of fathers.
Scripture reference: Psalm 68:5
Written and directed by Phil Lollar
Production engineer: Dave Arnold
(Original air date: 5-15-93)

Lawrence Hodges is a creature of imagination. One moment, he's a major-league baseball player, and the next, he's a mad scientist working on his latest Frankenstein-like creation. But lately, an odd element keeps creeping into Lawrence's imagination—his father. Or, more precisely, his *lack* of one.

Lawrence's dad is on the road a lot—never around when Lawrence really needs him. So Lawrence turns to what he believes is the best substitute—the Bones of Rath. Rusty recruits him, and soon Lawrence begins taking on the Bones's unfavorable characteristics. This all culminates in Lawrence vandalizing several flowerpots sitting on the Barclay's front lawn. Mrs. Hodges is mortified, but George recognizes that Lawrence really needs a father figure in his life. George offers to be there for Lawrence whenever he needs someone. Lawrence happily agrees. He is on his way to learning what the love of God—the *perfect* father—is all about.

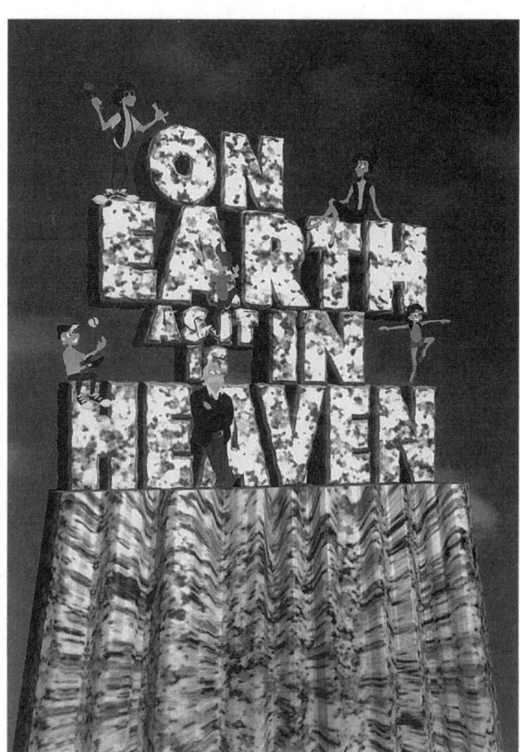

STUDY QUESTIONS:

1. Why was Lawrence so disappointed when his father couldn't show up for his baseball game?
2. Why did Lawrence think the Bones of Rath might be a good substitute for his family?
3. Why are fathers important?

Episode #231 "Hallowed Be Thy Name"

Theme: God's name; the holiness of God.
Scripture references: Mark 14:55-62; Luke 1:26-38; John 18
Written and directed by Phil Lollar
Production engineer: Bob Luttrell
(Original air date: 5-22-93)

In the Bible Room, Connie finds Whit putting the finishing touches on a new invention—the Bible Education Audio/Video Research System, or "BEAVRS." Whit explains that it is an advanced educational tool designed to help the user with Bible questions. First, you pick a topic—in this case, the "names of God." Type it in, hit a button, and all the names of God appear on the screen.

Intrigued, Connie remarks that she didn't know that God had so many names. She just thought He was called Lord, God, Almighty, and that all the names meant the same thing. But Whit explains that each name has a specific meaning designed to reveal something about God. So Connie spends the rest of the episode learning specifics about such holy names as "Elohim," "Adonai," "Elah," "Jesus," "Immanuel," and, of course, "Yahweh."

The point is made: Whether we're singing, praying, or even just talking about God, we must remember that in the Lord's Prayer, Jesus said, "Hallowed be thy name."

STUDY QUESTIONS:

1. Why does God have so many names?
2. How can you talk about God in a way that lets your friends and family know how important He is to you?
3. Have you ever used God's name in a flippant or blasphemous way? Why is it wrong to do that?

Episode #232 "Thy Kingdom Come"

Theme: The kingdom of God.
Scripture reference: 2 Corinthians 4:18
Written and directed by Paul McCusker
Production engineer: Dave Arnold
(Original air date: 5-29-93)

Whit is trying to put together a Kid's Radio program on Jesus' parable about the kingdom of heaven. Whit's having a difficult time of it, so he asks Eugene for help. Eugene declines, stating he's too busy at present. After a brief conversation, Whit deduces that Eugene actually doesn't want to help out because of his recent negative experience in the Imagination Station (see "The Mortal Coil," episodes #211 & 212).

Whit wants to talk about the experience with Eugene, but that is the last thing Eugene wants to do. He beats a hasty retreat. Connie learns of the situation and tries to broach the subject with Eugene. But this only makes matters worse, so Whit and Connie decide to leave Eugene alone.

Later, Whit sends Connie to pick up a sound effects record at the public library. Once there, she encounters Eugene—with an armload of books about Christianity. Eugene has been doing research on the subject after all. He is confused over several aspects of the Christian faith, especially the meaning of the phrase, "the kingdom of heaven." Connie sends him back to Whit. Whit uses the Kid's Radio project to help Eugene understand as well as he, being a non-Christian, can understand.

"I think I want to believe," Eugene admits, "but I need help with my unbelief."

Whit smiles and responds, "That's as good a start as any, Eugene."

STUDY QUESTIONS:

1. Whit told Connie they needed to be careful about how they proceeded with Eugene. What did Whit mean by that?
2. Eugene thought he could find the answers he sought in books. Was he right? Why or why not? Which book would *you* have given Eugene to read?
3. What does Whit think Jesus meant by the phrase, "the kingdom of heaven"?

Episode #233 "Thy Will Be Done"

Theme: Knowing God's will.
Scripture reference: Matthew 6:10
Written and directed by Paul McCusker
Production engineer: Bob Luttrell
(Original air date: 6-05-93)

At Whit's End one afternoon, Whit, Connie, and Lucy discuss God's will. Whit tells them that Christians are agents of God's will when they bring light into the world by showing the Lord's love and spreading the truth of His word. Excited about that, both Lucy and Connie look for opportunities to test this theory.

Lucy has been asked to write for a new school newspaper, the *Odyssey Voice,* which espouses many views Lucy doesn't support. Whit advises her to write a "test" article for the paper to see if her beliefs are compatible with the paper's.

Meanwhile, Connie has decided she is God's agent to bring Eugene to Jesus. First, she makes him listen to a fire-and-brimstone tape on the necessity of believing in Christ. Then, she asks him to help her memorize Bible verses—all on the theme of salvation. Finally, she programs BEAVRS to spout several verses at Eugene on the subjects of evangelism and conversion.

The results of Connie's and Lucy's experiments? Connie's pressuring tactics don't go over well with Eugene. And Lucy soon discovers that the *Voice* only believes in freedom of speech as long as its view is being portrayed. Both the girls learn an important lesson about what it means to truly say "*Thy* will be done."

STUDY QUESTIONS:

1. Why was Lucy concerned about writing for the *Odyssey Voice*? Should she have been?
2. What was wrong with the way Connie tried to bring Eugene to Jesus?
3. How can you know what God's will is for your life?

Episode #234 "Our Daily Bread"

Theme: Seeking God first; trusting in His protection and provision.
Scripture reference: Matthew 6:31-33
Written and directed by Phil Lollar
Production engineer: Bob Luttrell
(Original air date: 6-12-93)

At the Barclay home one afternoon, Mary, Donna, and Jimmy are talking excitedly about a promotion and raise they all expect George to receive at work that day. Each one of them has elaborate plans for future purchases: Mary wants to go on a cruise to some exotic location and then remodel the kitchen. Donna plans on buying an entirely new wardrobe and also hints that maybe Mom and Dad could get her a used car. And Jimmy talks about going to several baseball camps this summer.

Then George enters, subdued. In typical Barclay fashion, the family immediately grills him for answers. They ask when George will be receiving his increase, while telling him about all of their plans. George, however, just goes silently into the living room and sits on the sofa, stunned. Mary asks him what's wrong. George takes a deep breath and tells them that there won't be any increase—because he got laid off. He doesn't have a job.

The family all reacts differently. George is depressed. Mary is calm and rational. Jimmy and Donna panic at first, then decide to get jobs. Mary decides to go to work as well. The only one who can't find work is George. He is despondent until the family comes up with a solution: George will be the managing director of "BarclayCo," a new firm which offers unconditional support from his family. George accepts the job—and gives his family a big hug.

STUDY QUESTIONS:

1. Why was the family so stunned when George lost his job?
2. What do you think about the family's solution for George?
3. Has your family ever faced a situation like the Barclays'? How did you handle it?

Episode #235 "Forgive Us as We Forgive"

Theme: Forgiveness.
Scripture reference: Luke 6:37-38
Written and directed by Phil Lollar
Production engineer: Dave Arnold
(Original air date: 6-19-93)

Ernie Myers is finally getting out of prison. Julie, Brooke, and Eric are excited about Ernie's release and return home, as are Whit and Tom. Ernie wants to get on with his life and hopes his family will accept him back. Whit offers him a job at Whit's End. This sits well with everyone—except Eric.

Eric thinks such a job is beneath his dad, but his mom explains that the whole family will need time to adjust to having Ernie back home from prison. Eric is much happier when he learns that Tom has pulled a few strings and gotten Ernie a new job—until he finds that Ernie's new job is working as the janitor of Eric's school.

Now Eric doesn't want to have anything to do with his father. But Whit counsels Eric. Whit guesses correctly that the real problem is that Eric hasn't truly forgiven his father for going to jail in the first place. Eric realizes the error of his ways and apologizes to his father. The two of them begin to build a new foundation of love, trust, and forgiveness.

STUDY QUESTIONS:

1. Why didn't Eric want his father to work at Whit's End?
2. Why was Eric embarrassed that his father became the school janitor?
3. Why did Eric find it so difficult to forgive his dad? Have you ever found it hard to forgive someone? How did you handle the situation?

Episode #236 "Into Temptation"

Theme: The folly of giving into temptation.
Scripture reference: 1 Corinthians 10:13
Written and directed by Phil Lollar
Production engineer: Bob Luttrell
(Original air date: 6-26-93)

Jimmy Barclay is in the midst of a dilemma. It's his birthday, and he wants to buy himself a new, portable video game. The problem is, his mom doesn't think the purchase is a good use of his money. Jimmy takes the problem to Whit—who helps him solve it through the use of a new invention: the Room of Consequence. Whit programs Jimmy's dilemma into the room's computer, then Jimmy enters and "plays out" the scenario to its conclusion.

In this case, Jimmy decides to go against his mother's wishes and buy the game, which sets off a rash of bad decisions by Lawrence and everyone else who comes in contact with him. Jimmy tells Lawrence not to play the game. But Lawrence does and breaks it. To cover up his mistake, Lawrence tells Donna that he found the game. So Donna decides to take the game to the lost and found at the police station. But then Donna changes her mind and plans to give it to Jimmy for his birthday. She hides the game in the next-door neighbor's mailbox. The neighbor finds the game and gives it to George. George shows it to Mary—who thinks that George bought it for Jimmy. Mary concludes that George is the best father ever.

Each one of them gives in to the temptation to do wrong—and at Jimmy's birthday celebration that night, everything falls apart. Jimmy exits the Room of Consequence, realizing that it's best to resist temptation.

behind the scenes:

"'Into Temptation' introduced the Room of Consequence—which was originally my idea for a separate series. In the series, a crazy inventor creates a room designed to teach young people that their actions *do* have consequences. When it was initially proposed as one of Whit's inventions, some thought that it was too similar to the Imagination Station. But the difference was, the Imagination Station sent kids back in time to experience the *past*, and the Room of Consequence sent them *forward* in time to play out possible futures. We used it in this episode, and it ended up being a strong device for the show."

—Phil Lollar

STUDY QUESTIONS:

1. Why did everyone give in to temptation?
2. Is it wrong to be tempted? Why or why not?
3. Have you ever been tempted? Did you give in to the temptation or resist it? What would you have done in Jimmy's place?

Episode #237 "Deliver Us from Evil"

Theme: Biblical history: Daniel; God's protection.
Scripture reference: Daniel 1-3
Written and directed by Phil Lollar
Production engineer: Bob Luttrell
(Original air date: 7-03-93)

Marsha wants to use BEAVRS to look up a story she calls "The Fiery Furnace Rescue." Unfortunately, the machine isn't working. Eugene, who is attempting to repair it, doesn't know how long it will take to fix. Marsha is not happy, but just then, Bernard Walton appears. Bernard knows the story well and offers to tell it to Marsha. She accepts. But whenever Bernard starts talking, Eugene interrupts with corrections and more information than Marsha needs. Finally, Eugene and Bernard compromise and become a story-telling duo. Marsha hears their unique, exciting, and insightful rendition of four young Hebrew men named Daniel, Shadrach, Meshach, and Abednego. Marsha learns how the Lord God protected the four Hebrews from unlawful food, unscrupulous political climbers, a fiery furnace, and a powerful, egotistical king.

the 

archives:

"Deliver Us from Evil" was the only show that Hal Smith appeared in where he didn't play the character of Whit.

STUDY QUESTIONS:

1. Why did Daniel and his friends refuse to eat the king's food?
2. What did the king's strange dream mean?
3. Why did Shadrach, Meshach, and Abednego refuse to bow down before the statue? Would you have bowed down or gone instead into the fiery furnace?

Episode #238 "For Thine Is the Kingdom"

Theme: God's lordship in our lives.
Scripture reference: Romans 8:28
Written and directed by Paul McCusker
Production engineer: Dave Arnold
(Original air date: 7-10-93)

Courtney is a young ballerina with a brilliant future. But on the eve of her big tryout for the state ballet company, she steps off a curb at the wrong time and walks right into the path of an oncoming car. Her knee is badly damaged. Though she will walk again, all her hopes of having a career as a ballerina are gone forever. Courtney refuses to believe it at first, but she is finally forced to admit that painful truth. As a result, she stops caring about everything—her friendships, her family, even God.

Whit convinces Courtney to take a trip in the Room of Consequence to see how tragic her life will be if she turns completely from God. Courtney finally understands that just because one gift was taken from her doesn't mean her life is over—it is far better to be placed in God's hands.

the Adventures in ODYSSEY archives:

"For Thine Is the Kingdom" was inspired by Chuck Bolte's daughter, Sage. Like the character of Courtney, she, too, had twisted her knee and had to give up many of her favorite activities.

STUDY QUESTIONS:

1. Was it wrong for Courtney to keep hoping she could still perform ballet after her accident? Explain.
2. Courtney said that God would heal her knee "if He loves me." Was she right? Why or why not?
3. What does Romans 8:28 mean in saying that "God can work all things for good"?

Episode #239 "The Power"

Theme: The abuse of power.
Scripture reference: Matthew 6:13
Written by Marshal Younger and Paul McCusker
Directed by Phil Lollar
Production engineer: Bob Luttrell
(Original air date: 7-17-93)

Sam and Isaac are suspicious. Everyone is getting bad test grades in Miss Gardener's math class except Nicky and Rusty. Nicky's good grades are understandable—he's a child genius. But Rusty is a member of the Bones of Rath. They seem to foam at the mouth if they even hear the word "study."

Something obviously isn't right. Sam and Isaac are determined to find out the problem. Their search for truth causes them to tickle information out of Charles—who also uncharacteristically got a good grade on a pop quiz. Under pressure, Charles tells them that Nicky has access to the school's computer files. Isaac goes to the principal, but Nicky finds out about it before Isaac can get there. Nicky gets back at Isaac by making him look ridiculous.

Nicky seems unstoppable. With his computer skills, he can make or break anyone. But just as he gets ready to take care of Isaac once and for all, a freak storm causes a power outage—ruining his computer. Nicky's power is gone, and Sam and Isaac learn about the source of true power.

the Adventures in ODYSSEY archives:

"The Power" contained the first appearance of Nicholas Adamsworth since "A Prisoner for Christ," *AIO* #80. In that show, Nicholas was a good guy. Unfortunately, in "The Power," Nicholas's character turned a bit shady.

STUDY QUESTIONS:

1. Why did Nicky think he could get away with manipulating things?
2. Should Sam and Isaac have gotten information out of Charles? Why or why not?
3. Where does ultimate power lie?

Episode #240 "And the Glory"

Theme: Giving glory to God.
Scripture reference: Galatians 1:5
Written by Marshal Younger and Paul McCusker
Directed by Paul McCusker
Production engineer: Bob Luttrell
(Original air date: 7-24-93)

The Odyssey Coyotes are closer to the championship than they've ever been, thanks to Pete Flanagan's pitching. Pete has been working hard on his skills. In fact, he's even skipped Sunday school just to get in some pitching practice. Whit warns Pete he needs to spend time with God, who gave him his pitching talent. Pete promises to get back to church—just as soon as the season is over.

Later, in a decisive game, Pete dives to catch the ball for the win. He injures his arm in the process. The Coyotes's only available backup pitcher is Henry Thomas. Pete takes Henry under his broken wing and teaches him how to be a great pitcher. Henry rises to the occasion magnificently—and promptly forgets that Pete was the one who taught him how to win games.

The championship arrives. Henry struggles through it, barely hanging on to the Coyotes's lead. Pete tries to give Henry advice that will win the game, but Henry will have none of it. He decides to forget Pete completely and do what he wants. As a result, the Coyotes lose the game. Pete realizes that just as Henry turned his back on Pete, he turned his back on the Lord. He was guilty of ignoring the one who should receive all the glory—God.

behind the scenes:

"When I first handed off this script, Paul called me and said, 'Chuck laughed at this script—and he never laughs out loud.' I found out later that Chuck laughs at nearly everything—Paul was probably trying to boost my self-esteem by making me think my script was really funny. But at the time, I thought Chuck's reaction was pretty cool."

—Marshal Younger

STUDY QUESTIONS:

1. Why did Pete stop going to Sunday school? Was it for a good reason? Is there ever a good reason to ignore God? Explain your answers.
2. Why did Henry start ignoring Pete?
3. Why is it important to always give God the glory for everything? How can you do that today?

BERNARDISMS

Bernard Walton is one of the most colorful characters in Odyssey. One of the things that makes him so engaging is the way he speaks. What follows are some of the more ... uh ... unusual turns of phrase Bernard has employed over the years.

"He should be in agriculture, he's sold so many lemons."
—referring to his brother-in-law, in "By Any Other Name"

"See you tomorrow—if we don't die in our sleep."
— a farewell to Whit, in "By Any Other Name"

"They try a con job here and a con job there—here a con, there a con, everywhere a con-con."
—an exchange with Whit, in "By Any Other Name"

"Well, paint me red all over and send me to a four-alarm fire sirens blazin'!"
—to the gang at Whit's End upon learning that Whit may be getting married, in "Curious, Isn't It?"

"I'll bet people have nightmares about you."
—to Eugene, after one of his lengthy explanations, in "Curious, Isn't It?"

"You been out on maneuvers, or are you here to take hostages?"
—to Connie, on why she is wearing greasepaint, in "Suspicious Minds"

"Your brain is missing in action, but your heart is in the right place."
—to Connie, in "Suspicious Minds"

"You must have been a joy to have around as a child."
—to Eugene, upon learning that he hooked up electrical wires to the family refrigerator to help his parents diet, in "Suspicious Minds"

"I haven't had this much fun since I had my corns removed."
— to Whit, while watching Connie and Eugene scheme, in "Suspicious Minds"

"I wonder if I can get combat pay for this job."
—after getting smashed in the face by a door opened by Artie Powell, in "Bernard & Joseph"

"You know, woolly, white things that go 'baaaaa'?"
—explaining sheep to Artie Powell, in "Bernard & Joseph"

"I guess throwing somebody in a well can work up quite an appetite."
—explaining why Joseph's brothers sat down to eat after they threw Joseph in a well, in "Bernard & Joseph"

Continued on page 165.

Episode #241 "Forever...Amen"

Theme: God's love for us; dealing with loss.
Scripture reference: Matthew 19:13-14
Written and directed by Phil Lollar
Production engineer: Bob Luttrell
(Original air date: 7-31-93)

Danny Schmidt is excited. His mom is going to have a baby—and the Schmidts already know it will be a boy named Billy! Dr. Morton tells them that the ultrasound is occasionally wrong, but Danny and his father have made up their minds. Danny can't wait for Billy to arrive—Danny will be the best big brother ever. But his excitement turns into apprehension when he talks to Harvey. Harvey informs Danny that having a little brother is probably the worst thing that could happen to him.

"You'll have to give up all your privileges," Harvey says, "and you'll even have to do the 's' word—*share*! Before, you were special. Now, you're just one of the herd."

Danny doesn't like the sound of that at all, and he secretly wishes that Billy won't come. Just then, Danny's mother nearly collapses in pain. They rush her to the hospital, where she later loses the baby.

Danny believes it's his fault. Whit takes Danny home with him. That evening, Danny has a nightmare that his parents will hate him when they find out about his terrible wish. Whit comforts Danny. They pray that Jesus will help Danny see that he's not responsible for the loss of the baby, and that no one will hate him for his wish. And Jesus *does* comfort Danny, in a way that he—and even Whit—would never have imagined.

STUDY QUESTIONS:

1. Was Harvey right about how Danny's life would change once his little brother arrived? Explain.
2. Why did Whit want Danny to pray after his bad dream?
3. Can wishes come true? Is it good or bad to wish for things? Explain your answers.

Episode #242 "Hymn Writers"

Theme: Christian composers; the importance of singing hymns.
Scripture reference: Psalm 96:1-2
Written and directed by Phil Lollar
Production engineer: Bob Luttrell
(Original air date: 9-04-93)

Another Kid's Radio program called "A Moment in Time" is premiering, and it looks at important historical events. Whit, the host, informs us that the topic of this program is hymns. The guests are three people who wrote some of the greatest and best-loved hymns.

First, we go to Wittenberg, Germany, in the year 1517. There, we meet the author of the hymn "A Mighty Fortress Is Our God," Martin Luther. The hymn was an anthem for the Reformation—which was brought about when Luther nailed his 95 theses to the door of the church at Wittenberg—one of the most significant events in church history.

Next, we go to Ashtabula, Ohio, in the year 1876 to visit a remarkable musician named Philip Bliss. He wrote some of the church's most memorable hymns. Bliss was a contemporary of the great preacher D. L. Moody and wrote many of his hymns for Moody's evangelistic crusades. We hear the story behind perhaps his most famous hymn, "My Redeemer."

Finally, we move to Connecticut in the year 1915 to visit with the most prolific hymnist ever, a lady known as "the Queen of Hymns," and "the Happiest Creature in all the World," Fanny J. Crosby. Fanny shares snatches of just a few of her more than 8,000 hymns. She wrote classics such as "All the Way My Savior Leads Me," "Rescue the Perishing," and "Blessed Assurance."

As "A Moment in Time" concludes, we understand why the Bible says we should speak to one another in psalms, hymns, and spiritual songs.

STUDY QUESTIONS:

1. Why did Martin Luther nail the 95 theses to the church door at Wittenberg?
2. Why was Fanny J. Crosby known as "the Happiest Creature in All the World"?
3. Why is it important for us to sing hymns? Do you sing them in your church?

FAVORITE EPISODES
Dave Arnold's Top 10 Favorites

1. The Mortal Coil, 1 & 2
2. The Time Has Come
3. Isaac the Chivalrous
4. Gone . . .
5. Family Values
6. First Love
7. A Thanksgiving Carol
8. It Happened at Four Corners
9. Someone to Watch Over Me
10. Pilgrim's Progress Revisited, 1 & 2

Episode #243 "Family Values"

Theme: The importance of strong families.
Scripture reference: 1 Timothy 5:8
Written and directed by Phil Lollar
Production engineer: Dave Arnold
(Original air date: 9-11-93)

Whit is behind the counter at Whit's End when Bart Rathbone rushes in, panicked. Bart explains he needs advice on how to make his family stronger. Whit says that's not an easy thing to do and tries to explain that it's a lengthy process. Bart cuts him off, though. He needs to know how to make his family stronger by *Monday.*

Apparently, Bart's son, Rodney, entered an essay contest sponsored by a statewide magazine. The essay is about family values. The winner and his family will receive the honorable title "Family of the Year." Rodney's essay was picked as one of the finalists! The judges are coming to Odyssey to talk with the Rathbones.

The only problem is, the Rathbones don't know *how* to be a family—at least not how the magazine views a family to be. That's why Bart needs Whit's help. Whit again tries to explain that it takes more than just a few days to make a family strong. But Bart begs so hard, Whit finally directs him to several books on the subject. Bart tries to implement some of the suggestions in the book—but it's impossible to change the Rathbones. So, in typical Rathbone style, they decide that the only way they can win the contest is by making the other finalist, the Johnson family, *lose.*

As generally happens with the Rathbones' schemes, everything backfires just when they think they've reached success. The contest judges arrive, and everyone learns that, in his essay, Rodney wrote that Bart was a doctor, and Doris was a trial lawyer! While the rest of us pick up a lesson about *real* family values, the Rathbones carry on as always.

Adventures in the ODYSSEY archives:

"Family Values" was the first time Doris Rathbone—Bart's wife and Rodney's mother—appeared on the program. "Family Values" was also the first time we cut part of the episode out of the broadcast version—but included the whole thing in the album cassette. So if you've only heard the episode on the radio, you haven't heard the *entire* show.

STUDY QUESTIONS:

1. Why did Bart think he could change the way his family treats each other in just a few days?
2. What was wrong with the way the Rathbones went about trying to change themselves? What are some good ways to improve family relations?
3. Why did the Johnsons decide to withdraw from the contest? Do you think it was the right decision? Why or why not?

BERNARDISMS

(Continued from page 163)

"Don't try to figure it out—you'll just hurt yourself."
—to Mrs. Grayson, after suffering through one of Eugene's speeches, in "Last in a Long Line"

"Seems like you can't swing a dead cat these days without hitting somebody who's trying to save some plant or animal."
—to Lucy, on endangered species, in "Last in a Long Line"

"I'd rather pull out my fingernails with a pair of rusty pliers."
—to Lucy, on the possibility of being related to Eugene, in "Last in a Long Line"

"I'd rather leave that to someone like Robert Redford or Charlton Heston or James Stewart."
—Bernard's idea of who should play him in the movie, in "A Day in the Life"

"I've had some cases that'd curl your chest hair."
—to Whit, on how dirty some windows can get, in "A Thanksgiving Carol"

"Your windows have more fingerprints than the easels at a convention of six-fingered hand-painters."
—to Whit, in "Room Mates"

"You're the only guy I know who could ruin gratitude by saying thank you."
—to Eugene, in "Room Mates"

"I built it from the ground up—started with just a rag and a bucket, and now I've got . . . a squeegee and a bucket."
—to Edwin Blackgaard, on the success of Walton's Janitorial Service, in "My Fair Bernard"

"It's as uncooperative as my Uncle Jed's mule and more temperamental than my sister-in-law."
—to Eugene, on computers, in ". . . It Ended with a Handshake"

"Unless you can make microchips out of cow chips, there's not going to be a computer repair shop for probably 200 miles."
—to Eugene, on learning his computer is broken, in "Second Thoughts"

"Give the man a hammer, and he goes power crazy!"
—referring to a judge, after being sentenced for contempt of court, in "Third Degree"

"What kind of a town is this when you drive thousands of miles to look at a tennis court?"
—on Beverly Hills, in "The Fifth House on the Left"

"I haven't been this excited about anything since those self-adjusting squeegees came out."
—to Tom, on becoming his campaign manager for mayor, in "Tom for Mayor"

Episodes #244 & 245

"The Mysterious Stranger," Parts One & Two

Theme: Greed.
Scripture reference: Exodus 20:17
Recommended maturity level: 10 and up
Written and directed by Paul McCusker
Production engineers: Dave Arnold and Bob Luttrell
(Original air dates: 9-18-93 & 9-25-93)

PARENTAL WARNING: This is a mystery, crafted in the traditional style of mysteries—which means there are a few scary spots. While older children should be able to handle the suspense, this story is not intended for younger listeners.

Whit and Connie are sorting through the mail one afternoon when they come across a letter. It is written in response to an article Whit wrote for *Home & Town* magazine about Whit's End. Whit remarks that he's received at least a dozen such letters. They're all requests from folks wanting to stay at the discovery emporium.

Whit is just about write the magazine and tell them that Whit's End isn't a hotel when suddenly a strange young man, Kent Wakefield, walks through the front door. He is visibly stunned as he stands in the center of the room and looks around. Whit asks if he can help the young man—and Kent tells Whit that Whit's End is just like he remembered it. Whit assumes Kent saw the article, and Kent says he did. But he also knows the place because Whit's End was his home! He used to live there!

Whit explains to Kent that it is impossible. He couldn't have lived there. Before being turned into Whit's End, the building was a recreation center. It had never been a home or, at least, it hadn't been in Kent's lifetime. Kent is insistent that it *was* his home and gives Whit the strong impression that he is mentally unbalanced.

Kent explains that his parents died tragically in a fire when he was a child. He was raised in Pittsburgh by his adopted uncle. Until now, Kent didn't even know *where* his parents had been living when they died—his uncle had kept the information from him.

After Kent leaves, Whit begins to investigate Kent's claims. Soon, certain pieces to the puzzle fall into place—and someone keeps making anonymous threatening phone calls telling Whit to "beware." Whit also meets Kent's uncle, James Wakefield, who begs Whit not to indulge his nephew's fantasies. He tells Whit that Kent is seriously ill because of what had happened to his parents.

Whit is ready to give up his sleuthing when he learns that Kent's parents were the heirs to the Wakefield family fortune. They really did live in Odyssey once, in a mansion outside of town called the Tate House. Whit talks to the original architect of the mansion and finds out that the basic design was copied and used in the early part of the twentieth century for the mayor's house, which is now Whit's End.

Whit and Lucy, who is writing an article for the *Odyssey Times*, visit the burned-out shell of the Tate House. It looks exactly like Whit's End! Inside, they hear a creepy howling sound. Suddenly, debris is dropped onto Whit. He narrowly escapes unharmed. Whit and Lucy then meet a woman who lives in a cottage behind the old mansion. She is cautious and unfriendly and refuses to talk to Whit about the house.

Whit persists with his investigation, even though James Wakefield insists that he stop. Whit refuses. With all Whit's found out, he believes Kent's not as crazy as he seems. Whit takes Kent to the Tate House, where Kent sees and recognizes the caretaker. She's Mrs. Ullman, a woman who'd been the housekeeper there when Kent was a child. She screams and runs.

Whit learns that Kent's father did, in fact, survive the fire. But he was seriously burned and disfigured. He was first institutionalized, then released into the care of James Wakefield and moved to Tate *Lodge*—the house behind the burned-out mansion.

In a climactic confrontation at the lodge, we learn that Kent's father was mentally incapacitated by the fire. He lived as a servant with Mrs. Ullman. Ullman has been working for James Wakefield all these years. Wakefield is not Kent's adopted uncle, but his *real* uncle on his mother's side. Wakefield has been manipulating the lives of Kent and his father for years so that he would inherit the family fortune. The entire tragic scheme was merely a ploy to get money—and a living lesson that "the love of money is the root of all evil" (1 Timothy 6:10).

STUDY QUESTIONS:

1. Why was it so easy for James Wakefield to manipulate Kent?
2. Why was Kent's uncle so bent on keeping Kent locked away?
3. What are some of the consequences of greed? How can you avoid becoming greedy?

166 THE COMPLETE GUIDE TO ADVENTURES IN ODYSSEY

Episode #246 "My Fair Bernard"

Theme: Doing your best; the value of hard work.
Scripture reference: 2 Chronicles 15:7
Written and directed by Phil Lollar
Production engineer: Dave Arnold
(Original air date: 10-02-93)

Bernard Walton pulls up at one of his buildings downtown to wash some windows—and discovers that Bart Rathbone has expanded the Electric Palace to include janitorial services. Thanks to Bart's hot, new radio ads—which feature his lower prices—several of Bernard's customers are switching to Bart's services. Bernard furiously goes to Whit's End to try and produce some radio ads of his own. The result is less than satisfactory. So Bernard decides he needs acting lessons to improve the ads.

The only place to get acting lessons in Odyssey is at the Harlequin Theatre, taught by Edwin Blackgaard. But, surprisingly, Edwin agrees to not only take on Bernard as a student, but to put Bernard's plight on stage! Edwin explains that Bernard's struggle is right out of classic theatre: The little man strives against enormous odds to hold on to what he has built. It's a story of good vs. evil, right vs. wrong. It takes some convincing, but Bernard is finally bitten by the theatrical bug and agrees to do the play.

When he leaves, Shakespeare wonders if Edwin has lost his mind. Edwin reveals that Bernard's play will be just the kind of depressing, avant-guarde play that Rosecrantz Guildenstern, a local critic, will like! It will be excellent publicity for the Harlequin—and will help save Bernard's business to boot!

Just before the performance, Bart tells Bernard that everyone may like his play—but it won't bring him any new business. Bernard realizes that Bart is right. So Bernard ruins the play by inserting plugs for Walton's Janitorial Service after every other line. Edwin tries to stop him by literally pulling the curtain on Bernard. The play is a disaster.

As it turns out, Bernard's business was safe anyway. Bart's shoddy work causes his customers to switch back to Bernard. As for Edwin, Rosecrantz Guildenstern tells him to produce nice family shows like he usually does. As Shakespeare said, "All's well that ends well."

STUDY QUESTIONS:

1. Why did Bart decide to go into janitorial service? Why did Edwin want to do a play about Bernard's life? Were either of their reasons good ones? Why or why not?
2. Why did Bernard mess up the play?
3. Should Bernard have tried to fight off Bart's new business the way he did? What should he have done? What would *you* have done?

Episode #247 "Why Don't You Grow Up?"

Theme: Being content; maturity; acting your age.
Scripture reference: Philippians 4:6-7,11
Written by Charlie Richards and Paul McCusker
Directed by Phil Lollar
Production engineer: Bob Luttrell
(Original air date: 10-09-93)

Erica is tired of being a kid. She doesn't get to do *anything* fun. She can't drive a car, make long-distance phone calls, or eat and buy whatever she wants. Erica would much rather be an adult who gets to do *all* of those things. She complains to Whit about her plight, and Mr. Whittaker takes her to the Room of Consequence.

After a bit of quick programming, Erica finds that, on the outside at least, she is the ripe old age of 22. She is pleased—at first. But she soon learns that with adulthood comes enormous responsibility—getting and keeping a job, paying bills, being on time, eating properly, managing finances. The lessons Erica learns are difficult. In the end, she realizes that there is a good reason she's still a kid—Erica's not ready to be an adult yet.

STUDY QUESTIONS:

1. Why did Erica want to be older?
2. Why did she fail so miserably at it?
3. Have you ever wished you were older? What are some good things about the age you are right now?

Episode #248 "Terror from the Skies"

Theme: Don't believe everything you hear.
Scripture reference: 1 Thessalonians 5:21
Written and directed by Paul McCusker
Production engineer: Dave Arnold
(Original air date: 10-30-93)

Edwin Blackgaard has teamed up with one of the local radio stations in Odyssey to produce and air a fun, fictional program called "Terror from the Skies." The show is aired live to add to its spookiness, but it is all in good fun. Unfortunately, through a series of incidents and accidents, Lawrence and Jimmy miss the fact that it's just a show. They think the program is for real and are terrified that aliens from outer space are invading the earth! Lawrence takes off in a panic with Jimmy close behind him.

After a series of madcap mishaps, the two of them manage to burst in on the climax of the production. This gives it a poignant, if unintended, ending. Lawrence again learns that he shouldn't let his imagination run away with him—and Jimmy finds that you can't believe everything you hear.

STUDY QUESTIONS:

1. Why was it silly for Jimmy and Lawrence to be frightened of outer space aliens invading the earth? Explain.
2. Would *you* have been afraid? Why or why not?
3. What is the best way to handle fear?

Episode #249

"The Case of the Delinquent Disciples"

Theme: The importance of Bible study; commitment.
Scripture reference: 2 Timothy 2:15
Written and directed by Paul McCusker
Production engineer: Dave Arnold
(Original air date: 11-06-93)

Harlow Doyle is prowling around Whit's End, looking for a case. Nothing seems to be cropping up—until Connie walks in and tells Whit that she's not going to teach her Tuesday night Bible study anymore. Her students have been disappearing over the past few weeks. Harlow gets interested. Missing persons cases were a specialty of his back in detective school. So he takes off to find Connie's students, with typically goofy results.

But Whit does a little detective work of his own. He discovers that there is a good reason why Connie's students haven't been showing up lately: Connie hasn't been preparing her lessons well. Whit is able to show Connie that she may have the gift of teaching, but she still needs to study. Studying would show Connie to be a worker approved by God (2 Timothy 2:15). As Whit puts it, just because the Red Sea was miraculously parted doesn't mean we don't need to build bridges.

After "The Case of the Delinquent Disciples," we decided that Harlow Doyle was better suited as a secondary character. From this episode on, we used Harlow in small doses.

STUDY QUESTIONS:

1. Why did Connie's students quit coming to her Bible study? Were they wrong to stop? Why or why not?
2. Connie thought that having the gift of teaching meant she didn't have to study. Why is that untrue?
3. Have you ever thought of quitting a Bible study or a church? Why should you keep going? Is there ever a good reason to stop attending a Bible study or church? If so, what would be a good reason?

Episodes #250 & 251

"Pilgrim's Progress Revisited," Parts One & Two

Theme: The Christian life.
Scripture reference: 1 Corinthians 9:24-27
Written and directed by Phil Lollar
Production engineers: Bob Luttrell and Dave Arnold
(Original air dates: 11-13-93 & 11-20-93)

The gang at Whit's End presents a Kid's Radio version of John Bunyan's "Pilgrim's Progress." It's the story of young Christian

(played by Sam Johnson) and his journey to the Celestial City. Along the way, Christian encounters various people who serve as obstacles to his quest: Mr. Worldly Wise (played by Eugene), Ms. Busywork (played by Connie), Giant Despair (played by Bart Rathbone), and Apollyon, son of the devil (played by, believe it or not, Whit!). It's a funny, touching, and reverent program, showing the allegorical path a believer must often take to reach heaven.

the Adventures in ODYSSEY archives:

"Pilgrim's Progress Revisited" was originally titled "Lawrence's Progress." These episodes were intended to be an Imagination Station adventure for Lawrence—in order to bring him to Christ. But the team felt it was better to make these shows a Kid's Radio broadcast. That way, the characters could uniquely act out Bunyan's story. That is why the Giant sounds like Bart Rathbone, Mr. Worldly Wise is played by Eugene, Mr. Pliant is Harlow Doyle, and so on.

The character of Ms. Busywork does not appear in Bunyan's book. It was added to accomodate another role for Katie Leigh Pavlakovich, who plays Connie.

behind the scenes:

"To make Apollyon's voice, we slowed down Hal Smith's voice tracks and added various animal noises to make him sound like a dragon. The giant's footsteps were actually sonic booms mixed in with earthquake sounds.

"When we recorded the background voices for the 'demons-in-hell' scene, we used the regular cast members to provide the voices. But right in the middle of it, Will Ryan humorously suggested that we also record the demons using Goofy's voice (the Disney character). So now, we have a tape with a bunch of Goofy-sounding demons on it."

—Dave Arnold

STUDY QUESTIONS:

1. Why did Christian want to reach the Celestial City?
2. What is an allegory?
3. "Pilgrim's Progress" is the *second* best-selling book of all time. What's the first?

Episode #252 "The Bad Hair Day"

Theme: False accusations; taking the law into your own hands.
Scripture reference: Proverbs 22:24-25
Written and directed by Phil Lollar
Production engineer: Bob Luttrell
(Original air date: 12-11-93)

Henry is upset—his comic books are missing. He and Sam tell Whit about it, and Henry immediately accuses Rodney Rathbone. Whit actually defends Rodney. But there's no need because Rodney bursts in a few moments later with accusations of his own. He left his favorite pocketknife at the Wonderworld tree house. When he returned for it, it was gone. It appears Odyssey has a thief on the loose. Whit tells everyone to calm down and report the losses to the police.

Later, Rodney has different ideas. He gathers the Bones of Rath and Henry. They all take off to find the culprit and punish the person. After hunting for a while, they come across Charles Thompson, whom they believe is the guilty one. Charles loudly professes his innocence, but Rodney does not listen. He starts to brand Charles's hair with blue paint. But when Henry acts nervous about Rodney doing that, Rodney threatens him as well. Rather than stand up for Charles, Henry backs down.

Meanwhile, Sam and Harlow Doyle discover that the comic books and the pocketknife were actually taken by a scavenger raccoon. When Henry discovers this, he gets physically ill. He tells Whit, who also grieves for Charles. But Whit comes up with a unique way for Henry to make it up to Charles. And Henry does.

Adventures in ODYSSEY — the archives:

This episode—inspired by the classic book and movie *The Oxbow Incident*—was originally titled "The Incident." But Dave Arnold came up with a much better title—"The Bad Hair Day."

STUDY QUESTIONS:

1. Why were Henry and Rodney so quick to accuse other people of stealing their things?
2. Why was Whit so quick to dispute both the boys' theories?
3. What does the phrase "Innocent until proven guilty" mean? How could the boys have implemented that even while they were searching for the thief?

Episode #253 "A Time for Christmas"

Theme: The history of the Christmas holiday.
Scripture reference: Luke 2
Written and directed by Paul McCusker
Production engineer: Dave Arnold
(Original air date: 12-18-93)

It's Christmastime, and Courtney is busy rushing around buying presents for everyone. In fact, she's so busy, she doesn't have any time to help Jenny put on a Christmas show for her school, participate in the nativity program at city hall, perform in the holiday pageant at church, or even get involved with the Angel Tree project at Whit's End.

Whit feels it's time Courtney discovered what Christmas is truly about. He takes her on several trips in the Imagination Station so she can see into the hearts of others who have celebrated the birth of Christ. The trips are effective. As the Station winds down, Courtney wishes she could help those in history who are less fortunate than herself. She opens the door and steps into Jenny's house. Jenny is upset that Courtney couldn't find the time to help her with a simple holiday program. Suddenly, Courtney realizes just how selfish she has been.

Just then, the Station winds down again—for real this time—and Courtney is back at Whit's End. The real Jenny is sitting there. Courtney quickly volunteers to help her friend—for she finally understands the true meaning of Christmas.

Adventures in ODYSSEY — the archives:

Like "Back to Bethlehem," this episode was based on a musical of the same name by Paul McCusker.

STUDY QUESTIONS:

1. Why didn't Courtney want to help Jenny?
2. What did the play *St. George and the Dragon* represent?
3. Why was Christmas outlawed in England in the seventeenth century?

1994

By the end of 1993, *Adventures in Odyssey* was still growing by leaps and bounds. Both the weekly and daily network continued to add stations and releases. Five animated videos had been produced, and three more were in various stages of development and production. On the publishing side, Paul McCusker had written six novels, and three more were already prepared for publication. Other, different types of publications—including this book—were planned.

We were also looking at implementing other spin-off products as well, such as *AIO* trading cards, T-shirts, and backpacks. And the radio show wasn't exactly winding down, either. It was shaping up to be a year of unprecedented productivity.

Then on Thursday evening, January 27, tragedy struck. Hal Smith, voice of John Avery Whittaker, passed away. Appropriately, he was at his home in Santa Monica, California, listening to radio dramas on a local station.

The *AIO* team was shocked and grief-stricken. Not only was Hal a talented actor, he was also a dearly loved friend.

The future of the program now weighed heavily on our minds, and we met to consider how to proceed. A recording session was scheduled for the following week, and Hal was in all of the eight shows slated to be recorded. We immediately altered the episodes we could, then temporarily shelved others. Fortunately, we had finished several episodes with Hal in them that had not yet been aired. We decided to intersperse the Whit and non-Whit shows to give ourselves time to strategize.

In early February, the *AIO* team met together in California to brainstorm ideas. Our integrated episodes would take us as far as June—but then what? We discussed our options. The ideas ranged from having the character of Whit die, to creating a spin-off program for *Adventures in Odyssey.* For various reasons, none of those ideas was acceptable. So we then tried to figure out how Whit could leave Odyssey. It would be difficult to do without drawing attention to the fact that Whit wouldn't be able to explain *why* he was leaving town.

Finally, after much discussion, Paul came up with the answer: We would send Eugene and Bernard out of town on a road trip. This would take the program out of Odyssey, giving Whit enough time to make his decision to leave.

We also decided to develop a few new characters while Bernard and Eugene were on their summer adventure. Those characters were Jason Whittaker, Whit's son; and Jack Allen, one of Whit's oldest friends. But we started off the year by introducing another new character to the series—Katrina Shanks, Eugene's love interest and a pivotal player in Eugene's spiritual life.

Finally, the plans were in place. We just had to make them happen.

Episode #254 "Truth, Trivia & 'Trina"

Theme: Competition; pride; relationships
Scripture reference: Proverbs 13:3
Written and directed by Paul McCusker
Production engineer: Dave Arnold
(Original air date: 1-08-94)

It's a typical afternoon at Whit's End—Eugene and Connie are at each other's throats again. This time, they're arguing over several disparaging inferences Eugene has made about Connie's intellect. Their disagreement is so intense that both of them get suckered into Bart Rathbone's latest scheme—a game show called "Truth and Trivia," sponsored by the Electric Palace. Connie wants to prove to Eugene—on television—that she is no dummy.

Both Connie and Eugene start studying. Connie uses the library at Whit's End. Eugene goes to the library at Campbell County Community College, where he meets a pretty young lady named Katrina Shanks. She is working at the library. Eugene quickly realizes that Katrina is equally as smart as himself. Eugene is intrigued by this gray-eyed beauty and tries to spend as much time with her as possible, even inviting her to the game show.

Katrina shows up—but not as a spectator. She's also a contestant! The race has begun! Connie does surprisingly well and earns Eugene's respect. Eugene and Katrina battle until Bart asks Eugene the final question: "What color are Katrina's eyes?"

Eugene stammers, then answers, "Brown."

But he's wrong. Katrina's eyes are gray. Bart then asks Katrina about Eugene's eyes.

Without hesitation, she answers, "Periwinkle blue."

Katrina is right. She wins the contest—and Eugene realizes he doesn't have to try so hard to impress everybody with what he knows.

Adventures in
the ODYSSEY archives:
"Truth, Trivia & 'Trina" introduced Katrina Shanks, Eugene's love interest.

behind the scenes:

"Listeners were divided in their feelings about Katrina's arrival. Those who thought that Eugene would eventually marry Connie didn't like Katrina. But other listeners were charmed by her. We maintained a 'wait-and-see' attitude before we decided what would happen next."

—Paul McCusker

STUDY QUESTIONS:

1. Why did Eugene think Connie wasn't very intelligent? Was he right?
2. Why was Connie so eager to prove that she wasn't dumb?
3. There are many ways that people can be intelligent. Can you name some? What are some ways in which you are smart?

Episode #255 "The Boy Who Cried 'Destructo!'"

Theme: Controlling your imagination.
Scripture reference: Proverbs 14:7
Written and directed by Phil Lollar
Production engineer: Bob Luttrell
(Original air date: 1-15-94)

Lawrence Hodges is stuck in a fantasy world. This time, he imagines himself to be a secret agent on a mission to save a doctor from the science lab of Destructo—an evil, subversive organization that wants to take over the world. Lawrence ends up causing Eugene (the doctor) to mix the perfume chemicals he is working with into a chloroform solution. This causes Eugene to pass out.

Later, Lawrence bumps into Harlow Doyle and draws him into this fantasy world. They head off on Harlow's moped to destroy the evil Destructo headquarters. They come across two men unloading boxes from their van into a secret cave near Trickle Lake. They decide to split up to spy on the men, and when Lawrence returns to their meeting point, he hears a strange noise. The van, the men, and Harlow have disappeared, leaving behind only the moped!

Lawrence rushes to tell Whit that Harlow has been kidnapped, but Whit is skeptical, and Eugene thinks it is just a fabrication of Lawrence's imagination. Whit goes to the cave with him to check things out anyway. Seeing no tire tracks, Whit sends Lawrence to search for the missing moped. Whit goes into the cave to search for the boxes. Lawrence hears the same noise he heard when Harlow was kidnapped—but when he runs to warn Whit, he finds only Whit's flashlight. He runs back to Whit's End to tell Eugene, but Eugene still doesn't believe Lawrence and won't let him call the police. Finally, Eugene agrees to take Lawrence to the cave on the way to the college to have his chloroform perfume examined.

Meanwhile, Jones and Smith—the two men Lawrence saw—turn out to be bootleggers who have captured Whit and left him tied up in the cave with Harlow, next to a distiller. While trying to untie Whit, Harlow knocks over a broom and hits a valve on the distiller that causes it to overheat. Jones and Smith load up the "booze" in their van and head out through a gate—disguised as bushes—to their hideout. This explains the grinding noise Lawrence heard. Eugene hides in the van, and when the men return, he knocks them out with the chloroform. Eugene arrives inside just in time to put out the fire before the distiller blows up, saving Whit and Harlow. Eugene apologizes to Lawrence for not believing him—and Lawrence says he has learned that if he lets his imagination run wild, no one will ever believe him.

the ODYSSEY archives:

Many elements in this program were remade from *AIO* #70 & 71, "The Return of Harley." This show subtly furthered Eugene's interest in Katrina: In the beginning, he was making perfume, and although it's not stated, the fragrance was almost certainly for Katrina. It's also notable that Lawrence actually *stopped* himself from going on one of his imaginary jaunts for a change.

STUDY QUESTIONS:

1. Why was Whit one of the few people who believed Lawrence?
2. Should Lawrence and Harlow, then Lawrence and Whit, have split up to investigate matters? Why or why not?
3. Why is it important to control your imagination?

Episodes #256–258

"Aloha, Oy!" Parts One, Two & Three

Theme: Family togetherness.
Scripture reference: Psalm 68:6
Written and directed by Phil Lollar
Production engineers: Dave Arnold, Bob Luttrell, and Mark Drury
(Original air dates: 1-22-94, 1-29-94, 2-05-94)

Jimmy and Lawrence go to Rathbone's Electric Palace to buy some fuses for George, and they end up getting a big surprise. As soon as Jimmy enters the store, bells ring, whistles blow, alarms sound, and music plays. Bart rushes up to Jimmy. Rathbone proclaims Jimmy to be the 10,000th customer to enter the Electric Palace. He and four of his friends and family members have won a free trip to Hawaii!

Back at the Barclays' home, George confirms that the trip is legitimate—the family and Lawrence really are going to pineapple paradise. But when they arrive at the airport, they discover that Bart, Doris, and Rodney Rathbone are joining them. Bart has finagled extra tickets for his family.

The Barclays experience their wackiest vacation ever as Bart's cost-cutting measures lead them to a strange boat captain who gets them lost at sea. Meanwhile, Rodney goes to drastic measures to impress Donna (including having a wild parasailing experience). And Lawrence's efforts to find his father lead to several near-discoveries and a disastrous debut as a busboy.

Circumstances remarkably connect, however. Rodney learns a lesson about going to extremes to impress people, and Lawrence has a touching reunion with his father—thanks to the Barclays, who learn to *never* travel with the Rathbones again.

The part of Don Iowa was inspired by Randy Crenshaw's impression of the legendary Hawaiian singer Don Ho. Captain Quid was my tribute to the character the late Robert Shaw played in the movie *Jaws*. "Aloha, Oy!" part three was also Mark Drury's first solo production for *AIO*.

STUDY QUESTIONS:

1. Why didn't the Barclays want to go to Hawaii with the Rathbones?
2. What did Lawrence really want out of his trip to Hawaii? Did he get it?
3. Why is family togetherness so important?

Episode #259 "The Potential in Elliot"

Theme: Encouragement.
Scripture reference: Romans 12:10,15
Written by Marshal Younger
Directed by Paul McCusker
Production engineer: Bob Luttrell
(Original air date: 2-12-94)

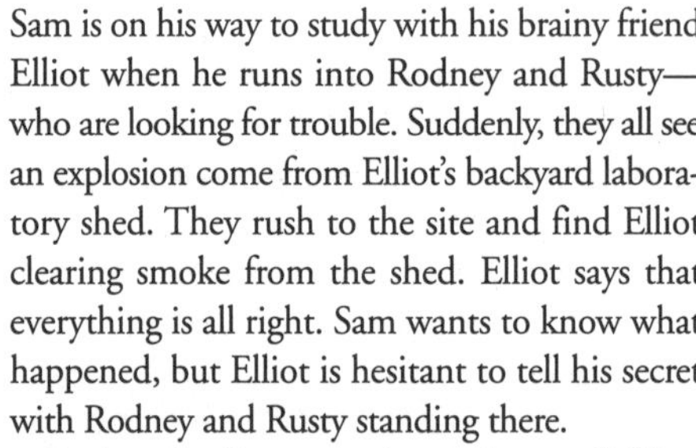

Sam is on his way to study with his brainy friend Elliot when he runs into Rodney and Rusty—who are looking for trouble. Suddenly, they all see an explosion come from Elliot's backyard laboratory shed. They rush to the site and find Elliot clearing smoke from the shed. Elliot says that everything is all right. Sam wants to know what happened, but Elliot is hesitant to tell his secret with Rodney and Rusty standing there.

Rodney finally coaxes the truth out of Elliot. Apparently, Elliot is working on a cure for cancer. Rodney and Rusty laugh hysterically at that concept. They leave the future mad scientist to his experiments. Even Sam is skeptical—after all, Elliot is just a kid. At least, that's what he tells Whit later at Whit's End. Whit says that Sam should be more supportive. Then Whit invites Sam to take a ride in the Imagination Station to prove his point.

Sam journeys back to Port Huron, Michigan, in the year 1856. There, he meets another young experimenter named Thomas. Sam helps him with several failed experiments. Sam ends up convincing Thomas that he should give up experimentation and just enjoy being a kid. But he discovers too late that he has just talked Thomas A. Edison out of becoming an inventor! Suddenly, everything goes dark. Sam realizes that without Edison's youthful precociousness, there would be no light bulb, no phonograph, no telegraph. His many inventions make our lives easier. Sam learns about history and the importance of encouragement.

STUDY QUESTIONS:

1. Why were Rodney, Rusty, and even Sam skeptical about Elliot's attempt to find a cure for cancer?
2. How could Sam have encouraged Elliot more?
3. Who can you encourage today? How?

Episode #260 "Naturally, I Assumed . . ."

Theme: Don't make assumptions.
Scripture reference: Philippians 4:8
Written and directed by Paul McCusker
Production engineer: Dave Arnold
(Original air date: 2-19-94)

Connie's curiosity is getting the best of her again. She tells Whit that Eugene has been acting strangely lately. He leaves just before four o'clock every day so he can race to the college. Whit says that's natural—Eugene is going to class. But Connie knows better. It isn't school Eugene is thinking about—it's Katrina. Sure enough, just then, Eugene speeds by on his way out the door. Connie teases Eugene as he leaves, then decides to find out how his relationship with Katrina is progressing.

As it turns out, Eugene is having a slight problem. Eugene really likes Katrina, but she hasn't given him any sign that the feelings are mutual. In fact, she tells Eugene that she can no longer meet at their usual time. She has another appointment and doesn't want to keep *him* waiting.

Eugene is understandably upset about having to vie for Katrina's affections. Connie coaxes the whole story out of him and immediately takes Eugene under her wing. She offers Eugene all sorts of suggestions about what girls like—small gifts, romantic language, flowers, candy. Eugene tries them all, with comically disastrous results. To make matters worse, Whit walks in on Connie and Eugene several times at the wrong moments. Soon Whit begins to think romance is brewing between his two employees!

Finally, Katrina discloses that her mysterious appointment is with a young boy from England named Darren. Katrina is tutoring him. The merry mix-up is solved—and everyone is reminded of why it is foolish to make assumptions.

STUDY QUESTIONS:

1. Should Eugene have told Katrina how he felt about her? Why or why not? How could he have shared his feelings?
2. How could all of these misunderstandings have been avoided?
3. Why should you never assume things about people? Have you assumed anything about anyone lately?

Episode #261 "Afraid, Not!"

Theme: Conquering fear.
Scripture reference: Isaiah 41:10
Written by Paul McCusker
Directed by Phil Lollar
Production engineer: Bob Luttrell
(Original air date: 2-26-94)

Danny Schmidt doesn't want to go to school today—or any *other* day, for that matter. He puts up a huge fuss, but his parents inform him that he *is* going. Danny reluctantly rises, gets dressed, and leaves.

Later, at school, Danny's teacher, Mr. Richards, dismisses the class for recess—everyone except for Danny. Mr. Richards wants to know why Danny is wearing sunglasses. Danny hems and haws and finally reveals that the glasses are covering up an enormous bruise. Danny is sent to the nurse, and his mother is called. Finally, everyone gets to the root of the problem: Danny is being chased and beaten up by a *female* bully.

That part of the problem is solved quickly, thanks to a phone call from the Odyssey police to the girl's parents. Unfortunately, Danny's fear of walking to school continues—to the point where he almost has a heart attack when Whit runs into him on the way home from school. Danny explains his problem to Whit. He offers a wonderful solution: memorizing a scripture verse.

Danny feels better. The next morning, he has an opportunity to try out his new "weapon." Rusty tries to bully him out of his lunch money, and Danny fairly shouts the verse at Rusty. Rusty cowers and runs in the face of the Word—providing Danny with proof about where the source of true courage lies.

STUDY QUESTIONS:

1. Why didn't Danny want to tell anyone what happened to him?
2. Why was Danny so afraid, even after the police had taken care of everything?
3. Where does real courage come from?

Episode #262 "A Prayer for George Barclay"

Theme: God's call to the ministry; dealing with change.
Scripture reference: 1 Corinthians 9:14,16
Written and directed by Paul McCusker
Production engineer: Dave Arnold
(Original air date: 4-02-94)

George Barclay has been out of steady work for some time. He's kept himself busy doing odd jobs, but mostly he has been waiting on the Lord to direct his life. That's not good enough for Jimmy and Donna, though. They decide the Lord needs some extra pushing, so they pray earnestly for their father. The next day, George's old company offers him a new job, one with better benefits.

The family is ecstatic—until George says that he's not sure if he should actually take the job. After lots of prayer, George drops the bombshell that he's not accepting the job. Instead, he believes that

God is calling him into ministry. Jimmy and Donna are stunned. But there is yet another surprise: Mary is pregnant! Change is in store for the Barclays. They have little choice but to place themselves in God's hands.

the *Adventures in* ODYSSEY archives:

In 1993, we threw a wrench into the Barclays' lives by having George lose his job. But since then, we hadn't done much of anything else with them—except send them to Hawaii. It was time to move the family forward, so we sent George into the ministry. But in doing that, we were also determined to make sure his experience was realistic—which meant we would have to do a lot of research.

STUDY QUESTIONS:

1. Did Jimmy and Donna pray for their father in the right way? Why or why not?
2. What does it mean to be called into the ministry? Is it a choice you make? Explain.
3. How do you think George knew that God wanted him to be a minister? How can you best determine what God's will is for your life?

Episode #263
"When Bad Isn't So Good"

Theme: Goodness is its own reward.
Scripture reference: Psalm 1:1-5
Written and directed by Phil Lollar
Production engineer: Bob Luttrell
(Original air date: 4-09-94)

Sam can't believe it. Thanks to Whit's Student Incentive Program, Rusty is enjoying an ice-cream sundae fit for royalty—just because he passed a test! Sam feels cheated: He works hard. He gets A's on everything. He is a good and responsible student. But Sam hardly gets noticed. Rusty gets one B minus on a test, and the teacher treats him like he's brillant, and Whit gives him a free sundae.

Sam says he thought rewards were supposed to come when you work hard and do the right thing. But he's done that all his life, and no one has ever rewarded him for it. Rusty responds that everyone *expects* Sam to be good. Rusty suggests that maybe if Sam were bad once in a while, he'd get free ice cream, too. Sam decides to try it, but Rusty tells him not to bother—he doesn't have the knack for being bad.

Meanwhile, Edwin Blackgaard is suffering from a similar situation. He has learned that his evil brother, Regis, is doing well in Europe. But Edwin is barely keeping his theatre afloat in Odyssey. Edwin is so upset about this that he vents his anger at "the system" during an interview on the Cryin' Bryan Dern radio show. Instantly, Edwin becomes a hit with Dern's listeners! Dern asks Edwin to become a regular political commentator on the show. Edwin does, and he subsequently blasts everyone possible.

While this is going on, Rusty takes Sam under his wing. Rusty tells Sam that he can prove his badness by breaking a large window Bernard Walton is cleaning. Bernard catches Sam in the act and talks sense into him. Sam then realizes what a dope he's been. He takes off to stop Rusty from setting off some dangerous firecrackers in the Harlequin Theatre. Rusty is getting back at Edwin for blasting city workers—among them Rusty's father—on the radio.

Sam arrives to discover the theatre being picketed by the local volunteer fire department, whom Edwin also criticized in a recent broadcast. Unfortunately, Rusty goes through with his act. He inadvertently sets fire to a backstage curtain. Edwin is certain that the firemen will let the theater burn down because of the way he has insulted them. Much to his surprise, the fire squad rushes in and puts out the fire.

Edwin learns that "the system" isn't too bad after all, and Sam finds that doing good is its own reward.

the *Adventures in* ODYSSEY archives:

"When Bad Isn't So Good" was the first show that had to be adjusted due to Hal Smith's death. The parts Eugene and Bernard played here were originally written for Whit.

STUDY QUESTIONS:

1. Why did Sam think he'd have to be bad before he got any attention?
2. What was wrong with Edwin's radio commentaries?
3. Is there anything wrong with being noticed for doing good things? Should you do good things only if you'll be noticed for them? Why or why not?

Episode #264 "Making the Grade"

Theme: Personal discipline; the importance of education.
Scripture reference: Proverbs 12:1
Written and directed by Paul McCusker
Production engineer: Mark Drury
(Original air date: 4-16-94)

The Barclays are celebrating Mary's pregnancy and George's acceptance into seminary. At the celebration, Jimmy tells his father that he thinks he'd like to be a paramedic someday. George thinks it's a wonderful idea and wholeheartedly encourages Jimmy.

The next day, Jimmy meets with a career counselor who enters Jimmy's career goal into a special computer. It matches Jimmy's goal with his current educational status. The counselor will present the results to a paramedic, whom Jimmy and others in his class will later visit. To prepare for the meeting, Jimmy borrows a dummy to practice CPR.

Then Lawrence shows up to talk with Jimmy. Lawrence is upset. Lately, he's had trouble getting his schoolwork done. Now, his mother is really badgering him about doing his science homework. Jimmy empathizes with Lawrence, but he continues practicing mouth-to-mouth on the dummy.

At the meeting, one of the first things the paramedic tells Jimmy and the others is that the job involves much more than driving around in ambulances and giving people mouth-to-mouth. Later, the paramedic also informs Jimmy that the profession involves a lot of math and science. Jimmy doesn't believe him until the paramedic grills Jimmy with several math- and science-related questions that are frequently used in paramedic work.

Jimmy returns home that night, feeling defeated. George comforts him. George reveals that he, too, is unsure of himself, especially now that he's heard how demanding seminary is. But George has resolved to just buckle down and develop the discipline to do the job. He wants to be the best minister possible. Jimmy understands. He agrees to take math and science more seriously—and he starts by going over to Lawrence's house and helping him with his homework.

STUDY QUESTIONS:

1. Why didn't Lawrence want to do his homework? Have you ever felt that way? What's the best way to develop discipline?
2. Why does it take so much math and science to be a paramedic?
3. What do you want to be when you grow up? Are you studying hard for it right now? Why or why not?

Episode #265 "War of the Words"

Theme: Swearing; using bad language.
Scripture reference: Proverbs 21:23
Written by Marshal Younger
Directed by Phil Lollar
Production engineer: Bob Luttrell
(Original air date: 4-23-94)

Charles and Henry are eavesdropping on one of Connie and Eugene's more lively "discussions." Their ears especially prick up when they hear Eugene tell Connie her "choices have left her somewhat . . . maladroit." Neither Connie, Henry, nor Charles knows what maladroit means. Henry and Charles (who think Eugene said "mallatroid") think Eugene used a dirty word.

Whit breaks up the disagreement. Connie and Eugene go their separate ways, and Henry suddenly has a new "bad" word to use. He uses it with increasing regularity and mispronounces the word until it becomes "milajoit." Unfortunately, he refers to the local librarian in this manner. The librarian responds by calling his parents.

Henry's dad demands to know where Henry heard such a word. When Henry finally reveals that he heard it at Whit's End, his father grounds him from the emporium. When Whit hears about this situation, he corners Charles and asks where he and Henry originally heard the word. Charles points the finger at Eugene. Eugene denies ever having said such a word as "milajoit." They all finally arrive at the truth, but by then, the damage is done. Henry's dad thinks Whit's End is a place where kids learn bad words. Whit is grieved. He pays a visit to Henry's dad to explain and apologize. Everyone learns an important lesson about the power of words.

the ODYSSEY archives:

"War of the Words" was the last episode Hal Smith recorded with us before he died. This script also contained the first mention of Robert Skeed, a character who never appeared on the program but who is referred to in several programs—usually when we needed to blame someone. In real life, the name "Robert Skeed" belongs to a friend of writer Marshal Younger.

behind the scenes:

"This show was a challenge to write. It was difficult to show the folly of using bad words without actually using bad words. I spent half the time writing this script just trying to come up with the right made-up bad word. I had some pretty good ones—but I finally ended up with 'milajoit.'"

—**Marshal Younger**

STUDY QUESTIONS:

1. Should Henry and Charles have listened to Connie and Eugene's argument? Was it Eugene's fault that the boys overheard what they thought was a bad word? Why or why not?
2. Why did the boys think "maladroit" was a bad word? If you heard a word you didn't know the meaning of, what would you do?
3. Why is it wrong to say bad words? What does the Bible say about the words we use?

Episode #266

"It Began with a Rabbit's Foot . . ."

Theme: Redemption; salvation.
Scripture references: Romans 3:10,23; 5:8; 10:8-10
Written by Paul McCusker
Directed by Phil Lollar
Production engineer: Dave Arnold
(Original air date: 4-30-94)

Katrina arrives at Whit's End in an agitated, though outwardly calm, state. The college is making cutbacks, and her job has been cut. Effective immediately, she has no work. Connie comforts her, then comes up with an idea: Katrina can work at Whit's End! Once Whit walks up, Connie tells him about Katrina's situation. Whit promptly hires Katrina. Then, Whit leaves with Lucy to give her information for an *Odyssey Times* article she's doing on the creation of the Bible Room.

When Eugene finally appears on the scene, Connie excitedly tells him the wonderful news about Katrina. But instead of being pleased, Eugene is uncomfortable. Strangely enough, he immediately rushes out to buy a newspaper. So Connie gives Katrina the grand tour. In the process, they comes across Whit and Lucy. Katrina is as intrigued by the Bible Room's creation as Lucy is, so Whit and Connie proceed to tell both Lucy and Katrina the story of its creation.

In the midst of this, Eugene returns with his newspaper. He shows Katrina the many jobs she could take instead of working at Whit's End. Everyone is confused by Eugene's actions. Whit makes it clear to Eugene that, for now, Katrina will stay. Katrina asks to hear the rest of the Bible Room story. But before Whit can continue, Eugene asks to speak to him privately.

In Whit's office, Eugene reveals why he is so reticent about having Katrina work there: He's in love with her, and he's afraid she will be affected by the place's prevailing views on Christianity. Eugene's concerns are confirmed when Connie enters a few moments later to retrieve a book on the basics of Christianity. Katrina is captivated by the story of the Bible Room. As it turns out, she is interested in Christianity. Eugene is too late.

Connie and Katrina leave to continue their discussion. Eugene sighs heavily and goes back to work. Lucy gets a final quote from Whit for her column: "The Bible Room is a wonderful example of what Whit's End is all about: Redemption—taking that which appears to be useless and making it useful once again. Just like Jesus does with our lives."

the Adventures in Odyssey archives:

The Bible Room was originally introduced in "Gotcha!" (*AIO* #24), but that episode was pulled from release because of scenes featuring Officer Harley. This episode gave us the opportunity to bring back—via flashbacks—the creation of the Bible Room.

STUDY QUESTIONS:

1. Why do you think Eugene was so concerned that Christianity would affect Katrina?
2. Why did Eugene say he doesn't really understand what love is? What would you say love is?
3. What does it mean to "redeem" something? Why was Jesus' redemption so important?

SAY WHAT?

Eugene Meltsner prides himself on his communication skills. Unfortunately, there are times when hardly anyone else can understand a word he's saying. Here are some of his more picturesque verbal gymnastics, along with their normal-language translations.

"Greetings and felicitations." (Translation: "Hello.")

"It is a superior and distinct honor to make your acquaintance, sir." (Translation: "Greetings and felicitations.")

"I would be proud and honored to offer my meager ministrations as your most obsequious journeyman for whatever course of time you deem necessary." (Translation: "I'd like the job, if it's okay with you.")

"I consider it an honor that you would bestow your trust upon us to watch over your establishment." (Translation: "We'd be happy to watch the place.")

"I hope you won't feel that I mistrust your powers of discernment, but if you could elaborate on the circumstances in a sequential enumeration, perhaps we could shed some light on our dilemma." (Translation: "What are the facts?")

"We're still very unsure of our facts, and therefore, feel it prudent to forgo any declarative stance until either the existing data can be thoroughly analyzed, or we receive further conclusive proof in this matter." (Translation: "We're not talking until we're sure about this.")

"Attention! Our quarry is on the approach! I believe it would behoove us to seclude ourselves, posthaste!" (Translation: "Hey! Here they come! Hide!")

"Got you, you premeditated pilferer!" (Translation: "Gotcha, thief!")

"To borrow the colloquialism: I am without perspiration." (Translation: "No sweat.")

Continued on page 179.

Episode #267
"... It Ended with a Handshake"

Theme: Communication; love.
Scripture reference: 1 Corinthians 13:5,7
Written and directed by Paul McCusker
Production engineer: Bob Luttrell
(Original air date: 5-07-94)

It's a few moments after Katrina has become a Christian. Connie is excited about this—but Eugene is confused. He is in the kitchen, typing on his laptop, pouring out his heart to his journal. Not only are Eugene's feelings for Katrina unclear, he also is uncertain of how Katrina feels about him now that she has become a Christian. He decides they need to be friends—nothing more.

Eugene leaves to help Bernard with his new computer. As he goes out the back, Frederick Holstein walks inside. He's the owner of Holstein's Books and is looking for Katrina to offer her a job! Katrina is ecstatic. Immediately, she leaves to check out Fred's store.

Meanwhile, Eugene is so agitated that he can't concentrate on Bernard's computer. Not only that, but he is late for class. He leaves his laptop with Bernard and runs off to school. A short while later, Bernard rushes into Whit's End, looking for Eugene. Bernard can't figure out the laptop. Whenever he turns it on, the screen tells him he has a disk error. Connie discovers that there is a disk in the "A" drive that is preventing the computer from booting up—a disk titled "Katrina, etc." Connie is dying to look at the contents of the disk, but she restrains herself. She merely tells Bernard to keep the disk with the computer. Bernard goes up to Whit's office to work.

Later, Katrina comes back in, excited about her new job. She bursts into Whit's office to thank him. There, she finds Bernard hard at work. After they briefly introduce themselves, Bernard hands Katrina the disk with her name on it—the disk filled with Eugene's journal, private thoughts, and undelivered love letters to her!

Eugene discovers that Katrina has the disk and is beside himself. He races to Katrina's room to tell her not to take anything she read seriously. Katrina agrees to this, and they shake on it. But then Katrina reveals that she didn't read anything on Eugene's disk. Eugene leaves, embarrassed. He realizes that he may have blown a potentially great relationship. It's a bittersweet day—Eugene is humiliated, yet Katrina has discovered that Eugene's feelings for her go deep.

Adventures in the ODYSSEY archives:

"It Ended with a Handshake" introduced the comical character Fred Holstein, who has trouble with popular expressions. The episode also showed Katrina's first steps as a Christian and how they would affect her relationship with Eugene.

Hal Smith passed away between the recordings of "It Began with a Rabbit's Foot . . ." and ". . . It Ended with a Handshake." This explains why Whit was off "running errands" in the latter episode.

STUDY QUESTIONS:

1. Why was Eugene so (rightly) convinced that once Katrina became a Christian, things would change between them?
2. Why did Eugene decide to stop talking to Katrina? What do you think about the way Eugene handled the situation? Katrina?
3. What does it mean to respect someone's privacy?

Episode #268
"Pet Peeves"

Theme: Responsibility; dealing with change.
Scripture reference: Hebrews 13:8
Written by Paul McCusker and Chris Fabry
Directed by Paul McCusker
Production engineer: Bob Luttrell
(Original air date: 5-14-94)

Changes, changes, changes. The Barclays have gone through nothing but changes lately, and Donna is unnerved by them all. At Whit's End, she tells Connie that she'd like things to be normal for once. Connie is about to respond when suddenly they hear a crash from the kitchen. They investigate and find a stray dog wreaking havoc among the pots and pans. Donna instantly falls in love with the canine. She wants to take it home, but Connie tells Donna to get her parents' permission first. Meanwhile, the stray is going to the pound.

Back at home, Donna has a family meeting, where a vote is taken about whether to keep the dog. George says definitely "no" (which counts for two votes—Barclay family rule), and Jimmy and Donna give two "yesses." This leaves Mary to cast the deciding ballot . . . a "yes." And so the Barclays have a dog! Or more precisely, *Donna* has a dog. George makes it clear that "Harry," as Donna has named the mutt, is her total responsibility. Donna must feed, water, clean, and care for him all by herself. And she does—at first.

Soon it becomes apparent that Harry is more than a handful, though. He tears up everything, barks at all hours of the day and night, and generally makes Donna's life a nightmare. She goes to Whit's End, frustrated by the dog and still unnerved by all the changes in her life. Connie comforts Donna and tells her that change *is* normal, but the one constant you can

depend on in the world is Jesus. Donna realizes Connie is right.

Donna is almost ready to take Harry back to the pound when he runs away. The Barclays look everywhere for him, but Harry is nowhere to be found. Donna is despondent.

The next day, she goes back to Whit's End to talk to Connie. Suddenly, they hear a familiar crash from the kitchen. They rush in, and Harry is playing in the garbage. Connie suggests Donna rename her dog "Normal." And she does.

the *Adventures in* ODYSSEY archives:

"Pet Peeves" went through five different script versions before we finally settled on this one. The early versions had Whit in them, but by the time we hit the last version, Hal Smith was gone. So Connie was purposely put in the position of helping Donna. The intent was to start Connie's "growing up" process.

Also, Production Engineer Bob Luttrell has the distinction of producing the two *AIO* episodes that prominently feature animals: a dog (this episode) and a cat ("All's Well with Boswell," *AIO* #125).

STUDY QUESTIONS:

1. Why did Donna feel like things weren't normal anymore? Have you ever felt like that?
2. The Barclays took a family vote to decide whether they should get a dog. How does your family make big decisions?
3. Do you have a pet? Is it your responsibility to take care of it? Do you?

SAY WHAT?

(Continued from page 177.)

"Let's punch the highway!" (Translation: "Let's hit the road!")

"Simply make your pronouncement." (Translation: "Just say the word.")

"I fail to comprehend your dilemma. The primary principle behind the Rule of Gold is simply to aid and/or otherwise assist, in a charitable fashion, those who live and work around us." (Translation: "What's the big deal? The Golden Rule means you be nice to people.")

"I was powering my two-wheeler along this concrete pathway when your personage suddenly appeared directly in front of me, blocking my course. My reflexes immediately sprang to life in an attempt to navigate an evasive maneuver around you while still maintaining my course and speed, but I overcompensated and my Schwinn careened off of the hardened path, taking me with it, and upended us both in this shrub—a rhododendron of the heath family, I believe, deducing from the lengthy evergreen leaves as distinguished from the deciduous azalea." (Translation: "I crashed my bike into this bush because you got in my way.")

"In a certain era, there lived a trio of swine who sought to construct protective domiciles from the imminent attack of a malevolent canis lupis. . . ." (Translation: "Once upon a time, there were three little pigs . . .")

Episode #269 "Fences"

Theme: Communication; dealing with disappointment.
Scripture reference: Ecclesiastes 4:9-12
Written by Marshal Younger
Directed by Phil Lollar
Production engineer: Mark Drury
(Original air date: 5-21-94)

Connie is ecstatic—her dad is coming for a visit! She's so happy, she even compliments Eugene on his shirt. But when she gets home that afternoon, her father calls—delivering bad news. He won't be able to make it. Connie is bitterly disappointed—so much so, she delivers a blistering talk about the evils of men to the girls at her Tuesday night Bible study. Her talk is so scathing that the girls nearly attack Eugene the next day, and they actually hang Charles up in a tree by his belt loop.

Whit wants to know what in the world is wrong with her. But Connie refuses to tell him. She says she can work out her problem by herself. She is still stewing at home that evening when a delivery person comes to the door. The delivery person is wondering if Connie or her mother will sign for a package their elderly next-door neighbor, Mr. Mitchell, has been sent. Apparently he's not there.

Connie thinks that's strange since Mr. Mitchell rarely goes anywhere. Connie goes to look over the new fence Mr. Mitchell has had built around his backyard. She discovers that Mr. Mitchell is lying unconscious on his back porch! Connie rushes to him, and her mother, June, calls for an ambulance.

The next day, Connie tells Whit that Mr. Mitchell had tripped and hit his head. He knocked himself out. Unfortunately, the fence around his property prevented anyone from seeing him. Whit points out that Mr. Mitchell isn't the only one who has put up a fence. Connie has built a wall of resentment against her dad that is keeping everyone away from her as well. Connie sees the point and apologizes. And just in time, too. The girls in her Tuesday night Bible study are now threatening to lock all men into closets!

STUDY QUESTIONS:

1. What was wrong with what happened at Connie's Bible study?
2. Why was it bad for Connie to not talk about what was bothering her?
3. Are you keeping anything pent up that you need to talk about with someone?

Episode #270 "The War Hero"

Theme: Heroism.
Scripture reference: Romans 12:1
Written and directed by Phil Lollar
Production engineer: Mark Drury
(Original air date: 5-28-94)

Dale Jacobs is writing a special series of articles for the *Odyssey Times* about Odyssey's war heroes. Naturally, he's including Whit, but he's also found out about several other heroes that fought in World War II—including Connie's Uncle Joe Finneman. According to the Veterans of Foreign Wars Association, Joe Finneman received both the Purple Heart and the Medal of Bravery. He single-handedly fought off a Japanese attack and led a group of children to safety during the Battle for New Guinea.

Connie is impressed. She and Dale try to convince Joe to tell the story. But Joe not only refuses, he insists there is no story. Despite Connie and Dale's encouragement, Joe refuses to talk about his experience.

Then Dale receives word that someone else is looking for Joe—Terence Bougainville, one of the children that Joe rescued! Dale arranges for Terence and Joe to meet. Joe still refuses to acknowledge not only the story, but also Terence. Finally, Connie, Dale, and Terence coax the story out of Joe. Joe doesn't think of himself as a hero—he believes he is a coward. He saved the children while he was running away, deserting. Joe can never forgive himself for it.

But no one else sees it that way, especially Terence. He and all of the other children from that night always have thought and always will think of Joe as a hero. That's what Dale Jacobs writes in the paper the next day, and Connie tells Uncle Joe that she will always see him that way as well. She excuses herself to go watch the Memorial Day parade. Uncle Joe stops her . . . and asks if there is room for him, too.

"The War Hero" was originally written about Whit, not Uncle Joe.

STUDY QUESTIONS:

1. Why did Uncle Joe think he was a coward? Was he right? Explain.
2. What does it mean to be a hero?
3. Do you have a father or grandfather who fought in a war? Have you ever talked to them about their experiences?

Episode #271

"The Secret Keys of Discipline"

Theme: Self-discipline.
Scripture reference: Proverbs 13:8
Written and directed by Phil Lollar
Production engineer: Dave Arnold
(Original air date: 6-04-94)

Danny excitedly rushes into Whit's End. Whit is putting on a talent show in the Little Theatre, and Danny wants to be the first one to sign up for it. Whit tells Danny that he needs his parents' permission before he can be in the show.

Danny's folks aren't so sure this is a good idea, though. Lately, Danny has been promising to do a lot of things and not following through on them. Danny promises that this time will be different. After much pleading, Danny's parents finally concede. But when they go to sign up, Whit tells them that so many people want to be in the show, he'll have to hold auditions. Danny must practice the piano every day to be good enough for the show. Danny promises he will and tries his best to do just that.

Unfortunately, Danny gets distracted with baseball, soccer, and other games. When audition time comes, Danny plays only marginally well. He's put on the alternates list. Later, someone drops out of the show. Whit puts Danny in it. His parents again try to make him understand that he must practice.

When it looks like he's going to blow it again, Danny's father shows him the "secret keys of discipline"—which are sitting down and not letting anything distract you from your task. Danny finally makes the commitment. Despite great potential distractions, Danny practices and improves every day. He plays flawlessly at the show. Everyone applauds him loudly, and his school principal asks Danny to play at the PTA banquet. Danny happily agrees. He immediately takes off to go practice at home.

the Adventures in ODYSSEY archives:

Amber Arnold, who plays the character of Brooke, recorded the piano piece played by Danny.

STUDY QUESTIONS:

1. When Brooke asked Danny to play baseball and soccer, what should he have said?
2. What are the "secret keys of discipline"?
3. Is there something that you need to be more disciplined about doing? How can you follow through?

Episodes #272 & 273

"Two Brothers . . . and Bernard," Parts One & Two

Theme: Bible history: Esau and Jacob; brotherly love.
Scripture references: Genesis 25:20-34; 27-33
Written and directed by Phil Lollar
Production engineers: Dave Arnold and Bob Luttrell
(Original air dates: 6-11-94 & 6-18-94)

Erica is having trouble with her little sister, Hayley. Bernard Walton tells Erica the story of a *real* sibling rivalry—one of the greatest in history, in fact—between twin brothers named Esau and Jacob. It's a story filled with treachery, jealousy, thievery, hatred, thoughts of murder—and, ultimately, brotherly love.

STUDY QUESTIONS:

1. What did God mean when He told Rebekah that "two nations struggle in her womb"?
2. What is a birthright? Why was a father's blessing so important?
3. Why didn't Esau kill Jacob like he vowed?

Episode #274 "First-Hand Experience"

Theme: Friendship; doing things for God's glory.
Scripture reference: Colossians 3:17
Written and directed by Paul McCusker
Production engineer: Bob Luttrell
(Original air date: 7-23-94)

Bernard Walton is off to San Diego, California, to buy a new truck. As he heads out of town, he comes across Eugene. Eugene is also heading out of town for his summer break. He has bought an open-ended bus ticket, and Bernard agrees to take him to the station. Once there, Eugene randomly picks out his destination. It turns out to be Bakersfield, California. Eugene comments that he and Bernard may see each other on the road. They part to head off on their respective journeys.

But a few hours down the road, Bernard's truck starts giving him trouble. He pulls over to see what the problem is. A little while later, Eugene's bus speeds past Bernard. Eugene sees Bernard stranded. Eugene pulls the emergency cord, grabs his knapsack, and bolts from the bus. The two manage to make it to a truck-stop diner. Bernard gets his truck fixed. He takes off, leaving Eugene to wait for the next bus.

While Eugene is waiting, a policeman walks up with a woman from the previous bus. The woman accuses Eugene of stealing her knapsack. Things are confusing for a few moments until the policeman deduces that Eugene grabbed the wrong knapsack when he got off the bus. Unfortunately, the lady's ticket was non-refundable and non-transferable. She's stuck. The police officer suggests that Eugene buy her a new ticket. After all, it was his fault she had to retrieve her knapsack and get off the bus. But Eugene doesn't have the money for that. So he gives up his open-ended ticket to make everyone happy. Now Eugene is stranded.

Hours later, a waitress at the truck stop tells Eugene he can't stay there forever. The waitress suggests that Eugene mingle with the plumbers at their annual convention. It's convening at the hotel across the street. Eugene agrees—and runs into Bernard. Bernard offers to take Eugene along with him to California. Eugene accepts. He has found that sometimes you don't know who your friends really are . . . until you need them.

STUDY QUESTIONS:

1. What do you think about Eugene's decision to buy an open-ended ticket, one without a clear destination? Was that brave or foolish? Explain.
2. If someone like Eugene sat down next to you on a bus, how would you treat him? Why?
3. Why didn't Bernard want to admit that he had done something nice for Eugene?

Episode #275 "Second Thoughts"

Theme: Family relationships.
Scripture reference: John 15:17
Written by Marshal Younger
Directed by Paul McCusker
Production engineer: Mark Drury
(Original air date: 7-30-94)

Bernard and Eugene are tooling down a lonely stretch of highway in Iowa on their way to San Diego. Suddenly, a deer runs across the road! They swerve to avoid it and end up running off the road. Bernard's truck is damaged. Fortunately, a mechanic/farmer named Kyle drives by them. Kyle tells them he can fix their truck. He also offers his home as lodging for Eugene and Bernard while they wait for the truck's replacement parts to arrive.

Once there, Kyle introduces them to his wife, Sandra; his daughter, Carrie; and his son, Graham. Right away, it is obvious that there is tension between Kyle and Graham. Graham is interested in computers and big cities, while Kyle wants Graham to one day take over the garage and the farm. This conflict intensifies over the next several days. Things get bad when Graham puts his prize pig in his father's station wagon and heads off down Route 24 to find a buyer. Graham is underage—so it doesn't take the police long to pull him over and bring him and the pig home.

Graham and his dad have another fight. Graham is grounded indefinitely. Bernard and Eugene discuss the matter and agree to talk separately with father and son. Bernard tells Kyle that maybe he is overreacting—Graham is trying to tell him something. Kyle would be wise to listen. Meanwhile, Eugene talks with Graham. The two of them figure out how to blend Graham's love of computers with working in his father's garage. At first Kyle is unsure. But he soon realizes that Graham is trying to mend the relationship—and that he can do no less. After all, they *are* father and son.

STUDY QUESTIONS:

1. Why did Kyle and Graham find it so difficult to talk to each other?
2. Why did Graham want to run away from the farm? How else could he have handled the situation?
3. Do you sometimes have trouble talking to your mom or dad? What should you do about it?

Episode #276 "Third Degree"

Theme: Friendship; making proper choices.
Scripture reference: Proverbs 27:17
Written by Marshal Younger
Directed by Paul McCusker
Production engineers: Bob Luttrell and Dave Arnold
(Original air date: 8-06-94)

Next stop, Colorado. Bernard and Eugene are truckin' down the highway at a turtle's pace—Bernard's truck doesn't handle high altitudes well. Suddenly, they hear a siren behind them. A policeman pulls them over and tickets them for going too slowly! Bernard concludes it's a scam. He decides to fight it in the Municipal Court of Oak Park.

While setting up the court date, Bernard and Eugene become acquainted with a young man named Bryant. Bryant talks a lot like Eugene. In fact, most of the people in Oak Park talk like Eugene. This is especially obvious when Bernard and Eugene attend a party that night at Bryant's house. Bernard feels out of place among all the intellectuals. But he doesn't mind using their smarts. They all help Bernard prepare his defense for traffic court. Unfortunately, when he appears in court, his mind is full of too much information. Bernard gets flustered. He ends up in contempt of court and gets thrown in jail for 72 hours!

Meanwhile, Bryant likes having Eugene around town. Bryant gets his uncle, who runs a computer company, to offer Eugene a job in the programming department. Eugene is tempted to stay—especially when an inmate convinces Bernard to fight the system and remain in jail beyond his three-day sentence. But Bernard realizes that would be a big mistake, and Eugene realizes that he doesn't want to live permanently among people who are just like him. Bernard pays his fines, and the two of them continue their trip to San Diego.

STUDY QUESTIONS:

1. Do you think Bernard handled his court appearance in the best way? Why or why not?
2. Why did Eugene ultimately decide not to stay in Oak Park?
3. What are the benefits of befriending people who are different from you? What is good about having friends who are similar to you?

Episode #277 "It Happened at Four Corners"

Theme: Greed.
Scripture reference: Proverbs 1:19
Written and directed by Phil Lollar
Production engineer: Bob Luttrell
(Original air date: 8-13-94)

Bernard and Eugene approach a place called Four Corners, Arizona. Bernard suggests they pass the time by telling stories. Eugene can't think up one, so Bernard tells a tale about two guys who are traveling together across country. But as soon as he begins, a car suddenly whizzes around them. It nearly runs them off the road. The driver loses control of his vehicle. The car careens off the highway and tumbles down an embankment.

Bernard and Eugene make their way down to the car. They pull the man from the wreckage. He is badly hurt and nearly comatose. The man manages to tell them about a river of gold that flows underground. He pulls out the map that leads to it. Just before he conks out, he tears the map in two. He gives half to Bernard and half to Eugene. The man says they can have the fortune—if they stay together. When Bernard and Eugene are finally sure that the map is real, they get greedy. They each try to get to the gold first. Their chase leads them through some incredible twists and turns. Eugene and Bernard are left with a surprise ending and an important lesson on the evils of greed.

the Adventures in ODYSSEY archives:

"It Happened at Four Corners" was a tribute to two movie classics: Stanley Kramer's *It's a Mad, Mad, Mad, Mad World* and Eric Von Stroheim's silent film *Greed.* The episode ran too long for broadcast, so we had to cut a hilarious scene of Eugene telling the story of "The Three Little Pigs." Fortunately, we were able to use it in a later episode, "I Want My B-TV" (*AIO* #298).

STUDY QUESTIONS:

1. What should Bernard and Eugene have done when they first got the map?
2. How did greed take over Bernard and Eugene? What should they have done to stop it?
3. Name some examples of greed in the Bible, in history, or even in your life. What were the consequences of that greed? What could have been done to prevent it?

Episodes #278 & 279
"The Fifth House on the Left," Parts One & Two

Theme: Trusting God in all situations; salvation.
Scripture reference: Matthew 6:19-21
Written and directed by Paul McCusker
Production engineer: Dave Arnold and Bob Luttrell
(Original air dates: 8-20-94 & 8-27-94)

Bernard and Eugene finally make it to San Diego. Bernard purchases his new truck, and Eugene figures out the expenses of their trip. Eugene finds that the trip has eaten up almost all of the savings Bernard supposedly made on the truck deal. Instead of driving straight back, Bernard wants to make a detour to see Hollywood and visit the stars' homes—especially the home of cowboy film star Hip Hobson.

Once they get there, they can't find the house or the star, who has long since moved. Instead, there is just a locked gate to a large estate. Bernard and Eugene walk up to it. Bernard is ready to give the owners of the house a piece of his mind. Suddenly, a car screeches around the corner. It heads straight toward them—nearly hitting Eugene!

Their adventure in Hollywood has started—Eugene has an interesting screen test, Bernard soaks in a hot tub, a devastating earthquake occurs, and a little girl finds Christ. California may never be the same!

STUDY QUESTIONS:

1. Why were Kelsey and Tammi so spoiled?
2. Why was Foster so opposed to Bernard telling Tammi about Jesus?
3. Have you ever had a major emergency in your town? How would you react if you did?

Episode #280 "Gone . . ."

Theme: Dealing with loss.
Scripture reference: 1 Corinthians 15:51-52
Recommended maturity level: 8 and up
Written and directed by Paul McCusker
Production engineer: Dave Arnold
(Original air date: 9-03-94)

PARENTAL WARNING: This is a highly emotional episode. It may raise several questions about why Whit had to leave. This episode could be used as an opportunity to talk about death with your child.

Home at last! Bernard and Eugene drive onto the main street of Odyssey. But things are strange: Banners are hanging across the street that say things like, "Good-Bye and God Bless," and "We'll Miss You!" Curious, they park in front of Whit's End. Connie frantically runs outside. She grills Bernard and Eugene: Where have they been? Why didn't they keep in touch? They calm Connie down and ask what's wrong. Her answer hits them like a punch in the stomach: Whit has left! He's gone!

Right after Bernard and Eugene left town, Whit got an urgent call from the board of directors at the Universal Press Foundation in Chicago. Universal Press sponsors different kinds of Christian missions projects all over the world. One of them—an archaeological mission in the Middle East—was run by Whit's close friend and mentor, Dr. Baynes. Dr. Baynes passed away suddenly from a heart attack. Universal Press was looking for a replacement. And Whit's name came up as the best man for the job. Whit thought about it, prayed about it, and talked to several people about it. Then he decided to go.

Eugene nearly falls over from the news. He decides that Whit can't leave without

Whittaker Named "Archaeologist of the Year"

JERUSALEM/APS - John Avery Whittaker (better known as Whit here in Odyssey) has been named "Archaeologist of the Year" by the National Association of Middle Eastern Academics. "His work, wisdom and overall diligence at various sites around Israel compel us to present him with this award," Mort Schwabb said in a ceremony at the Jerusalem Museum of Antiquities.

The Chicago-based organization presented Whit with a plaque and a check for an undisclosed sum of money to help further his work in the Middle East. "You're worth a lot more than this," Schwabb said.

Obviously surprised and touched by the award, Whit accepted it with a humble "thank you" and expressed his desire that funding for archaeological work would increase rather than decrease. "We're here because we know that to rediscover our past is to guide us into the future. Technology changes, but the human spirit doesn't. Learning what we can about those who came before us will assist our understanding of ourselves in the present."

Whit was nominated for the award after the publication of his internationally acclaimed paper, *Biblical Proof in the Dust of Time*, an objective examination of how archaeological evidence validates miracles in the Bible.

Those gathered gave Whit a two-minute standing ovation.

Weather

Today will see seasonal temperature averages played out under partly sunny skies. Tonight will be dark and cooler with some unexpected thunderstorms and scattered rain. Tomorrow's weather was unavailable at press time.

saying good-bye to him! Connie calls the airport and discovers that there is a slight chance that Eugene could get there in time. Eugene leaves. He does everything humanly possible to get to the airport before Whit leaves. Eugene even nearly gets arrested for running out on the runway after Whit's plane. But it's no good. The plane departs.

Eugene is disappointed—but he's not the only one. Jack Allen, one of Whit's old friends, has arrived on a different plane to see Whit. Jack and Eugene go back to Whit's End. They watch a videotape of Whit's farewell speech to the town and hear a few of Jack's stories about the early days. Eugene goes back to his dorm room, alone with his thoughts. He peruses his mail and finds a note from Whit. It expresses how much Eugene means to him. The note leaves him with one last, hopeful thought—"The best is yet to come."

the *Adventures in* ODYSSEY archives:

"Gone . . ." contained the biggest change in the program since its inception: the exit of Whit and the introduction of Jack Allen. Dave Arnold culled through all of our past programs, looking to find clips of Whit to insert into Whit's conversations with Tom and the stewardess on the plane. Whit's farewell speech on the videotape was actually a tape Hal Smith made after his wife died, thanking everyone at Focus on the Family for the cards and letters they had sent to him. We were sad that Hal had passed away, but we were also excited to have Alan Young—best known as "Wilbur" on the TV series *Mr. Ed*—join our cast as Jack Allen.

STUDY QUESTIONS:

1. Why did Whit feel the need to go to the Middle East?
2. Why was Eugene so frantic about saying good-bye to Whit? What do you think Whit meant in his letter to Eugene, "The best is yet to come"?
3. Have you ever had a good friend move? How did you handle it?

Episode #281 ". . . But Not Forgotten"

Theme: Dealing with loss; change.
Scripture reference: Deuteronomy 31:8
Written and directed by Phil Lollar
Production engineer: Dave Arnold
(Original air date: 9-10-94)

Connie arrives at Whit's End—late, as usual. She finds Eugene almost having a nervous breakdown. He has been working all alone, and the kids practically mobbed him. Connie calms him down, then Tom enters. They discuss the situation. They realize that none of them have the time to always be there like Whit was.

They start to clean up and discover Jack Allen! He's been sitting there all afternoon—waiting for a sundae he ordered several hours earlier. Jack listens to their complaints about running Whit's End—then he leaves.

A few days later, Jack and Tom talk. Tom asks Jack if he would mind running Whit's End for the afternoon until Connie arrives. Jack gladly agrees. Tom curiously asks Jack why he accepted this time, but didn't do so when he previously had the chance. Jack says it is because no one *asked* him previously.

Everything runs smoothly until Connie arrives. She sees Jack behind the counter, wearing Whit's apron and immediately concludes that Jack is trying to take Whit's place. This suspicion is confirmed for her later that week. Tom, who is running the place until Jason Whittaker arrives, appoints Jack to manage Whit's End. Connie goes ballistic! She is sure Jack is pulling some kind of scam. She loudly proclaims this as she rushes out in tears.

Jack follows to talk to her. Then Scrub runs up, upset about his loose tooth. Jack consoles Scrub. Jack says that change can be painful, but it is also sometimes God's way to prepare us for something better. Connie understands the lesson was meant for her as well. She and Jack develop a new friendship under one condition—that Jack doesn't wear Whit's apron anymore. Jack agrees.

the *Adventures in* ODYSSEY archives:

Where "Gone . . ." emphasized the surprise and loss that Eugene (and our audience) felt about Whit's departure, ". . . But Not Forgotten" helped us see the situation through Connie's eyes. Connie represented those in our audience who felt confused and resentful about the disappearance of such an important character. We wanted to assure our listeners that Jack was not going to replace Whit, but serve as a character of his own. Thus, the scene between Jack, Connie, and Scrub was actually about Hal Smith dying and all the changes that occured.

STUDY QUESTIONS:

1. At first, Jack didn't offer to help around Whit's End because he wasn't asked. Why do you suppose he wanted to be asked?
2. Why was Connie so suspicious of Jack?
3. Jack told Scrub and Connie that sometimes change is "God's way of preparing us for something better." What did he mean by that? Do you agree with him?

Episode #282 "The Fundamentals"

Theme: The importance of learning and wisdom.
Scripture reference: Proverbs 1:5
Written and directed by Marshal Younger
Production engineer: Mark Drury
(Original air date: 9-17-94)

It's basketball season. Camp What-a-Nut is putting on a clinic. Dale Jacobs and Tom Riley are coaching. Jimmy, Phil, and Rusty are participating. Phil is a hot-dog player—and not a bad one. He makes every shot he tries, but his style leaves little to be desired. Unfortunately, he *thinks* he plays great. Phil stubbornly refuses to listen to any instruction from Tom. Then Tom asks Rusty to play against Phil. Rusty is bigger—and better—than Phil. Rusty ends up blocking every one of Phil's shots.

Phil is so humiliated that he steals Rusty's expensive shoes and hides them in a locker. Jimmy lies about it for Phil. When Rusty's father finds out, he is so upset about this, he doesn't let Rusty come to the camp the next morning. But Rusty does return that afternoon, again showing up Phil.

Phil finally realizes that he doesn't know as much about basketball as he thought. He seeks out Tom's help. Finally, Phil's shooting improves to the point that he actually scores on Rusty!

Meanwhile, Dale talks with Jimmy about the lie he told to protect Phil. Dale explains that Phil isn't a Christian. His father hoped that sending him to the camp would be a good influence on him. Jimmy realizes that he's made a mistake. In front of Phil, Jimmy apologizes to Rusty. The camp ends—and both Phil and Jimmy realize that sometimes the only way you can improve is by getting back to the fundamentals.

behind the scenes:

"I've always loved sports, and I love writing sports episodes. 'The Fundamentals' was similar to an experience my ninth grade basketball team had. Our best player always made every shot, but he had a strange technique—so the coach told him to change it. I wanted to say, 'Leave him alone! He's doing great!' But the kid did what the coach said, and his skills improved.

"'The Fundamentals' was the first episode I directed. The show we recorded before this one had a lot of well-known actors in it, and I was blown away by how experienced and professional everyone was. I was nervous about having to follow that show, but everything went well. The next day, I directed 'The Truth About Zachary,' and one thing after another went wrong in the studio. It took away all the glory of 'The Fundamentals.'"

—Marshal Younger

STUDY QUESTIONS:

1. Why did Jimmy lie for Phil?
2. Why did Phil finally seek out Tom's help?
3. Why should we watch our actions and attitudes at all times?

Episode #283 "A Book by Its Cover"

Theme: Judging others.
Scripture reference: Matthew 7:1-2
Written by Paul McCusker
Directed by Phil Lollar
Production engineer: Bob Luttrell
(Original air date: 9-24-94)

Katrina writes a letter to her folks, explaining some interesting events around town. The first involves her and a new student named Melissa. In a flashback, Katrina reveals that Melissa needs help with her studies. Melissa appears to be mature enough to handle Katrina's assignments—but as they talk, Katrina realizes that Melissa is not an older teen but is actually in middle school. Not only that, but whenever Katrina tries to start the lesson, Melissa avoids the subject. She tries talking about Katrina and her family.

Later, Katrina gives Melissa a pop quiz—which Melissa flunks. Melissa turns on Katrina. She accuses Katrina of purposely making her fail. Finally, Melissa threatens Katrina with her job if she gives another pop quiz. Katrina takes control of the situation. She scolds Melissa and tells her to keep studying. Melissa eventually complies. She breaks down and cries like the little girl she is.

In her letter, Katrina also describes an incident that took place with Jack, Eugene, and Connie. Jack has begun painting and has just finished a work to be put on display at the local library. Connie is dying to see it. When Jack leaves for the day to run a few errands, Connie coaxes Eugene up to the office for a quick peek. But the painting they see is awful! If Jack presents this, he'll be humiliated. Connie and Eugene gently try to prevent Jack from displaying his painting. But they discover that what they thought was Jack's painting is actually a scratch canvas. He was using it to clean off his brushes.

Katrina explains in her letter that Connie and Eugene were set straight—and next time, they will all (Katrina included) be careful not to judge a book by its cover.

the Adventures in ODYSSEY archives:

This episode was actually the last of the "Whit adaptations," having been written for our February recording session. It was brought back and rewritten to explore Jack's character a little bit more.

STUDY QUESTIONS:

1. Why did Melissa keep distracting Katrina?
2. Was Katrina right to get angry with Melissa? What would you have done? Explain your answers.
3. Should Connie and Eugene have tried to prevent Jack from displaying his painting? Why or why not?

Episode #284
"The Election Deception"

Theme: Honesty; integrity.
Scripture reference: 3 John 11
Written by Marshal Younger
Directed by Paul McCusker
Production engineer: Dave Arnold
(Original air date: 10-01-94)

It's election time at Odyssey Middle School. Courtney is running for class president against Shannon. But while Courtney is working on election slogans with Erica, she picks up a copy of the *Odyssey Owl* school newspaper. There, one of Courtney's poems is in print. A poem that she'd written in her private diary is now attributed to "Anonymous." Courtney rummages through her locker. She can't find her diary anywhere. It's been stolen!

Courtney gets another shock at a political rally a few days later. The speech Shannon delivers is word for word the same one that Courtney is about to deliver! Courtney accuses Shannon of stealing her diary. Shannon denies the charge and accuses Courtney of letting the pressures of the election send her off the deep end.

Strangely, more and more of Courtney's journal contents keep appearing. Private thoughts she's written about her friends are revealed—making Courtney look bad. Finally, Courtney decides to drop out of the race. When she tells the principal, though, he produces Courtney's journal. The school janitor found it in the trash. Then the principal tells Courtney that he's figured out a way to trap the journal thief. He puts his plan into motion and traps the culprit—Shannon.

Courtney decides to re-enter the election. And she focuses her campaign on the importance of ethics.

STUDY QUESTIONS:

1. Did Courtney have reason to suspect Shannon of stealing her diary? Explain.
2. Why was Erica mad at Courtney for writing what she did in her diary? Did Erica have a right to be angry? Explain.
3. Is it wrong to write things about people in a private diary? Why or why not?

Episode #285
"George Under Pressure"

Theme: Family togetherness; dealing with stress.
Scripture reference: Colossians 1:9-13
Written and directed by Paul McCusker
Production engineer: Dave Arnold
(Original air date: 10-08-94)

George is in the thick of his seminary studies—so engrossed that he falls asleep right at the dinner table. His studies and the demands on his life are taking him away from his family—and severely straining their finances. All of this is putting tremendous pressure on George. So Jimmy, Donna, and Mary decide to force George to relax by kidnapping him and taking him on a picnic. Unfortunately, the afternoon is a disaster—one of the worst afternoons they've ever spent together.

Later, George complains to Jack. Jack tells George that he and his family are not alone. Jack says every book he's ever read about great preachers describes the same pressures. It's just God's way of preparing all of them for the ministry. George says that all sounds good—but he can't believe God would want him to destroy his family by pursuing his ministry dream.

George goes home and tells the family he's given up on the idea of being a minister. Mary, Donna, and Jimmy mean too much to him—he doesn't want to see them suffer anymore. But they've had a meeting of their own and have come to the opposite conclusion. The Barclays all realize they need to rally more around George. They must lift him up in prayer and support him. God almost immediately blesses that decision, for George is offered an interim pastorate at the local church. With God's help, things look like they'll work out after all.

STUDY QUESTIONS:

1. Why do you think it is so hard for George to get through seminary?
2. Should the family have taken George away from his studies? Should George have tried to enjoy the afternoon? Explain.
3. How has God taken care of you and your family lately?

Episodes #286 & 287

"Tom for Mayor," Parts One & Two

Theme: God's guidance in times of trouble.
Scripture reference: John 17:11
Written and directed by Paul McCusker
Production engineers: Dave Arnold and Bob Luttrell
(Original air dates: 10-29-94 & 11-05-94)

Odyssey's mayor has suddenly and mysteriously resigned. So Bernard and the gang at Whit's End convince Tom Riley that he is the best man for the job. Tom accepts their endorsement and announces his candidacy for mayor. But he isn't running unopposed. Bart Rathbone also has his sights set on the office. Bart is convinced that he would make a better mayor than Tom would. Immediately, Bart starts campaigning against Tom.

Bart's opposition ends up being the least of Tom's worries. In the midst of all this, Philip Glossman shows up, bringing with him two thugs from the Environmental Detection Agency. They have come because of the Edgebiter Chemical Company spill, which occurred a few years back. The result of the spill was that several bushels of contaminated apples were accidentally shipped from Tom's farm. The agents have complete authority to scour Tom's farm. They want to collect evidence to try and implicate Tom in some sort of scandal.

Along the way, it's revealed that Glossman is not acting on his own but is on orders from a mysterious person "higher up." Despite Glossman's best efforts, Tom clears his name and wins the election. But even as Tom celebrates his victory, Glossman vows that Odyssey hasn't seen the last of him or his mysterious boss.

the Adventures in ODYSSEY archives:

Many things set the stage here for future episodes: Tom's political career, the Edgebiter scandal from "One Bad Apple," the mysterious "higher up" person for whom Glossman works. But one of the most interesting things is that Ed Walker played both Tom Riley and Bart Rathbone—characters who actually debated each other in Part Two. Ed is so talented, he actually switched his voice back and forth throughout the scene in *real time*. We did very little editing in post-production.

STUDY QUESTIONS:

1. Do you think Christians should run for public office? Explain.
2. What was wrong with the way Bart ran his campaign?
3. Could Tom have done anything to avoid the scandal? Why was Glossman so intent on ruining Tom? Explain.

Episode #288 "The Twilife Zone"

Theme: Addiction; self-control.
Scripture reference: 1 Corinthians 6:12-13a.
Recommended maturity level: 10 and up
Written and directed by Phil Lollar
Production engineer: Dave Arnold
(Original air date: 10-22-94)

PARENTAL WARNING: This episode is about the dangers of addiction. Although presented in a comical and non-threatening way, we suggest you listen with your children and use the episode as an opportunity to discuss the subject of drug abuse with them.

It's Kid's Radio time again at Whit's End, and Connie narrates an unusual story. A young boy is walking to school one day when a friend coaxes him into an alley. The friend shows him something unusual: a talking toy chicken who tells goofy jokes. The young boy, played by Sam, is intrigued by the chicken. He ends up meeting the friend, played by Rusty, after school at a secret location. There, a bunch of boys are gathered to hear more from this chicken.

Sam is so intrigued, he begs Rusty to let him have a chicken of his own. Rusty agrees to do this—for a price. Sam pays it. But soon, he becomes addicted to the chicken! He can't even go to school without listening to its goofy jokes and hearing the chicken's recorded voice say, "I like you. You're my best friend."

Sam still thinks it's harmless—until the chicken actually starts talking specifically to him! Sam can't believe it. The chicken, Henny, remarks that he can only come to life for Sam—but only if Sam does everything Henny tells him to do. One of the things Henny wants Sam to do is steal some money from a school fund-raiser!

Sam nearly gives in, but he is rescued in the nick of time by his good friend—and his conscience! He finally sees the light and rejects Henny for what he is: a sick addiction, which destroys people.

behind the scenes:

"This allegory about the dangers of drug addiction originally described Courtney's addiction to a talking toy doll named Mary Jane. But after reviewing the script, we realized the show might scare children away from playing with their dolls and action figures.

"The chicken idea came from one of the voices I could always get a laugh with around the office, especially from Chuck Bolte. It was from Jay Ward's cartoon Super Chicken. Chuck suggested that the way to make the story lighter and funnier—but still remain effective—was to change the doll to a talking toy chicken. So I used that voice for Henny."

—Phil Lollar

STUDY QUESTIONS:

1. When Rusty wanted Sam to try out the chicken, what should Sam have done?
2. Why was Sam so hooked on Henny?
3. What should you do if anyone ever offers you drugs? How could you help a friend who was on drugs?

NOBODY'S PERFECT!

Blunders, Bloopers, and Bungles from the World of *Adventures in Odyssey*

Okay, okay, as much as it pains us to admit it, we're not perfect. Far from it, in fact. We've made *lots* of mistakes over the years, but what can we say? After 370-plus shows (and counting), it's hard to keep track of every little detail. But because we believe that confession is good for the soul, listed below are some of the more obvious goofs, gaffes, and inconsistencies that have appeared on *Adventures in Odyssey* during its first 10 years. (A special thanks goes to Marshal Younger for helping to catch these.)

Perhaps the most frequent inconsistencies have to do with people's ages. Most notable among these is Connie Kendall. Connie has been 16 years old throughout the run of *Adventures in Odyssey*, despite the fact that many of the kids around her (like Jack Davis) have grown up and even, in some cases, *surpassed* her in age.

Rodney Rathbone is another perpetual teenager who also seems to skip around age-wise. When he was introduced in "Isaac the Courageous," he was 16. Three months later, in "An Act of Mercy," he was 15. Then, two years later, in "Isaac the Chivalrous," he was still 15. Perhaps Rodney has discovered the fountain of youth.

Then there's Tom Riley. He stated early in the series that he has been friends with Whit for more than 20 years. But this is quite impossible. The show has, as of this writing, been on the air for 10 years. Tom became friends with Whit only after Jenny died fighting for the Fillmore Recreation Center, which was four years before "Recollections," the show that tells that story. Therefore, Tom can only claim Whit's friendship for 14 years *at most* (at least as of this writing). It's not that Tom is a liar . . . he's just given to occasional flights of exaggeration.

Last names are another area of inconsistency. Bones of Rath member Rusty has the surname Gordon in several shows, while in others, his last name is Malone. There are also two Fishbines in Odyssey: a Mr. Fishbine, who is a jeweler, in "Gifts for Madge & Guy," and a Mrs. Fishbine, who owns Boswell the cat, in "All's Well with Boswell." Despite their unusual and identical last names, they're not related—rather unlikely in a town as small as Odyssey.

But the big winner in the inconsistent names contest is Lucy Cunningham-Schultz. Lucy's father was killed in a car accident when she was five, and her mom remarried a man named Schultz. Thus, her name is Lucy Cunningham-Schultz. But in "Our Best Vacation Ever," her stepfather's name is Hal Cunningham. In "The Truth About Zachary," we attempted to fix this discrepancy by having Lucy say that Hal Cunningham was the one killed in the car accident. The only problem with that is, it couldn't have happened when she was five, because she is much older than that when "Our Best Vacation Ever" takes place. Go figure!

Whit himself is the subject of a few goofs, some of which come from his own lips. In "Thank You, God!" he says that when he was young, his family "moved to Raleigh, North Carolina, where my father . . . taught at Duke University." Unfortunately, Duke is actually located in *Durham*, North Carolina. In "The Case of the Secret Room," Whit and Tom are working in the basement at Whit's End when Whit remarks, "I haven't done this much digging since I was in the army." But of course, Whit was *never* in the army. He served in the *navy*—which is made clear in "Rescue from Manatugo Point" and "Operation: DigOut!"

Speaking of "Operation: DigOut!" . . . in that episode we hear how Whit was severely wounded in the leg and head while helping to unload a troop transport in World War II. Obviously, you can't "hear" the scar

NOBODY'S PERFECT!

(Continued)

from a head wound, but what about the leg? If the wound was that bad—which it was—shouldn't we hear Whit walk with a limp? The answer is yes, but we never do.

The geography of Odyssey and its surrounding environs is also a source of inconsistency. For instance, in several episodes we established that Trickle Lake is a fairly long drive from town. But in "Small Fires, Little Pools," Lucy and Sam ride to the lake on their bikes with apparent ease. And in "The Return of Harley" and "The Boy Who Cried 'Destructo,'" neither Jack nor Lawrence have any trouble *running* the entire distance from Trickle Lake to Whit's End in a very short time.

The Barclay family apparently lives in two different places—either 1612 Maple or 320 Sycamore, depending on which show you listen to. Of course, if they reside on Sycamore, then they live up the street from the Rathbones, whose address is 4242 Sycamore. But Sycamore must be a terribly *long* street, because the Barclays clearly live in a suburban neighborhood, while the Rathbones live in a wooded area. Sycamore is also on the way to Tom Riley's farm and just around the corner from the Electric Palace . . . which is close to city hall. Quite a street, eh?

Then there's Whit's End, which seems to expand and contract with each passing episode. For instance, the counter in the main room is next to the front door in some shows, while in others, it's all the way across the room from the front door. And when exactly was the Whit's End building constructed? In "Recollections," Jenny Whittaker says that "the Fillmore Recreation Center [the building that eventually became Whit's End] was built in 1934 as part of a Depression relief effort." But in "The Curse," Eugene discovers that "in 1910, Almon McCalister installed the first telephone switchboard in the Fillmore Recreation Center."

Which brings us to perhaps the single most glaring error in the *Adventures in Odyssey* canon: the ownership of the land around Whit's End. In "Recollections," Tom tells Connie how Whit burst into a city council meeting and saved the building that eventually became Whit's End by buying it—"and its adjoining land"—for 3.5 million dollars. But in "Moving Targets," Philip Glossman tells Connie and Jason that "the land Whit's End sits on is owned by the city. The building belongs to you, that's all."

Of course, it could be argued that Glossman was lying, and that in the eight years between the two incidents, Connie and Tom just forgot. But the truth is . . . we goofed.

By the way, we know this list is far from complete, and that there are probably *lots* of other goofs in the series. If you ever come across one . . . please *don't* tell us about it. Our faces are red enough as it is.

Episode #289

"A Call for Reverend Jimmy"

Theme: God's calling.
Scripture reference: Isaiah 30:21
Written by Marshal Younger
Directed by Paul McCusker
Production engineer: Mark Drury
(Original air date: 11-19-94)

After one of George Barclay's sermons one Sunday morning, one of the church members plants the idea in Jimmy's head that he should become a pastor. Jimmy is intrigued by the idea. When his father asks him to teach a Sunday school class, and Lawrence tells him he handled a crisis with Donna just like his father would—Jimmy begins to take the idea seriously.

Meanwhile, Donna is getting mad. Her dad keeps using stories about her in his sermons. The stories are humorous and good illustrations, but they are embarrassing to Donna—especially one where George describes how Donna made goo-goo eyes at a boy during an awards ceremony the family attended for Jimmy. Donna is irate.

Jimmy joins Donna's foul mood when his Sunday school teaching experience is terrible. He is so boring that the kids practically walk out on him during the class.

Later, George and Mary counsel their children. Jimmy realizes that he doesn't really want to be a preacher, and George apologizes to Donna for using her so often as a sermon illustration. He promises to ask permission before he tells stories about her in the future. It's not easy being a preacher's kid.

behind the scenes:

"We got the ending of 'A Call for Reverend Jimmy' from the movie *Patriot Games*. Paul and I were in his cubicle at Focus, trying to figure out how to end the episode. We didn't know if we should reveal the sex of the Barclay baby, so we worked it out so that the noise of an airplane covers up the answer—which is similar to the way *Patriot Games* ended. We had so much fun in the process, laughing about our ideas. People in the cubicles around us must have thought we were crazy! With this ending, we had more time to decide whether Baby Barclay should be a boy or a girl."

—Marshal Younger

STUDY QUESTIONS:

1. Why did Jimmy think he'd make a good preacher?
2. Why did Donna have a problem with George's stories about her?
3. What do you think God wants you to do with your life? What's the best way to find out?

Episodes #290 & 291

"A Name, Not a Number," Parts One & Two

Theme: God's protection.
Scripture reference: Psalm 27:5-6
Recommended maturity level: 10 and up
Written and directed by Phil Lollar
Production engineers: Dave Arnold and Bob Luttrell
(Original air dates: 11-26-94 & 12-03-94)

PARENTAL WARNING: These episodes are about international political intrigue and the threat of biological terrorism. While presented in a way that most youngsters will find enjoyable, these episodes may be too intense for younger listeners.

The place: Geneva, Switzerland. Where? A toy shoppe. A great deal of activity is happening there. Papers are being burned in an incinerator. Things are quickly getting cleaned. Equipment is hurriedly being dismantled—equipment that doesn't belong in a toy shoppe.

This toy shoppe is owned by Tasha Forbes, who works with the United States National Security Agency. The shoppe is a front for Agency activities—and Tasha has just learned that they've been discovered. She and her assistant, Molly, are destroying everything. Tasha has informed her boss, Donovan, that their cover is blown. They must escape to a secure location.

Tasha sends Molly on ahead. Tasha tells Molly to mail a special package on her way—a package postmarked to. . .Odyssey! Just as Molly leaves, the front door opens. One of Tasha's regular customers walks in the door—a man she calls "Doctor." He wonders if a doll he's ordered for his granddaughter has arrived. Tasha quickly helps him out, then suggests that he leave immediately. But before he can, the door opens once again. A harsh and cruel man named Mustafa walks inside.

Mustafa immediately knocks out Doctor. Then Mustafa tells Tasha that he knows who she is. Tasha tries to cover for herself, but Mustafa won't listen. He knocks Tasha out as well, then one of his men carries her away. They leave. Mustafa walks over to Doctor and asks if he is all right. Doctor opens his eyes. He rises and, in a brief conversation, reveals that he is. . .Dr. Regis Blackgaard! While Mustafa is a member of a radical group called Red Scorpion, Dr. Blackgaard is carrying out an entirely separate scheme of his own.

Meanwhile, back in the United States, Jason Whittaker prepares for his move to Odyssey. Since his father had gone to the Middle East to run an archaeological dig, Jason agreed to run Whit's End. He figures the peace and quiet will be a welcome change from his hectic life as an analyst for the government. But Donovan, his former "boss," informs him that things have gone terribly wrong overseas—an agent has been kidnapped by Red Scorpion. Red Scorpion is prepared to use a virus called Rukuta on innocent victims to advance the group's cause. Jason is unimpressed until he learns that the kidnapped agent is Tasha, his closest friend in the Agency. Jason springs into action.

Back in Switzerland, Jason follows a trail left by Tasha that takes him through a labyrinth of political and biochemical warfare. He discovers where she is being held and arranges to rescue her. The plan backfires, and he's taken prisoner, where he meets up with Tasha—and Dr. Blackgaard, who is also an agent and acts as if he's trying to *help* them. Jason is also surprised to find out that Dr. Blackgaard knows his father. Mustafa arrives and decides to make Jason a victim of the Rukuta virus. Mustafa is about to inject it into Jason's arm when Dr. Blackgaard suddenly attacks Mustafa, preventing him. A fight ensues until Donovan and his agents suddenly burst inside. They capture Mustafa, but not before he jabs Blackgaard with the needle. Everyone is shocked as Jason pronounces Dr. Blackgaard dead.

Later, we learn that Rukuta is indeed a virus but is fairly harmless until it is connected to a mysterious "TA-418" formula, which makes it far more deadly. Jason learns from Tasha that the "T" stands for her name and the "A" stands for "Avery"—Whit's middle name! Whit had been working with the Agency to figure out the formula. With Mustafa in custody and the threat of world domination over, Jason says good-bye to Tasha and heads for Odyssey.

Jason isn't in Odyssey long, however, before he discovers a mysterious package from Switzerland—with Tasha's handwriting on it—in a stack of unopened mail. He is then surprised when Tasha herself appears. The package contains the complete formula for TA-418. She'd mailed it off as a precaution, and now she's come to retrieve it. Jason persuades her to stick around for a few days to enjoy the peace of Odyssey.

A week later, we see that Jason and Tasha have a deep affection for each other. Their time together has been blissful. But it's interrupted by news from Donovan that Mustafa has escaped! Before Jason can warn Tasha, she has been captured by Mustafa. The deal is simple: He'll trade Tasha for the formula. They agree to meet at Whit's End where Filby, one of Donovan's agents, arrives to capture Mustafa. Jason realizes, however, that Filby is a double-agent. Jason creates enough of a diversion at Whit's End to save himself and Tasha. Mustafa escapes by leaping through the window.

But Mustafa is only free for so long. He is captured not by the police, but by Dr. Blackgaard, who had faked his death. Blackgaard, who knows all about the power of the TA-418 formula, murders Mustafa and leaves. This adventure is only part of Blackgaard's bigger plan.

Meanwhile, Jason says good-bye to Donovan and Tasha—his days as a secret agent are over.

the *Adventures in* ODYSSEY archives:

"A Name, Not a Number" highlighted the return of Dr. Blackgaard and re-introduced Jason to the series. Jason had appeared only once before (see "The Mortal Coil," *AIO* #211 & 212)—although he was played by a different actor.

In the discussions about life in Odyssey without Whit, we decided to "divide" Whit's personality between Jack and Jason: Jack Allen would be wise, discerning, and compassionate—and Jason would be intelligent, assertive, and rambunctious. Together, both characters would complement one another—a device which we would use in subsequent stories.

We also wanted to give Jason a love interest—thus bringing Tasha to *AIO*. Jason is played by Townsend Coleman, who also plays on the TV show *The Tick* and is one of the Teenage Mutant Ninja Turtles as well. Alan Young played Donovan—employing the accent he used in the motion picture *The Time Machine*. In that movie, Alan played the role of Filby—which is where the name of the British agent originated.

behind the scenes:

"Tasha was played by Christie Nimitz. We had booked another actress to play the part of Tasha, but she sounded too young. In a panic, we called yet another actress we had worked with, but she couldn't make it.

"The owner of the studio where we record had Christie booked for another session. He recommended her for the job, and we liked her voice, so she spent the day shuttling back and forth from one studio to the other. Christie helped us out in a pinch and made a fine Tasha in the process."

—Dave Arnold

STUDY QUESTIONS:

1. Do you think what Jason did for a living is good or bad work for a Christian? Explain your answer.
2. Is there such a thing as a synthetic virus in real life? Explain.
3. Why do you think some people want to do things to hurt their own country?

Episode #292 "Siege at Jericho"

Theme: Bible history: Rahab and the spies; Joshua and the walls of Jericho.
Scripture reference: Joshua 1:10-6:27
Written and directed by Phil Lollar
Production engineer: Mark Drury
(Original air date: 12-10-94)

We interrupt this book to bring you a special bulletin: Brink Chetley, Lucy Cunningham-Schultz, Lawrence Hodges, and the rest of the Kid's Radio Old Testament Action News Team report on a crisis in the Middle East! They follow the incredible story that unfolds in the year 1406 B.C. The people of Israel are getting ready to invade the land of Canaan—specifically the city of Jericho, the Canaanite stronghold. Lucy is with the Israelites as they prepare to attack. Lawrence is inside the city, talking with a prostitute named Rahab, who lives in a house built in the city walls. And Chet is back in the newsroom. He is trying to make sense of it all with Middle East expert Hassn Ben-Sober. Don't miss this late-breaking historical news story! We now return you to your regularly scheduled book reading.

the *Adventures in* ODYSSEY archives:

One funny thing in "Siege at Jericho" is the Middle East expert's name, Hassn Ben-Sober (played by Don Long, who was also the voice of Jack Davis). I got the name from an old Three Stooges short film. Just keep saying it over and over to yourself. You'll get it.

STUDY QUESTIONS:

1. Why was Joshua so certain the Israelites would take Jericho?
2. Why do you think God had the Israelites march around the city instead of attacking it directly?
3. How was Rahab rewarded for helping out Israel? Why did Rahab agree to hide the spies?

Episode #293 "A Code of Honor"

Theme: Doing good works.
Scripture reference: Ephesians 2:10
Written and directed by Paul McCusker
Production engineer: Dave Arnold
(Original air date: 12-17-94)

While going through Whit's workroom, Jack and Jason come across an old book filled with what seems to be a handwritten code. Jason is intrigued and decides to decipher it. It is a logbook for a group that called themselves "the Israelites." But some entries don't make sense. Many have names with words beside them like "paint" or "clean." Now Jack, who has picked up the book, is intrigued. He asks Connie if she recognizes any of the names in the book. At first, she says no—but then she sees the name "Emma Douglas."

Connie remembers that Emma used to work at Whit's End before Connie came. Jack goes to Emma. After a lot of coaxing, Emma tells Jack what she knows. She says the Israelites were a "gang" formed by Whit to do anonymous good deeds around Odyssey. Emma remembers one boy in particular: Billy MacPherson.

Jack and Jason go looking for Billy the next day. They find him working in a gas station near Connellsville. Billy is happy to talk about his involvement with the Israelites and inadvertently reveals that he hasn't been to church much lately. Jack encourages him to go—then hands over the Israelite Chronicles. Jack feels that with all the gangs these days who do *evil* deeds, maybe a gang who does *good* deeds is an idea that needs to come around again.

the *Adventures in* ODYSSEY archives:

The idea of a "good gang" called the Israelites was first developed in the *Adventures in Odyssey* novels. It was based on a real-life "good gang" that secretly helped people around town. Another aspect of Jack's character was introduced here—his dreams, which we played out in later episodes.

STUDY QUESTIONS:

1. Why did Jack feel it was so important to unravel the mystery of the Israelites?
2. Do you think Jack's dreams meant anything? Have you had dreams like Jack did?
3. Do you think a "good gang" is a good idea? Why or why not? Would you like to belong to a group like the Israelites?

FAVORITE EPISODES
Paul McCusker's Top 10 Favorites

1. The Mortal Coil, 1 & 2
2. The Time Has Come
3. Gone . . .
4. Unto Us a Child Is Born . . .
5. (tie) A Touch of Healing, 1 & 2; Where Is Thy Sting?
6. On Solid Ground
7. Best Intentions
8. BTV: Compassion
9. Hidden in My Heart
10. The Perfect Witness, 1, 2 & 3

Episode #294 "Unto Us a Child Is Born"

Theme: The Christmas story.
Scripture reference: Luke 2
Written and directed by Paul McCusker
Production engineer: Mark Drury
(Original air date: 12-24-94)

It's Christmastime in Odyssey. This year, Jimmy Barclay has gotten ambitious with the annual Christmas production. Jimmy wants to perform the biblical account of Jesus' birth—live on the radio. He coerces his family and the gang at Whit's End to help. As a new Christian, Katrina is especially enthusiastic about the whole thing.

The rehearsals come off mostly without a hitch—except for whenever there is a stop or a break. Then George runs off to call the church; Mary has to lie down because she's pregnant; Donna takes off to go shopping; and Connie, Jason, and Jack run out to the front counter to wait on customers. Only Eugene and Katrina stay at their posts. Eugene runs the board and Katrina handles the sound effects. But soon Eugene takes off, too. He's anxious because Katrina has bought him a Christmas gift—and he hasn't gotten one for her. So, at Connie's suggestion, Eugene buys Katrina what he feels is an appropriate present.

The night of the broadcast rolls around. Everything is running smoothly—until Mary Barclay goes into labor, and George and Donna have to rush her to the hospital. Fortunately, Eugene and Katrina are there to fill in the roles of Joseph and Mary. During the final scene of the broadcast, Eugene's feelings for Katrina blossom and grow. After the program, the two exchange gifts. They're pleased and amused to see they've bought each other the same thing—a Bible. Meanwhile, at the hospital, the Barclays coo over the newest addition to their family: a baby boy named Stewart Reed. "For unto us a Child is born. . . ."

the Adventures in ODYSSEY archives:

In keeping with the names of the Barclay family (all named for characters and actors in the film "It's a Wonderful Life"), the baby's name was taken from the last names of the actors who played the leads: Jimmy Stewart and Donna Reed.

STUDY QUESTIONS:

1. What is the purpose behind gift-giving? Should Eugene have bought Katrina a gift merely because she had bought him one? Why or why not?
2. Why was Katrina so excited about participating in the Christmas production?
3. How do you celebrate Christmas at your church?

Episode #295 "Soaplessly Devoted"

Theme: Discernment.
Scripture reference: Proverbs 17:24
Written by Marshal Younger
Directed by Phil Lollar
Production engineer: Dave Arnold
(Original air date: 12-31-94)

Erica lives and breathes a certain soap opera called "Medical Center of Love." Her parents don't know this, but Erica plans her whole day around watching the soap. She reveals her devotion to Jason—and he comes up with a plan to show her how trashy and immoral soap operas really are.

Jason reprograms the Room of Consequence so that Erica actually becomes her favorite character in "Medical Center of Love," Holly. Erica has a blast—at first. But soon, the excitement and glamour wear off, and the soap opera life becomes tiring and tedious. Before long, it becomes downright silly and stupid! When all of the other characters rob, cheat, and betray her, Holly (Erica) has finally had enough—of both the Room of Consequence program and of soap operas. She goes back to being Erica—and that's more than good enough for her.

the Adventures in ODYSSEY archives:

Jason's character was further developed in this episode. Here, he exhibited Whit's penchant for tinkering, inventing, and programming.

"Soaplessly Devoted" revealed the third or fourth variation on the Room of Consequence. Each time, the room had a different approach, unlike the Imagination Station, which was more consistent with how it worked.

behind the scenes:

"My best lines always seem to be in the background of scenes—only someone who has their ears pinned to the speaker could hear some of those background lines. 'Soaplessly Devoted' has a great line coming from the TV in the background. The soap opera announcer says, 'For every heartache . . . don't self-medicate. Check into the 'Medical Center of Love.' "

—Marshal Younger

STUDY QUESTIONS:

1. Why was Erica so caught up in "Medical Center of Love"?
2. Why was Jason so concerned about Erica's obsession with the program?
3. Do you watch soap operas? How about other television shows? Do you listen to radio programs? Are you as addicted to them as Erica was to her show?

1995

We were all getting tired. Paul McCusker and I had been working on *Adventures in Odyssey* as its primary writers and directors for approximately eight years. Both of us felt drained and empty—the stress of doing a weekly program with minimal breaks was beginning to take its toll. Dave Arnold and Bob Luttrell felt the same way on the production side. We had often talked about taking a hiatus from the series, but it never seemed to materialize.

Right around this time, Paul and I began discussing how we could bring the program to a close. We had already set the stage with the arrivals of Jack and of Jason, Tom Riley's election as mayor, the Katrina/Eugene stories, and Connie's career choice dilemmas. What we needed to do now was play all of those elements out over the course of the next year until everything came together in a dramatic climax. Would that, then, spell the end of the program? We would decide when we got to that point.

When our dramatic 11-part series was finally wrapped up in October 1995, Bob Luttrell left the show to fulfill his lifelong dream of owning a restaurant. Bob's exit was followed by Marshal Younger's in November, who became a freelance writer for *AIO.*

No one knew what the future held for either the *Adventures in Odyssey* staff or for the actual program.

Episode #296

"Red Wagons and Pink Flamingos"

Theme: Friendship; forgiveness; resolving conflicts.
Scripture reference: Matthew 5:23-24
Written and directed by Marshal Younger
Production engineer: Bob Luttrell
(Original air date: 1-07-95)

Erica's birthday is around the corner. She and her best friend, Kim, are planning a party at Whit's End. Kim suggests that the theme for the party be flamingos, but Erica pooh-poohs the idea. While they plan, Jason wheels in his new invention—a Bible video game. Jason plugs it in and turns on the power. Much to Jack's dismay, it's an instant success. The invention is loud and obnoxious. But the kids seem to like it, so Jack keeps his thoughts to himself.

A few days later, Erica has her party. Kim shows up extremely late. In fact, the party is almost over when Kim arrives. Kim explains that on the way to the party, she passed Greenblatt's Department Store. It was having a huge sale, so she had to stop. Erica can't believe that Kim missed the party to go *shopping*. Kim apologizes, but Erica is irate. She and Kim get into an argument that ends up nearly destroying their friendship.

Meanwhile, Jack gets so annoyed by the video game's noise, he unplugs it. Erica comes in and tells Jack about her fight with Kim. Jack can relate to Erica because he once experienced a similar situation. But Jack says he realized that the friendship was more important than the disagreement. He helps Erica see that her friendship with Kim is worth saving. Erica leaves to find Kim.

Then Jason enters. He and Jack talk about the video game, and they agree to put the game in a soundproof room. And as Jack and Jason resolve their differences, so do Erica and Kim.

the Adventures in Odyssey archives:

"Red Wagons and Pink Flamingos" established an element of conflict between Jack and Jason that we would explore in future episodes.

behind the scenes:

"Judging from the negative letters we got, introducing video games—even Bible-based ones—into Whit's End was not an idea that the average listener's parents liked. Later, we got rid of them."

—Marshal Younger

STUDY QUESTIONS:

1. Why was Erica so angry at Kim? What did Kim's actions say to Erica about their friendship?
2. Why didn't Erica want to forgive Kim?
3. Why didn't Jack want to tell Jason how he really felt about the video game? Should Jack have said something sooner? Why or why not?

Episode #297

"Blackbeard's Treasure"

Theme: Greed.
Scripture reference: Proverbs 21:25-26
Written and directed by Phil Lollar
Production engineer: Bob Luttrell
(Original air date: 1-14-95)

While going through some of his dad's things, Jason comes across a plastic box. On the bottom is an inscription: "Jack and Whit, Cove Cave, Bath, N.C." Inside is an old gold coin. Jack can't believe it—Whit actually kept one of them!

In a flashback, Jack tells Jason all about the summer when he and Whit were kids, vacationing in the historic little community of Bath, North Carolina. Whit's Uncle Randy is the sheriff of the town. Whit and Jack sail up and down the coast of Pamlico Sound, exploring the area. One day, they come across a cave in the middle of a small cove. The cave is accessible at low tide, so the boys decide to explore it.

Inside, they have a series of scary and exciting adventures which lead them to a buried cache of Spanish doubloons—valuable gold coins! But as they look for more coins, they suddenly hear strange noises from further inside the cave. They turn, and

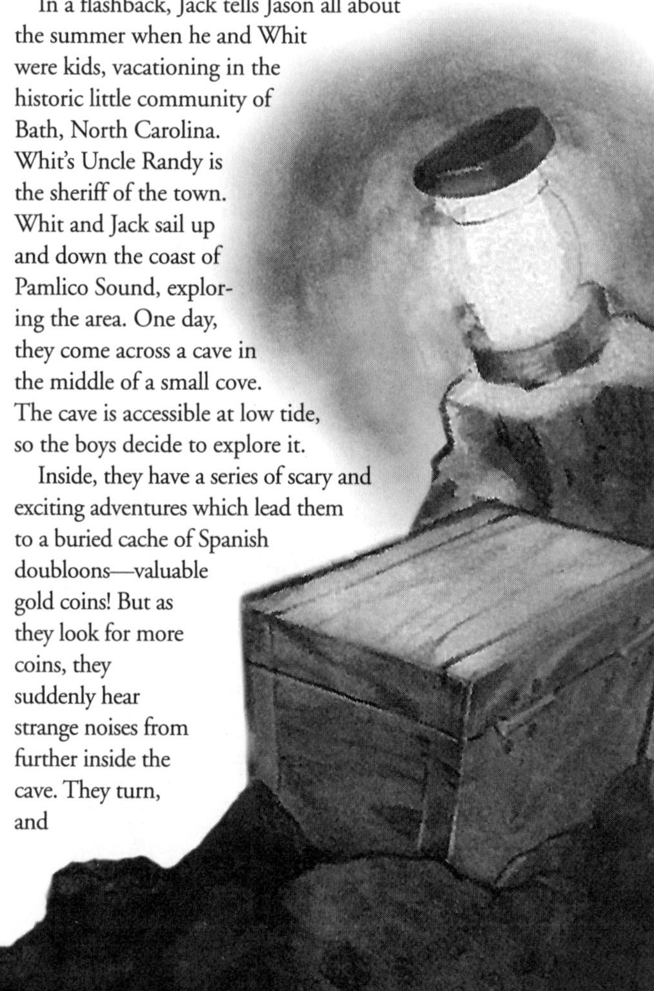

coming straight toward them is what appears to be the ghost of Blackbeard the Pirate, who's roaring that they have uncovered his treasure!

Whit and Jack run for their lives and head back to Uncle Randy's office. He's gone, but Whit checks some of his uncle's books about rare coins. Whit is sure they have discovered Blackbeard's lost treasure and is determined to go back to the cave. Jack thinks Whit's crazy, considering their experience. Deputy Arnie shows up—and is quick to tease the boys about their wild imaginations, so they make excuses and leave. What the boys don't know is that their entire conversation was overheard by Ewell Mosby, a lowlife who'd been jailed overnight for being drunk and disorderly. Deputy Arnie had thought Ewell had learned his lesson and set him free earlier.

Taking a shortcut from the library where they'd been doing further research, Whit and Jack bump into Ewell and his partner, Jocko. They grab the boys and force them to lead the way to the cave. On the way, Whit succeeds in scaring Jocko about the "ghost," but Ewell won't hear of it. Once inside the cave, Jocko ties Whit and Jack to the ground—where they'll likely drown when the tide comes in! Whit tries to persuade Jocko that, the first chance Ewell gets, he will double-cross Jocko for the money. Jocko tries to ignore Whit's warnings. Ewell and Jocko go into another part of the cave to look for the money.

While they're gone, Whit uses a knife that fell out of Jocko's pocket to cut himself free. But not before the "ghost" of Blackbeard can be heard in the hollows of the cave. Jocko and Ewell return and are terribly nervous about the sounds. Then the apparition appears, and Jocko and Ewell run for their lives—right into a cave wall, knocking themselves out cold. The "ghost" comes closer and closer and, rather than attack the boys, commands them to follow him. The "ghost" ties up Ewell and Jocko and leads Whit and Jack to safety.

Whit and Jack learn that the "ghost" is an old hermit who lives near the cave and uses a "Blackbeard" get-up to scare away trespassers. Even though the boys disobeyed by going into the cave, the hermit simply gives them a warning and allows them to keep some of the coins they'd found. Jack learns from Whit an important truth about having faith in something greater than legends and ghosts—a lesson worth far more than money.

STUDY QUESTIONS:

1. Should Whit and Jack have gone exploring in the cave? Why or why not?
2. What did Whit mean when he said that he isn't afraid of ghosts because he is a Christian?
3. When was the last time you talked to a friend about Jesus?

Episode #298 "I Want My B-TV"

Theme: Foundations; cooperation; the importance of watching and listening to quality programs.
Scripture reference: Philippians 4:8
Written and directed by Phil Lollar
Production engineer: Dave Arnold
(Original air date: 1-21-95)

Bernard is cleaning the local television station and overhears a conversation between the station manager and his program supplier. The station manager is unhappy with the quality of the programs the supplier is sending him. They all seem to be about dinosaurs. Bernard tells the manager that he knows of several local people who could probably put on an entertaining show.

The station manager loves Bernard's idea. Bernard goes back to Whit's End, gathers the gang, and tells them that they are now all part of a television variety show. They brainstorm ideas and come up with a variety of sketches, jokes, and fascinating facts about many subjects. The gang even amusingly retells an old fairy tale. Welcome to "B-TV"!

Adventures in the ODYSSEY archives:

We had talked for months about doing a new program. Finally, the variety show "B-TV" was born. Originally, I wanted to call it "C-TV" and have it be hosted by Connie. But the team felt that the best person to fill that role was Bernard, a natural storyteller.

STUDY QUESTIONS:

1. Why is it important to be careful about what you listen to and watch? How can TV, movies, and music affect people?
2. What do you think the Dudley and Mudley sketch was really about?
3. Think about the Percival sketch. What's the best way to study the Bible?

Episode #299 "The Truth About Zachary"

Theme: Friendship; encouragement.
Scripture reference: Romans 15:1-3
Written by Marshal Younger and Paul Malm
Directed by Marshal Younger
Production engineer: Mark Drury
(Original air date: 1-28-95)

Zachary Sellers is the new kid in town. He's unusual—in more ways than one. The most obvious characteristic about Zach is that he's in a wheelchair. But Zachary is also very intelligent. He's able to fix the electric train when even Eugene can't repair it. Unfortunately, Zachary is so bitter about being crippled that he treats everyone around him with rudeness and, sometimes, cruelty.

Lucy wants to get to know him, but she mistakenly tries to get Zach to open up in front of their entire class. Zach embarrasses himself and everyone in the class. He marks Lucy down as one of his enemies. This makes Lucy's next assignment for the *Odyssey Owl*—interviewing the newest kid in school, Zachary Sellers—all the more difficult.

Unfortunately, Zach is insulted by Lucy's natural curiosity about how Zach became crippled. He rightly tells Lucy that it's none of her business. He even turns the tables on her by demanding to know why she has two last names: Cunningham-Schultz. But Lucy ignores his question. She continues to press Zach until he finally blurts out the truth: A drunk driver hit their family car. It killed Zach's dad and crippled Zach.

Later, Jack tells Lucy she needs to come up with a way to show Zach that she's his friend. The next day, Lucy visits Zach. He is still cold to her—until Lucy explains why she has two last names. Her dad was also killed in a car accident, and her mom remarried. Zach warms up to Lucy, and the two of them talk about their fathers.

Adventures in Odyssey the ODYSSEY archives:

Of course, the *real* reason Lucy has two last names is because of our writing inconsistency.

STUDY QUESTIONS:

1. Why was Zach so bitter?
2. Should Lucy have suggested that Zach tell the class about himself? Why or why not?
3. What should you do when someone you're trying to make friends with treats you badly?

Episode #300 "Preacher's Kid"

Theme: Being a preacher's kid; being Christlike; being imperfect.
Scripture references: Romans 3:23; Ephesians 5:1
Written and directed by Marshal Younger
Production engineer: Mark Drury
(Original air date: 2-04-95)

Old Mrs. Erskine is at it again. She is sitting behind Donna and her friends during the Sunday morning worship service. George is preaching, and something happens to make all the kids giggle. Mrs. Erskine is annoyed. She threatens to move up a pew and sit between all of them if they don't quiet down. Not only that, but she tells both George and Mary about Donna's behavior after the service.

George and Mary come down on Donna, who is beginning to have serious doubts about being a preacher's kid. Nowadays, it seems that no matter what she does, someone is scrutinizing her. Donna feels she can't make even the slightest mistake. George and Mary try to sympathize with her, but George tells Donna that now she is expected to be a role model—simply because she is his daughter.

But Donna feels imposed upon, especially when she has to attend pastor functions like a senior citizens' dinner and a home Bible study on parenting. Donna decides enough is enough. On the night of the Bible study, she skips out to go on a hay ride with her friends. Only, her friends don't go on a hay ride. Instead, they go to the old Donovan house near Gower's Field—and accidentally burn it down!

No one is hurt, but the police bring Donna home in disgrace. George is called to an emergency meeting of the pastor's committee at the church. He is sure he will be fired for not being able to control his rebel daughter, but the committee is anything but condemning. Even Mrs. Erskine is understanding. The committee just wants to know what they can do to help George.

In the end, Donna apologizes for her actions—and everyone realizes that just because you're a preacher's kid doesn't mean you're perfect.

STUDY QUESTIONS:

1. Were Donna and her friends misbehaving in church? How should they have behaved?
2. Were George and Mary putting too much pressure on Donna to behave a certain way? Explain.
3. Donna did something she knew she shouldn't just because her friends talked her into it. Have you ever been in a similar situation? How did you handle it?

Episode #301
"The Good, the Bad & Butch"

Theme: Making proper choices; choosing friends wisely.
Scripture reference: Psalm 1:1-2
Written and directed by Marshal Younger
Production engineer: Bob Luttrell
(Original air date: 2-11-95)

Sam and his mother are shopping for new school clothes when they run into Brian, one of Sam's old friends, and Brian's mother. While the two moms talk, Sam and Brian, who now likes to be called "Butch," also carry on an awkward conversation. Butch now hangs out with the Bones of Rath. Sam rightly feels that the two of them have little in common.

Later, the Bones decide to pull a major prank at an academic awards banquet. Butch is forced to pal around with Sam again because Sam has an extra ticket to the banquet—a ticket that Butch needs to let the Bones into the building where the banquet is being held. The only problem is, Sam and Butch start to rebuild their friendship. Sam pulls out several mementos he's kept from their previous friendship. Butch is genuinely touched by them—and by the fact that Sam has kept them.

Things seem to be progressing nicely between the two of them when Rodney and the Bones again rear their ugly heads to get Butch to help them with another scheme. Now Butch is torn between his friendship with Sam and wanting to remain with the Bones of Rath. What Butch is really dealing with, though, is his perception of himself. Is he a "good kid" like Sam, or does Butch belong with the "bad kids" like the Bones of Rath? He ultimately makes a difficult choice that teaches Sam a hard lesson about friendship and loyalty.

the Adventures in ODYSSEY archives:
This episode introduced Butch, who plays a prominent role in later episodes.

STUDY QUESTIONS:
1. Why was Sam hesitant to talk to Butch?
2. Sam agreed to go to a Bones meeting if Butch would go to church with him. Was this a smart bargain? Why or why not?
3. Why did Butch go with the Bones instead of with Sam? What would you have done in Butch's place?

Episode #302
"Share & Share Alike"

Theme: Sacrifice.
Scripture reference: Hebrews 13:16
Written by Marshal Younger
Directed by Paul McCusker
Production engineer: Mark Drury
(Original air date: 2-18-95)

It's Kid's Radio's first annual Share-a-Thon, hosted by Connie and Jack. Their goal is 3,000 items—that is, 3,000 toys, items of clothing, or food to be donated to the Odyssey Shelter for the Homeless. To entertain listeners while they call in and pledge during the Share-a-Thon's last half hour, Connie and Jack narrate three short stories about the importance of sharing.

The first is about a young girl named Jane who is so selfish she won't even give her little sister a ride to Whit's End on her bike. Jane's behavior is atrocious—until everyone else starts treating Jane the same rude way she treats them. Her mom won't give her any food, her classmates won't help her out in a crisis, and her father won't even give her a ride home in his car. Jane sees the error of her ways.

Story number two is about a man named Roy who is the manager of an apartment building. The owner of the building gives Roy a great sum of money to refurbish the place. Instead of fixing things up, Roy spends the money on himself. The owner returns. He fires Roy, evicts him, and takes all of the things he bought back to the store.

Finally, the third story is about a boy named Daniel. Although he is hungry and poor, he gives up five loaves of bread and two fish to feed others—five *thousand* others, to be exact. The lessons on the importance of sharing are well learned. The first annual Kid's Radio Share-a-Thon is a rousing success!

STUDY QUESTIONS:
1. Why is it important to share?
2. Why did the apartment building owner fire and evict Roy?
3. If you had been Daniel, would you really have given up your day's food to Jesus?

Episode #303

"All the Difference in the World"

Theme: What it means to be a Christian.
Scripture reference: Colossians 1:21-23
Written and directed by Paul McCusker
Production engineer: Dave Arnold
(Original air date: 2-25-95)

Danny spends the night at his new friend Jeff's house. The two of them decide to watch a movie—one which Danny isn't allowed to watch. Danny tells his parents about it the next day, and they are upset with him.

But Danny is even more upset at his strict parents. He feels they won't let him do anything that the other kids get to do—just because his parents are Christians. So Danny decides he doesn't want to be a Christian anymore. Not only that, but the next time he spends the night Jeff's house, *Danny* is the one who suggests that they watch an inappropriate movie. This time, both Jeff's and Danny's parents walk in, right in the middle of the movie.

Back at home, Danny's folks are furious with him. They explain that they are trying to lead Jeff's parents to Jesus. But it's difficult when Danny—a boy who calls himself a Christian—blatantly disobeys his parents, causes his friend to disobey *his* parents, and watches a video that he knows he's not supposed to see. Danny's parents remind him that Christians are called to witness about how Jesus changes lives. Danny says he understands. He agrees to, once again, start living like a follower of Christ. After all, being a Christian makes all the difference in the world.

STUDY QUESTIONS:

1. Danny felt that he didn't get to do the things all the other kids could do. Was he right? Explain your answer.
2. Have you ever felt like Danny? What did you do about it?
3. Why is it important for Christians to watch how they behave?

Episodes #304 & 305

"St. Paul: The Man from Tarsus" & "St. Paul: Set Apart by God"

Theme: Bible history: the story of St. Paul.
Scripture reference: Acts 24-28
Written and directed by Phil Lollar
Production engineers: Bob Luttrell and Dave Arnold
(Original air dates: 3-04-95 & 3-11-95)

Rodney Rathbone and Sam Johnson inadvertently take a trip together in the Imagination Station back to the first century. There, they meet a martyr named Stephen, experience and participate in the early days of the Christian church, and watch firsthand as a religious fanatic named Saul has a remarkable conversion and becomes an apostle named Paul.

the Adventures in ODYSSEY archives:

Though these episode have different titles, they are really two parts of the same program—and only half of the whole story about the apostle Paul. The rest of the story—also done in two parts with two titles—was done later (see *AIO* #346 & 347).

These episodes highlighted a change in the nature of the Imagination Station. Up until now, when kids went back in time, they were obviously out of place. We even made jokes about their clothes and their manner of speaking. But in these episodes, the kids actually became a part of the story from the beginning. These episodes also marked the first time Rodney Rathbone was in the Imagination Station.

STUDY QUESTIONS:

1. Saul forced Rodney to throw the first stone at Stephen. What would you have done if you were Rodney? Explain.
2. Why was Ananias afraid to go see Saul?
3. Many people didn't believe Saul's story of his conversion. Would you have believed him? Why or why not?

Episode #306

"A Victim of Circumstance"

Theme: Taking responsibility for your actions.
Scripture reference: Genesis 3
Written and directed by Phil Lollar
Production engineer: Mark Drury
(Original air date: 3-18-95)

Jack and Jason are in the office one evening, looking at the moon through their new skylight. Suddenly, they hear creaking and groaning from the ceiling. Before anyone knows what is happening, the skylight comes crashing down almost on top of them! They discover that the skylight didn't cave in by *itself*. Rodney Rathbone stepped through it! He has a severe cut on his head and a broken arm.

200 THE COMPLETE GUIDE TO ADVENTURES IN ODYSSEY

Later, at the hospital, he admits to Jack, Jason, and Bart that he was setting up a water-balloon trap on the roof. Bart tells Jack and Jason he's grateful they're not pressing trespassing charges against Rodney. But as soon as Jack and Jason leave, a new visitor steps into the room—a lawyer named Howard J. Weizel. Weizel convinces Bart and Rodney that they have a strong lawsuit against Jason Whittaker and Whit's End! Jack and Jason can't believe it. They try everything possible to get the case dismissed. They even send Weizel on a strange ride in the Room of Consequence to show him the disastrous results of his work. But Weizel and Rodney press charges—and they actually win.

Fortunately, the jury only awards them one dollar. The damage is still done, though. From now on, Whit's End will have to put warning signs on everything.

STUDY QUESTIONS:

1. Was Rodney *really* in the wrong for being on the roof? Why or why not?
2. Should Whit's End have had a sign telling kids to stay off the roof? Explain.
3. Why is it wrong to not take responsibility for your mistakes? Have you ever done that?

Episode #307 "Poetry in Slow Motion"

Theme: Don't be afraid to ask for help when you need it.
Scripture reference: Proverbs 15:22
Written by Marshal Younger
Directed by Phil Lollar
Production engineer: Bob Luttrell
(Original air date: 3-25-95)

It's poetry time in Charles and Courtney's English class, much to Charles's dismay. Charles absolutely hates poetry. Not only that, but he just doesn't get it. The symbolism goes right past him, and he wouldn't know rhythm and meter from a parking meter. But despite this, he will not admit that he needs help. He refuses all offers of assistance from his teacher, Courtney, and even Rusty, who somewhat understands poetry.

What makes matters worse is that Charles and the others in his class must write a poem for their final assignment. The best Charles can come up with is a mini epic called "I Like Pants." He reads it to Jack, who tries to put on a good face about it, but Charles sees right through Jack and tears up his opus.

Charles still needs a poem, though. The day the assignment is due, he buys a poem from Rusty. Big mistake! The poem was copied from a Mother's Day card that Charles's teacher received from her son the previous Mother's Day! Charles gets a failing grade on the assignment, but his teacher does manage to get the reason for his actions. She explains that occasionally everyone needs help with something. For example, she's terrible at working with anything mechanical. Charles understands. He agrees that from now on, when he needs help, he'll simply ask for it—and he does ask Courtney at lunchtime.

STUDY QUESTIONS:

1. Why did Charles say he understood the poems in the assignment when it was obvious he didn't?
2. Have you ever felt like Charles—unwilling or afraid to ask for help when you needed it? How did you correct the situation?
3. Why do we study poetry in school?

Episode #308 "Subject Yourself"

Theme: Obeying those in authority.
Scripture reference: Romans 13:1
Written and directed by Paul McCusker
Production engineer: Mark Drury
(Original air date: 4-01-95)

Lawrence is unhappy—so unhappy, even his renowned imagination can't change things. The cause of this unhappiness? Braces. He has a mouthful, along with the medieval-torture-device headgear he must wear at night. Of course, he also has a list of foods he can't eat as well—all his favorites: pizza crust, candy, and caramel apples. The mere thought of it makes him want to scream. Jack tells him to use his imagination to solve his problem. While Lawrence is doing that, his mother, Maureen, is facing problems of her own.

Maureen is a school teacher, and the board has voted in a new history curriculum—one that eliminates Christianity's contribution to the development of the United States and western civilization. Maureen can't in good conscience teach this to her students. After much soul searching—and persuasion and encouragement from Jack and others—she decides to take on the school board.

Meanwhile, Lawrence has come up with a creative way to handle his braces problem—he wants fashionably-colored braces. Unfortunately, he's not willing to wait to let the dentist do it. Instead, he paints them himself using the paint from his model car kit. He shows Jack, who immediately rushes him to the hospital. Lawrence learns a valuable lesson about being patient and also about listening to his mother and those in authority.

And Maureen? Her stance against the curriculum is successful—and she learns that there are times when you have to go *against* what the authorities say—namely, when the authorities contradict God.

the *Adventures in* ODYSSEY archives:

"Subject Yourself" was the last time Lawrence Hodges appeared on *AIO*. He was phased out of the show, much like Jack Davis, Robyn and Melanie Jacobs, and other kids who grew up on the program. Everything has a life—even in Odyssey.

STUDY QUESTIONS:

1. Why was Maureen so opposed to the history curriculum?
2. What is "revisionist" history?
3. When is it appropriate to go against those in authority over you? Can you think of any other examples of when it might be okay?

Episodes #309–311
"The Perfect Witness," Parts One, Two & Three

Theme: God judges people by their hearts, not their physical appearance.
Scripture references: 1 Samuel 16:7; Mark 7:1-23; 2 Corinthians 5
Recommended maturity level: 8 and up
Written and directed by Paul McCusker
Production engineers: Dave Arnold and Mark Drury
(Original air dates: 4-08-95, 4-15-95, 4-22-95)

PARENTAL WARNING: This three-part mystery includes an armed robbery and kidnapping, which are played and replayed throughout all three parts. Although no one gets hurt in the episodes, they may be too intense for younger listeners.

At Holstein's bookstore, Fred Holstein is showing Katrina Shanks a rare book, which he has acquired for Professor Marcus at Campbell College. Jenny Roberts, who is blind, comes inside. She is frustrated because people treat her like an invalid. Suddenly, two robbers, Russell Kosh and Martin Johns, lock the door and steal the money in the cash register. They also steal Katrina's backpack, which holds her college supplies. When the robbers realize Mr. Holstein has pushed the silent alarm, they grab Jenny—thinking she is a perfect hostage because she is blind. They take off with her.

The kidnappers eventually return Jenny to the police station. After Dr. Morton pronounces her all right, she is interviewed by Captain Richard Quinn and visiting Detective Pat Ethan. Detective Ethan tells Jenny that because of her blindness, she can help them paint a "sound picture" of the criminals and their hideout.

Meanwhile, Eugene Meltsner rushes to Holstein's, frantic about Katrina and Jenny. He had heard about the robbery while he was at the police station, reporting that his laptop computer and car were stolen. Captain Quinn comes in and informs Eugene that his car was used as a getaway in the robbery.

While Jenny is questioned, she remembers things that lead the investigators to believe that it was the rare book, not the money, that was the motivation for the robbery. Captain Quinn and Eugene go over Eugene's car for clues. Then the captain urges Eugene to go back to his room to see if anything else was stolen. Eugene discovers that a box of computer disks is missing, and the hard drive on his computer has been erased.

With Jenny Roberts's help, Detective Pat Ethan begins to unravel the mystery. Ethan returns to Holstein's to ask about the stolen, rare Haugaard book, which Holstein had ordered for Dr. Marcus. Captain Quinn and Detective Ethan meet. The detective explains how Eugene Meltsner's stolen car was recovered at a gas station in a nearby town.

Ethan continues to question Jenny, who remembers more details about the surroundings of the kidnappers' hideout. Using sound effect discs, Jenny is able to identify the sound of an industrial pneumatic chisel, used at demolition sites. Quinn says Eugene's car had concrete dust on it, perhaps from a demolition site.

Katrina Shanks and Eugene work together to discover why someone stole his laptop computer and disks and erased his hard drive. They also wonder why the robbers would steal her knapsack, which also contained computer information.

Eugene remembers that he'd had information for a secret analysis report on his computer and disks. He and Katrina also remember that he'd given a copy to her, which she'd put in an envelope in her knapsack. Then they realize the thieves were after the report—not the money or the rare book. Eugene rushes off to warn Dr. Marcus because Eugene had given the professor a copy of the report. If that's what the culprits were after, then Dr. Marcus may be in danger. Dr. Marcus is skeptical and unconcerned.

Later, in his office, Dr. Marcus argues with Russell Kosh. Marcus is furious that Kosh and Johns complicated what was supposed to be a simple robbery. Eugene suddenly arrives. Kosh hides while Eugene tells Dr. Marcus that he's found another copy of the report. Dr. Marcus is pleased and tells Eugene what a brilliant report it is. The professor says he'll be happy to use his influence to see that it's published. Later, Marcus instructs Kosh to get to Eugene's dorm room to steal the copy of the report. Kosh arrives, but the police are waiting there to arrest him. Dr. Marcus is also arrested.

In the end, Detective Ethan explains that Dr. Marcus had planned the whole scheme to steal Eugene's report and take credit for its authorship. Dr. Marcus was convinced that the publication of the report would ensure his tenure at the university. It was supposed to be a simple plan but was foiled—thanks especially to Jenny. Jenny understands now how her blindness isn't always a liability and she was, indeed, "The Perfect Witness."

behind the scenes:

"This show had to be written backward. First, Paul McCusker and I discussed and previewed which sound effects to use, then Paul wrote the script around that."

—Dave Arnold

STUDY QUESTIONS:

1. What was the big mistake the robbers made in taking Jenny hostage?
2. Why would Dr. Marcus stage an elaborate robbery simply to get tenure at the college where he worked?
3. Have you ever misjudged anyone by their outward appearance? If so, what did you learn from your mistake?

Episode #312 "Rewards in Full"

Theme: Having pure motives.
Scripture reference: Matthew 6:1
Written and directed by Phil Lollar
Production engineer: Mark Drury
(Original air date: 4-29-95)

Jack has started a new social program around town called "Food for the Hungry." He's made a poster for advertising and is just leaving to get it copied when Bart Rathbone enters. Connie explains the program to Bart. After some persuading, Bart agrees to put up a poster in the corner of one of his store windows. That afternoon, Jack encourages Erica to begin a poster campaign of her own about bicycle helmet safety.

A few days later, though, Bart ends up taking credit for Jack's idea when he discovers that the program is good for his business—and Erica's friend Brenda winds up getting praised in front of the whole school for Erica's bicycle helmet safety posters. Erica storms into Whit's End, fuming. She tells Jack what happened, but Jack has trouble understanding why she is so upset. After all, the point of Erica's campaign is to help keep kids from getting hurt. He says, as long as she is helping kids, what does it matter if she doesn't get credit?

Just then, Connie enters. She tells Jack that Bart is hogging all the credit for the "Food for the Hungry" program. Erica believes that Jack will finally understand how she feels now—but Jack still doesn't see the problem. As he puts it, he didn't start the program to get credit. He started it to gather food for the hungry. And since Bart is helping the hungry, why should Jack be upset if the program is working?

A few moments later, Bart makes a fool out of himself on television by revealing that he knows next to nothing about "Food for the Hungry." Then Brenda comes and apologizes to Erica for taking credit she didn't deserve. All is well in Odyssey again.

the Adventures in Odyssey archives:

The name "Harry Wainwright" came from two of the characters in the film *It's a Wonderful Life.* We also got part of the Electric Palace's address—1313 Mockingbird Road—from the TV series *The Munsters.*

STUDY QUESTIONS:

1. Why didn't Bart want to have anything to do with the "Food for the Hungry" program at first? What changed his mind?
2. What should Erica have done to keep the principal from making the mistake he did?
3. Have you ever done work someone else took credit for? What did you do about it? Have you ever taken credit for someone else's work? Why is that wrong?

FAVORITE EPISODES
Phil Lollar's Top 10 Favorites

1. Someone to Watch Over Me
2. A Name, Not a Number, 1 & 2
3. It Happened at Four Corners
4. It Is Well
5. The Treasure of Le Monde!
6. (tie) On Solid Ground; Pilgrim's Progress Revisited, 1 & 2
7. Coming of Age
8. (tie) The Tangled Web; The Twilife Zone
9. Hidden in My Heart
10. Castles & Cauldrons, 1 & 2

Audio Dramas 203

Episode #313 "Top This!"

Theme: Unhealthy competition; putting God first.
Scripture reference: Jeremiah 9:23-24
Written and directed by Marshal Younger
Production engineer: Bob Luttrell
(Original air date: 5-06-95)

Courtney's cousin, Hannah, has moved into town. Suddenly, Courtney is acting strange. She's much more competitive than usual—mainly because Hannah is much more competitive with Courtney. The two cousins have been rivals for a long time. Hannah always feels she needs to top Courtney, which makes Courtney feel that she needs to top Hannah.

Things get even worse when Hannah visits Courtney's Sunday school class. When Hannah learns that Courtney is in charge of a bake sale fund-raiser for the church youth camp, Hannah immediately springs into action. She comes up with an alternate idea—a car wash. Both ideas work well, but that's not good enough for either girl. Soon they are both involved in a flurry of fund-raising ideas—everything from door-to-door gardening to five-mile runs to softball marathons.

Courtney and Hannah aren't the only ones doing marathons, though. When Cryin' Bryan Dern's radio station decides to become a 24-hour, all-polka channel, Dern goes nuts. He takes over the place, doing a marathon session to save the station! Dern nearly kills himself on the air. But to no one's surpise, the station's change to polka and Dern's on-air marathon are revealed to be publicity stunts—thought up by Cryin' Bryan! The stunts work. The station manager thinks Dern is a genius. But Bryan is nearly dead with exhaustion!

Meanwhile, Jack tells Courtney that this constant competition with Hannah isn't doing either of them any good. Courtney agrees, but isn't sure how to stop it. Jack suggests a novel approach—let Hannah win. Courtney tries Jack's idea. It seems to work, and instead of being constant rivals, they turn into fast friends.

behind the scenes:

"I asked John Campbell to ad-lib a musical clip from a rock star—to sing words that no one could understand. John came up with this Bruce Springsteen-type clip, which was completely hilarious. We used the clip for Cryin' Bryan Dern's 'What Is He Saying?' contest. I would listen to it over and over again, rewind it, and laugh harder each time."

—Marshal Younger

STUDY QUESTIONS:

1. Why were Courtney and Hannah so competitive with each other?
2. Have you ever felt that way about someone? How did you handle the situation?
3. Jack suggested that the way for Courtney to stop the competition would be to let Hannah win. Can you think of another way?

Episodes #314–316 "The Underground Railroad," Parts One, Two & Three

Theme: God in history; the sanctity of life.
Scripture reference: Psalm 82:3
Written and directed by Marshal Younger
Production engineers: Bob Luttrell, Dave Arnold, and Mark Drury
(Original air dates: 5-13-95; 5-20-95; 5-27-95)

Jack arrives at Whit's End one morning to find a visitor waiting for him to open. The visitor's name is Carl. He says he's the curator for a museum in Chicago. He wants to look around because he believes that Whit's End may have historical significance. Jack is intrigued.

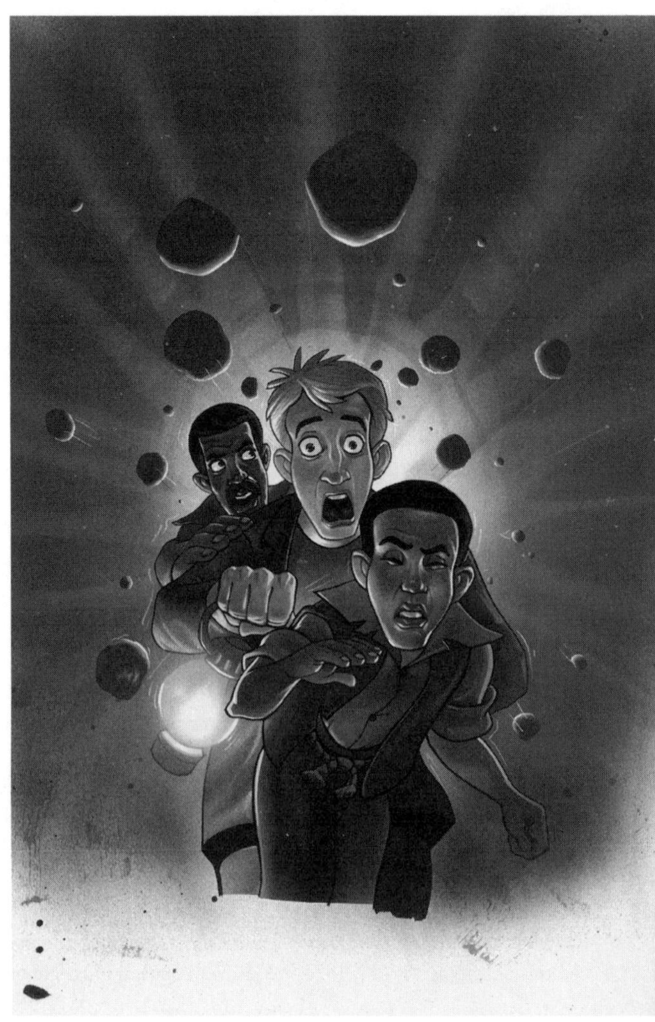

Carl asks if the building has any tunnels underneath it. Jack explains that there is a little-known tunnel that connects the downstairs workroom with the middle of the woods on the edge of McCalister Park.

Hearing this, Carl looks as if he's about to faint. Jack asks if he is all right, and Carl explains the reason for his excitement: The tunnel and Whit's End itself may have been a stop on the Underground Railroad! Jack shows Carl the tunnel and asks why Carl believes it played a part in freeing runaway slaves. In response, Carl shows Jack an old book—an original manuscript written before the Civil War. The book describes a slave family's run for freedom. The landmarks and the cities described in the book seem to show that Odyssey was one of the places the family stopped.

Jack asks Carl to tell him the story, and Carl imparts the tale of the Ross family—Henry; his wife, Caroline; and William, their 17-year-old son. They were Tennessee slaves who broke their bonds and escaped to freedom in the North on the Underground Railroad.

behind the scenes:

"These were the most emotional scripts I ever wrote for *AIO*. Judging from the way everything came together, God was obviously at work. Unlike our usual routine, we did a read-through with all the actors first. We had never worked with most of these people before, and we wanted them to have some chemistry going into the recording. I was incredibly nervous when they started reading, but right at the first scene—wow!—it sounded like the actors had worked together for years."

—Marshal Younger

"These episodes were by far the toughest we had ever done production-wise. They required two to three days per episode for foley (our process of creating custom sound effects), compared to the one half to one day we normally take.

"We got the sound of running across ice by running on a hard surface sprinkled with broken, florescent tube glass and corn flakes. Walking through the snow was done by hauling buckets of snow into the studio and . . . well, *walking* on it. We really created a mess in the process."

—Dave Arnold

STUDY QUESTIONS:

1. Why was the Underground Railroad necessary?
2. Why is slavery wrong? What does the Bible say about it?
3. If you had lived in the pre-Civil War South, would you have helped slaves run away? Why or why not? What were some of the risks associated with helping slaves escape?

Episode #317 "B-TV: Envy"

Theme: The dangers of envy.
Scripture references: Genesis 4:1-16; 2 Samuel 11:1-12:23; 1 Kings 21
Written and directed by Phil Lollar
Production engineer: Bob Luttrell
(Original air date: 6-03-95)

"B-TV" is back! Yes, it's another episode of that fast-paced, wacky show. The topic this time: envy. This episode includes an Oprah-like talk show. The show features a man named Cain who murdered his brother, Abel, and a king named David who committed adultery and murder—all because of envy. "B-TV" also shows a crime drama called "N.V.P.D. Squad." On this drama, a detective named Elijah and his partner, Lippowicz, solve the murder of a vineyard owner named Naboth, who was killed because King Ahab and Queen Jezebel envied him! The point of this episode of "B-TV"—Don't let envy get *you*!

STUDY QUESTIONS:

1. Why is envy a bad thing? What does Jesus say about envy?
2. Have you ever envied someone? What did you do about it?
3. Bernard gave us a great way to conquer envy. Can you think of any other methods?

Episodes #318 & 319

"A Touch of Healing," Parts One & Two

Theme: Accepting things beyond our control.
Scripture reference: 1 John 5:14
Recommended maturity level: 8 and up
Written and directed by Paul McCusker
Production engineers: Mark Drury and Dave Arnold
(Original air dates: 6-10-95 & 6-17-95)

PARENTAL WARNING: This is a story about life, dashed hopes, and the death of a loved one. It may be too sensitive for younger listeners.

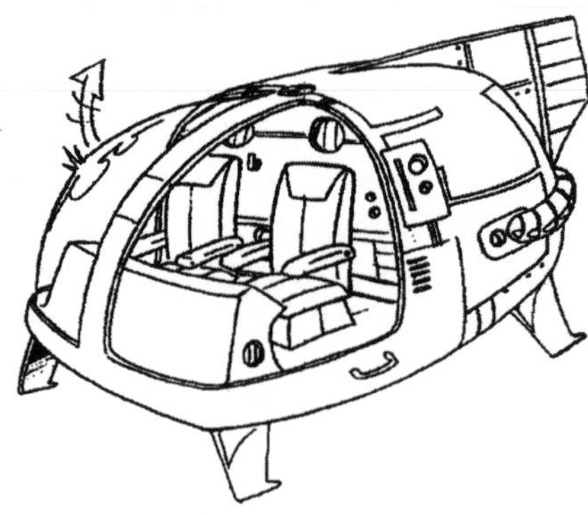

Connie Kendall comes to Whit's End to ask Jason Whittaker for time off to spend with her grandma, Mildred Kendall. Grandma has come to live with Connie and her mom while she recuperates from heart trouble. Jason listens, then tells Connie about his plan to reprogram the Imagination Station. He wants to see if Jenny, who is blind, and Zachary, who is unable to walk because of a car accident, would be able to imagine themselves healed in the Imagination Station. Jack Allen is against the idea, just as he was against the Bible-based arcade games that Jason had put in Whit's End. Jason gives Connie extra time off work.

Connie and Mildred talk about Connie's dad's need for salvation and how glad they are that they have stayed close in spite of the divorce. Later, Connie waits in the doctor's office while Mildred is being tested. Finally, she approaches a nurse and is told that the doctors believe Mildred has had a heart attack. When she is finally allowed to see her, Mildred expresses her desire to see Bill (Connie's father) before she dies. Mildred also shares some prayers with Connie that she has written in her Bible.

At Whit's End, Jenny is the first to try the altered Imagination Station and ends up in the town of Bethany with Lazarus, Martha, and Mary. Jenny is still blind in the story but is encouraged by Lazarus, who tells her that he died and rose again so that Christ would be glorified—and that Jenny's blindness can be used in the same way. Jason is disappointed that Jenny wasn't "healed" of her blindness in the Imagination Station. He reluctantly agrees to let Zach try the next program and decides to get in *with* Zach to witness the results.

The Imagination Station sends them both to America during the Revolutionary War. They are both surprised and excited when Zach can not only walk, but also run—just as he could before the car accident. Their adventure ends abruptly when Zach's mom, Eileen, arrives to take him home. She is disturbed by Jason's program and insists that Zach go home with her immediately. But Zach doesn't want to leave—he wants to stay in the Imagination Station because he is able to walk in there. He throws a tantrum, and his mother has to drag him out.

Later, Eileen tells Jason and Jack that Zachary no longer wants to go to therapy because he wants to spend all his time in the Imagination Station. She complains that Jason's program has given Zach false hope. They've argued nonstop because she won't let him go in there anymore.

But Jason is still excited about his Imagination Station program and, in spite of Jack's objections, even agrees to do an interview with Cryin' Bryan Dern about it.

After the interview, Whit's End becomes madhouse—it seems every kid in Odyssey wants to try the Imagination Station. Some of the children are disappointed and upset that they haven't been "healed" of their problems. Zach arrives on the scene and insists on being allowed to enter the Station. He gets into a fight with his mother, saying that he hates everyone who gets in the way of the Station adventure.

Realizing the damage he's been doing, Jason closes down the Imagination Station until further notice. Privately, Zach tells Jack he is sorry he ever tried the Imagination Station. Now, he's worried that he may never walk again. Jack encourages Zach to concentrate on the *spiritual* healing that needs to take place. Jack prays with him and his mother, Eileen, to receive Christ.

At the hospital, Connie's grandmother feels her time has almost ended. She urges Connie to pray, not for healing, but for strength. Mildred slips into a coma. Jack visits Connie at the hospital, and Connie expresses her confusion over Mildred's suffering. It seems her prayers haven't been answered. Jack says he can't really explain it, but although suffering is an inevitable result of our fallen world, it is still important to pray. That way we can better understand the mind of God and feel His comfort. Connie and her mom continue their vigil at the hospital, and Connie urges her mom to accept the Lord and His strength for herself—just as Mildred dies.

STUDY QUESTIONS:

1. Why was Jack opposed to Jason's new Imagination Station program? Do you agree with Jack's reservations? Why or why not?
2. Why is it important to persist in praying, even when it seems God isn't answering your prayers?
3. What did Connie learn through her grandmother's illness?

Episode #320 "Where Is Thy Sting?"

Theme: Dealing with the death of a loved one.
Scripture references: 1 Corinthians 15:54-57; 1 Thessalonians 4:13; 1 Timothy 6:17-19
Written and directed by Paul McCusker
Production engineer: Dave Arnold
(Original air date: 6-24-95)

Connie's grandmother has died, and everyone at Whit's End is sympathetic—even Eugene. Connie and her mother are trying to make arrangements for the funeral. They are also waiting for Connie's dad to arrive. When they pick him up at the airport, he is agitated, surly, and depressed—and he goes downhill from there.

First, Bill Kendall bristles when Connie suggests that instead of having a morose funeral service, they celebrate her grandmother's life on earth and her new life in heaven. Bill retorts that they're not going to turn his mother's funeral into some sort of party. He storms out of the room. Later, he and June get into an argument about the service, and Bill storms out again. He's so upset that, at the viewing that night, he shows up drunk. June and Connie try to find out why Bill's behaving so badly, but he won't tell them.

The service is the next day, and it is beautiful. Jack and George Barclay read from the Scripture and Grandma's pastor from her home church in New York gives a wonderful eulogy. After the service, Bill, June, and Connie are left alone to say good-bye to Grandma. Bill finally explains his bad behavior: His marriage to April is finished. His life is a mess. He breaks down in tears and leaves—completely without hope.

But for June, it's a different story. She realizes that she's been living on the coattails of Connie's faith—June needs to have a faith of her own. She knows the time is right, so she asks Connie to introduce her properly to Jesus. Connie is only too happy to oblige.

the Adventures in Odyssey archives:

"Where Is Thy Sting?" was the longest single-part *AIO* program to date. More than 12 minutes of dialogue had to be cut for the broadcast version, and six minutes were cut for the album version. One of the scenes we lost dealt with Jack's and Eugene's various perspectives on death—Jack related the Christian viewpoint, while Eugene gave his non-Christian perspective on death.

STUDY QUESTIONS:

1. Why was Bill Kendall so upset about his mother's death?
2. Why was Connie so peaceful about it?
3. Have you ever had anyone close to you die? How did you feel about it? Why did you react in the way you did?

Episode #321 "Hidden in My Heart"

Theme: Memorizing Bible verses.
Scripture reference: Psalm 119:11
Written and directed by Marshal Younger
Production engineer: Bob Luttrell
(Original air date: 7-01-95)

Kid's Radio is on the air, and Connie introduces a new show called "Rescue 1-1-9." William Shattered narrates this program of "true-to-life" spiritual emergencies, showing how the folks at Rescue 1-1-9 resolve those crises.

This particular episode involves a young boy named David Hornsby who is home alone one evening when there is a knock on his door. He answers it and finds two cult members standing there. Immediately, they launch into a powerful speech, trying to persuade David to join their organization. The cult members almost have him convinced—until they ask him to do something that goes against what God teaches in the Bible. The trouble is, David can't remember where God says this in the Bible. That's when he calls up Rescue 1-1-9. The Rescue 1-1-9 operator gives David the proper verse. David cites it to the cultists, and they leave feeling dejected and defeated—never to return.

The other major story, "Star Trip," is a spoof on the TV series *Star Trek*. We join the crew of the Starship Aerobocise as they rescue the beautiful Princess of Tibia from the evil Ding-Dongs on the planet Ulna. The Ding-Dongs have only one weapon: deception. They can turn themselves into any kind of being—people, animals, snack cakes, *anything*. The Ding-Dongs act like they're somebody or something else—then use temptation and deception to lure people to do the wrong things. Once those people become vulnerable, they are destroyed. The Captain and Mr. Schlock arm themselves with temptation detectors and Scripture phasers and head off in search of the princess. After a bit of trouble, they find and rescue her—showing why it's important to memorize God's Word.

STUDY QUESTIONS:

1. Why was David so easily taken in by the cultists?
2. Why is it important to memorize Scripture? What are the benefits of Scripture memorization?
3. What would you say to someone who challenged your faith?

Episode #322 "The Turning Point"

Theme: God's plans for individuals.
Scripture reference: 2 Corinthians 6:14
Written and directed by Paul McCusker
Production engineer: Dave Arnold
(Original air date: 7-08-95)

Eugene has come to work dressed in a nice suit, and for a good reason. Katrina's father, Armitage, is coming into town to visit Katrina—and to meet Eugene. Eugene is understandably nervous about this meeting. He wants everything to be perfect. Unfortunately, he is working on a display that collapses and showers him with drywall dust—just as Katrina and her father arrive. This marks the beginning of a disastrous lunch. Eugene spills water all over himself and argues about his career goals with Armitage. Then Eugene insists on paying for lunch, not realizing that he has left his wallet behind at Whit's End.

But Eugene is even more distressed by the real reason Armitage is here. Lately, Katrina has been distracted—not keeping up with her studies at college—and Armitage wants to know if Eugene is the cause. Katrina finally admits that he is. She loves him but faces a dilemma: Eugene is not a Christian. Katrina doesn't know what to do. Her father suggests that Katrina get some perspective on the situation. Armitage thinks she should leave Odyssey, move back home, and go to school there for a while.

Katrina realizes that her father is right, and she tells Eugene, who is devastated. He reveals his love for her but states his unwillingness to become a Christian. Katrina explains that they have no alternative. She expresses her love for him, then leaves. Is this the end of Katrina and Eugene? Only time will tell. . . .

Adventures in Odyssey the ODYSSEY archives:

The name Armitage Shanks came from a porcelain/plumbing company in England.

STUDY QUESTIONS:

1. Why was Eugene so concerned about impressing Katrina's father?
2. Why did Katrina realize it was wrong for her to date Eugene?
3. Both Jack and Katrina told Eugene that he wasn't making a decision about Jesus because he didn't have to. What did they mean by that?

Episode #323 "A Little Credit, Please"

Theme: Stewardship.
Scripture reference: Luke 16:10-12
Written and directed by Paul McCusker
Production engineer: Mark Drury
(Original air date: 7-15-95)

Connie comes down to breakfast one morning and gets a wonderful surprise: Her mother has gotten her a gift—her first credit card. June makes it clear that Connie must use the card responsibly. Connie agrees to do so.

Meanwhile, at Whit's End, Bernard enters with a new window-washing assistant—Simon, a young man from Australia. Bernard then asks Eugene how he is doing now that Katrina has left, but Eugene sidesteps the issue. Bernard goes to work as Connie enters. She, too, asks about Eugene's state of mind. Eugene also avoids her and sets off to work. Later, Tom enters to find Connie on the phone, ordering clothes from a catalog and putting them on her credit card. Unfortunately, Connie has started making many purchases with her new card, "just to see if it's working."

Across town, Simon tells Bernard that he's been reading up on Bernard's power spray washer. Simon would really like to use it. Bernard tells Simon that the power spray washer is tricky—Simon needs to learn the basics before he moves on to the more advanced stuff.

That evening, Connie is shopping at the mall when she runs into Eugene. After some small talk, Connie manages to pry out of Eugene that he is miserable now that Katrina is gone. Connie invites Eugene out for dinner (which she pays for with her credit card). Eugene admits that his life feels empty without Katrina. In fact, his life stinks. Connie tries her best to comfort him.

The next day, however, Connie needs comforting herself. She remembers that she needs to buy her mother a birthday gift. When she tries to purchase one at the Electric Palace, though, she is told that her credit card is over the limit. Connie leaves the store in a huff and runs into Simon outside.

Simon is preparing to wash the Electric Palace's front windows with Bernard's power washer—against Bernard's orders. Things go from bad to worse for both of them when Simon asks Connie to hold the washer while he turns on the power. Neither he nor Connie can control the mechanism. It gets away from them, smashing one of the windows! Simon and Connie learn valuable lessons about handling responsibility, while Eugene decides to do something radical to give his life a change: He grows a mustache.

Adventures in Odyssey the ODYSSEY archives:

Simon Birtles was played by an honest-to-goodness Australian boy, Sam Falson, who lost most of his accent from living in America. We later heard from listeners who complained they wished we'd hired a *real* Australian to play the part.

STUDY QUESTIONS:

1. Why did June get Connie a credit card? Was it a good idea? Explain.
2. Why was Eugene so unhappy when Katrina left?
3. What does the Bible say about credit?

PARENTAL WARNING: The following 11-part series deals with Satan's attacks on Odyssey. Those attacks manifest themselves in ways ranging from stolen bicycles to vandalism to a bomb exploding at Whit's End. While these things are handled carefully and are integral to the plot, the series still gets extremely intense in places, and is therefore not recommended nor intended for younger listeners.
Recommended maturity level: 10 and up

Episode #324
"Small Fires, Little Pools"

Written and directed by Phil Lollar
Production engineer: Bob Luttrell
(Original air date: 7-22-95)

The trouble starts with a wave of vandalism against Odyssey First Church, Whit's End, and other places. Everyone is wondering what in the world is happening.

Meanwhile, Jack is again beset with strange dreams. He specifically dreams that he's in a forest. Little fires suddenly shoot up all around him, then are quickly put out by little pools of water. Jack realizes what the fire part of the dream means when Whit's End is vandalized. Later, in a conversation with Connie, Jack guesses that the little pools in his dream might be a symbolic way to fight the crime wave that has suddenly befallen the town. Jack takes action.

While all this is going on, Sam and Lucy head up to Trickle Lake for an outing. When they try to go back, they discover their bikes have been stolen. A strange phone call leads Sam to the Wonderworld tree house. There, a mysterious figure gives Sam back the bikes. Sam jumps the figure, pulls off his disguise, and finds that it is Butch! Sam pumps Butch for information—he guesses the Bones of Rath must be behind all this. Butch wants to do the right thing, but he is also influenced by the Bones. He turns from Sam and leaves. And, as if all this weren't enough, Bart Rathbone now uses the vandalism around town as an excuse to attack Tom Riley's abilities as mayor. What is going on around Odyssey?

the *Adventures in* ODYSSEY archives:

This episode and the next 10 are contained in the album "Darkness Before Dawn." Each episode is interconnected, and all deal with the spiritual warfare that hits Odyssey. For this reason, none of the programs in this series has a specifically outlined scripture reference or theme.

Also, the 11-parter was originally designed for us to wrap up some major story lines we had left hanging for so long. At this point, we were even considering finishing off the entire *Adventures in Odyssey* program. We played out the series, hoping that some things would be answered by the end of this 11-part show.

STUDY QUESTIONS:

1. Why did Jack think his dream was significant?
2. Why did Butch give back the bicycles? Why wouldn't he go with Sam?
3. What is the best way to fight evil?

Episode #325 "Angels Unaware"

Written and directed by Phil Lollar
Production engineer: Mark Drury
(Original air date: 7-29-95)

As Sam Johnson and Butch part, Sam is grabbed by Jack Allen and his friend Billy MacPherson to ask for Sam's help. Butch also runs into Rusty and Rodney—who tell Butch that the Bones of Rath are planning to vandalize Odyssey Middle School that evening. Butch meets up with Sam later on, and they swap information . . . and concoct a plan.

Later, Lucy Cunningham-Schultz receives a mysterious phone call telling her to look in her driveway. Her stolen bike is sitting there. When she asks Sam about it, he acts suspiciously.

That night, the Bones show up to vandalize Odyssey Middle School. Butch notices that there is a police car parked down the street, watching them. The Bones of Rath call off their vandalism.

But not all the happenings around town are bad. Brock Peterson, Channel 10 News reporter, interviews Alma Stump, whose fence was mysteriously mended. Mayor Tom Riley tells of an anonymous phone call the police received, warning them of planned vandalism at Odyssey Middle School. Ralph Foreman, a city worker, describes how bushes were mysteriously trimmed, making an intersection safe for the community. He describes it as a random act of goodness.

Connie Kendall hears the news report and begins to wonder if Jack Allen has anything to do with these mysterious occurrences. When confronted, Jack won't admit to any involvement with the good deeds.

Bart Rathbone also hears the news report and yells at Rodney. Bart warns Rodney that people are beginning to think everything is all right in Odyssey. Someone from "higher up," who signed loan papers for Bart, is putting pressure on him to make waves. Rodney promises he has something evil planned for that night.

Connie and Lucy compare notes—they are both suspicious about Sam and Jack's strange behavior, so they decide to follow Sam that evening. The girls follow Sam into the woods, where they are caught by Sam and a strange man. The stranger orders Connie and Lucy to come with he and Sam. This story is continued in "Gathering Thunder."

STUDY QUESTIONS:

1. Should Sam have told Lucy how he got their bikes back? Should Lucy have questioned him about it? What would you have done if you were in Sam's place? Lucy's? Explain your answers.
2. Why do you think the mysterious "higher up" person wanted to cause chaos around Odyssey?
3. Should Lucy and Connie have followed Sam? Why or why not? What would you have done?

Episode #326 "Gathering Thunder"

Written by Marshal Younger
Directed by Paul McCusker
Production engineer: Mark Drury
(Original air date: 8-05-95)

Lucy and Connie have been nabbed by a group called "the Israelites." It's a "good" gang that Whit used to run around town. Jack has brought the group back to take action against the Bones's crime wave. Their leader is Billy MacPherson, a member of the original Israelites. Jack has also recruited Sam, which explains why he has been acting so strange lately. And Sam has made Butch their informant. This enables the Israelites to prevent the Bones's next rotten plan: vandalizing a war monument in McCalister Park.

Meanwhile, based on instructions from "higher up," Bart heats up his attacks on Tom Riley's mayorship. He implies there is a connection between the crime wave and Tom's lack of leadership.

Then, a new leader is brought in to guide the Bones—Jellyfish, who instantly suspects that there is a traitor in their midst. Jellyfish gives the gang their next line of attack: Part of the Bones will meet at the movies and cause a diversion while the rest of them will attack Whit's End again. Butch tells Sam about the plan. But Sam is worried about Butch and tells him to be careful. At the movies that night, Butch learns that Jellyfish wants part of the Bones to attack the Harlequin Theatre instead of Whit's End. Butch tries to sneak out to make a phone call to warn Sam and the Israelites. But Jellyfish catches him, and the Bones beat him up—badly. When Jack learns about this, he is horrified. He never meant for things to get this out of hand. As a result, he disbands the Israelites.

the *Adventures in* ODYSSEY archives:

The character of Billy MacPherson was first introduced in the *Adventures in Odyssey* novels. The name "Jellyfish" came from a San Francisco-based rock group.

behind the scenes:

"In the movie theater scene, there's a parody of the movie *Rocky*. Rocky, who's now an older man, is trying to prove that he can still fight so that his family won't put him in a nursing home."

—Marshal Younger, on one of his favorite parts in "Gathering Thunder"

STUDY QUESTIONS:

1. Do you think it was a good idea to create a good gang in order to battle an evil one? Why or why not?
2. Why did Bart keep hammering away at Tom Riley's lack of leadership?
3. What would you have done if you were in Butch's place?

Episode #327 "Moving Targets"

Written and directed by Paul McCusker
Production engineer: Dave Arnold
(Original air date: 8-12-95)

Jason, who has been out of town, and Eugene, who has been busy at the college, reunite at Whit's End and catch up on all the mayhem that's been happening around Odyssey. Jason has decided that the Underground Railroad tunnel under Whit's End would make a great display for the kids. He has asked an inspector to come in and make sure it's safe.

Jack arrives. He is bothered by this idea. The timing isn't right, especially with all the problems around town lately. He has had another strange dream. In this last one, the tunnel was a way to let evil into Whit's End. But Jack's reticence about the tunnel is frustrating to Jason. He feels that every time he has a new idea for Whit's End, Jack has a problem with it. This leads to friction between the two of them.

The tunnel is causing more problems than those between Jack and Jason. The city inspector defers to state authorities on the tunnel issue, and later, Professor Bovril shows up as a state consultant—with Philip Glossman, everybody's favorite weasel, right behind.

Alone in the tunnel, Bovril and Glossman are pleased to find that the mysterious mineral they've been looking for is there. Now they need to get Whit's End cleared out so they can have total access to the mineral. To do this, they bring in more "experts" to prove the tunnel is a safety hazard. Glossman can do this because the city owns the land under Whit's End. If the tunnel proves hazardous, the city council can close down the shop.

Eugene conducts his own test on the mineral, but it is inconclusive. He promises to keep investigating matters.

Meanwhile, further friction develops between Jason and Jack. Jason has learned that Jack started up—and then disbanded—the Israelites. Jack defends his decision. He says the battle is way too serious when kids start getting hurt. But Jason disagrees. He says that getting hurt is the nature of battle—you must fight fire with fire. Jack believes that something far more sinister is going on—and using the Israelites isn't the way to fight it. Jason responds by saying that if Jack won't keep the Israelites going, then *he* will. Their disagreement becomes so heated, Jack feels he has no choice but to resign his job. Effective immediately, he will no longer work at Whit's End.

Bovril is the British equivalent of Ovaltine.

STUDY QUESTIONS:

1. Why was Jack so opposed to Jason's plans for the Underground Railroad tunnel and the Israelites? Do you agree or disagree with Jack? Explain.
2. Have you ever had dreams like Jack's? Do you believe that God still talks to us through our dreams? Why or why not?
3. Jason felt it was important to fight fire with fire. Was he right or wrong?

Episode #328 "Hard Losses"

Written and directed by Phil Lollar
Production engineer: Bob Luttrell
(Original air date: 8-19-95)

Bart Rathbone's misinformation campaign against Tom Riley is getting more intense. Dale Jacobs at the *Odyssey Times* has just learned that Tom's campaign was helped financially by Edgebiter Chemical Company. This makes it look like Tom was backing the very company he was supposed to be against. Bart and Cryin' Bryan Dern make a big deal out of this, questioning Tom's honesty.

But in a surprising turn of events, former wrongdoer Richard Maxwell shows up to tell Tom that something big is happening—and Richard wants to find out what it is. Tom has never really forgiven Richard for burning down his barn several years ago, though. Tom refuses Richard's help and won't even listen to him.

Meanwhile, we discover that Jellyfish and Philip Glossman are working together. Jellyfish tells Glossman about Jack Allen's resignation from Whit's End and reports that Jason has taken over the Israelites. Glossman is delighted that their plan is working so nicely—everything is falling apart for the good guys. Jason's reckless decision making will work in the Bones's and Glossman's favor.

On his way out, Jellyfish bumps into Richard Maxwell in the elevator. They recognize each other from their jail days. Their meeting gives the impression that Jellyfish and Richard were enemies while in prison. It seems that Jellyfish often tried to get Richard into trouble—and that Richard would like nothing better than to put Jellyfish in his place.

That night, Bart frantically wakes up Rodney and tells him they need to hurry with the "recall Tom Riley" petitions because "he's" coming. It's time.

The next day, Richard meets Jack at Whit's house. Richard pleads with Jack to persuade Tom to listen. Richard has important information about who is behind the whole mess in Odyssey. Richard says the responsible party is Dr. Regis Blackgaard. But Tom stubbornly refuses to listen. Tom believes that Richard is probably working with Blackgaard again.

Meanwhile, the city council is voting on the issue of Tom's recall. The vote is close, but the council decides to allow the city to vote. The city will decide whether Tom should be recalled as the mayor of Odyssey. Tom sadly vows to fight to clear his name.

STUDY QUESTIONS:

1. Why wouldn't Tom listen to Richard Maxwell?
2. Why were Bart and Rodney so afraid of the news that "he is coming"?
3. Why was it so dangerous for Jason to be making reckless decisions, especially at that time?

Episode #329 "The Return"

Written and directed by Phil Lollar
Production engineer: Dave Arnold
(Original air date: 8-26-95)

Things are getting even more strange in Odyssey. Jason approaches Jack about coming back to Whit's End. Jack refuses. He is determined to spend his time exploring the *spiritual* nature of this battle—through prayer, instead of through violence, the way Jason has wanted to proceed.

Meanwhile, Edwin Blackgaard is terrified. He has just learned that his evil twin, Regis, is back in town. Regis threatens his twin, telling Edwin he must help Regis with his plans or leave town right away. Edwin timidly skips town.

On Cryin' Bryan Dern's radio show, Dr. Blackgaard announces that he is running for mayor. He wants to prove he is innocent of the evil deeds attributed to him several years ago. Regis knows he can be the kind of mayor Odyssey needs. Jason is shocked to hear Blackgaard's voice—he thought that Blackgaard had died in Switzerland (see "A Name, Not a Number" *AIO* #290 & 291).

To make matters worse, the Bones of Rath are vandalizing the town again. Now they're committing crimes while dressed up as the Israelites. Jason visits Dr. Blackgaard to talk to him about what is happening—but ends up playing into Blackgaard's hands. He has recorded their conversation and plans to blackmail Jason later.

Finally, on Blackgaard's orders, Philip Glossman leads the campaign to get the city council to agree to close down Whit's End because of the mysterious mineral in the Underground Railroad tunnel. Glossman says the mineral is a public health hazard. The council agrees, and Glossman hangs up the sign announcing that Whit's End is closed.

STUDY QUESTIONS:

1. Why did Edwin and Shakespeare leave town so quickly?
2. Should Jack have come back to work at Whit's End? Why or why not?
3. Should Jason have visited Blackgaard? Explain your answer.

Episode #330 "The Time Has Come"

Theme: Salvation.
Written and directed by Paul McCusker
Production engineer: Dave Arnold
(Original air date: 9-02-95)

In the midst of the evil encompassing Odyssey, Eugene's spiritual journey has been moving full steam ahead. He's been stripped of everything he's ever cared about: Whit is gone, Katrina has left Odyssey because of Eugene, and now Whit's End has closed and is in the hands of Glossman and Dr. Blackgaard. Eugene wants to help in the battle, but Jack wisely points out that Eugene can't. It's a spiritual battle Eugene isn't equipped to fight. Jack challenges Eugene. Jack says that if Eugene thinks over all his experiences in Odyssey, he'll see that everything points to the inevitable: Sooner or later, Eugene must make a decision about Jesus Christ.

Fortunately, Eugene and the other employees of Whit's End aren't banned from the emporium. Thanks to Jason's pleading and political connections, they have permission to come to the shop. So Eugene decides to use the Imagination Station's data banks to "search" Odyssey's history for any references about the mysterious mineral under Whit's End.

To test his search program, Eugene decides to take Jack up on his challenge—to search through his own life in Odyssey. Eugene does, and he re-lives many scenes from his past that have pointed him toward Jesus Christ. Eugene comes out of the Imagination Station ready to say "yes" to the Lord's call. And what begins as a tender moment of prayer between Jack and Eugene turns comical as Connie, Bernard, and Tom show up to share in Eugene's decision. The only one missing is Whit. But even he is represented when, on the downstairs phone, he calls and leaves a message of encouragement on the answering machine. Finally, Eugene Meltsner becomes a new creation.

behind the scenes:

"I compiled the sequence where Eugene searches through his life from numerous *AIO* shows. I pulled 30 minutes worth of material, then Paul and I sifted through most of it. Because the sound design was so complicated, it took eight hours to mix that one scene with Eugene. Normally, it takes no more than one hour."

—Dave Arnold

"No two *AIO* characters have come to God the same way. So, of course, we wanted to handle Eugene's salvation differently from Connie's. Connie needed to ultimately understand how much God added to her life thanks to Whit and Whit's End—though she kept trying to escape and move back to California. For Eugene, it was the opposite. He had to be stripped of everything he held dear in order to clear the way for God to work in his heart. So while Connie's conversion meant a trip to California, the means for Eugene's conversion was a computer program. I believe God often uses the object of our resistance as the means of His grace."

—Paul McCusker

STUDY QUESTIONS:

1. Why did Eugene feel so uninvolved with the battle for Odyssey?
2. Why did Jack think that the only way Eugene could become effective in the fight was to become a Christian?
3. Why was it so obvious to Eugene that after looking over his life, he needed to accept Christ?

Episode #331 "Checkmate"

Written by Phil Lollar and Paul McCusker
Directed by Phil Lollar
Production engineer: Mark Drury
(Original air date: 9-16-95)

Evil still abounds in Odyssey. Dr. Blackgaard is livid that Whit's End hasn't been completely evacuated. He blasts Glossman for his incompetence. Meanwhile, Jason has restructured the Israelites in order to spy more aggressively on the Bones of Rath. He wants the Bones to know that the Israelites aren't predictable—by having Billy and Sam go to the Bones's hideout and clean it. Butch has informed the Israelites that the Bones will be bowling that night, so the Israelites should hit the hideout then. To keep tabs on the Bones, Lucy follows them to the bowling alley. Rodney sees Lucy and decides to take matters into his own hands. He is annoyed that Jellyfish has taken over the Bones so effectively. He lures Lucy to the Bones's *new* hideout in a cave where he hopes to get information from her about the Israelites.

While this is going on, Eugene continues his work in the Imagination Station. He's searching through Odyssey's history for information about the Underground Railroad tunnel. In the Imagination Station, Eugene is just about to find out an important piece of the puzzle about the mineral from Reverend Andrew (see "The Underground Railroad" *AIO* #314-316) when the power suddenly goes down. Eugene comes out of the Station and finds that Whit's End is being attacked by the Bones of Rath.

Later, during the cleanup, Jason and Sam realize that Butch either got his information wrong, or he has double-crossed them. (They later discover that it is the latter—after Butch was beaten up by the Bones, he opted to spy on the Israelites. For his own protection, Jason gets Butch out of town.) Sam and Jason also realize that Lucy is missing. Jellyfish is furious that Rodney brought Lucy to the Bones's new hideout, but Rodney persuades Jellyfish that he can get some useful information from her. Fortunately, Richard Maxwell intercedes and saves Lucy.

But that doesn't help Whit's End. Claiming that it's for the public's safety, Glossman throws everybody out—leaving Blackgaard to gloat that Whit's End is finally, truly, *his*.

STUDY QUESTIONS:

1. Was Jason right in believing that the Israelites should be more aggressive against the Bones? Why or why not?
2. Should Lucy have followed Rodney and Rusty to the Bones's new hideout? Explain.
3. Do you think Butch should be blamed for his decision to tell on the Israelites? Why or why not?

Episode #332 "Another Chance"

Written by Phil Lollar
Directed by Paul McCusker
Production engineer: Bob Luttrell
(Original air date: 9-23-95)

Word has gotten out that the soil under Whit's End is unsafe, and Tom is accused of hiding that information from the townspeople. Blackgaard takes advantage of the situation. He says he wants to protect the children of Odyssey from problems like this—but he collapses in the middle of his press conference.

Even worse, though, is that Bart Rathbone's Electric Palace was vandalized, and Bart claims the Israelites did it.

Eugene is still trying to find out Whit's End's history through the Imagination Station. After the power outage, he tries to salvage what he can from the Station's data banks. Now Eugene is willing to try anything. He accepts Richard Maxwell's help in attempting to sort out the code. All they can replay from the conversation with Reverend Andrew is that the local Indians called the mineral "the Silent One."

While this is happening, Richard has another brief confrontation with Tom. Unfortunately, Tom is still unwilling to forgive Richard—even though it's obvious that Richard is just trying to help.

At the same time, Rodney is furious that Jellyfish is running the Bones of Rath without consulting him. Jellyfish is also keeping a record of all that's happening on a laptop computer—just in case things go wrong. Jellyfish pulls the Bones together for a meeting. Rodney interrupts Jellyfish and unsuccessfully challenges his leadership. Betrayed, Rodney storms out of the meeting. Later, Rusty tells Rodney about Jellyfish's laptop. Rodney, in return, tries to get revenge by making a deal with Richard Maxwell to get Jellyfish's computer.

Richard and Rodney sneak into Whit's End and overhear Dr. Blackgaard talking with Professor Bovril and Philip Glossman. There's a close call as Blackgaard demands Jellyfish's laptop so the professor can finish some calculations. Certain that Blackgaard will find Jellyfish's files, Richard creates a diversion so Rodney can escape. Richard gets caught by Blackgaard. The professor and Jellyfish drive away, determined to dispose of Richard, but Richard throws himself out of the car! Jellyfish and the professor panic and quickly leave. But Richard is not left on the road for long. Jack drives by on his way back from Trickle Lake and finds Richard by the side of the road. He's taken to a hospital, where he slips into a coma.

STUDY QUESTIONS:

1. Why was Jellyfish keeping a record of everything that happened on his computer?
2. Why didn't any of the Bones of Rath stand up for Rodney against Jellyfish?
3. Why do you think Rodney and the Bones were having so many problems with their leadership?

Episode #333 "The Last Resort"

Written by Phil Lollar
Directed by Paul McCusker
Production engineer: Mark Drury
(Original air date: 9-30-95)

Jason, Tom, and Eugene go to the hospital to see Richard. Jack is there, too. Together, they all speculate on what happened. Tom is still wary of Richard. Jason solidly reprimands Tom for his suspicious attitude. Jason and Eugene leave the hospital and, on their way out, they run into Rodney in the elevator. Rodney says he's come to see how Richard is doing. Jason and Eugene force Rodney to tell them what happened to Richard. Rodney blabs everything he knows about Jellyfish, the laptop computer, and all that has been happening in Odyssey.

Jason decides to get his hands on the contents of Jellyfish's laptop. Jason plans to do it through a sophisticated piece of infrared equipment. The equipment makes it possible to download the laptop's hard disk onto Eugene's computer. Jason and Eugene enlist Bernard Walton's help. Together, they sneak into Blackgaard's headquarters at the Harlequin Theatre and set up the infrared device. Bernard successfully sets up the equipment next to a laptop on Blackgaard's desk.

But when Eugene downloads the information, he realizes that what he's seeing on his computer is nothing like the information they know Jellyfish has. He realizes he, Jason, and Bernard are downloading the wrong laptop. Eugene recognizes some of the information. It has something to do with the mineral in the Underground Railroad tunnel! Eugene reads this new information. Suddenly, Eugene understands that Glossman is working for Blackgaard, who is trying to get to the mineral.

Jason also realizes that the Indian word for "the Silent One"—"Ruka"—is very close to the "Ruku" in the Ruku virus he and Blackgaard were involved with in Switzerland (see "A Name, Not a Number," *AIO* #290 & 291). Jason tells Eugene to make copies of the information. But shortly after, Jason gets picked up by the police for questioning. Apparently, a cassette tape has gotten out that reveals Jason making threats against mayoral candidate Regis Blackgaard!

Back at the hospital, Tom finally learns about all that Richard has done for him. He goes to Richard's bedside to ask his forgiveness. Richard grants it. Meanwhile, Jack goes to the police station to deal with Jason's arrest. Jason has told the police everything he knows about the problems around town. He uses his former position with the Agency to help prove his case. While the police check into it, Jason also tells Jack about his work with the Agency. Then Jason adds that he realizes now that he's been wrong. He shouldn't have so blindly rushed in to fight the evil. He apologizes to Jack, and they pray together.

While this is going on, Blackgaard holds a press conference to make a statement about Jason's "arrest"—once again collapsing in the middle of it. Blackgaard is rushed to the hospital. Things are really heating up around Odyssey!

STUDY QUESTIONS:

1. Why did Tom finally forgive Richard Maxwell?
2. Should Jason have secretly downloaded information from Blackgaard's computer? Why or why not?
3. Jason admitted that he had been acting arrogant, prideful, and reckless. Do you agree? Do you think Jack was in the wrong at all?

Episode #334 "The Final Conflict"

Written by Phil Lollar and Paul McCusker
Directed by Phil Lollar
Production engineer: Bob Luttrell
(Original air date: 10-07-95)

Jason reveals to Jack that the mysterious mineral is a component of a compound called TA-418, which was part of a deadly virus called Ruku. This Ruku was used by a terrorist group Dr. Blackgaard was connected with in Switzerland (see "A Name, Not a Number," *AIO* #290 & 291). It's clear now that *everything* that has happened in Odyssey—the vandalism, Tom's recall as mayor, Blackgaard's candidacy, the scandals—has been part of Blackgaard's scheme to gain unlimited access to the mineral under Whit's End.

Jason has the Israelites, Eugene, and Bernard surround Whit's End to keep a close eye on the mineral. They wind up capturing Jellyfish and Rodney Rathbone as they break into, then try to escape from the discovery emporium.

Meanwhile, at the hospital, Dr. Blackgaard tells Glossman that his illness was simply a scam to get out of running for mayor. (A doctor, however, contests this.) Regis now plans to slip out the back of the hospital. Then he'll go to Whit's End with Professor Bovril and Jellyfish to get the last of the mineral and escape while Whit's End is blown to bits. Blackgaard has ordered Glossman to set up a press conference at the hospital, which will put the plan in action.

But things soon backfire. Blackgaard announces his withdrawal from the mayoral race, but he doesn't endorse Bart Rathbone as his successor. Bart retaliates by blaming Glossman for the things that have been happening around Odyssey. At the police station, Jellyfish tries to get himself off the hook. He confesses to everything—including Blackgaard's plan to blow up Whit's End! Jason and the police race to the scene.

At Whit's End, Blackgaard realizes that something has gone wrong. He sends Professor Bovril off with a van filled with the mineral. But Eugene and Bernard are lying in wait for the professor and catch him. Blackgaard goes down into the Underground Railroad tunnel to set off the explosives—and comes face-to-face with Jack.

They have a final confrontation in which Jack appeals to Blackgaard to come to Christ. Blackgaard threatens Jack with death, but Jack says he is willing to sacrifice his own life to lead Blackgaard to Jesus. Blackgaard reveals that it is already too late. He really does have the Ruku virus—Regis is dying anyway. He has nothing to lose, so he pushes the button. The bomb goes off, collapsing the tunnel. Miraculously, Jack is thrown clear of the explosion. He is all right. But Blackgaard is not.

Later, Jack reflects sadly on the whole affair. He had hoped to help Blackgaard change, but he was so corrupt, now there could only be one destination for him—an eternity without God.

the Adventures in Odyssey archives:

A lot of questions and stories were wrapped up with the end of this 11-part series: the whole Blackgaard saga, Eugene's salvation, the relationship between Jack and Jason—among other things. Unfortunately, we also *raised* a lot of unanswered questions: What would become of Eugene and Katrina's relationship now that Eugene had become a Christian? What would everyone would do after this huge adventure? Would Whit ever return to Odyssey?

We decided we couldn't stop the program, especially now. Instead of wrapping things up, we had done just the opposite—we had created more work for ourselves than ever.

STUDY QUESTIONS:

1. Why did Bart expose Glossman at the press conference?
2. Why was Jack so willing to sacrifice his own life for Dr. Blackgaard's?
3. Dr. Blackgaard said that it was "too late" for him. But was it really? Is it ever too late to come to Jesus?

Episodes #335 & 336

"Love Is in the Air," Parts One & Two

Theme: Love; romance; God's will for our lives.
Scripture reference: 1 John 4:7-12
Written and directed by Paul McCusker
Production engineers: Dave Arnold and Mark Drury
(Original air dates: 10-28-95 & 11-04-95)

Love is in the air around Odyssey. First of all, Jason is working at the counter at Whit's End when the front door opens. In walks an old friend—Tasha Forbes! At the same time, Eugene has shaved off his measly mustache, anticipating the arrival of *his* sweetheart, Katrina. The two of them have been corresponding since she left for Chicago.

Unfortunately, when Katrina arrives, she walks in on Eugene and Connie in the middle of an innocent hug. (Connie is trying to show Eugene what an "it's-good-to-see-you" hug feels like.) Eugene blows Katrina's lack of a reaction out of proportion. He stumbles all over the place to convince her that there is nothing between Connie and himself. Katrina tells Eugene to call her later and leaves.

Meanwhile, Tasha and Jason are visiting the Connelsville zoo. Their conversation turns to their relationship and their feelings for each other. They both express their mutual love, and Jason takes things a step further: He asks Tasha to marry him!

While this is going on, Eugene and Katrina meet at their favorite restaurant for an intimate conversation. Eugene wants to know where the two of them stand. Katrina says she doesn't know and doesn't want to decide the question right now. Eugene continues to probe and uncovers his worst fear: Katrina is dating another guy!

To further complicate things, Connie has been acting strange ever since Tasha came to Odyssey—and it worsens when Jason and Tasha inform everyone that they are engaged. Tasha tells Jason that Connie has a crush on him. Jason talks to Connie about it, but she assures him that she doesn't.

Meanwhile, Eugene is so confused about Katrina that he is also acting irrationally. Katrina calms Eugene down. She explains that Brandon, the other man in her life, is more of a spiritual mentor than a boyfriend. Katrina still doesn't know where that leaves Eugene. She feels they should be apart for a while and pray for God's guidance. Eugene agrees.

Jason and Tasha continue to talk about their future plans. They have a big disagreement, though. Tasha wants to go back to Washington for work, but Jason wants her to quit her job.

By now, Jack has noticed Connie's strange behavior. He asks if she has a crush on Jason. Connie admits that she does. Jack suggests that Connie could be feeling left out—things are developing for both Jason and Eugene, but not for her. Jack counsels Connie to be patient and seek God's will.

Later, Jason and Eugene sit sadly together at Whit's End. Both Katrina and Tasha are leaving. Neither Jason nor Eugene knows exactly where he stands with his sweetheart. Jack tells them both to stop moping around, and they listen. Eugene and Jason rush off to the airport to say good-bye to Katrina and Tasha.

At the airport, Jason finds Katrina, while Eugene finds Tasha. Katrina admits to Jason that she loves Eugene. She tells Jason to relay the message. Eugene also finds out from Tasha that she is in love with Jason. Taking things one step further, Eugene pulls a ring from Jason out of his pocket. Now Jason and Tasha are officially engaged. The ladies rush off to meet their flights, and Jason and Eugene are happy once again.

the *Adventures in* ODYSSEY archives:

After the intense 11-parter, which included Blackgaard's death and the near destruction of Whit's End, we needed several lighter-hearted programs to balance out things. But although they were lighter, these episodes raised several serious questions about Eugene and Katrina, Jason and Tasha, and Connie and her future plans—which would be answered in future episodes.

STUDY QUESTIONS:

1. Jack said he felt that Connie was missing something in her life. Why did he say that?
2. Do you think Jason and Tasha should get married? How about Katrina and Eugene? Explain your answers.
3. What are some good reasons to get married? What are some bad reasons for getting married?

Episode #337 "W-O-R-R-Y"

Theme: Worry.
Scripture reference: Matthew 6:25-34
Written by Marshal Younger
Directed by Phil Lollar
Production engineer: Bob Luttrell
(Original air date: 11-11-95)

Erica is getting a haircut in anticipation of her annual class picture. She wants the haircut to be perfect. Every other year, she's looked like a geek in her picture. Unfortunately, the stylist isn't paying attention, and Erica ends up with the worst haircut in history. She is worried about how things will turn out—and she isn't the only one.

Sam Johnson has entered the Academic Olympics at school and is stunned—the last subject is spelling, and Sam is *terrible* at it. Both Sam and Erica panic and worry about their respective problems—then decide to pray about them. Later, Erica's mother turns her disastrous cut into a wonderfully stylish 'do. Meanwhile, Sam learns that if he can score well enough on his other subjects, he may not have to worry about the spelling section.

But on the day before the pictures, Sam and Erica race their bikes through the park. Erica loses control of her bike and crashes, scratching her face! A new problem to worry about! Then Sam learns that his scores going into the spelling test are only high enough to tie him for first place. More worrying. Jack notices their attitudes and advises each of them to pray again. He tells Erica to leave her problem in God's hands—she can't do much about it anyway. But Jack tells Sam to get busy and start studying for the test.

Sam wonders why he has to study when Erica gets to pray. Jack explains that their situations are different. Erica has no control over her situation, but Sam *does* have control over his. Sam understands and begins preparing. He ends up placing third in the Academic Olympics. As for Erica, she gets her picture taken, and it ends up being completely normal! And both of them learn not to worry about tomorrow, for tomorrow will take care of itself.

STUDY QUESTIONS:

1. Why is it so bad to worry? What does Jesus say about it?
2. Why did Jack give different advice to Sam and Erica?
3. Is there something you are worried about? Do you have any control over your situation? What should you do to stop worrying?

Episode #338 "Easy Money"

Theme: Gambling; responsibility.
Scripture reference: 1 Timothy 6:10
Written and directed by Marshal Younger
Production engineer: Dave Arnold
(Original air date: 11-18-95)

Butch and Sam both want to play on a neighborhood roller-hockey team. The only problem is, they don't have the money to buy the equipment necessary to play. So they decide to get jobs cleaning up at a local automotive garage—where they'll have to get up extremely early to get their work done before school. Butch decides that kind of work is for the birds. When he finds a friend who likes to make bets, Butch decides doing that is a better way to make easy money.

Meanwhile, Sam continues to work at the garage. He becomes so obsessed with working that he begins neglecting almost everything else—including his homework, his friends, and his family. In fact, Sam can't even stay awake in church. Butch wins enough bets to buy his equipment, but soon he starts losing and gets deeply in debt. Before long, Sam decides that he really needs to give up his job. Butch is forced to stop gambling when his bookie comes looking for payment and winds up taking Butch's new roller-hockey equipment. Both Sam and Butch learn the hard way that there is no such thing as easy money.

STUDY QUESTIONS:

1. Where did Sam go wrong?
2. Why did Butch feel he had to bet on the big game?
3. Is gambling wrong? Why or why not? What are the dangers of gambling?

Episode #339 "Do, for a Change"

Theme: Pride; humility; patience.
Scripture reference: Luke 18:9-14
Written by Marshal Younger
Directed by Phil Lollar
Production engineer: Mark Drury
(Original air date: 12-02-95)

Odyssey is full of new Christians. Among them are Zachary Sellers; his mother, Eileen; and, of course, Eugene. But like many new Christians, Zach seems to be having trouble adjusting to his new life. He still gets angry and flies off the handle at the smallest things. Eugene, on the other hand, seems to have just the opposite problem. He is so academic in his approach to Jesus that he doesn't experience any trials, tribulations, or conflicts in his life at all.

Things worsen for Zach. Finally, he gets to the point where he considers giving up Christianity altogether. But Jack and Connie counsel and comfort him. They tell him that the Christian life is not an event, but a *process*. Little by little, Zach will get better at controlling himself—in ways that he may not even notice.

Zach's real test of patience comes on a class trip. There, he is pestered by an annoying kid named Glenn. Zach tries to be patient, but he ends up yelling at Glenn and pushing him into a volcano display. Zach tells Jack that he simply can't be a Christian anymore. But Jack explains that Zach is trying too hard to be perfect. He needs to stop relying on himself and start relying on God's grace. Zach agrees to keep trying, and soon he sees results.

As for Eugene, Jack also confronts him. He tells Eugene that knowledge is meaningless if it doesn't penetrate your heart. Eugene understands and agrees to approach his faith with less intellect and more spirit.

STUDY QUESTIONS:

1. Why did Mrs. Sellers think that she and Zach should behave differently now that they're Christians? Was she right? Why or why not?
2. Zach said he didn't think he could be a Christian anymore. Do you think it's possible for someone to stop being a Christian? Explain your answer.
3. Why did Jack feel that Eugene needed to learn more about grace and humility?

1996

It was a year of upheaval—starting with several more departures from the *AIO* staff. At the end of January, Paul McCusker resigned his position as producer to work on other writing projects. Like Marshal Younger and myself, Paul didn't leave *AIO* completely—he continued freelancing and consulting for the program.

Then, in March, Chuck Bolte resigned his position as executive producer of *AIO* and vice president of Focus on the Family to become president of Child-Help USA, an organization that helps troubled children. His departure came as a surprise. Chuck had been the executive producer ever since he came to Focus in 1988—and he left his stamp on *Adventures in Odyssey* in innumerable ways.

After these departures, Dave Arnold became the show's new producer. Mark Drury filled Dave's position as production manager, and Focus on the Family Vice President Kurt Bruner and Book Publishing Director Al Janssen became executive producers of the show.

Several huge changes had occurred—and they were only the beginning. The program itself was also undergoing a transformation because, along with the staff departures, we also said good-bye to some of our most popular characters—the Barclays, who we moved from Odyssey to Pokenberry Falls.

But Whit was one character whose departure we hadn't entirely addressed. After Hal Smith's death, one of the questions we almost continually dealt with was if Whit would ever return to Odyssey. The Focus leadership wanted a new Whit, as did the video crew—after all, Whit is the centerpiece of the *AIO* franchise. We also received hundreds of letters from listeners, many of them almost begging us to bring Whit back.

But there was a slight problem—namely, finding a voice to replace Hal Smith's. Not that we hadn't tried. We had auditioned many, many fine actors. But we discovered that Hal's voice was pretty unique . . . or so we thought.

In the fall of 1995, Chuck got a call from a radio station manager in Seattle. This man had heard a commercial on a local general market station, featuring what he thought was Hal Smith's voice—which he knew was impossible, since Hal had died nearly two years earlier. The station manager contacted the station, which gave him the name of the ad agency that produced the commercial. The ad agency then put him in touch with the actor, whose name was Paul Herlinger. The manager passed this information on to Chuck, who gave it to Paul McCusker, who telephoned Paul Herlinger in Seattle.

Paul McCusker remembers that "from the first 'hello,' chills went up and down my spine." The voice he heard was the voice of Hal Smith.

The two talked, and Paul Herlinger agreed to do an audition with Chuck in Seattle. The tape Chuck brought back was stunning. It wasn't exact in every respect, but it was incredibly close to Hal—so close, in fact, it seemed to answer the question of whether or not we could bring back Whit.

We made immediate plans to introduce Paul Herlinger into an episode as Whit. But we didn't want to commit to bringing Whit back indefinitely, so first, we ran a show with Whit in the Middle East, "The Search for Whit." The performance was so strong, and the response was so positive, we decided to have Whit return for good.

The final two shows of 1996 were designed to take *AIO* back to where it was when it first started—with Whit at Whit's End and Odyssey back to normal.

Episodes #340 & 341

"Pokenberry Falls, R.F.D.," Parts One & Two

Theme: God's providence.
Scripture references: Romans 8:28; Philippians 1:6
Written by Paul McCusker
Directed by Phil Lollar
Production engineers: Mark Drury and Dave Arnold
(Original air dates: 1-06-96 & 1-13-96)

The Barclays are audio-taping a story for the newest member of their family, Stewart Reed. The story is about them—George, Mary, Donna, and Jimmy—and how they visited a little town called Pokenberry Falls.

It starts just after George graduates from seminary. He's ready to be a pastor. He has an immediate offer: senior pastor at Odyssey First Church. But George isn't sure that's the offer he should accept—especially when he gets a postcard from Pokenberry Falls that says simply, "Wish you were here." The postcard is followed up by a visit from a colorful character named Ellis Birch. He has come to ask George and the Barclays to consider moving to Pokenberry Falls so George can pastor their church. Ellis flies them there in a private plane owned by Pokenberry Falls's leading citizen, Barry Lionel. Once there, they see what the town has to offer—or at least what Ellis and his wife, Vivian, *want* them to see of the town.

It seems Pokenberry Falls is a town in decline—run down and going even further downhill. Its teenagers—as evidenced by Ellis's granddaughter, Amy—live in hopelessness and despair. They long for the day when they can leave the town. Meanwhile, they turn to alcohol, which helps them forget where they live. It's a town in need of a heart and a soul—a town that needs Jesus. After much thought and prayer, the Barclays decide that this town is where God wants them to be. They say good-bye to Odyssey and hello to Pokenberry Falls.

"Pokenberry Falls" was created to end the Barclay family's story line. We felt that they had grown beyond *Adventures in Odyssey.* Jimmy and Donna were both dealing with teen issues—which we really couldn't address on *AIO*—and George and Mary had progressed as well. The Barclays needed a new outlet for continued growth, so we moved them to Pokenberry Falls.

behind the scenes:

"The name 'Pokenberry Falls' came from Chuck. The name was going to be 'Bedford Falls,' the town in 'It's a Wonderful Life.' But Chuck couldn't remember that name, so in the story meeting he blurted out, 'Pokenberry Falls, or whatever the name is!' The name stuck.

"Also, these shows were narrated differently. Instead of being narrated from a person's point of view, the narration came from a microphone's perspective."

—Dave Arnold

STUDY QUESTIONS:

1. Why did George hesitate to take the pastor's job in Odyssey?
2. Why did Amy and the kids of Pokenberry Falls feel the need to drink alcohol?
3. George told Mr. Lionel that it wasn't up to either one of them whether George became their new pastor, but it was up to God. What did he mean? How would the Barclays know if God said "yes" to the job?

Episode #342

"Welcome Home, Mr. Blackgaard"

Theme: Forgiveness.
Scripture references: Matthew 6:14-15; 18:21-22
Written and directed by Phil Lollar
Production engineer: Dave Arnold
(Original air date: 1-20-96)

Things are rough for Edwin Blackgaard. Having recently fled Odyssey, Edwin has spent his time with Shakespeare, doing a two-man *Hamlet* in Hooterville and Pecanburg, where we catch up with him. After a particularly disastrous performance (in which the town's livestock actually outnumber the people in the audience), Edwin is visited backstage by Morton Dunkey, attorney at law. Morton informs Edwin that he has been named in Regis's will!

Edwin has inherited a piece of property in Odyssey—a store called the Electric Palace! At first, Edwin refuses his inheritance, but the stipulations of the will force him to accept. Shakespeare doesn't understand why Edwin is so hesitant to go back to Odyssey. Edwin explains that the townspeople will probably never forgive him for running away during his brother's takeover. Now he'll have to face the music.

They head back to Odyssey. Edwin braces himself for the trouble he is sure he will encounter. But he doesn't come across any problems. In fact, the people of the town—including Jack and Tom—welcome Edwin back with open arms. Edwin is so grateful, he feels he must do something for everyone. He decides to give away all of the merchandise in the Electric Palace!

After the store is cleaned out, Jack visits Edwin and convinces him that it isn't the people of Odyssey who need to forgive him—Edwin needs to forgive *himself.* Edwin realizes Jack is right. That night, Edwin gets proof that the town isn't holding a grude against him. Everyone throws him a party and brings back all the merchandise they took from the store. Edwin is again grateful—so much so, he decides to treat everyone to a one-man performance of *Hamlet.* Which is almost bad enough to make them take back their merchandise again.

STUDY QUESTIONS:

1. Why was Edwin so certain that the townspeople of Odyssey would hate him?
2. Why *didn't* the townspeople hate him?
3. Jack told Edwin he needed to forgive himself. What did Jack mean? Have you ever done anything for which you needed to forgive yourself?

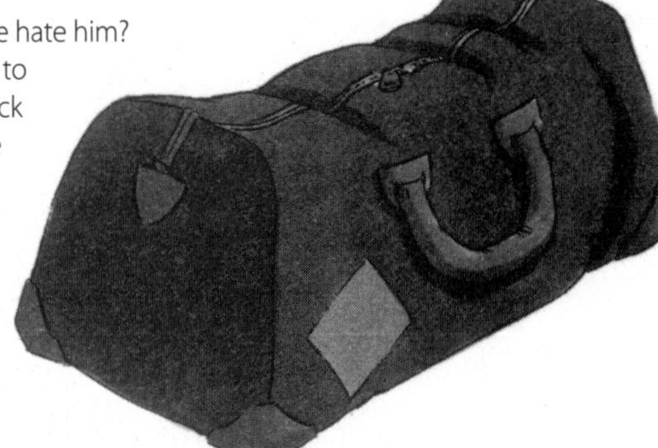

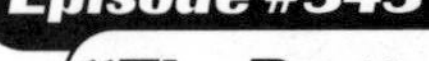

Episode #343

"The Pretty Good Samaritan"

Theme: Treating others with kindness.
Scripture reference: Luke 10:30-37
Written and directed by Marshal Younger
Production engineer: Mark Drury
(Original air date: 1-27-96)

Connie has assigned a project to her Sunday school class: They must come up with original presentations of Bible stories. Brenda decides to do a puppet show of the story of Jesus and the 10 lepers. Charles plans to use popsicle sticks to present the story of the good Samaritan. They start on their projects, not realizing that they'll both have opportunities to act out those stories in real life that week.

Charles's turn comes when he is assigned to sit next to Glenn in study hall. Glenn is terribly obnoxious. He nearly drives Charles crazy, and even gets Charles in trouble. But the next day, Charles is faced with a dilemma—Glenn has decided that Charles is the best friend he's made since moving to Odyssey. Glenn invites Charles to his birthday party that Thursday after school.

Later, on the bus, Charles tells Brenda to invite him somewhere—anywhere!—so he won't have to go to Glenn's party. Brenda does, and Charles is relieved—until that Friday when he discovers that *no one* showed up for Glenn's party. Charles feels terrible about it—so terrible, he relates himself to the bad guys in the good Samaritan story.

That Sunday, Brenda gives her presentation of Jesus and the 10 lepers. Then Connie provides the class with a treat—homemade ice cream. Everyone enjoys it, except Charles, who decides to make amends with Glenn. When Charles leaves, Brenda realizes that Connie isn't there either. She rushes out to Connie's car to thank her for the ice cream. Connie tells Brenda that she was the only kid to do so, just like in the story of the 10 lepers.

As for Charles and Glenn, they have a nice game of catch. Charles realizes that even though he wasn't exactly a good Samaritan, at least he was a *pretty* good Samaritan. And for now, that's good enough.

STUDY QUESTIONS:

1. How should Charles have handled Glenn in study hall?
2. Do you know anybody like Glenn? How do you treat that person?
3. Why is it important to be a "good Samaritan"? Can you think of other ways to be one?

Episode #344 "Letting Go"

Theme: Dealing with loss.
Scripture reference: Psalm 147:3
Written and directed by Marshal Younger
Production engineer: Mark Drury
(Original air date: 2-03-96)

It's not news that Zachary Sellers is having a hard time getting over his dad's death. But just when he seems to be coping, a new wrinkle develops: His mom, Eileen, begins seeing a new man. His name is Blake, and he works with Eileen. Blake has a daughter, Jill, who is Zach's age, and Blake's wife died of cancer two years ago. Zach tries to be pleasant to Blake, but he is still clinging to the memory of his father.

Blake tries to win Zach over and seems to make a little headway. Blake takes Zach to the mall in Connelsville. When Blake sees a Fast Pitch game, he tells Zach that he was a star pitcher in college. To prove it, Blake shows off his fast ball—wrenching his shoulder in the process. Zach cracks up and starts to warm up to Blake—until Blake suggests that the two of them go see a baseball game together sometime. Suddenly, Zach turns cold as ice again because his dad used to take him to baseball games.

Later, Zach talks with his mom about Blake. Zach wants to know if Eileen and Blake are going to get married. Eileen says she likes Blake, but it's too soon to talk about marriage. She also reassures Zach that just because she may like—and even love—another man doesn't mean she will ever stop loving Zach's father. She hasn't forgotten the past, she just doesn't want to live there anymore. Eventually, Zach realizes his mom is right—and he even begins to admire Blake when he drives them to Zach's dad's grave site, two hours away. Zach knows it's time to let go and move forward.

STUDY QUESTIONS:

1. Blake told Zach, "There are more people involved here than just you." What did he mean by that?
2. Is it wrong to try to keep memories of a deceased loved one fresh in your mind? Explain your answer. What's the difference between cherishing the past and living in it?
3. Read Psalm 147:3. Has God healed your broken heart? How?

Episode #345 "B-TV: Compassion"

Theme: Compassion.
Scripture reference: Galatians 5:14
Written and directed by Phil Lollar
Production engineer: Dave Arnold
(Original air date: 2-10-96)

It's another episode of "B-TV!" The topic this time is compassion. The sketches include the story of a poor shoemaker named Marty who wants to see Jesus; a game show called "Who's Got Compassion?" where contestants pit their knowledge against one another to answer the question, "Who's got compassion?"; and a blind man named Bartimaeus who was in dreadful need of some compassion—and received it from a savior named Jesus.

STUDY QUESTIONS:

1. What is compassion?
2. Why is it important that we have compassion for others?
3. Name some ways that Jesus has shown you compassion.

Episodes #346 & 347 "St. Paul: Voyage to Rome" & "St. Paul: An Appointment with Caesar"

Theme: Bible history: The life and ministry of St. Paul.
Scripture reference: Acts 24-28
Written and directed by Phil Lollar
Production engineers: Todd Busteed and Mark Drury
(Original air dates: 3-02-96 & 3-09-96)

It's Kid's Radio time again. This time, Jack is telling the story. The story he's chosen is about a young Roman boy named Antoninus; his father, a centurion named Julius; and the remarkable adventure they have when Julius is assigned to take a prisoner—the apostle Paul—to Rome to see Caesar himself!

the Adventures in ODYSSEY archives:

These episodes concluded the first two stories about the apostle Paul (see *AIO* #304 & 305). These two are Kid's Radio stories instead of Imagination Station adventures for practical purposes. The first two dealt with a short period in Paul's life—so they were best told in the here-and-now, Imagination Station type of format. But the last two parts encompassed several years of Paul's life. It would have been awkward to try and make those leaps seem logical in the Imagination Station. So we turned them into narrated stories.

STUDY QUESTIONS:

1. Why did Julius have such a problem with Paul and Luke telling Antoninus about Jesus?
2. How did Paul know that no one would be killed in the shipwreck?
3. Julius offered to let Paul go, but Paul refused. Why? If you had been Paul, would *you* have refused? Why wasn't Paul afraid of Nero?

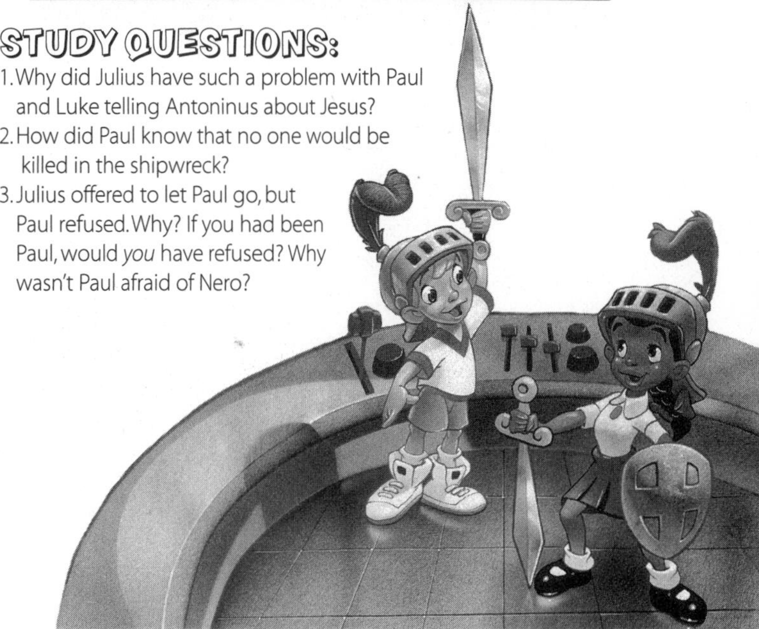

Episode #348

"With a Little Help from My Friends"

Theme: Peer pressure.
Scripture reference: Romans 12:2
Written and directed by Phil Lollar
Production engineer: Dave Arnold
(Original air date: 3-16-96)

At Whit's End one afternoon, Connie, Jason, June, and Sam talk about their recent run-ins with peer pressure. Sam starts off by telling about something that happened the previous day. On the way home from school, he was stopped by Courtney and several other kids who were on their way to the park to pick up trash. Courtney asked Sam to go with them. Sam refused, saying that his parents always want him to come straight home from school before he goes anywhere else. But Courtney and the others kept pleading and pressing until he finally gave in and went. Before he knew it, an *hour* had passed! Now he feels dopey for letting Courtney and the others talk him into disobeying his parents.

Sam's not the only one who's given in to peer pressure, though. The previous weekend, Connie went to the mall with her friends Blair and Carla. These snobby girls all but dragged Connie into a store so they could avoid talking with one of their geeky schoolmates, Larry Melwood. Moments later, Blair and Carla managed to pressure Connie into basically blurting out that Larry is the biggest geek in school—right as Larry walked up to them. He was hurt and ran off before Connie could apologize. Now, Connie feels just awful about it.

But much to everyone's surprise, June says she knows just how both Connie and Sam feel. The previous week, she succumbed to peer pressure herself. She had just gotten a promotion at work. June was attending her first executive meeting when the big boss asked for comments on one of his pet proposals. June felt she should say something about how bad the proposal was, but Harry, the co-worker who pushed for June's promotion, advised against saying anything. In fact, Harry put so much pressure on June that she went along with the crowd, just like Sam and Connie did.

Jason sympathizes with them. Then he tells Sam, Connie, and June what Whit used to say—"You plus Jesus are always a majority." Whit meant that the next time they're tempted to go with the crowd, they should pray. Jesus will help them stand up for what is right.

The following week, Connie, Sam, and June each have the opportunity to do that. Sam resists Courtney's coaxing to sneak off school grounds. Connie apologizes to Larry despite Blair and Carla's pressure for Connie not to do it. June diplomatically tells her boss what she really thinks of his proposal—and gets demoted for her frankness. Each one is still happy they did the right thing. And Connie, Sam, and June now know the best way to combat peer pressure.

Adventures in Odyssey the archives:

One of the most interesting things about this episode was the way Connie deflected the peer pressure *away* from herself and onto Blair.

STUDY QUESTIONS:

1. Why is it sometimes so hard to not give in to your friends?
2. Jason told everyone that Whit used to say, "You plus Jesus are always a majority." What does that mean?
3. What is positive peer pressure? Give an example of how you could use it.

Episode #349

"Blessings in Disguise"

Theme: Trust; friendship.
Scripture reference: Proverbs 12:19
Written by April Dammann and Marshal Younger
Directed by Marshal Younger
Production engineer: Mark Drury
(Original air date: 3-23-96)

Brenda is busy writing a letter to her pen pal, Thor-Douglas. Only, it's no ordinary letter. This note is filled with all sorts of colorful things like how busy Brenda is, how brilliant and accomplished she is, and what a bright and rosy future she has. In other words, it's a big exaggeration. Her friend Sean points this out to her. Brenda explains that Thor-Douglas is so accomplished, handsome, and athletic that she pales by comparison. She has to stretch the truth a little to keep him interested in her. Sean notices that stretching the truth includes Brenda inserting an air-brushed and doctored photo of herself in with the letter. Sean tells Brenda she is foolish and remarks that the amazing Thor-Douglas is probably just a regular guy.

Brenda soon decides that her letters shouldn't be an exaggeration, so she decides to become the person she writes about in her letters. Unfortunately, she discovers this is a lot easier said than done. After nearly killing herself on the tennis court, she decides enough is enough. Why keep up all the lies? She reasons that, after all, Thor-Douglas is just a pen pal. It's not like she'll ever meet him face to face.

Brenda heads over to Whit's End for a cool drink, and Sean meets her at the door. He tells her Thor-Douglas is inside! Brenda decides to rush to the nearest beauty parlor to have herself made up like the glamour photo. But before she can, the door to the beauty parlor opens. Thor-Douglas walks inside. He is putting up posters to publicize a tennis tournament he's playing in.

Brenda is humiliated. Thor-Douglas has seen her looking so plain! But as they talk, Thor-Douglas says he likes Brenda the way she is. He asks where he can put up more posters. Brenda tells him to go back to Whit's End, where he just was. But Thor-Douglas says he hasn't been to Whit's End. Something strange is going on, and a little while later at Whit's End, Brenda discovers what it is.

Thor-Douglas is really—twins! One is named Thor, and the other is named Douglas. In their letters, they combined themselves to impress Brenda—the same way Brenda stretched the truth about herself to impress them. Everyone apologizes and finds that it's much better to be who you are.

STUDY QUESTIONS:

1. Why did Brenda exaggerate the truth about herself?
2. Why is trust so important in a friendship?
3. Have you ever exaggerated the truth about yourself to anyone? What was the outcome?

Episode #350 "The Time of Our Lives"

Theme: Making the most of your time.
Scripture reference: Ephesians 5:15-17
Written by Marshal Younger
Directed by Paul McCusker
Production engineer: Mark Drury
(Original air date: 4-13-96)

Do not adjust your radio. We are in control. You are about to enter a dimension of sight, sound, and mind; a land of shadow and substance; and a lot of weirdness. This is the "Twilife Zone," hosted by Connie, or "Rodlyn Serly."

In this presentation, Connie introduces two young kids. The first is Kathy, who is popularly known as a "mallie." Kathy spends all her time in the mall, shopping. She loves to shop. She *lives* to shop—until she enters a very special store and emerges 10 years older! Yes, she has wasted 10 years of her life in the mall! Now her friends have all grown up, gotten married, and started careers. Her parents have moved away. Her brother has gone off to war—and Kathy has missed all of it!

The second story concerns a young man named Jeremy, who is addicted to television. He loves TV. He *lives* for TV—until two policemen break down his door one afternoon, threatening to arrest him. According to the police, television viewing has been outlawed. They take away Jeremy's TV, but he finds an old black-and-white portable in the garage and takes it on the run! Now he is a fugitive! He'll do anything to watch TV, little realizing that he is wasting his life.

The story jumps to years later. Now age 30, Kathy and Jeremy are at a Time Wasters Anonymous meeting, sharing their testimonies. Rodlyn Surly, our "Twilife Zone" announcer, is in charge of the meeting. She tells them to go back, confront their pasts, and make up for the time they've lost in their lives. Kathy and Jeremy realize that the only way to do that is to go to the mall. There, they encounter their younger selves—begging them to change their time-wasting ways and to make the most of their time. The ending is not entirely happy—but the lesson of this episode is for us, the listeners. We learn not to waste our time on frivolous activities that sap us of our futures.

STUDY QUESTIONS:

1. Why is it wrong to waste time?
2. Are watching TV and going to the mall really bad in themselves? What makes those activities bad?
3. Do you do something that wastes time? What is it? What's the best way to overcome your habit?

Episode #351 "What Are You Gonna Do with Your Life?"

Theme: God's plans for our lives; career plans.
Scripture reference: Isaiah 42:16
Written and directed by Paul McCusker
Production engineer: Dave Arnold
(Original air date: 4-20-96)

Connie is facing a dilemma. She doesn't know what she wants to do with her life, and it seems that everyone around her has his or her life completely planned. She asks Jason about how he and Whit decided what they wanted to do. Jason tells her that it was a combination of interests and opportunity. That doesn't help Connie much, so Jason suggests that she explore and examine her life to find out what she likes to do. Careers have often been made that way.

Connie starts on her quest. First, she tries working at the perfume counter for a local department store. That job ends when she starts disagreeing with customers' choices. Then, she tries being Harlow Doyle's secretary, which is a disaster. After that, Eugene gives her a homemade aptitude/personality test, which reveals that Connie has no personality and is best suited for a career gluing corrugating to cardboard boxes. Finally, Connie believes that working at Whit's End should be her career—but when she tries to take on more administrative duties, she fails miserably at that, too.

Jason gives her the rest of the day off to contemplate her future. Connie visits Tom Riley. He tells her that, despite what her career guidance counselors and school friends are telling her, she shouldn't be in such a rush to make a lifetime decision in just a few days. She needs to give it time, play around with different options for a bit, and most of all, pray. If she does those things and keeps her eyes and ears open, God will help her work out everything.

the *Adventures in* ODYSSEY archives:

"What Are You Gonna Do with Your Life?" was an attempt to steer Connie in a new, more "grown-up" direction—which we hoped to explore in future episodes.

STUDY QUESTIONS:

1. Why did Connie think she had to make such a quick decision about her career goals?
2. Do you think God really cares about what kind of a career you have? Why or why not?
3. Do you know what you want to do with your life? If so, what is it?

Episode #352 "Memories of Jerry"

Theme: Doing what's right; courage.
Scripture reference: Psalm 73:23-26
Written and directed by Phil Lollar
Production engineer: Mark Drury
(Original air date: 4-27-96)

Connie is looking for a book in Whit's office one afternoon. Suddenly, the bookshelf slides open, and Jason steps out of the hidden computer room behind it. They both are startled to see each other, and Connie accidentally knocks several books off the shelf. As they replace the fallen books, Jason comes across a novel called the *Terminus Factor.* He thinks it odd that his dad kept such a book—Whit always said he hated it.

Jason flips through the paperback. An old postcard addressed to Jason falls out of it! It's from his older brother, Jerry, who sent it from Vietnam. This is the first time Jason has seen the card. He reads it, and it brings back a flood of memories for him—which he relays to Connie via flashback . . . .

Jerry is an instantly likable guy and wonderful big brother. He helps Jason with his high-jump performance, then the two of them go to the university to get a soda. There, they run into Leonard Plateman, aka "Plato," a hard-core hippie. Plato confronts Jerry about his volunteering to go to Vietnam and tries to talk him out of it. But Jerry says there is nothing to discuss. Plato leaves to attend an anti-war rally, and Jerry and Jason go to the ROTC building to drop off some papers. But when they exit, they see that the rally has turned into a riot. Jerry and Jason escape unharmed, but Jason is bothered by the rioters and by the fact that Jerry is going to 'Nam in general.

Jerry comforts him, and the two of them go up to the Whittaker family cabin on Lake Michigan for a long weekend. They have a great time. On the night before they're supposed to come back, Plato shows up at the door! He's received his draft notice—and he's decided to run away to Canada. Jerry and Plato argue over the morality of Plato's decision, but Plato has made up his mind. He's leaving, and he wants Jerry to go with him.

That night, Jason awakens from a fitful sleep to hear Jerry praying and wrestling with his convictions. The next morning as Jerry sees Plato off across the lake, Jason runs up and begs Jerry to go with him. Jason doesn't care if it's wrong—he just wants Jerry to stay alive! Jerry calms and comforts Jason. Jerry tells his brother that he wouldn't really be living if he were to betray his commitments to his country, his family, and to God. He must honor those commitments, all the way to the end, just like Jesus did. Jason isn't convinced and starts crying. Jerry again comforts him, telling him there is no need to fear—God is with him.

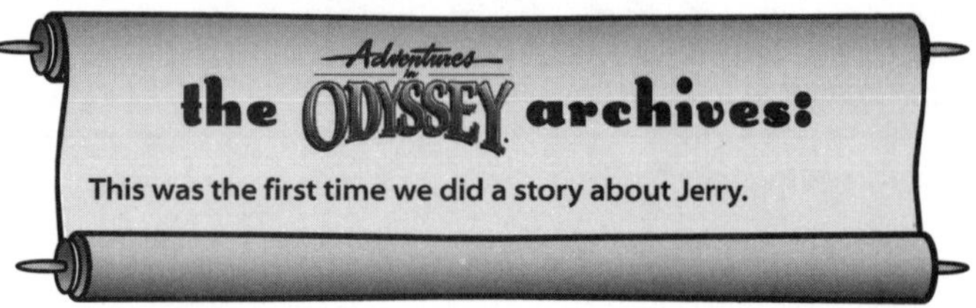

This was the first time we did a story about Jerry.

behind the scenes:

"T.J. Lowther, who played young Jason, is an accomplished child actor who has worked with major stars like Katherine Hepburn, Charlton Heston, Clint Eastwood, and Kevin Costner. T.J. is also a big *AIO* fan. He actually contacted us to talk about the program. When we asked him if he would be willing to work with us, he said, '*Would* I? *Yeah*!'

"A lot of what we learn about Jason in this episode comes from my own life. I was nicknamed 'The Judge' when I was small because I didn't smile until I was two years old. I broke a high-jump record in junior high. I've never really liked camping outside if there's a cabin readily available. My uncle was a languages specialist, just like Jerry. I was also Jason's age when the Vietnam War was raging—and got caught up in a riot on a university campus. You know the old saying, 'Write what you know.'"

—Phil Lollar

STUDY QUESTIONS:

1. Plato said that he was going to go "change the world." What did he mean?
2. Why didn't Plato want to go to Vietnam? Why did Jerry feel he had to go to Vietnam? Why didn't Jason want Jerry to fight in the war? Between the three of them, who was right? Explain your answer.
3. Is it wrong to fight in a war? Why or why not?

Episode #353 "A Question About Tasha"

Theme: The importance of Christian marriage.
Scripture reference: 2 Corinthians 6:14-18
Recommended maturity level: 10 and up
Written and directed by Phil Lollar
Production engineer: Dave Arnold
(Original air date: 5-04-96)

PARENTAL WARNING: This is an emotional story about the importance of Christian marriage. It is sensitively told, but may be too mature for younger listeners.

Connie is elated. Jason and Tasha are on their way to Whit's End from the airport. The time has come for them to get married! The happy couple arrives, everyone extends warm and heartfelt greetings, and then Jason drops a bombshell. Since Tasha has to be back at work to train her replacement, and they have only a week in town, they've decided to get married tomorrow!

Needless to say, this tightens the schedule. Everyone rushes off into a flurry of activity. Jason goes to shop for a gift for Tasha and to scout out jewelry stores. Connie, who in her search for a career is learning to be a wedding coordinator, helps Tasha pick out her dress and flowers.

Then Connie assists Tasha in making arrangements for the ceremony and reception. Connie starts to call up Odyssey First Church, but Tasha stops her. She explains that they want to have the ceremony and reception right there at Whit's End. Connie agrees, then says she still has to find out if the pastor is available. But Tasha again stops her. She and Jason have decided to use a justice of the peace instead of a pastor. This surprises Connie until Tasha asks her to be the maid of honor. Connie is flattered and flabbergasted, and she immediately agrees.

Later, while Jason and Tasha are ring shopping, Connie tries to get in touch with the justice of the peace. Jack wants to know why, and Connie tells him it's for Jason and Tasha's wedding. Jack finds this strange. When Jason returns later, Jack asks him point blank if Tasha is a Christian. Jason is taken aback—he says he really doesn't know, but he assumes she is. Jack tells Jason that he should find out for sure before they get married. But Jason feels that everything will work itself out after they get married.

This leads to a heated discussion that ends up with Jack refusing to participate in the wedding, and Jason taking Tasha and storming out of Whit's End. Jack grieves for them, and while he is doing so, Connie bursts into the office with more upsetting news: Jason and Tasha have run off to elope!

Jack is heartbroken. Connie comforts him and says maybe Tasha will come to Jesus after they get married. Jack says maybe she will—and maybe she won't. His wife didn't. Connie is stunned. Jack's wife wasn't a Christian? Jack says no, and he tells Connie about his wife's last moments. Just before she died, Jack tried one last time to get her to accept Christ. But because a stroke had robbed her of speech and movement, Jack won't know if she's saved until he goes to heaven. He doesn't want Jason to have to go through that pain and uncertainty. Jack says all they can do is pray.

Outside the justice of the peace's house, Jason opens up about why he was so upset with Jack. Tasha says she doesn't know what she believes about Jesus—and she doesn't want to make any decisions now, either. The justice appears at the car window, wondering if they're coming inside. Jason sighs, and then he says no. They're not ready to be married yet. Jason takes Tasha to her hotel, then he returns to Whit's End to apologize to Jack. Thankfully, Jack always encourages Jason to do the right thing.

the *Adventures in* ODYSSEY archives:

Jack's story about his wife's death was inspired by a similar story Shirley Dobson told about her father.

behind the scenes:

"We did this episode because we realized that Jason couldn't marry Tasha—we hadn't yet dealt with her lack of faith. In order to give a consistent message to our listeners, we knew that Jason and Tasha would have to break up—but we knew it wouldn't be easy."

—Paul McCusker

STUDY QUESTIONS:

1. Why were Jason and Tasha so anxious to get married?
2. Why did Jack counsel Jason to wait?
3. Why is it important for Christians to marry Christians? What does the Bible say about Christian marriage?

Episode #354 "Blind Justice"

Theme: Justice; peer pressure.
Scripture references: Isaiah 59; Micah 6:8
Written by Marshal Younger and Paul McCusker
Directed by Paul McCusker
Production engineer: Todd Busteed
(Original air date: 5-11-96)

Bernard and Eugene learn a lesson in civic duty as they are called to sit on the same jury. They—and the 10 other jurors—must decide the guilt or innocence of a young man named Donald who is accused of breaking-and-entering and burglary. Donald has confessed to the breaking-and-entering, but does not admit to the burglary.

In the jury room, the vote is 11-to-1 to convict him of both crimes. The lone holdout? Eugene! He simply isn't convinced of Donald's guilt in the burglary and demands that they review all the facts until they can be sure. The jury argues and argues. Slowly but surely, Eugene convinces nearly everyone that Donald is innocent. Only a hateful juror, Victor, holds out. Under pressure, Victor reveals that he has a personal vendetta against Donald. A mistrial is declared, and justice triumphs in Odyssey after all.

STUDY QUESTIONS:

1. Why was Eugene so adamant against voting Donald guilty?
2. Was Victor right or wrong in his feelings about Donald?
3. Why is justice so important?

Episodes #355–357
"The Search for Whit," Parts One, Two & Three

Theme: Knowing what you believe; the joy of reunion.
Scripture reference: James 1:16-18
Written and directed by Paul McCusker
Production engineers: Dave Arnold and Mark Drury
(Original air dates: 5-18-96, 5-25-96, 6-01-96)

Jason is behind the counter at Whit's End, trying to fix the phone answering machine when Eugene enters. Suddenly, the machine rewinds, sputters, and plays a muddled recording of . . . Whit! He has called to tell Jason of a significant find he's made at the archaeological site where he's working. He's brought the find back to Chicago for tests. He's also sending Jason a package for safekeeping. Whit says he doesn't have time to explain further—he has to rush off somewhere.

Eugene retrieves the mail, and they find the package from Whit. It's a microcassette containing Whit's diary of his finds at the dig. But at the end of the cassette is the huge surprise: Whit reveals excitedly that he may have found "the Q." He goes on to say that he needs to tighten security around the site. Suddenly, the recording turns into what sounds like gibberish.

The cassette is a definite mystery, and Jason and Eugene first try to figure out what "the Q" is. After pondering it for a while, Eugene postulates that it may actually be "the Q Parchment"—which many scholars believe was a source document for the gospels of Matthew, Mark, and Luke. In fact, it may actually be a *fifth* gospel! If Whit has found it, it is, indeed, the find of the century.

Jason feels they need to go to Chicago to unravel the rest of the mystery. Once there, the mystery grows even more mysterious. The professor Whit worked with at the university in Chicago, Steven Charles, is missing—and so is Whit! The lab where they were working has been ransacked. Jason feels it's time to bring in some experts, and he calls Tasha. Ironically enough, she and the Agency are also looking for Whit, but she won't tell Jason anything she knows. Further, Tasha tells him to back off the investigation. Jason is annoyed and tries a couple of other contacts in the government for information. He learns that Whit has flown to Tel Aviv, where he has disappeared. The Agency now thinks that Whit may be a double agent. Jason decides that the only way to solve this mystery is to go to the Middle East. He invites Eugene along.

On the flight to Tel Aviv, Eugene reveals that the garbled message from Whit actually says, "How I do is nothing great." It makes no sense to either Jason or Eugene, but they're certain it's another clue.

Tired and jet-lagged, Jason and Eugene are met at the airport by Whit's associate, Alfred Brownlee, who says they are being watched. He carefully explains that the stakes have risen even higher. The parchment seems to indicate that Jesus Christ died on the cross, but *wasn't* resurrected! It claims that the disciples had bribed the Roman soliders and stolen the body. Worse, this document details exactly *where* His body was buried! This possibility throws Eugene into a crisis of his newfound faith.

Brownlee takes Eugene and Jason Whittaker to Aharoni—the site of Whit's archeological dig—to look for clues to Whit's disappearance. Jason is amused to see that his father still has a cross-stitch sampler his sister had made for him. On it is an acronym which spells out "Trust."

Their visit is interrupted by Brownlee's assistant, Benjamin. Benjamin turns on them and kidnaps Jason at gunpoint. Jason is taken to an abandoned warehouse where Benjamin grills him about the meaning of the message, "How I do is nothing great." Benjamin and his cohorts imply that they have Whit held hostage and will hurt him if Jason doesn't cooperate. But Jason realizes the meaning of the message and concludes that these villains don't have his father. He marches out of the warehouse. Benjamin is furious, but an unknown voice says to him over an intercom, "Be patient."

Back at their hotel, Jason explains that the message was an acronym for "Hiding." Whit was telling Jason that he'd gone into hiding. Tasha arrives and asks Jason on behalf of the Agency to back off his search for Whit. Jason is angry to discover that the Agency lied to Whit about the work they'd contracted with him to do in the Middle East. The Q Parchment he was supposed to find was a fake—part of a government ploy to catch those who illegally export valuable archeological treasures. But Tasha thinks that Whit may have actually discovered the *real thing*—now his life is in danger from two terrorist organizations called the Symposium and First Things!

Later, in the hotel elevator, an old man demands money from Eugene. It is Whit in disguise! Whit explains that he found a first-century parchment which appears to be a gospel. It has directions to a tomb that supposedly holds the bones of Christ. Eugene is alarmed, but Whit cautions him not to base his faith on archaeological finds—especially since they don't know if the parchment is genuine. He confides his plans to search for the tomb and arranges for Eugene and Jason to meet him at 3:00 that afternoon. Whit also warns Eugene that their hotel room is probably bugged by someone. After Whit leaves the elevator, Eugene is joined by the long-lost Professor Steven Charles, who is also looking for Whit. Eugene is suspicious of Charles and tells him nothing.

Later, Eugene fills Jason in on his talk with Whit and his encounter with Professor Charles. Alfred Brownlee suddenly shows up and questions Jason and Eugene about Whit's whereabouts. Brownlee also acts suspiciously. After he leaves (without getting any information), Jason and Eugene decide that it's best not to trust anyone.

Jason and Eugene meet Whit in the hotel stairwell and arrange to meet him later at the Egged bus terminal on Joppa Street. They leave, not realizing they've been watched by a cleaning woman, who reports their whereabouts to someone via walkie-talkie.

Before Jason can meet Whit, he bumps into Tasha in the hotel lobby. They argue about her job and the fact that it doesn't bother her to lie to Jason or Whit. Jason indicates that their relationship is in danger over this issue.

Later, Jason, Eugene, and Whit meet at the bus terminal and get on a bus for the Kidron Wadi (valley), the site of the dig where Whit found the parchment. They are followed by someone in a helicopter, but escape into a hidden underground site. It is filled with a series of tombs. Whit explains that the site was formerly a commune of the Sadducees, who hated Jesus and wanted Him dead. The parchment Whit found was supposedly written by Judas Iscariot. It claims that the disciples had bribed the Romans so they could take Jesus' body and hide it, allowing them to claim He had risen from the dead. They then buried His body somewhere in the Kidron Valley. The body was supposedly placed in a tomb marked with a sign of suffering.

They eventually find the tomb and start the laborious process of breaking through the wall. Just as they're about to get through, Professor Charles, Benjamin, then Alfred Brownlee appear and insist on being the first to see what's inside. But Eugene is more worried that they may actually find bones. Whit reminds Eugene that his faith must be based on the Bible, which is true—not on what they may find in this tomb. Inside, they find an ancient coffin and open it. The coffin is filled not with bones, but containers encasing yet *more* parchments. Charles, Benjamin, and Brownlee try to take possession of the parchments, but Tasha suddenly appears (having tracked them with a homing device she'd put on Jason's belt when she saw him in the lobby) and forces them to surrender.

Later, after Charles, Benjamin, and Brownlee are in custody, we learn that Charles and Brownlee were the leaders of The Symposium and First Things. They weren't part of a terrorist group, but are smugglers.

While waiting for government scientists to determine the contents of the tomb parchments, Jason and Tasha decide to call off their engagement. They realize that Tasha loves her job and would be unhappy giving it up to live in Odyssey.

Whit calls them in and explains the truth about all the parchments. He says one of the parchments was a letter from the High Priest Ananias to Gesius Flores, the Roman governor in the '60s. Ananias offered to create false accounts of Jesus' death to appease the Romans. Documents were created and were intended to be distributed to counter the Christians' claims that Jesus had risen from the dead. But later, the Romans virtually destroyed Israel in A.D. 66. The parchments were buried and almost forgotten. Eugene is relieved, though Whit reminds him that his faith should not have been so easily swayed.

At the story's end, Eugene decides to stay in the Middle East for a couple of weeks to visit with Whit. Jason flies back to Odyssey. When asked if he'll ever return to Odyssey, Whit smiles and says, "You just never know."

the Adventures in Odyssey archives:

Paul Herlinger's performance (as Whit) in "The Search for Whit" was so strong, we decided to bring Whit back to Odyssey. But we knew we couldn't simply have Whit show up and say, "I'm back"—for the producers of Odyssey, it can never be that easy. So the next collection of episodes explored several existing story lines and introduced a few new ones as Whit made his return.

STUDY QUESTIONS:

1. Why were people so willing to commit violence to find Whit and get to the Q Parchment?
2. Why was Eugene so concerned about what the parchment would say? Why was Eugene so afraid they might actually find the bones of Jesus?
3. Upon what should we base our faith?

Episode #358 "The Secret Weapon"

Theme: Leadership; believing in the right thing.
Scripture reference: John 8:32
Written and directed by Phil Lollar
Production engineer: Todd Busteed
(Original air date: 9-21-96)

It's baseball season again, and Sam is less than enthusiastic about it. He doesn't think he's a very good player, and he doesn't think the Coyotes are a very good team. And basically, he's right. But Jack has a feeling that this season may be a little different—the Coyotes have a new coach: Connie Kendall! Connie gives the team a brief pep talk, and they head out to the field. Jack questions Connie about her wanting to be a coach—does she really think she can handle it? Connie confidently tells Jack to just watch and see.

The Coyotes's practices go well for everyone—except Sam. He just can't seem to do anything right, especially hit. So he's decided to leave the team. But Connie comes up with a plan to instill some confidence in him. She asks him to meet her at Whit's End. When he does, she gives him a special bat—a slugger that once belonged to Lefty Grizzell, a Major League home run hitter. Connie convinces Sam that the bat is a secret weapon with great power and accuracy—and has what seems like a mind of its own. To prove it, she has Sam hit a few pitches outside. He ends up whacking them nearly out of the park!

Sam has a renewed interest in the game and is now ready to play. But Connie tells him that he must practice with the bat every day if he really wants to learn to control the bat. Sam agrees and runs off to the batting cage.

Connie Kendall Named Coach

The Odyssey League of Public Sports announced today that the new Coach for the Coyotes will be Connie Kendall, a high-school student and employee of Whit's End.

"This will surprise some of you," Chuck Ahern, head of the League, said. "But we want to demonstrate how diverse and tolerant we are of placing young ladies into traditionally male-dominated positions."

Connie Kendall said she was honored to be chosen by the League. "I'll do my best to bring victory to our team and our town. Most of all, I hope we'll learn teammanship and how to be courteous players, whether we win or lose."

When challenged by Bart Rathbone, a spectator at the announcement, that Connie wasn't qualified to coach because she knew nothing about baseball, Kendall replied that "ignorance certainly hasn't gotten in your way, Bart."

Kendall will take over the reigns of the team immediately. Former Coach Tom Riley had previously resigned due to his responsibilities as Mayor.

Odyssey League of Public Sports

Jack admires Connie's solution to the problem of Sam quitting but is concerned that she has given Sam a false security. Connie tells Jack that she knows what she's doing—and it seems she's proven right when the Coyotes win not only their first game, but also their entire season! They've made the playoffs, and it's all because of Sam's batting, using the secret weapon. But on the day of the big game, the secret weapon is stolen! Sam panics and rushes to Whit's End, looking for Connie. Jack tells him that Connie is already at the game. Sam is frantic. Jack calms him down long enough for him to explain what's wrong, then they both head to the game.

At the game, the coach for the opposing team stops Connie and hands her the secret weapon. One of the other players took it. Connie takes the bat to Sam—but tells him that he can't use it. The bat is just a piece of wood. It doesn't have any special powers or abilities. Sam was able to hit those home runs because he practiced. Connie affirms that the Coyotes need Sam—not the bat.

Sam regains his confidence and strides to the plate. Two strikes fly by . . . but then Sam hits a home run that wins the game! The Coyotes are Little League champions.

STUDY QUESTIONS:

1. Why was Sam unhappy about playing for the Coyotes?
2. Was it a good idea for Connie to give Sam a "secret weapon"? Why or why not?
3. Have you ever put too much faith in something? If so, what was it? Was it *really* lucky?

Episode #359 "The Merchant of Odyssey"

Theme: Mercy.
Scripture reference: James 2:13
Written and directed by Phil Lollar
Production engineer: Ramsey Drexler
(Original air date: 9-28-96)

Bart Rathbone is finally off the hook for the crimes he committed during the Blackgaard scandal. A judge has decided to show him some mercy by reducing his sentence to time served and allowing him to work again.

Immediately, Bart rushes out to try and get the Electric Palace away from Edwin Blackgaard. He offers Edwin a down payment of $5,000 and the balance in monthly installments. But Edwin turns down his proposal. He won't sell because he's become fond of his inheritance and, for personal reasons, he *can't* sell.

Bart is disappointed—until he comes up with a plan. He picks up the phone and calls the IRS to rat on Edwin about the inheritance tax Edwin has due on the Electric Palace. An IRS field agent visits Edwin. The agent informs Edwin that he owes a grand total of $10,000, payable in two installments of $5,000 each. Edwin doesn't have $5,000, and the only person he knows who does is Bart Rathbone!

Edwin foolishly borrows the money—certain that he'll be able to pay off the loan with the proceeds from his new show, *The*

Merchant of Venice. But Bart causes Edwin to have a little accident, trying to make sure the play won't open! According to their deal, if Edwin doesn't repay his debt, Bart will take over both the Electric Palace and the Harlequin Theatre.

Edwin thinks he's doomed. But Jack comes up with a plan to make Bart change his mind. Jack brings Bart to a rehearsal, where Bart is persuaded to play a role in a terrifying scene. In the scene, Bart must repay a debt or lose a pound of flesh! The trick works. Bart is scared silly by the play. He reluctantly agrees to give Edwin more time to repay the loan. Unfortunately for Bart, the IRS agent has learned that he didn't pay taxes on the $5,000 he loaned Edwin. Now *Bart* has an appointment with the Internal Revenue Service.

the *Adventures in* ODYSSEY archives:

This was our attempt to adapt William Shakespeare's *The Merchant of Venice* to *AIO*. Originally, Whit supposedly wrote a series of books, which adapted Shakespeare's plays into modern stories that people could more easily understand. This episode loosely followed that concept.

By the way, this episode featured a new production engineer—Ramsey Drexler—a pseudonym we got from Mark Drury's mother, the former Mrs. Ramsey, and Dave Arnold's mother, the former Mrs. Drexler.

STUDY QUESTIONS:

1. Why did Bart want the Electric Palace back so much?
2. Bart told Edwin a contract is a contract. Was he right? Should he have shown mercy to Edwin? Why or why not?
3. Describe a time in which you have shown someone mercy or when someone else has been merciful to you.

Episodes #360 & 361

"Three Funerals and a Wedding," Parts One & Two

Theme: Bible history: Ruth; loyalty.
Scripture reference: the book of Ruth
Written and directed by Phil Lollar
Production engineers: Mark Drury and Todd Busteed
(Original air dates: 10-05-96 & 10-12-96)

Courtney and Jenny haven't been attending Connie's Bible study lately, and Connie wants to know why. The girls tell her that the Bible seems to be full of exciting, action-filled adventures about men—but hardly anything about women. So Connie narrates one of the greatest and most romantic stories ever written: She tells the biblical story of a young maiden named Ruth, and how her loyalty to her mother-in-law and her love for the Lord God made her the great-grandmother of King David and a part of the lineage of the king of kings, Jesus.

STUDY QUESTIONS:

1. Why did Ruth insist on staying with Naomi?
2. Have you ever felt like the Bible doesn't relate to you? What should you do when you feel that way?
3. Name some other great women of the Bible.

Episodes #362 & 363

"The Right Choice," Parts One & Two

Theme: God's plans for our lives; waiting on the Lord.
Scripture reference: Psalm 27
Written and directed by Paul McCusker
Production engineers: Mark Drury and Todd Busteed
(Original air dates: 10-19-96 & 10-26-96)

Whit and Eugene are finally coming home from the Middle East. Jason meets them in Chicago. Whit has to make a presentation on his time spent in Israel to the board of directors at Universal Press, and Jason is a member of that board. The board also has an offer for Whit—to go on a worldwide missions tour!

The layover in Chicago gives Eugene the opportunity to spend some time with Katrina. But when he tries calling her, no one answers the phone at her dorm room. Eugene thinks that's weird, so he tries her roommate's workplace, the University Bookstore. Katrina's roommate, Janice, tells Eugene that Katrina has gone on a trip to the Lake Shore Lodge. She went with Brandon, whom Katrina admitted to be dating when she was last with Eugene (see "Love Is in the Air," *AIO* #335 & 336). Eugene actually drops the phone and nearly faints when he hears Janice's next revelation: Katrina and Brandon went to the Lake Shore Lodge to get engaged!

Nov. 12.

Dear Chris,
In the episode The Right Choice. I was sooooooooooooooooooooooooooooooodisappointed that Catrina is not going to marry Eugene. I think in the episodes to come you should have Eugene meet a girl like me. Smart, little wild, and likes to tell jokes. I also think Mr. Witicer should get married again. Love,
Kayla

P.S. I Love Adventers in Oddesy.
I never miss a week!

No one can believe that Katrina would take such a big step without telling Eugene. Whit suggests that Eugene call up the lodge to see if Katrina is there. Eugene does and is hit with another bombshell: Not only is Katrina there, she is part of the Shanks wedding party! Katrina is getting married to Brandon! Eugene doesn't know what to do. Jason tells Eugene to rent a car, drive up to Lake Shore Lodge, and fight for her—show her that he's not willing to let her go so easily! Eugene rushes off to follow Jason's advice.

At the Lake Shore Lodge, Eugene quickly deduces where the Shanks wedding party is and bursts in on them—just in time to hear the happy couple say "I do." But Eugene has burst in on Mr. and Mrs. Shanks renewing their vows. Eugene humiliates himself and ends up apologizing to Katrina. Eugene wants to talk with Katrina about their relationship, but Katrina wants to wait until they are both more rational. She turns and leaves.

Eugene becomes even more irrational. He acts crazy, logging into the Lodge's computer, and almost gets arrested. Katrina is so upset by this, she asks Brandon to take her home to Chicago. On the way home, Brandon and Katrina talk, and their affection grows. Brandon screws up his courage—and asks Katrina to marry him.

Eugene races back to Chicago to find Katrina. He asks Armitage, Katrina's father, for permission to marry his daughter. Armitage says yes—but he has also given Brandon permission. Eugene races to Katrina's college. There, she explains that she hasn't said yes to Brandon's proposal. She needs time to think about it—because she's in love with Eugene. Hearing this finally brings Eugene to his senses. He realizes he has been totally self-absorbed—not thinking about what's best for Katrina. He asks her to marry him.

Katrina ends up saying no. But everything is okay. Her and Eugene's hopes for a future relationship are in God's hands.

behind the scenes:

"The simple fact about Katrina and Eugene was that we couldn't decide whether or not they should get married. When 'Love Is in the Air' was written, we thought they might—it made sense because Eugene had become a Christian. But then, after the comical episode 'The Right Choice,' we decided they shouldn't get married—which took us back to square one. We decided that for the time being, it was best for Eugene to mature a little—spiritually and in other ways."

—Paul McCusker

"The Lounge Lizard scene had to be cut for the broadcast, but we decided to leave it in for the album version. But after the recording, we realized that the songs we were going to use were copyrighted—we'd have to pay lots of money to use them. So Jim Adams came in and redid the Lounge Lizard, who was originally played by Steve Bridges. I then blended Jim's new stuff with the existing Katrina/Eugene material."

—Mark Drury

STUDY QUESTIONS:

1. Should Katrina have been angry with Eugene? Explain.
2. Do you think Katrina overreacted? Why or why not?
3. Why was it important for Brandon and Eugene to get Mr. Shanks's permission to ask Katrina to marry them?

Episode #364 "Home, Sweet Home"

Theme: The joy of reunion; the importance of home.
Scripture reference: Psalm 84:3
Written and directed by Phil Lollar
Production engineer: Mark Drury
(Original air date: 11-02-96)

Connie is excited—Whit is finally coming home! She and the rest of the town have planned a huge homecoming bash for him. Jack urges her to go meet Whit at the airport—but Jack has decided to stay behind. Connie rushes out excitedly, and Jack says quietly, "Good-bye, Connie. It's been nice knowing you."

Meanwhile, the plane carrying Whit, Jason, and Eugene touches down in Odyssey. They are all glad to be home and looking forward to rest and relaxation, peace and quiet. But as soon as Whit steps into the terminal, he is met with cheers and applause! Bernard and several others have gathered to welcome Whit home. Whit is grateful, but really doesn't want this kind of celebration. Bernard tells him to relax and enjoy it, then starts to make a speech.

Before he can, though, he is interrupted by Bart Rathbone, who provided the decorations, the balloons for the event, and a loudspeaker, which announced the delay of the flight. Then Harlow Doyle also interrupts. He lets it slip that there is a special motorcade waiting to take Whit to city hall. There, Mayor Tom Riley and the whole town are waiting with a big celebration for Whit! Before Whit can protest, they whisk him away, leaving Eugene and Jason behind with the bags. Jason collects his and Whit's, but Eugene's are on the delayed flight.

Jason leaves, and Connie runs up, late as usual. She's just missed Whit. Connie offers to drop Eugene off at the college on her way downtown. They leave.

Meanwhile, Whit arrives to an incredible celebration. Tom greets him warmly. He gives Whit the key to the city and proclaims the following day "John Avery Whittaker Day!" Then Bart Rathbone and the Electric Palace provide a fireworks spectacle—only, something goes wrong, and all of the explosives go off at the same time. Everything gets chaotic, and Whit, Tom, and Bernard leave for a celebration at Whit's End.

Of course, Connie arrives just as the fireworks burn themselves out. She can't believe she's missed Whit again—but when she tries to take off for Whit's End, she blows out a tire and has no spare! She desperately hitches a ride on the back of Harlow Doyle's moped. But his police scanner picks up a crime in progress. Instead of going to Whit's End, they take off for the crime scene. Connie hops off the moped and runs to Whit's End. There, she discovers that Whit was so tired, Tom took him home! She races there, but Tom tells her that Whit has already gone to bed. Connie can see him in the morning. This is the final straw. Connie breaks down crying. Tom starts to take her home, when she hears a familiar voice behind her. She turns . . . and there stands Whit. She rushes into his arms, and they embrace warmly. Whit is finally home.

the Adventures in ODYSSEY archives:

Connie's race to catch Whit as he comes back into town was parallel to the scene in "Gone . . ." (*AIO* #280), where Eugene raced to catch Whit before he left Odyssey. The two scenes sort of "bookend" everything together.

behind the scenes:

"The crowd scene in this show was especially difficult to produce. I pulled together a group from the Focus on the Family Correspondence Department and a group of visitors who were touring the Focus facilities. Those folks especially enjoyed being the whistlers.

"Also, to get the sound of Connie's tires squealing, I went into the Focus parking lot, set up a microphone on a boom, and spun out in my new van. Unfortunately, a police officer saw me and pulled me over. But after he found out what I was doing, both of us had a good laugh, and I saved myself from a ticket."

—Mark Drury

STUDY QUESTIONS:

1. Why was Connie so anxious to see Whit?
2. Have you ever participated in a homecoming before?
3. How will going to heaven be like a homecoming?

Episode #365 "Clara"

Theme: Forgiveness; friendship.
Scripture reference: Proverbs 17:17
Recommended maturity level:9 and up
Written and directed by Phil Lollar
Production engineer: Dave Arnold
(Original air date: 11-09-96)

PARENTAL WARNING: This is an emotional show about love, loss, and adoption. It may be too mature for younger listeners.

Jack is at the Odyssey airport, picking up his one-way ticket to Chicago. Eugene walks up, looking for his flight-delayed bags. Eugene wants to know what Jack is doing there. The clerk behind the counter says that Jack is leaving Odyssey. Eugene asks where Jack is going and why he is leaving, but Jack doesn't want to talk about it. He tries to walk away.

Fortunately, Eugene isn't easily dissuaded. He follows Jack, pleading with him to explain what is happening. Eugene remarks that Jack should at least stay until he talks with Whit! But Whit is the last person Jack wants to talk to. The last time they were together, Whit said he never wanted to see Jack again. Eugene can't believe it, and Jack tells his tale.

It happened right after Jenny, Whit's wife, died. Jack takes Whit to Nebraska, where he is running an orphanage. Whit doesn't really want to be there—until he meets Clara, a beautiful, hazel-eyed, red-haired, angel-faced six-year-old. The two of them immediately hit it off and soon become inseparable. Jack is pleased to see Whit smiling and laughing again and is also pleased that Clara is finally opening up to someone.

Whit falls in love with Clara. He is so taken with her, in fact, that he wants to adopt her. But Jack hasn't told Whit an important piece of information about the little redhead: She's already slated for adoption by another couple—and *was* even before Whit got there. Whit is extremely angry with Jack over this. Clara doesn't want to go with the couple. This causes an emotional and tearful separation for Whit and Clara. She leaves with her new parents . . . and Whit says he never wants to see Jack again.

Back to the present. Jack says he's always intended to contact Whit and try to seek his forgiveness, but something always got in the way. Now, he's lost his nerve. He's just about to leave when Whit calls his name. Jason had told Whit that Jack was at the airport. Whit produces a letter from Clara. In it, she thanks both Whit and Jack for finding her some wonderful parents and giving her a great start in life. Whit also apologizes for what he said to Jack and asks him to stay. There is a pause, and Jack agrees to remain in Odyssey. The two old friends hug, united once again.

STUDY QUESTIONS:

1. Do you think what Jack did was wrong? Do you think Whit was wrong to be angry? Explain your answers.
2. Clara thanked Whit and Jack for giving her a great start in life. What did she mean by that?
3. Why is forgiveness so important?

Episode #366 "Solitary Refinement"

Theme: The importance of solitude.
Scripture reference: Philippians 4:6-7
Written by Paul McCusker and Dave Arnold
Directed by Phil Lollar
Production engineer: Todd Busteed
(Original air date: 11-16-96)

After his last incident with Katrina, Eugene realizes he is spiritually immature. He decides to do something about it. So Eugene considers joining a monastery! Bernard and Jason can't believe it. Eugene, a *monk*? But Eugene is serious. He even visits the Oak Hills Monastery & Retreat Center to see if God is calling him to a monastic life.

At the monastery, Eugene realizes that he hasn't completely worked out his problems with Katrina, and he even talks to her in a dream. In the dream, Katrina assures Eugene that he is making positive strides in his spiritual maturity. Eugene is comforted by that.

Meanwhile, Whit has been rushing around so much lately, he hasn't had time to consider whether he will accept the Universal Press Board's offer to go on the world missions tour. He, too, decides to spend some time at the monastery to contemplate his decision.

behind the scenes:

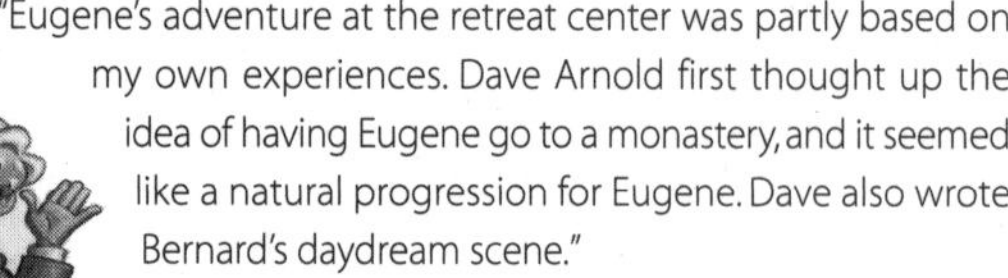

"Eugene's adventure at the retreat center was partly based on my own experiences. Dave Arnold first thought up the idea of having Eugene go to a monastery, and it seemed like a natural progression for Eugene. Dave also wrote Bernard's daydream scene."

—Paul McCusker

STUDY QUESTIONS:

1. Why did Eugene want to join a monastery?
2. Katrina spoke to Eugene in a dream. Do you think people can really communicate that way? If not, then who do you think was actually speaking in the dream? Explain your answers.
3. Why are solitude and silence important?

Episode #367 "The Decision"

Theme: Seeking God's will for our lives.
Scripture reference: Proverbs 3:5-6
Written and directed by Phil Lollar
Production engineer: Dave Arnold
(Original air date: 11-23-96)

In her search for a career, Connie has started a new program on Kid's Radio called "Candid Conversations with Connie." Her guest on this particular edition is John Avery Whittaker. He is describing some of his adventures in the Middle East when a caller asks if it's true that he is going on another world missions tour. Connie scoffs at the idea, but Whit admits that it's a possibility—the board of directors at Universal Press have extended the offer.

This upsets Connie—especially when she learns that nearly everyone in town knew about this but her! Whit apologizes, and Eugene walks up and announces that a visitor is there for John Avery—Joanne Woodston, one of the UPF board members. Whit goes to talk with her. Connie tells Eugene they need to figure out how to keep Whit in Odyssey. Eugene disagrees with Connie—he prefers to leave things in God's hands. But Connie feels that Odyssey needs Whit, he just doesn't *know* they need him. She sets out to make him see just how valuable he really is.

Meanwhile, Joanne tells Whit she needs an answer soon because a situation has arisen at one of the missions in South America that requires immediate attention. Whit promises to give her an answer quickly. Just then, Jack walks in—and when he meets Joanne, there is obviously a mutual attraction between them.

Hoping to influence Whit before he makes his decision, Connie puts her plans into action, trying to show Whit that he is needed. To further complicate things, Jason tells Whit that he is thinking of going on the missions tour because he misses the excitement of life in the Agency. Next, Eugene expresses desire to go on the tour as a means of spiritual growth. Then Jack enters and tells Whit he has to go on the tour, or the Board will send Joanne! Everyone starts talking at once. Whit calms them down and tells everyone to go downstairs. He'll reveal his decision then.

Downstairs, Whit says that everyone has great reasons why they should go, but no one has mentioned the most important reason anyone should become a missionary—God's calling. No one can honestly say that God has called them to South America—and neither can Whit. So he's not going either. Instead, he's called Dan Isidro, a missionary friend already in the region, to handle the problem. Whit says, "It's good to be home again."

STUDY QUESTIONS:

1. Why did Whit have so much trouble trying to decide whether or not to go on the trip?
2. Why is it important to seek God's leading before making decisions?
3. How can you seek God's will when making an important decision?

Episode #368 "The Other Woman"

Theme: The danger of spreading rumors; dealing with the mentally ill.
Scripture references: Proverbs 16:28; 1 Peter 3:12
Written by Paul McCusker
Directed by Phil Lollar
Production engineer: Todd Busteed
(Original air date: 11-30-96)

News flash! Tom Riley stuns Odyssey by insinuating that he may not seek re-election! He tells Dale Jacobs that he really would like to get back to the peace and quiet of his farm, which creates a media firestorm. Unfortunately, Bart Rathbone is listening to the television report on Tom, and it gives Bart the idea that he should run for mayor again. Bart's wife, Doris, and Rodney think Bart's nuts. They say no one would ever vote for Bart. But Bart still thinks he has a real chance—as long as Tom doesn't run again. So Bart tells Doris and Rodney it's their job to make *sure* Tom doesn't run again.

That opportunity presents itself a few days later when Doris and Rodney see Tom driving and decide to follow him. They all end up at a place called Hillingdale Haven—where Doris and Rodney take pictures of Tom sitting and holding hands with a blonde woman! Rodney is certain that Tom's wife isn't blonde and deduces that they have a major scandal on their hands.

Doris and Rodney take the pictures back to Bart, who gives them to a new rag sheet tabloid newspaper called the *Odyssey Tattler*. The editor of the *Tattler* surmises that the pictures were taken at Hillingdale Haven Hospital—a mental health facility! He readily prints the pictures, setting off a media frenzy.

But it ends up that the story is much less scandalous than it appears. The woman is Tom's wife, Agnes. She has manic depression and must frequently stay at Hillingdale Haven. Tom calls a press conference to tell everyone this—and to add that he officially won't seek re-election as mayor.

Later, at Whit's End, Whit and Eugene discuss Tom's decision. Eugene wonders why Tom never mentioned Agnes's problem to the church so they could pray for her. Whit says Tom did at first, but when Agnes didn't get better, he stopped. He says many Christians have trouble with unanswered prayer. And the only thing to do is to keep praying for people like Tom and Agnes.

behind the scenes:

"'The Other Woman' was written to answer the long-standing question—whatever happened to Tom's wife? She appeared in 'Thank You, God!' (*AIO* #49) and then seemed to disappear without a trace. Considering the tragedies both Tom and Agnes experienced, we thought the best explanation was that she suffered from some form of manic depression."

—Paul McCusker

STUDY QUESTIONS:

1. Why did Tom keep his wife's illness quiet? Should he have? Why or why not?
2. Why do you think God heals some people and doesn't heal others?
3. Whit told Eugene that "Christians who can't cope are poor advertising." What did he mean by that?

Episode #369 "It's a Wrap!"

Theme: God's role in everyday life.
Scripture references: Psalm 118:24; Proverbs 27:1
Written by Paul McCusker
Directed by Phil Lollar
Production engineer: Todd Busteed
(Original air date: 12-07-96)

We're back on Kid's Radio again. This time, Lucy Cunningham-Schultz takes the microphone to Whit's End for a day to follow John Avery Whittaker as he adjusts to life *off* the mission field. Lucy and Glenn, who is also reporting, catch up with Whit at breakfast, where he eats and reads his Bible. From there, he goes to Whit's End, where Connie and Eugene are waiting for him—and getting into one of their famous "discussions." After helping to resolve things, Whit talks to Lucy about Connie and Eugene. He describes how Connie has matured and how Eugene's faith has changed him for the better.

Next, we follow Whit as he helps Sam Johnson solve a problem, as he works on the Imagination Station, then deals with Harlow Doyle, and finally takes Connie to the doctor when she cuts her finger and needs stitches. Whit wraps things up by telling Lucy how he thanks God for letting him share with the families who come to visit at Whit's End, for his enriching friends, and for another day of living in God's grace. As for what the next day will be like? Whit says it will probably be pretty typical—meaning unpredictable. Which is just the way he likes it.

behind the scenes:

"'It's a Wrap!' was the last show recorded before the team took a much-needed break to rethink and regroup for the future. It also contained innovations, recording- and production-wise. The whole style of this show was different from anything we had yet done. Instead of trying to record things by having everyone right 'on mic' all the time, we had them walk on and off mic, jostle the mic, and make mistakes on purpose. Oh, and Dave Arnold was stellar as the grouchy owner of Hal's diner."

—**Mark Drury**

STUDY QUESTIONS:

1. Whit reads his Bible at breakfast. When do you read your Bible each day?
2. Why is it important to have a regular quiet time? What kinds of things can you do in your quiet time?
3. Whit said that he thanks God for allowing him to live another day in God's grace. What does that mean?

Episodes #370 & 371 "Christmas Around the World," Parts One & Two

Theme: Christmas.
Scripture reference: Luke 2
Written and directed by Paul McCusker
Production engineer: Dave Arnold and Mark Drury
Music by John Campbell
Music producer: Tim Jaquette
(Original air dates: 12-14-96 & 12-21-96)

Erica and Sam need to do a report for school on how other cultures celebrate Christmas. So Whit sends them, along with Tom and Eugene, on an adventure in the Imagination Station to experience Christmas around the world. The surprise? Other countries celebrate our Lord's birth basically the same way we do.

the Adventures in ODYSSEY archives:

"Christmas Around the World" was actually recorded in 1994—and it wasn't originally a *program*, but our annual Christmas special for that year. It was produced in "split-track" so kids could sing along.

STUDY QUESTIONS:

1. What is the true meaning of Christmas?
2. What is the best way to celebrate it?
3. Why do we traditionally give gifts on Christmas? Think of some other Christmas traditions. Do you know how they originated?

The Expanding World of *Adventures in Odyssey*— Books and Videos Bring More Adventure

FROM THE MIND'S EYE TO THE SMALL SCREEN

Adventures in Odyssey on Video

In early 1989, talks began on how *Adventures in Odyssey* could be expanded to video. Steve Stiles, executive producer of the *AIO* videos, remembers, "Focus on the Family saw the marketplace open up with the *McGee & Me* videos. That was our first series, and the terrific response opened doors for what followed. It made perfect sense to follow the success of the *McGee* videos with a series based on *Adventures in Odyssey*, which already had thousands and thousands of fans."

The next decision was whether the videos should be live action or animation. Budget constraints and casting problems pointed toward animation. Production began in late 1989, and in 1990, Focus premiered the first in a series of fully-animated videos based on the *AIO* radio series.

The videos feature Whit, Eugene, Whit's End, and several new characters in a vivid cartoon style reminiscent of classic Disney. The *Adventures in Odyssey* videos are only loosely based on the audio program, which allows for the many adaptations needed to accommodate an animated genre. For that reason, some of the characters from the audio series were left out or changed and, in many respects, geared to a younger audience. The first video, "The Knight Travellers," introduces the Taylor family—Dad; Mom; their son, Dylan; and his younger sister, Jesse.

Episode #1
"The Knight Travellers"

Theme: Materialism vs. lasting treasure.
Scripture reference: Matthew 6:19–21
Written by Ken C. Johnson
Directed by Mike Joens and Ken C. Johnson

When John Avery Whittaker's prize invention, the Imagination Station, is stolen from Whit's End, his dog, Sherman, is the only witness. Whit is baffled until he finds a business card that accidentally fell to the ground at the scene of the crime. It belongs to the notorious and greedy used car dealer Fred J. Faustus.

Meanwhile, in another part of town, the Taylor household is in an uproar because Dylan and his sister, Jesse, are fighting over a gift catalog. Their parents calm them down and, after a talk with his dad, Dylan is sent outside to think things over.

Alongside the river, Dylan spies Faustus's thugs, Niles and Edgar, who are about to do away with Sherman because he knows too much about the previous night's robbery. Dylan rescues the dog and winds up following him back to Whit's End. There, he meets Whit and wrangles his way along on a visit to Faustus's used car lot.

By the time they get there, Faustus has transformed the Imagination Station into the "Manipulation Station," which allows him to capitalize on peoples' greed by offering cheap thrills that further enslave them to their need for more. Whit's attempt to intervene is cut short when Faustus traps Whit and forces him into the Manipulation Station so Faustus can send Whit back to the Dark Ages. But Dylan complicates matters when he knocks Faustus, Sherman, and himself into the machine, and they all travel back in time to the site of a medieval joust.

Faustus, now a menacing knight on a black horse, challenges Whit to a joust. But before he can get outfitted, Whit is knocked out by a wayward lance. Faustus seizes the opportunity to tempt Dylan with "all the things the world has to offer" if he'll turn his back on Whit and go with Faustus. Dylan, however, remembers that his father once told him to consider only things that are truly important: "friends, family, and the gifts of God." He refuses Faustus's offer and must now joust with him. It's a David-and-Goliath-like battle with the same results . . . sort of. Faustus is defeated, present day is restored, Dylan has learned a valuable lesson about lasting treasure . . . and he gets to keep the dog, too.

the Adventures in ODYSSEY archives:

Tony Jay, who plays the evil Fred J. Faustus, was also the voice of Shere Khan in Disney's *The Jungle Book* and Frollo in *The Hunchback of Notre Dame.*

STUDY QUESTIONS:

1. Why were Dylan and Jesse fighting over the magazine?
2. Why did Fred Faustus want the Imagination Station?
3. What is the greatest treasure of all?

Episode #2
"A Flight to the Finish"

Theme: Loving your neighbor.
Scripture reference: Matthew 19:19
Written by Don Goodman and Ken C. Johnson
Directed by Mike Joens and Ken C. Johnson

Spring has arrived, and the Tri-County Junior Grand Prix is coming to Odyssey. Normally, Dylan would be thrilled by that, but a fiery new neighbor named Holly has just moved in next door, and she is giving Dylan grief. Holly has a conniving cat named Jasper, Dylan has a dog named Sherman—and the two don't mix.

Dylan believes that the Grand Prix will take his mind off his troubles. Hoping Whit will sponsor him in the race, Dylan finds Whit at Whit's End, testing a new compound that makes things spin—a "Rotation Compound." The trouble is, it's unstable and tends to lose control. Whit needs to test it more. Whit agrees to sponsor Dylan and offers to help him with his car, but Dylan decides he wants to design and build it himself.

Later, at the junkyard, Dylan runs into Holly and is humiliated when a bucket gets jammed on his head. She laughs at him, announcing that she is also entering the race. Dylan decides that this is war! Just wait until he's standing in the victor's box, holding the trophy!

But the race trials are a disaster for Dylan—his rickety soapbox springs apart like a bad watch, and Holly wins. Back at the drawing board, Dylan seeks Whit's advice and help to rebuild his car.

Things are looking up for Dylan until Holly's cat, Jasper, picks on Sherman—provoking him to attack Jasper. In the melee, the animals knock over a bystander, and Holly threatens to turn in the "vicious" Sherman to the authorities. So they make a deal: If Dylan wins the race, he can keep Sherman —but if Dylan loses, Sherman must go. Only after the bet is in place does Holly tell Dylan that she's a former Grand Prix champion.

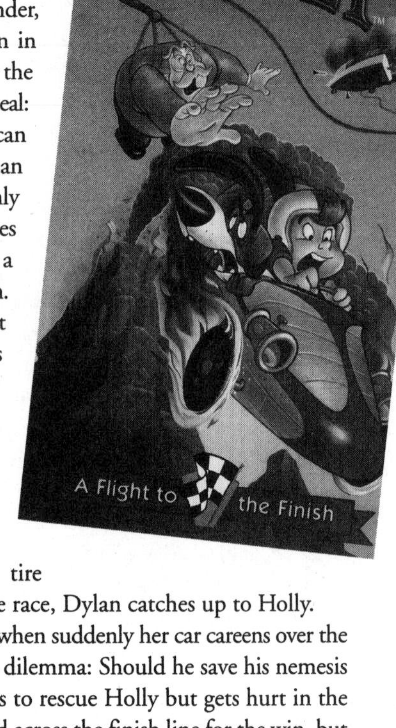

Race day arrives and, at the gun's signal, Holly takes a commanding lead. At first, Dylan's car won't even budge, but then it takes off like a rocket! He mistakenly painted Whit's Rotation Compound on his tires, thinking it was tire black. Halfway through the race, Dylan catches up to Holly. He is about to overtake her when suddenly her car careens over the edge. Dylan is faced with a dilemma: Should he save his nemesis or win the race? He decides to rescue Holly but gets hurt in the process. She manages to skid across the finish line for the win, but it's a hollow victory as she watches Dylan leave by ambulance.

Later, Holly pays a visit to the hospital and awards the trophy to Dylan. Holly acknowledges Dylan's sacrifice and extends her hand in friendship. They've both learned a valuable lesson about looking beyond their own concerns and caring for others.

the Adventures in ODYSSEY archives:

The old Focus on the Family radio theme can be heard coming from a radio in the Taylors' kitchen.

STUDY QUESTIONS:

1. Why was Dylan so upset with Holly? How should they have treated each other?
2. What does it mean to love your neighbor as yourself?
3. It is wrong to be competitive? When does it go too far?

Episode #3
"A Fine Feathered Frenzy"

Theme: Responsibility and the consequences of actions.
Scripture reference: Luke 16:10-12
Written by Ken C. Johnson
Directed by Mike Joens and Ken C. Johnson

Dylan's curiosity gets the best of him one day when he fiddles with a remote control device on a lawnmower that Whit had told him to leave alone. That starts the trouble! The lawnmower destroys neighborhood sprinkler heads and hedges—and the immaculate, prize-winning gardens of the harsh and persnickety Mrs. Evelyn Harcourt.

Dylan's honest attempt to patch up her flower bed falls short, and Mrs. Harcourt accuses Whit of tutoring vandalism. But they reach a settlement, and Dylan is to report in the morning for instructions on taking care of her house while she is gone for a day. That night, he has a nightmare that suggests things may not go smoothly at Mrs. Harcourt's.

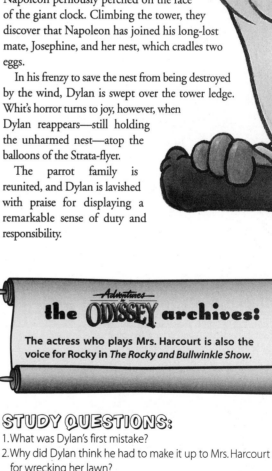

The next morning, Mrs. Harcourt's list of things for Dylan to do is exhaustive, but she says that nothing is as important as the safety of her beloved parrot, Napoleon. She tells Dylan that there used to be two parrots, but one vanished. She will return at 6:00 P.M. sharp and expects to find everything in order.

Before long, Napoleon escapes from his cage, and just when Dylan is about to capture the bird, Whit opens the front door—allowing Napoleon to fly into the wild blue yonder. Aided by Eugene and the Strata-flyer, Whit and Dylan mount a desperate effort to find Napoleon and return him to his cage before Mrs. Harcourt comes home.

Their search leads them to the clock tower at the center of town. In the midst of a windstorm, they spot Napoleon perilously perched on the face of the giant clock. Climbing the tower, they discover that Napoleon has joined his long-lost mate, Josephine, and her nest, which cradles two eggs.

In his frenzy to save the nest from being destroyed by the wind, Dylan is swept over the tower ledge. Whit's horror turns to joy, however, when Dylan reappears—still holding the unharmed nest—atop the balloons of the Strata-flyer.

The parrot family is reunited, and Dylan is lavished with praise for displaying a remarkable sense of duty and responsibility.

The actress who plays Mrs. Harcourt is also the voice for Rocky in *The Rocky and Bullwinkle Show*.

STUDY QUESTIONS:

1. What was Dylan's first mistake?
2. Why did Dylan think he had to make it up to Mrs. Harcourt for wrecking her lawn?
3. Should Dylan have gone after Napoleon the way he did? What would you have done?

Episode #4
"Shadow of a Doubt"

Theme: Faithfulness to friends and God.
Scripture reference: Proverbs 18:24
Written and directed by Ken C. Johnson and Mike Joens

The peaceful town of Odyssey is shocked by a string of sensational burglaries. Everyone is baffled until a surveillance camera from the Watchdog Security Company captures the cat burglar red-handed and the police haul him off to jail. Who would have thought that *Mr. Whittaker* was capable of such offenses?

Dylan is dumbfounded and doesn't know what to believe. But his father gently encourages him to stand by his friend no matter what everyone else thinks. When Dylan questions Eugene about the mystery, he concludes that someone must be impersonating Whit in order to frame him with the crimes. Dylan decides that he must track down the real burglar and exonerate his friend.

Video camera in tow, Dylan searches the local park in vain, taping everyone who passes by. Finally, he stumbles onto a character named Phineas, who says he used to work for Scotland Yard and might be able to help Dylan solve the crime.

Meanwhile, at the courthouse, the case against Whit looks grim. The jury is entranced by the slick district attorney's courtroom theatrics: "John Avery Whittaker is guilty, guilty, GUILTY!"

Dylan enters Phineas's apartment, intending to look at mug shots of likely impostors, only to discover that Phineas is the impostor who has been using a mask to pose as Whit and leaving clues that will incriminate him. Dylan wrestles the mask away from Phineas and heads for the courthouse, with Phineas in hot pursuit. The chase takes them through back alleys and down into the drainage system beneath Odyssey. Dylan and Sherman resurface right in front of the courthouse and manage to clobber Phineas with the manhole cover.

They dash into the courtroom just as the verdict is being read and present the mask as proof of Whit's innocence. Whit's integrity is saved thanks to the faithfulness of his friend.

STUDY QUESTIONS:

1. Why did Dylan believe Whit was innocent? Have you ever stood by a friend who was accused of doing something wrong but who you knew was innocent?
2. Should Dylan have trusted the man in the park? Why or why not?
3. Why is justice so important? According to the Bible, what is greater than justice?

Episode #5
"Star Quest"

Theme: Jealousy vs. teamwork.
Scripture reference: 1 Corinthians 12:12–31
Written by Rob McFarlane and David N. Weiss
Directed by Robert Vernon and Steve Stiles

When Dylan and his friend, Sal, learn that their favorite science fiction TV show is coming to Odyssey to film, they can hardly contain themselves. Captain Quirk! Mr. Spot! The Starship Synergize! What's more, Mr. Whittaker has been commissioned to build a robot for the episode.

Racing to Whit's End, Dylan and Sal find Whit and Eugene tinkering with a bunch of hardware and computer parts. Eugene is "testing" a video game cartridge called "Kong." As Whit explains how the robot works, the famous and flamboyant *Star Quest* director, Ian McIan, sweeps into the room to check on the progress of his robot. Whit unveils his huge creation and tells Dylan that he's built the robot with Dylan in mind as the pilot and Sal as the engineer. But McIan reverses the roles and chooses Sal to pilot, leaving Dylan with the unglamorous task of monitoring oil pressure in the engineering bay.

Whit takes Dylan aside and assures him that he'll be performing a crucial role and that all parts of a body are important. Dylan only shrugs.

When filming begins, Sal gets all the credit and glory for the robot's actions. Reporters want to interview him, and kids ask for his autograph, while no one seems to notice Dylan at all. So when Sal gets trapped in his dressing room one day, and McIan calls "Action!" Dylan secretly decides to show the world that he can pilot the robot, too. But things go haywire when he accidentally inserts the "Kong" video game cartridge into the robot's computer, and the robot becomes a huge gorilla with an attitude.

Pandemonium breaks out as the robot goes on a rampage, swooping Sal up in its giant paw and marching through town. Dylan is frantic to stop it and save his pal. Whit and Eugene give chase in the Strata-flyer. Finally, at the top of a radio tower, and in a desperate, last-ditch attempt to stop the mechanical monster, Dylan and Sal descend into the belly of the beast and together destroy its mechanism. Just as the robot begins to fall, they leap across to the hovering Strata-flyer and soar homeward.

Safe back in their tree house, Dylan and Sal renew their friendship, having gained a new appreciation for how much more can be accomplished by avoiding jealousy and working together.

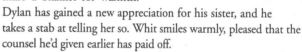

the *Adventures in* ODYSSEY archives:

This episode contains a parody of the TV show *Star Trek*.

STUDY QUESTIONS:

1. Dylan and Sal were big fans of *Star Quest*. Is it wrong to be a big fan of a television program? When might it become wrong?
2. Why was Sal so worried that he would make a mistake? Have you ever felt that way? What did you do about it?
3. Why did Dylan become jealous of Sal? Did Dylan have a good reason? Why does God dislike jealousy so much?

Episode #6
"Once Upon an Avalanche"

Theme: Kindness/brotherly love.
Scripture reference: John 15:13
Written by Paul E. McCusker
Directed by Robert Vernon and Steve Stiles

The local chapter of the Odyssey Junior Woodscouts is holding its winter retreat at Camp What-a-Nut in the mountains. Whit and Eugene are in charge of the contingent of boy Woodscouts, which includes a new friend of Dylan's named Carter.

When Jesse strays over from the girls' camp and begins to impose on Dylan's fun, Dylan decides to give her a little scare on the toboggan. The result is a near disaster as the toboggan goes out of control and deposits Dylan, Jesse, and Carter into Avalanche Canyon and out of reach of immediate rescue. Eugene and Sherman begin looking for them, while Whit organizes an official search party.

Dylan, Jesse, and Carter end up spending the night in the canyon, surviving a small avalanche, encountering a bear, and learning to appreciate each other. Meanwhile, Eugene's rescue attempts turn into misadventure as he valiantly stumbles his way down the mountain. Whit and the rescuers are stalled at the bottom of the canyon because of the unstable avalanche conditions. Eugene, covered with snow and ice from his escapades, produces a mighty sneeze that sets off a gigantic avalanche.

The kids' death-defying escape down the mountain via an old logging flume deposits them at the foot of the rescue party and a much-relieved Whit. The happy reunion is complete when Eugene and Sherman arrive a few moments later encased in a giant rolling snowball.

Back at camp that night, Carter recounts the harrowing adventure for the whole group, as Dylan and Jesse share a blanket for warmth. Dylan has gained a new appreciation for his sister, and he takes a stab at telling her so. Whit smiles warmly, pleased that the counsel he'd given earlier has paid off.

the *Adventures in* ODYSSEY archives:

To replicate the sound of walking in snow, a sound effects man recorded the noise his fists made when he shoved them into a deep tray of baking soda.

STUDY QUESTIONS:

1. Why was everyone so scared of Hatchet Jack?
2. Why did Dylan want to get back at Jesse?
3. How should brothers and sisters behave toward each other?

Episode #7

"Electric Christmas"

Theme: The true meaning of Christmas—Jesus' birth.
Scripture references: John 3:16; Luke 12:15; Ephesians 2:8
Written by Steve Stiles
Directed by Robert Vernon and Steve Stiles

Dylan and Jesse shop for Christmas presents in downtown Odyssey. As Dylan complains about the greed and commercialism that is taking over Christmas, he brushes off a small boy who is selling something to raise money for camp. Jesse shows Dylan the cordless razor she wants to buy for their dad, but Dylan is struck by the sight of an XR-7 limited edition speedster bicycle.

Later, at Whit's End, Dylan draws the name of Matt Williams in the Angel Tree drawing and agrees to buy him a bike helmet for Christmas. He tries to convince his dad to give him the XR-7 for Christmas, but Mr. Taylor tells him it is too expensive for their budget.

When Dylan learns that the XR-7 is the grand prize of the Christmas yard decorating contest, he decides to enter. As Dylan and Jesse set up a simple manger scene, Doug, the neighborhood bully sets up an extravaganza next door. Intimidated by Doug, Dylan spruces up his display with lights and gadgets, creating a display to rival Doug's two T-Rexes and Elvis snow sculptures. Dylan is so preoccupied by the contest that he lets Whit down by forgetting his Angel Tree gift.

The rivalry intensifies as Dylan and Doug sabotage each other's displays. The contest comes to a crashing halt when a cat inadvertently destroys both displays—just as the judges arrive—leaving only the simple manger scene they started with. As Jesse sings "Silent Night," Dylan is reminded of the real meaning of Christmas. The grand prize—the XR-7—is awarded to Jesse, who unselfishly gives it to Dylan. When he admits he doesn't deserve it, Jesse agrees, but reminds him that God gave us the gift of His Son, even though we didn't deserve it. Dylan suddenly remembers his Angel Tree obligation and bikes over to Matt's house. He realizes that Matt is the little boy he pushed aside earlier and, having learned his lesson, gives him not only the bike helmet he asked for, but the XR-7 as well.

the Adventures in ODYSSEY archives:

This is the only video to feature characters from the series performing songs: Eugene singing "Seasonal Felicitations" and Jesse singing "Silent Night."

STUDY QUESTIONS:

1. Why was it wrong for Dylan to want the bike so much?
2. How should Dylan have treated Doug?
3. Why did Jesse win the contest?

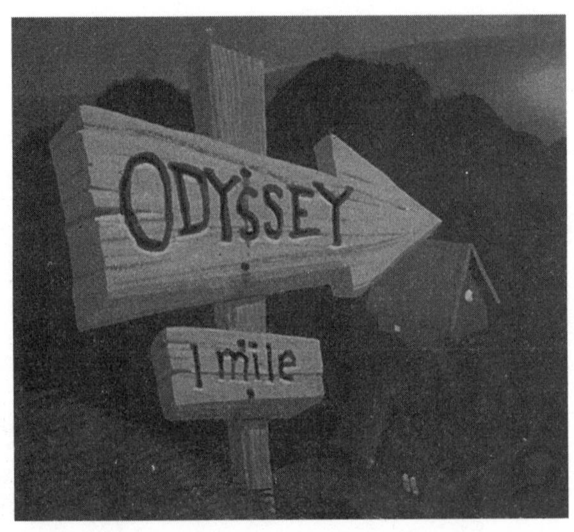

Episode #8
"Go West, Young Man"

Theme: Personal integrity; keeping your word.
Scripture references: Acts 24:16; Matthew 5:37
Written by Robert Vernon and Paul McCusker
Directed by Robert Vernon and Steve Stiles

Whit can't join Dylan on an adventure in the new Imagination Station because Whit promised to attend Mrs. Harcourt's piano recital, so Eugene agrees to go along. Dylan and Eugene arrive in Tuttleville, an Old West town, just in time to thwart a bank robbery by Amos Dalton and save the mayor's daughter, Lily, who immediately falls for Eugene.

When the mayor makes Eugene the sheriff and Dylan his deputy, Dylan promises that he and Eugene will run all the criminals out of Tuttleville. But Dylan didn't realize that Angus Dalton, Amos's older brother, has come to town and broken Amos out of jail in order to steal the town's gold shipment. What's worse, Angus destroys the Imagination Station's remote control, stranding them in Tuttleville. Dylan wants to quit and run away, but Eugene reminds him of his promise to the townspeople, so Dylan devises a plan to save the town from the Dalton gang.

As high noon approaches, Eugene joins Dylan at the gold mine with the repaired remote control, but Dylan is determined to keep his promise and refuses to return to Odyssey. Inside the mine, the boys outwit the outlaws, saving the gold shipment and Miss Lily. As they prepare to go home, Dylan starts to promise to return but stops because he's learned a lesson about making empty promises.

If you listen carefully, you can hear Whit whistle the musical theme from *The Last Chance Detectives,* another video series produced by Focus on the Family.

STUDY QUESTIONS:

1. Should Dylan have made the promise to clean up the town? What does the Bible say about making promises?
2. If you were in Dylan's place, would you have run or stood your ground?
3. Does having courage mean you're not afraid? What is the true source of courage?

Episode #9

"Someone to Watch Over Me"

Theme: God's sovereignty.
Scripture references: Psalm 23:4; Hebrews 2:14; 1 Peter 5:8
Written by Robert Vernon
Directed by Robert Vernon and Steve Stiles

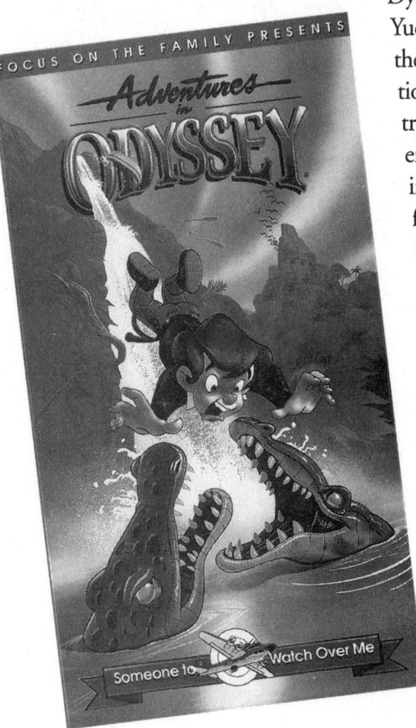

Dylan and Jesse's adventure in the Yucatan jungle ends abruptly when the Imagination Station malfunctions. As Whit and Eugene are trying to fix the machine, Dylan enters and is suddenly catapulted into another adventure. Dylan finds himself in a World War II bomber flying over Nazi territory. He discovers from his companions, a navigator, and Lieutenant Nagle, that he is *Captain* Taylor. He recalls reading about the craft in a book Mr. Whittaker gave him and assumes he is in the Imagination Station.

The plane is damaged, and they detour to take a direct route home, but their path lies over the sector of Dylan's arch enemy, Grimmstaad. The plane is hit, and Grimmstaad demands that Dylan bail out. He jumps out the door and lands in the snow, and Nagle is there to meet him, calling him Agent 014 and hurrying him to a waiting car. Nagle's plan is to smuggle Dylan past a blockade set up by his arch rival, Grimkov, but before he can do so, their car is fired upon and crashes. The only escape is to jump into a manhole next to the car, and Dylan finds himself falling again, this time landing on the star cruiser *Wonder*.

Now he is *Admiral* Taylor, with Nagle piloting the spacecraft. Dylan gets tired of the recurring theme of these adventures and yells to Whit that he has had enough. Nagle comes out of character to inform Dylan that Grimm is angrier than ever after the previous three defeats and tells Dylan he is not in the Imagination Station, and Whit cannot get him out of this adventure. Before he can explain further, the star cruiser is attacked. Grimm demands Dylan's surrender, but Nagle secures Dylan in the escape pod and sacrifices himself to save Dylan. Nagle appears to Dylan on the escape pod and urges him to remember something before he leaves the vessel. Dylan develops a headache and slowly remembers that he had been in the Imagination Station and fell, hitting his head. He has been in a coma for three days, and the Grim Reaper—death—has been pursuing him. God sent Nagle to protect Dylan because it was not yet his time to die.

the Adventures in Odyssey archives:

This is the only video to be adapted from an *Adventures in Odyssey* radio drama. Dylan Taylor fills the role originally written for Jimmy Barclay.

STUDY QUESTIONS:

1. Why did Dylan never have anything to fear from Grimm?
2. Can you think of a time when one of God's angels protected you?
3. Do you think what happened to Dylan could *really* happen?

Episode #10
"In Harm's Way"

Theme: Seeing others through God's eyes.
Scripture references: 1 Samuel 16:7; Matthew 25:40
Written by Robert Vernon
Directed by Robert Vernon and Steve Stiles

Dylan has had it! Elliot, the new kid in town, is always messing things up, and this time Elliot has caused Dylan to lose the bike race down Suicide Hill. So when Elliot offers to teach Dylan to catch butterflies, Dylan forcefully tells Elliot, "Just leave me alone!"

Hurt, Elliot walks outside, where he is "befriended" by Doug, the neighborhood bully. Doug suggests that the best way Elliot can impress all the other kids is to ride his bike down Suicide Hill.

Meanwhile, Whit is unhappy with Dylan. Whit saw the way Dylan treated Elliot and sends Dylan on an Imagination Station adventure in Victorian London. There, Dylan finds himself locked in a carnival cage, displayed as the main attraction. He is released, but even his rescuer is only interested in showing off Dylan, the "freak." Dylan flees. Unfortunately, everyone he meets is horrified by the sight of him. He is chased down the streets of London. Finally cornered, Dylan looks into a puddle and sees a terrifyingly disfigured face looking back at him. He sinks to the ground, begging his pursuers to see that he is just like them. He looks up to find himself back in Whit's End.

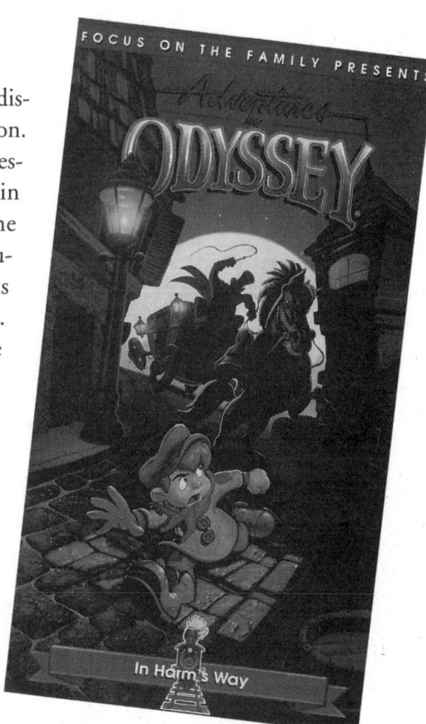

But Dylan is given no chance to recover from his adventure, for Holly suddenly bursts into the room and tells Dylan that Elliot is at the top of Suicide Hill with Doug. Holly and Dylan race there on bike, and Whit and Eugene follow in the Strata-flyer. But before anyone can reach the top, Doug pushes Elliot's bike down the hill. Elliot swoops past Holly and Dylan, and they realize that Elliot's brakes aren't working. Dylan takes off after Elliot, but he crashes and is thrown into Elliot's basket. Racing down Suicide toward the train tracks, Dylan and Elliot narrowly escape an oncoming truck. They jump onto a train, but the engineer falls out, leaving Dylan and Elliot alone in the engine. And as the train rushes down the hill, Dylan discovers that Elliot has a special ability that just might save them—teaching Dylan an unforgettable lesson about acceptance and the value of all people.

the Adventures in ODYSSEY archives:

The young boy who played the character Elliot was not a professional actor. He was located through a school for the hearing impaired.

STUDY QUESTIONS:

1. Why was it wrong for Dylan to yell at Elliot?
2. Do you know anyone like Elliot who seems different or weird? How should you treat them?
3. What does the Bible say about how God looks at us?

Episode #11
"A Twist in Time"

Theme: You will reap what you sow.
Scripture reference: Galatians 6:7-9
Written by Steve Stiles
Directed by Robert Vernon and Steve Stiles

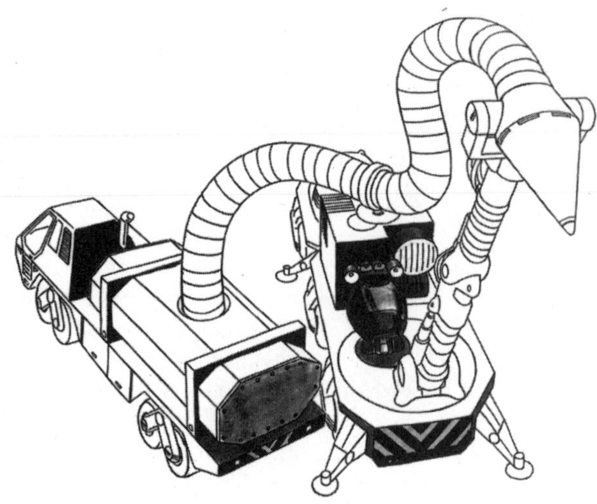

Whit is working on a mysterious new invention at Whit's End and has asked for privacy until it is completed. He's instructed Dylan and Sal to please stay away, but their curiosity gets the best of them, and they sneak into the area to take a quick look. What they find is a river of cables, conduits, and diagnostic equipment, which all lead to a room-like chamber marked with the letters "ROC."

Once inside, Dylan and Sal accidentally engage the room's computer and cause it to malfunction. The results are disastrous. Alarms sound, the control panel begins to spark, and with a mighty jolt, the boys are thrown to the ground and left in darkness.

When they pry the door open, they find that 50 years have passed and that Whit's End lies in shambles from years of neglect. What's worse, a developer is bent on tearing down the beloved Whit's End and replacing it with something more modern. Eugene, now 70 years old, is the only one left fighting to keep it standing.

The rest of the story is an account of the boys' frantic attempt to reverse the process and undo the wrong they have done. Along the way, they experience a series of near disasters with runaway futuristic vehicles, mechanical watchdogs, and the pending destruction of Whit's End.

Never in their wildest dreams did the boys ever think that one little act of disobedience could lead to this. In the end, they learn that even the littlest actions can have big consequences which can't be avoided or ignored.

the *Adventures in* ODYSSEY archives:

The actor who plays Vern also supplies the current voice for the Tazmanian Devil featured in the Warner Bros. cartoons.

STUDY QUESTIONS:

1. Why was it important for Dylan and Sal to obey Whit's instructions to stay away from the work area?
2. Have you ever done something that seemed small at the time but led to big problems? What happened?
3. Why do we sometimes grow tired of doing what's right? What does the Bible say about this?

ADVENTURES IN ANIMATION

How *Adventures in Odyssey* Videos Are Made

The process of creating *Adventures in Odyssey* videos can be an adventure in and of itself. Each step requires hours of work—and everything is done by hand. But, much like the *Adventures in Odyssey* radio drama, the results are magical. Here's a closer look at how we bring characters like Whit, Eugene, and Dylan to life:

The Story

It all begins with a script, which tells a story and describes the characters. Scripts always contain some main characters, like Dylan, Whit, Eugene, and Jesse. But every script introduces some new characters as well. Every person involved in the animation process gets a script. It acts as a guideline for everyone who works in the production of the video, since the drawings, dialogue, and sound all must complement the script.

The Models

The script helps to design the new characters. Artists draft many drawings so that the finished character looks just right. The finished drawings act as reference models, showing everybody (the storyboard artist, the animator, and the people working on color) how to draw a particular character.

Once the models are finished, the drawings are colored. The colored drawings also act as guidelines for when the final animation is painted. Backgrounds and locations are also designed at this point. These drawings are used to place the characters in the location where the action of the story takes place.

SIZE COMPARISON CHART

Recording Dialogue

While the artists are designing the new models, voiceover actors are hired to play the parts of various characters. Sometimes an actor will play two parts at once. The recording is done in a studio, where the actors act out the dialogue from the script. An actor often has to perform his lines many times—it takes time to find the right voice for Jesse or Dylan. Each character's voice is recorded separately—unlike the radio broadcast, which usually records all the actors together. Then the sound editor edits the best "takes" together, creating the dialogue track.

Storyboards

Storyboard artists take all of this information—the script, models, background, and the dialogue track—and create a storyboard, a comic-book version of the script. The story is usually broken into three acts—with a different artist for each act. More complex shows are broken down further.

These artists divide the script into different scenes—sometimes as many as 500. Each of these scenes contains a small drawing that portrays the characters, the action, and the dialogue from the particular scene. Once the storyboard is finished, it helps everyone involved in the production see the story unfold.

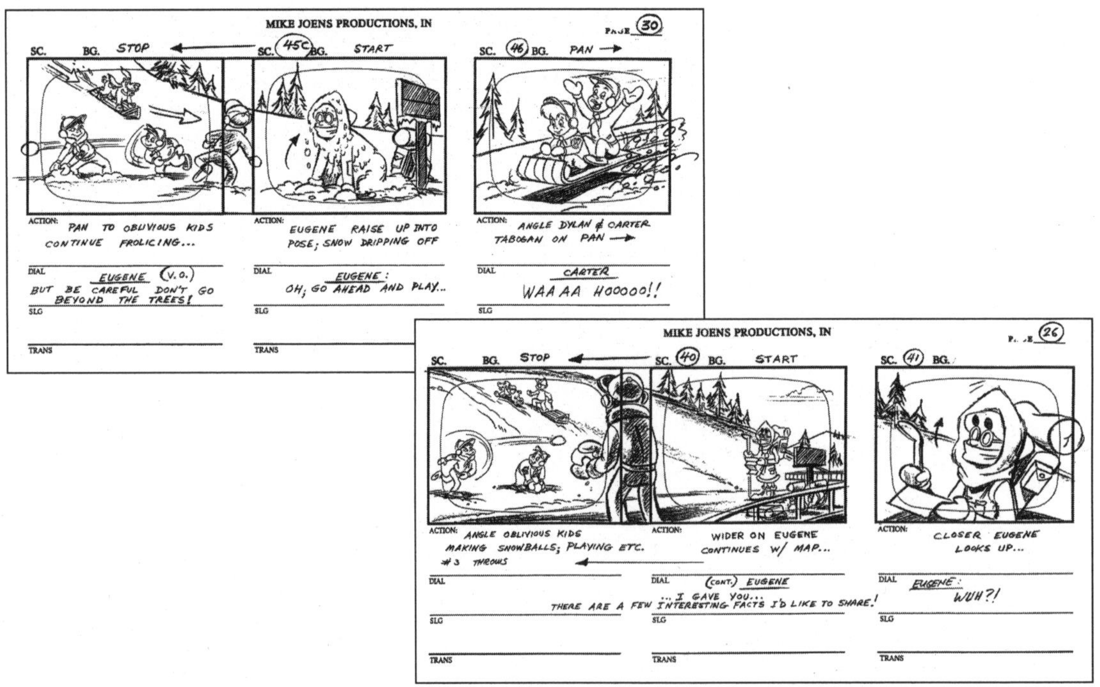

Exposure Sheets

How do animators make Dylan look as if he's walking with his dog or sledding down Avalanche Mountain? By sketching countless drawings.

A typical show will use more than 20,000 drawings. Because there are so many drawings, the animators need a detailed account of all the action. They also need to know how the camera captures this action. So the sheet director takes all of the script, dialogue, and storyboard information and places it on a large graph-like piece of paper: an exposure sheet. This gives the animator all of the information he or she needs for each drawing.

Layouts

Using animation paper (which is simply regular paper with registration holes at the bottom), the layout artist stages the scene. He or she breaks down the storyboard into major poses, showing the key positions of movement for each character. For example, the layout person might say, "Whit needs to be placed next to the Imagination Station in frame one."

The layout artist will also set the background of a scene—showing where Eugene needs to walk or whether Jesse is sitting on a chair or lying on the couch. This is important because it allows the animator to know where the specific boundaries are for his or her drawings. If the layout artist indicates that Jesse is sitting on a chair, the animator will draw her around that background (the chair). A layout artist will act as a type of director to the animators.

The background art from a scene in "Once Upon An Avalanche"

Characters are drawn around the background for animation purposes.

Animation

Next comes the actual animation process. Armed with the models, storyboard, exposure sheets, and layouts, the animator creates the illusion of movement—one drawing at a time. The storyboard and layouts tell the animator where each of the characters needs to be on the paper, the models tell the animator exactly how the character needs to look, and the exposure sheet tells the animator how many drawings he or she needs. As with the other steps, it often takes many drawings to get the character's motion just right.

Color

Once each of the line drawings—the animated characters—is finished, each page is photocopied onto clear plastic sheets called cels. Next, the cels are painted. The cel painters refer to the models so they know exactly what colors to use on the characters.

Film

When the paint is dry, the camera is loaded with film. Because the cel is clear—except for the characters in the scene—the characters can be photographed against a painted background. The photographer places one cel after another in front of the background painting. For example, every time Sherman's tail changes position, the photographer must take a new picture. Thousands of pictures are taken. This is done for all 20,000 cels!

Finishing Touches

When the animation is on film, the sound is added. Here, the dialogue, sound effects, and music are combined. Finally, the film—with the finished sound effects—is copied to a videotape. And, after a 10-month process, another *Adventures in Odyssey* video is ready to be viewed.

Books

A NOVEL IDEA

How *Adventures in Odyssey* Books Came to Be

Spinning off the audio series, the *Adventures in Odyssey* novels feature new and original stories. The first six focus on Mark Prescott, a young boy who moves to Odyssey after his parents separate. Hurt and lonely, Mark faces the difficulty of making new friends, feeling accepted, and coping with the many changes in his life.

Paul McCusker, author of the *Adventures in Odyssey* novels, explains, "If you're familiar with the *AIO* radio series, you might be surprised to find that some characters from the audio series aren't in the books. That was done on purpose. Since the radio show was produced weekly, the characters went through changes more frequently than the books could keep up with. Therefore, the first 10 books feature the *pre*radio-show time period. In other words, the books center on stories set in a time *before* the radio era. Thus, some of the characters on the radio programs haven't even arrived in Odyssey yet. But rest assured, Whit and Whit's End are there."

Book #1
Strange Journey Back

Mark Prescott believes it is his fault when his dad leaves home. After moving to Odyssey and hearing of the Imagination Station at Whit's End, Mark is sure he can go back to the day his father left and patch things up. But first, he must get past Mr. Whittaker. As Mark's adventures unfold, he learns lessons about friendship, responsibility, and living with change.

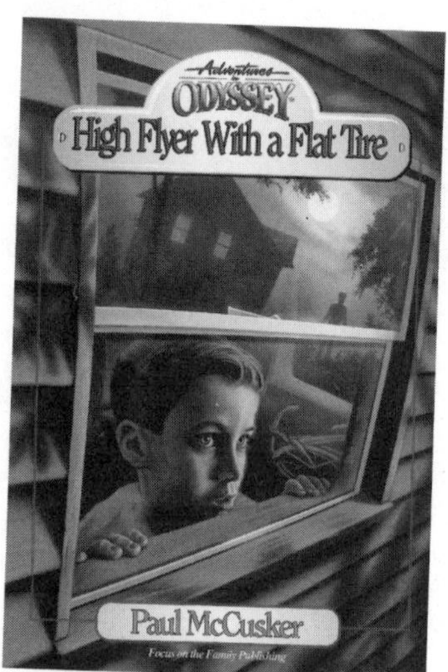

Book #2
High Flyer With a Flat Tire

Mark Prescott is in trouble. He has gotten in a fight with Joe Devlin, and now Joe is accusing Mark of slashing the tire on his new bike. Mark realizes the only way to prove his innocence is to find the real culprit.

He and his best friend, Patti, encounter a crowd of potential villains: Rachel, a girl Joe teased about being fat; Chad, the boy who had an argument with Joe; and even Patti. With the help of his wise friend Whit, the eccentric inventor, Mark untangles the mystery and learns new lessons about friendship and family ties.

Book #3
The Secret Cave of Robinwood

Mark Prescott promises his friend Patti that he'll never reveal the secret of her hidden cave. But when the Israelites, a gang Mark wants to join, are looking for a new clubhouse, Mark thinks of the cave. He's positive they would make him a member if he told them about it. Patti doesn't want to share the cave, though, and she doesn't want to join the Israelites. Mark is torn between the gang and his friendship with Patti. As he makes his choices, Mark learns about faithfulness, the need to belong, and the gift of forgiveness.

Book #4
Behind the Locked Door

Mark Prescott goes to stay with John Avery Whittaker while his mother visits his father in Washington, D.C. Whit not only opens his home to Mark, but also shares with him about his family. Whit tells about how he met his wife and how her death was tied to the establishment of Whit's End.

But when the caretaker of the Odyssey cemetery informs Mark that Whit's wife is not really buried beneath her memorial marker, and after Whit forbids Mark to enter the attic, Mark grows curious. Fueled by thriller comic books, his mind conjures up dark possibilities, and he determines to get beyond the locked attic door to learn Whit's secret.

The secret he finds is a boy's bedroom with old mementos and a newspaper article announcing the death of Whit's son Jerry in Vietnam. In his surprise at hearing Whit come home early, Mark breaks a paperweight Jerry had made for his father. Mark realizes he will have to be honest with Whit about sneaking into the attic. He also learns the importance of guarding his thoughts and being able to apologize. Whit's angry response to Mark convinces the usually affable man that he also has a lesson to learn: It isn't healthy not to allow old wounds to heal.

Book #5
Lights Out at Camp What-a-Nut

When he and his mother return to Odyssey from a trip to Washington, D.C., to visit his father, Mark Prescott finds the town practically deserted. He learns that his two best friends, Patti Eldridge and Mr. Whittaker, have gone to Camp What-a-Nut. A lonely Mark convinces his mother to send him to join his friends.

Upon arrival, Mark quickly discovers that he has some real challenges ahead of him. His bunk is next to Odyssey's worst bully, Joe Devlin, and Patti has fallen in love with a teenage counselor. Before the day is finished, Mark and Joe end up in the camp director's office for having a food fight. To Mark's amazement, the director is Whit, who shows him no leniency even though they're friends. After a series of scrapes, the boys are warned that they will be sent home if they step out of line again.

Mark decides he's had enough when he finds out that his partner for the camp treasure hunt is Joe Devlin. Whit won't give Mark a new partner, though, so Mark and Joe fight their way through the clues, arguing about who is right. Joe's wrong guess takes them to an abandoned bomb shelter, where they are locked inside by an air-tight door. Unable to get out, the boys begin to talk about their families. Mark discovers that Joe is insecure because his parents are getting a divorce. Able to empathize with Joe, Mark explains how his own parents' separation has hurt him.

After the boys are finally found, things begin to go better for Mark. And a surprise when he gets home ends the week perfectly for Mark: His dad is there, and his parents have worked out their differences.

Book #6
The King's Quest

Mark Prescott isn't sure he wants his parents back together if it means he has to return to Washington, D.C., to live. When he expresses this to Mr. Whittaker, Whit sends him on a journey in the Imagination Station to learn about God's control over his life.

Mark is propelled back in time to the era of brave knights, great castles, an evil nobleman, and a good king. He finds himself in the middle of a quest to help the king retrieve a valuable ring. He survives the schemes of many evil forces, and in the end, he and the good Sir Owwen battle a dangerous dragon to retrieve the ring. As Mark moves from adventure to adventure, he discovers how God uses even the most difficult experiences to accomplish His will.

Book #7
Danger Lies Ahead

Jack Davis's first day of school is an eventful one. First, Mark Prescott moves out of Odyssey. Then Jack meets the new kid, Colin Francis, ends up in a fight with him, and is sent to the principal's office. Then, a convict escapes from the Connellsville Detention Center and heads right for Odyssey.

Colin is a strange kid who claims no one is really who they claim to be. He begins to drive a wedge between Jack, Lucy, and Oscar by telling each of them lies about one another. Colin also says that his family is part of the FBI witness protection program, that the escaped convict is a hit man looking for his dad, and that his parents have moved and left him with his abusive, alcoholic aunt and uncle.

Jack and Lucy discover that not only is Colin lying, but he is also stealing from the other kids in class. Jack decides to tell his parents. With the help of his dad and Whit, Jack discovers the truth about Colin—that he's a chronic liar and very troubled young man. Jack vows to apologize to his friends for not trusting them.

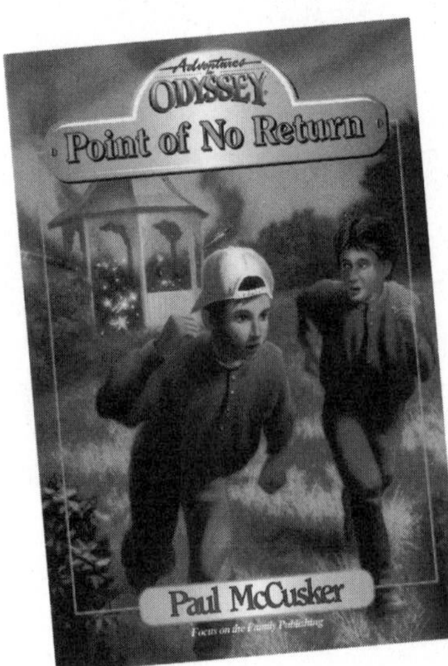

Book #8
Point of No Return

Ten-year-old Jimmy Barclay seems to have a knack for hanging around troublemakers and getting into trouble. When he turns his life over to Jesus, though, Jimmy is sure things are going to be different. Unfortunately, things seem to go from bad to worse as Jimmy continues to be influenced by his non-Christian friends, gets into trouble, loses his friends, and feels the sorrow of his grandmother's death.

The only Christians Jimmy knows suddenly leave Odyssey, and Jimmy begins to doubt God's goodness. When things seem to be at their worst, Jimmy is ready to give up his newfound faith. But John Avery Whittaker explains to Jimmy that sometimes God takes things away to keep us relying on Him, but He always replaces them with things that are just as good—or better!

Book #9
Dark Passage

In this adventure about the Underground Railroad, Jack Davis and Matt Booker are exploring a cave behind Whit's End when they find themselves in the basement at Whit's End. There, they discover the Imagination Station, invented by John Avery Whittaker. Curious, the boys climb inside and push an inviting red button, which plunges them back into the same cave—only this time they emerge in 1858!

When they come out of the cave, they find themselves inside a church, where they encounter Reverend Andrew, a participant in the Underground Railroad. Andrew is trying to help Clarence, a runaway slave, and his little girl, Eveline. As the boys watch from the shadows, another African-American man posing as a runaway slave leads slave catchers into the room, and the chase is on.

The boys escape with Eveline to a graveyard, a prearranged meeting place chosen by her father. While Jack goes into Odyssey to find help, Matt and Eveline see her father being taken away by the slave catchers and take off in pursuit. As they travel south, toward the plantation they escaped from, Matt, an African-American, is forced to face the reality of slavery. Jack joins Reverend Andrew on a journey south to rescue their friends, but they get there too late to save them from being sold to another plantation owner. As they try to find them, Jack suddenly finds himself transported back to Whit's End—and the present—in the Imagination Station. Matt is also sent back, but both boys beg Whit to let them go back so they can save their newfound friends from danger and tragedy. Whit agrees, and the book ends as the boys are transported back. To be continued in the next volume. . . .

Book #10
Freedom Run

In this sequel to *Dark Passage,* Matt and Eveline are taken to the Ross plantation and put to work. Jack and Reverend Andrew Ferguson head for the Mason plantation, where they find Clarence and make plans to help him escape. At the Ross plantation, Matt tells Colonel Ross the truth about who he is and where he's from. Matt is whipped as a liar but refuses to give up trying to help Eveline escape. Jack and Andrew arrive, posing as bird watchers. They discover that Clarence has escaped from the Mason plantation and find themselves arrested as accomplices!

Just in time, Clarence appears at the courthouse and turns himself in. With the help of some of Colonel Ross's slaves, they all escape and meet in the forest, where they are pursued by a pack of dogs and the slave hunters. They finally reach safety in Odyssey, where the debate over slavery and abolition is just beginning. Eveline and Clarence continue on the Underground Railroad to Canada, where they are reunited with their mother and wife, Lucy. Back in present-day Odyssey, Matt discovers that Eveline and Clarence are his ancestors. He develops a greater appreciation for the freedom he enjoys.

Index

Subject Index

Scripture Index

Appendix

Cast Listing

Editors' note: Over the years, hundreds of actors and actresses have appeared in the *Adventures in Odyssey* radio drama, playing roles both large and small. We attempted to contact each person, but over time some people have moved. In the interest of privacy, others prefer not to be included in this book. Therefore, this is not a complete listing of the actors and actresses who have been the voices of *Adventures in Odyssey.*

NAME	CHARACTER	EPISODE
Whitney Aaron	Jill	Letting Go
Spencer Allen	Al Larson	Harley Takes the Case, I, II
	Bill Kendall	Father's Day; Where Is Thy Sting?
	Father (Jack)	The Return of Harley, I, II
Alicia Anderson	Amy	Pokenberry Falls, I, II
Marlene Lizzio Aragon	Esther	A Mission for Jimmy
Amber Arnold	Brooke Myers	All the Difference in the World; Forgive Us as We Forgive; Game of Compassion; The Marriage Feast; Where's Your Daddy?; The Secret Keys of Discipline
Dave Arnold	Chase	Lincoln, I
	Conductor	Train Ride
	Dad	Clara
	Doctor	The Battle, I
	Grace	Sixties-Something
	Harry	You Go to School Where?
	Head of Deacons	Preacher's Kid
	Jesus	The Imagination Station, I, II;
	Jocko	Blackbeard's Treasure
	Messenger	A Single Vote
	Mr. Benson	Good Business
	Pastor	No, Honestly!
	Police Officer	By Faith, Noah; No, Honestly!
	Radio Announcer	Peace on Earth
	Security Officer	Hold Up!
	Teacher	Isaac the Procrastinator
	TV Reporter	Waylaid in the Windy City, I
Janna Arnold	Mother	Nothing to Fear
Landon Arnold	Cousin "Scrub"	. . . But Not Forgotten
	Moseley	The Mysterious Stranger, I; Like Father, Like Son; Red Wagons & Pink Flamingos
Janan Assaf	Sheri	Rights, Wrongs & Reasons
Laura Assaf	Brenda Perry	W-O-R-R-Y
	Kim	Count It All Joy
	Maggie	It Is Well
	Woman Bystander	Red Wagons & Pink Flamingos
Thom Babbes		The Right Choice, I, II
Natalie Babbitt	Jenny Roberts	Count It All Joy; For Thine Is the Kingdom; Hymn Writers; Pen Pal; The Perfect Witness, I,II, III; Rights, Wrongs & Reasons; Three Funerals & A Wedding, I, II; A Time for Christmas; A Touch of Healing, I
	Girl	Caroling, Caroling
Parley Baer	Joe Finneman	And the Last Shall Be First; East Winds, Raining; The Meaning of Sacrifice; The War Hero
	Balthazer	The Star, I, II
	Capt. Anderson	East Winds, Raining
	Elijah	Elijah, I, II
	Hezekiah	Back to Bethlehem I, II, III
	Jeduthum	An Adventure in Bethany, I
	Mr. Burglemeister	Eugene's Dilemma
	Mr. Grayson	Eugene's Dilemma
	Old Man McKinney	The Return of Harley, II
	Reginald	Operation DigOut; The Very Best of Friends
Gloria Bell	Customer	Top This!
	Mrs. Hogan	Poetry in Slow Motion
	Teacher	Top This!
Brooke Bellessi	Traci Needlemeyer	The Barclay Ski Vacation; Emotional Baggage; A Model Child; What Happened to the Silver Streak?; The Winning Edge
	Martha	You Go to School Where?
	Sandra	The Reluctant Rival
Chris Berg	Librarian	War of the Words
	Mike	A Game of Compassion
Chuck Bolte	George Barclay	Aloha, Oy! I, II, III; And When You Pray; Bad Company; The Barclay Ski Vacation; A Call for Reverend Jimmy; Caroling, Caroling; Castles & Cauldrons, I, II; Coming of Age; Curious, Isn't It?; Easy Money; Family Vacation, I, II; George Under Pressure; A Good and Faithful Servant; Heroes; Into

262 THE COMPLETE GUIDE TO ADVENTURES IN ODYSSEY

NAME	CHARACTER	EPISODE
		Temptation; Isaac the Chivalrous; The Jesus Cloth; Making the Grade; Let This Mind Be in You; The Meaning of Sacrifice; A Mission for Jimmy; Modesty Is the Best Policy; Moses; The Passover, I, II; No, Honestly!; One-in-Ten; Our Best Vacation Ever; Our Daily Bread; Our Father; Peace on Earth; Pet Peeves; Pokenberry Falls, I, II; A Prayer for George Barclay; Preacher's Kid; The Prodigal, Jimmy; Thanksgiving at Home; Treasures of the Heart; The Trouble with Girls; Two Sides to Every Story; Unto Us a Child Is Born; The Visitors; The Vow; Where There's a Will; Wonderworld; Wishful Thinking
	Amasiah	Elijah, II
	British Soldier	The Day Independence Came
	Dale Jacobs	Mayor for a Day; Muckraker; The Second Coming
	Father (Billy)	By Faith, Noah
	Francis Scott Key	By Dawn's Early Light
	Joseph	Back to Bethlehem, II, III; The Star, I, II
	Mr. Baehr	A Single Vote
	Mr. Dillard	Kid's Radio
	Mr. Hart	A Change of Hart
	Pastor Williams	V.B.S. Blues
	Pharoah	Bernard & Joseph, II
	Profesor Ronan	Hold Up!
	Sheriff	Pipe Dreams
	State Trooper	Harley Takes the Case, II
Erin Bolte	Melanie Jacobs	Backwoods Jacobs; Bernard & Esther, I, II; Dobson Comes to Town; Melanie's Diary; A Model Child; Pen Pal; The Second Coming; A Test for Robyn
	Laurie	You Go to School Where?
Sage Bolte	Robyn Jacobs	All's Well with Boswell; Backwoods Jacobs; Bad Luck; Bernard & Esther, I, II; Better Late than Never; But, You Promised; Connie Goes to Camp, I, II; The Courage to Stand; Elijah, I, II; Good Business; The Greatest of These; Heat Wave; Melanie's Diary; Pen Pal; The Second Coming; A Test for Robyn; The Treasure of Le Monde!; The Winning Edge; A Worker Approved; You Go to School Where?; You Gotta Be Wise
	Girl	A Matter of Obedience
	Karen	Karen
	Laura Freemont	Honor Thy Parents

NAME	CHARACTER	EPISODE
	Linda	Doing Unto Others
	Shirley	Nothing to Fear
	Suzie	Bad Company
	Wendy	Family Vacation, II
Steve Bridges	Anchorman	Gathering Thunder
	Ding-Dong	Hidden in My Heart
	Expendable Crewman	Hidden in My Heart
	Ford	The Time of Our Lives
	Gilligan	The Time of Our Lives
	Howard J. Weizel	A Victim of Circumstance
	Jesus	B-TV: Compassion
	John Madden	Easy Money
	Kyle	The Time of Our Lives
	Manager	Gathering Thunder
	Mechanic	Easy Money
	Ogre	Our Father
	Park Man	Gathering Thunder
	Pete Johnson	Easy Money; Family Values
	Sales Clerk/ Operator	The Right Choice, I, II
	Sanders	Blind Justice
	Steven	Hidden in My Heart
	Teenage Boy	The Time of Our Lives
	Van Scuddy	Our Father
	Vin Scully	Easy Money
Brian Brinegar	Meshach	Deliver Us from Evil
Kurt Bruner	Bailiff	The Merchant of Odyssey
Leland Bruno	Chad Pearson	This Is Chad Pearson?
	Jerry Whittaker	The Mortal Coil, II
	Pastor	For Thine Is the Kingdom
David Buller	Billy MacPherson	Checkmate; A Code of Honor; The Final Conflict; Gathering Thunder
Steve Burns	Rodney Rathbone	Aloha, Oy! I, II, III; An Act of Mercy; Angels Unaware; Another Chance; The Bad Hair Day; The Case of the Candid Camera; Checkmate; Family Values; The Final Conflict; Forgive Us as We Forgive; Gathering Thunder; Hard Losses; Isaac the Chivalrous; Isaac the Courageous; The Last Resort; Like Father, Like Son; The Living Nativity; Missing Person; No, Honestly!; The Potential in Elliot; A Rathbone of Contention; The Scales of Justice; St. Paul: Set Apart by God; Thank You, God; A Victim of Circumstance; You Gotta Be Wise; The Other Woman
	Dan	First Love
	Howie	The Prodigal, Jimmy
	Joe	A Rathbone of Contention
	Robert	Go Ye Therefore
	Thor-Douglas	Blessings in Disguise
	Tony	That's Not Fair!
Corey Burton	Adam	B-TV: Envy

NAME	CHARACTER	EPISODE
	Adult Kathy	The Time of Our Lives
	Advisor	Moses: The Passover, I
	Angel	On Solid Ground
	Ann (First)	Terror from the Skies
	Attendant	Home Sweet Home
	Babcock	The Merchant of Odyssey
	Barker	Thy Kingdom Come
	Beavers	Hallowed Be Thy Name
	Benai	The Marriage Feast
	Boaz	Three Funerals & a Wedding, I, II
	(Cryn') Bryan Dern	Hard Losses; Real Time; The Return; Small Fires, Little Pools; Tom for Mayor, I, II; A Tongue of Fire; Top This!; A Touch of Healing, II; Treasure Hunt; When Bad Isn't So Good
	British Soldier	A Touch of Healing, II
	Brock Peterson	Angels Unaware; Hard Losses; Small Fires, Little Pools
	Bully	Hidden in My Heart
	Caller	On Solid Ground
	Chief Priest	The Star, II
	Dad	The Time of Our Lives
	Dave Saburo	East Winds, Raining
	Director	B-TV: Envy
	Dr. Franklin	A Touch of Healing, I, II
	EDA Agent	Tom for Mayor, I, II
	Elijah	B-TV: Envy
	Emcee	The Conscientious Cross-Guard
	Employee	Top This!
	Feldskin	I Want My B-TV!
	Franz Gruber	Joy to the World
	Gaspar	The Star, I, II
	God	On Solid Ground
	Group Leader	The Time of Our Lives
	Hank	Terror from the Skies
	Hank Bonsall	The Return
	Herald	The Marriage Feast
	Jacob	Hallowed Be Thy Name; Two Brothers . . . and Bernard, I, II
	James	An Act of Nobility
	John Q. Public	Welcome Home, Mr. Blackgaard
	Joshua	Moses: The Passover, I, II
	Judas	St. Paul: Set Apart by God
	King Ferdinand	Columbus: The Grand Voyage
	Larry	Blind Justice
	Loud Speaker	Home Sweet Home
	Man	On Solid Ground; Thy Kingdom Come
	Marquis	The Marriage Feast
	Mayor	Tom for Mayor, I
	Motorist	Top This!
	Mr. Burton	The Election Deception; A Question of Loyalty; The Truth About Zachary
	Mr. Jones	My Fair Bernard
	Mr. Umprees	The Conscientious Cross-Guard
	Mudley	I Want My B-TV!
	Narrator	Thy Kingdom Come
	Nabor	On Solid Ground
	Nathan	B-TV: Envy
	Officer Phelps	Small Fires, Little Pools

NAME	CHARACTER	EPISODE
	Picasso	I Want My B-TV!
	Policeman	Home Sweet Home
	Randall	Blind Justice
	Robosaur	I Want My B-TV!
	Satrap	Hallowed Be Thy Name
	Scotty	Hidden in My Heart
	Scripture Phaser	Hidden in My Heart
	Servant	A Time for Christmas
	Servant	Thy Kingdom Come
	Shadrach	Deliver Us from Evil
	Shepherd	A Time for Christmas
	Sir Richard	A Time for Christmas
	Smart Guy	Hidden in My Heart
	Stephen	St. Paul: The Man from Tarsus
	Trevor	Soaplessly Devoted
	Walter Shakespeare	B-TV: Compassion; A Class Act; Double Trouble; The Merchant of Odyssey; My Fair Bernard; The Return; Terror from the Skies; Welcome Home, Mr. Blackgaard; When Bad Isn't So Good
	Young Joe	East Winds, Raining; The War Hero
Sara Buskirk	Courtney Vincent	B-TV: Compassion; B-TV: Envy; The Case of the Delinquent Disciples; The Election Deception; For Thine Is the Kingdom; I Want My B-TV!; Poetry in Slow Motion; Red Wagons & Pink Flamingos; Three Funerals & a Wedding, I, II; A Time for Christmas; Top This!; With a Little Help from My Friends
	Girl	B-TV: Envy
	Hayley Clark	Count It All Joy
	Kathy	The Time of Our Lives
Amick Byram	Chilion	Three Funerals & a Wedding
Joseph Cammarato	Oscar	Front Page News; That's Not Fair!; Two Sides to Every Story; The Very Best of Friends; A Worker Approved
	Boy	A Matter of Obedience
	Jay	Harley Takes the Case, I
	Leo	The Price of Freedom
	Ted	Family Vacation, II
	Sherman	Kid's Radio
	Young Whit	Thank You, God
Joe Campanella	Ernie Myers	Forgive Us as We Forgive
	Haban	Two Brothers . . . and Bernard, II
	Horatio Spafford	It Is Well
Nathan Carlson	Richard Maxwell	Another Chance; An Encounter with Mrs. Hooper; The Battle, I, II; Checkmate; Eugene's Dilemma; Hard Losses; The Homecoming; The Last Resort; The Nemesis, I, II; Waylaid in the Windy City, I, II
	Admiral Cockburn	By Dawn's Early Light
	Cordova	The Cross of Cortes, I, II
	Courier #2	The Underground Railroad, II

NAME	CHARACTER	EPISODE
	Customer	A Bite of Applesauce
	Dan	Go Ye Therefore
	Father (Lucy's)	Choices
	Grover	The Ill Gotten Deed
	John Mark	The Imagination Station, I, II
	Judah	Back to Bethlehem, I, II, III
	Len Barclay	Castles & Cauldrons, I, II
	Nathan	The Imagination Station, I, II, III
	Phil Bliss	It Is Well
	Young Reginald	Operation DigOut; Rescue from Manatugo Point
Townsend Coleman	Jason Whittaker	Another Chance; Blackbeard's Treasure; Checkmate; A Code of Honor; The Final Conflict; The Last Resort; Love Is in the Air, I, II; Memories of Jerry; Moving Targets; A Name, Not a
Number,		I, II; A Question About Tasha; Red Wagons & Pink Flamingos; The Return; The Search for Whit, I, II, III; Soaplessly Devoted; St. Paul: The Man from Tarsus; St. Paul: Set Apart by God; A Touch of Healing, I, II; Unto Us a Child Is Born; A Victim of Circumstances; What Are You Going to Do with Your Life?; With a Little Help from My Friends; Home Sweet Home; Solitary Refinement; The Decision; The Right Choice, I, II
	Ananias	St. Paul: Set Apart by God
	Ewell Mosby	Blackbeard's Treasure
Randy Crenshaw	Airport Security Officer	Gone . . .
	Don Iowa	Aloha, Oy! I, II, III
	Lance Lincoln	The Fifth House on the Left, I, II
	Maintenance Man	Gone . . .
	Plato	Memories of Jerry
Jim Custer	David Herold	Lincoln, I, II
	Hunk	Lincoln, I, II
	Joseph	Bernard & Joseph, I, II
	Mr. Adams	Kid's Radio
	Mr. Bostich	Family Vacation, II
	Mr. Henderson	Cousin Albert
	Soldier	Lincoln, II
	Young Whit	Operation DigOut; Rescue from Manatugo Point
Joe Dammann	Eric Myers	Forgive Us as We Forgive; A Game of Compassion; Like Father, Like Son; Preacher's Kid; Where's Your Daddy?
Jennifer Day	Brenda Perry	Blessings in Disguise; The Pretty Good Samaritan; Rewards in Full
	Shannon Everett	The Election Deception
Ryan Devin	Foster	The Fifth House on the Left, I, II
	Lawyer	Welcome Home, Mr. Blackgaard
Mark Drury	Aaron	Unto Us a Child Is Born
	Guard	Real Time
	Man	The Right Choice, I
	Officer Spector	The Perfect Witness I, II, III
John Eldridge	Caiaphas	The Imagination Station, I, II
	Jim Norton	Muckraker
Kyle Ellison	Sam Johnson	And the Glory; Angels Unaware; The Bad Hair Day; Best Intentions; Blackbeard's Treasure; B-TV: Compassion; B-TV: Envy; Checkmate; Easy Money; Family Values; The Final Conflict; Gathering Thunder; I Want My B-TV!; It's a Wrap; Joy to the World; No, Honestly! The Potential in Elliot; The Power; The Secret Weapon; St. Paul: Set Apart by God; Small Fires, Little Pools; Tom for Mayor, I, II; The Twilife Zone; When Bad Isn't So Good; Why Don't You Grow Up?; With a Little Help from My Friends; W-O-R-R-Y
	Boy	B-TV: Envy
	Caleb	Share and Share Alike
	Chipmunk	The Time of Our Lives
	Christian	Pilgrim's Progress Revisited, I, II
	Daniel	Share and Share Alike
	David	Hidden in My Heart
	Jeremy	The Time of Our Lives
	Timmy	Hidden in My Heart
	Young Whit	Blackbeard's Treasure
Gabriel Encarnacion	Lawrence Hodges	A Call for Reverend Jimmy; Siege at Jericho; Subject Yourself; Terror from the Skies; Treasures of the Heart; The Twilife Zone; Wonderworld
Bernard Erhard	Armitage Shanks	The Turning Point; The Right Choice, I, II
	Ashpenaz	Deliver Us from Evil
	Mr. Chapman	Timmy's Cabin
	Pharoh	Moses: The Passover, I, II
Sam Falson	Simon Birtles	A Little Credit, Please
Joan Gerber	Cora	Honor Thy Parents
	Ethel	Gifts for Madge and Guy
	Eula Fremont	Honor Thy Parents
	Grace	Family Vacation, II
	Mabel (computer)	A Bite of Applesauce
	Mary Hooper	An Encounter with Mrs. Hooper
	Mrs. Bavaqua	Pipe Dreams
	Mrs. Erskine	Preacher's Kid
	Mrs. Nelson	Connie, I, II
	Mrs. Rossini	The Day After Christmas
	Mystery Lady	The Case of the Secret Room, II
	Vivian	Pokenberry Falls, I, II
John Giali	John Giali	Dobson Comes to Town
Andrew Gillespie	Henry Thomas	And the Glory; The Bad Hair Day; War of the Words
	P. D.	Greater Love

NAME	CHARACTER	EPISODE
Luke Graham	Antoninus	St. Paul: An Appointment with Caesar; St. Paul: Voyage to Rome
James D. Griffin	Jimmy Barclay	"A" . . . Is for Attitude; Aloha Oy! I, II, III; An Act of Mercy; And the Glory; And the Last Shall Be First; And When You Pray; The Barclay Ski Vacation; The Big Broadcast; A Call for Reverend Jimmy; Castles & Cauldrons, I, II; Coming of Age; Connie Goes to Camp, I, II; Family Vacation, I, II; The Fundamentals; George Under Pressure; A Good and Faithful Servant; Heroes; Into Temptation; Let This Mind Be in You; Lincoln, I, II; Making the Grade; The Meaning of Sacrifice; A Member of the Family, I; A Mission for Jimmy; Moses: The Passover, I, II; Our Best Vacation Ever; Our Daily Bread; Our Father; Peace on Earth; Pet Peeves; Pokenberry Falls, I, II; A Prayer for George Barclay; Preacher's Kid; The Price of Freedom; The Prodigal, Jimmy; Someone to Watch Over Me; Terror from the Skies; Thanksgiving at Home; A Tongue of Fire; Treasures of the Heart; The Trouble with Girls; Two Sides to Every Story; Unto Us a Child Is Born; The Very Best of Friends; The Visitors; The Vow; Where There's a Will; Wonderworld; Wishful Thinking
	Billy	By Faith, Noah
	Bobby	Bobby's Valentine; Connie Comes to Town; Lights Out at Whit's End
	Freddy	The Life of the Party
	Jeremy	The Tangled Web
	Johnny	Doing Unto Others
	Mike	Mike Makes Right
	Steve Larson	Harley Takes the Case, I
	Young Bernard	The Conscientious Cross-Guard
D. J. Harner	Jana Whittaker-Dowd	A Member of the Family, I, II; Monty's Christmas; The Mortal Coil, II; The Reluctant Rival
Jack Hayford	Jack Hayford	Dobson Comes to Town
Paul Herlinger	Whit	Home Sweet Home; It's a Wrap; Solitary Refinement; The Decision; The Other Woman; The Search for Whit, I, II, III; The Right Choice, I, II
Julie Herron	Mom	Clara
	Penny	Hard Losses
	Stewardess	Home Sweet Home
Bob Hoose	Commander	Rescue from Manatugo Point
	Commander Donovan	Operation DigOut
	Confederate Officer	Lincoln, II
	Father (Pamela's)	Pamela Has a Problem
	Lewis Payne	Lincoln, I
	Mr. Jenkins	Cousin Albert
	Mr. Stanton	Lincoln, I, II
	Sergeant	Lincoln, II
	Simeon	Bernard & Joseph, I, II
	Wine Taster	Bernard & Joseph, II
Charles Howerton	Rev. Thomas Rowe	Where Is Thy Sting?
	Salmon	Siege at Jericho
Matt Hurwitz	Alan Ginsmore	Thy Will Be Done
	Andrew	Share and Share Alike
	Arich	An Adventure in Bethany, I
	Delivery Man	What Are You Going to Do With Your Life?
	Doctor	It Is Well
	Everett	Share and Share Alike
	Fireman	It Is Well
	Gentleman at counter	What Are You Going to Do with Your Life?
	Herald	The Marriage Feast
	James	The Underground Railroad, II
	Jerel	The Marriage Feast
	Mahlon	Three Funerals & a Wedding, I
	Man	Hallowed Be Thy Name
	Mike	The Perfect Witness, I, II, III
	Mr. Kramer	It Is Well
	Nathan	Share and Share Alike
	Robber	Share and Share Alike
	Rodney	Like Father, Like Son
	Roy	Share and Share Alike
	Satrap	Hallowed Be Thy Name
	Scribe	The Marriage Feast
	Stu Prentice	The Perfect Witness, III
	Tattler/Announcer	The Other Woman
	Thomas	An Adventure in Bethany, I, II; The Underground Railroad, II
A-Jay James	Margaret	The Underground Railroad, III
	Ms. Anita Clair	Making the Grade; Subject Yourself
Hunter Jamison	Young Terence	The War Hero
	Zachary Sellers	The Truth About Zachary
David Kirkwood	Henry Ross	The Underground Railroad, I, II, III
	Pastor	The "No" Factor
Chris Lansdowne	Madge	Gifts for Madge and Guy
	Mrs. Grayson	Last in a Long Line
	Rachel	The Ill-Gotten Deed
Peter Laurence	Boaz's Foreman	Three Funerals & a Wedding, II
	Festus	St. Paul: Voyage to Rome
	George	The Underground Railroad, II
	Matthias	Siege at Jericho
	Ned Tatch	Blackbeard's Treasure
	Old Man	It Happened at Four Corners
	Oren	Three Funerals & a Wedding, I, II
	Owen	Pokenberry Falls, I, II
	Saul/ Paul	St. Paul: An Appointment with

NAME	CHARACTER	EPISODE
		Caesar; St. Paul: The Man from Tarsus; St. Paul: Set Apart by God; St. Paul: Voyage to Rome
	Sidney	The Underground Railroad, II
	State Trooper	It Happened at Four Corners
	Uncle Randy	Blackbeard's Treasure
	Victor	Blind Justice
Bryan Leder	Steve Anderson	The Mysterious Stranger, II
Katie Leigh Pavlakovich	Connie Kendall	"A" . . . Is for Attitude; Addictions Can Be Habit Forming; An Act of Mercy; And the Last Shall Be First; And When You Pray; Angels Unaware; Auld Lang Syne; Back to Bethlehem, I, II, III; Bad Company; The Battle, I, II; Best Intentions; Better Late Than Never; A Bite of Applesauce; Blessings in Disguise; Bobby's Valentine; A Book by Its Cover; The Boy Who Didn't Go to Church; . . . But Not Forgotten; But, You Promised; Caroling, Caroling; The Case of the Delinquent Disciples; The Case of the Missing Train Car; The Case of the Secret Room, I, II; Castles & Cauldrons, I, II; Checkmate; Choices; A Class Act; A Code of Honor; Coming of Age; Connie, I, II; Connie Comes to Town; Connie Goes to Camp, I, II; The Courage to Stand; Curious, Isn't It?; The Curse; A Day in the Life; Do, for a Change; Dobson Comes to Town; Doing Unto Others; Double Trouble; East Winds, Raining; Emotional Baggage; First Love; Father's Day; Flash Flood; Gathering Thunder; Gifts for Madge & Guy; Go Ye Therefore; Gone . . . ; A Good & Faithful Servant; Gotcha!; The Greatest of These; Hallowed Be Thy Name; Harley Takes the Case, I; Have You No Selpurcs?; Heroes; Hidden in My Heart; Hold Up!; I Want My B-TV!; Ice Fishing; Isaac the Benevolent; It Began with a Rabbit's Foot . . . ; . . . It Ended with a Handshake; The Jesus Cloth; Karen; Let This Mind Be in You; A License to Drive; A Little Credit, Please; The Living Nativity; Love Is in the Air, I, II; Memories of Jerry; Missed It by That Much; Monty's Christmas; The Mortal Coil, I, II; Moving Targets; Muckraker; The Mysterious Stranger, I, II; Naturally, I Assumed . . . ; The Nemesis, I, II; The "No" Factor; Not One of Us; Nothing to Fear; On Solid Ground; One Bad Apple; Operation DigOut; Over the Airwaves; Pamela Has a Problem; Peace on Earth; Peacemaker; Pet Peeves; Pipe Dreams; Pranks for the Memories; The Pretty Good Samaritan; The Price of Freedom; Promises, Promises; The Quality of Mercy; A Question About Tasha; Real Time; Recollections; The Reluctant Rival; Rescue from Manatugo Point; The Return; The Return of Harley, I, II; Rewards in Full; Rights, Wrongs & Reasons; Rumor Has It; The Sacred Trust; The Scales of Justice; Scattered Seed; The Secret Weapon; Share and Share Alike; The Shepherd and the Giant; A Single Vote; Sixties-Something; Small Fires, Little Pools; The Star, I, II; Stormy Weather; Suspicious Minds; Tales of Moderation; The Tangled Web; That's Not Fair!; Thank You, God; A Thanksgiving Carol; This Is Chad Pearson?; Three Funerals & a Wedding, I, II; Thy Kingdom Come; Thy Will Be Done; The Time Has Come; The Time of Our Lives; Tom for Mayor, I, II; A Touch of Healing, I, II; Train Ride; The Treasure of Le Monde!; The Trouble with Girls; The Truth About Zachary; Truth, Trivia & 'Trina; The Turning Point; The Twilife Zone; Unto Us a Child Is Born; The War Hero; War of the Words; Waylaid in the Windy City, I, II; What Are You Going to Do With Your Life?; What Happened to the Silver Streak?; Where's Your Daddy?; A Worker Approved; What Are We Gonna Do About Halloween?; Where Is Thy Sting?; With a Little Help from My Friends; Home Sweet Home; It's a Wrap; The Decision
	Angel	B-TV: Envy
	Cheerful Lady	A Thanksgiving Carol
	Girl	The Midnight Ride
	Clerk	The Time of Our Lives
	Cynthia	Share and Share Alike
	Eve	B-TV: Envy

NAME	CHARACTER	EPISODE
	Julie	The Time of Our Lives
	Katherine	Hidden in My Heart
	Maid	B-TV: Envy
	Malanga	Rescue from Manatugo Point
	Milcah	On Solid Ground
	Ms. Busywork	Pilgrim's Progress Revisited, I
	Peter	An Act of Mercy
	Porter	Pilgrim's Progress Revisited, I
	Shirley	Hidden in My Heart
	Teeny Tim	A Thanksgiving Carol
	Trudy	Share and Share Alike
	Tumweiler Twin	Pipe Dreams
Kay Lindley	Marjorie Sadler	Muckraker
	Mary	Back to Bethlehem, II, III
	Miss Primblush	Mayor for a Day
	Mrs. Fishbine	All's Well with Boswell
	Public Relations Rep.	One Bad Apple
Phil Lollar	Dale Jacobs	And the Glory; Backwoods Jacobs; Bad Luck; Better Late Than Never; But, You Promised; Caroling, Caroling; Curious, Isn't It?; Dobson Comes to Town; Double Trouble; The Fundamentals; Good Business; Harlow Doyle, Private Eye; Isaac the Procrastinator; The Jesus Cloth; Melanie's Diary; A Model Child; The Mysterious Stranger, I, II; The "No" Factor; No, Honestly!; Pen Pal; Small Fires, Little Pools; Terror from the Skies; The War Hero; The Winning Edge; You Go to School Where?; You Gotta Be Wise
	Ann (Second)	Terror from the Skies
	Arney	Blackbeard's Treasure
	Benjamin	The Search for Whit, II, III
	Big Ed	Isaac the Benevolent
	Bill	East Winds, Raining
	Blarney the Rhinosaur	I Want My B-TV!
	Butler	B-TV: Envy
	Captain	Hidden in My Heart; It Is Well; Rescue from Manatugo Point
	Contestant	Treasure Hunt
	Dad	B-TV: Envy
	Driver	Waylaid in the Windy City, I
	Dr. Munroe	An Act of Nobility
	Dudley	I Want My B-TV!
	Father (Jeremy)	The Tangled Web
	Father (Sally)	Whit's Flop
	Father (Scott)	The Quality of Mercy
	Guard	Moses: The Passover, I
	Henny	The Twilife Zone
	Herald	The Marriage Feast
	Homer	Our Best Vacation Ever
	Inspector McGreavy	Train Ride
	Japheth	By Faith, Noah
	Jehosabad	Elijah, I, II
	John Skinner	By Dawn's Early Light
	Jones	The Return of Harley, I, II; A Single Vote
	Lawrence Chalmers	Train Ride
	Lieutenant	Lincoln, I
	Lippowicz	B-TV: Envy
	Man	B-TV: Envy; By Faith, Noah; Harley Takes the Case, II
	Meres	Bernard & Esther, I
	Mr. Altman	The Price of Freedom
	Mr. Cole	Where There's a Will
	Mr. Southworth	The Greatest of These
	Photographer	W-O-R-R-Y
	Police Officer	The Cross of Cortes, I; No, Honestly!
	Principal	Pipe Dreams
	Professor Cyril	Eugene's Dilemma
	Reuben	Bernard & Joeph, I, II
	Rider	Moses: The Passover, II
	Robert E. Lee	Lincoln, II
	Rod Serley	Better Late Than Never
	Scotland Yard Detective	The Last Great Adventure of the Summer
	Security Guard	One Bad Apple
	Sergeant	Pipe Dreams
	Servant	Moses: The Passover, II
	Slave Driver	Moses: The Passover, I
	Soldier	Lincoln, II
	Thomas	The Midnight Ride
	Timon	St. Paul: The Man from Tarsus
	William Shattered	Hidden in My Heart
	Worker	The Curse
Donald Long	Jack Davis	Auld Lang Syne; The Boy Who Didn't Go to Church; By Faith, Noah; A Call for Reverend Jimmy; A Class Act; Connie Goes to Camp, I, II; Double Trouble; Elijah, I, II; Good Business; Heat Wave; Isaac the Insecure; Let This Mind Be in You; Modesty Is the Best Policy; The "No" Factor; Return to the Bible Room; The Return of Harley, I, II; Rumor Has It
	Brad Dillard	Kid's Radio
	Freddy	A Change of Hart
	Herald	The Marriage Feast
	Irwin Springer	The Day Independence Came
	Jay Brandt	Missing Person
	Jonathan	Isaac the True Friend
	Prince	The Marriage Feast
	Sam	One-in-Ten
	Tanyer Hyde	The Conscientious Cross-Guard
	Young Man	Waylaid in the Windy City, I
Genni (Mullen) Long	Lucy Cunningham-Schultz	An Adventure in Bethany, I, II; An Encounter with Mrs. Hooper; And the Last Shall Be First; Angels Unaware; Auld Lang Syne; The Battle, I, II; The Big Broadcast; The Boy Who Didn't Go to Church; But, You Promised; By Any Other Name; By Dawn's Early

NAME	CHARACTER	EPISODE
		Light; By Faith, Noah; The Case of the Candid Camera; Checkmate; Choices; Connie Goes to Camp, I, II; Cousin Albert; The Curse; Double Trouble; Front Page News; Gathering Thunder; It Began with a Rabbit's Foot . . . ; Have You No Selpurcs?; Home Is Where the Hurt Is; The Homecoming; Hymn Writers; Isaac the Benevolent; Isaac the Courageous; Isaac the Insecure; Isaac the Procrastinator; It Is Well; It Takes Integrity; It Sure Seems Like It to Me; It's a Wrap; The Jesus Cloth; Last in a Long Line; Let This Mind Be In You; The Living Nativity; Missing Person;Muckraker; The Mysterious Stranger, I, II; The Nemesis, I, II; Not One of Us; On Solid Ground; Over the Airwaves; Pranks for the Memories; A Question of Loyalty; A Rathbone of Contention; Return to the Bible Room; Rumor Has It; The Sacred Trust; The Scales of Justice; Scattered Seeds; Siege at Jericho; Small Fires, Little Pools; Thy Will Be Done; The Truth About Zachary; The Twilife Zone; Wishful Thinking;
	Hope	Pilgrim's Progress Revisited, I, II
Erin Love	Erica Clark	Do, for a Change; The Election Deception; Red Wagons & Pink Flamingos; Reward in Full; Share and Share Alike; Soaplessly Devoted; This Is Chad Pearson?; Top This!; Two Brothers . . . and Bernard, I, II; Why Don't You Grow Up?; W-O-R-R-Y
	Heather	Rights, Wrongs & Reasons
	Jane	Share and Share Alike
T. J. Lowther	Young Jason	Memories of Jerry
Bob Luttrell	Alan Booth	A Day in the Life
	Ambrose Schnook	The Ill-Gotten Deed
	Attorney	By Faith, Noah
	Baker	Bernard & Joseph, II
	Benjamin	By Dawn's Early Light; Moses: The Passover, I
	Bill Kendall	Connie, II
	Bookstore Clerk	Harlow Doyle, Private Eye
	Chief	You Go to School Where?
	Col. Conant	The Midnight Ride
	Customer Service Rep.	One Bad Apple
	Dr. Bloomberg	Muckraker
	Duke	The Marriage Feast

NAME	CHARACTER	EPISODE
	Flavius	A Prisoner for Christ
	Harry	No, Honestly!
	Harvey Nelson	Mayor for a Day
	Homer	A Single Vote
John Lynd	Father (Courtney's)	For Thine Is the Kingdom
Dave Madden	Bernard Walton	Bad Luck; Bernard & Esther, I, II; Bernard & Joseph, I, II; Blind Justice; B-TV: Compassion; B-TV: Envy; By Any Other Name; Caroling, Caroling; The Conscientious Cross-Guard; Curious, Isn't It? A Day in the Life; Deliver Us from Evil; Feud for Thought; The Final Conflict; First Hand Experience; Fifth House on the Left, I, II; Flash Flood; Gone . . . ; I Want My B-TV!; . . . It Ended with a Handshake; It Happened at Four Corners; Last in a Long Line; The Last Resort; A Little Credit, Please; My Fair Bernard; Room Mates; Second Thoughts; Suspicious Minds; A Thanksgiving Carol; Third Degree; The Time Has Come; Tom for Mayor, I, II; Two Brothers . . . and Bernard, I, II; When Bad Isn't So Good; Home Sweet Home; Solitary Refinement
	Bigthan	Bernard & Esther, I
	Chester	Family Vacation, II
	Evangelist	Pilgrim's Progress Revisited, I, II
	Melchior	The Star, I, II
	Mr. Heath	Honor Thy Parents
	Nabesh	B-TV: Envy
	Police Officer	B-TV: Envy
	Stooge	A Thanksgiving Carol
	Von Warberg	An Act of Nobility
Bill Maier	Jim Reeves	Sixties-Something
	Pilate	The Imagination Station, II
	Paul Revere	The Midnight Ride
	Thomas, the Doubter	The Imagination Station, II
	Witness	The Imagination Station, I
Maggie Malloy	June Kendall	Connie, I; Emotional Baggage; Father's Day; Fences; Go Ye Therefore; A Little Credit, Please; The Nemesis, I, II; The "No" Factor; Stormy Weather; That's Not Fair!; Thank You, God; A Touch of Healing, II; Where Is Thy Sting?; With a Little Help from My Friends;
	Mary Barclay	Family Vacation, I, II
	Mary, Mother of John Mark	The Imagination Station, I, II
	Noah's Wife	By Faith, Noah
	Rebekah	Back to Bethlehem, I, II
	Woman at Triumphal Entry	The Imagination Station, I

NAME	CHARACTER	EPISODE
Shifra Margolis		The Other Woman
Brad McMurray	Steven Schmidt	Afraid, Not!; Forever . . ., Amen; The Secret Keys of Discipline
Heather Mehl	Ashley	Share and Share Alike
	Carrie	Second Thoughts
	Hayley	Share and Share Alike
Diane Michelle Thine	Dr. (Mrs.) Morton	Best Intentions; Fair-Weather Fans; Forever . . ., Amen; For Is the Kingdom; The Mortal Coil, II
	Molly	Blind Justice
	Orpah	Three Funerals & a Wedding, I
	Sarah	On Solid Ground
Erin Morales	Jessie Morales	All's Well with Boswell; The Meaning of Sacrifice; Melanie's Diary; Peacemaker; That's Not Fair!; The Trouble with Girls; The Very Best of Friends; The Vow
Curt Morse	Curt Morse	Another Chance; The Last Resort
Rosemary Morton	Mrs. McGillicutty	You Go to School Where?
Bill Myers	Blake	Letting Go
	Ron Marsden	All the Difference in the World
Natalie O'Hare	Grandma Kendall	A Touch of Healing, I, II
	Jenny Whittaker	The Mortal Coil, I, II; Recollections
	Mrs. McGillicutty	Mike Makes Right
	Naomi	Three Funerals & a Wedding, I, II
	Secretary	Mike Makes Right
Jeff Parker	Gary Burkhead	The Search for Whit, I
	Robb	The Barclay Ski Vacation
Myeisha Phillips	Giselle Foster	The Case of the Deliquent Disciples
Thom Pinto	Harvey	Our Daily Bread
	Jason	The Mortal Coil, II
William Pomeroy	Captain	A Time for Christmas
	Dudley	War of the Words
	Kent Wakefield	The Mysterious Stranger, I, II
	Minstrel	A Time for Christmas
	Shepherd	A Time for Christmas
	Steven Schmidt	All the Difference in the World
Michael Portillo	Denver Thorpe	The Case of the Candid Camera; Pipe Dreams
	Stable Boy	The Midnight Ride
Bonnie Reed	Mrs. Littleton	Blind Justice
Gary Reed	Daniel	Deliver Us from Evil
	Donald	Blind Justice
	Jeffrey	First Love; Third Degree
Chad Reisser	Billy Borton	Mike Makes Right
	Bruno	The Secret Weapon
	Chas Wentworth	Camp What-a-Nut, I, II
	Craig	The Life of the Party
	Danny	Nothing to Fear
	Derek	Fair-Weather Fans
	Digger Digwillow	Heat Wave; The Imagination

NAME	CHARACTER	EPISODE
		Station, I, II
	Horace Higgenbotham	A Single Vote
	Leonard	Kid's Radio; What Are We Gonna Do About Halloween?
	Mac	Easy Money
	Monty Whittaker-Dowd	Ice Fishing; A Member of the Family, I, II; Monty's Christmas; The Reluctant Rival; Scattered Seeds
	Mugsy Mumford	V.B.S. Blues
	Nick	The Conscientious Cross-Guard
	Phil	The Fundamentals
	Ralph	Whit's Flop
	Young Tom	A Matter of Obedience
Terri Reisser	Anne Jacobs	A Worker Approved
Lydia Reissmueller	Marsha	Deliver Us from Evil; The Midnight Ride; The "No" Factor; Preacher's Kid; Timmy's Cabin
Charles Knox Robinson	Father (Terry's)	The Last Great Adventure of Summer
	Flavius	St. Paul: An Appointment with Caesar
	Hank Murray	Treasure Hunt
	Horace	The Ill-Gotten Deed
	Kyle Barnett	Second Thoughts
	Medicine Man	The Curse
	Nagle	Someone to Watch Over Me
	Nathan Hale	The Day Independence Came
	Stranger	Hold Up!
Scott Rummell	Ensign Roberts	East Winds, Raining
	Larry	East Winds, Raining
	Martin Luther	Hymn Writers
	Soldier	East Winds, Raining
Maureen Davis Russack	Cafeteria Lady	Share and Share Alike
	Carla	With a Little Help from My Friends
	Carol	Share and Share Alike
	Gabby Libbens	Rewards in Full
	Hairdresser	W-O-R-R-Y
	Jezebel	B-TV: Envy
	Kelsey	The Fifth House on the Left
	Martha	Share and Share Alike
	Mom	B-TV: Envy
	Mrs. Clark	W-O-R-R-Y
	Opera	B-TV: Envy
	Salesperson	Share and Share Alike
	Victoria	Soaplessly Devoted
	Wife	B-TV: Envy
Will Ryan	Eugene Meltsner	Another Chance; Auld Lang Syne; Back to Bethlehem, I, II, III; The Battle, I, II; Best Intentions; The Big Broadcast; A Bite of Applesauce; Blind Justice; A Book by Its Cover; The Boy Who Cried "Destructo!"; B-TV: Compassion; . . . But Not Forgotten; Caroling, Caroling;

NAME	CHARACTER	EPISODE
		Checkmate; A Class Act; Connie, I, II; The Cross of Cortes, I, II; Curious, Isn't It?; The Curse; A Day in the Life; The Decision; Deliver Us from Evil; Do, for a Change; Dobson Comes to Town; Eugene's Dilemma; Fences; Feud for Thought; First Hand Experience; The Fifth House on the Left, I, II; Flash Flood; Gone . . . ; A Good and Faithful Servant; Harlow Doyle, Private Eye; Hold Up!; The Homecoming; Home Sweet Home; Ice Fishing; It's a Wrap; I Want My B-TV!; Isaac the Benevolent; Isaac the Chivalrous; It Began with a Rabbit's Foot . . . ; . . . It Ended with a Handshake; It Happened at Four Corners; Joy to the World; Last in a Long Line; The Last Resort; Let This Mind Be in You; A License to Drive; A Little Credit, Please; The Living Nativity; Love Is in the Air, I, II; Melanie's Diary; The Mortal Coil, I, II; Moving Targets; A Name, Not a Number, I, II; Naturally, I Assumed . . . ; The "No" Factor; On Solid Ground; The Other Woman; Over the Airwaves; Peace on Earth; The Perfect Witness, I, II, III; Pipe Dreams; A Rathbone of Contention; The Return of Harley, I; The Right Choice, I, II; Room Mates; The Sacred Trust; The Scales of Justice; Scattered Seeds; The Search for Whit, I, II, III; Second Thoughts; Solitary Refinement; The Star, I, II; St. Paul: Set Apart by God; Suspicious Minds; Tales of Moderation; Terror from the Skies; A Test for Robyn; A Thanksgiving Carol; Third Degree; Thy Kingdom Come; Thy Will Be Done; The Time Has Come; Tom for Mayor I, II; Tongue of Fire; Train Ride; Treasure Hunt; The Trouble with Girls; Truth, Trivia, & 'Trina; The Turning Point; Unto Us a Child Is Born; War of the Words; What Are You Going to Do with Your Life?; When Bad Isn't So Good; Where Is Thy Sting?
	Arley	A Thanksgiving Carol
	Athiest	Pilgrim's Progress Revisited, II
	Big Ed	Doing Unto Others

NAME	CHARACTER	EPISODE
	Bill	The Life of the Party
	Boss	Why Don't You Grow Up?
	Caiaphas	St. Paul: The Man from Tarsus
	Cain	B-TV: Envy
	Charlie	A Tongue of Fire
	Col. Whalley	A Time for Christmas
	Crook	Pipe Dreams
	David	B-TV: Envy
	Disc Jockey	A Test for Robyn
	Doc Miles	Backwoods Jacobs
	Euben	St. Paul: Set Apart by God
	Eubulus	The Imagination Station, I
	Frank Faylen	The Perfect Witness, II
	General Grant	Lincoln, I, II
	Guard at Jail	The Imagination Station, II
	Harlow Doyle	. . . But Not Forgotten; Terror from the Skies; What Are You Going to Do with Your Life?; Truth, Trivia & 'Trina; Home Sweet Home
	Jamison Shoemaker	A Single Vote
	Joab	B-TV: Envy
	Joe	B-TV: Envy
	John Wilkes Booth	Lincoln, II
	Jonah	Return to the Bible Room
	Jones	The Time of Our Lives
	Judah	Bernard & Joseph, I, II
	King	Return to the Bible Room
	Man at Triumphal Entry	The Imagination Station, I
	Marco Dibiasi	Camp What-a-Nut, I,II
	Mark	Sixties-Something
	Memucan	Bernard & Esther, I
	Minstrel	A Time for Christmas
	Monk	Columbus: The Grand Voyage
	Mr. Dierdorf	The Twilife Zone
	Mr. Gutwrench	It Sure Seems Like It to Me
	Mr. Lang	A Single Vote
	Mr. Worldly Wise	Pilgrim's Progress Revisited, I, II
	Mustafa	A Name, Not a Number, I, II
	Officer David Harley	Addictions Can Be Habit Forming; Lights Out at Whit's End; Missed It by That Much; Peace on Earth; Promises, Promises; The Quality of Mercy; Recollections; The Return of Harley, I, II; Rumor Has It; The Tangled Web
	Officer O'Ryan	Pipe Dreams; Pranks for the Memories
	Officer Symczek	An Act of Mercy
	Official	Bernard & Esther, I
	Peter	The Imagination Station, I, II; St. Paul: The Man from Tarsus; St. Paul: Set Apart by God
	Photographer	Heroes
	Pliant	Pilgrim's Progress Revisited, I
	Professor	The Time of Our Lives
	Sailor	Return to the Bible Room
	Salesman	Heroes
	Sam Houston	A Single Vote
	Servant	Bernard & Esther, I, II
	Shepherd	A Time for Christmas

NAME	CHARACTER	EPISODE
	Strange Man	The Last Great Adventure of Summer
	Teacher	Back to School
	Ted	The Time of Our Lives
	Wretched	A Thanksgiving Carol
Danny Schmittler	Danny Schmidt	Afraid, Not!; All the Difference in the World; Forever, Amen; The Secret Keys of Discipline
Mark Shillinger	Charles (Chunky) Edward Thompson	Blackbeard's Treasure; Pipe Dreams; Poetry in Slow Motion; The Power; The Pretty Good Samaritan; War of the Words
	Howard	Fences
	Young Jack	Blackbeard's Treasure
Amy Slivka	Joey	Addictions Can Be Habit Forming
Betsy Speer	Det. Aldridge	The Mysterious Stranger, I
	Mrs. Hughes	Afraid, Not!
Michelle Stacy	Blair	With a Little Help from My Friends
	Hannah	Top This!
	Homeowner	Top This!
	Melissa	A Book by Its Cover
	Molly	A Name, Not a Number, I
Fabio Stephens	Curt Stevens	Mayor for a Day; One Bad Apple; Pranks for the Memories; The Trouble with Girls; What Happened to the Silver Streak?
	Benjamin	Elijah, I, II
	Calvin	The Ill-Gotten Deed
Kara Stokke	Cheryl McCormick	"A" . . . Is for Attitude; First Love; Go Ye Therefore
	Suzie	Connie, I
Shawn Svoboda	Rusty Gordon	Angels Unaware; Another Chance; Checkmate; The Election Deception; Our Father; Poetry in Slow Motion; The Potential in Elliot; The Power
	Carl	A Game of Compassion
	Leonard	Greater Love
Isaac Keith Swan	Adult Terence	The War Hero
Mike Trout	Mike Trout	Dobson Comes to Town
Bobbie Valentine	SPCA Woman	By Faith, Noah
Janet Waldo	Maureen Hodges	Making the Grade; Our Father; Pipe Dreams; Subject Yourself; Terror from the Skies; Wonderworld; W-O-R-R-Y
	Joanne	The Decision
	Mrs. Clydesdale	What Are You Going to Do With Your Life?
	Tumweiler Twin	Pipe Dreams
	Woman	Terror from the Skies
Jimmy Weldon	Dr. Newcastle	The Mysterious Stranger, II
	Fireman Grady	Real Time
	Lou	Real Time

NAME	CHARACTER	EPISODE
	Mr. Peterman	With a Little Help from My Friends
Josh West	Bryant	Third Degree
Jordan Wood	Young Julie	The Time of Our Lives
Marshal Younger	Benjamin	Unto Us a Child Is Born
	Caller	Top This!
	Guy	B-TV: Envy
	Mr. Clark	The Pretty Good Samaritan
	Officer Spector	The Perfect Witness, I, II, III
	Postal Clerk	Blessings in Disguise
	Servant	B-TV: Envy
Alan Young	Jack Allen	All the Difference in the World; Blackbeard's Treasure; . . . But Not Forgotten; A Code of Honor; The Decision; Do, for a Change; The Final Conflict; George Under Pressure; Hard Losses; Home Sweet Home; I Want My B-TV!; The Last Resort; Love Is in the Air, I, II; The Merchant of Odyssey; Moving Targets; Poetry in Slow Motion; A Question About Tasha; Red Wagons & Pink Flamingos; The Return; Rewards in Full; The Secret Weapon; Share and Share Alike; Small Fires, Little Pools; St. Paul: An Appointment with Caesar; St. Paul: Voyage to Rome; Subject Yourself; The Time Has Come; Tom for Mayor, I, II; Top This!; A Touch of Healing, I, II; The Truth About Zachary; The Turning Point; The Underground Railroad, I, II, III; Unto Us a Child Is Born; A Victim of Circumstance; Welcome Home, Mr. Blackgaard; Where Is Thy Sting? W-O-R-R-Y
	Elihu	Share and Share Alike; Solitary Refinement
	Mr. Harding	Share and Share Alike
	Titulinus	St. Paul: An Appointment with Caesar

Adventures in Odyssey *Radio Dramas, Books, and Videos*

ALBUM COLLECTIONS

Each album collection of six audiocassettes or four CDs features 12 radio broadcast adventures.

The Early Classics (1)
AL 702 (audiocassette only)
"Whit's Flop"
"The Life of the Party"
"Connie Comes to Town"
"Recollections"
"Gifts for Madge and Guy"
"The Day After Christmas"
"Promises, Promises"
"Nothing to Fear"
"An Act of Mercy"
"The Tangled Web"
"Isaac the Benevolent"
"The Trouble with Girls"

Grins, Grabbers and Great Getaways (2)
AL 703 (audiocassette only)
"Family Vacation" I
"Family Vacation" II
"The Day Independence Came"
"Stormy Weather"
"Kids' Radio"
"V.B.S. Blues"
"Camp What-A-Nut" I
"Camp What-A-Nut" II
"The Case of the Secret Room" I
"The Case of the Secret Room" II
"Return to the Bible Room"
"The Last Great Adventure of the Summer"

Secrets, Surprises and Sensational Stories (3)
AL 704 (audiocassette only)
"Back to School"
"The Shepherd and the Giant"
"Mike Makes Right"
"Rumor Has It"
"A Single Vote"
"Heroes"
"Thank You, God"
"Karen"
"Connie" I
"Connie" II
"A Sacred Trust"
"Peace on Earth"

Puns, Parables and Perilous Predicaments (4)
AL 705 (audiocassette only)
"By Faith, Noah"
"The Prodigal, Jimmy"
"A Matter of Obedience"
"A Worker Approved"
"And When You Pray..."
"The Boy Who Didn't Go to Church"
"Let This Mind Be in You"
"A Good and Faithful Servant"
"The Greatest of These"
"Bad Company"
"Choices"
"Go Ye Therefore"

Daring Deeds, Sinister Schemes (5)
AL707 (audiocassette only)
"The Imagination Station" I
"The Imagination Station" II
"A Bite of Applesauce"
"Eugene's Dilemma"
"Connie Goes to Camp" I
"Connie Goes to Camp" II
"The Nemesis" I
"The Nemesis" II
"Our Best Vacation Ever"
"Heatwave"
"The Battle" I
"The Battle" II

Terrific Tales, Mysterious Missions (6)
AL708 (audiocassette only)
"The Ill-Gotten Deed"
"The Treasure of Le Monde!"
"The Price of Feedom"
"That's Not Fair!"
"Good Business"
"An Encounter with Mrs. Hooper"
"A Prisoner for Christ"
"A Mission for Jimmy"
"Rescue from Manatugo Point"
"Operation DigOut"
"Elijah" I
"Elijah" II

Courageous Characters, Fabulous Friends (7)
AL709 (audiocassette only)
"Isaac the Insecure"
"The Very Best of Friends"
"The Reluctant Rival"
"Monty's Christmas"
"The Visitors"
"The Barclay Ski Vacation"
"Ice Fishing"
"Scattered Seeds"
"Front Page News"
"Isaac the Courageous"
"Lincoln" I
"Lincoln" II

Cunning Capers, Exciting Escapades (8)
AL710 (audiocassette only)
"By Any Other Name"
"Bad Luck"
"'A'...Is for Attitude"
"First Love"
"Curious, Isn't It?"
"Suspicious Minds"
"Pranks for the Memories"
"Missing Person"
"Castles and Cauldrons" I
"Castles and Cauldrons" II
"The Winning Edge"
"All's Well with Boswell"

Amazing Antics, Dynamic Discoveries (9)
AL711 (audiocassette only)
"The Big Broadcast"
"Two Sides to Every Story"
"Whatever Happened to the Silver Streak?"
"Better Late Than Never"
"Wishful Thinking"
"Have You No Selpurcs?"
"Bernard & Joseph" I
"Bernard & Joseph" II
"Cousin Albert"
"Not One of Us"
"The Vow"
"Over the Airwaves"

Other Times . . . Other Places (10)
AL712 (audiocassette only)
"Back to Bethlehem" I
"Back to Bethlehem" II
"Back to Bethlehem" III
"Someone to Watch Over Me"
"Melanie's Diary"
"Isaac the Procrastinator"
"The Second Coming"
"Emotional Baggage"
"Waylaid in the Windy City" I
"Waylaid in the Windy City" II
"The Homecoming"
"Last in a Long Line"

It's Another Fine Day . . . (11)
AL713 (audiocassette only)
"By Dawn's Early Light"
"Mayor for a Day"
"A Day in the Life"
"Where There's a Will..."
"...The Last Shall be First"
"The Meaning of Sacrifice"
"A Rathbone of Contention"
"Muckraker"
"Bernard & Esther" I
"Bernard & Esther" II
"Coming of Age"
"Home is Where the Hurt Is"

It All Started When . . . (12)
AL714 (audiocassette only)
"You Gotta Be Wise"
"Isaac the Pure"
"It Takes Integrity"
"Scales of Justice"
"Tales of Moderation"
"Isaac the Chivalrous"
"A Question of Loyalty"
"Conscientious Cross-Guard"
"An Act of Nobility"
"The Courage to Stand"
"No, Honestly!"
"Modesty Is the Best Policy"

At Home and Abroad (13)
AL715 (audiocassette only)
"The Cross of Cortes" I
"The Cross of Cortes" II
"A Model Child"
"The Curse"
"A Test for Robyn"
"Room Mates"
"A Thanksgiving Carol"
"Hold Up!"
"East Winds, Raining"
"Where's Your Daddy?"
"The Star" I
"The Star" II

Meanwhile, In Another Part of Town (14)
AL716 (audiocassette only)
"Moses: The Passover" I
"Moses: The Passover" II
"Peacemaker"
"Sixties-Something"
"A Tongue of Fire"
"A License to Drive"
"Father's Day"
"Harlow Doyle, Private Eye"
"The Midnight Ride"
"Treasure Hunt"
"Feud for Thought"
"Timmy's Cabin"

A Place of Wonder (15)
AL717 (audiocassette only)
"Double Trouble"
"Fair-Weather Fans"
"Wonderworld"
"The 'No' Factor"
"Pen Pal"
"The Case of the Candid Camera"
"Flash Flood"
"Pipe Dreams"
"On Solid Ground"
"Rights, Wrongs & Reasons"
"A Class Act"
"Real Time"

Flights of Imagination (16)
AL718 (audiocassette)/CC706 (CD)
"The Mortal Coil" I
"The Mortal Coil" II
"Best Intentions"
"Columbus: The Grand Voyage"
"The Living Nativity"
"Like Father, Like Son"
"It Is Well"
"Treasures of the Heart"
"This is Chad Pearson?"
"A Game of Compassion"
"An Adventure in Bethany" I
"An Adventure in Bethany" II

On Earth As It Is in Heaven (17)
AL719 (audiocassette)/CC719 (CD)
"Our Father"
"Hallowed Be Thy Name"
"Thy Kingdom Come"
"Thy Will Be Done"
"Our Daily Bread"
"Forgive Us As We Forgive"
"Into Temptation"
"Deliver Us From Evil"
"For Thine Is the Kingdom"
"The Power"
"And the Glory"
"Forever...Amen"

A Time of Discovery! (18)
AL721 (audiocassette)/CC721 (CD)
"My Fair Bernard"
"Hymn Writers"
"Greater Love"
"The Jesus Cloth"
"The Case of the Delinquent Disciples"
"The Marriage Feast"
"Family Values"
"Why Don't You Grow Up?"
"Terror From the Skies!"
"Count It All Joy"
"The Mysterious Stranger" I
"The Mysterious Stranger" II

Passport to Adventure (19)
AL722 (audiocassette)/CC722 (CD)
"Pilgrim's Progress Revisited" I
"Pilgrim's Progress Revisited" II
"The Bad Hair Day"
"A Time for Christmas"
"Truth, Trivia & 'Trina"
"Naturally, I Assumed . . ."
"Aloha, Oy!" I
"Aloha, Oy!" II
"Aloha, Oy!" III
"The Potential in Elliott"
"A Prayer for George Barclay"
"The Boy Who Cried 'Destructo!'"

A Journey of Choices (20)
AL723 (audiocassette)/CC723 (CD)
"When Bad Isn't So Good"
"Making the Grade"
"Fences"
"Afraid, Not!"
"Pet Peeves"
"War of the Words"
"The War Hero"
"The Secret Keys of Discipline"
"Two Brothers...and Bernard" I
"Two Brothers...and Bernard" II
"It Began With a Rabbit's Foot..."
"...It Ended With a Handshake"

Wish You Were Here! (21)
AL724 (audiocassette)/CC724 (CD)
"First-Hand Experience"
"Second Thoughts"
"Third Degree"
"It Happened at Four Corners"
"The Fifth House on the Left" I
"The Fifth House on the Left" II
"Gone..."
"...But Not Forgotten"
"The Fundamentals"
"The Election Deception"
"A Book By Its Cover"
"The Twilife Zone"

The Changing Times (22)
AL725 (audiocassette)/CC725 (CD)
"Tom for Mayor" I
"Tom for Mayor" II
"Siege at Jericho"
"George Under Pressure"
"A Name, Not a Number" I
"A Name, Not a Number" II
"A Code of Honor"
"A Call for Reverend Jimmy"
"Soaplessly Devoted"
"Blackbeard's Treasure"
"Red Wagons & Pink Flamingos"
"Unto Us a Child is Born"

Twists and Turns (23)
AL726 (audiocassette)/CC726 (CD)
"I Want My B-TV!"
"The Truth About Zachary"
"Preacher's Kid"
"The Good, the Bad & Butch"
"Share and Share Alike"
"All the Difference in the World"
"St. Paul: The Man from Tarsus"
"St. Paul: Set Apart by God"
"A Victim of Circumstance"
"A Perfect Witness" I
"A Perfect Witness" II
"A Perfect Witness" III

Risks and Rewards (24)
AL727 (audiocassette)/CC727 (CD)
"Poetry in Slow Motion"
"Subject Yourself"
"Rewards in Full"
"Top This!"
"The Underground Railroad" I
"The Underground Railroad" II
"The Underground Railroad" III
"B-TV: Envy"
"A Touch of Healing" I
"A Touch of Healing" II
"Where is Thy Sting?"
"The Turning Point"

Darkness Before Dawn (25)
AL728 (audiocassette)/CC728 (CD)
"A Little Credit, Please"
"Small Fires, Little Pools"
"Angels Unaware"
"Gathering Thunder"
"Moving Targets"
"Hard Losses"
"The Return"
"The Time Has Come"
"Checkmate"
"Another Chance"
"The Last Resort"
"The Final Conflict"

Back On the Air (26)
AL729(audiocassette)/CC729(CD)
"Welcome Home, Mr. Blackgaard"
"Do, for a Change"
"Love Is in the Air" I
"Love Is in the Air" II
"The Pretty Good Samaritan"
"W-O-R-R-Y"
"Hidden in My Heart"
"Easy Money"
"St. Paul: Voyage to Rome"
"St. Paul: An Appointment with Caesar"
"Pokenberry Falls, RFD" I
"Pokenberry Falls, RFD" II

The Search For Whit (27)
AL730 (audiocassette)/CC730 (CD)
"BTV: Compassion"
"Letting Go"
"With a Little Help From My Friends"
"Blessings in Disguise"
"The Time of Our Lives"
"What Are You Gonna Do With Your Life?"
"Memories of Jerry"
"A Question About Tasha"
"Blind Justice"
"The Search for Whit" I
"The Search for Whit" II
"The Search for Whit" III

Welcome Home (28)
AL731 (audiocassette)/CC731 (CD)
"The Secret Weapon"
"The Merchant of Odyssey"
"The Right Choice," I
"The Right Choice," II
"Home Sweet Home"
"Clara"
"Three Funerals and a Wedding," I
"Three Funerals and a Wedding," II
"Solitary Refinement"
"The Decision"
"The Other Woman"
"It's a Wrap!"

Adventures in Odyssey Classics: Welcome to Odyssey (Introductory Set)
AL732 (audiocassette)/CC732 (CD)
"Connie Comes to Town"
"Recollections"
"Promises, Promises"
"Stormy Weather"
"Kid's Radio"
"Karen"
"The Shepherd and the Giant"
"Thank You, God"
"Connie," I
"Connie," II
"The Imagination Station," I
"The Imagination Station," II

Adventures in Odyssey Classics: Chronicles, Kings and Crosses (Classic Bible Stories)
AL720 (audiocassette)/CC720 (CD)
"The Imagination Station" I
"The Imagination Station" II
"Elijah" I
"Elijah" II
"Bernard and Joseph" I
"Bernard and Joseph" II
"Back to Bethlehem" I
"Back to Bethlhem" II
"Back to Bethlehem" III
"On Solid Ground"
"Moses: The Passover" I
"Moses: The Passover" II

ANIMATED VIDEOS

The Knight Travellers (1) (VI081)
A Flight to the Finish (2) (VI082)
A Fine Feathered Frenzy (3) (VI083)
Shadow of a Doubt (4) (VI084)
Star Quest (5) (VI085)
Once Upon an Avalanche (6) (VI086)
Electric Christmas (7) (VI087)
Go West Young Man (8) (VI088)
Someone to Watch Over Me (9) (VI089)
In Harm's Way (10) (V1090)
A Twist in Time (11) (VI091)

NOVELS

Strange Journey Back (1) (CB151)
High Flyer With a Flat Tire (2) (CB152)
The Secret Cave of Robinwood (3) (CB153)
Behind the Locked Door (4) (CB154)
Lights Out at Camp What-a-Nut (5) (CB155)
The King's Quest (6) (BF532)
Danger Lies Ahead (7) (BF546)
Point of No Return (8) (BF561)
Dark Passage (9) (BF564)
Freedom Run (10) (BF566)
The Stranger's Message (11) (BF570)
A Carnival of Secrets (12) (BF588)

NOTE:
AIO Audio Album Collections #1-15 are available only from Focus on the Family (Call 1-800-A-FAMILY to order). All other AIO products are available from Focus on the Family or at your local Christian bookstore.

OTHER PRODUCTS

ADVENTURES IN ODYSSEY BIBLE
(Word Publishing) (CB294)

ADVENTURES IN ODYSSEY PUZZLES, ACTION FIGURES, PEEL AND PLAY SET, "AT WHIT'S END" FAMILY BOARD GAME
(Rainfall Educational Toys, an Imprint of Chariot-Victor Publishing: 719 536-0100)

ADVENTURES IN ODYSSEY SHIRTS, CAPS AND BACKPACKS
(LAS Creations, 800 886-6555)